VIETNAM VANGUARD

THE 5TH BATTALION'S APPROACH
TO COUNTER-INSURGENCY, 1966

VIETNAM VANGUARD

THE 5TH BATTALION'S APPROACH
TO COUNTER-INSURGENCY, 1966

EDITED BY RON BOXALL
AND ROBERT O'NEILL

This book is dedicated to all who died in service
with the 5th Battalion, the Royal Australian Regiment,
during its first tour of duty in Vietnam, 1966–67.

Published by ANU Press
The Australian National University
Acton ACT 2601, Australia
Email: anupress@anu.edu.au

Available to download for free at press.anu.edu.au

ISBN (print): 9781760463328
ISBN (online): 9781760463335

WorldCat (print): 1137863512
WorldCat (online): 1137863899

DOI: 10.22459/VV.2019

This title is published under a Creative Commons Attribution-NonCommercial-NoDerivatives 4.0 International (CC BY-NC-ND 4.0).

The full licence terms are available at creativecommons.org/licenses/by-nc-nd/4.0/legalcode

Cover design and layout by ANU Press.

Cover photograph: Lance Corporal Gordon Meredith leading 9 Platoon in the shake-out after dismounting from Armoured Personnel Carriers into open terrain during the dry season, by Neil Ordner.

This edition © 2020 ANU Press

Disclaimer

The Commonwealth Government has not participated in the research or production of, or exercised editorial control over, this publication or its contents. The views expressed and conclusions reached herein do not necessarily represent those of the Commonwealth, which expressly disclaims any responsibility for the content or accuracy of the publication.

CONTENTS

Foreword ix
Major General Steve Gower

5th Battalion Roll of Honour xi

List of Maps and Figures xiii

List of Illustrations xv

Acknowledgements xix

Preface xxv
Ron Boxall

Introduction: The Purpose of this Book 1
Robert O'Neill

1. The Challenge 9
   Robert O'Neill

2. Why was 5 RAR Stationed at Nui Dat? 21
   David Horner

3. Facing New Realities: From Holsworthy to Nui Dat 45
   Stan Maizey

4. 5 RAR on Operations, May–September 1966 55
   Max Carroll, Peter Isaacs, Roger Wainwright and Robert O'Neill

5. Intelligence Work in Phuoc Tuy after Long Tan 81
   Robert O'Neill

6. Into the Hills: Operations Canberra and Robin – October 1966 93
   Max Carroll and Peter Isaacs

7. Operation Queanbeyan – October 1966: Unfinished Business
   from Operation Canberra 123
   Max Carroll, Michael Deak (Michael von Berg)
   and Barry Campbell

8. A Platoon Commander's War – Part 1 151
    Roger Wainwright and Terry O'Hanlon

9. Contact with the Enemy – Through Soldiers' Eyes 175
    Bob Kearney, Ted Harrison, Dan Riley and John O'Callaghan

10. A Platoon Commander's War – Part 2 191
    John Hartley and Harry Neesham

11. Advisers? Activities Beyond the Battalion 217
    Ron Boxall and Ron Bade

12. Fire Support: 103 Field Battery Royal Australian Artillery in Action ..253
    George Bindley, John Griggs, Peter Aspinall, Doug Heazlewood
    and Brian Mortimer

13. The Medical Problems of Operations in the Hills 273
    Tony White and Ian McDougall

14. The Challenges of Air Support 285
    Jim Campbell, Bob Supple, Bob Askew, Robert O'Neill
    and Bill Davies

15. The Development of the Reconnaissance Platoon 301
    Michael Deak (Michael von Berg)

16. John Warr as Commanding Officer: His Approach to the War 319
    Max Carroll, Peter Isaacs, Michael Deak (Michael von Berg)
    and Mark Warr

17. Conclusion: The Development of a 5 RAR Approach 335
    Robert O'Neill

Appendix A. 5th Battalion Decorations and Awards: Vietnam 1966–67....347

Appendix B. Authors' Biographical Notes.........................349

Appendix C. Cordon and Search Operations 361
John Warr

Appendix D. The Enemy: Uncontested Tenancy Prior to the Arrival
of 1 ATF 393
Ernest Chamberlain

Appendix E. Glossary of Military Terms..........................425

Appendix F. Map Symbols 427

Appendix G. Bibliography 429

Index 431

FOREWORD

Major General Steve Gower

I regard it as a singular honour to be asked to write the foreword to this book. I write it not as a member of the battalion, as such, but as an attached artillery forward observer.

In the period September to December 1966 I was part of A Company on Operations Canberra, Robin, Queanbeyan, Bundaberg, Yass, Hayman and Canary with Peter Cole, then Max Carroll as the company commander. It was an intense operational period, and it gave me a good insight into the 5th Battalion, the Royal Australian Regiment (5 RAR), approach to countering the VC (Viet Cong) insurgency, as well as the chance to observe closely the fighting capability of the battalion and its spirit. I was impressed.

With my parent battery (101st Field Battery) moving into direct support of 6 RAR, my time as 103rd Field Battery's fourth forward observer in A Company came to a close. I was sorry to leave, as I had developed a great respect, indeed affection, for the battalion and those who served in it.

I regard this book as very important. It is much more contemplative and a more detailed record of the first half of the battalion's tour of duty than has been available before. I hasten to say that observation is in no way a criticism of Bob O'Neill's unit history, a copy of which has long graced my bookshelf. Rather, the contributions in this book have resulted from the passage of time and the opportunity to contemplate, reflect and think more deeply about what was achieved and perhaps what might have been.

The battalion's tour of duty was unique in a number of ways. It was the first battalion to be deployed with national servicemen, and the first to be deployed to occupy the Task Force's operational base at Nui Dat within an autonomous area of operations. Among other things, the battalion came to develop a very effective technique for conducting cordon and search operations, a fundamental way of disrupting the VC hold on surrounding villages. It was also innovative in other ways, such as forming a battalion reconnaissance platoon. To me, the battalion's approach could be characterised as deliberate but flexible rather than doctrinally rigid, based on intelligence assessments complemented by its own analyses and not one that needlessly took risks.

5 RAR's tour was very successful by any measure, but its resilience was to be tested severely when it suffered the loss of two company commanders and other officers, non-commissioned officers and soldiers in a series of tragic mine incidents in early 1967. These incidents could have broken a lesser group of men.

This book contains many worthwhile lessons, particularly those relating to the challenges of facing a capable and determined enemy. It is a tribute to all members of the battalion who served so valiantly in Phuoc Tuy Province. Over 50 years later I remember, commemorate and celebrate their service.

Congratulations to those involved in producing this book, especially Bob O'Neill, Ron Boxall and Roger Wainwright, and to all the authors.

Steve Gower AO AO(Mil)
Director, Australian War Memorial (1996–2012)

> Steve Gower graduated from the Royal Military College, Duntroon, in 1961 with the Sword of Honour and the Queen's Medal. In 1966 he went to Vietnam as a forward observer in the 1st Field Regiment. A highlight of his time in Vietnam was being the forward observer attached to A Company of 5th Battalion, the Royal Australian Regiment, before leaving mid-tour to move to the 6th Battalion. On returning to Australia, he had several artillery appointments and was Commanding Officer of 8th/12th Medium Regiment. He had numerous other training and policy appointments before becoming General Officer Commanding Training Command, then Assistant Chief of the Defence Force for Logistics, and later for Personnel. He retired from the Army as a major general to accept the Directorship of the Australian War Memorial in Canberra, a position he held for 16 years.

5TH BATTALION ROLL OF HONOUR

Vietnam 1966–67

Private	**Errol W Noack**, 21, of Adelaide, South Australia, died 24 May 1966
Private	**John R Sweetnam**, 20, of Melbourne, Victoria, died 9 June 1966
Corporal	**Brendan F Coupe**, 23, of Sydney, New South Wales, died 10 June 1966
Private	**Leslie T Farren**, 20, of Reservoir, Victoria, died 10 June 1966
Private	**Robert J Lubcke**, 23, of Whyalla, South Australia, died 2 July 1966
Lance Corporal	**Marinko Tomas**, 21, of Nannup, Western Australia, died 8 July 1966
Private	**Raymond J Kennedy**, 26, of Canley Vale, New South Wales, died 15 August 1966
Private	**Graham FA Warburton**, 21, of Warrnambool, Victoria, died 1 October 1966
Corporal	**Norman J Womal**, 28, of Bowen, Queensland, died 17 October 1966
Private	**Gordon H D'Antoine**, 20, of Derby, Western Australia, died 18 October 1966
Private	**Bryan P Watson**, 21, of Norseman, Western Australia, died 10 November 1966

Private	**Erald H Nilsen**, 20, of Dunwich, Queensland, died 14 November 1966	
Private	**Noel A Pracy**, 20, of Sydney, New South Wales, died 14 November 1966	
Private	**Paul C Sullivan**, 21, of Lane Cove, New South Wales, died 27 December 1966	
Major	**Donald M Bourne**, 35, of Tamworth, New South Wales, died 14 February 1967	
Captain	**Robert J Milligan**, 30, of Taree, New South Wales, died 14 February 1967	
Private	**Donald M Clark**, 21, of Northampton, Western Australia, died 21 February 1967	
Private	**Michael D Poole**, 20, of Fitzroy, Victoria, died 21 February 1967	
Private	**Richard W Sandow**, 20, of Broken Hill, New South Wales, died 21 February 1967	
Private	**James C Webster**, 22, of Perth, Western Australia, died 21 February 1967	
Lance Corporal	**George B Green**, 21, of Granville, New South Wales, died 21 February 1967	
Lieutenant	**John Carruthers**, 28, of Mount Morgan, Queensland, wounded 21 February 1967, died 24 February 1967	
Major	**M Bruce McQualter**, 29, of Braidwood, New South Wales, wounded 21 February 1967, died 5 March 1967	
Private	**Richard E Lloyd**, 21, of Weston, New South Wales, died 6 April 1967	
2nd Lieutenant	**Kerry P Rinkin**, 21, of Taree, New South Wales, died 7 April 1967	

LIST OF MAPS AND FIGURES

Map 1: Phuoc Tuy Province 1966 xxiii

Figure 1: 5 RAR in Vietnam, 1966..................................3

Map 2: Phuoc Tuy Province 1966: Main Viet Cong locations
and district boundaries.......................................15

Map 3: Operation Hardihood – Phase 1: 24–31 May 1966..............60

Map 4: Operation Hardihood – Phase 2: 1–3 June 1966...............62

Map 5: Operation Sydney: 6–17 July 1966..........................67

Map 5A: Nui Nghe artillery incident: 8 July 1966..................68

Map 6: Operation Sydney Two: 19–20 July 1966.....................71

Map 7: Operation Holsworthy: 7–8 August 1966.....................75

Map 8: Operation Canberra – Phase 1: 6–8 October 1966.............96

Map 9: Operation Canberra – Phase 2: 8–10 October 1966...........103

Map 10: Operation Robin: 11–16 October 1966.....................108

Map 11: Operation Queanbeyan: 17–26 October 1966................126

Map 12: Anti-Tank and Assault Pioneer Platoons enemy contacts:
17–18 October 1966..139

Map 12A: Anti-Tank and Assault Pioneer Platoons enemy contacts:
17–18 October 1966..140

Map 13: 10 Platoon attack: 21 October 1966......................142

Map 13A: 10 Platoon attack: 21 October 1966.....................146

Map A.1: Operation Sydney Two: 19–20 July 1966..................366

Figure A.1: 5 RAR Interrogation Compound........................374

Map A.2: Operation Holsworthy: 7–8 August 1966 379
Map A.3: Operation Yass: 6–7 November 1966 388
Figure A.2: VC organisation in Phuoc Tuy Province in mid-1966 415

LIST OF ILLUSTRATIONS

1. February 1966, on exercise at Canungra before departure for Vietnam 111
2. October 1966: Two C Company members, Lance Corporal Ron Shoebridge (left) and Lance Corporal David 'Stretch' Bryan (right), support Private David Riik after 8 Platoon suffered casualties from booby traps during Operation Canberra. 111
3. May 1966: The Commander US Military Assistance Command Vietnam, General William C. Westmoreland, and the Commander Australian Forces Vietnam, Major General Ken Mackay, talk with Private Kevin Cavanagh, C Company, aboard HMAS *Sydney* at Vung Tau 112
4. April 1966: Brigadier David Jackson, Commander 1 ATF, and Lieutenant Colonel John Warr, commanding officer 5 RAR, soon after the latter's arrival at Tan Son Nhut airport 113
5. July 1966: 5 RAR medical officer, Captain Tony White, sutures a machete gash for one of his medical assistants, Corporal Ian McDougall. 114
6. October 1966: Soldiers of C Company, at a landing zone on Nui Thi Vai with captured materiel. Operation Canberra. 115
7. September 1966: The Australian Army Chief of the General Staff, Lieutenant General Tom Daly, visits D Company during Operation Toledo, September 1966. 116
8. May 1966: Lieutenant Colonel John Warr (centre) discussing helicopter training with Lieutenant Charles Brinnon of the US Army's 68 Assault Helicopter Company (left) and Major Richard Hannigan (right), operations officer, 1 ATF, at Vung Tau 116
9. October 1966: Private Bruce Mason, A Company, makes a brew beside a local charcoal burner's oven during Operation Robin 116

10. December 1966: Members of 8 Platoon admiring Private Robin Lestrange's Christmas treats sent by his former employers. 116

11. October 1966: 5 RAR's Signals Officer, Captain Brian Le Dan, with his damaged Owen machine carbine which deflected and shattered an enemy sniper's bullet thus saving him from serious wounding or death during Operation Queanbeyan 117

12. September 1966: The Commander 1 ATF, Brigadier David Jackson (left), greets the Commander Australian Forces Vietnam, Major General Ken Mackay, and the Australian Army's Chief of the General Staff, Lieutenant General Tom Daly, on their arrival at his HQ at Nui Dat . . 117

13. October 1966: A 9 Squadron RAAF Iroquois delivers ammunition, equipment and water to a landing zone between hills Jan and Julie during Operation Canberra 118

14. 5 RAR's second in command, Major Stan Maizey, setting a good example 118

15. Early October 1966: Men of 4 Section, 8 Platoon 118

16. Villagers watching a distribution of food aid by 5 RAR soldiers 119

17. Villagers collecting food aid 120

18. October 1966: Nui Thi Vai from the west during Operation Robin . . . 121

19. October 1966: Second Lieutenant John McAloney MC who was awarded the Military Cross for leading the Assault Pioneer Platoon's attack on a defended enemy cave system during Operation Queanbeyan. 121

20. Late 1966: Prime Minister Air Marshal Nguyen Cao Ky visited 5 RAR 121

21. October 1966: A 9 Squadron RAAF Iroquois delivers resupplies to the pagoda landing zone during Operation Queanbeyan 122

22. November 1966: 5 RAR's medical officer, Captain Tony White, examines a dead baby in Long Son village 122

23. 5 RAR soldiers patrolling through the secondary growth of an unworked rubber plantation 239

24. A platoon of C Company filling water bottles from a jungle stream while the surrounding area is secured by the rest of the company 240

25. November 1966: Helicopter insertion into Long Son Island on Operation Hayman. 240

LIST OF ILLUSTRATIONS

26. Lance Corporal Gordon Meredith leading 9 Platoon in the shake-out after dismounting from Armoured Personnel Carriers into open terrain during the dry season 241

27. October 1966: Preparing for the evacuation by Sioux helicopter of Captain Brian Le Dan who was wounded during Operation Queanbeyan. 242

28. November 1966: Captain Ron Boxall, in command of D Company during Operation Hayman. 243

29. Second Lieutenant Bob Askew and Captain Jim Campbell DFC 244

30. November 1966: D Company's artillery forward observer, Lieutenant Barry Campbell, and 10 Platoon's commander, Second Lieutenant Dennis Rainer MC, who had worked closely together during 10 Platoon's attack on 21 October. 244

31. Second Lieutenant Michael Deak MC at work. 244

32. This photograph of the Reconnaissance Platoon typifies the fighting soldiers of 5 RAR's first tour of Vietnam in 1966–67 245

33. January 1967: The officers of 5 RAR at Nui Dat 246

34. November 1966: Dai Uy (Captain) Nguyen Van Be and Captain Ron Bade at Binh Ba. Private Ron 'Frenchy' Delaurey-Simpson is standing between the two bare-chested soldiers on the left 247

35. Late 1966: Second Lieutenant John Deane-Butcher on patrol with his platoon 247

36. October 1966: Battalion Headquarters on operations on Nui Thi Vai . . . 248

37. February 1967: Major Ivor 'Blue' Hodgkinson (5 RAR's second in command from December 1966), Captain Bob O'Neill (intelligence officer), Captain Peter Isaacs (adjutant) and Major Ron Hamlyn (officer commanding Administration Company) after a conference with the Commanding Officer, Lieutenant Colonel John Warr 249

38. 5 RAR's Operations Officer, Major Max Carroll, and the commander of 103 Field Battery, Major Neville Gair, at a time when that battery was allocated in direct support of the battalion. 249

39. July 1966: Wet season conditions were experienced for several weeks during construction of 5 RAR's base at Nui Dat. 249

40. Intelligence Officer Captain Bob O'Neill briefing soldiers in 5 RAR's open-air theatre, 'The Mayfair' 250

41. October 1966: Pilot Second Lieutenant Bill Davies, being stretchered to a waiting aeromedical evacuation helicopter for transportation to a US neurosurgical facility in Saigon after being shot down in his Sioux Helicopter, the wreckage of which is strewn along Route 15. . . . 250
42. 'The Rat Pack', a group of 9 Platoon members 251
43. Late 1966: Corporal Bob 'Dogs' Kearney, reflecting while on a break from patrolling in the jungle. 251
44. December 1966: The Commanding Officer serving Christmas dinner to men of C Company 251

ACKNOWLEDGEMENTS

This book is the result of a major team effort. It arose out of the several draft accounts written 50 years after the events that they describe. Max Carroll led the way, demonstrating in his late 80s that he had retained the quality of memory and the analytical mind that had enabled him to produce the well-constructed, detailed operation orders that guided us through our first six months in Phuoc Tuy. His accounts were followed by Peter Isaacs, the adjutant, and Mick von Berg, our Reconnaissance (formerly Anti-Tank) Platoon commander.

It was not difficult to find others willing and able to write of their own experiences of war in Vietnam. Soon we had 30 contributors all keen to write, and more material than we could cope with in a single volume. We are thankful both for their willingness to write, and then for the spirit in which they accepted the need for cuts so that we could fit the story into a book of medium size. We are fortunate to have the range of rank levels, and hence of perspectives, which this team offers. A good battalion allows for and encourages a two-way flow of ideas and information, but command in war remains a top-down system. Difficult decisions need to be taken by commanders at various levels, and we have tried to convey an understanding of where the hard choices lay in the way in which John Warr, and his company and platoon commanders, conducted our operations.

Our battalion, 5 RAR – 5th Battalion, the Royal Australian Regiment – and our sister unit, 6 RAR, were the first two Australian battalions in Vietnam to be composed of both regular (volunteer) soldiers and conscripted national servicemen. Given the controversial nature of the Vietnam War, there was ample potential for friction to occur between national servicemen and regulars. Due to good fortune and careful management, the two units were harmonious in the way in which they functioned. There were times when some of the national servicemen let it be known that there were other ways in which they would rather be occupied than being in the army. However, we were spared the disciplinary crises that some of our allies had to endure. The battalion functioned as a team, and its members saw to it that the dividing line between conscript and volunteer was not accentuated. We all knew that we needed the full team, with its many components, if we were to survive the year and achieve something useful. Hence, we have put together a team of authors that includes both regular and conscript soldiers. We are grateful to those, both officers and soldiers, who contributed their recollections of testing experiences to Chapters 8, 9, 10 and 15.

Our rifle company soldiers were grouped into sections, small teams of nominally 10 men, who were right at the point of most of our actions and contacts with the enemy. Three sections and a four-man headquarters made up a rifle platoon, so we have some chapters written by young officers, again both conscript and volunteer, in their first command appointments. These young men were seldom older than the soldiers they commanded, so they had to make a major adjustment in how they related to the people that they led, and for whose lives they were directly responsible.

Moving up the chain of command, we have been assisted by our operations officer, Major Max Carroll, who also served as a rifle company commander, and Captain Peter Isaacs, the adjutant and assistant operations officer. Sadly, our commanding officer, Lieutenant Colonel John Warr, died in 1999, but his family have rallied to give us their thoughts and comments, particularly concerning John's wider thinking on how to meet our responsibilities most effectively. We are particularly grateful to John's widow Shirley, and their daughter Anne and sons Peter and Mark, for their contributions, especially Mark for his part in writing Chapter 16.

Working closely with John Warr were our second in command, Major Stan Maizey, and our multi-skilled regimental medical officer, Captain Tony White, who both had unusual and enlightening perspectives to give us. Stan passed away in 2018, but he has left his readers with a rare picture of a battalion that went to war under-equipped and that had to 'live off the land' in order to be able to function properly in terms of food, tentage, radios and weapons. Tony, a young graduate medical officer, had to keep over 800 young Australians fit and healthy, and treat all the injuries and sicknesses that are regular occurrences in war. Sometimes he was called upon to expose himself to danger in order to assist those who had been seriously wounded. He and some of the rifle company medical assistants have given us their perspectives on what it was like to meet the same challenges over lengthy periods.

Other battalion members who have contributed to the book include Captains Ron Bade and Ron Boxall, who served separately at Binh Ba for several weeks. Ron Boxall's detachment from the battalion saw him involved with a CIA-sponsored charade. Ron Bade later mentored a South Vietnamese Regional Force company in the same environment.

The battalion could not have functioned without the assistance of other parts of the army, and the Royal Australian Air Force. We thank three of our supporting Sioux helicopter pilots, aided by Captain Bob Supple, and our supporting artillery team, led by Captain George Bindley, who have contributed their perspectives on their problems and how they increased their effectiveness during our very testing first months of operations. And finally, there are two friends who, although both army officers, did not serve in 5 RAR during 1966–67. They are Brigadier Ernest Chamberlain CSM, an intelligence specialist who has studied and written on the Viet Cong over many years, and Colonel Professor David Horner AM, who knows more than most people about how the Australian commitment to the Vietnam War was made in 1965–66 and why we were stationed in Phuoc Tuy Province. We are very grateful to them both for their major contributions.

There are also many other individuals who have contributed to the book behind the scenes. The members of the Executive Committee of the 5 RAR Association, chaired by Colonel Roger Wainwright, have helped with the financing of this publication and its general administration. Roger, who is in his 15th year as the Association's president, has been of invaluable assistance to us. Our perfect backstop, he has been an inveterate chaser of information through his innumerable contacts and is an ever-reliable source of detailed knowledge about the battalion from its earliest days up to the present. Other association members, particularly Gary Townsend and Ted Harrison, have helped with the illustrations. Author and Vietnam veteran Major Bruce Davies MBE (Retd) magically provided pristine military map coverage of Phuoc Tuy Province in 1966; and Alan Mayne of Mayne Maps cleverly used it to produce the maps which support our authors' narratives.

We are grateful to Ashley Ekins and other members of the staff of the Australian War Memorial for their assistance, especially in obtaining access to photographs and official records of our operations. We appreciate also the very helpful way in which members of the staff of ANU Press, and our copyeditor Beth Battrick, have assisted us in the publication process.

We also gratefully acknowledge the assistance of the Commonwealth Government's 'Saluting Their Service' Commemorations Program, which provided a significant grant towards the funding of the project. Any benefits that accrue from the project will be dedicated to the support of 5 RAR veterans or serving members of 5 RAR.

Finally, we wish to thank our wives, Sally O'Neill and Joan Boxall, for their comments and support of our work and their tolerance of the time commitment it has imposed on us for almost three years. They are well qualified for the task, having been our partners for over 50 years, including our various times in Vietnam. Sally helped Bob to produce *Vietnam Task*, based on his letters to her of 1966–67. Joan's management of all family affairs throughout Ron's two tours of duty was a source of helpful reflection, and her many years as a soldier's wife provided invaluable scrutiny which helped reduce the use of arcane 'military speak'.

Ron Boxall
Robert O'Neill

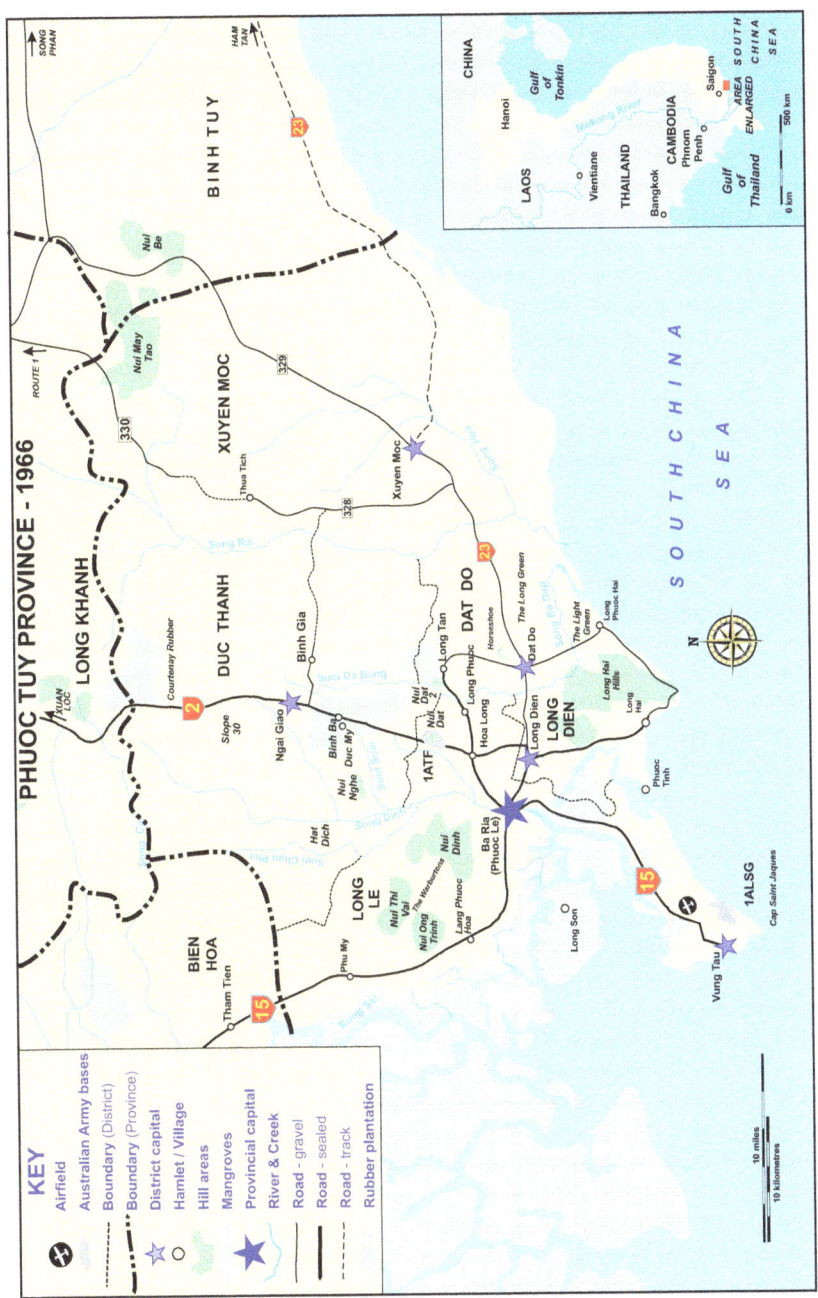

Map 1: Phuoc Tuy Province 1966.

Source: Designed by Ron Boxall and produced by Alan Mayne from a map provided by the Army History Unit.

PREFACE

Ron Boxall

Professor Robert O'Neill, the intelligence officer of the 5th Battalion of the Royal Australian Regiment (5 RAR) during its first tour of duty in South Vietnam in 1966–67, proposed this book. The battalion was the leading element of the 1st Australian Task Force (1 ATF) when it was inserted into Phuoc Tuy Province, the area which was to remain Australia's principal area of land operations for the next six years. His book, *Vietnam Task*, published in 1968, was the original firsthand account of an entire tour of operations by an Australian infantry battalion in Vietnam. It immediately became an important reference for those who were to follow 5 RAR. Some 50 years later, in retirement, he could see that there was more that should be told in detail about 5 RAR operations in the western mountains of Phuoc Tuy Province during late 1966.

Bob suggested that such details would best be revealed by a selection of willing contributors from among 5 RAR's participants, together with a few others; some who had been providers of close combat support and yet others who, while not directly involved, could provide expert overview material. Discussions inevitably questioned whether such a book was needed, what its purpose might be, who could best contribute to it and so on. Among many wise voices, one opined, 'Who would write about these finer details if we don't? It is *our* history!' And so, the die was cast. It is notable that the first national servicemen to be committed to combat in Vietnam made up half of the battalion's strength, so it was important that they should be represented among the contributors.

A collegial approach to solving operational problems pervaded the original 5 RAR. These traits again came into play 50 years later during the gestation of this book. The inward flow of discussion and contributions propounded the idea that the book should also give an account of the battalion's preparations for deployment to Vietnam and how it settled into its initial operations in the vanguard of 1 ATF, before highlighting its pathfinding incursions into the Nui Thi Vai hills.

This book's contributors share the prized common thread of having been full-time soldiers at some time in their lives and are at ease about being veterans of Australia's most unpopular war, Vietnam. In canvassing potential contributors for each chapter, a formidable hurdle arose. Survivors of the battalion's first tour in Vietnam who might readily contribute were declining in number; a sobering reality which lent a touch of urgency to the project.

Accordingly, nearly every part of this book has been written by men ranging in age from their early 70s to their late 80s. They have all led happy and productive postwar lives and the keenness of their memories, undimmed by intervening years, is remarkable. Unsurprisingly, each of them has completed his task with a blend of discernment and sagacity acquired through 50 years of reflection. Their reflections, well-tempered by the time-bestowed benefits of detachment and perspective, are valuable insights. Their writings help to flesh out the necessarily broader approach of the official history which records that war.

The comprehensive article republished in Appendix C was written by the battalion's commanding officer, John Warr, in 1967, soon after the return of 5 RAR to Australia. John passed away in 1999. His account shows how cordon and search operations were rapidly developed in Vietnam by 5 RAR. It highlighted and temporarily filled a vacuum in Australian Army doctrine on tactics and techniques that needed to be employed in a much more virulent type of warfare than that experienced in the previous two decades. Since the end of the Korean War in 1953, the army's focus had been the low-level counterterrorist operations of the Malayan Emergency and the Indonesian Confrontation of Malaysia. Thus, 1 ATF was the first Australian Army formation since the Second World War committed to operations in circumstances where it was largely free of allied tactical dictates. It fell to John Warr, as the commander of the first battalion to be inserted into 1 ATF's assigned area of operations, to interpret, adapt and invent the essence of his battalion's modus operandi. Contributors to Chapter 16 have provided a memoir that gives readers a revealing look at a well-respected Australian infantry battalion commanding officer.

PREFACE

Apart from its more prosaic purposes, a book of this kind is both a nod of acknowledgement to old mates and, especially, a respectful salute to those who left our sight on the battlefield over 50 years ago. It is to them that this book is dedicated. In crafting a tribute, we could not render a better summation than that given by the great Athenian warrior-statesman, Pericles. Around 430 BC he delivered a lengthy tribute to his dead soldiers. It included a peroration of a mere 50 words in which he neatly compressed the deepest of soldierly reflections. His few, plain words require no elaboration:

> They gave their bodies for the common good and received, each for his own memory, praise that will never die; and with it, the grandest of all sepulchres – not that in which their mortal bones are laid, but a home in the minds of men where their glory remains fresh.[1]

The writings of this book's contributors may well be their last hurrah in terms of adding detail to the proud history of 5th Battalion, the Royal Australian Regiment, widely known as the Tiger Battalion. Their hearty and indomitable camaraderie will be apparent to the reader. Their more elusive literary motives are suggested by lines adapted from Banjo Paterson's *The Daylight is Dying*:

> Now, we still half hearing
> An old-time refrain,
> With memory clearing
> To hear it again,
> Bring tales, roughly wrought of
> Young men and their ways,
> That call back much thought of
> Our soldiering days,
> And, blending with each
> In the mem'ries that throng,
> There haply shall reach
> You a clear-ringing song.

---

1   Thucydides, *The Peloponnesian War*, II, 43.

INTRODUCTION: THE PURPOSE OF THIS BOOK

Robert O'Neill

This book focuses on a series of operations carried out by the 5th Battalion, the Royal Australian Regiment (5 RAR), during the Vietnam War in 1966. They were challenging and keenly fought by both sides. They were also productive because we developed careful new methods – hence the title of this book, *Vietnam Vanguard*. These operations had the strategic purpose of making a major road and its surrounding countryside secure for allied troop and supply movements. The Viet Cong had exerted control over this region, western Phuoc Tuy Province, for many years.

The country north of the road was mountainous, and several villages were situated along the road itself. It was a real test of our abilities to drive the Viet Cong off the mountains while avoiding damage to the villages and loss of life to the local people. In April and May 1966, some 800 young Australians arrived in South Vietnam for a year of war service. I was one of them, a captain, then second in command of B Company of 5 RAR. Half of the battalion were national servicemen, conscripted by the government. The other half was made up of regulars who, for the most part, were pleased to be doing the job that they had enlisted for – sustaining the defence of our nation. I think it is fair to say that we all felt that Australia was in greater peril than it actually was at that time. We certainly applied our best efforts, and we all put our lives on the line.

We were a year or two in advance of the wave of dissent which drove Australian public opinion on the war. All members of 5 RAR thought that we had an important job to do, and we pressed ahead with it. We were not riven by internal debates over the morality of the whole undertaking. Those debates impacted on us all once we returned to Australia, but more in the context of our civil social life than our work in the army or our comradeship with former members of our battalion once they had been discharged. Ex-members of 5 RAR have remained reasonably united in believing that what we did in Vietnam was honourable. Had the wider war gone successfully for the South Vietnamese Government and the United States, good would have come out of our actions in 1966–67. But that was not the case, and we have all had to struggle with the fact that we fought in a war which was ultimately very unpopular and largely disowned by the Australian people, and many of our national governments since the early 1970s.

Because of the war's unpopularity, public interest in what Australian servicemen and servicewomen did in Vietnam has been low, and focused largely on a few short, spectacular events such as the battles of Long Tan, Binh Ba and Fire Support Bases Balmoral and Coral. While these were well-fought, successful actions by Australian soldiers, they were of brief duration and did not typify the careful, continuing tussle which went on throughout Phuoc Tuy Province, the Australian area of responsibility, for over five years. This contest, for control of territory and for Vietnamese public support, was conducted by both sides, on a continuous basis. This book attempts to shed light on an Australian battalion's engagement in that kind of war, over a period of several months, to give Australian readers who were not directly involved in the war a fuller understanding of what we did, why we did it and what we felt about all that we had to endure.

That this book is being published in 2020, 54 years after the events it describes, is due largely to the recent occurrence of the 50th anniversaries of these events. From mid-2016 onwards I found myself receiving many letters, personal accounts and diary entries from former 5 RAR members, asking me to check them for accuracy. This awoke in me a feeling of regret that we did not already have all this material available in some enduring and publicly accessible form. I had written a book on the battalion's year in Vietnam, 1966–67, *Vietnam Task*, while out on operations or back at our Nui Dat base while we were in Vietnam. However, it was relatively brief, covering our year in 256 pages; it was written over 50 years ago and it was the work of a single author (assisted by the editorial skills of his wife). The interesting nature of the evidence from the 1960s that I was reading 50 years later made me think that we ought to publish it soon. There was clearly a strong desire on the parts of surviving ex-5 RAR members to have their memories restocked with fuller, up-to-date descriptions of what we had been doing for that year in Vietnam.

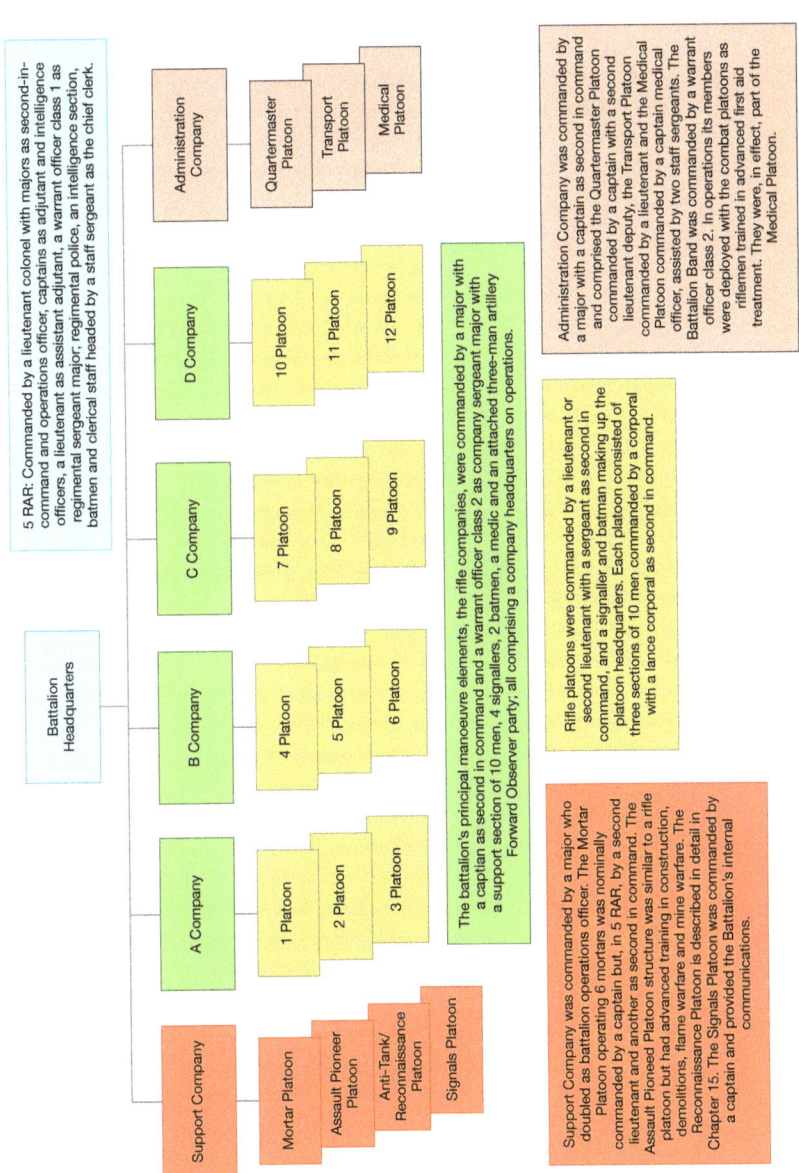

Figure 1: 5 RAR in Vietnam, 1966.
Source: Diagram designed and produced by Ron Boxall.

A second factor stimulated me further in this direction: the accuracy and scope of the memories of many of those who had been showing me material were quite remarkable. I soon came to believe that out of the surviving group of 5 RAR veterans, we could put together an interesting book, with chapters written by a team of some 30 authors. I wanted this team to include people who had held ranks from private to major, and others who, while not being members of the battalion, played vital roles in our operations, especially the gunners who supported us in heavy actions, and the helicopter pilots who had to take great risks in evacuating our wounded and supplying us in action. I was fortunate in being able to enlist the cooperation of Captain (later Brigadier) Ron Boxall as co-editor. He has been very busy helping with selection of authors, decisions on what to include in the book and editing the contributions that the individual authors delivered to us. It has been a great pleasure for me to have worked again with Ron. We found that we were 'on net' over many issues of historical fact and editorial policy that could have caused problems in the production of the book.

The book has been structured and written with three sets of readers in mind: the Australian public, readers elsewhere and the surviving members of the battalion's first tour of duty in Vietnam. We have been fortunate in being able to select a fine team of contributors from the ranks of surviving members of 5 RAR, and of other units who worked directly with us during 1966–67. Having edited several other multi-authored books during my professional life, I feel particularly blessed by this team who have been willing to accept guidance from Ron, myself and other editorial assistants who have worked on the text with us.

I need to pay a special tribute to Major (later Colonel) Max Carroll, our operations officer for the first six months in Phuoc Tuy, and then a rifle company commander for the remaining six months. He undertook to write three central chapters on how our operations were conducted in the period May to October 1966, and he achieved this goal splendidly. There was nothing wrong with his memory at the age of 87, or with his judgement in selecting events to write on!

The first issue that we have focused on is the nature of the challenge that we faced in Vietnam. Was it primarily a military challenge or was it more of a social and political one? How did we prepare ourselves to face both over the course of the year ahead of us? Next we consider why we were sent to Phuoc Tuy Province rather than other parts of Vietnam.

Who made the choice and for what reasons? How far was it an American decision and how far was it driven by Australian preferences? It is a large and complex topic, deserving a chapter on its own and calling for an accomplished historian to tackle. From Australia's perspective, the chief person involved in the selection of Phuoc Tuy as our area of responsibility was General Sir John Wilton. His distinguished biographer, Professor (Colonel) David Horner, was the obvious person to invite to write such a chapter: Chapter 2.

So that readers could have a more detailed picture of what the Viet Cong had been doing in Phuoc Tuy before we arrived, we invited former director of military intelligence Brigadier Ernest Chamberlain to contribute Appendix D. Ernie not only spent many years focusing on the Viet Cong and North Vietnamese from an intelligence perspective, but also is a Vietnamese linguist and historian, and has translated and published several histories originally produced by the Viet Cong regiments and battalions that we faced when on operations.

Chapters 3 to 17, except Chapters 12 and 14, are all written by former 5 RAR members. Chapter 12 is the work of our supporting gunners of 103 Field Battery, Royal Australian Artillery, led by Captain George Bindley. Captain Jim Campbell, Second Lieutenant Bob Askew and Second Lieutenant Bill Davies of 161 (Independent) Reconnaissance Flight helped Captain Bob Supple with Chapter 14, on the challenges of flying helicopters into enemy fire in all types of terrain.

One point on which we all agree is that we were very lucky to have faced the challenges of being at war for a year under the outstanding leadership of John Warr. It has not been difficult to find several authors capable of throwing light on why he was such a good commanding officer. I am particularly grateful also to members of the Warr family, John's widow Shirley, and their three children Anne, Mark and Peter, for their contributions to the words and the thoughts behind Chapter 16. John's thoughts on making counter-insurgency more effective, written soon after our return to Australia in 1967, are set out in Appendix A, which is a republication of an article he contributed to the *Australian Army Journal*, No. 222, November 1967.

As I try to make clear in Chapters 5 and 17, the war in Vietnam was partly an intellectual struggle. In some ways it was a continuation of the frequently occurring nationalist, anti-colonialist conflicts of the mid-

20th century. Yet in one key aspect it was different: it was conducted by the insurgent side with public opinion on the opposing, potentially dominant, side as their main target. General Vo Nguyen Giap, the former North Vietnamese commander, had learned during the early 1950s to attack the resolve of the French Government by shaping French public opinion to believe that their army was suffering heavy losses without making appropriately compensating gains.

By 1967–68, when the North Vietnamese and National Liberation Front leaders were planning their decisive Tet Offensive of 1968, Giap had lost much of his power, being displaced by Communist Party Secretary-General Le Duan and his assistant Le Duc Tho. They decided to hit hard, regardless of the damage this policy would do to the North Vietnamese economy and the casualties that their forces would suffer. Giap, Ho Chi Minh and several other leaders did not want to intensify the war to this extent. They could see that much of their work of the 1950s and '60s would be placed at risk by the weight of American counter-attacks in response to a major Viet Cong and North Vietnamese offensive. The spectacle of so much chaos in South Vietnam, and the loss of control by the South Vietnamese Government and American forces were a great stimulus to the anti-war movement throughout Western countries. Political turmoil resulted, forcing US and allied governments to review their policies in Vietnam and open negotiations, which led to allied, including Australian, withdrawal in the early 1970s.

Of course, this was not all obvious in 1966–67, but John Warr could see that we were in an unusual kind of conflict, and that we needed to keep two things in mind. First, heavy casualties on our side would be very counter-productive because they would turn Australian public sentiment more firmly against the war. Second, we needed to foster support among the Vietnamese people in our area of operations if we were to have any prospect of enduring success. He gave me his thoughts, both on the details of current operations and on the larger strategic issues, when we talked together every day during the nine months for which I was his intelligence officer. As a battalion commander, he had limited freedom in which to plan his operations, but he was careful throughout our time in Vietnam to pay due regard to the needs of the local people, and to engage the Viet Cong in such a way that we had a good chance of success without losing Australian soldiers. Soon every officer on Battalion Headquarters and all his company commanders came to know and understand the way that John Warr thought, and the finely balanced path that he trod.

His personality, his mind and his evident concern for the welfare of his soldiers played a great role in keeping the battalion together and in good spirits for this very testing year.

A final author that I will mention is our regimental medical officer, Captain Tony White. We are fortunate to have a chapter in which he describes the tough challenges he repeatedly had to face when we were operating in the Nui Dinh hills and along Route 15. These few months were typical of Tony's entire year. Whenever casualties occurred, Tony would be involved in treating them. Usually he was not far from the spot where the injuries were suffered, but sometimes they occurred simultaneously in multiple places. Then the company medics would come into their own, but usually with guidance from Tony by radio. Tony's courage must be mentioned. Time after time he had to expose himself to danger, from snipers, from Viet Cong soldiers manning prepared defences, and from concealed mines and booby traps. I have several memories of him moving through minefields to reach badly wounded soldiers before they bled to death. We were all so glad to have him as our doctor, and that he has recorded his experiences at war in his 2011 book *Starlight: An Australian Army Doctor in Vietnam*.

This book focuses on our operations in western Phuoc Tuy, conducted between August and November 1966. This was a crucial period for 5 RAR, as we sought to put into practice what we had learned in our training in Australia. These lessons were polished up by application in our opening few months of operations, described by Max Carroll and Peter Isaacs in Chapter 4. In September we began a series of operations with an important strategic purpose: to regain the use of Route 15 and enable incoming American formations to move large numbers of men and quantities of materiel through to their intended bases in the Bien Hoa area. For the following three months we operated in mountainous terrain which had been used by the Viet Cong for several years. It was a period in which many members of 5 RAR distinguished themselves both in battle and in relating to the local Vietnamese people.

In inviting authors to contribute to the volume, we have tried to make a balance between those who were in command of the major aspects of our operations and those who were at the sharp end, carrying out their orders. We have 30 authors, ranging in rank from private to brigadier, to give us their differing perspectives on what we were doing. We are particularly glad to have among them nine officers and one non-commissioned officer from other units who were supporting 5 RAR operations, particularly the gunners and helicopter pilots. We also welcome the contributions of key persons on Battalion Headquarters, especially our operations officer, Max Carroll, and our adjutant, Captain Peter Isaacs. Captain Ron Bade, second in command of A Company, also contributed a half-chapter. I have already referred to Captain Tony White's contribution. Parts of the book have been written by my co-editor Ron Boxall and myself. We are particularly grateful for the foreword to Major General Steve Gower, former director general of the Australian War Memorial, and in 1966 a captain, forward observation officer with 101 Field Battery, Royal Australian Artillery, who took part in several 5 RAR operations.

The 5 RAR Association warmly embraced the proposal to publish this book, and I am grateful to the Executive Committee and members of the association for their support and cooperation, particularly for the help of the president, Colonel Roger Wainwright, and also of the president of the Royal Australian Regiment Association, Mick von Berg. Both of them were distinguished platoon commanders in 1966–67.

I hope that the readers of this book will come to have a fuller understanding of what we were doing in Vietnam in 1966–67. We have the several large volumes of the official history of Australia's part in the Vietnam War for comprehensive reference, but, as with our involvement in the two world wars, it is now time for the publication of shorter books on how individual battalions fought and what their members thought about their part in the Vietnam War. The epithet 'Lest we forget' applies not only to our memories of our fallen comrades but also to our memories of events as they occurred in Vietnam and the reasons for their being undertaken.

1

THE CHALLENGE

Robert O'Neill

What were the challenges we would be facing in Vietnam and how should we meet them? These were the dominant thoughts in the minds of most members of the 5th Battalion, the Royal Australian Regiment (5 RAR), in early 1966. The battalion was raised for service in Vietnam on 1 March 1965 at Holsworthy, south of Sydney. Nothing firm was said publicly about its mission until January 1966, and its destination was not revealed until March 1966. However, word had been spreading since August 1965, from discreet but reliable sources within the army, that we were destined for Vietnam. The government wanted to send a two-battalion task force to support the Americans. We all knew from one source or another that we had to be ready for operational service by early 1966. New members of the battalion came in through 1965, and by the beginning of 1966, we were clearly entering the final phases of training. We expected to be in Vietnam in May.

What were we heading for? How did we feel about it? Nobody in 5 RAR believed that this commitment was going to be a relatively short one—all over in two or three years—for Australia. We were about to enter a long struggle between communist and anti-communist forces in Vietnam, a conflict which had flowed naturally out of the defeat of the French in Indo-China in 1954. This struggle had been going on for a long time before 1954, when the Viet Minh inflicted their decisive defeat on the French at Dien Bien Phu. Nationalists, including communists, had been in action against the French since the 1920s and '30s. The outside world looked on but then became embroiled in the Second World War.

For a brief time at the end of this war, some younger Americans in the US State Department looked favourably on the Viet Minh, the nationalist–communist force which intended to step in to govern their own country once the Japanese had left. Things did not work out that way. The great powers became caught up in the Cold War, in which it was natural for the Americans to want to resist all communist encroachments around the world, despite the differing causes and consequences of the many regional security problems that the United States faced. By 1964 the balance of power in East and South-East Asia looked to some, particularly the governing parties in Washington and Canberra, to be sliding into a crisis. The danger was summed up by the 'Domino Theory'. If Vietnam went communist, Laos and Cambodia would follow. The threats to the anti-communist government in Thailand would then intensify and bifurcate, flowing on to Malaya, Singapore and Indonesia. Then communists would be on Australia's doorstep.

As history has shown, there were many weaknesses in this theory but that was the prevailing wisdom in 1964–65. Official adherence to it as a basis for policy had been strengthened by the forthright way in which the Americans had entered the war in Vietnam with their own forces. We, as soldiers, were aware that our government was strongly committed to this point of view, so we took our final phase of preparation for combat very seriously. From our perspective, the Vietnam War was one of counter-insurgency. Many of the senior members of the battalion, both by rank and by length of service, had taken part in controlling the Malayan Emergency and in resisting Indonesian Confrontation of Malaysia in Borneo. They knew that the essence of success in counter-insurgency was to win the political and social support of the civilian population, both in the major cities and in the rural areas. There was a key military dimension to the war, but without the support of the local people, any success in the military dimension would not translate into a lasting victory. In Malaya, our major allies, the British, understood this well and had been successful. In Vietnam, we had to hope that our major allies there also understood this basic truth of counter-insurgency. We were optimistic that the Americans would apply a 'hearts and minds' approach – it was their term after all – and that success would follow. It might take a long time but it would come – or so we thought in early 1966.

Against this backdrop of strategic purpose the battalion began a demanding program of acquiring skills in training and then applying them in tactical exercises in distant training areas. In the four months before we departed for Vietnam, we spent around seven weeks in testing exercises, including two or three weeks at the army's rigorous Jungle Training Centre at Canungra, Queensland. We also spent a fortnight in the Gospers Mountain training area, in rugged sandstone country, essentially a continuation of the Blue Mountains. However, the trees were sparse and the weather turned cold. We were soon carrying out what we nicknamed 'jungle exercises in the snow'. By late April we were all slimmed down, physically fit and keen to do our job. 5 RAR was made up of both regular (volunteer) soldiers and national servicemen, in roughly equal proportions. The national servicemen were in the army for two years, which allowed for a year's training and then another year's active service. Although the average age of the national servicemen in the battalion was around 21 – a year or more older that many of our regular infantrymen – the two types of soldier melded very smoothly. The national servicemen performed as well as the regulars of similar experience. There were some national servicemen who would rather not have been in the army at that time of their lives, and they made their thoughts known occasionally. But they all accepted military service as a legitimate obligation, and we were spared most of the problems which ate at the structure of authority in the US Army during the Vietnam War.

An infantry battalion is not simply a military organisation. It is also a linkage of many families. Soldiers, when they are abroad on active service, think of their families and loved ones a lot. It therefore matters to the harmony and confidence of the battalion abroad that their family members at home should be in touch with each other and offer support when it was needed. Thus, in the first few months of 1966, some of us devoted a significant part of our off-duty time to getting to know each other's families, particularly the wives, girlfriends and children of the people that we would be working most closely with. It made a great difference, when we had been on operations for a few months, to be able to circulate family news and photos to others with whom we were working. And when the sad news of a soldier's death or severe wounding came through to his family in Australia, there were other friends ready at hand to give practical help and emotional support to those who were grieving.

As our preparation time moved on, there were indications that we might not have the full and active support of the Australian people in this war. The principal issue which brought dissent to the surface was conscription for overseas service – hardly surprising given the intense political confrontations which had taken place on this issue during the two world wars. By the middle of 1965 an organisation of dissenting mothers had been founded called 'Save our Sons'. By the time of our departure for Vietnam they were still a relatively small force in Australian politics, but we were aware of their protest meetings and occasional picketing of barracks where national servicemen were being trained. While Australia was still two or three years away from the massive moratorium assemblies and marches that took place in the major cities, there was something here to keep a weather eye upon. In 1966, through personal contacts, I became more aware of dissent in our universities. But at that point, Australian public opinion overall was strongly supportive of Australia's commitment in Vietnam, and the opposition that was expressed did not weigh on our morale or undercut our belief that we were doing the right thing in Vietnam. Little did I know that I would be dealing with this opposition for many years to come once I had entered into the academic world professionally.

Another index of public attitudes to Australian participation in the Vietnam War was the nature of the questions that journalists put when visiting our barracks on the outskirts of Sydney, or when accompanying us on exercises. Overall, the media were supportive of the government's policy to accept commitment with the United States, but some of our leading writers such as Denis Warner could see problems ahead and wanted to test our own thinking on what we expected from the Americans, given their own unfamiliarity with this kind of conflict. Did we believe that American prospects of success were as great as those of the British in the 1950s in Malaya? Such questions gave us pause for thought.

As the opening months of 1966 passed by, we all became sharply focused on the nature of the dangers and difficulties we would soon be facing on the ground in Vietnam. Our commanding officer (CO), Lieutenant Colonel John Warr, saw the conflict in historical depth and wanted the battalion to have some understanding of the social and political complexities of what we were embarking upon, as well as the military problems that we would face. I, by then a captain and second in command of B Company, had recently returned from studying international relations at Oxford, so the CO detailed me to give a series of lectures to the companies on the course and nature of the conflict since 1945. We were also receiving current intelligence information via army channels, and some of this was passed on to us directly by the battalion intelligence officer, Captain Don Willcox.

By April 1966 we knew exactly where we would be stationed in Vietnam – in the central part of Phuoc Tuy Province, around the hill Nui Dat. This was an area which included only a few hamlets, but which had several large villages around the edge, and included the province capital of Ba Ria, whose population exceeded 10,000. Ba Ria was some 60 kilometres south-east of Saigon and 25 kilometres north of the port of Vung Tau, which was about to become our logistical support area. The population of the province plus Vung Tau was approximately 150,000 people, and they were occupying a key strategic area for whoever happened to be the governing power in Saigon. The National Liberation Front, or Viet Cong as we knew them, had strong base areas to the east and north-east of Saigon. Saigon itself had the Saigon River to connect it with the sea, but this route was vulnerable to intercepting attacks, leaving the main road from Saigon to Vung Tau, Route 15, as one of the principal logistical links between the capital and the ships of distant allies. Making Route 15 secure for the passage of reinforcing American soldiers and their supplies was the first major task of the Australian battalions coming into the area around Nui Dat.

The economy of Phuoc Tuy was made up of peasant agriculture, market gardening, rubber plantations, timber-getting, charcoal production and fishing. Phuoc Tuy fed some of its produce into the markets of Saigon and Vung Tau. There was a poor road network to carry all the produce and people necessary to move goods to market. Route 15 to Saigon had a bitumen surface with two traffic lanes, but for the most part when we arrived, the other roads were earth-surfaced and usually single lane, augmented by passing places. Because of the climate, there were many streams and rivers dissecting the road network, therefore there were many small bridges which were relatively easy for the Viet Cong to cut and inflict additional costs on the people whose livelihoods were thereby placed at risk. Some of the roads were well suited to the placing of temporary Viet Cong tax-gathering points. The Viet Cong also exercised direct control in some of the villages by demanding a substantial portion of their agricultural production or some of their young men, to serve as conscript soldiers or porters for their comprehensive supply system.

Before we could tackle the long-term problem of gaining support for the Saigon government from the people of Phuoc Tuy, we needed to establish security for our bases and ourselves against the military threat posed by the Viet Cong. We were therefore particularly keen in early 1966 to be briefed on our direct opposition and what they had been doing in recent times. We learned that we, a two-battalion task force, would be opposed by a division consisting of two regiments of what we termed 'Main Force' Viet Cong. These regiments, 274 and 275, had three battalions each and had been built up over the past two years from smaller Viet Cong units – platoons and companies of village-based guerrillas – which had then expanded into full-sized regiments of 2,000 men or more, who served on a full-time basis. A key enabling factor in this growth of Main Force regiments was the increasing availability of equipment from the North, especially machine guns, mortars, artillery and radios. It had taken some time for the two major supply routes from North Vietnam, the Ho Chi Minh Trail and the 'sea channel' via the coast of Phuoc Tuy, to become effective. But by 1966 the military strength of the Viet Cong in the south-eastern sector of South Vietnam had to be taken seriously by an intervening force of two Australian infantry battalions plus supporting arms (See Figure A.2 in Appendix D).

The Viet Cong combined their two regiments to form the Fifth Infantry Division of around 4,500 men in 1965, so that by the time of our arrival in Phuoc Tuy they could pack a powerful punch, and we needed to take that into account, particularly in the early months of our operations in Phuoc Tuy. We knew that it would take time to build secure fixed defences around Nui Dat, and until we had, we would be vulnerable to testing attacks. If our enemy was willing to take a major risk with his own forces in an all-out battle with a couple of thousand of his own men against a few hundred of ours, we could have been in a serious predicament. What seemed more likely was that the Viet Cong would seek to attack one of our companies when it was on patrol outside of our base area, as happened to D Company of 6 RAR at Long Tan in August 1966.

1. THE CHALLENGE

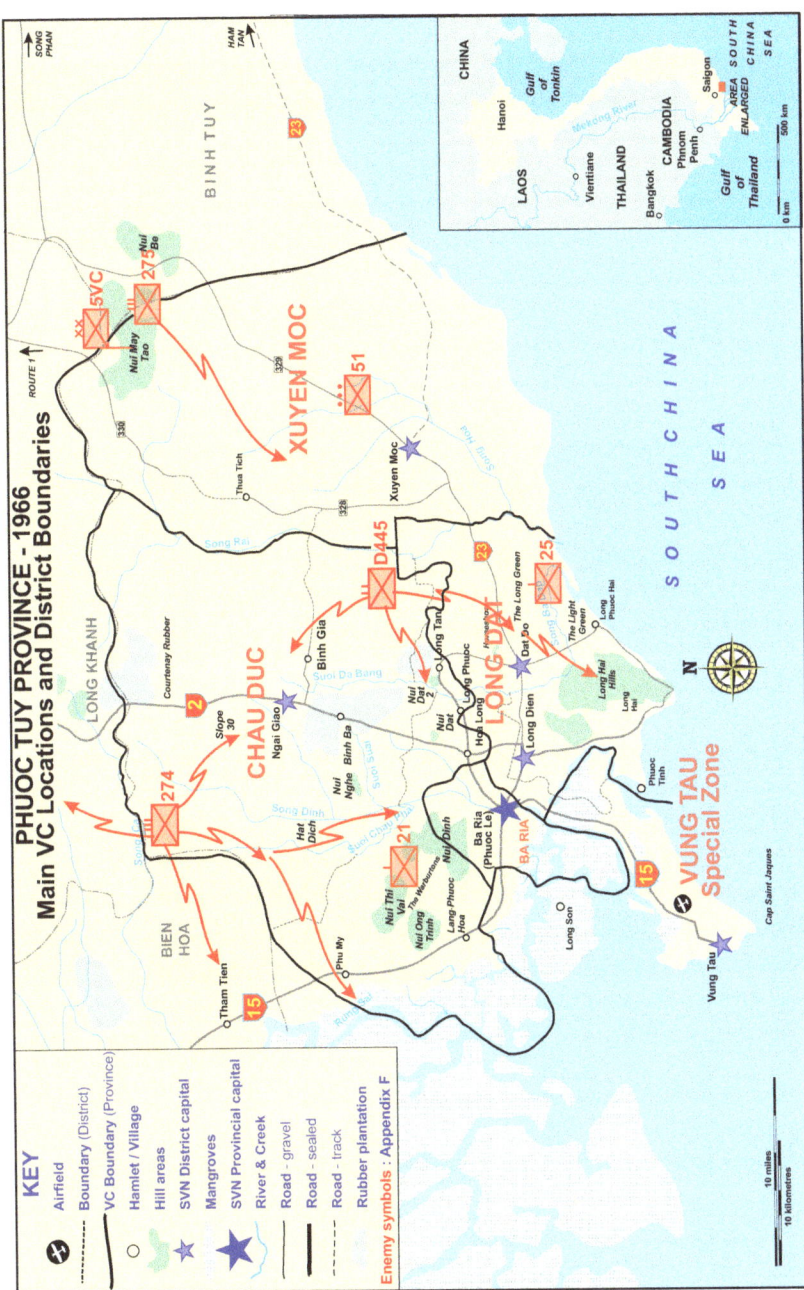

Map 2: Phuoc Tuy Province 1966: Main Viet Cong locations and district boundaries.

Source: Drawn and produced by Ron Boxall from data provided by Ernest Chamberlain.

The Viet Cong relied on three major base areas in Phuoc Tuy. The largest of these was the May Tao Secret Zone, in north-eastern Phuoc Tuy. It was spread around Nui May Tao (*nui* means hill or mountain), and it could normally support a Main Force regiment. By 1966 the base could take the whole Viet Cong Fifth Infantry Division when there was need to concentrate it. Viet Cong jungle bases were not like those of their opponents. They were much less visible from the air, and their sheds were built of materials ready to hand in the jungle. The second Viet Cong base, in north-west Phuoc Tuy, was the Hat Dich area, built near a small village of that name. The third was in the Long Hai hills in south-eastern Phuoc Tuy, extending northwards into the Minh Dam area. This base was more of a resting and replenishing point for the Viet Cong battalions than a major supply source. However, as it was close to the coast, some supplies could be brought in by sea. The other two bases were supplied from the north by the Ho Chi Minh Trail directly from North Vietnam, or by the 'sea trail' direct from North Vietnam or from the more northerly coastal areas of South Vietnam, which were themselves supplied by the Ho Chi Minh Trail.

Although the Main Force Viet Cong forces were reasonably well equipped for fighting under the protection of jungle-clad mountains and hills, they were not well suited for fighting in the more open areas. Here they had to divide into small groups which lacked the firepower and support that we could rely on in the event of a major engagement. Where they were strongest was in the jungles to the east and north-east of Nui Dat, closer to the Nui May Tao base area. However, as the Battle of Long Tan was to show, even in that relatively favourable situation, 275 Regiment suffered heavy casualties while trying to overwhelm one company of 6 RAR. The weight of supporting artillery, airpower and armoured personnel carriers from other elements of the Task Force was telling.

We knew from the operations conducted by the US 173 Airborne Brigade (including 1 RAR) earlier in 1966 that the Main Force Viet Cong soldiers were brave and able fighters. Their marksmanship with rifles and machine guns was good, and they could usually rely on mortar support. They thickened their defences by copious use of minefields and booby traps, often using ammunition they had obtained from South Vietnamese sources. They were also supported effectively by their own locally recruited and supplied platoons and companies. Several of these local companies had been combined to form D445 Provincial Mobile Battalion, a force of some 400–450 men, whom we constantly had to take into account

1. THE CHALLENGE

in our operational planning. D445 Battalion published its own history, *The Heroic 445 Battalion: Its History and Tradition,* in 2004, and it has been translated and republished by Brigadier Ernie Chamberlain, a senior Australian intelligence officer, and one of the contributors to this volume. This history of D445 Battalion is one of the major sources for Brigadier Chamberlain's contribution to this volume (Appendix D).

The Viet Cong could also draw on the people of the areas under their control (fully or in part), for recruits, supplies, porters and medical assistance. The contest for the hearts and minds of the people of Phuoc Tuy had been in progress for several years before our arrival. Initially the Viet Cong were able to work out informal 'coexistence' arrangements with several of the smaller, local subunits (companies or platoons) of the Army of the Republic of Vietnam (ARVN) that were stationed nearby. The province remained nominally under the control of the Saigon government, but we knew that its writ did not run far from the province capital, Ba Ria, or the several district administrative centres of Phuoc Tuy. ARVN forces and vehicles could move around by day, although they were occasionally attacked or ambushed. The Viet Cong had a fairly free rein at night but kept out of sight of the ARVN forces by day. Provincial administration was controlled largely by the ARVN, which provided the province chief and his staff, and the district chiefs and their small headquarters.

Our main challenge, therefore, was to turn this situation around, so that the Viet Cong no longer had the necessary support from the civil population of the province to maintain the flow of recruits that they needed or to weaken the administrative grip of the South Vietnamese Government and drive out its administrators, military and police personnel. Before we could begin work on achieving this change, we had to ensure our own security in a military sense. We were vulnerable to attacks, raids and ambushes which could result in significant Australian casualties, and therefore undermine the Australian Government's ability to stay the course.

Obviously the quality and capacities of the South Vietnamese civil authorities and armed forces would have a substantial influence on our prospects for success. We knew very little about these issues until we had been active in Phuoc Tuy for several months. What we did hear, from our friends in 1 RAR and from others who had been members of the Australian Army Training Team Vietnam during the past year, was disturbing. Corruption in the local administration was rife, justice

17

was often dispensed on a partial basis to favour those in authority, and it was very much a 'top-down' system of rule. The decrees came from on high, but not a lot of notice was taken of the complaints and wishes of Vietnamese civilians, particularly in the rural areas. Consequently, although there were some districts which were well governed, there were others in which the Viet Cong found it easy to gain a footing and to recruit supporters. As we had limited resources, one of our key tasks in the early stages of our deployment was to get to know the individual villages and districts, so that we could concentrate first on the ones in which we were likely to be more successful.

One of the most helpful groups of people in the province were the Catholic clergy in the villages. These were men who had to live without any guarantee of their own security. They were protected and helped by their parishioners because they exercised useful leadership, and often could get people to work effectively together when nobody else could. They were anti-communist but they could also be nationalist to the extent of wanting an open, honest, independent system of government which was rather different from what they had in 1966. Getting to know these men and establishing relationships, which were viable and useful in both directions, was one of the most interesting challenges of our time in Phuoc Tuy. It helped that they also spoke French or English.

The language barrier was another challenge we had to tackle. The process began with elementary classes in Vietnamese while we were still in Australia in early 1966. Of course in a brief instruction period of a few hours a week, not a lot could be accomplished. But for those who were minded to communicate directly with the local Vietnamese once we arrived in Phuoc Tuy, it made a difference to be able to offer basic greetings, using the masculine and feminine forms correctly as appropriate, and to be able to say please and thank you. Once that initial barrier had been surmounted, some of us were able to progress more deeply into the Vietnamese language. That step made a powerful psychological difference on both sides once we made progress in the language. It was very easy, in fact natural, for local people to be afraid of us and therefore unwilling to help in important ways, but breaking through the language barrier enabled them to see us in a very different light and our relations became much more productive for both sides.

1. THE CHALLENGE

When we set off for Vietnam in April and May 1966, some went via the 'grey funnel line' – that is, the former aircraft carrier HMAS *Sydney* – and others went via Qantas jet. By that stage, the challenge was looming, large and threatening, for most of us and our families, our nearest and dearest. We had those final intense hugs that departing soldiers and their families have been exchanging for hundreds of years. Then, alone with our thoughts, we began coming to terms with the fact that a year is a long time in warfare, and who knew what our fortunes, both individually and collectively as a battalion, would be? We had a certain amount of confidence as a result of our training and our faith in each other's natures and capacities. But there was no knowing who might be the target of a well-aimed enemy shot or who would be blown up by a mine whose activating trigger we had failed to see. And then there were the other risks – not so obviously fatal – that came with service in South-East Asia, such as insect-borne diseases and poisoning by Agent Orange. We did not know about post-traumatic stress disorder in those days, but it came to affect some of us in later years.

Fortunately, by the time we had reached deeply into that imagined trail of the personal dangers and challenges we had to face, we had arrived in Vietnam. We were then diverted by the demands of having to cope with our settling into the most basic of accommodation, tents on a sandhill near Vung Tau. Here we came to know one of our principal supporting units in coming months, the US Army 68 Assault Helicopter Company, our helicopter transport. They gave us a particularly warm welcome, because, in the words of their liaison officer, Lieutenant Charles Brinnon, 'You are not here just as advisers. You are here to *do* something about the situation!' As we spent many hours over the following week climbing into and out of the ubiquitous Iroquois helicopters, better known as Hueys, we seemed to enter a new world. Our recent anxieties fell away as we focused on meeting our most direct challenges in the very near future. Operation Hardihood was about to begin!

2

WHY WAS 5 RAR STATIONED AT NUI DAT?

David Horner

Phuoc Tuy Province and Nui Dat are two names that resonate strongly with Australian Vietnam veterans. More Australian soldiers served in Phuoc Tuy than in any other part of Vietnam and, while operating in the province and sometimes in nearby provinces, they were based at Nui Dat in the centre of the province. Certainly, members of the Australian Army Training Team Vietnam (AATTV) served throughout South Vietnam, and the 1st Battalion, the Royal Australian Regiment (RAR), was based at Bien Hoa in the province of the same name in 1965–66. But from 1966 to their withdrawal at the end of 1971, 15 Australian infantry battalions, along with supporting arms and services, served in Phuoc Tuy. The Australian Logistic Support Group and the helicopters of No 9 Squadron RAAF (Royal Australian Air Force), based at nearby Vung Tau, were not located within the province, but elements were deployed to Nui Dat, and the helicopters operated throughout the province.

So why was Phuoc Tuy selected as the focus of Australian operations, why was the 1st Australian Task Force (1 ATF) based at Nui Dat, and who was responsible for locating it in the province? The answer to the last question is clear – it was the chief of the general staff (CGS), Lieutenant General Sir John Wilton. But what were the factors behind Wilton's decision? This chapter seeks to answer these questions. It also examines why Australia sent a two-battalion, rather than a more balanced three-battalion, task force to Vietnam in 1966.

General Wilton

Appointed CGS in January 1963 at the age of 52, Wilton had extensive command, operational and staff experience.[1] After graduating from the Royal Military College (RMC) in 1930, he served in the British artillery in India before joining the Indian Mountain Artillery in Burma. By May 1939 he was back in Australia, serving in the coast artillery until May 1940 when he joined the Australian Imperial Force. He was brigade major of the 7th Division Artillery in the Syrian campaign in 1941 and attended the Middle East Staff School. From August 1942 to August 1943 he was chief operations staff officer of the 3rd Division in the advance towards Salamaua in New Guinea. He then joined the Australian Military Mission in Washington DC, before returning to operations in May 1945 as a key member of General Sir Thomas Blamey's headquarters on Morotai and, for a while, in Manila.

After the war, Wilton moved to Army Headquarters (AHQ) Melbourne, and by 1947 was director of military operations and plans (DMO&P). In July 1950 he visited Malaya as part of a mission reporting on the British Commonwealth campaign against communist terrorists in that country. He attended the Imperial Defence College, London, in 1952 and then took command of the 28th Commonwealth Brigade in Korea. Part of the 1st Commonwealth Division, the brigade consisted of two Australian and two British battalions. It occupied a key defensive area, covering Seoul, along the battle-line that stretched across the Korean peninsula.

By November 1955 Wilton was brigadier, general staff at AHQ, concentrating on the defence of South-East Asia, including issues surrounding the Malayan Emergency, Vietnam and the South-East Asia Treaty Organization (SEATO). Promoted to major general in March 1957, he was commandant of the RMC until June 1960, when he became chief of the Military Planning Office in SEATO headquarters, Bangkok. There he dealt with the alliance's strategic problems in the region, especially the conflicts in Laos and Vietnam. From that position he was appointed CGS.

---

1   For Wilton's career, see David Horner, *Strategic command: General Sir John Wilton and Australia's Asian wars*, Oxford University Press, Melbourne, 2005.

Wilton was well suited for his task as the government's principal military adviser. Reserved, self-disciplined and tactful, he easily won the confidence of ministers. He had a vision for the services and he had clear and considered ideas about the importance of alliances in the defence of Australia. Above all, he was a man of strong character; he believed in what he was doing and could not be seduced by personal ambition. He seemed less suited for command in the field. Nonetheless, he had much command experience, having had continuous regimental postings for the first decade of his service, and he had performed well as a brigade commander in Korea. But he did not reveal an engaging personality when dealing with soldiers or more junior officers. Known as 'Smiling Jack' and later as 'Sir Jovial', he was renowned for his lack of small talk. Soldiers would follow him because they had confidence in his judgement and knew that he cared for their welfare, not because of his charisma.

Few heads of the army have faced such a range of challenges as Wilton did in his three-year tenure as CGS. A major concern was the deteriorating strategic situation in South-East Asia. Indonesia began its confrontation of the new state of Malaysia in 1963, and sent 'volunteers' to fight in Sabah, Sarawak and even mainland Malaysia. Australian troops were based in Malaysia and the government deployed army engineers to Sabah. The AATTV had been sent to Vietnam in 1962 and in 1964 the government approved the employment of team members as advisers in the field.

As the pressure for more deployments mounted, Wilton advised the government that the army was too small to meet the commitments. Eventually, in November 1964, the government announced a huge expansion of the army, to be achieved by the introduction of a selective national service scheme. The increased manpower was matched by the purchase of new weapons and equipment, and the construction of additional accommodation. Wilton changed the army from the Pentropic organisation, with five large battalions per division, and no brigade structure, to a 'Tropical' organisation, with a division consisting of nine smaller infantry battalions and intermediate task force headquarters. This, and the national service scheme, allowed the army to grow from four battalions in 1964 to nine in 1967. In March 1965, 3 RAR and a Special Air Service (SAS) squadron were sent to Borneo, and in June 1965 1 RAR arrived in South Vietnam.

Wilton did not shy away from these operational commitments. Indeed, he believed that, provided that the Australian Government was clear about its purpose, a combat commitment to Vietnam was necessary. But based on his past experience, he was determined to ensure that 1 RAR was not exposed to suffering unnecessary casualties.

1 RAR's role

To understand why 1 ATF was deployed to Phuoc Tuy in May/June 1966, it is necessary to understand how 1 RAR was employed in the previous year. When the Cabinet approved the deployment of 1 RAR in April 1965, Wilton advised Sir Edwin Hicks, Secretary of the Department of Defence, that as the Australian battalion would operate as part of a US force, it required a compatible role; in no circumstances could it be given 'responsibility for a separate area as it is not large enough nor is it organised to handle such a situation'.[2] On 20 April the Defence Committee discussed Wilton's concerns.[3] During the meeting Sir James Plimsoll, Secretary of External Affairs, questioned Wilton closely, and stated that:

> Australian troops should not be used on their own in exposed positions. If Australia's only battalion in Vietnam was completely lost, our presence there would be gone, quite apart from other considerations. The expression of this to the Americans would need to be handled carefully, and we must avoid any suggestion of mollycoddling our forces, but something could be said orally between the relevant Commanders.[4]

On the following weekend, Wilton reviewed the plans with Brigadier Ken Mackay, the DMO&P at AHQ. Mackay was later to play a major role in the decision to base 1 ATF in Phuoc Tuy Province. The 48-year-old Mackay was a highly qualified officer. After graduating from the RMC in 1938 he had served in both artillery and infantry appointments in the Second World War. He had valuable experience in joint staff positions.

---

2   Letter, Wilton to Hicks, 15 April 1965, CCOSC (Chairman of the Chiefs of Staff Committee) files, box 16, file 513.
3   Defence Committee Minute, 20 April 1965, CCOSC files, box 16, file 513. Chaired by the Defence Secretary, the Defence Committee included the Chairman of the Chiefs of Staff Committee (COSC), the service chiefs and the permanent heads of External Affairs, Treasury and the Prime Minister's Department.
4   Note for File re: Defence Committee minute 21/1965, M, 22 April 1965, NAA (National Archives of Australia): A1838, TS 696/8/4 pt 8.

Towards the end of the Second World War he served in the small secretariat responsible for providing up-to-date briefings to the chief of the imperial general staff, Field Marshal Brooke in London. He was joint secretary of the Joint Chiefs of Staff in Australia during the establishment of the British Commonwealth Occupation Force in Japan and served at Australia House in London during the 1956 Suez Crisis.

Wilton directed Mackay to begin planning to send a full battalion group, including a battery of artillery and a troop of engineers, to Vietnam. It was the first step in building the force beyond the initial battalion.[5] Although the government had decided to send a battalion it had still not formally committed it, and the army's planning was kept secret until the evening of 29 April 1965, when prime minister Robert Menzies announced in parliament that 1 RAR would be deployed to Vietnam.

Three days later, Mackay and a small planning team arrived in Saigon where General William Westmoreland, commander of US Military Assistance Command, Vietnam (US MACV), welcomed them. They learned that the Americans planned for 1 RAR to become the third battalion in the 173rd Airborne Brigade that was to defend the Bien Hoa airbase, near Saigon. They discussed 1 RAR's proposed roles and conducted a reconnaissance of Bien Hoa and Vung Tau, which would be the entry point for the battalion. At Wilton's direction, Mackay examined the US 173rd Brigade and satisfied himself that 1 RAR would be joining a first-rate organisation. By then the commander of the AATTV, Colonel David Jackson, had been appointed Commander, Australian Army Force Vietnam (AAFV), and together they agreed on a Military Working Arrangement with the Americans that Mackay signed on 5 May.[6]

Returning to Canberra, on 13 May Mackay accompanied Wilton to the Defence Committee, which endorsed his report, approved draft directives for the Commander AAFV and the battalion commander, and approved the command arrangement whereby Westmoreland, not the South Vietnamese, would exercise operational control over the Australians.[7] Wilton and Mackay also attended the meeting of the Foreign Affairs and Defence Committee of Cabinet on 18 May that approved the Defence

---

5 Letter, AM Morris (External Affairs representative on Joint Planning Committee) to Jockel, 27 April 1965, NAA: A1838, TS 696/8/4 pt 8.
6 Report, Mackay to CGS, 'Report by the Leader of Planning Team Visit to Saigon', 11 May 1965, NAA: A1945, 248/4/114.
7 Defence Committee Minute, 13 May 1965, AWM (Australian War Memorial) 121, 161/A/4.

Committee's report.[8] Mackay recalled that he and Wilton came under intense questioning about the security of 1 RAR's position at Bien Hoa. Menzies even asked about 'adequate fields of fire'.[9]

With 1 RAR preparing for operations at Bien Hoa, it was time for Wilton to check that all was in order there. He arrived in Saigon on 22 June determined to ensure there would be no problems integrating 1 RAR into an American brigade. He had clear views of his own on this issue, but before leaving Canberra, his deputy, Major General Frank Hassett, had reminded him of the pressures he (Hassett) had borne in Korea when commanding the lone Australian battalion there in 1951.[10] Wilton would have been less concerned if it had been an Australian brigade in a US division, but a battalion was a relatively small command and he did not want the brigade commander thinking he could 'treat an Australian battalion in the same way as he can an American battalion'. He told Westmoreland and the brigade commander that 'we wouldn't agree to it', and as tactfully as possible said he disapproved of the way some US brigade commanders had acted in Korea. This was, he recalled:

> a delicate situation; I received assurances all round that this wouldn't happen, but that the battalion commander would be brought in and consulted in planning arrangements for the employment of his battalion, they wouldn't just be committed at five minutes notice to a badly organised and planned operation. So with that sort of 'preparation', shall we say, things went off smoothly because they said: 'Look we'll just get the task agreed upon and let them do it in their own way'. I said: 'That's fine, you won't be disappointed'.[11]

Having resolved these command concerns, Wilton departed for Australia, leaving Colonel Jackson to ensure the directives concerning the security of the Australians were followed and 1 RAR's operations conformed to its agreed role.

---

8   Cabinet Minute, Decision No 975 (Foreign Affairs and Defence), 18 May 1965, NAA: A1945/43, 248/4/116.
9   Interview, K Mackay with author, 7 April 1986; letter, McMahon to Paltridge, 23 June 1965, NAA: A1945/39, 248/4/19.
10 Interview, FG Hassett with author, 14 March 2003.
11 Army Historical Programme, interview with Gen Sir John Wilton, 9, 13, 14 September 1976, p 12, AWM 107 (hereafter: Wilton interview).

Wilton had been back in Canberra less than two weeks before there was an apparent attempt to change 1 RAR's role. On 4 July Jackson informed him that Westmoreland planned to form a general reserve based on the 173rd Brigade that could be deployed anywhere in Vietnam and he recommended the inclusion of 1 RAR.[12] Wilton did not agree, explaining in a letter to the Minister for the Army, Jim Forbes, that 1 RAR's inclusion would involve it in 'a succession of hazardous operations which would inevitably result in heavy casualties'.[13] Jackson (now promoted to brigadier) replied that Westmoreland wanted to conduct offensive operations, particularly in the II Corps Tactical Zone, and although 1 RAR was located in the III Corps Tactical Zone, he thought it should be permitted to take part, as the proposed operations would allow the Australians to 'have the greatest impact' on the war. Wilton was unmoved; he considered that Jackson would not be able to watch over Australian national interests effectively and there was the possibility of higher casualties.[14]

The restrictions on the use of 1 RAR were still in force when Wilton, accompanied by Major General Tom Daly, General Officer Commanding Eastern Command, visited Saigon for two days at the beginning of September on the way to a British Army conference in London. On the morning of 2 September, he called on Westmoreland who recorded in his diary that Wilton was apologetic that certain constraints had been placed by his government on the deployment of his troops.

> I informed him that the last proposal that his forces could be used in operations contiguous to Bien Hoa was acceptable at this stage of the war. General Wilton suggested, and I heartily agreed, that we should try to solve these problems in military channels and try and keep them out of diplomatic channels, which serve only to complicate or confuse the situation.[15]

Next morning, Wilton signalled Hassett in Canberra that, after discussion with Westmoreland, he believed 1 RAR should be permitted to operate anywhere in the III Corps area. He directed Hassett to put this proposal through the Chairman of the Chiefs of Staff Committee (Air Chief Marshal Sir Frederick Scherger) to the Defence Minister, adding that

---

12 Signal, Jackson to Wilton, 4 July 1965, AWM 121, 161/A/4.
13 Letter, Wilton to Army Minister, 6 July 1965, AWM 121, 161/A/4, and NAA: A1945, 248/4/124.
14 Signal, Wilton to Jackson, 9 July 1965, AWM 121, 161/A/4.
15 Entry for 2 September 1965, Westmoreland Papers, History File No 2, US Center of Military History.

1 RAR should now 'have a more active role. It is the best battalion in the theatre and its morale will suffer if it is not used to best effect in the mobile offensive role'.[16] Securing the extension to 1 RAR's area of operations took longer than Wilton had hoped, mainly because the Defence Minister, Shane Paltridge, had fallen ill, and because of the need to get agreement from the Minister for External Affairs.[17] It was 1 October before Wilton signalled Jackson that 1 RAR was 'available for operations more distant from Bien Hoa'.[18]

The importance of this episode lies in what it reveals about the attitude of the Australian Government, and particularly of Wilton, who was determined to limit casualties and not expose Australian troops to capricious American operations. Wilton and the Australians had a different philosophy to the Americans, believing that the Americans favoured a direct approach, using plentiful firepower to kill as many enemy soldiers as possible. Such an approach might result occasionally in heavy allied casualties, and Australia could not afford to take the risk that its sole battalion might be the one that took the casualties. In any case, the Australians preferred a more methodical approach to counter-revolutionary warfare.

Considerations on expanding the Australian force

Wilton played the key role in planning to expand the force in Vietnam. Indeed, as soon as 1 RAR arrived in Vietnam, Wilton and his advisers began considering how the force could be built up to an independent task force, so the Australians could apply their own doctrine for counter-revolutionary warfare. At a meeting of the Chiefs of Staff Committee on 15 July, he argued that they should begin planning to build up the commitment to a task force of two infantry battalions with supporting elements, plus a detachment of RAAF Iroquois helicopters.

---

16   Signal, Wilton to Hassett, 3 September 1965, NAA: A1945/42, 248/4/128.
17   Signal, Mackay to Wilton, 13 September 1965, AWM 121, 161/A/5.
18   Ian McNeill, *To Long Tan: The Australian Army and the Vietnam War 1950–1966*, Allen & Unwin, Sydney, 1993, p 121.

Meanwhile, information arrived that the US Government might soon request Australia to increase its force contribution. Setting out how Australia might respond, Wilton explained to Scherger on 20 July:

> The war in Vietnam is essentially an infantry war and the requirement for additional forces is basically for more infantry battalions. Other supporting arms such as artillery, APCs and engineers are important but have a less vital part to play in the present situation.[19]

He continued that 3 RAR had just completed a 'strenuous two-year tour in Malaya and Borneo and is due for relief and return to Australia'. It was to be relieved by 4 RAR, which was about to deploy to Malaysia. On return from Malaysia, 320 members of 3 RAR were to transfer to the embryonic 7 RAR to help form the new battalion. The only available battalions were 2 RAR, 5 RAR and 6 RAR; each had a strength of about 550, but these included some 100 soldiers who were ineligible for service overseas because of under-age or medical classification reasons. The earliest these battalions would be ready for operations would be February 1966. If another infantry battalion were sent to Vietnam at short notice it would seriously disrupt and delay the national service program and should only be contemplated if it were 'a matter of dire operational necessity'. Wilton concluded:

> I believe that we should plan now to build up our existing force to a Task Force of two infantry battalions plus the required scale of combat and logistic support units, together with a detachment of army light aircraft and a detachment of RAAF Iroquois utility helicopters.[20]

Noting this advice, on 29 July the Defence Committee recommended increasing the force by an artillery battery and an engineer troop in the short term, with another infantry battalion to be made ready by February or March 1966.

With these plans in mind, in early August Brigadier Mackay visited Saigon where Lieutenant General John Throckmorton, acting commander US MACV, and Throckmorton's chief of staff, Brigadier General William DePuy, told him that president Johnston was requesting additional

---

19 Letter, Wilton to Scherger, 20 July 1965, and attached paper, 'An assessment of the Army's ability to expand its force in Vietnam', AWM 121, 161/A/4.
20 Ibid.

Australian forces, and asked what Australia had in mind.[21] Johnston had approved the deployment of a further 125,000 troops to Vietnam, and the Republic of Korea was expected to dispatch a division.[22] Anxious to reserve an area for an Australian task force, Mackay called on DePuy before he left to return home. As he recalled:

> I said, you know, old Bill, 'Just put a ring around Phuoc Tuy Province. If we're going to come in with a force, this is the place I believe we ought to come in to … Now flog off this other area, flog off this and that, do what you like, but don't let this one go.' He laughed and said: 'OK, we'll put a thumb mark on it for you'.[23]

This was just prudent planning. While Wilton wanted to expand the force to two battalions, he recognised such a force could not yet be sustained. But clearly the idea of a larger force was being discussed; for example, on 12 August Wilton advised the Defence Minister, Senator Shane Paltridge, that:

> if it became necessary to provide forces in the field in addition to the proposed task force of 3,500 plus existing commitments in Malaysia and New Guinea, we would be very close to the stage when a defence emergency should be declared.[24]

On 17 August the Cabinet agreed to send an additional 350 troops to Vietnam, but directed that the army not undertake any further planning to deploy a task force.[25] The additional 350 troops enabled the battalion to be reinforced with a battery of artillery and a troop of engineers to form a battalion group – the force first suggested by Wilton on 27 April.

The army ceased planning for a two-battalion task force for the remainder of the year. On 29 November, however, the US Secretary for Defense, Robert McNamara, told the Australian Ambassador in Saigon that a request for a second battalion would be made shortly.[26] On 7 December Hicks advised the Acting Defence Minister, Alan Hulme, that:

---

21 Letter, Wilton to Forbes, 19 August 1965, AWM 121, 161/A/1.
22 Report, Mackay to Wilton, 9 August 1965, AWM 121, 161/A/4.
23 Army Historical Programme, interview with Maj Gen K Mackay, 8 March 1972, p 12, AWM 107 (hereafter: Mackay interview). McNeill, *To Long Tan*, pp 182–4.
24 Letter, Wilton to Hicks, 12 August 1965, AWM 121, 161/A/4.
25 Letter, Secretary, Department of Defence to CGS, 18 August 1965, AWM 121, 161/A/5.
26 Report by the Joint Planning Committee at a meeting on 7 February 1966, CCOSC files, box 16, file 513, pt 3.

if an additional Australian contribution in Vietnam is judged to be the most effective Australian contribution, then it would seem that nothing short of a task force of at least two battalions with appropriate supporting units (say a total of 3,500 men) would meet the requirement.[27]

In the preceding months General Westmoreland had been anticipating the deployment of an Australian task force. For example, on 12 August Brigadier Jackson reported to Wilton that Westmoreland had said he would 'be very pleased to know … how the possibility of an Australian task force was progressing'.[28] While there is no record, it is likely Westmoreland discussed this issue with Wilton when he visited on 2 September. Jackson was present for their meeting. Jackson recalled later that in the three to four months preceding the arrival of the Task Force, Westmoreland sought his views as to where an Australian task force could be deployed:

> I think the sort of thing I tried to get across to him was that Australian troops were trained for operations in jungle and mountain warfare. They were trained particularly in patrol type operations and I didn't think they would be really suitable in the [Mekong] Delta unless they were given considerable support, particularly equipment support, as we had not really examined this sort of fighting in flooded paddy fields and miles and miles of water, and very heavy rain, and dense population.[29]

Jackson also recalled that when he visited the US Marines near the demilitarised zone at the far north of South Vietnam, the Marine commander said he would be delighted to have an Australian force there. Another suggestion was to base the Australian Task Force at Bien Hoa airfield, but there was not sufficient room as the 173rd US Brigade was already based there. Phuoc Tuy Province was also mentioned because it was 'sufficiently close' to Saigon.

> It was an area which had gone bad in recent years. The VC [Viet Cong] were pretty much in control of it and it was therefore a thorn in the side of the Saigon defence … It was an area in which there were no other major forces deployed so we had the position where allied forces were needed there and there was really nobody else likely to be available to go there – at that stage any rate.[30]

---

27 Letter, Hicks to Acting Defence Minister, 7 December 1965, NAA: A1945/42, 248/4/138.
28 Signal, Jackson to Wilton, 12 August 1965, AWM 121, 161/A/4.
29 Army Historical Programme, interview with Brig OD Jackson, 9 March 1972, AWM 107 (hereafter: Jackson interview).
30 Jackson interview, p 45.

Brigadier Mackay visited Vietnam between 14 and 20 December 1965, but before he departed Australia he was specifically briefed 'not to give any indication that Australia would be prepared to supply additional units for service in Vietnam at this stage'.[31] Nonetheless, during Mackay's visit Jackson received the 'first firm information' that the Australian effort might be increased to the task force level.[32] Mackay recalled that he discussed possible areas with General Westmoreland:

> I don't know which visit it was on, but I can remember he had a very good grasp of the situation. He wanted a spread of forces into areas where the VC had not been challenged, and it was important that he have the various provinces covered, particularly where the ARVN [Army of the Republic of Vietnam] just had no forces at all.[33]

As Mackay indicated, he was not sure when he met Westmoreland. In fact, he visited Vietnam three times in 1965, in May, August and December, and on the latter two occasions Westmoreland was absent from Saigon. In December Mackay certainly had discussions with Westmoreland's deputy, as well as his chiefs of operations, plans and logistics.[34]

Mackay was clear about the alternatives being offered: the Phan Rang area in central South Vietnam, the Mekong Delta and Phuoc Tuy Province. Phan Rang was 'pretty easy to eliminate because it was too isolated, there wasn't much enemy activity up there, and you'd be open to all sort of criticism, not pulling your weight etc.'. The problems with the Delta have already been mentioned. According to Mackay, the Americans were 'very keen to have our forces in Phuoc Tuy'. Considering the geography of the province, he thought:

> it would be relatively easy to put our force, small as it was, between say 100,000 people in Phuoc Tuy and the VC who were out in the bush ... if we with a national force could sit in the centre of things here we could play an important role in the liberation and defeat of the VC.[35]

---

31 Minute, Secretary, Department of Defence to Wilton, 16 December 1965, AWM 121, 161/A/5.
32 Jackson interview, p 42.
33 Mackay interview, p 10.
34 Report, Brigadier K Mackay, 'Report on visit to South Vietnam by DMO&P', 27 December 1965, NAA: A1945/42, 248/4/138.
35 Mackay interview, pp 10–11.

Approving a two-battalion task force

While Mackay was still in Saigon, on 18 December the Minister for External Affairs, Paul Hasluck, who was also visiting Saigon, cabled Canberra that the South Vietnamese prime minister, Nguyen Cao Ky, had made 'almost a request' for additional army and air force assistance.[36] The head of the Australian Defence staff in Washington, Major General Charles Long, followed this on 23 December with advice that Westmoreland had said he envisaged an ANZAC brigade with two Australian and one New Zealand battalions plus supporting arms and services, logistic support units and a SAS squadron.[37] Moving quickly, on 4 January Hicks sent Hulme two papers – one prepared by Scherger in consultation with the military chiefs, the other by Hicks's staff – outlining the forces that could be sent to Vietnam.[38] The Cabinet considered them on 5 January; although it took no decision, it permitted the Chiefs of Staff to prepare a formal proposal.[39]

The Joint Planning Committee, chaired by the Director of Joint Service Plans, Major General Mervyn Brogan (a later CGS), now prepared a detailed report on what forces could be made available for service in Vietnam. The committee stated that the ground war was 'essentially an infantry war with brigade-sized forces securing major bases throughout the country'. In view of later criticism that Australia should have provided a three-battalion task force, as this would have allowed two battalions to operate throughout Phuoc Tuy Province while the third protected the Nui Dat base, it should be noted that Australia was responding to a specific US request for a second battalion. Further, at this stage 4 RAR was still on operations in Borneo, and the committee considered that while Indonesia was 'unlikely to step up confrontation ... the possibility of limited war cannot be excluded'. Both 5 RAR and 6 RAR would be ready for operations by May/June 1966, but 3 RAR, which had returned from operations in Borneo, and 7 RAR, which had recently been formed, would not be ready until September 1966. In addition, 1 RAR was still in Vietnam and it, and 2 RAR, would not be ready for operations until October 1966. The final battalion, 8 RAR, which was being raised, would not be ready until

---

36 Peter Edwards, *A Nation at war: Australian politics, society and diplomacy during the Vietnam War 1965–1975*, Allen & Unwin, Sydney, 1997, p 86.
37 Cable WA1666, Washington to Canberra, 23 December 1965, NAA: A1945/42, 248/4/138.
38 The papers are in NAA: A1945/42, 248/4/138 and 248/4/145.
39 Cabinet Minute, No 1467, Melbourne, 5 January 1966, NAA: A1845/42, 248/4/138.

March 1967. Planning needed to be based on 'the possibility that the operations may have to be sustained for an indefinite period'. That is, at this stage only a two-battalion task force could be supported. There was no suggestion of sending tanks to Vietnam – such a proposal does not seem to have been even considered.[40]

The Defence Committee endorsed this report on 10 February 1966.[41] Wilton was adamant that if further forces were requested for service in South Vietnam it would not be practical 'to meet such a request in a situation short of a defence emergency'.[42] Air Chief Marshal Scherger noted that a brigade was 'the optimum unit which operates alone' in Vietnam. If Australia did not deploy 'one national force incorporating all Australian units in the theatre' it risked the loss of national identity, the loss of valuable experience, especially in command appointments, the 'repetition of the problems which General Monash had in World War I and General Blamey in World War II of getting national units together under national command', and 'subjection to tactical doctrine to which we may not subscribe'. A national force would preserve 'national identity', provide essential military experience particularly in command and, because it would use Australian tactical doctrine, provide a force that was militarily more effective.[43]

These issues went to the heart of the problem of a small country operating in a larger coalition and were brought home just a few days later when Jackson reported that the Americans planned to use 1 RAR in operations close to the Cambodian border. Jackson objected and 1 RAR was withdrawn. Wilton agreed with Jackson's action and advised Hicks that this was 'the first occasion on which it has been necessary for Brigadier Jackson to exercise his responsibility, laid down in his Directive for the safety and well-being of AAFV'.[44]

On 2 March the Cabinet considered the Defence Committee's report and approved the deployment of a task force of two infantry battalions, an SAS squadron, combat and logistic support units, and eight RAAF

---

40   Report by the Joint Planning Committee at a meeting on 7 February 1966, CCOSC files, box 16, file 513, pt 3.
41   Minute by the Defence Committee at a meeting on Thursday, 10 February 1966, NAA: A1945/42, 248/4/145.
42   Letter, Wilton to Hicks, 3 February 1966, NAA: A1945/42, 248/4/145.
43   Paper, Sir Frederick Scherger, 'South Vietnam—Australian Military Assistance', 10 February 1966, CCOSC files, box 16, file 513, pt 3.
44   Letter, Wilton to Hicks, 18 February 1966, NAA: A1945/42, 248/4/145.

Iroquois helicopters. The total contribution of about 4,500 would include national servicemen.[45] Much of the initiative for expanding the force had come directly from Wilton, who saw sound military reasons for it. As he said later:

> When we sent our first battalion up, it was the most we could do in terms of the size of the force. We'd always, I think, known in the backs of our minds that when our manpower and other resources permitted this would have to be increased.[46]

Wilton selects Phuoc Tuy Province

On 12 March, just four days after prime minister Harold Holt announced that the Task Force was going to be deployed, Wilton departed for Saigon for meetings with Westmoreland and the Chief of the Vietnamese Joint Chiefs of Staff, General Cao Van Vien. Wilton had prepared a brief, setting out what he hoped to achieve in Vietnam, and he forwarded this through Scherger to the Defence Minister for his concurrence. In preparing the brief Wilton had discussed his proposals with the new Minister for the Army, Malcolm Fraser, explaining the advantages of finding a separate 'piece of geography' for the Australian Task Force.[47] Accompanying Wilton were Brigadier Bob Hay, shortly to take over from Mackay as DMO&P, and Lieutenant Colonel Alan Stretton, from the Directorate of Staff Duties. Soon after departing from Sydney, Wilton called Hay and Stretton into the aircraft's private compartment usually reserved for off-duty crew and, as Stretton recalled, 'set about planning the details of the Australian build-up in Vietnam'.[48]

Accompanied by his advisers from Canberra, as well as Brigadier Jackson, in Saigon Wilton went straight to a meeting with Westmoreland. They agreed that, on all matters concerning the Australian forces, Westmoreland would deal directly with the Commander, Australia Force Vietnam (COMAFV), who would be an officer of major general rank. Mackay was shortly to be promoted to fill this position. Operational control of the 1st Australian Task Force (1 ATF) would be through the commanding general of II Field Force, who was co-located with the commander of

---

45 Cabinet Minute, Decision No 60, 2 March 1966, NAA: A1945/42, 248/4/145.
46 Wilton interview, p 13.
47 Interview, JM Fraser with author, 18 November 2002.
48 Alan Stretton, *Soldier in a storm*, Collins, Sydney, 1978, p 181.

II Vietnamese Corps near Bien Hoa. 1 ATF would be located in Phuoc Tuy Province, while the Australian Logistic Support Group would be at nearby Vung Tau.

Subsequent discussions between their staffs established the roles for 1 ATF. First, it was to secure and dominate the assigned tactical area of responsibility in Phuoc Tuy Province. Second, it was to conduct operations related to the security of the highway linking Vung Tau and Saigon as required. Third, it was to conduct other operations in the province. Fourth, it was to conduct operations anywhere in the III Corps Tactical Zone and also to conduct operations anywhere in the adjacent province of Binh Tuy (in the II Corps Tactical Zone) as agreed between Westmoreland and COMAFV. Thus, Australia placed clear limits on the geographic extent of 1 ATF's operations.

The key decision was the allocation of Phuoc Tuy Province to 1 ATF. As we have seen, Mackay had already identified it and Wilton had probably discussed possibilities with Westmoreland when they had met in September. Wilton, Mackay and other staff at AHQ considered the requirements for an Australian operational area, which Mackay described later in a presentation to the CGS Exercise in 1971. These were that the operational area should have significant enemy activity so there need be 'no thought by any party that Australia was pulling less than its share'; the area should not be contiguous to the borders with Cambodia, Laos or the demilitarised zone; it should be a geographically distinct area which could be left largely to the Task Force and with which the Australian national effort could be readily identified; and it should offer reasonably secure access to shipping and overseas aircraft.[49]

Wilton recalled later that the choice was between Phuoc Tuy and Bien Hoa. Although for military reasons 1 ATF had to be under US operational control, he 'preferred not to be brigaded with an American position. I wanted to have as much independence within the force limitations as I could, so I could keep a closer eye on it'. He thought 'our two-battalion task force was worth any US three-battalion brigade', and that placing it in the province gave 'us the best opportunity to make the most impact nationally—which is always an important consideration in a war like this'. He wanted 'to get clear of the American densely populated

---

49 Maj Gen Mackay, Chief of the General Staff's Exercise 1971, Notes for Speaker – Maj Gen Mackay. Papers from the CGS Exercise in author's collection (hereafter: CGS Exercise 1971).

area, and get into a place where they could operate, in a way we thought was most effective'. Another disadvantage in selecting Bien Hoa was that Australian resupply ships would have to sail right into Saigon where they might be delayed for some time. Phuoc Tuy could be resupplied through Vung Tau.[50]

But the most important reason concerned the safety of the force. Vung Tau was on a nearby and isolated peninsula, so 1 ATF could be evacuated or reinforced by Australian national resources should the situation in the province deteriorate. As Wilton explained, 'if the war went really bad and some frightful disaster was impending, we could look after ourselves'. Considering all these reasons, Wilton said: 'all right, we'll go to Phuoc Tuy Province'.[51] Then, according to Stretton, they went through 'a face-saving exercise with the South Vietnamese', visiting various generals who each said that he had decided to allocate the province to the Australians. Stretton thought that in selecting the province 'Wilton showed remarkable military judgement and that there would have been a greater loss of life if the Australian force had been allocated to any other province'.[52]

The decision to base the Australian Logistic Support Group at Vung Tau caused more problems. The only available site was a windswept sandy area east of the city, but the local mayor told Wilton and Jackson that a senior military officer in Saigon had to give his approval. So, they went back to Saigon and, as Wilton described it, he 'nailed this fellow down at a reception a couple of nights' before they left Saigon. Wilton said, 'Now look, this is the place we want. Can you give me your assurance that this will now be allocated without delay?' 'Oh yes', replied the general, 'that will be done'. Wilton accepted this assurance but reminded the general that if the area was not made available 'we can't bring in our force'.[53] As it happened, Jackson secured final approval when the first ship carrying supplies was only a week from Vung Tau, and only after he threatened to have the ship turned around.[54]

---

50   CGS Exercise 1971.
51   Wilton interview, p 21.
52   Stretton, *Soldier in a storm*, pp 182–3.
53   Wilton interview, p 24.
54   Jackson interview, p 48.

Why Nui Dat?

Wilton's decision to locate 1 ATF in Phuoc Tuy Province has not been seriously questioned, but the decision to base 1 ATF specifically at Nui Dat in the centre of the province has been criticised. Brigadier Jackson, who had been nominated to command 1 ATF, selected Nui Dat, and his decision was confirmed by Wilton when they flew over the area in the afternoon of 14 March. As Jackson recalled:

> I remember flying over the Nui Dat with General Wilton and he looked down there and he said, 'Well one day there'll be an empire down there won't there?' And we had in other words pretty much agreed that that's where the Task Force would go.[55]

Jackson later explained that he selected Nui Dat because it was located between the enemy's Main Force bases and the areas of most dense civilian population. The base had to be capable not only of being held by a minimum force but also of providing for a small airfield, a task force maintenance area, and tactically located unit base areas with room to fight should the base come under heavy attack. There were three other factors. It had to be on ground which would be above water level during the wet season, which was due to begin one week after forward deployment began. It needed to be in relatively open ground and not too close to densely settled areas to enable maximum use of firepower rather than manpower for its defences. And it should be located close enough to the Vung Tau–Ba Ria area to avoid diversion of forces for line of communication security duties or alternatively to allow maintenance by air.[56] After the war Jackson still believed it was right to base 1 ATF at Nui Dat.[57]

Stretton thought the decision to base 1 ATF at Nui Dat was one of the 'cardinal blunders' made by the Australian commanders in Vietnam.[58] The huge complex that was eventually developed had to be defended, thus reducing the numbers of troops that could be deployed on operations. If the troops had been located at Vung Tau fewer would have been needed to defend the base.

---

55   Ibid, p 50.
56   Brig OD Jackson, CGS Exercise 1971, Presentation Operation Hardihood – Deployment of 1 AF to Nui Dat.
57   Jackson interview, p 52.
58   Stretton, *Soldier in a storm*, p 213.

Wilton's successor as CGS, Daly, thought 'with the advantage of hindsight' that 'it would have been a better proposition to develop Vung Tau as the Task Force base. In any future operation such as that, I think it would be most unwise to set up two permanent bases'.[59] Further, the construction of the Nui Dat base required a large-scale engineering effort that was not appreciated at the time it was selected. As Brigadier Philip Greville, historian of the Royal Australian Engineers, has argued, there was no one 'accompanying General Sir John Wilton who understood engineering matters upon which the well-being of the forces would largely depend'.[60]

Lieutenant General Sir Donald Dunstan, who was deputy commander of 1 ATF in 1968, COMAFV in 1971–72, and later CGS, thought the army made a:

> fundamental mistake when we went into Phuoc Tuy in that we sat at Nui Dat in the manner in which we did. Nui Dat was always a pain in the neck; it was a large base, it became a relatively sophisticated base and it was always a heavy consumer of manpower.[61]

He thought if the base had been at Vung Tau there would have been a saving of personnel and the defensive task would have been far less demanding. Then, with the number of people the army had in Vietnam, it would have been possible to raise a force of four battalions. At any time, three battalions could have operated continually in Military Region 3 or Phuoc Tuy. To operate in Phuoc Tuy it was only necessary to provide fire support bases: 'I don't believe that you have to put the base there to separate the enemy from the civil population.'[62]

Wilton rejected this argument. He wanted the troops based away from a populated area. Placing the base in the centre of the province posed a continuing threat to Viet Cong operations. And importantly, if the troops had been at Vung Tau the American high command might have wished to deploy them away from the province on the sort of deep operations that, from the beginning, he had wanted to avoid.

---

59   Army Historical Programme, interview with Lt Gen Sir Thomas Daly, 22 November 1974 and 4 June 1975, p 22, AWM 107.
60   PJ Greville, *The Royal Australian Engineers 1945 to 1972: Paving the way*, Corps Committee of the Royal Australian Engineers, Moorebank, NSW, 2002, p 721.
61   Army Historical Programme, interview with Maj Gen DB Dunstan, 4 October 1973. Copy of transcript given to the author by Dunstan at an interview on 23 December 1985.
62   Ibid.

Major General Mackay, who took up his appointment as COMAFV in May 1966, thought the idea of basing 1 ATF at Vung Tau was 'ridiculous':

> You can't go in as the big bold boys to sort this problem out and sit back ... at Vung Tau and then get in your damned trucks or helicopters every day and go for miles out in the bush and do something and come back [to] live in a villa or live by the seaside.[63]

But Mackay claimed the Nui Dat base he had in mind 'bore no relation to the hideous monster that developed later on'. He thought the task force maintenance area should have been at Vung Tau rather than Nui Dat.

> When I went up there as QMG [quartermaster general] I almost blew a valve. I think there were about 290 fellows sitting on their backsides with a bloody great engineer's stores yard there with refrigerators and logs and timber and stuff ... I didn't envisage this enormous area of bitumen where you could bring in half the American air force.[64]

The historian Greg Lockhart has provided the most detailed criticism of the decision to locate 1 ATF at Nui Dat.[65] He points out that Australian Army counter-revolutionary warfare doctrine encouraged the establishment of a forward operational base, and indeed this concept had been practised during Exercise Sky High near Singleton in NSW in November 1963.[66] Lockhart argues that Wilton and Jackson (and for that matter Mackay also) misunderstood the nature of the war in Vietnam in claiming that a base at Nui Dat would separate the enemy from the population in central and south-western Phuoc Tuy. Lockhart points out that many residents in Ba Ria and Long Dat, which the Nui Dat base was supposed to separate from the Viet Cong, supported or were actual members of the Viet Cong. Lockhart sees the decision as evidence of Wilton's 'barrier mentality'. He and successive 1 ATF commanders never 'understood the web of mutually supportive relations between the local semi-regular and regular guerrilla units and national PAVN [People's Army of Vietnam] main forces'. Lockhart argues that Wilton 'never fully comprehended' that the ground of tactical importance in Phuoc Tuy Province was in the south, in the Long Hai Hills, where substantial

---

63 Mackay interview, pp 17, 18. Mackay was QMG from 1968 to 1973.
64 Ibid.
65 Greg Lockhart, *The minefield: An Australian tragedy in Vietnam*, Allen & Unwin, Sydney, 2007, ch 2.
66 McNeill, *To Long Tan*, pp 18, 19.

Viet Cong forces had been based for many years.⁶⁷ That is, Wilton and the other Australian Army leaders not only failed to understand the nature of the war in Vietnam, but had no knowledge of the history of the Viet Cong in Phuoc Tuy Province.

There is, however, a contrary view. Ian McNeill, author of the official history, has shown that senior North Vietnamese and Viet Cong officers agreed that the location of 1 ATF at Nui Dat presented a great obstacle to their operations.⁶⁸ Further, in discussing the Battle of Long Tan in August 1966, McNeill concluded:

> The decision to place the task force at Nui Dat and the subsequent operations had been designed to separate the guerrillas from the people, a fundamental tenet of Australian counter-insurgency doctrine. These activities had apparently taken effect, forcing the enemy to confront the task force as Jackson had anticipated.⁶⁹

Major General Bob Hay, who as a brigadier accompanied Wilton and Jackson on the reconnaissance to Phuoc Tuy in March 1966 (and was COMAFV in 1969–70), agreed that the Task Force should have been located at Nui Dat:

> It was better to put this on the ground between the main centres of population and true jungle area, which were dominated by the VC and NVA [North Vietnamese Army] ... In the long term I think this proved to be a wise move, although it did mean a substantial base was, in fact, developed in Nui Dat, and this really was not, I am quite sure, the thought in 1966.⁷⁰

While Wilton and Jackson's decision to locate 1 ATF at Nui Dat can be understood in terms of creating a presence in the province, in retrospect perhaps there was another alternative. As Dunstan suggested, the Task Force could have been based at Vung Tau with a large fire support base located forward at Nui Dat, but still much smaller than the eventual 1 ATF complex. This is a variation on Mackay's idea. Later in the war,

---

67 Greg Lockhart, 'Extracts from *The Minefield*', *The Vietnam Veteran Newsletter*, September 2003, pp 18, 19.
68 McNeill, *To Long Tan*, p 200. For further criticism of the decision, see Ian McNeill and Ashley Ekins, *On the offensive: The Australian Army in the Vietnam War, January 1967–June 1968*, Allen & Unwin, Sydney, 2003, pp 63–4.
69 McNeill, *To Long Tan*, p 366.
70 Army Historical Programme, interview with Maj Gen RA Hay, 22 November 1971, p 7, AWM 107.

battalion fire support bases were established at Courtenay Hill and the Horseshoe for months on end. They had the desired effect of dominating the surrounding areas.[71]

Important decisions

The decision to locate 1 ATF in Phuoc Tuy Province and specifically at Nui Dat reveals Wilton's determination not to place the lives of Australians at risk in more adventurous American operations. He also wanted to ensure that 1 ATF had the best possible opportunity to conduct operations according to Australian tactical doctrine. He had been reminded of the differences between Australian and American doctrine when, on the afternoon of 13 March 1966, he visited 1 RAR on Operation Silver City, deep in War Zone D, where the 173rd Brigade was engaged in destroying the headquarters of the Viet Cong 7th Military Region. Three days later three Viet Cong battalions attacked one of the US battalions and Australian gunners fired continuously for four hours to break up the Viet Cong assaults.[72]

Wilton concluded his visit to Vietnam in the morning of 17 March, when he signed a Military Working Agreement with Westmoreland, who noted in his diary that the 'Australians are pleased to deal with us and there is apparently a mutual friendship between the officers of our two nations and a common outlook'.[73] Wilton then headed home and on 23 March the Chiefs of Staff Committee endorsed the arrangements that he had made in Vietnam.[74]

Wilton's visit to Vietnam in March 1966 was the most important by any Australian military chief during the Vietnam War and, according to Malcolm Fraser, it was carried out 'brilliantly'.[75] Lockhart and others would argue, however, that the decision to place 1 ATF at Nui Dat was flawed. Whatever the judgement on this issue, Wilton's decision established 1 ATF in Phuoc Tuy Province and set guidelines for its

---

71 For a description of 1 ATF fire bases see Bruce Picken, *Fire support bases Vietnam: Australian and allied fire support base locations and main support units*, Big Sky Publishing, Newport, NSW, 2012.
72 Bob Breen, *First to fight: Australian diggers, N.Z. kiwis and U.S. paratroopers in Vietnam 1965–66*, Allen & Unwin, Sydney 1988, p 233.
73 Westmoreland Diary, 17 March 1966, US Army Center of Military History.
74 COSC Minute, 23 March 1966, CCOSC files, box 25, file 1910.
75 Interview, JM Fraser with author, 18 November 2002.

employment that were to continue for the remainder of the war. These guidelines were a clear reflection of the Australian Government's policy of minimising the chances of excessive casualties. His visit also established the command arrangements. The decision to appoint the COMAFV, who reported to the Chiefs of Staff Committee through its chairman, set a precedent for appointing an Australian national commander with joint service responsibilities. This approach has persisted to the present day. As for the two-battalion task force, in December 1967 it was expanded to three battalions. Confrontation had ended in August 1966 and 9 RAR was raised in November 1967.

Before 1 ATF arrived at Nui Dat, Wilton had taken over from Scherger as Chairman of the Chiefs of Staff Committee, and when he was promoted to general in September 1968 he was the first Australian Army officer to reach this rank since General Sir Thomas Blamey was promoted in September 1941. In his new position, Wilton would continue to provide oversight of Australia's Vietnam commitment until he retired in November 1970. At that time 1 ATF, based at Nui Dat and reduced again to two battalions, was still operating in Phuoc Tuy Province.

3

FACING NEW REALITIES: FROM HOLSWORTHY TO NUI DAT

Stan Maizey

Editors' introduction

Stan Maizey was second in command of 5th Battalion, the Royal Australian Regiment (5 RAR), from January 1966 until December 1966, when he was posted as the senior operations staff officer at Headquarters, 1st Australian Task Force (HQ 1 ATF). He spent 16 months in Vietnam, eight months each with 5 RAR and HQ 1 ATF. Stan, sadly, died on 18 June 2018, while this book was still being written. Fortunately, several years ago, he had written an article about his experiences with 5 RAR and he agreed that this could be published in *Vietnam Vanguard*.

This chapter is about 5 RAR's preparations for its first tour of duty in Vietnam, and the inherent logistic difficulties encountered. Getting ready for a lengthy period of war service is a complex process, especially in terms of assembling the necessary equipment. As second in command of the battalion, it was principally Stan's responsibility to see that we went to war with all our necessary equipment. If we could not get all that we needed in Australia, he then had to negotiate with the Americans to make up for the deficiencies in equipment and other essential supplies. Bearing in mind that Australia had not sent a multi-battalion-sized force abroad on operations since the Korean War of the early 1950s, there was much to be done in terms of equipping and supplying 5 RAR and 6 RAR before they went to Vietnam in April 1966. Here is Stan's account of how he met the challenges confronting him in 5 RAR's initial year of service in Vietnam.

Stan Maizey

I was posted as second in command (2IC) of 5 RAR in December 1965, arriving at Gallipoli Barracks, Holsworthy, in early January 1966. The commanding officer (CO), Lieutenant Colonel John Warr, was visiting 1 RAR at Bien Hoa, South Vietnam, but had left instructions for the training he required until his return.

At this stage, the battalion was a nucleus of regular army officers, non-commissioned officers and men. Reinforcements started to arrive from September 1965 and included many national servicemen (NS) from the Officer Training Unit, Scheyville (near Windsor, NSW), and from the various NS recruit training battalions.

While no official announcement had been made, it was understood that 5 RAR would replace 1 RAR in Vietnam in April/May 1966. Correspondence between counterparts of the battalions was taking place and the logistic information included: bring as much timber/flooring as possible; scale holdings of consumable items for at least six months, not three months as shown in the various equipment tables; get a fisheye lens for the movie projector; be aware of the various US codes and code words (such as *Dustoff*, for casualty evacuation), and requisition procedures; and get used to US rations.

The battalion's training concentrated on shooting, platoon drills, company movement, helicopter familiarisation and getting to know one another. During February and early March 1966, each company was phased through a company training exercise in the Gospers Training Area, near Rylstone, NSW, and evaluation at the Jungle Training Centre, Canungra, Qld. Finally, in March a battalion exercise under the direction of the CO took place in the Gospers Training Area to be followed immediately by an assessed exercise under the direction of HQ 1st Task Force at Holsworthy.

During this training, the quartermaster's (QM) staff were extremely busy ensuring that the battalion was properly equipped. Unfortunately, the army's supply depots refused to accept our requisitions as we submitted them in a multi-listed format, and not by single items (that is, one item to one page). Achieving this level of detail required all the battalion's clerks to be seconded to the QM for about 10 days to rewrite the paperwork. Then, because no formal announcement had been made regarding 5 RAR replacing 1 RAR in Vietnam, our requisitions for any items in the infantry battalion equipment tables – which were designated as restricted warlike stores – were endorsed 'Not Approved' and returned to us. Lastly, when we tried to follow 1 RAR's advice to scale our holdings for six months (instead of the customary three months), the staff officers at HQ Eastern Command either refused to approve an extra holding or replied, 'the items are to be taken over from 1 RAR *in situ*'. It was not until late February or early March 1966, after the announcement that the Australian commitment was to be significantly increased to a two-battalion task force with supporting arms and a logistic support group named 1st Australian Logistic Support Group (1 ALSG), that our demands were reluctantly processed. However, with the introduction of national service in June 1965, many items of clothing and equipment were in short supply and the army's procurement system proved sadly inadequate. For example, some soldiers had only one set of jungle green uniforms (other than protective dress, which was usually an outdated but recycled khaki summer uniform). Most soldiers had only one pair of calf-length general purpose (GP) boots with protective stainless-steel inserts in the soles, so each soldier was issued with a pair of 1944-era tropical studded ankle boots and a pair of canvas gaiters (leggings). All soldiers had their full entitlement of personal load-carrying equipment and there was little or no reserve in the battalion QM Store.

The final training exercise saw the battalion using a range of equipment recently received and still in protective packaging. The exercise was held in foul weather so, with the connivance of the regimental medical officer (RMO), we managed to get a rum issue for all ranks through the supply system.

During the preparatory phase, and on advice from 1 RAR, we tried to shed our anti-tank (ATk) weapons: an 84 mm rocket launcher (Carl Gustav) held by each of the rifle companies; and six 106 mm recoilless rifles (RCLs) held by the Anti-Tank Platoon. Sadly we were unsuccessful in this endeavour. The RCLs were mounted on modified Land Rovers and, after discussion within the battalion, our armourer, Sergeant Mick Henrys, suggested that we mount a machine gun on each vehicle, primarily for convoy protection. These six vehicles became known as 'Sports Cars' and were invaluable in their adapted, albeit technically illegal, role. We were required to take the anti-tank equipment to war where it languished in the QM Store, except for two 106 mm RCLs, which were located on either side of the flag pole 'guarding' Battalion Headquarters in the base area. At the same time, and with a submission by 1 RAR to support our request, we tried to amend the equipment table to obtain more M60 general purpose machine guns (M60 GPMG), radios and telephones for base area defences, but this was refused with the comment 'not until the CO has personally established the need'. How we overcame these deficiencies is told later in this chapter.

During the build-up of men and materials, as bad as the ordnance stores supply system was, the engineer and medical systems were magnificent. The engineer system provided us with a good supply of timber and the School of Military Engineering at Casula provided instructors for training in the use of mines and booby traps, barbed wire fencing and sandbagging. The medical system, particularly 2 Camp Hospital at Ingleburn, provided instructors for first aid, health and hygiene training, and vital associated stores. They also gave high priority to members of the battalion with respect to inoculations.

In April 1966, the battalion Advance Party flew out, to be initially fostered by 1 RAR at Bien Hoa, then to proceed to the sand dunes at Vung Tau to establish a camp for the battalion prior to the occupation of the 1 ATF base at Nui Dat. C Company and all the battalion's stores, equipment and vehicles departed in mid-April 1966 on HMAS *Sydney*, while the remainder of the battalion flew out from Richmond Royal Australian Air Force (RAAF) base in Boeing 707s over a period of three weeks. In mid-May 1966 the last element of the battalion, including myself, departed for South Vietnam. On arrival at Saigon's Tan Son Nhut airport, we disembarked and collected our weapons and equipment. We then embarked on a US C123 Provider transport aircraft for the flight to Vung Tau. We waited nearly two hours inside the aircraft, in atrocious heat and humidity, before take-off.

On arrival in Vietnam, it was immediately obvious that some of the stores and equipment we were required to take over from 1 RAR were unserviceable from 12 months of hard use, especially tentage and M16 rifles. The rifles arrived without cleaning accessories and our armourers were required to fashion cleaning rods from heavy gauge fencing wire.

Life at Vung Tau was hectic as we acclimatised, and got to know our supporting troops and their jargon, and conducted aerial reconnaissance of Phuoc Tuy Province (some of these flights were decidedly hair-raising). The US Army's 68 Assault Helicopter Company, based at Vung Tau air base, deserves special mention because this unit provided wonderful support whenever required. Prior to leaving Vung Tau, we had an officers' dining-in night at the Pacific Hotel (a big French colonial hotel taken over by the US troops as officers' quarters) where the aviators were present. The battalion provided the cooks and stewards and the Battalion Band played a tremendous rendition of 'Those Magnificent Men in their Flying Machines', which brought the house down.

Operation Hardihood, the clearing and then occupation of the Task Force's operational base at Nui Dat, began in mid-May 1966, initially conducted by the US 173 Airborne Brigade with, in late May 1966, 5 RAR placed under its command for the final phase of the operation. The battalion was assisted by a company of 1 RAR. During the operation, the battalion was very active to the north of Nui Dat and had many contacts, mostly with groups of three to five Viet Cong (VC).

In early June 1966, our contacts with the enemy diminished, and it was decided to commence occupation of the Task Force base at Nui Dat. Prior to the administrative echelons of the battalion and the Task Force moving into the area, we were warned of a likely assault by 274 Viet Cong Regiment. The CO called for an urgent resupply of ammunition, particularly belted ammunition for the M60 machine guns, Claymore mines and mortar rounds. While the ammunition was being gathered, I asked for helicopter support, from the US Army's 68 Assault Helicopter Company to lift the heavy loads forward. Our QM Platoon had removed most of the packaging to reduce weight and bulk, but there was still considerably more to move. When the helicopters arrived, I asked a pilot how much weight could be carried by each aircraft. With typical US nonchalance, the pilot replied, 'Fill it [the aircraft] up'. When we could put no more aboard, he gave the thumbs up, lifted off about one metre, bounced the aircraft to about three metres then moved forward, settled, bounced again and was finally airborne.

Life at Nui Dat was a constant struggle – against the elements (the wet monsoon season had started), the stores and equipment shortages, the discomforts of 'home', the inability to defend the base adequately when the battalion was out on an operation – all endured while developing the base's defence works.

Many problems complicated our efforts. With the wet season, each time a weapon pit was dug and before any overhead cover/protection could be found, the pit filled with water. Thank goodness the weather was not cold. Trying to fill sandbags with wet clay, the predominantly available filling material at Nui Dat, was extraordinarily difficult so, whenever possible, I would send a convoy of Land Rovers and trailers to Vung Tau to fill sand bags with sand. Whenever the battalion was on operations there were only three radios (mine and those of the officer commanding (OC) Administration Company and the QM) left in the battalion's base area. Our field telephones were required on operations, therefore we literally used message sticks for communications between company positions at Nui Dat until the 'Scrounging Platoon' (formed in country for obvious reasons and consisting of company 2ICs, company quartermaster sergeants and most of Administration Company) found, by the side of the road, an unattended switchboard, some telephones and radios. The other, and most worrying, deficiency was a lack of machine guns for the defence of the base. Administration Company had a handful of heavy-barrelled rifles, capable of magazine-fed automatic fire, but nothing more by way of defensive weapons. Again, the Scrounging Platoon, by exchanging a couple of slouch hats and some butter with our allies, gained several .30 and .50 calibre machine guns. The former were immediately mounted onto the Sports Cars and the latter were positioned in bunkers in the company areas. Further defence and other base stores were obtained when the Scrounging Platoon under my command, and using our Land Rovers and trailers, visited the US Supply Depot at Vung Tau. We left the Depot with all trailers full of borrowed stores, a stores truck and a water truck. After we spent most of the day at the 'supermarket', the new guard on duty demanded written authorisation, which of course we did not have. As it was getting very late and because the road to Nui Dat was classified black (unsafe) at night, I explained as courteously as possible that it was late and we could sort out the paperwork later. I sent the convoy on its way and when the Sergeant went into the guardroom for advice, I took off. The Sergeant fired at us but fortunately his aim was not accurate. After this foray, we became more secure and more comfortable.

By about July 1966 shortages were causing significant problems. We had no replacement clothing, boots and personal equipment for our men; the 1944-era tropical-studded boots had provided nourishment for the rubber ants, the clothing had succumbed to wear and tear and could not be replaced, and although we took personal equipment from our administrative elements, we could only put about two thirds of the fighting troops into an operation. During a visit by the Commander, Australian Force Vietnam (COMAFV), Major General Ken Mackay, the CO was wearing a very tattered and torn shirt. When the Commander learned of our plight, he had his headquarters QM Store in Saigon scoured, and we received about 100 sets of clothing and a box of equipment.

Many of the soldiers were not living in tents because the new tents arrived without tent poles, and an RAAF C130 transport aircraft due to bring poles arrived full of toilet paper. The transport ship HMAS *Jeparit* arrived with many crates empty. We could only construe that there had been sabotage somewhere!

Because of problems with belted ammunition for the M60 GPMG, it was decided to make a sheath for each 100-round belt from inflatable inserts for the field mattresses we usually slept on. This precaution kept rubbish from fouling the belts. However, the ammunition sweated and the steel links, which joined each round to the next, rusted very quickly; so we decided to use regimental funds (non-government moneys owned collectively by the battalion's members) to obtain a gross of WD40 aerosol cans of anti-rust spray. After a few weeks, when the goods had not arrived, we started to investigate and found them, together with crates of GP boots and green floppy hats, on the garbage tip at Vung Tau! Some people at 1 ALSG needed to lift their game.

Food became our next major concern; Australian combat rations were not readily available, and we were forced to use the bulky and unpopular US combat rations. When the battalion was due to return from operations, we would order fresh rations, but most of the time the arrival of fresh rations would seem to signal a need for the battalion to return to operations, where packaged, individual combat rations were consumed. As there was a delay in the installation of cool rooms in our base, the fresh rations quickly became inedible. Indeed, the CO received, in August, a bill for US$25,000 for fresh rations; but these were the spoiled fresh rations that had been written off by our RMO and the QM. One soldier asked the CO not to order fresh rations because with their arrival the battalion would be ordered back onto operations. Towards the end of July 1966, the fresh rations system broke down completely and we ate nothing but frankfurts and sweet corn for about five weeks. We had them baked, boiled, fried, grilled and minced. I even sent our warrant officer caterer to fly 300 kilometres to Dalat (in central South Vietnam's highlands) to buy some fresh vegetables; again using money from our regimental funds. The dysfunction of the system was demonstrated by the repeated delivery to our base of fresh rations and ice cream when the battalion was out on operations and while we had no refrigerated storage in base.

By about mid-September 1966, 'home' was becoming more habitable and, while the battalion was on operations, its rear elements built and consolidated the base area. A large movie screen was erected (we were fortunate to find a fisheye cinemascope lens in a US Amenities Unit in Saigon). Also, in the outdoor theatre, named 'The Mayfair', we built a small kitchen to serve steak sandwiches, the inevitable hot dogs plus the CO's favourite, goffers (flavoured milk in a can which could be enjoyed hot or cold – canned soft drinks went by the same nickname). The screen was a beauty, somewhat like the old drive-in theatre screens, I am not sure if any VC, lurking outside the wire, liked our selection of movies! The tents were erected, the cool rooms and refrigeration arrived and were installed. When a couple of Nissen huts arrived, these were allocated to the RMO and padres (chaplains). The rain was dissipating, the weather was cooler at night, the company kitchens and canteens were up and running, and the QM Store started to get some replacement clothing and equipment. During operations and whenever any maintenance resupply to our troops in the field was required, we had the company cooks prepare a meal of hot soup, which we sent out in plastic jerrycans (5-gallon cans similar in appearance to those used by the Germans for the safe carriage of petrol during the Second World War) and steak sandwiches. These fresh meals, delivered during operations, gave our men a welcome break from the monotony of combat rations.

On 18 August 1966, D Company of 6 RAR fought the Battle of Long Tan and used RAAF Iroquois helicopters for combat resupply in late afternoon amid torrential rain. The RAAF performed very well. Prior to this battle, the RAAF seemed to be constrained by hangover peacetime regulations which applied in Australia. After Long Tan we felt that they were full members of the team. However, during Operation Queanbeyan in October 1966, the battalion was required to clear the Nui Thi Vai hills. As the operation progressed, we found occupied caves, live booby traps and determined VC opposing us. The CO decided to clear the caves using flame-throwers. The necessary equipment and incendiary fuel were assembled at Nui Dat and the RAAF Iroquois arrived to fly them across to Nui Thi Vai. The pilot then said he was not permitted to carry fuel in his aircraft. After discussion between myself and the pilot, I consulted higher authority, namely the task force commander, who then brought the RAAF component commander and COMAFV into the discussion. The result was that the RAAF agreed to carry the fuel if the steel jerrycans were packed in wooden crates. In the meantime our troops in close contact with the enemy had to wait while the issue was resolved!

In November 1966, I acted as operations officer while Max Carroll was on rest and recreation leave. During this period, 5 RAR undertook a cordon and search of a small village, Phuoc Hoa, north-west of Ba Ria on Route 15. Immediately following this task, we were required to clear Long Son Island, which was used by the VC as a stepping stone between the Mekong River and the Nui Thi Vai hills. During this operation, the task force commander decided to deploy his headquarters onto the island. These operations gave me a break from administrative duties and provided some operational experience for my next posting as the operations officer at Task Force Headquarters.

I was to leave the battalion in mid-December 1966 after a most eventful year, but one right off the top shelf.

Editors' conclusion

We have included this chapter, essentially on administrative and logistic matters, to give readers an understanding of how important they are in determining operational capability. As has been demonstrated in the early years of other wars, it takes a long time to prepare a peacetime army for service in war. Moving from a standing start to full operational capability takes a huge effort and demands great determination and ingenuity. We in 5 RAR were very fortunate to have Stan Maizey as our 2IC and principal logistics officer. He had a deep insight into what we needed to have available once we were in operations in Vietnam. He then showed high resolve and negotiating abilities to get what we needed, both in Australia and Vietnam. Once he had seen that we had enough stores and equipment to be able to go to war with confidence, he kept all our stocks of food, fuel, ammunition, tentage and other essential supplies up to the level that we required. In personal terms he was one of the battalion's great characters, with a formidable sense of humour, a warm affection for sport, particularly if it offered betting opportunities, and a strong determination to improve the day-to-day lives of our soldiers when they were not on operations by making sure that they were given decent meals and a place in which to relax and enjoy a drink or two. Underpinning his desire to give outstanding service to those who had to rely on him was a very strong personal commitment to 'the Regiment', meaning the Royal Australian Regiment. He saw operational service with a battalion of the Regiment as his highest aspiration and the most satisfying time of his professional life.

4

5 RAR ON OPERATIONS, MAY–SEPTEMBER 1966

Max Carroll, Peter Isaacs, Roger Wainwright
and Robert O'Neill

Editors' introduction

The Battalion Headquarters (BHQ) staff officers principally responsible for operational planning and assisting the commanding officer (CO) in all aspects of 5th Battalion, the Royal Australian Regiment (5 RAR), battlefield activity were the operations officer, Major Max Carroll, and his deputy, Captain Peter Isaacs, who was also the battalion's adjutant. In this chapter they describe how 5 RAR entered the fray and embarked on the steep learning curve which confronted all members of the battalion.

Max Carroll

5 RAR was complete on the ground at Vung Tau by 13 May 1966. The Battalion Advance Party, of which I, as officer commanding (OC) Support Company and battalion operations officer, was a member, had arrived on 20 April 1966. We were fostered by our sister battalion 1 RAR, which was part of the US 173 Airborne Brigade based at Bien Hoa, where we dispersed to learn the ropes. This attachment was invaluable for all of us. It enabled me to meet the brigade headquarters staff with whom I would be working, and to accompany the 2nd Battalion, 503 Airborne Infantry Regiment (2/503), on a helicopter-mounted assault and subsequent ground sweep through War Zone D, north of Phuoc Tuy.

By giving us this firsthand knowledge of how they conducted battalion level operations, our American hosts were very generous and assisted us in every way they could. Operationally our styles differed, but they respected the professionalism of the Australian Army; both through their association with 1 RAR and from the high reputation of the Australian Army Training Team Vietnam (AATTV).

US Army assistance continued at Vung Tau where the US Army's 68 Assault Helicopter Company provided us with excellent training in essential techniques for infantry helicopter-mounted insertions and assaults, resupply by helicopter and the rapid aeromedical evacuation of casualties. They also flew several of our officers on reconnaissance sweeps over Phuoc Tuy Province, the area with which we were soon to become intensely familiar. Additionally, 173 Airborne Brigade invited Captains Peter Isaacs and Brian Le Dan to accompany the HQ of 1st Battalion, 503 Airborne Infantry Regiment (1/503), on their forthcoming operation.

Peter Isaacs

The last group of 5 RAR troops to deploy to South Vietnam arrived at Saigon's Tan Son Nhut airport aboard a Qantas charter flight in the middle of May 1966. The battalion second in command (2IC), Major Stan Maizey, and I were part of that final group. Several hours later I was sitting on a box in the tent I was to share with my assistant adjutant, Lieutenant Ralph Thompson. He briefed me on happenings over the past month as the battalion had arrived by air and sea. Having been the battalion's adjutant for the preceding 16 months and usually at the centre of everything, I was a touch bewildered! This lasted no more than 24 hours as there was a tremendous amount of work to be accomplished before the battalion deployed to its operational area in Phuoc Tuy province. This included our 'baptism of fire' during an air reconnaissance, when all four helicopters in which our four-man reconnaissance party flew were fired on. The fire was returned with much enthusiasm!

Ever since being appointed adjutant, I had been determined that my role would be predominantly operational and not chiefly concerned with personnel management and administration, for which adjutants within the army's former Pentropic infantry battalions had been primarily responsible. In this I was helped in having a reliable assistant adjutant, an exceptionally capable chief clerk in Staff Sergeant Merv Fridolf, and an experienced orderly room sergeant, Sergeant John Leaman. My principal role therefore was assistant operations officer and deputy to the operations officer who was also the OC Support Company. My job entailed responsibility for running the battalion command post (CP) and the organisation of all the battalion's air support activities, including helicopter movements and offensive air support.

In preparation for our roles I and the signals officer, Brian Le Dan, who was to be commander of the deployed BHQ Group, were both attached to the 173 Airborne Brigade for a two-battalion air assault into the area of Phuoc Tuy Province. 1st Australian Task Force (1 ATF) was to establish itself here about a week later. We joined the 1/503 at Bien Hoa airbase shortly before dawn, having spent the night before the operation with 1 RAR, which was soon to return home after its 12-month tour of duty as part of 173 Airborne Brigade.

The three-day operation was exhilarating. We flew south in an armada of helicopters, landed in an assembly area close to our supporting artillery battalion, and then flew with an assaulting rifle company into the objective landing zone (LZ), preceded by air strikes, artillery fire and, finally, by the machine guns and rockets of our accompanying helicopter gunship heavy fire teams. There was no opposition! This was the second time that 173 Airborne Brigade had carried out 'search and destroy' operations in the province to prepare for the arrival of 1 ATF; and on this occasion, during a series of heavy engagements, had inflicted considerable casualties on the Viet Cong (VC). By the time this operation had concluded, our friends had incurred a further eight dead and 23 wounded. Brian and I spent the whole time at the BHQ of 1/503, and watched closely how Lieutenant Colonel Coad and his immediate staff handled operations during the several contacts with VC. During one heavy contact, about four rounds of friendly artillery fire somehow dropped onto a platoon of their B Company, killing and wounding several American soldiers. At no time was there any panicky reaction to whatever was happening, especially when, during our first night, VC were reported as being within the BHQ perimeter. The next morning, a large Chinese-made, command-detonated, directional mine was found just outside the perimeter, which fortunately for us had failed to detonate. On return to Vung Tau, we continued preparations for our own airborne assault into LZ Hudson.

Max Carroll

5 RAR's shooting war started when we were placed under command of 173 Airborne Brigade on 24 May 1966. The Brigade was involved in Operation Hardihood, which was intended to insert 1 ATF into Phuoc Tuy Province. The first phase of the operation involved the Vietnamese authorities removing all inhabitants from within a 4,000-metre radius of Nui Dat, 1 ATF's selected base area, and resettling them elsewhere in the province. This was only partially achieved. The second phase, involving 173 Airborne Brigade, including us, was to clear the area surrounding 1 ATF's proposed base of any enemy forces. The brigade, less 5 RAR, conducted a helicopter assault onto LZ Hudson, which was a couple of thousand metres north of the Nui Dat hill feature. This took place on 17 May 1966, so we, 5 RAR, had a secure LZ for our insertion by helicopter. Our American colleagues had not had an easy time before our arrival. On the first day of their insertion, 1/503 had a heavy engagement and lost 12 killed in action (KIA) and 35 wounded in action (WIA). By 21 May 1966 the brigade had sustained a total of 19 KIA and 75 WIA. The attrition continued. As we were flying in, while clearing the bitterly fought-over village of Long Phuoc, the 2/503 had lost another 19 KIA and 90 WIA. It is not widely known what total casualties 173 Airborne Brigade sustained to get us lodged; and all before we had fired a shot! This was the seldom acknowledged background to 1 ATF's insertion into Phuoc Tuy Province.

At this point in my narrative, I should acknowledge that 5 RAR operations from May to August 1966 are already well documented in Bob O'Neill's *Vietnam Task*; as are those of both 5 RAR and 6 RAR in Ian McNeill's official history volume 1, *To Long Tan*. Therefore, I have no intention of reprising their excellent coverage, but I hope to provide material from a personal experience viewpoint, which will put additional flesh onto the bones of their histories of this period.

Our arrival at LZ Hudson went smoothly and our companies rapidly deployed into their assigned areas of search. We did not want our people tarrying at LZ Hudson as it was congested with the Brigade Headquarters and their protective elements, and the operation's fire support base. By early afternoon our Battalion Command Group also moved off to a preselected location, from where we could better control our mobile companies. During that first day, several fleeting, indecisive contacts with VC occurred so all were on full alert. On the evening of 24 May 1966, our first day in operations, we lost our first fatal battle casualty, Private Errol Noack. For the next 10 days or so we probed further to the east, with all our companies having contacts and killing VC without further loss to ourselves. The enemy we encountered were what we termed 'Local Forces' (district companies); and it appeared that the D445 Provincial Mobile Battalion, with which 1/503 and 2/503 had been heavily engaged, had withdrawn to sanctuary areas to regroup. Our American colleagues may have taken casualties, but they had badly mauled the VC, particularly at the villages of Long Tan, which they had levelled to the ground, and Long Phuoc.

A further recollection by Peter Isaacs of an incident in this period is of interest. Peter recalls that, while we were still with 173 Airborne Brigade, one of our companies had a contact shortly before last light and captured two badly wounded VC. The company commander decided not to call for them to be evacuated, as to do so would compromise his company's night position. Both died during the night. The following day the 173 Brigade commander, Brigadier General Smith, visited our BHQ. He took our CO Lieutenant Colonel John Warr aside and said that while 5 RAR was under his command, we would treat VC wounded in exactly the same way we would treat our own wounded. It was an unexpected rebuke by a general from an army frequently described as being ruthless in pursuit of body count. I must amplify Peter's account at this point by continuing the story and setting the record straight. I made the decision not to evacuate the VC casualties. After closely questioning the OC A Company, Major Bert Cassidy, I was told the VC were mortally wounded, unconscious and close to death. At the time it was dark, so I refused to risk a *Dustoff* (medical evacuation) helicopter and crew with a hazardous night extraction for dying VC, although I would have done it for our own people. Another important consideration was that the VC did not recognise the sanctity of the Red Cross and fired at all low-flying aircraft. A further factor to be weighed was that of revealing A Company's location, where some lights would have to have been displayed to bring in the *Dustoff*. I told Bert to keep the casualties comfortable with morphine until they died. I later informed John Warr of what I had done and he reluctantly agreed with my decision. He accepted General Smith's rebuke for my decision! I respected General Smith very much and he was a good commander; but I still think, in view of the circumstances at the time, my decision was correct. The safety and security of our people and those of our allies came first.

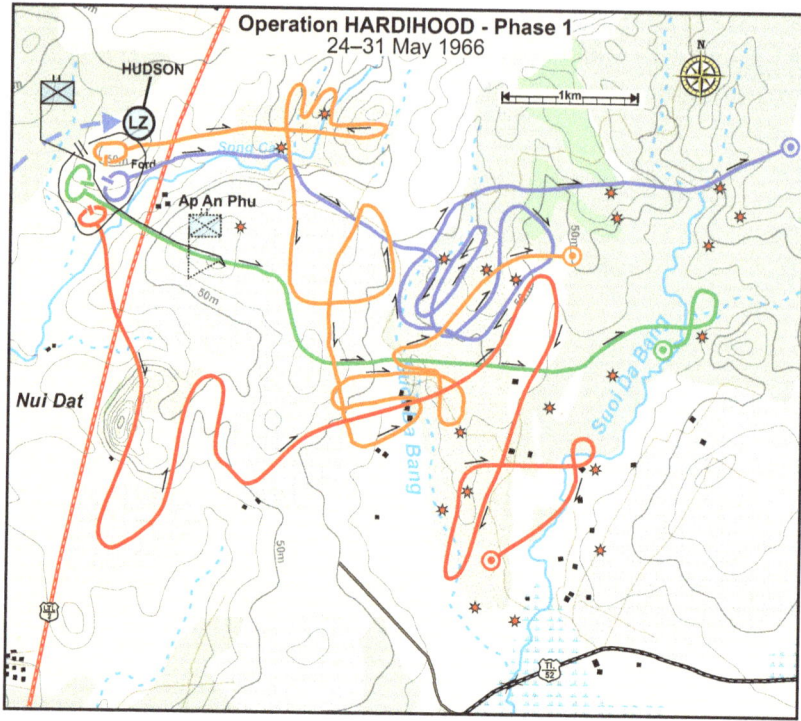

Map 3: Operation Hardihood – Phase 1: 24–31 May 1966.

Source: Designed by Ron Boxall and produced by Alan Mayne from circa 1966 US military maps provided by Bruce Davies.

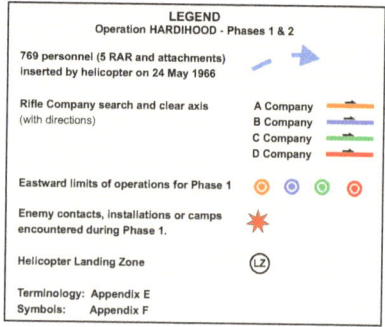

4. 5 RAR ON OPERATIONS, MAY–SEPTEMBER 1966

Peter Isaacs

After his remonstration about enemy casualties, General Smith then referred to his map and said, 'Colonel, there is a VC battalion there! Go get 'em!' The commander of 1 ATF, Brigadier David Jackson, was standing nearby listening. He took John Warr aside and said, 'On no account are you to tangle with a VC battalion'. Our A Company was close to the position indicated by the 173 Brigade commander. Max Carroll swiftly gave instructions to OC A Company, Bert Cassidy, to move – rapidly! Bert was apparently eating at the time, having just completed a resupply. His lunch was abandoned as A Company took off at high speed.

Max Carroll

To add to Peter's account of this incident, I think it is a good example of the chain of command problem for John Warr, which was always in the background at that time. While we were part of 173 Airborne Brigade, General Smith was our operational commander. However, national interests were very much the concern of Brigadier Jackson, the commander of 1 ATF, to whose command we were to revert a few days later. The recent political concerns following our first fatal battle casualty, Private Errol Noack, a national serviceman, would also have been fresh in Brigadier Jackson's mind when he spoke to John Warr.

On 2 June 1966, 5 RAR began to concentrate on what was to be the 1 ATF Base Area at Nui Dat. On 3 June 1966, the next operational phase of Operation Hardihood commenced and we occupied a temporary defensive position around Nui Dat. By 5 June we had provided a patrol screen to cover the arrival of the remainder of 1 ATF from Vung Tau. On 5 June 1966, HQ 1 ATF assumed command of the area from HQ 173 Airborne Brigade. We, 5 RAR, were the only Australian infantry battalion on the ground as 6 RAR was still assembling at Vung Tau after arriving from Australia and, consequently, our companies were rather widely spread. Then, on 8 June 1966, 173 Airborne Brigade moved on to conduct Operation Hollandia in the Long Hai hills, which stretch from 10 kilometres south of Nui Dat to the southernmost coast of Phuoc Tuy. This meant that we were on our own.

VIETNAM VANGUARD

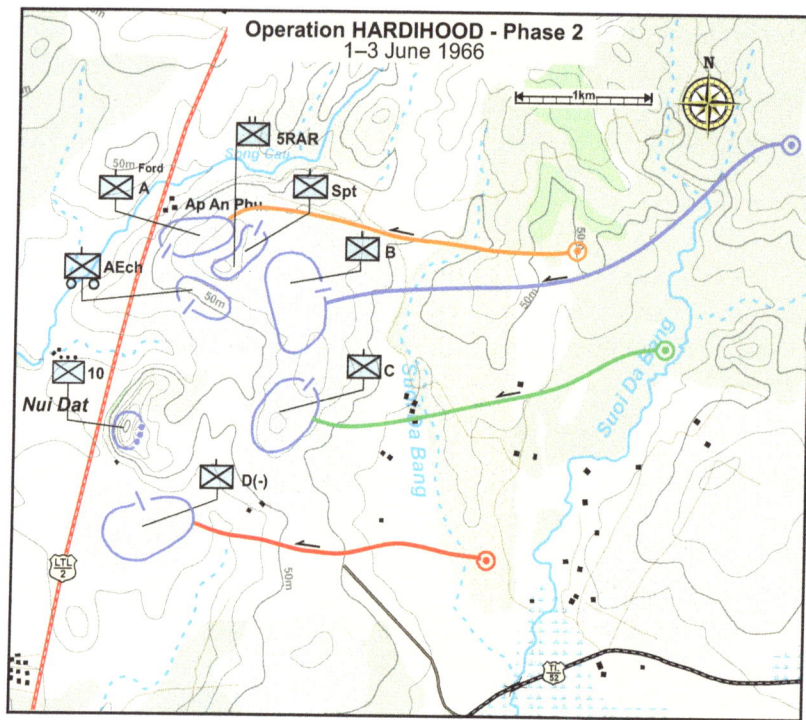

Map 4: Operation Hardihood – Phase 2: 1–3 June 1966.

Source: Designed by Ron Boxall and produced by Alan Mayne from circa 1966 US military maps provided by Bruce Davies.

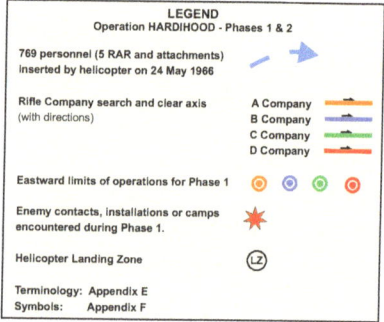

We continued with a heavy program of aggressive patrolling and night ambushing in order to dominate our thinly held area. It was a very tense time. The departure of 173 Airborne Brigade had been noted by the VC and consequently, for several nights, our various dispersed company perimeters were probed by their reconnaissance patrols, who tried to establish our general dispositions and especially the locations of our machine guns. These patrols were very professional in their conduct and were obviously carried out by an enemy of higher calibre than we had encountered to date. We expected to be hit heavily as allied intelligence sources had warned HQ 1 ATF of this VC intention but, for reasons unknown to us at that time, the attack did not eventuate.

On a later operation in October 1966, we captured documents which confirmed that the VC Main Force 274 Regiment had in fact intended to attack us in June. They had moved to a position near the large hill Nui Nghe, about 6 kilometres north-west of Nui Dat, while their patrols reconnoitred our positions. However, on 9 June 1966, a US light observation aircraft which had been supporting us had disappeared on its return flight to Bien Hoa. We were tasked to provide a company on standby to go to the assistance of the crew, but aerial searches along their flight path found no trace of the missing *Birddog* and our company was not deployed. The captured documents also revealed that the VC 274 Regiment had shot down this aircraft and the enemy commander decided that there would be more advantage in placing an ambush around the wreck and destroying the rescue force than in attacking our rapidly developing base. Perhaps we were lucky not to locate the crash location until six months later when A Company, which I was then commanding, found the missing aircraft and the remains of the crew. In the light of a strengthening enemy presence in Phuoc Tuy, which became evident in early June, 6 RAR were hastened forward to join us on 14 June, a week earlier than intended. With their arrival, Operation Hardihood concluded.

We were glad to see 6 RAR arrive so that we could regroup our companies into our final battalion defensive position in the now-established 1 ATF Base, and have them share the patrolling load. Our people were getting rather tired from three weeks of constant, hard operations with no respite. When they were not out on patrol or ambushing by night, the digging-in and construction of our base was a high priority for their labours. This work had to be done by hand with the field tools we carried, as no engineer earth-moving plant support was available at that time. Throughout this period the incessant, heavy monsoon rain turned the area into a quagmire of deep, sticky red mud. Everyone was constantly wet from rain or sweat, and clothing and boots soon began to rot. The hoochies (one-man shelters), which each man carried, provided barely adequate protection from rain when trying to sleep. These conditions, coupled with monotonous US combat rations, started to take their toll and we all became rather lean and mean.

We welcomed the arrival of our administrative echelon from Vung Tau. They completed our unit on the ground, and brought a lot of the gear we needed to establish ourselves. Essential barbed wire, steel pickets, sandbags and other defence stores were followed by marquee tentage to protect kitchens and QM (quartermaster) Stores and, later, accommodation tentage followed. To our annoyance, the latter arrived without their wooden poles. The army's initial logistic support for our deployment had acute problems which were exacerbated by contemptible trade union sabotage on the wharves in Australia.

For the rest of June, 5 RAR clashed with VC and sustained casualties as we patrolled the approaches to the Task Force base; but the casualty ratio was heavily in our favour. We also continued the development of the defences of our own base area. In addition, we had to provide a company on standby as 1 ATF's immediate reserve and another company to secure 6 RAR's base area while they were deployed on their Operation Enoggera. This task required them to search Long Phuoc village and destroy an extensive tunnel system. It was a dangerous village and 6 RAR razed it to the ground. Throughout our year of operations there was no respite for either of the two battalions. When one was on a battalion operation, the other had to remain at Nui Dat in the base protection and construction role. A third battalion was obviously needed for 1 ATF, but none was available. It was not until December 1967 that a third battalion was provided, together with a squadron of Centurion tanks. In the meantime, we got on with the job despite being continually stretched.

Another problem, which had not been resolved before we left Australia, now arose. This was a shortage of M60 general purpose machine guns. The number of guns was adequate when the unit was together as in our defensive role in base. However, when we left the base and went on battalion-sized operations, the bulk of the M60s went with the combat troops, leaving the base denuded of machine guns. A theatre increment of additional weapons was needed for base defence and, for some months, we had been pressing for this to no avail. Survival demanded that we help ourselves. Our inimitable battalion 2IC, Major Stan Maizey, entrepreneur and trader extraordinaire, and his personally selected and talented team, designated the 'Scrounger Platoon', duly 'acquired' a number of .30 calibre Browning light machine guns (LMGs) and .50 calibre Browning heavy machine guns (HMG) and about 50,000 rounds of ammunition from an American source. We sited the latter in key bunkers on our perimeter and the smaller weapons were mounted on vehicles. Their significant additional firepower made the people who remained in base during operations a lot happier and more secure. The theatre increment was eventually approved and we received more M60s; but we kept the .50 calibre HMGs and passed them on to 7 RAR who relieved us in May 1967. While the army's inadequately prepared logistics system was sorting itself out, Stan and his team also 'found' many of the items essential for our base security, such as telephones, switchboards, radios, and even a US 2.5-ton, 6-wheel-drive truck. We left these items for 7 RAR as well.

The remainder of the month was busy for me as I was coordinating our patrol and ambushing activities, developing my own Support Company base area and working with the CO on plans for our next operation. This was to follow 6 RAR's scheduled return to Nui Dat on 5 July 1966, after completing their Operation Enoggera. There was no let-up in the tempo of Task Force operations as we departed the base on 6 July to mount our Operation Sydney until 17 July 1966. We were tasked to clear and extend the 1 ATF-controlled area to the north and north-west, including Nui Nghe. This feature, located about 6 kilometres north-west of Nui Dat, was a prominent jungle-clad hill with numerous radiating ridges, rising about 160 metres above the surrounding flat terrain and covering about 1.5 square kilometres. It dominated the surrounding country out to several kilometres in all directions but had not been cleared of VC during Operation Hardihood. We were going into unknown enemy territory, so were prepared for trouble.

Our planning for Operation Sydney had been thorough, as the area we had to cover was large and included a variety of terrain, and tracks which had to be checked for signs of enemy activity. Although the enemy we anticipated encountering were local and district VC units, the appearance of the Main Force battalions of 274 and 275 Regiments could not be discounted. It was desirable, indeed essential, that our companies could assist each other if one struck trouble, but the formidable obstacle of Nui Nghe could prevent this. Also, some distances to which we proposed to penetrate were at extreme range for our supporting artillery. The CO and I spent a lot of time examining the problems, first by personal aerial reconnaissance, followed by tasking ground patrols to reconnoitre the areas to be covered. We were looking for possible artillery fire support bases, and suitable ground routes for the passage of armoured personnel carriers (APC). We then conducted the time-honoured military assessment known as 'an appreciation of the situation'. I found John Warr to be a good and easy man to work for. He had a keen intellect and a good tactical brain which quickly assessed the value of views and ideas I put to him, before he gave me his outline plan.

My job was then to get down to the detail and produce a draft operation order, which Warr then cleared. In this instance, we established our BHQ with a fire support base (FSB) code-named Tennis. FSB Tennis was located a few kilometres north-west of the Task Force base to provide artillery fire support to our northernmost elements, who might need to move out of range of the 1 ATF guns at Nui Dat. From FSB Tennis our direct support artillery, 105 Field Battery, could easily support our companies when they were at the planned limits of their assigned search areas. We also had one company held in reserve at FSB Tennis, together with the APC troop of 12 tracked armoured fighting vehicles which was allotted to us, to rapidly react should any of the searching companies get into trouble. The Anti-Tank Platoon and Pioneer Platoon were also at FSB Tennis to protect the guns and BHQ, should our reserve company have to be deployed in support of the searching companies.

Bob O'Neill gave a good account of this successful operation in his book *Vietnam Task*. There is little to add, except to record the loss of a good soldier to friendly fire. Our supporting gunners were excellent; and their control and accuracy had always been spot on. On this occasion, the target was on the summit of Nui Nghe; and for reasons which can only be explained by artillerymen, three rounds in a salvo of six went high, just cleared the crest of Nui Nghe, and unfortunately landed among C Company's 9 Platoon who were operating on the north-western side of the hill and killed one of their soldiers.

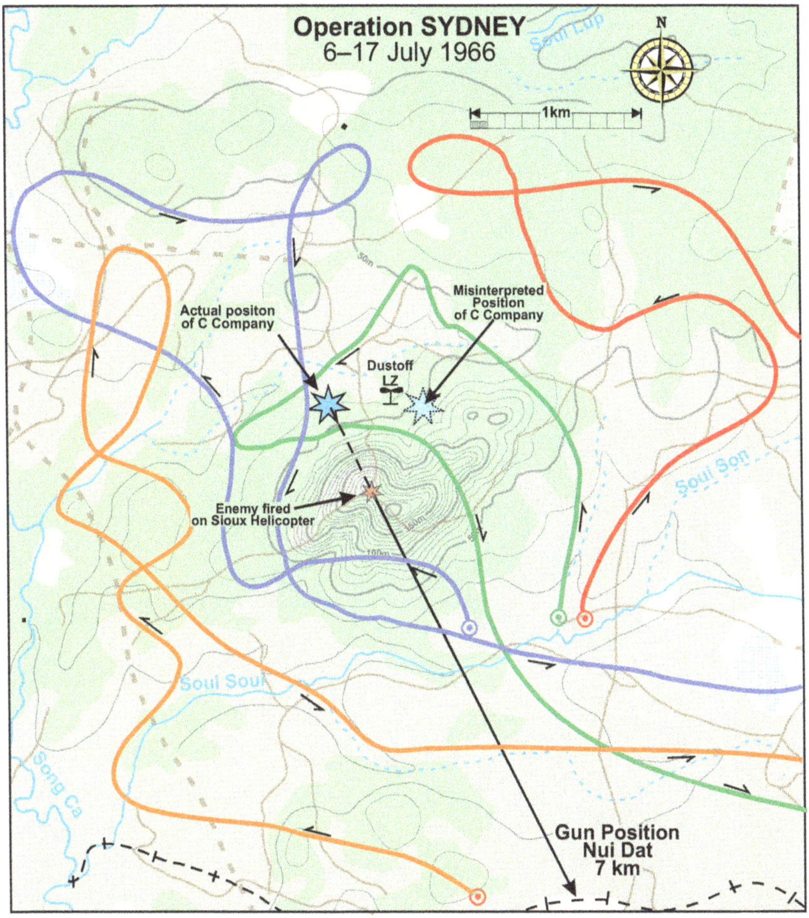

4. 5 RAR ON OPERATIONS, MAY–SEPTEMBER 1966

Map 5: Operation Sydney: 6–17 July 1966.

Source: Designed by Ron Boxall and produced by Alan Mayne from circa 1966 US military maps provided by Bruce Davies.

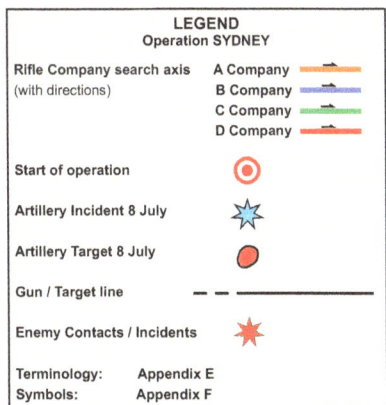

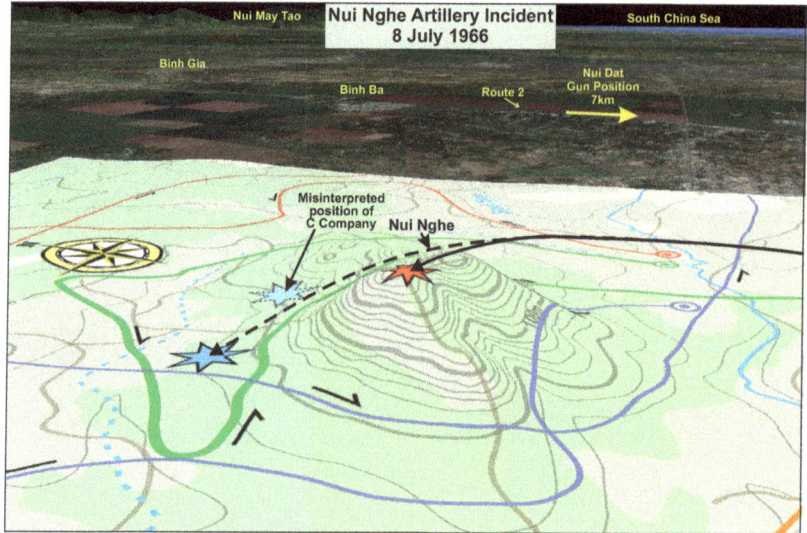

Map 5A: Nui Nghe artillery incident: 8 July 1966.

Source: Designed by Ron Boxall and produced by Alan Mayne from circa 1966 US military maps provided by Bruce Davies.

We were angered and shocked, our gunners were mortified and an investigation followed. Enemy ground fire had been directed at a Sioux helicopter from the summit of Nui Nghe and clearance had been given for the target to be engaged by artillery located at the Task Force base at Nui Dat. One round 'fire for effect' from each of the tasked battery's six guns was fired simultaneously. Three of these rounds cleared the crest being targeted and landed in C Company's area. One of them struck a tree near 9 Platoon scattering lethal shrapnel and killing Lance Corporal Marinko 'Titch' Tomas.

Roger Wainwright

Artillery fire control procedures required that the locations of nearby friendly troops had to be confirmed before clearance to fire was given. The location of C Company had been incorrectly decoded at the battery headquarters due to misinterpretation of a signaller's handwriting in a log book. The error placed C Company 600 metres further to the east and well out of danger from the fire mission. If C Company's position had been accurately interpreted, clearance to fire would not have been given. The circumstances of this occurrence are shown in Maps 5 and 5A. In war, such incidents can be the result of one or more of many variables or, as in this case, a momentary lapse in a team of highly dedicated professionals working under pressure. Fortunately, for 5 RAR these proved to be rare.

Max Carroll

During Operation Sydney it became clear that we would have to do something about the village of Duc My, which was on the north-eastern flank of our area of search. We knew that most of the village's inhabitants were forcibly resettled indigenes known as Montagnards, gathered together from throughout Phuoc Tuy several years earlier in a badly managed South Vietnamese Government attempt at population control. These people, originally hill tribes from Central Vietnam, did not like the government and were susceptible to VC influence. We also knew that there was a village squad of about 15 VC in Duc My to keep the population in line, and to extort taxes and food from the already impoverished people. A major tenet of counter-insurgency warfare is to separate the civilian population from enemy control and influence and open the way for re-establishment of government control. We now had a good opportunity to put this into practice and eliminate the village's VC squad. With this in mind, the CO gained approval from the Commander 1 ATF to extend our present operation by several days to conduct a cordon and search operation of Duc My on the night of 19/20 July 1966. This extension was named Operation Sydney Two.

At that time cordon and search operations had not been conducted at battalion level in Vietnam. Indeed, Allied forces of that size rarely moved operationally at night, but the VC did! What we were about to undertake would break new ground in Vietnam. I had limited knowledge of what was involved. When I was at Staff College in 1965, this subject had been considered briefly and its many problems discussed. Both directing staff and students agreed it was a difficult tactical exercise. John Warr had read widely on the subject and knew what his battalion had to do, so it was with keen interest we did the preliminary map study, aerial reconnaissance and the customary military appreciation of the situation. As a result, a ground reconnaissance was then deemed necessary to confirm the suitability of approach routes we had selected for the battalion to move in by night and establish the cordon before the village became aware of our intentions. This was a complex operation and we endeavoured to keep the final plan as simple as possible. As always seems to happen when getting down to the fine detail, we found problems which meant compromises had to be made.

There was a stream running through the village from north-east to south-west, then on towards our location at FSB Tennis. This initially appealed as a good directional guide to assist our night approach to the south side of the village, and from there our companies could diverge to their assigned cordon positions. A night reconnaissance patrol, which included all four of the rifle company 2ICs, found this approach unsuitable so we had to think again. The village houses were widely scattered on the western side of Route 2 within an area about 600 metres square. The allocation of troops to each identified task then had to be carefully considered.

At that time 5 RAR could place about 550 men in the field. We decided each company forming a side of the cordon would have two platoons forward, in line, with men in pairs every 20 metres. The third platoon was to be positioned back in depth 70 metres or so for rear security. Each company cordon frontage could cover about 450 metres, and even if all four companies were placed in the cordon, we could not secure the whole village. We therefore decided we would have to exclude some of the outer houses. In broad outline, our final plan was that three of the companies would move at night to a position to the rear of their intended cordon positions, C Company from the west, while B and D Companies and the CO's party came in from the east, with all three companies to move forward into their final cordon positions and link with each other immediately after first light.

A Company, BHQ, two sections of mortars and the Anti-Tank Platoon, all mounted on APCs, were to close from the south at the last possible moment. A Company, while mounted on APCs, acted as the battalion reserve during the move-in. They then dismounted and rapidly moved to their cordon position on the south flank while the Anti-Tank Platoon also dismounted and took over the role of battalion reserve. We then had A Company closing off the south with B Company doing the same on the east, C Company was on the west and D Company temporarily on the north, in open young rubber trees, until relieved by the APC troop. D Company then became the search company for the village. In the event it worked well, with some exciting moments. During their night approach, the leading D Company soldier, Private Fred Clarke, in Stygian darkness, fell 10 metres down a disused well. After he was quietly and safely retrieved using toggle ropes, D Company's clandestine insertion resumed.

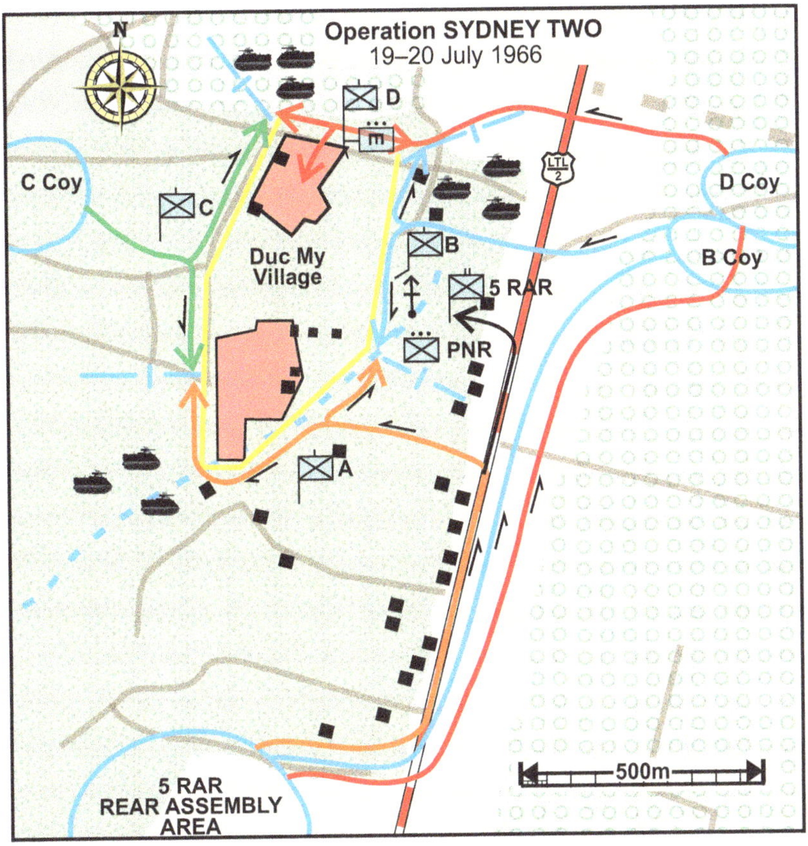

Map 6: Operation Sydney Two: 19–20 July 1966.

Source: Designed by Ron Boxall and produced by Alan Mayne from circa 1966 US military maps provided by Bruce Davies.

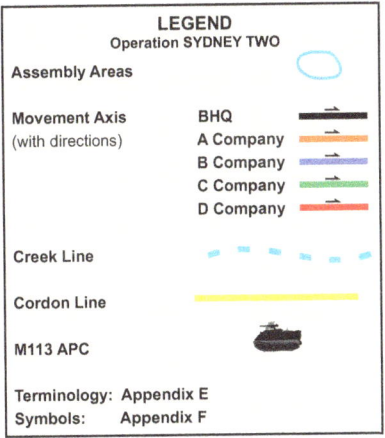

When the cordon was closed, several firefights erupted as VC attempted to escape. With the enemy who were killed, wounded and captured, we had cleaned out the place without loss to ourselves. Good fire discipline was essential to safeguard civilians, and our carefully thought-out rules of engagement, issued before the operation, were adhered to during its execution. After the village was cleared and the population screened, civil affairs aid in the form of medical and dental treatment was given to the villagers, which favourably impressed them. Our soldiers were firm but friendly and courteous, and they were well received. We withdrew from the village during the afternoon of 20 July 1966 to mount clearing operations in the surrounding areas, where we killed one VC and wounded another before harbouring (deploying defensively and adopting night routine) in separate company groups. We also set four overnight ambushes on likely approaches to the village to engage any VC who tried to re-enter it. During company sweeps on 21 and 22 July, we killed another VC and wounded two, one of whom escaped and the other was captured. The CO then got task force approval for C and D Companies to remain in the area for a further day, while the remainder of the battalion withdrew to Nui Dat to relieve 6 RAR for their Operation Hobart, due to commence on 24 July; there still being no let-up in the tempo of 1 ATF operations. We were well-satisfied with Operations Sydney and Sydney Two, both having been quite successful.

Operation Sydney Two was the first of nine cordon and search operations that 5 RAR conducted during our year in Vietnam. We learnt from each one and progressively refined our execution. Our methods were subsequently adopted as standard procedures in 1 ATF. John Warr wrote an excellent article for the *Australian Army Journal*, published in November 1967 in its Edition No 222, entitled 'Cordon and Search Operations in Phuoc Tuy Province'. It can be read in its entirety in Appendix C. His paper became a very significant input into the ongoing development of Australian Army doctrine on counter-revolutionary warfare.

After our success with Operation Sydney Two, the CO was keen to go again, with the much larger complex at Binh Ba as the target. The task force commander concurred, but 6 RAR's next operation had priority. From 24 July, we had to provide a company to protect their operational fire support base, as well as another to protect 6 RAR's base area at Nui Dat, plus another as 1 ATF's immediate reserve. We became used to this sort of situation. Then the picture changed when 6 RAR struck trouble, necessitating a second company of ours joining them. Our people remained under command of 6 RAR until the whole force was recalled to base due to reports of a serious enemy threat unfolding to the west. Our B Company, with the Anti-Tank Platoon under command, was then dispatched to check out the report of a large enemy build-up. They returned late on 31 July having found a two-day-old, company-sized VC camp. D Company of 6 RAR conducted a similar patrol to the north-east, and returned on 2 August with nothing to report. Assessing the reliability of reports of VC movements from Vietnamese and other allies was a real problem for our intelligence people at that time. Nevertheless, we could not move until the situation clarified, so we did a lot of planning and were well prepared to commence our Operation Holsworthy, the cordon and search of Binh Ba.

With the lessons we learnt from our dress rehearsal at Duc My, we were far better equipped to handle the much larger complex of Binh Ba and the adjacent hamlet of Duc Trung, with an all-up population of about 2,000. We also were tasked to 'revisit' Duc My, so we were faced with a two-phased operation which went well with only a few minor hitches. We had two companies of 6 RAR under command, along with many others from various combat arms and combat support services units, both Australian and US. These latter included air support, interpreters and Vietnamese police. The operational functions of all elements had to be tied together and, as the operation's success indicated, we achieved a satisfying level of combined professionalism. Our preliminary reconnaissance commenced on 5 August when C Company established a patrol base to the south-west of Binh Ba. On the night of 5/6 August, reconnaissance patrols checked the suitability of proposed assembly areas, routes and timings. The CO issued his orders on 7 August, and at 0800 hours on the following day, Captain Peter Isaacs departed with a patrol of company guides to lay out and secure the assembly area for the five rifle companies and BHQ who would be approaching the cordon area from the west. B Company was moving separately and approaching their cordon position from the east.

Peter Isaacs

I was responsible for laying out the battalion's assembly area to the south-west of Binh Ba village. Comprised of platoon guides from each of the 5 RAR and 6 RAR cordon companies, this 15-man crew set off 90 minutes before the rest of the battalion and proceeded north towards our objective. Feeling rather vulnerable, with only my trusty shepherd's crook and a 9 mm pistol, I was less than pleased to be handed an 81 mm mortar round to carry as my patrol left our base! Nothing occurred until we came to the edge of a track close to the assembly area. The lead scout indicated by silent hand signals the presence of what he thought were four VC approaching along the track. I gave the silent signal to establish an immediate ambush, drew my pistol and cocked it. The battalion was by now strung out in a long 'snake' not far behind us and contact with a small group of VC at this stage would compromise our cordoning and searching of the large village of Binh Ba. The VC turned out to be rubber tree tappers returning home. Fortunately, they gave no sign of having seen us.

Max Carroll

We applied the many lessons learnt from Duc My and had the cordon in position and closed by 0530 hours, which was 25 minutes before first light. In this we were assisted by having moonlight and a clean rubber plantation to move through. The result was that, without having to fire a shot, we apprehended and interrogated 169 males of military age, of whom 17 were confirmed VCs and 77 were suspects. Route 2 was opened to civilian traffic to Ba Ria and the province chief was eventually able to establish a Vietnamese military presence in Binh Ba. Until the so-called Provincial Reconnaissance Unit became available for this task, we left a company at Binh Ba. Subsequently, one of our officers, Captain Ron Boxall, acted as commander/adviser with this non-ARVN (Army of the Republic of Vietnam) unit. Its replacement, an ARVN unit, was then advised by another of our officers, Captain Ron Bade. Boxall's group were armed civilians, all either Montagnards or Nungs (Vietnamese Chinese), and were recruited, armed and paid by a CIA agency engaged in irregular military activities in Phuoc Tuy province. Their replacements, Bade's group, were an ARVN Regional Force company provided by the Duc Thanh district chief, Captain Be. Boxall and Bade relate their experiences in Chapter 11. Bade's functions were eventually taken over by AATTV members in late November.

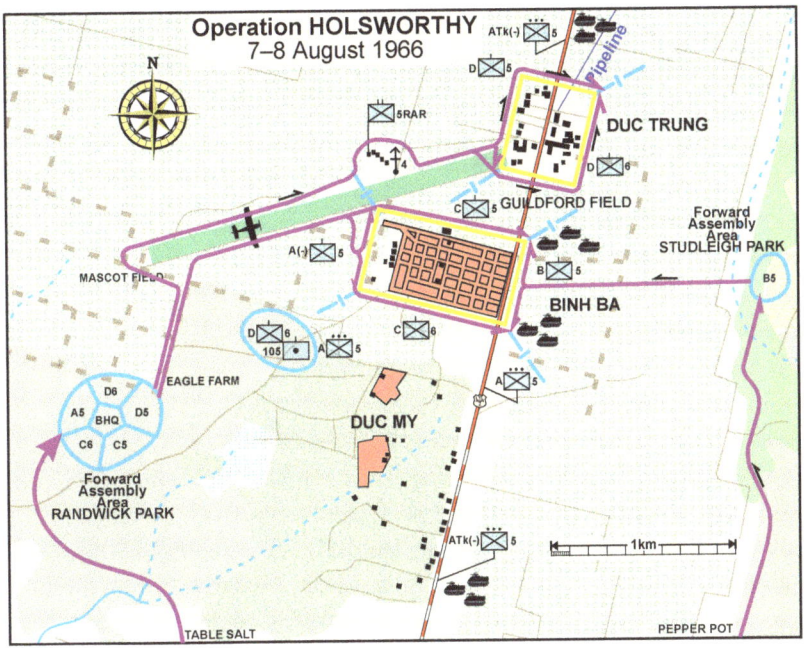

Map 7: Operation Holsworthy: 7–8 August 1966.

Source: Designed by Ron Boxall and produced by Alan Mayne from circa 1966 US military maps provided by Bruce Davies.

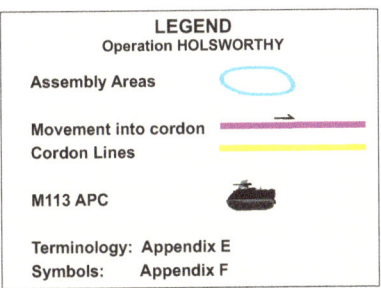

5 RAR remained at Binh Ba for several days after the cordon and search, in which time we secured Route 2 for civilian traffic to Ba Ria and carried out civil affairs tasks helping the people. We established a good rapport with the local Vietnamese Catholic priest and the resident French rubber plantation estate managers, whose lives under the VC must have been very difficult; and a large stockpile of their treated rubber was able to be moved down the road to Ba Ria. We also established liaison with the isolated ARVN outpost at Duc Thanh to the north of Binh Ba; and made the acquaintance of the very lonely US Army adviser, Major Bill Prescott, who was stationed there. Then we visited the large Vietnamese Catholic village of Binh Gia further to the north-east of Duc Thanh and established valuable liaison with the village leaders. It was a busy, productive time.

Before we were to return to Nui Dat, we were tasked to investigate an intelligence report that a VC HQ was located to the east of Binh Ba. We subsequently searched the area for several days and found no trace of VC presence. During the search, I made a liaison flight to Duc Thanh to brief Bill Prescott on our activities so that he could keep his people out of the way. While in his office I saw his battle map on the wall showing a big sweeping red arrow, indicating VC troop movements, leading from the VC-held May Tao Mountains in the far north-east of the province, south then west to Nui Dat. I asked him where he had obtained the information and whether it was accurate. He replied that it had come from the provincial ARVN HQ in Ba Ria where 1 ATF had a liaison officer, and that he believed it to be accurate. I immediately returned to our BHQ and contacted 1 ATF. It transpired that they knew of the report but believed the source was questionable. In view of the numerous false alarms we had been subjected to, this approach is perhaps understandable. However, that very night, 16/17 August 1966, the 1 ATF base was subjected to substantial mortar, recoilless rifle and light artillery fire from the east, which caused 24 wounded casualties, of whom two were serious. 1 ATF artillery responded with counter-fire and the next morning, on 17 August, 6 RAR dispatched patrols to locate the enemy firing positions. 5 RAR less C Company, who remained at Binh Ba, were recalled to Nui Dat as soon as our search for a VC HQ east of Binh Ba was concluded. We arrived back at Nui Dat on the afternoon of 18 August at about the time D Company, 6 RAR, became heavily engaged at the start of the Battle of Long Tan.

I flew over the battlefield next day in a Sioux light observation helicopter, as our OC D Company, Major Paul Greenhalgh, and his men were under command of 6 RAR for the clearance of the battlefield. The scene was like France in the First World War, with smashed trees, churned-up earth and desolation surrounding the small area where D Company, 6 RAR, had made their stand. It was a sobering but exhilarating scene, as we knew that the VC had suffered a significant defeat despite their greatly superior strength at the point of battle.

After Long Tan, immediate pursuit of the retreating enemy was hampered by other credible VC Main Force threats to both Nui Dat and Binh Ba. We did not have the strength on the ground at that time to both pursue and defend, so the Americans mounted a long-running operation, code-named Toledo, in which 5 RAR later became involved. We named our initial involvement Operation Darlinghurst and departed on 26 August for five days of operations in conjunction with US forces who were operating to our north. We slowly and carefully searched areas to the north then east of the 1 ATF Base, then turned south to Long Tan, then home. We did not encounter any VC nor fire a shot, although some VC mass graves were discovered, and abandoned equipment and ammunition indicated an enemy in hasty withdrawal.

We departed again on 2 September, to continue in Operation Toledo as a blocking force to the west of Binh Ba, while US forces swept an area to our north. We patrolled extensively around Nui Nghe, an area familiar to us, where we killed two VC and captured another, all of whom were trying to escape the Americans. We considered this to be a poor result for the effort expended and we all were rather tired and frustrated when we returned to base on 8 September 1966.

Our return from Operation Toledo allowed 6 RAR to depart on their Operation Vaucluse in the Nui Dinh hills; they were out from 8 to 24 September. We slipped back into the routine of one company on standby as task force immediate reserve, one company to secure 6 RAR's base area at Nui Dat, continual patrolling in the 1 ATF Tactical Area of Responsibility (TAOR) and, of course, the ongoing development of our own base area. During these activities, we did several one-day company-sized 'County Fair' operations in which we provided cordons of selected areas while the ARVN searched. We also did a 'Road Runner' operation (APC-mounted infantry) along Route 44 down to Long Hai, to show the VC and the locals that we could still use the road when we wanted to.

There was no let-up and, after 6 RAR returned to Nui Dat, we departed on Operation Crow's Nest on 1 October to follow up on information provided by a VC Main Force soldier of 274 Regiment, who had surrendered at Binh Gia on 28 September. We were out for three days to establish a small command element within the Duc Thanh compound, where we were hosted by Captain Be, the district chief, and his US Army adviser, Major Bill Prescott. At the same time, two of our companies and supporting APCs searched the areas to the north, up to and around a village called Ngai Giao. This was outside the northern extremity of the 1 ATF TAOR and had not been searched before. We did not strike any 274 Regiment elements, although D Company lost Private Graham Warburton to a sniper. We discovered a cache of over six tonnes of rice and a hoard of meat, which we confiscated. We gave the meat to Captain Be, who distributed it to the needy in his area. We then had to withdraw due to our imminent involvement in a major US operation, code-named Robin, along Route 15, the main road between Vung Tau and Saigon.

Robert O'Neill and Peter Isaacs

War is one of those human activities which continue by day and night. We tend to remember those parts of wars that happen in daylight. Then they are so arresting, and often spectacular. Most war films are set in daytime. Books, newspapers and magazines also focus on the actions of the day rather than those of the night. Yet, warfare continues both by day and night. At night, when on operations, our troops left their defended positions to patrol intensively, either quietly to gain information, or more openly to dominate the battlefield, and push their opponents back and demoralise them.

During the Vietnam War, Australian night operations included patrolling, ambushing and tactical concealment manoeuvres such as setting cordons or moving covertly into a new area. As several of the chapters of this book show, physical and mental exhaustion were continuing problems that members of the battalion accepted as part of their daily burden. When not moving at night, whether in the field or in base, each section and platoon would have several men on sentry rotation around the clock. Platoons and companies on patrol at night rarely had an opportunity for adequate sleep. They were on the alert continuously. When patrolling at night, most stood, crouched or moved carefully, listening and peering to catch any available hint of enemy movement among trees, rocks or over open ground in front of them. When they identified possibly hostile movement, they had to choose between remaining concealed or moving carefully before taking offensive action against intruders in our area of operations. All had to be aware that a night encounter with ill-informed friendly forces or innocent civilians, as well as the enemy, was always a possibility.

For a small group of us, the three captains on BHQ – Peter Isaacs, the adjutant, Brian Le Dan, the signals officer, and myself, the intelligence officer – the nights brought another set of responsibilities: we were the available pool of BHQ command post (CP) duty officers. So that the CO and the operations officer could get some uninterrupted sleep when

BHQ was not on the move at night, we divided the period from stand-down after sunset (around 2030) to stand-to before dawn (around 0500) into three 'watches' of around three hours each. Any action occurring between those hours in the battalion's area of responsibility was reported by radio to whoever of the three of us was on duty, and our first thought in response was whether to wake the CO or Max Carroll to take over conduct of the action. Most incidents reported to us were minor contacts or observation reports, and we could allow our seniors to continue sleeping. However, every now and then there were medium or higher-level clashes or ambushes in which our soldiers required artillery or mortar support. In response we would go first to Max, and he would make the decision on whether to handle the situation himself or awaken the CO.

When BHQ deployed on operations outside the Nui Dat base area, the actual CP usually occupied two parallel trenches dug into the earth, about two metres long and half a metre deep. The ground between the two provided a surface for maps, log books and radio sets. At night, a rudimentary and supposedly lightproof and waterproof shelter enclosed the duty officer and duty signallers. At stand-to periods, the CO and Max, plus the operator of the radio link to 1 ATF HQ, would cram into this restricted space too. Lighting was by hand torch – usually red-lensed to minimise the visibility of scattered light amid the green foliage that normally surrounded us. The commander of our direct support artillery battery, the mortar platoon commander and their signallers occupied a similar double trench close by. Occasionally, the CP was located within a deserted building or an armoured command vehicle and, on one occasion, a borrowed US Army air-conditioned caravan!

This system of night-time control worked well, but at the cost of constant tiredness during the day for each of the three of us, until we could get away for a couple days and catch up on lost sleep. Of course, we were not the only members of the battalion affected by daytime tiredness. It was a constant problem that all had to learn to manage, for we really needed to be sharp both by day and by night. Returning to peacetime routine in Australia was a great blessing in more ways than one.

Max Carroll

Peter Isaacs, who had come to the Australian Army from the British Army, observed that he considered himself fortunate in working in an outstanding battalion; a sentiment shared throughout the whole of 5 RAR. Despite the burdens of being in the 1 ATF vanguard from the outset, the shortages and oversights noted earlier and the need to conjure solutions to unforeseen operational problems, the morale of the battalion was holding up well following its first four months of hard service. Without doubt John Warr had forged a fine, aggressive fighting battalion of which we were all immensely proud.

Editors' conclusion

This chapter has described 5 RAR's early forays into the unique mix of military and civilian aspects of operations in Vietnam; and how, through necessity, this mixture settled quickly into differing types of operation and devised its own initiative-driven systems of problem-solving and improvisation. This approach inevitably became the dominant mode in 5 RAR's deployment in the first wave of 1 ATF's battalions in Phuoc Tuy. The next chapter describes the effects of the expanding presence of 1 ATF on the lives of both the VC and the province's civilian population, and the role of intelligence in shaping our relations with these two groups.

5

INTELLIGENCE WORK IN PHUOC TUY AFTER LONG TAN

Robert O'Neill

As Brigadier Chamberlain has written in Appendix D, the Viet Cong and their predecessors, the Viet Minh, had long had a substantial presence in Phuoc Tuy. In May 1966, when 1st Australian Task Force (1 ATF) began to arrive and build a substantial and defensible base at Nui Dat, we were at a serious disadvantage in terms of local knowledge. The Viet Cong knew the country and people of Phuoc Tuy well, they had some political leverage over the local people, and they were indigenous. We were newcomers to the country and people. Very few of us spoke Vietnamese. And at some point we would be withdrawing. The big question was who would we be leaving in charge – the Viet Cong or the Saigon-based Government of the Republic of Vietnam?

We all thought that to be successful, Australia would have to make a long-term military commitment to Vietnam. Therefore, its costs had to be acceptable to the Australian public for whatever time it took for this effort to become effective. We needed early successes that were judged to be significant by the Australian Government and people, and we had to complete the process of settling into Phuoc Tuy without suffering heavy casualties. The Viet Cong and North Vietnamese leadership, having been through a long war with the French, ending only 12 years before our arrival in Phuoc Tuy, had drawn their own lessons from costly experience. They had to deny any appearance of early victory to their enemies and inflict heavy casualties on them, even at the cost of suffering a commensurate number themselves.

The first priority for the Viet Cong forces in Phuoc Tuy after our arrival was to reconnoitre our positions. How strong were we at Nui Dat and in Vung Tau? How well equipped were we? How well were our defences laid out and built? How reliant were we on the Americans? How capable were we in operational terms? How well did we understand counter-insurgency warfare in South-East Asia? How effective were we in more conventional operations? Were we likely to collapse when under direct attack? Could we be ambushed and kept confined and ineffective by relatively moderate, province-based forces, such as the district companies and D445 Battalion?

These were all compelling questions to which the Viet Cong had to have answers fairly quickly. So, we were in for a period of being reconnoitred, inspected, tested and assessed by our enemy, beginning on day one of our arrival in Phuoc Tuy. We were fortunate in being accompanied by the US 173 Airborne Brigade, but we saw that local Viet Cong forces were out and about, probing and searching from the commencement of Operation Hardihood on 24 May 1966. We could tell from their numbers, weapons and uniforms that these local units were only light forces. But we also knew that heavier forces were available, especially 274 and 275 Regiments, over 3,000 troops in all, who were capable of inflicting heavy blows on us. Once 173 Airborne Brigade had departed from Phuoc Tuy, the real testing would come. As Brigadier Chamberlain has recorded, in June 274 Regiment, the stronger of the two Main Force Viet Cong regiments that we faced, came in close to check us out. They probably would have made an attack if they had thought the chances of inflicting a heavy blow on us were good. However, perhaps over-cautiously, they chose not to make a major attack in June or July but to set an ambush for us, around a recently crashed US aircraft. Our perimeter at Nui Dat was tested by small Viet Cong patrols at night during June and July, and when they felt that they had our measure, they came in on 17 August with a large attacking force: 275 Regiment assisted by D445 Provincial Mobile Battalion. We were fortunate that the Viet Cong revealed their presence by rather premature mortar, light artillery and recoilless rifle fire against the Task Force base on 17 August. Next day, 275 Regiment encountered a relatively strong Australian reaction force, D Company of 6th Battalion, the Royal Australian Regiment (6 RAR), our sister battalion. In a determined action fought out on the afternoon of 18 August, just north of the village of Long Tan, the Viet Cong attack was contained, D Company of 6 RAR was reinforced late in the day, and held its ground and inflicted heavy losses on 275 Regiment, 245 confirmed dead and an estimated several hundred wounded.

These losses led their commander to break off the action and withdraw his force from the battlefield. Follow-up patrolling by a joint Australian–US force discovered that the Viet Cong had fully withdrawn from the eastern approaches to Nui Dat. 5 RAR took part in this phase of the clearance of eastern Phuoc Tuy, sweeping 8 kilometres east of Binh Ba, then 8 kilometres south, before returning to Nui Dat, another 8 kilometres to the north-west. In five days, the battalion patrolled over 40 kilometres on foot, carefully searching the jungle we were passing through, digging defences to hold off any night attack by the Viet Cong, and sending out small reconnaissance patrols to check whether there was continuing enemy movement close to the base. The searching was made more difficult because we were still in the wet season. At around 2 pm on most afternoons a mass of dark grey clouds would build up overhead, soon to send down heavy rain showers, which saturated our clothing and equipment and turned the ground into muddy porridge. Several days and nights of those conditions created muscular, skin and accumulated fatigue problems.

Of course the Viet Cong also had to deal with these challenges. Local resources and knowledge may have eased their discomfort relative to ours, but nonetheless, everybody, on both sides in this war, had to learn to cope with the effects of heavy rain, physical exhaustion and mental stress. While 275 Regiment had been concentrating for its mission against Nui Dat in mid-August, 274 Regiment had been active in western Phuoc Tuy, attempting to deny the use of Route 15 to the Americans by taking over some of the defended villages along the highway. Phu My was attacked several times in August 1966, and signals intelligence indicated that the commander of 274 Regiment, assisted by local Viet Cong companies and D445 Battalion, was determined to close the road to South Vietnamese Government and allied use.

This knowledge was particularly worrying for General Westmoreland and his senior intelligence and operations advisers. To reinforce the US position around the major US bases at Bear Cat, Bien Hoa, Long Binh and Saigon, they needed to move troops along Route 15. How much the Viet Cong knew about this American plan is difficult to say, but their increased level of activity in western Phuoc Tuy, especially on and close to Route 15, suggests that the Viet Cong had gained relevant intelligence, studied Westmoreland's priorities and were ready to take serious action to thwart him.

Certainly, Westmoreland knew that the Viet Cong had a heightened interest in controlling Route 15, and one of the main purposes in deploying 1 ATF into Phuoc Tuy was to be able to prevent the Viet Cong from dominating the road. For much of September, the Task Force was divided, with 6 RAR conducting clearing operations in the Nui Dinh hills, and 5 RAR conducting more clearing and defensive operations around and to the north of Binh Ba, including the district headquarters at Duc Thanh.

The American reinforcement of their position around Bien Hoa and Saigon in early October was planned to commence with the movement of a brigade of troops, by road, from Vung Tau to Bear Cat. Therefore, General Westmoreland left no doubt in the mind of Brigadier Jackson that the Viet Cong had to be driven off the high ground along Route 15. Given the Viet Cong strengths and dispositions and General Westmoreland's plans, I, as battalion intelligence officer, had my work well cut out for the next three months. Originally, I had been the second in command (2IC) of B Company, but on 6 August our intelligence officer, Captain Don Willcox, was moved to fill a vacant position on the Task Force headquarters. Colonel Warr then tapped me to take over from Don – a major new challenge, but a position which gave me an extremely interesting view of the war, of our enemies and allies, and particularly of the Vietnamese people for whose support the war was being waged.

The most important source of intelligence for the 'big picture' was the American corps-sized headquarters, II Field Force Vietnam (II FFV), located at Long Binh, not far from Bien Hoa. They were able to tell us, even before we had left Australia, who our principal military opponents were and what their record had been. American intelligence staffs were also able to provide some information on the level of political support that the Viet Cong had built up in the various villages and towns of Phuoc Tuy. There were two problems with this information. First, it tended to lag well behind events: each week an impressive-looking Intsum (intelligence summary), the size of a telephone directory, hit my in-box at Nui Dat, but it tended to be one or two weeks out of date by the time it came to me. Therefore, it was often not of great use for planning future operations. Second, the American-supplied information and analysis was better when focused at the higher Viet Cong levels than on the lower ones. They could discuss Viet Cong Main Force command issues and personalities, but they did not reach down very far into the kinds of forces we faced on most occasions, the provincial mobile battalion and district guerrilla companies. This pattern of strengths and deficiencies was dictated in part by the heavy dependence of the Americans on signals intelligence. It was up to us, away in Phuoc Tuy, to fill in the gaps, particularly to gain some insights into the political battlefield in the populated areas.

Nonetheless, the framework provided to us by II FFV was extremely valuable. I could circumvent the problem of slowness in transmission by making my own personal visits to HQ II FFV, assisted by the Australian liaison officer there, Major Bert Cassidy, formerly commander of A Company, 5 RAR. Normally a US battalion intelligence officer would not have been allowed inside the building, but because I was Australian, the Americans were curious, and in return for my appearance at their door, they would tell me things that I would otherwise not have known for a week or two, when the official papers reached me at Nui Dat. One early lesson I learned in the craft of intelligence was that people will share information with you if they like you. A second lesson was that what they told you, with the best of intentions, was not always correct: it was a *caveat emptor* situation – let the buyer beware.

We built up our current intelligence picture largely through our own activities: patrolling, village searches, my own frequent visits to villages of interest, and the stationing of small numbers of our own soldiers in villages for a few days at a time, on an occasional basis. One of our best assets in this regard was the Anti-Tank Platoon, soon to become the Reconnaissance Platoon, led by Second Lieutenant Michael von Berg (then known as Mick Deak). Mick had all the right qualities for leading this platoon. He was bright, intellectually curious and brave. He won a Military Cross in the coming actions on Nui Thi Vai in October 1966, and he had a great capacity to relate warmly and good-humouredly with others, including Vietnamese villagers, sometimes with and sometimes without an interpreter. He was in many ways the ideal counter-insurgent, and much of my effectiveness as intelligence officer was based on the information he continually brought me from his platoon's activities.

As Chapter 15 describes, the Reconnaissance Platoon was a 5 RAR innovation, introduced by our commanding officer, Colonel Warr, as a way of finding more useful employment for our Cold War–derived Anti-Tank Platoon. The Viet Cong did not have any tanks in our province, so we had a small force available for special tasks, such as intelligence gathering and ambushing Viet Cong patrols deep in the jungle. The members of this platoon were carefully selected and given specialised training. In fact, all of our platoons and companies, when they were out on patrol, were carrying out intelligence-gathering tasks. They relied on stealth and their own powers of observation to work effectively.

Another very important source for us was the local people. We had to feel our way carefully into developing reliable, secure contacts with the Vietnamese villagers. Initially we had little idea as to how strong their support was for the Viet Cong. We had to take personal risks in opening contact in a friendly, non-threatening way. We had to be careful not to identify Viet Cong opponents publicly through paying too much observable attention to them. This concern applied particularly to the village priests and anyone in the employ of local government agencies. They often preferred to come to visit us at Nui Dat – where we were accepting another risk, namely that they might be carrying out an intelligence mission inside our perimeter for the Viet Cong.

We offset the risks by beginning slowly and testing the quality and reliability of what we learned. We soon discovered that many villages were divided in their loyalties: some people favoured the Viet Cong, others preferred a more liberal regime. Not many were supporters of the Saigon government, which they saw as too remote, often corrupt, and not concerned with the big issues which affected every peasant farmer, such as the reform of land ownership laws. The Saigon government seemed to have too many people who were poorly trained and prepared for their tasks. The local Vietnamese wanted political leaders who were in touch with their supporters, not a group of generals who were more used to governing by giving orders than by gaining popular consent. This division within local public opinion raised special problems for information gathering. We got nothing from the Viet Cong supporters except misinformation. And some of the others told us things which, if we believed them, were flattering to our egos but misleading, and potentially dangerous to act on.

Eventually, by trial and error, we discovered whom to listen to and whom to trust. But we kept talking with everyone who was willing to talk in order to protect the security of our most valuable sources. We also took note of the willingness of people to talk with us and, as time went by, we had a better understanding of where truth lay. There was some advantage in being Australian in this process. Many villagers were afraid of the Americans because they had heard that they drove tanks across the village rice fields and even destroyed houses, storages and other facilities. They knew we were not American because of our uniforms and equipment. Some initially thought that we were French, returning to re-establish a colonial regime. They were soon disabused of that thought when they heard the way we spoke!

We were lucky in establishing good relations with many villages because our soldiers were open and friendly, and they exercised their powerful sense of humour, which proved able to cross international barriers with ease. Most importantly of all, we were fortunate that our company commanders and our operations officer, Major Max Carroll, had all served in the Malayan Emergency, where they had successfully applied the more nuanced approach of the British to a situation which, in its early years, had been deteriorating rapidly. They knew how a South-East Asian village worked, what the local people's concerns and desires were, and how crucial were their slender resources such as rice fields and fruit trees. The adjutant, Captain Peter Isaacs, formerly of the British Army, was another key contributor to our planning discussions. A further key supporter of our local relations program was our medical officer, Captain Tony White, who, with his very small staff, would put in many hours of consultation time, trying to help local people with their various illnesses and other health issues. And after searching a village, we would offer the inhabitants some compensation for the trouble we had caused by distributing clothing, sometimes with bizarre results as old men struggled into bright floral dresses supplied by donors in Australia, and intended for female recipients.

Despite all these gaffes, minor mishaps and sometimes downright inconveniences that the village people suffered at our hands, most of them could tell that on the whole we meant them well, wanted to be friendly and, like them, hoped for a better life for everyone in Phuoc Tuy after we had left the scene. From my perspective as the battalion's intelligence officer, it was a significant challenge to sift through all the often contradictory information that the villagers provided. Sometimes the information we gained was deliberately distorted by Viet Cong supporters, and on other occasions it would be out of date or just based on gossip. I had to assess what was wrong and what was solid and useful. Again, it helped to be able to debate findings with those of our officers and non-commissioned officers who had Malayan Emergency experience. They could sometimes sort the chaff from the grain better than I could.

Another major factor in building up our intelligence network was the personal interest of our commanding officer, Colonel Warr. He had not served in Malaya, but had been badly wounded in the Korean War, which had given him other insights into modern warfare. He was highly intelligent, liberal in relating to his subordinates, and for me he was like a good doctoral supervisor in a university graduate school. He would ask to see me on most days for a discussion on the Viet Cong: what they were doing, how strong they were, where they were and what their commanders might be intending to do over the next week or two. 'Bob, what have you got for me?' was usually his opening question. I would respond with a résumé of my views on the above topics. 'Yes, you might say that but what about …?', he would often reply, and the serious discussion would begin. My ideas and theses would be tested and pulled apart where they lacked strength. He would sometimes send me back to obtain more information on this or that topic, and occasionally to do a serious detailed analysis of a particular problem relating to our methods of operation and their effectiveness. Without his keen personal interest in and understanding of intelligence issues in that war, we would probably have suffered heavier casualties and achieved less impact on the Viet Cong than we did in 1966–67. It was not surprising when the University of New South Wales appointed him as deputy registrar a few years later.

Reinforcing my own capacities were the members of the battalion Intelligence Section – some five or six soldiers, led by Sergeant Ernie Madden, who systematically gathered, recorded and organised all the intelligence flowing in from our many sources. They kept me up to date with that material, producing marked-up maps showing enemy activity which we used for briefing platoons and companies going out on patrol. They built accurate three-dimensional models of the terrain that the battalion would cover in each future operation, from which I was able to brief the company commanders as part of the CO's orders before we set out. When we were out on operations, and I was walking along close to the CO and the operations officer, my section back at Nui Dat would keep me up to date on any new information that had come in, especially from signals analysis, and then devise a way to get it to me securely. The Viet Cong listened in to our radio traffic too, so delivery by hard copy on foot was usually the best method.

As one of the two battalions making up 1 ATF, 5 RAR's operations were part of a wider operational scheme. The task force commander, Brigadier David Jackson, allowed his two battalion commanders a great deal of initiative in planning and conducting their operations. Nonetheless they were planned jointly with the Task Force headquarters, and they were supported by the full resources of the Task Force, including those of its small intelligence staff, under the direction of Major Alex Piper. While this group was not able to mount its own intelligence-gathering operations, it was an important hub in the system because it received the results of analysis of Viet Cong and North Vietnamese radio traffic. My own contacts with Alex Piper and his assistant (and my predecessor as intelligence officer of 5 RAR), Captain Don Willcox, were particularly important, and I was in touch with them nearly every day, both to receive and to pass on intelligence information.

Let me give an example from one operation in the Nui Dinh hills in October 1966 of how our entire intelligence system worked: Operation Queanbeyan, from 17 to 26 October 1966.

First, we had to establish the size and locations of the Viet Cong forces in the hills. Our patrols soon encountered groups of up to 40 men, well equipped and probably Main Force soldiers, on the slopes of Nui Thi Vai. On 8 October Alex Piper flew in by helicopter to brief us. He had just learned that an enemy group higher up on Nui Thi Vai was led by the deputy commander of 274 Regiment, the better of the two Main Force regiments that we faced. They had a strong defensive position in rocks and caves above our level, and if we attacked without due preparation, the result could have been heavy Australian casualties. We had not expected to find as large a Viet Cong force as this, together with all the supporting and base facilities which went with a regimental presence in the area. After engaging a large number of enemy with airstrikes, helicopter gunships and artillery and mortar fire, we were ordered to withdraw closer to Route 15 to prevent the Viet Cong from setting up any ambush positions along the road.

Once the American reinforcement convoys had passed through, we were able to turn our efforts fully to driving 274 Regiment off the hills. Frequent visits by Brigadier Jackson and Major Piper kept us up to date with the signals intelligence picture of the Viet Cong activities on and around the hills. Over the 10 days from 17 to 26 October, we fought our way back up the steep slopes, encountering several Viet Cong delaying parties inside caves and tunnels, and among rocks. We discovered extensive base facilities and equipment, including a recently made Chinese radio transmitter and receiver and the diary of the deputy commander himself,

Nguyen Nam Hung. This diary was probably the most important single intelligence discovery we made during the whole year. He began each day's entry with his current location, so we could piece together the pattern of his movements during the first 10 months of 1966. After translation of the diary, it took much of my time over the following three months to extract all the available intelligence. The utility of the diary was reinforced by another discovery – a marked 1:50,000-scale map of western Phuoc Tuy which showed the complete Viet Cong track system and the location of base camps and fortified areas. From this map, we could plan reconnaissance and ambush missions over the next several months.

In essence this operation had succeeded because we had been able to build up a detailed picture of Viet Cong activities on either side of Route 15 before we began. We had not known the full size of the enemy group on Nui Thi Vai, but US and Australian signals intelligence soon gave us the essential information. Pressing on with the final wave of clearing attacks on the Viet Cong positions yielded further useful discoveries which strengthened our intelligence framework for our remaining time in Vietnam.

One problem that most intelligence officers must face when dealing with operational commanders is that the latter can often have in their minds a preferred tactical method of operating, and they look for intelligence to justify the use of that method. I learned about this issue in depth through a lucky personal coincidence. Not long after 5 RAR's arrival in Vietnam my first book, *The German Army and the Nazi Party*, was published in London by Cassells. Soon afterwards I received a letter from my production manager at Cassells, Ken Parker, to say that they were also publishing a book on the German bombing offensive against Britain in the First World War, *The First Battle of Britain,* by Raymond Fredette. Fredette, Parker wrote, was a major in the US Air Force, and was currently serving in Saigon in the headquarters of the US Military Assistance Command, Vietnam, better known as MACV, the headquarters of General Westmoreland. Fredette soon invited me to visit him in Saigon. We had a lot of common interests and a friendship developed, leading to further visits. This friendship has deepened and Ray and I are still in touch by telephone and email – he at the age of 95 and myself at 82. Of particular relevance to this chapter was what I learned from Ray about the functioning of the highest US headquarters in Vietnam. There was a broad spectrum of views among the senior commanders and staff on how to win the war, ranging from turning South Vietnam into a car park by physical destruction through to a huge civic action program which put public education ahead of military action. Each school of thought looked for intelligence information to prove that its approach was the most effective, and they suppressed information which favoured the advocates of other approaches. This influenced the intelligence staff, the J2 division of MACV, who also had their own theories on how to win the war, and these ideas could influence what they chose to pass on to their counterparts in the J3 (Operations) division. This J2/J3 rivalry did not end at the level of MACV, Ray told me. It existed at lower levels throughout the US forces in Vietnam. Once Ray had taken me through this analysis, I could see that it also had applicability to our much smaller Australian forces in Vietnam. Commanders could selectively use intelligence to justify a hasty choice of their favourite strategic or tactical idea, rather than making a conscious choice among all the available alternative approaches.

These were useful lessons, both for the shaping of our operations in Vietnam and for my own understanding of why various notable commanders of the past had stuck to unsuccessful strategies, despite intelligence available at the time which undermined the logic of their grand design. Fortunately, at the level of 5 RAR Battalion Headquarters, we had a commander and a group of principal officers who could see the dangers of a rigid strategic approach, and they were rigorous in their demands for full intelligence briefings rather than brief resumes of what I personally thought was important. It was, above all, that expert debating circle which set and maintained the standards of our intelligence gathering and analysis system during our year in Vietnam. The operations of October 1966 were a great schooling experience in how to combine intelligence and operational planning. These lessons have continued to be relevant and to shape the development of methods that are still in use today.

6

INTO THE HILLS: OPERATIONS CANBERRA AND ROBIN – OCTOBER 1966

Max Carroll and Peter Isaacs

Editors' introduction

The operational narrative resumes, following on from Chapter 4. In October 1966, 5th Battalion, the Royal Australian Regiment (5 RAR), was to embark on operations which entailed a host of new challenges involving an incursion into the jungle-clad, rocky and cave-riddled Viet Cong (VC) stronghold of the Nui Thi Vai hills. The enemy had been unmolested in this established sanctuary area for long periods before the arrival of 1st Australian Task Force (1 ATF). Clearing of the Nui Thi Vai hills was a necessary precursor to a forthcoming US Army operation code-named Robin in which 1 ATF was to participate.

Max Carroll

In the bigger picture, the war was escalating, and a major build-up of US forces was taking place. To ease the congestion at the up-river port of Saigon, newly arrived troops and stores were to disembark at Vung Tau, then move through Phuoc Tuy by road to bases at Bear Cat, Long Binh and Bien Hoa. These installations were serviced by Route 15, which was regularly interdicted by the VC. 1 ATF was to have the task of securing the road within Phuoc Tuy Province from Ba Ria to a hamlet named Phu My, about 22 kilometres distant to the north-west, where there was also an Army of the Republic of Vietnam (ARVN) post. Our old comrades, the US 173 Airborne Brigade, would then take over the task north of Phu My, through Bien Hoa Province to Bear Cat, some 26 kilometres further up the road, which was also the destination of the first formation we were providing cover for, the 3 Brigade of the 4 US Infantry Division.

In the 1 ATF sector, Route 15 was dominated by the hill massifs of Nui Dinh and Nui Thi Vai, which also had a subsidiary feature – Nui Ong Trinh – running south-west towards the road. There was yet a fourth peak, Nui Toc Tien, but this was further to the east and not considered to be a direct source of VC threat. The route clearance was a 1 ATF operation; and the road allotted to 5 RAR was about 15 kilometres in length, while 6 RAR's A Company covered the shorter section nearest to Ba Ria. 6 RAR had been successful in their recent Operation Vaucluse in the Nui Dinh hills, and D Company, 6 RAR, were to patrol that hill area again, as added security, while the road convoys were passing.

The task given to 5 RAR was a big one. We had to secure the road between 0900 hours and 1600 hours, from 11 to 16 October, during which period two 50-truck convoys would pass daily. This was Operation Robin, and the timings were inflexible. The 15-kilometre sector of Route 15 for which we were responsible dictated that our fire support base would have to be located about midway along the road, so we could provide artillery coverage for all our dispersed companies. The nature of the vegetation along the verges was such that we had to patrol a zone several hundred metres wide on either side of the highway. The dominating hill features of Nui Thi Vai and Nui Ong Trinh were within VC mortar range of the road, which meant these would have to be cleared beforehand. We were given five days, 6 to 10 October, to check out the summits and the western slopes. This was to be Operation Canberra, which would then flow on immediately into Operation Robin. Having returned from Operation Crow's Nest as late as 3 October, our preparations were in overdrive again.

For both Operations, Canberra and Robin, we established our fire support base close to the road near a hamlet named Ap Ong Trinh Dp. In addition to our normal direct support battery, 103 Field Battery, we had two 155 mm self-propelled guns from Battery A of 2/35 Artillery Regiment in support. This latter unit was part of the US artillery allotted to 1 ATF and

6. INTO THE HILLS

they were normally deployed in the Task Force base area. Because 6 RAR was fully committed to other activities, for Operation Canberra we had to use our own troops to protect the guns. 11 Platoon from D Company and the Anti-Tank Platoon were given this task under the command of Captain Ron Boxall, the second in command (2IC) of D Company. The remainder of D Company accompanied Battalion Headquarters (BHQ) as 'Palace Guard'. This deployment left us three companies for searching, and we also took two of the three sections of our Mortar Platoon with us into the hills. These were to be flown in on 7 October once the BHQ objective had been secured.

We moved to our start point by road and, leaving the armoured personnel carriers (APCs) on Route 15 south of Ap Ong Trinh Dp, we rapidly deployed to move to our target area to the north. This approach was not ideal, but the time available for the operation made it the best option. We proceeded for several thousand metres through thick scrub before reaching the foot of the hills, with B Company moving around the western side and C Company on the eastern flank of Nui Ong Trinh. A Company led the column, followed by BHQ and D Company, up towards the summit of Nui Ong Trinh. We did not reach the top on day one but did so on the morning of the second day, 7 October, with the search so far being uneventful. An unnecessary drama then occurred when I received a radio call from Captain Ron Boxall advising that the commanding officer (CO) of 1 Field Regiment had arrived at our fire support base (FSB), didn't like the location, and was moving the guns; and what should he, Boxall, do as he was responsible for protecting them? This was the first we knew of this nonsense. Neither John Warr nor Neville Gair, the battery commander, had been consulted. This was inexcusable because the guns could not adequately support us while they were moving. Some rather heated exchanges with HQ 1 ATF followed. Our CO ordered Ron's gun protection group to remain where they were, the Commander 1 ATF countermanded the CO 1 Field Regiment's illogical order; and we duly got our FSB back and continued with our task.

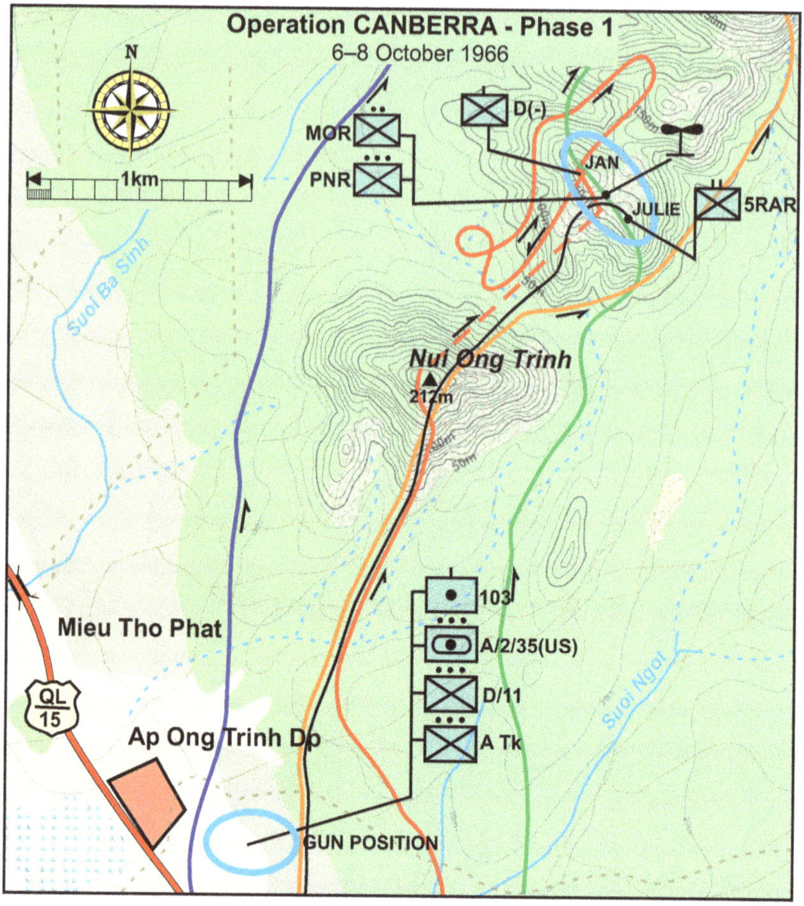

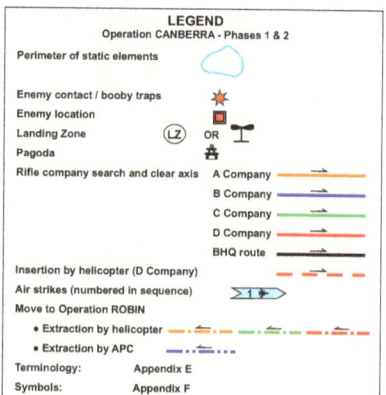

Map 8: Operation Canberra – Phase 1: 6–8 October 1966.

Source: Designed by Ron Boxall and produced by Alan Mayne from circa 1966 US military maps provided by Bruce Davies.

6. INTO THE HILLS

The selected objective for BHQ on 7 October was a twin-peaked feature which was about 1,500 metres, as the crow flies, north-east from Nui Ong Trinh. I had code-named the twin peaks Julie and Jan after two young teenaged friends of my family. C Company had crossed from the eastern flank of Nui Ong Trinh and had checked out the two peaks while moving to their day three search area, which was the southern slope of Nui Thi Vai. A Company initially led off from Nui Ong Trinh, descending into a steeply sloping, jungle-clad valley. On reaching the valley floor, A Company then left us, branching off further to the north-east and skirting Hill Julie, before they commenced their ascent of Nui Thi Vai. It had taken A Company some time to pick their way down the slope; and we were concerned that the BHQ Group and D Company would be hard-pressed to reach our objective before dark. We asked for Iroquois helicopter support to be on standby, should we find an extraction landing zone (LZ) on Nui Ong Trinh, to fly us to the LZ we knew was in the small saddle between the twin peaks. In any event, D Company found a suitable LZ on Nui Ong Trinh from which they flew to our destination. However, the lead scouts of the BHQ Group missed the track made by D Company where they turned off to the LZ from A Company's path, and we went the whole way on foot, cursing the hapless scouts and the hellish slopes and vegetation! At least the objective area was secure when we eventually arrived. We intended to stay there, so D Company occupied Hill Jan and the BHQ Group Hill Julie, while the pioneers enlarged the LZ, on the edges of which our two sections of mortars were located once they were flown in. We had a strong defensive position from which we could control our searching companies with good radio communications and provide mortar fire support.

The third day of our search, Saturday 8 October, started quietly; our command team was joined by the deputy operations officer, Captain Peter Isaacs, who had been on duty at Nui Dat.

Peter Isaacs

By the time I reached BHQ atop Hill Julie, Operation Canberra had been underway for 48 hours. I therefore avoided the long haul on foot from the flat plain beside Route 15 and the arguments about the FSB being moved on the orders of 1 Field Regiment's CO without prior consultation with CO 5 RAR. Captain Bob Supple, who was 2IC Support Company, stood in during my absence. I arrived by helicopter on the morning of 8 October. Early that morning we had received unconfirmed reports of a VC mobile battalion near our area of operations. At 1000 hours C Company became involved in a contact in which 8 Platoon was fired on from several different directions. Initially, Major John Miller, the officer commanding C Company, reported being in contact with a possible company-sized force. The VC withdrew but C Company sustained seven casualties from booby traps and an eighth man injured with a twisted ankle. All were evacuated by *Dustoff*, which took about an hour. At around 1400 hours, C Company reported that the rudimentary houses and livestock enclosures they were among were heavily booby-trapped. They had sustained another five wounded and requested further *Dustoff*. C Company was therefore engaged in difficult casualty evacuations from their jungle-clad mountainside location for several hours, and their strength was depleted by 13 men.

At 1400 hours B Company reported sighting a group of VC on the lower western slopes of Nui Thi Vai. 5 Platoon's forward scout, Private Colin Cogswell (aged 19) and his second scout, Private Doug Hillier, had located a booby trap, deloused it and a few minutes later heard voices of enemy close by. Covered by Hillier who remained stationary, Cogswell moved forward to investigate. He initially sighted 15 VC and, a short time later, even more close by. He remained in these positions for nearly an hour after Hillier had cautiously withdrawn to report the enemy presence. Cogswell moved to within five metres of the enemy, but he was not seen as he continued to observe. His performance entailed magnificent use of the cover offered by rocks and heavy vegetation and his highly developed movement and concealment skills; to say nothing of his coolness under pressure.

6. INTO THE HILLS

Colin Cogswell recalls this episode

I thought I might have trouble remembering everything about what happened on 8 October 1966 during Operation Canberra. When I started writing I was surprised how clearly memories flooded back. Of course, I have read the citation that accompanied the award of my Military Medal and have always felt surprised that I was rewarded for just doing my job as a forward scout and that my recollections don't precisely match that of the citation.[1]

B Company was moving up an east-to-west major ridgeline of Nui Thi Vai mountain. My platoon, 5 Platoon, was in the lead with me as first scout and Doug Hillier as second. As we got near the top of this ridgeline we crossed over a re-entrant. We were about 50 to 60 metres in front of the rest of 5 Platoon when we came across two huts about 25 metres to our front. What then attracted our attention was a group of 12 to 15 Vietnamese in well-fitting green uniforms who seemed to be holding an O Group. [Editor's note: a meeting where orders are distributed and coordinated by officers. The Conclusion to this chapter gives more details.]

We had moved too far forward and had lost sight of the rest of our section who were following us. We decided that I should remain where I was, and Doug would go back and let our section commander, Corporal Jim Hall, know what we had found so he could pass the information up the chain of command. My first instinct was to find better cover, so I moved very carefully about 10 metres away and behind some large rocks among foliage. In doing so I lost sight of the enemy group we had first seen. After about a minute I heard Vietnamese voices very close nearby.

I slowly looked over the rock and through the bushes and saw a Vietnamese, well dressed in a green uniform and wearing a cap with a red star on its front. I remember thinking his shoulder-slung AK47 looked immaculate. Fortunately, he was looking down and talking to someone I couldn't see. He didn't know that my M16 was pointed at the side of his head and I was about to squeeze the trigger.

One part of me wanted to shoot him and another thought that the shot would draw attention to the nearby presence of B Company who were probably planning some action to get me out and deal with the enemy. So, I slowly got back behind my rock and waited for something to happen. The enemy were so close that I could smell them and was concerned that they might smell me – or hear my thumping heart. They were only 4 or 5 metres from me. I guess they had their slack moments too.

I seemed to be there for ages waiting for the Company to do an attack or something. I knew that they were aware that I was still in position close to the enemy. By now I had pulled out my two M26 grenades and removed the striker lever safety tapes so that when something happened, I could throw one just over my covering rock and the other one as hard as I could towards where I'd seen the larger group. I hoped that my mates didn't brass me up – being a forward scout I'd had a few times when I was more worried about my mates behind me than any enemy in front of me.

As I waited, I got an uneasy feeling and looked up to my right where the boulders were about 6 metres high. I saw another neatly uniformed soldier standing there and looking straight out into a clearing in front of my rock. If he had looked down and to his left, he would have seen me, but he turned around and disappeared into what we found later was a cave in which a radio setup was housed. The same man came out again briefly, but still did not see me.

> I don't know how much time had passed before I realised I couldn't hear any more talking and was no longer sure where the enemy were. I felt it was time to get back to 5 Platoon one way or the other. I put my grenades back into their pouches and slowly backed out around another massive boulder hoping I would not be seen. At the same time, I'm looking for my section on the other side of the re-entrant. I saw Jim Hall waving me to come back and Joe Devlin, our M60 machine gunner, ready to give me covering fire.
>
> I thought 'it's now or never' and ran 30 metres down into the re-entrant and scrambled up the other side expecting to be shot at any stage. The moment I got back I realised that only my section was there, and Jim had them on their feet and moving as fast as they could back down the hill to where B Company had been ordered to pull back out of the way of an air strike. I don't know how Joe held onto that M60 while scrambling down that steep and rocky jungle slope.
>
> We didn't seem to have moved far when the first jet came screaming in with its Gatling cannon roaring and dropping two canisters of cluster bombs right where I had been not very long before. By the time we got back to B Company our artillery was getting in on the act. The daylight was fading, and B Company harboured for the night. All I wanted was to make a hot brew, but not before Doug and I had to go and see Major McQualter for a debrief. When we got back to our section, we were told that we were going out for the night to set up a listening post. There was no rest for the wicked – nor even for the lucky!
>
> After returning to Australia I was surprised to learn that I had been awarded a Military Medal for doing what I thought was my job of detecting the enemy and getting the information back. It was presented on my 21st birthday, at Government House in Sydney, by Sir Roden Cutler VC.

[1] Colin Cogswell's citation for the Military Medal can be viewed at the 5th Battalion The Royal Australian Regiment Association website, *Citation accompanying the award of the Military Medal to Pte. Cogswell*, www.5rar.asn.au/history/cite_cogswell.htm.

Major Bruce McQualter had begun quietly to position B Company for an attack. While he was doing so, we were advised by 1 ATF that the HQ of VC 274 Regiment was believed to be in our vicinity and that a task force intelligence officer was on his way to brief us on the situation. B Company was warned to be extremely careful in its movements and that if help was needed, A Company would provide it. C Company was closer to B Company but still engaged in casualty evacuation.

Major Alex Piper from HQ 1 ATF arrived shortly afterwards and confirmed that HQ 274 Regiment was indeed believed to be nearby. John Warr stepped away from the command group and considered what action to take. Allow the B Company attack to proceed, or order B and C Companies to move away and call in artillery and air strikes? Nobody knows what thoughts John Warr had in the short time he took to decide to order B Company to cancel their impending attack. Maybe he was remembering some advice that he had been given shortly before the battalion had commenced deployment for Vietnam. During his final inspection visit, the highly regarded General Officer Commanding Eastern Command, Major General Tom Daly, had told John that if ever he found himself in a position where he felt that by delaying an action he could achieve a similar result but would probably save soldiers' lives, then he should delay, as those lives were of paramount importance.

I must admit that, personally, I was disappointed that B Company was ordered to abandon its attack plan, but I have no doubt that had it proceeded some members of B Company would have died, and others could have sustained life-changing injuries. John Warr was correct – his soldiers' lives were of paramount importance in a conflict that was not concerned with Australia's national survival. The chief reason why John was held in such high esteem by all ranks of the battalion was because all knew of his concerns for us.

Max Carroll

B Company were chagrined at being ordered back to a safe distance to the west and C Company were also moved out of the way before both VC areas were subjected to heavy artillery fire from our FSB. Our four mortars also joined the attack and the clearly identified target areas must have been most uncomfortable for the VC. We had a US Army helicopter light fire team, consisting of two heavily armed Iroquois, code-named *Derringer,* available to support us, and they were called in during short breaks in the artillery and mortar fire to deliver high explosive (HE) rockets and high-volume fire from their multi-barrelled machine guns at opportunity targets. As they made their low-level passes they drew heavy ground fire, which was returned with effect by their side-door gunners. Obviously, the target areas were well defended, and it looked as though we were in for a long engagement. We requested an air strike to handle any hardened targets and in a short time a US forward air controller (FAC), code-named *Birddog,* was overhead in his small Cessna. He was briefed on the situation as he circled us, familiarising himself with our locations and the targets to be hit. His lazy drawl belied his professionalism for he obviously knew his trade. Soon a flight of four F100 Super Sabre fighter-bombers came screaming onto the scene and orbited while the FAC briefed them. Then the FAC went in low, marking the target area with his white phosphorous smoke rockets, before getting out of the way of the jets who followed him in. The first passes were from the west across our front and we had a good view from Hill Julie. The target was plastered with both 500-pound HE bombs and cluster bomb units. These were thin-cased canisters which burst above the ground, widely scattering many smaller fragmentation bomblets, which, in turn, exploded on impact or lay dormant, to explode when disturbed.

The F100s then varied their line of attack and came in low, above Hills Jan and Julie, and we were startled by the screaming roar as they passed. When they had expended all their heavy ordnance, they again went in low, strafing with their 20 mm cannon and firing salvos of HE 70 mm Mighty Mouse rockets. It was a most impressive use of ground attack air power. I had never seen such an amount of effective destruction in such a short time; and when the FAC offered us a second wave, of course we accepted. During the short break between sorties, our artillery and mortars kept up the bombardment so there was no break for the VC. The second wave continued the destruction but added napalm to the mix, which was quite sobering to watch as the burning petroleum jelly agent penetrated caves and any other apertures it hit or burst over. We thanked the FAC for the valuable assistance he and his colleagues had given us as he signed off and went home, by which time it was dusk. Regrettably, any VC survivors now had darkness to assist their escape.

Earlier in the afternoon the CO had been prescient in ordering 1,000 81 mm mortar bombs to be flown forward to our mortar line on Julie; these fortunately had been delivered. It appeared that this had caused some unhappiness along the supply line. These bombs had come from Task Force holdings at Nui Dat which, in turn, had to be replaced. Noting that most of his mortar bomb holdings at Nui Dat was being flown out to us, our brigadier called replacement stocks forward from 1st Australian Logistic Support Group (1 ALSG) at Vung Tau. We soon heard that some 1 ALSG pogos (an informal nickname applied by combat troops to others who work in safe billets behind them) were upset because they had to work their butts off getting the replacement ammunition forward in a hurry; and it was on a Saturday – a weekend! We weren't worried about what day of the week it was, or the preferred working arrangements in base areas – we demanded the bombs we needed and were soon to use them.

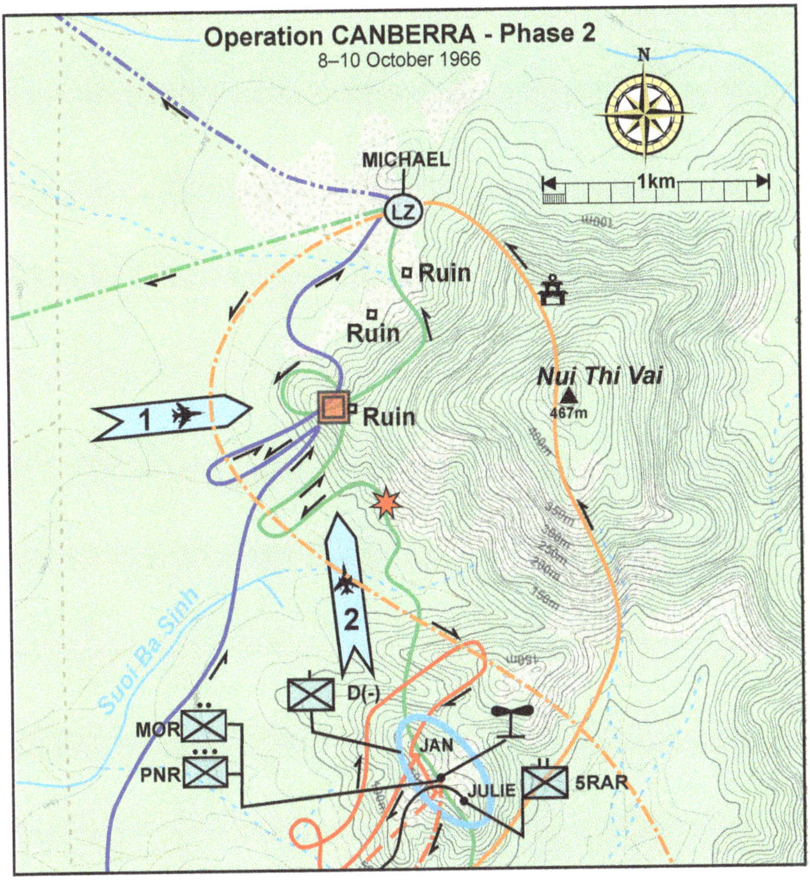

6. INTO THE HILLS

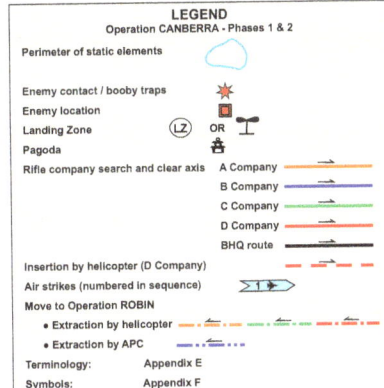

Map 9: Operation Canberra – Phase 2: 8–10 October 1966.

Source: Designed by Ron Boxall and produced by Alan Mayne from circa 1966 US military maps provided by Bruce Davies.

103

Editors' Note

Inevitably, differences in outlook arose when supporting troops were distinctly separated from combat troops both by distance and in terms of relative comfort and safety. In Chapter 2 the pros and cons of separating 1 ATF from its dedicated logistic support agency were discussed. Inevitably, the exigencies and tempo of operations lacked immediacy for many members of 1 ALSG, which primarily operated on a workaday routine and in much better-developed facilities. These were permanently ensconced beside a beach in Vung Tau; a large and quite safe urban area which was both remote from 1 ATF operations and protected from major enemy ground attack by its location at the end of a long, narrow peninsular. Combat soldiers who got to spend infrequent two-day breaks from operations at Vung Tau considered the atmosphere there to be akin to a seaside holiday resort; this was a bit harsh, but the perceived differences were telling and lasting. They felt a strong need to clearly distinguish themselves from their counterparts who worked in such a setting. Hence, an old British Army tag 'pogos' (standing for 'personnel on garrison operations') re-emerged to be applied routinely, and sometimes disdainfully when it was deemed deserving. Infantrymen laughingly accepted the inevitable comeback, 'grunts', which was copied from the Americans. Pogo was a far less derogatory term than its expletive US equivalent, which Australian combat soldiers peremptorily declined to adopt as descriptor for our base soldiers.

Max Carroll

The harassing fire we used to interdict likely VC withdrawal routes throughout the night had to be provided by our mortars, as it was not logistically possible to get large amounts of heavy artillery ammunition forward to our FSB in time. The four mortars we had with us fired about 960 rounds throughout the night and no one got much sleep. Early next morning B and C Companies moved back into the areas they had vacated on the previous afternoon and continued their search. The VC had gone and taken their casualties with them.

We now had to reassess the situation as we were on the fourth day of our five-day operation and had been engaged in a major encounter. This indicated a reasonably strong VC presence in the area and there was still a lot of ground to cover. It was obvious to us that we would have to return to Nui Thi Vai when we had completed Operation Robin, but in the meantime, we had to search and clear the slopes and crest to our immediate front.

The search by A Company of the Nui Thi Vai crest, and then down to the pagoda on the north-western spur, was uneventful, except they captured a suspect Buddhist monk, whom they passed on to Captain Bob O'Neill, our intelligence officer, for interrogation. B Company's search was gratifying. They were continuing carefully to cover the area of the airstrikes when they found a large VC camp, spread over several hundred metres including 15 huts, caves, a tunnel system, a water supply system, a quantity of medical supplies, ammunition, grenades, mines, rockets and clothing and equipment. They also recovered a quantity of valuable documents, which, among other things, gave details of the company which had administered the installation and listed the VC units and numbers which had passed through recently. This was a major VC base area. The discovery of this installation and its contents no doubt helped ease any disappointments that lingered in the company from earlier contacts. C Company's search was also most productive and revealed why the area where they had taken casualties had been covered by trail watchers and booby traps. They found two company-sized bases, containing a hospital and a quantity of medical stores, a booby trap factory, explosives, ammunition, general stores and equipment, many valuable documents and a large quantity of rice. Probably the most important item found was a 1:50,000-scale map, which showed the VC track system for western Phuoc Tuy and other bases and fortified areas.

Both companies reported that the airstrikes had been most effective with many direct hits making it difficult to count weapon pits and other defensive locations. We sent all the documents found and some of the medical stores back to Task Force for analysis. All other stores, ammunition, equipment and the rice were destroyed as they were too difficult to remove. Time was pressing, the destruction work took time and we could not complete destroying all installations we had found before moving on to meet our deadline for commencing our part in Operation Robin.

The final day was uneventful as the search companies moved to their extraction point, LZ Michael, at the north-western end of Nui Thi Vai. B Company then moved by APCs to their allotted position on Route 15 in readiness for Operation Robin, due to commence next day, while A,

C and D Companies were airlifted to theirs. BHQ, the mortars and pioneers were also airlifted back to the FSB. We were all repositioned on the afternoon of 10 October and Operation Canberra was concluded. We left Nui Thi Vai with mixed feelings. We had killed VC and wounded others during contacts, but C Company had suffered 12 wounded plus another man injured; and D Company had also had a man injured. However, the operation was considered highly successful as we had seriously disrupted major VC elements, forcing them to rapidly vacate a long-occupied sanctuary, as well as finding and destroying three large installations and associated stores and equipment. Also, the intelligence value of the documents captured was incalculable. The casualties suffered by the VC due to the airstrikes and our artillery and mortar fire, all of which were highly accurate, must have hurt them but to what degree we would never know. We knew we would be going back to Nui Thi Vai; and we also knew we would be expected! For the present, Operation Robin was about to begin.

The official history volume, *To Long Tan*, covers Operation Robin in just two sentences, which I will quote here:

> The clearance of the western side of the Nui Thi Vais ensured the smooth conduct of Operation Robin. One security patrol received ineffective sniper fire and several mines were detonated harmlessly while checking the roadway, but the US troop convoys went through unmolested.[1]

For those of us on the ground there was far more to it.

Our subunits were dispersed over the 15 kilometres of our assigned sector, from Phu My in the north, southwards in the order shown at Map 10: B Company, C Company, BHQ and Support Company (co-located with the FSB), then D Company and A Company, whose southern boundary linked with 6 RAR. Each rifle company had a section of APCs to assist with rapid redeployments, as well as their attached engineer combat teams to clear the road of mines and booby traps each morning. In the event, we started work as soon as we moved in on the afternoon of 10 October, and the first mines were found. We also lost a sapper wounded by a booby trap and an APC had a track blown off by a mine on the road verge. The same afternoon there was a further incident when the Sioux helicopter that

---

1   McNeill, Ian, *To Long Tan: The Australian Army and the Vietnam War 1950–1966*, Allen & Unwin, Sydney, 1993, p 391.

was supporting us crashed. The aircraft was flying at low altitude along the road between companies, when the rotor blade appeared to strike a roadside telegraph pole and disintegrate. A metal fragment struck the pilot, Second Lieutenant Bill Davies, in the head, seriously wounding him. Fortunately, both Davies and his passenger, the company quartermaster sergeant of B Company, Staff Sergeant 'Sailor' Mealing, survived, mainly because the crash occurred close to C Company where our regimental medical officer, Captain Tony White, was waiting to be picked up by the aircraft. As related by Bill Davies in Chapter 14, his immediate presence on the scene saved Davies' life, as Tony recognised the seriousness of his condition and directed the *Dustoff* to take him straight to a specialist hospital in Saigon for surgery. Mealing's injuries were less serious, but he still had to return to Australia. I knew him well, having served with him in 3 RAR in Malaya. All of this happened on the afternoon before Operation Robin officially started!

The danger of sniper fire was ever-present, and our patrols had to clear well back from the road, constantly, throughout each day. Map 10 shows helicopter pilot reports of locations from which they received enemy small arms fire as they flew over Route 15 and the areas to either side, before and during the operation. The road and its verges and culverts within each sector were checked daily for mines and booby traps before 0900 hours, then APC-mounted infantry road patrols throughout the day, between convoys, ensured there would be no interference by enemy activities.

There was considerable civilian activity in our area as there were several villages and hamlets along the road, together with numerous charcoal-producing ovens, which were a main source of income for local peasants. We took no chances and all movement and activity was carefully watched. Most of the locals were Buddhists and there were two villages inhabited by Catholic refugees from North Vietnam, Ap Ong Trinh Dp and Long Cat, which were well maintained and defended. We took the opportunity to establish good relationships with these people as they were anti-VC. We also assisted them with the provision of some barbed wire to strengthen their defences, and Tony White and one of the dentists from the Task Force Dental Unit spent a day providing much welcomed treatment.

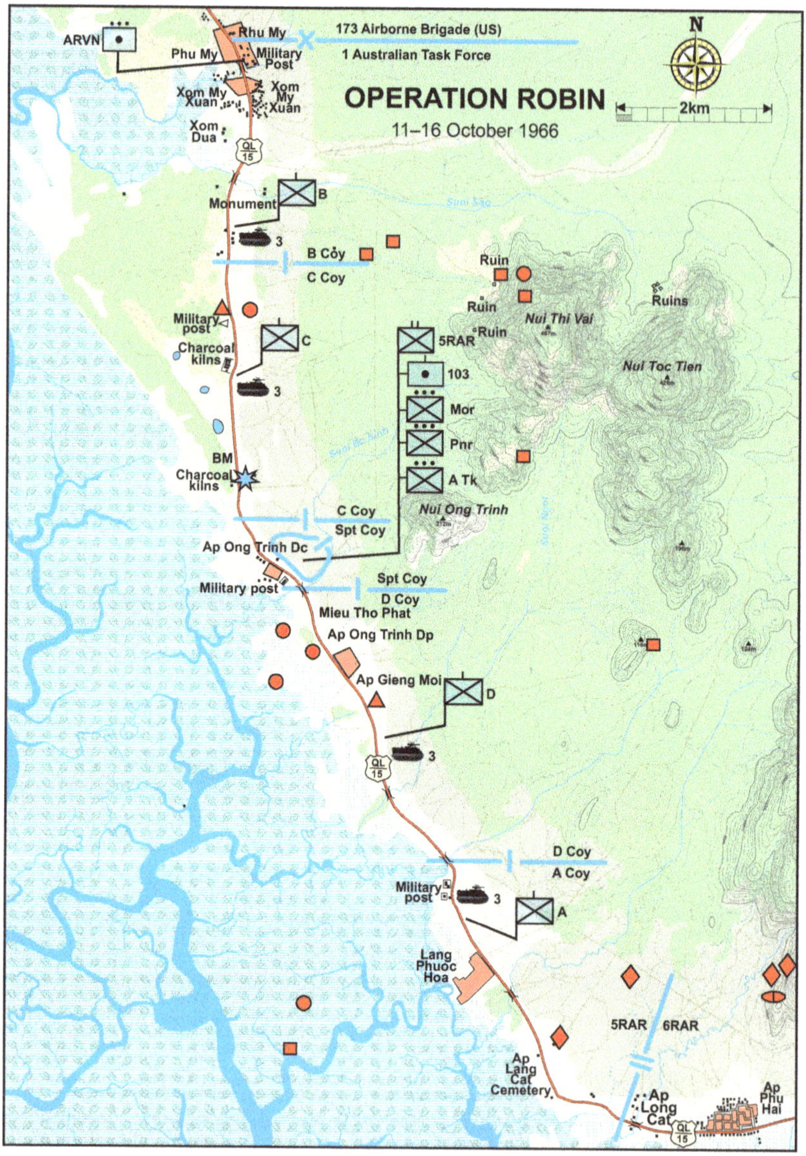

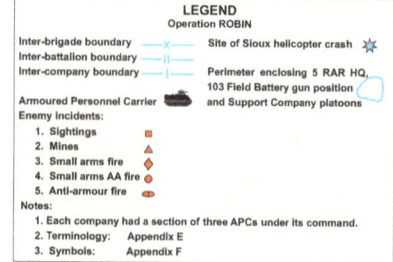

Map 10: Operation Robin: 11–16 October 1966.

Source: Designed by Ron Boxall and produced by Alan Mayne from circa 1966 US military maps provided by Bruce Davies.

The passage of the convoys was a sight to behold. The nominated limit of 50 vehicles at a time was often exceeded; and the stream seemed endless. I believe something like 1,200 men a day passed up the road during the operation. Each convoy was escorted by US Army APCs, while overhead was a command and control helicopter with fire teams of helicopter gunships constantly prowling the flanks. It was a most impressive display of American strength and we hoped that any VC observers who had returned to the hills behind us were duly impressed.

Editors' conclusion

The official history's passing reference clearly doesn't do justice to this period of intense activity, with many important facets of inter-allied cooperation and interaction with the civilian population living along the vital, inter-provincial Route 15. During Operation Robin, 5 RAR commenced planning a return to Nui Thi Vai and was able to clear a proposed plan with Brigadier Jackson, the task force commander. During one of his regular visits he granted John Warr's request that no time limit be imposed for completion of the operation. It was obvious from earlier experience that there was still a lot to be discovered on Nui Thi Vai, and flexibility to react to developing situations without time constraints was needed. Brigadier David Jackson had an excellent grasp of 5 RAR's approach to operations and, once he had approved a plan, he let the battalion get on with the job in hand. Orders for a new operation code-named Queanbeyan were prepared and the CO held his Orders Group (the assembly of subordinates to receive verbal orders, with hard copy confirmation, and to provide any needed clarification of details). On 17 October the battalion was ready to launch a much-desired return to the Nui Thi Vai hills, to follow up its successes during Operation Canberra.

1. February 1966, on exercise at Canungra before departure for Vietnam (left to right): WO2 Don McGregor, Corporal Bob Whillas, Major Paul Greenhalgh, Private Max Stringer, all of D Company HQ, and 5 RAR's chaplain, Father John Williams, taking a breather.

Source: Ron Boxall.

2. October 1966: Two C Company members, Lance Corporal Ron Shoebridge (left) and Lance Corporal David 'Stretch' Bryan (right), support Private David Riik after 8 Platoon suffered casualties from booby traps during Operation Canberra. Private Ian Foran at left monitors the company radio net and Private Robert Birtles kneels at right. The dense jungle and rugged terrain are visible in the background (see Chapter 8).

Source: Australian War Memorial, COA/66/0877/VN.

3. May 1966: The Commander US Military Assistance Command Vietnam, General William C. Westmoreland, and the Commander Australian Forces Vietnam, Major General Ken Mackay, talk with Private Kevin Cavanagh, C Company, aboard HMAS *Sydney* at Vung Tau.

Source: Australian War Memorial, CUN/66/0369/VN.

4. April 1966: Brigadier David Jackson, Commander 1 ATF, and Lieutenant Colonel John Warr, commanding officer 5 RAR, soon after the latter's arrival at Tan Son Nhut airport.
Source: Australian War Memorial, KEL/66/0362/VN.

5. July 1966: 5 RAR medical officer, Captain Tony White, sutures a machete gash for one of his medical assistants, Corporal Ian McDougall.
Source: Australian War Memorial, FOR/66/0484/VN.

6. October 1966: Soldiers of C Company, at a landing zone on Nui Thi Vai with captured materiel. Operation Canberra.

Source: Bill Parkes.

7. **September 1966:** The Australian Army Chief of the General Staff, Lieutenant General Tom Daly, visits D Company during Operation Toledo, September 1966. Here he speaks with Sergeant Bob Armitage (left) and Major Paul Greenhalgh.

Source: Australian War Memorial, FOR/66/0785/VN.

9. **October 1966:** Private Bruce Mason, A Company, makes a brew beside a local charcoal burner's oven during Operation Robin.

Source: Australian War Memorial, COL/66/0965/VN.

10. **December 1966:** Members of 8 Platoon admiring Private Robin Lestrange's Christmas treats sent by his former employers. Platoon commander Lieutenant Roger Wainwright (right) is keeping an eye on (left to right) Sergeant Ralph 'Rowdy' Hindmarsh, Private Dick Criss, unknown, Private Daryl McCombe (kneeling), Private Robin Lestrange, Private Bill Cavanagh, Private Phil Long and Private Alan Suckling (later Alan Hunter).

Source: Australian War Memorial, COL/66/1010/VN.

8. **May 1966:** Lieutenant Colonel John Warr (centre) discussing helicopter training with Lieutenant Charles Brinnon of the US Army's 68 Assault Helicopter Company (left) and Major Richard Hannigan (right), operations officer, 1 ATF, at Vung Tau.

Source: Australian War Memorial, FOR/66/0386/VN.

11. October 1966: 5 RAR's Signals Officer, Captain Brian Le Dan, with his damaged Owen machine carbine which deflected and shattered an enemy sniper's bullet thus saving him from serious wounding or death during Operation Queanbeyan (see Chapter 7).

Source: Australian War Memorial, CUN/66/0945/VN.

12. September 1966: The Commander 1 ATF, Brigadier David Jackson (left), greets the Commander Australian Forces Vietnam, Major General Ken Mackay, and the Australian Army's Chief of the General Staff, Lieutenant General Tom Daly, on their arrival at his HQ at Nui Dat.

Source: Australian War Memorial, FOR/66/0779/VN.

13. October 1966: A 9 Squadron RAAF Iroquois delivers ammunition, equipment and water to a landing zone between hills Jan and Julie during Operation Canberra.

Source: Australian War Memorial, VN/66/0074/13.

14. 5 RAR's second in command, Major Stan Maizey, setting a good example.

Source: 5 RAR Association website, www.5rar.asn.au.

15. Early October 1966: Men of 4 Section, 8 Platoon (left to right): Privates Bob Box, Dave Annells, Warren Pearson, Alan Suckling, Corporal Russell Quinn and Private David Riik. Russ Quinn is carrying an Owen machine carbine and Alan Suckling is carrying an M16. This photo was taken around the time when the Owen was beginning to be phased out.

Source: David Bryan.

16. Villagers watching a distribution of food aid by 5 RAR soldiers.
Source: David Bryan.

17. Villagers collecting food aid.
Source: David Bryan.

18. October 1966: Nui Thi Vai from the west during Operation Robin. The peak reaches 467 metres (1,532 feet) above sea level. The road at the foot (Route 15) was close to sea level, making the hill a long, steep climb for heavily laden infantry attempting to drive the enemy off the heights.

Source: Bill Parkes.

19. October 1966: Second Lieutenant John McAloney MC who was awarded the Military Cross for leading the Assault Pioneer Platoon's attack on a defended enemy cave system during Operation Queanbeyan (Chapter 7).

Source: Michael Deak (Michael von Berg).

20. Late 1966: Prime Minister Air Marshal Nguyen Cao Ky visited 5 RAR. Shortly after this photograph was taken, he was flat on the ground, covered by his security guards, because the bomb that had just been fired from the mortar in front of him had a faulty propellant charge and landed 50 metres away. Fortunately, the bomb itself failed to explode.

Source: Lloyd Miller.

21. October 1966: A 9 Squadron RAAF Iroquois delivers resupplies to the pagoda landing zone during Operation Queanbeyan.

Source: Lloyd Miller.

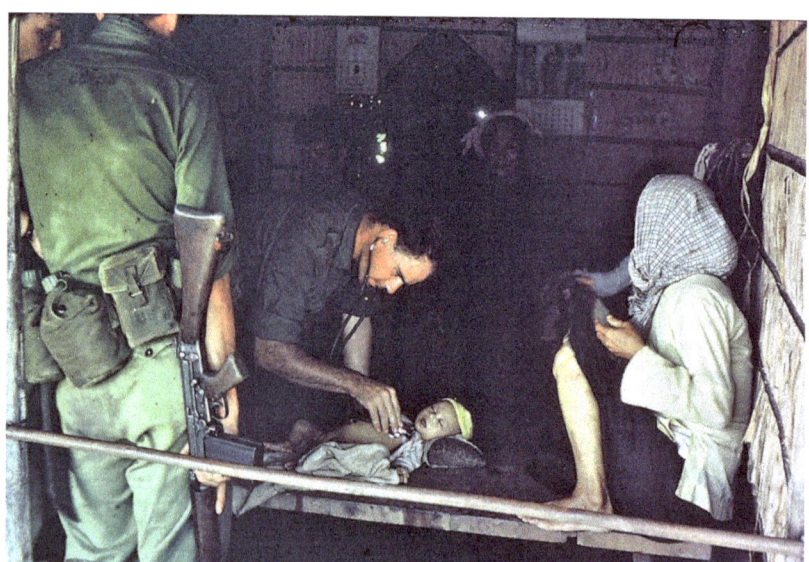

22. November 1966: 5 RAR's medical officer, Captain Tony White, examines a dead baby in Long Son village. The baby's distraught grandmother refused to relinquish the baby to her family for burial until a '*bac si*' (doctor) had confirmed that it had died.

Source: Ron Boxall.

7

OPERATION QUEANBEYAN – OCTOBER 1966: UNFINISHED BUSINESS FROM OPERATION CANBERRA

Max Carroll, Michael Deak (Michael von Berg) and Barry Campbell

Editors' introduction

Clearly, the need for 5th Battalion, the Royal Australian Regiment (5 RAR), to leave the Nui Dinh hills to play its part in Operation Robin left 1st Australian Task Force (1 ATF) with many unanswered questions about follow-up action to the events of Operation Canberra. As described at the end of the previous chapter, Brigadier Jackson understood that 5 RAR, having mounted the previous operation, was already familiar with the terrain and the enemy's tactics and was best suited to conduct a follow-up operation. He quickly endorsed the battalion's obvious desire to attend to what it considered to be unfinished business, and let it get on with the job.

Max Carroll

Deception was a major factor in our planning for Operation Queanbeyan. We knew that some Viet Cong (VC) were still up on Nui Thi Vai and that the passage of the road convoys would have been observed and reported, as would our security activities along Route 15. It was a fair assumption that our fire support base (FSB) location would also have been noted and the volume of traffic associated with it detected. Once the road convoys stopped it would be expected that we would regroup before moving again towards Nui Thi Vai. Time was critical, as we needed to be well clear of the road and concealed in the jungle before the VC realised we were gone. To this end we planned on approaching along four separate company routes with Battalion Headquarters (BHQ) and its protective Anti-Tank and Assault Pioneer platoons initially following A Company. B and C Companies could commence their insertions from their present locations on Route 15, but both A and D Companies had to be relocated from their southern positions. This was done over the last day of the convoy movements, as part of our normal armoured road patrols. D Company of 6 RAR, which was to protect our FSB, was inserted among the daily resupply convoys, so there was no obvious increase in our normal traffic movements. We also left our headquarters tents erected so there was no change in the appearance of the base.

Our intelligence assessment was that the best areas for our renewed search would be the western and northern sides of Nui Thi Vai. The general plan therefore was for two companies to search the north-western spur and the uncleared south-western slopes, a third company to cover the northern side, and a fourth company to establish ambushes on the track system further out to the north (these had been found marked on the VC map captured on Operation Canberra).

D Company was to be the furthest north of our subunits, entering the jungle from up near Phu My. They were to lay the ambushes on the approaches and escape routes to the north. B Company was next down the road and tasked to search the northern slopes and area, while A Company was responsible for the central north-western spur. The BHQ Group was to follow the A Company column before proceeding up the spur to the abandoned pagoda, from where it would control the searching companies, while protected by the two Support Company platoons. The pagoda grounds were big enough for a single Iroquois landing zone (LZ), and once secured, a section of our mortars was to be flown in. C Company was to the south of A Company and responsible for searching the uncleared western slopes.

Before, when writing operation orders, I had regularly used female names as nicknames for areas and features; these names were often of the wives, fiancées, girlfriends, friends or relatives of both myself and other officers of the battalion. However, after the gasping and irreverent expletives I heard uttered by my colleagues, directed at the hill feature Julie during Operation Canberra as we clawed our way up its extreme slopes, I decided it was not a good idea! For Operation Queanbeyan, the nicknames I used for areas were: A Company, Alvenia; B Company, Blanche; C Company, Christine; D Company, Doda; and our headquarters, Heidi. All these names were from *Playboy* centrefolds adorning many tents at Nui Dat. There were no personal connections, so any sensitive feelings we harboured were protected.

All our columns moved off from their respective harbours along Route 15 at 0300 hours on 17 October 1966, heading eastwards towards their assigned areas. All made good time and were well inside the jungle before halting for a short rest to await the dawn. We, the A Company and BHQ Group column, then followed a track which headed towards our destination, making best possible speed. It was not long before A Company found a large vacated VC camp across our front, which had well-constructed trenches with overhead protection. We were lucky it was not occupied! While checking this area a booby trap was exploded, fortunately without harming anyone, but it could have warned any VC further ahead. We continued carefully until we arrived at an unoccupied group of well-built houses located at the base of the north-western spur. While A Company was securing the area another booby trap was triggered, this time wounding four men, who had to be evacuated. It was obvious that A Company was going to be busy searching the houses and lower slopes for some time after their casualties were evacuated, so the Anti-Tank Platoon led the BHQ Group up the spur line leading to the pagoda. In places steps had been cut into the mountainside. However, for most of the climb it was very hard going, as our destination was over 430 metres above our start point.

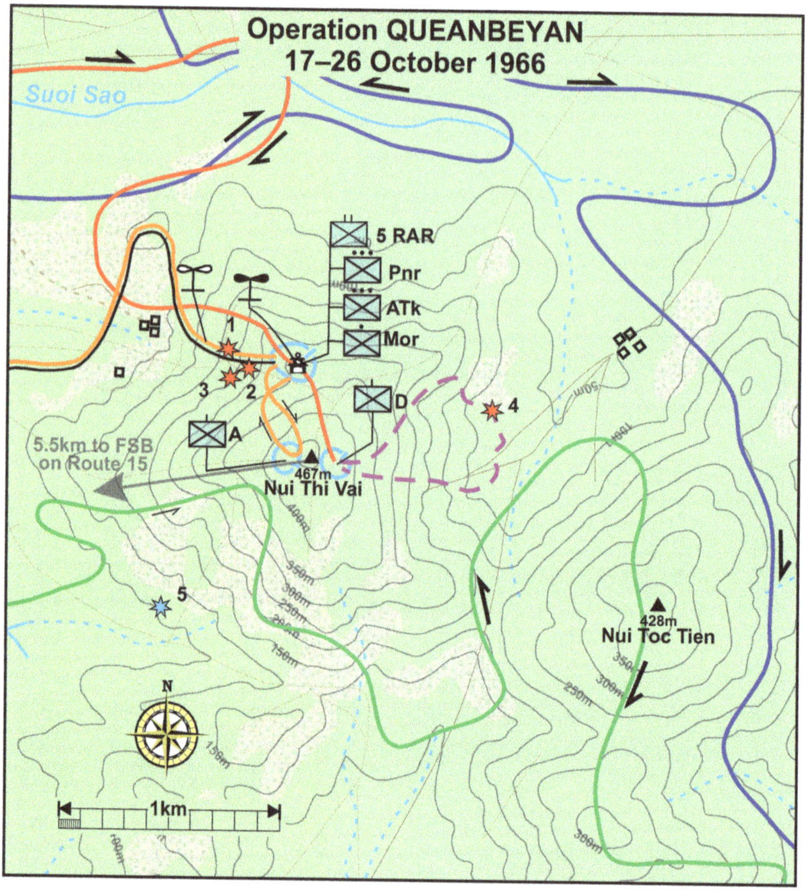

Map 11: Operation Queanbeyan: 17–26 October 1966.

Source: Designed by Ron Boxall and produced by Alan Mayne from circa 1966 US military maps provided by Bruce Davies.

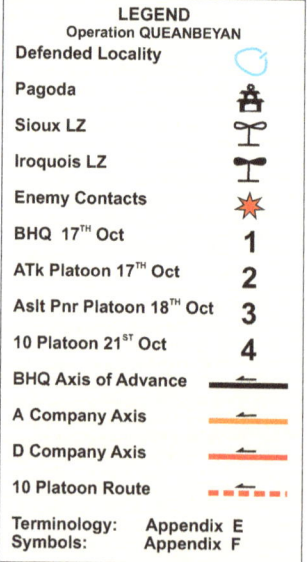

The ground was extremely broken, with a steep-sided re-entrant (deep gully) full of boulders and jungle on the right flank, and progress was slow and careful, with the Anti-Tank Platoon clearing the track in tactical bounds until they reached the pagoda. The BHQ Command Group and the Assault Pioneer Platoon had halted further down the track waiting for the radio call from the Anti-Tank Platoon that the track was clear. At this point the BHQ Reconnaissance Party, led by Captain Brian Le Dan, moved off to lay out the area ready for the arrival of our main body. Shortly after their departure several shots were fired from up the track, and their distinctive sounds told us they were not from our weapons! A strong volley of friendly fire followed, then we received a radio call from Brian Le Dan's operator that the Reconnaissance Party was under fire; Brian had been hit and could not get to the radio. The situation had become decidedly unpleasant. At this point it is appropriate to pass the narrative over to Second Lieutenant Michael Deak, as he and his Anti-Tank Platoon had a very busy afternoon. His graphic account, which follows, is a good example of a difficult platoon action.

Michael Deak

I've never quite understood why I have always had some sort of an attraction for hills and mountains. Was it my time in postwar Austria, living in the Alps, or later after immigrating to Australia, the Snowy Mountains, or nearer to home, Rocky and Willan's Hills near Wagga Wagga? There was a similar, perhaps naive, attraction for the mountain ranges to the west of our defensive position at Nui Dat. After Operation Canberra's first foray onto its rocky, jungle-clad slopes, we were about to reconfront Nui Thi Vai, which peaked at 467 metres and rose very steeply from the surrounding flat terrain.

On our ascent on 17 October the Anti-Tank Platoon, operating as a rifle platoon, was tasked with climbing the north-western spur of Nui Thi Vai to clear the area ahead of the BHQ Group, which intended to establish a command post at the pagoda located below and to the north-west of the summit. After receiving my orders from BHQ, I called my section commanders together to brief them on our mission and, most importantly, the enemy threat. When in Vietnam, many of us often forgot what day of the week it was because we were operating 24/7 and the days' names seemed unimportant. But I do remember that the day that we stepped off to climb this mysterious feature was Monday, the start of a working week back in Australia; and what a working week it was to be for the battalion.

I was most fortunate to have very experienced and capable section commanders and, once they had briefed their sections, we slowly headed up a small footpad led by Corporal Allan McLean's section, with my platoon headquarters behind him. Then followed the other two sections led by Corporals Norman Womal and Bill 'Sharpie' Drennan. No more than 15 minutes into the ascent at very slow patrol pace, we were confronted with a steeper climb with a gradient of 1 in 2. It wasn't so much the gradient that worried us, but the huge outcrops of boulders, rock slides and big trees with root systems intertwined through and around the footpad. These, with the platoon fully laden in hot, humid conditions, made it a very hard climb. It was made more difficult for all of us, with adrenaline pumping and super alert, by having the large re-entrant on our right with boulders and outcrops able to hide an enemy group of any size. Although energy sapping, we managed the climb without incident and I called a halt at the flat ground surrounding the pagoda to await the remainder of the BHQ Group and Assault Pioneers. Then a burst of fire was heard from down the track that we had supposedly cleared. To make matters worse, I heard on our radio that our signals officer, Captain Brian Le Dan, had been wounded in an exchange of fire between enemy and the BHQ Reconnaissance Party. Hearing of Brian's wound, I felt guilty in that we had supposedly cleared the area of enemy where they had been ambushed. These thoughts were rushing through my mind when the commanding officer (CO) ordered me to come back down the track and clear the enemy from above. This I was determined to do!

We were somewhat fatigued from the climb, but I ordered the platoon to drop our heavy backpacks in a pile, which we camouflaged, and took all spare ammunition with us. Corporal Norm Womal's section then led the platoon back down the track with the rest of us following, our descent being a lot faster and easier than the climb up. We approached the area where Brian had been wounded and I got a quick situation report from Warrant Officer Bruce 'Hughie' Hughson, the company sergeant major (CSM) of Support Company, who was close to where Brian was being treated by Captain Tony White, our battalion's medical officer. The information I received was somewhat sketchy as nobody could indicate from where the enemy fire was coming. It was continuing spasmodically from different directions and locations on the opposite side of the re-entrant which had concerned me on the way up.

7. OPERATION QUEANBEYAN – OCTOBER 1966

Close fire support from artillery or mortars was impractical due to the enemy being so close to us and the nature of the target area, with its many large boulders and trees. We had to resort to covering fire from within the platoon, trying to clear the enemy by conducting fire and movement drills in very difficult terrain down through the re-entrant. In a situation like this there was no opportunity to get the section commanders together for some form of coordination briefing on how we were going to tackle this situation. We were all under fire and any movement without covering fire was very dangerous. I simply had to convey my orders to everyone by shouting what I required to be done, using my loudest parade ground voice; which, thankfully, was clearly understood, even over the continual sound of small arms gunfire. In this sort of situation as a platoon commander you need to shout your orders very clearly. There can't be any misunderstanding or ambiguity. You tell your men what you want and, thankfully, all my men on the mountain that day reacted fearlessly and fought magnificently.

I ordered Corporal Allan McLean's section to be the supporting fire team back up the track where there was a rock projecting out from the footpad, and which had a good view and field of fire down along the re-entrant where we thought some of the enemy were located. Norm Womal's section was to clear the re-entrant, moving by fire and movement from the north-east to the south-west, accompanied by myself, my signaller and our stretcher bearer (medic). My platoon sergeant, Ray 'Skinny' Calvert, was with Sharpie Drennan's section behind us, acting both as my reserve and a covering fire team across the top of the re-entrant as we descended into it. I thought this combination of direct and enfilade fire would give the clearing section enough covering fire. I would call for it when, with each fusillade, Norm Womal and his section, using fire and movement, would advance from cover to cover to try and clear the re-entrant and up its steep other side where we thought the enemy was located. Suddenly there was a burst of enemy fire and Norm shouted 'Skip, I've been hit'. This immediately changed the dynamics of the situation. I had always briefed my men that if they were wounded or dead, we would do everything to get them out. This was now a primary task but, because of the nature of the terrain, none of us knew where Norm was located. Although seriously wounded, he was still shouting orders to his machine gun group and we began to fight our way towards where we had heard him but, soon after, he fell silent. We eventually found that he was lying on a large flat rock. However, we knew the enemy were using Norm as bait because every time

I or my stretcher bearer, Private Peter Fraser, tried to get to him there was a burst of fire hitting the flat rock where he lay. I simply could not risk anyone crawling out to assist Norm until we had been able to suppress the enemy fire. Not knowing where they were located made this extremely difficult. The enemy fire seemed to be coming from different directions and locations, indicating that it came from more than just a random track watcher. Of concern to me was the obvious fact that the enemy had identified my voice as that of the leader. Every time I shouted an order, fire would come my way, necessitating intuitive and rapid decisions about where to take cover before shouting orders.

This made the recovery of Norm extremely difficult and, contrary to my orders, I saw Peter Fraser, our stretcher bearer, crawling out to Norm to try and treat his wounds. My heart stopped at the thought of needing to extract two wounded soldiers, and the increasing possibility of running short of ammunition really concerned me. The platoon's covering fire somewhat suppressed that of the enemy but there were still bullets hitting the flat rock where both Norm and Peter lay. Then I saw an act of incredible courage, as Peter crawled to place his body between Norm and the enemy to protect him from further wounding. While communicating with Peter, I ordered a maximum amount of covering fire to give Skinny Calvert a chance to work his way to the edge of the rock with a stretcher party to drag Norm up the friendly side of the re-entrant to safety. There a makeshift helicopter landing pad had been organised by BHQ away from enemy fire. It took us almost two hours to extract Norm but, sadly, he died from a gunshot wound to the neck before he could be evacuated to hospital.

The next problem was to extract Norm's section, myself and my signaller from the killing ground. Again using our own platoon's covering fire, we managed to do so while the enemy were still spasmodically firing. It was now growing late in the day and our ammunition was becoming critically low and we were no further advanced. I had lost a good non-commissioned officer and the enemy were still in place and shooting at us, with relative impunity, from the opposite side of the re-entrant. The whole of the BHQ Group were held up on a steep mountain track and I was feeling somewhat desperate and frustrated. So much so that I grabbed an M60 machine gun from one of my gunners and fired a belt of ammunition into the trees on the other side of the re-entrant, thinking the snipers were up in the trees where we couldn't see them. This made me feel better to the point that my head cleared, and I set about making 'an appreciation of the situation' as I was taught to do in my officer training at the Officer Cadet School just one year ago. How would I get out of this mess? Then over the radio, Major Peter Cole, commanding A Company which was located at the base of a spur some 800 metres away, said that he could see where he thought the enemy were located and could try to neutralise them using some of the M60 machine guns in his company. I had a pretty good idea of the characteristics of the M60 and its beaten zone (size and shape of the area of fall of its multiple projectiles) at a range of 800 metres and, with my platoon still being very close to the enemy, I was not totally enthusiastic, but, being short of ammunition, I agreed, and we marked our locations using coloured smoke grenades. When we were all prepared, A Company opened fire and as soon as I heard rounds cracking over our heads and all around us I gave the order to STOP! My fears about the beaten zone had been correct but in no way was my order to halt A Company's supporting fire a reflection on the help offered by Peter Cole and his company. Serious problems need serious solutions, but this one was not the answer. As the enemy were still taking pot shots, making movement along the track impossible, I received a radio message that the 'cavalry' in the form of a US Army helicopter light fire team was being called in to assist us to clear out the enemy position. This was the best news I had had all afternoon; and the sounds of the two UH1 Iroquois gunships off in the distance ready to support us boosted the morale of everyone on that mountainside.

We again marked our positions using coloured smoke grenades and the choppers came in one after the other to a point where the pilots could see some tunnel openings we had not located and launch their rockets right into the mouths of those tunnels. This went on until all their ammunition and rockets had been expended. Although aware of the devastation that this firepower could cause, I was not sure what results this lot had achieved, if anything at all. I was dreading having to go back down and across that re-entrant where we were ambushed, but an assessment had to be made to establish whether there were any enemy casualties and whether there were more to be dealt with. We noticed that the enemy firing had stopped, and this encouraged us to get on with the job we had been given three and a half hours earlier. I left Allan McLean's section where they had been providing support throughout and, with a small group, slowly cleared from boulder to boulder and other forms of cover that could be used by the enemy. We made our way up the opposite side of the re-entrant without further enemy resistance. After the previous three hours this was quite a relief, and what we discovered confirmed why we had no idea of how many and from exactly where the enemy had been shooting at us. We found numerous interconnected tunnels in the rocks, blood-soaked bandages and pieces of equipment. But the area was booby-trapped and, therefore, not within my 'pay scale'. This was a major job for assault pioneers and combat engineers, so I withdrew my platoon and we were ordered to make our way back up to where we had left our heavy packs. We carefully made sure that they had not been discovered and booby-trapped. With that done successfully, we went into a harbour position around the pagoda with the rest of the BHQ Group and the Pioneer Platoon.

Once I had been debriefed I settled down to make a small meal and called my section commanders in to congratulate them on a job well done. I then quietly sat on my own to reflect and consider what had happened that afternoon. I was devastated at losing Norm Womal, an outstanding soldier and human being, married with four children. I did much soul searching then, and still do today, about what I might have done differently. That night I curled myself up in my hutchie and quietly wept. I needed to do that to mourn his loss and enable me to continue in my role with confidence and clarity. Everyone in the platoon on that day fought like men possessed. The way that Norm Womal fought to the end and Peter Fraser's astonishing courage on that rock will stay with me forever. Norm was subsequently awarded a Mentioned in Dispatches posthumously and Peter a Military Medal (MM), one of the few stretcher bearers so recognised. Years later Peter sadly succumbed to motor neurone disease. Before he died, he asked me to deliver the eulogy at his funeral in Perth, where I was honoured to applaud Peter's bravery for the benefit of his many civilian mates. Although recognised by the award of an MM, I still feel that his actions deserved a higher award.

Max Carroll

I shall backtrack to fill in the activities which occurred while the Anti-Tank Platoon was engaged. The BHQ Reconnaissance Party included the Regimental Sergeant Major, WO1 Les Foale, and the CSM Support Company, WO2 Hughie Hughson. When fired on, they immediately deployed defensively and, under cover of their own fire at suspected VC positions, recovered the wounded Brian Le Dan to a safe position from where he could radio the situation to us. He had been very lucky in that the enemy round had struck the safety slide of his Owen gun. The bullet had shattered, with fragments tearing into the right side of his chest inflicting nasty flesh wounds. When we learnt of Brian's wounding, the CO ordered Tony White, our doctor, and an escort to proceed up the track to provide medical treatment and evacuate him. I also called for a *Dustoff* helicopter to move to our FSB on Route 15 to standby, as there was nowhere at our present location suitable for the large helicopter to extract a casualty.

The prospect of a possible stretcher-carry down the horrendous track between us and A Company prompted a search of our area for a place nearby where it might be possible to land a Sioux light observation helicopter, so that he could be quickly extracted and transferred to the waiting *Dustoff*. Fortunately, there was a large flat rock overhang close by and the Pioneers rapidly removed some trees to enlarge the clear area. Even then there was only one line of approach for the Sioux and the pilot would need to reverse out as there was no room for him to turn the aircraft around on the rock. The flying skills needed to execute this extraction are difficult to describe. Second Lieutenant Bob Askew, who was well known to us, performed this extremely difficult feat of flying with amazing skill.

The serious firefight was still going on a short distance up the spur line and the possibility of enemy fire being directed at the Sioux was very real. Captain Bob Supple from our BHQ Group guided the Sioux's approach while kneeling, as the slope of the ground was such that he could have been decapitated by the rotor blades if standing. Bob Askew gently brought his aircraft in with doubtful clearance for his rotor blades on each side (his account is in Chapter 14). As Brian was 'walking wounded', he was strapped inside the cockpit next to Askew who very carefully lifted off from the rock shelf, reversed his aircraft until he had room to turn, then flew down the mountain to the waiting Iroquois *Dustoff*. Later in the afternoon, when we needed to extract Norm Womal's body, Askew was called back to do it all again. The Australian Army's 161 (Independent) Reconnaissance Flight pilots who supported us in operations were excellent, often demonstrating a combination of superb flying skills and fearless commitment.

It was late afternoon before the BHQ Group was able to proceed uphill to the pagoda, and ours was very careful movement, with everyone supremely alert. I was feeling uncomfortable, as this was the first operation where

I had been without my rifle. I had always carried an SLR (self-loading rifle) as well as my 9 mm pistol, much to the amusement of the CO, who had often teased me saying that we were well protected, and our job was to control the battalion. But now BHQ had been ambushed! Second Lieutenant John McAloney, the Assault Pioneer Platoon commander, had earlier damaged his SLR and it was with our armourer for repair, so I had loaned him mine. Now, here I was travelling up a narrow track between two clearly recognisable radio operators, with a map in my hand and armed with a useless pistol. Anyhow, we duly arrived at the pagoda and established our defensive position just on last light. It had been a long hard day for us, but I was told later that there were some jokers in the rifle companies who found delight in BHQ's discomfiture. On the plus side, it seemed we were no longer regarded as pogos!

After a tense night – the VC were certainly aware of our location – on the morning of 18 October 1966 we dispatched an Anti-Tank Platoon patrol to check out the peak of Nui Thi Vai, which was about 500 metres further uphill from the pagoda. On their return with nothing to report, a section of our mortars was flown in from the FSB on Route 15, and the assault pioneers were warned to be ready to move back down the track to clear booby traps from the tunnels and caves from which we had been ambushed. This was necessary before more detailed searching could be undertaken. From our recent experiences, we anticipated that more combat engineer support would be needed, in addition to their two-man mini-teams that were already attached to each rifle company. To this end, three combat engineer officers flew in as observers to accompany our assault pioneers on their initial cave clearance to assess the requirement for additional men and equipment. By the time this activity was completed it was early afternoon.

While the Support Company platoons were busy, the rifle companies were also proceeding carefully with their allotted tasks. A Company was searching the lower slopes of the north-west spur, B Company was doing the same to the north and D Company was in ambush positions on the northern tracks. Meanwhile, C Company's activities on the south-western slopes made for an interesting day.

On the morning of 18 October 1966, C Company needed combat engineer assistance to complete the demolition of installations started during Operation Canberra. A Royal Australian Air Force (RAAF) Iroquois was therefore tasked to fly in two combat engineers and a quantity of explosives to the LZ, which C Company had successfully used twice before on 8 October 1966 when a US Army Iroquois had evacuated their casualties without any problems. C Company were securing the LZ for the RAAF aircraft and some of its members witnessed the disaster which followed. The RAAF Iroquois crashed while trying to land. The RAAF version of the incident and accounts by army witnesses differ. George Odgers, in his book *Mission Vietnam, Royal Australian Air Force Operations 1964–1972*, states:

> When the helicopter reached the 5th Battalion position and hovered over the landing zone, Flight Lieutenant Cliff Dohle decided that the area was too small to land safely so he commenced an overshoot. A few seconds later the aircraft crashed into the jungle and caught fire. Flight Lieutenant Cliff Dohle had managed to warn the crew before the aircraft entered the trees, enabling them to brace themselves to a reasonable extent.[1]

Another account attributed the crash to engine failure, but the C Company witnesses believe that, while hovering, the tail rotor might have clipped a tree. The aircraft came down some 70 metres past the LZ, which seemed like the pilot was having difficulty in controlling a damaged aircraft. Cliff Dohle was a good and courageous pilot, known in the Task Force as the captain of one of the two RAAF 9 Squadron choppers which executed the hazardous ammunition resupply of D Company, 6 RAR, at the Battle of Long Tan. Thankfully, there were no fatalities in this crash. Lieutenant Roger Wainwright, whose 8 Platoon soldiers were nearby and appeared rapidly on the scene to assist, describes the rescue of the aircraft's occupants in Chapter 8.

Before leaving this accident, a couple of observations are warranted. First, I cast no aspersions on RAAF aircrew, having flown with them often during my tour of duty. Having experienced the aggressive, get-the-job-done approach of US Army helicopter support, we naturally felt that RAAF policies on aircraft safety were unrealistic in Vietnam operations and might have influenced Cliff Dohle's decision to abort the landing. There had been much debate with RAAF commanders in the early months of 1 ATF's deployment about helicopter support in ground operations. We had no concerns about the aircrews, who were obliged to abide by RAAF policy constraints and were as frustrated as

---

1 George Odgers, *Mission Vietnam, Royal Australian Air Force Operations 1964–1972*, Australian Government Publishing Service, Canberra, 1974, p 34.

we were. The LZ had been successfully used twice on 8 October 1966 for evacuation of C Company casualties by a US Army *Dustoff* Iroquois, so we naturally opted to use it again. Also, we considered it unusual that the RAAF crash investigators never interviewed Roger Wainwright, who was present and witnessed the crash, or his soldiers who played a major role in rescuing the copilot and helping others at the crash site. Inability at higher levels to resolve differences between the army and the RAAF on inter-operational matters inevitably led to comparisons between RAAF and US Army helicopter support, and caused unneeded, unnecessary and regrettable tensions between battlefield partners.

The two 8 Platoon soldiers Bill Cavanagh and Syd Shore had saved the copilot, Flight Lieutenant Peter Middleton, at significant risk to themselves. Their actions had been witnessed by Roger Wainwright and his recommendations for awards were successful, with them both being Mentioned in Dispatches. The RAAF crewman, Sergeant Gordon Buttriss, was cited by the RAAF and received the higher award of the George Medal. His citation describes how, after being involved in the crash and getting clear of the wreckage, he twice re-entered the burning aircraft to extricate the two injured army combat engineers, Sapper Dennis Schubert and Sapper Colin Hopper.[2]

To return to the demolition of the VC installations: at 1400 hours on 18 October, Second Lieutenant John McAloney and his party departed the pagoda for the caves and tunnels they were to investigate and clear of any booby traps. The patrol numbered 24 and consisted of McAloney, his signaller, a medic, two understrength sections of assault pioneers, two guides from the Anti-Tank Platoon and three engineer officer observers and their signaller.

They arrived at the cave area at 1440 hours after a careful approach, being very aware that a day had elapsed since the ambush and the VC might have reoccupied the site. Having posted sentries along the track and the remainder of the patrol in covering fire positions, McAloney, his signaller and a single Pioneer cover-man were led up to the cave site by the two Anti-Tank Platoon guides. He then posted the two guides as sentries above the first cave. He positioned his cover-man, Private Gordon D'Antoine, just

---

2   RAAF personnel records are stored in 'RAAF Personnel files – All Ranks', National Archives of Australia, A12372. In addition, see 'News of the award of the George Medal to A21702 Sergeant (Sgt) Gordon Dudley Buttriss, of Sefton …', 1967, Australian War Memorial, VN/67/0020/04, available at: www.awm.gov.au/collection/VN/67/0020/04/.

forward and downhill of the cave so that he could overlook the immediate area. The signaller remained under cover close by his platoon commander. John then commenced his search for booby traps and discovered the first one, just to the side of a cave entrance below a large rock. He was lowering himself down to look at it when a shot was fired. D'Antoine shouted that the round, which had passed close to him, had come from below and behind him from another cave entrance. John's signaller also reported that the shot had come from below the rock on which he was positioned. John then ordered his fire support group to cover the suspect area, but another shot fired from the same area below hit D'Antoine in the back, apparently from a range of only several metres.

The time between the two shots was about 45 seconds. John then ordered his M60 machine guns to fire into the area below D'Antoine's position, which was also just below his and his signaller's positions. After the first few bursts he had to call for the fire to cease as ricochets off the rocks were passing too close to him. Corporal Brian Burge, commanding the fire support group, fired a snap shot with his SLR from 20 metres at a VC face he saw peering out of a rock hole below McAloney. Burge was certain he hit his target and McAloney and his signaller heard tumbling sounds coming from the rocks beneath them. John then ordered fire into all caves and holes while he and the medic, who had moved forward with difficulty, recovered D'Antoine who had been very badly wounded and died shortly afterwards. At BHQ we had been monitoring the action and organised a platoon from A Company to secure an extraction LZ some way downhill and John sent a stretcher party of four and a protection party of six to evacuate Gordon D'Antoine's body.

About mid-afternoon John and the remainder of his patrol were able to go after the VC. Their first step was to get gas grenades into all tunnels and holes and into the entrance of the main cave. The uphill anti-tank sentries reported no resulting sounds or movement from potential rear exits, so 40 mm M79 grenades were fired into the cave mouth. John then requested flame-throwers be brought forward; but this entailed a delay of 30 minutes. The A Company platoon securing the extraction LZ was ordered to hold the Assault Pioneer party escorting D'Antoine's body at the LZ, in order to wait and return to John with the flame equipment when it was air delivered. This they did, arriving back at the cave site as it was growing dark. In the meantime, John had been slightly wounded while he was recovering D'Antoine's M16 rifle. He had been unable to reach it earlier when he and his medic were dragging the wounded man to safety. The flame-thrower equipment included eight gallons of fuel, some of which was used to saturate suspect holes around the main cave. With covering fire from his support section, John then led a frontal assault at the cave in which the flame-thrower was used to good effect. Flame and smoke were seen billowing out of some probable rear exits. By then fading light prevented any immediate follow-up action, so the patrol reassembled on the track and made good time moving back to the pagoda.

On the next day, 19 October, the assault pioneers returned to the cave area and found that the flame had been effective on the top level. However, this complex consisted of three levels, was overall about 16 metres deep and was large in volume, having some sections with wooden flooring. Seven backpacks which contained good information about the enemy were found and it was clear that the VC had been using this area for some time. The Pioneers continued their search in other caves, finding 60 kilograms of TNT and some grenades, both of Chinese origin, some small anti-tank rockets and a quantity of documents. During the search they lost two soldiers, Privates Trevor Lynch and David Goodman, wounded by a Chinese directional mine rigged as a booby trap. Trevor Lynch was shockingly wounded, losing both eyes as well as sustaining multiple fragmentation wounds to his head, body and limbs. It was surprising that he survived. After lengthy treatment in Vietnam until well enough, he was evacuated to Australia. The medic Corporal Ian McDougall's gripping account of the incident in which Trevor Lynch suffered his wounds is in Chapter 13.

The whole area that 5 RAR was searching was honeycombed with booby trapped caves and tunnels; and dealing with this situation required very steady nerves and extreme care. All soldiers, both those of the battalion and our supporting sappers (combat engineers), displayed both qualities together with exemplary courage. On this day, B Company on the northern slopes also encountered a group of five VC local guerrillas, wounding two before the group broke contact and fled. C Company on the western slopes later found and destroyed a cache of two tons of rice.

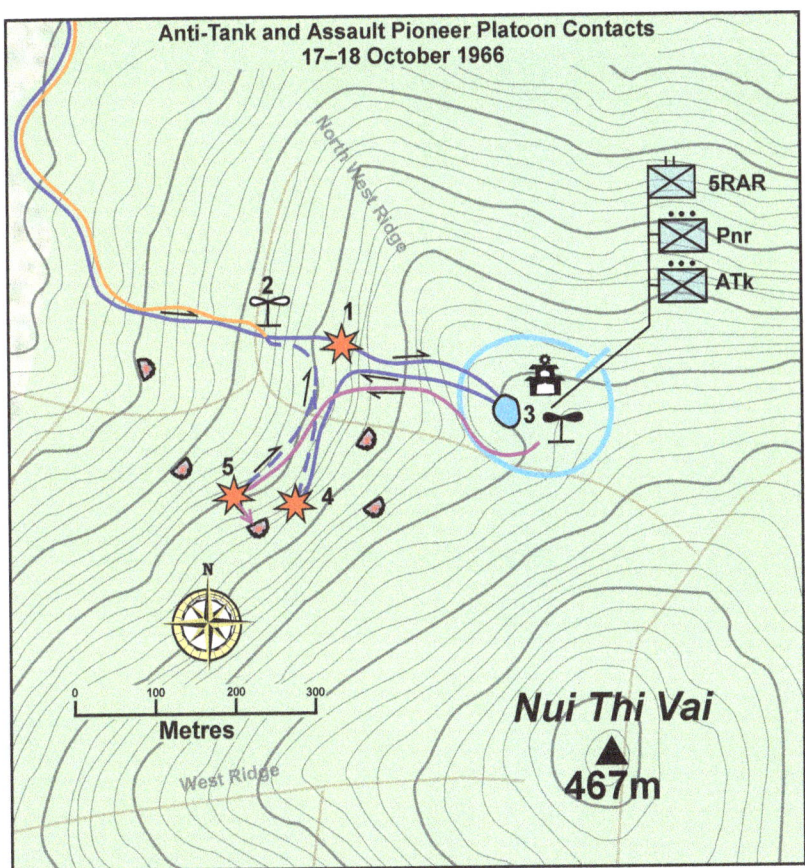

Map 12: Anti-Tank and Assault Pioneer Platoons enemy contacts: 17–18 October 1966.

Source: Designed by Ron Boxall and produced by Alan Mayne from circa 1966 US military maps provided by Bruce Davies.

VIETNAM VANGUARD

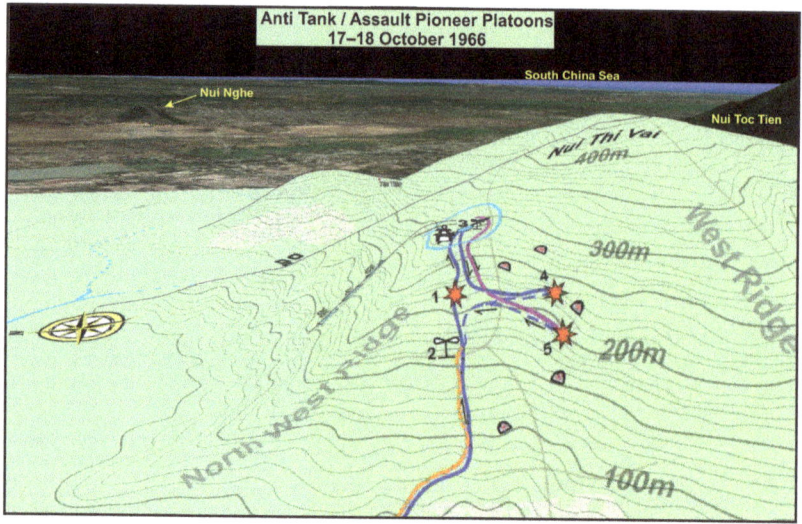

Map 12A: Anti-Tank and Assault Pioneer Platoons enemy contacts: 17–18 October 1966.

Source: Designed by Ron Boxall and produced by Alan Mayne from circa 1966 US military maps provided by Bruce Davies.

Over the following days, further engineer elements and stores were flown in to support us and our successes increased. A Company found, searched and destroyed some booby-trapped cave and tunnel complexes, recovering a variety of documents, training pamphlets and medical supplies including 200 phials of morphine and other drugs. There were also medical certificates from a doctor located in Ba Ria. Undoubtedly, he soon received a nasty visit from the provincial authorities. Apart from this, also found were various kinds of ammunition, stores and equipment, including some anti-tank mines and detonators, webbing and helmets, cooking oils, fish, rice, some paper money and, interestingly, some sets of clean and well-pressed civilian clothes. The most important find was a Chinese military radio transmitter/receiver, complete with its power plant, aerials, Morse key, operating instructions book, log books and other documents. With the radio was a diary belonging to Colonel Nguyen Nam Hung, the deputy commander of 274 Regiment, which provided invaluable intelligence material. The VC must have been in desperate haste to escape to abandon such essential items, even though they were well hidden. B Company discovered and destroyed a well-constructed water point, which had been hollowed out of the rock, and several multiple-company installations spread over large areas including a facility that had been used as a hospital. C Company found another large camp containing some huts, another cache of two tons of rice and a pen holding a sow and her litter of piglets. D Company was relieved of their ambush role by B Company and, on 21 October 1966, redeployed to search the eastern slopes of Nui Thi Vai.

On the afternoon of 21 October 1966, 10 Platoon of D Company, commanded by Second Lieutenant Dennis Rainer, was tasked to investigate any tracks in the saddle area between Nui Thi Vai and Nui Toc Tien, the hill complex further to the east. They found a well-used track leading uphill towards the Nui Thi Vai peak and followed it. They passed through an area that had been napalmed. Rainer halted his leading section to secure against any enemy movement down the main track while he investigated a small side track. This search revealed a sizeable rice cache and he was in the process of quietly destroying it when, by silent signal from his leading section on the main track, he was summoned forward. Initially Lieutenant Barry Campbell, the artillery forward observer with D Company, who was accompanying 10 Platoon on this patrol, went forward to investigate. Barry now takes up the narrative to give a firsthand account of the events that followed.

Barry Campbell

On 20 October 1966, D Company, to which I was attached as the artillery forward observer, ascended to the summit of Nui Thi Vai and occupied its rock-strewn crest. On the following day 10 Platoon, commanded by Second Lieutenant Dennis Rainer, was tasked to descend the eastern side of the feature to search the area of the pass separating Nui Thi Vai and Nui Toc Tien. I suggested that I should accompany the platoon to ensure that, if needed, they could be provided with fire support; and the OC D Company, Major Paul Greenhalgh, gave me the OK.

We descended several hundred metres to the east and proceeded parallel to a track while contouring the eastern face of Nui Thi Vai in a northerly direction. This route enabled us to cross the lower reaches of any re-entrants (gullies) on the eastern slopes of the mountain. At around 1400 hours, the platoon's leading section found a distinct track leading into a steep and narrow re-entrant. As we followed it uphill into the fissure we detected the distinct smell of smoke, scented with the aroma of cooking bamboo shoots. Clearly a VC encampment of unknown size was very close nearby.

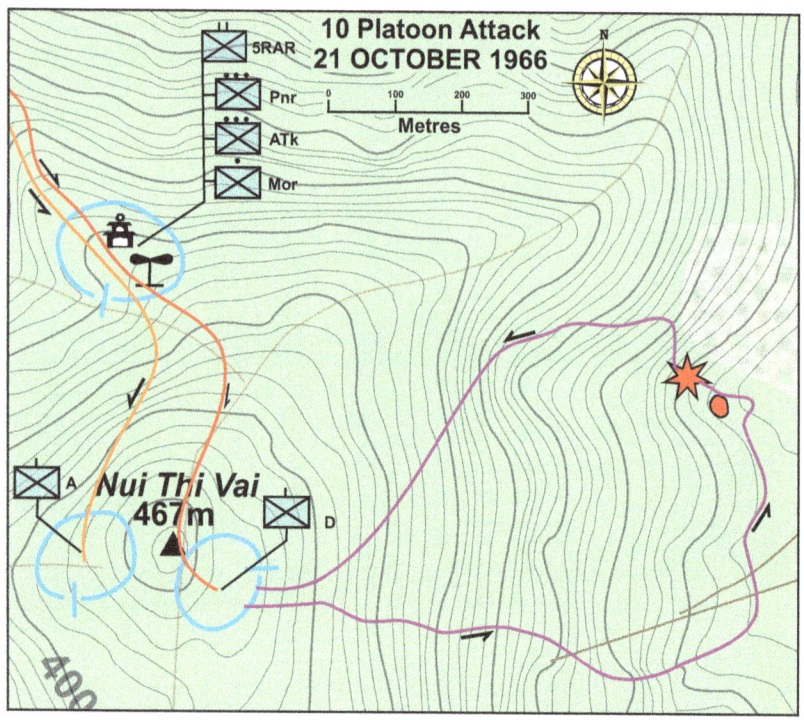

Map 13: 10 Platoon attack: 21 October 1966.

Source: Designed by Ron Boxall and produced by Alan Mayne from circa 1966 US military maps provided by Bruce Davies.

7. OPERATION QUEANBEYAN – OCTOBER 1966

As we silently and carefully followed the track uphill, we came across a large, dry cavern which contained a substantial cache of equipment, food and ammunition. Dennis busied himself with a search of the cache and we received the urgent hand signal message 'fetch officer' from our leading section. Passing the message to Dennis, I moved further forward and came across what was clearly an unoccupied sentry post. Within a short distance I met Corporal Dave Babbage and his great mate and 2IC, Lance Corporal Gary Leslie. They led me to the edge of what was obviously an area cleared of foliage to provide a defensive arc of observed fire. On the other side of this cleared area was a perimeter fence with a sign-posted gate to our left front. The gate's sign had a large skull and cross bones and a depiction of exploding mines or booby traps indicating their presence in the barrier obstacle which extended across the re-entrant. Beside the sign was a makeshift gong comprised of an artillery shell case and a metal striker, presumably for visitors to announce their arrival. We elected to forego such social niceties! Both ends of this barrier abutted the steep rock-faced sides of the re-entrant. The left rock face (to the south) was fronted by a fast-flowing mountain stream. Beside the stream a path led uphill to two huts from which smoke was issuing and dispersing under the heavy overhead tree canopy.

As we took in details of the scene before us, a monsoonal downpour started and under the cover of its noise I examined the mined barrier and found it to be heavily sewn with punji stakes, which were more numerous against the right (northern) side of the re-entrant (punji stakes were short wooden or metal stakes which had been pointed at one end and the other pushed into the ground so that an unwary foot could be impaled). Clearly there was not a second to lose and, on the shaky assumption that the area of thickest punji stakes probably contained fewer mines, I indicated to Babbage and Leslie that I should be followed by each man stepping into my footprints as we traversed the barrier.

It only took a few minutes to cross because the punjis were now set in deluge-softened soil and were easily pushed aside with a foot. Thus, in single file, we passed through the barrier, clambered up the right-hand escarpment and debouched onto the northern side of the encampment. A higher, rocky platform lay above us, so we deployed onto it and awaited Dennis's arrival. So far, so good! Dennis joined us and, with his wonderful eye for ground, indicated that he wished to get further into the re-entrant. For my part, I quickly recognised that the encampment was almost impervious to artillery and mortar fire from the south-west where our guns were sited. Two Army of the Republic of Vietnam (ARVN) 105 mm guns were located to the north-west but were an unknown quantity in terms of their proficiency and familiarity with our procedures. My assessment of the encampment's difficulty as an artillery target was subsequently borne out.

The area higher up into the re-entrant was still unknown to us but, with the benefit of surprise, Dennis thought that initiating an attack from that flank would stand a good chance of flushing the occupants downhill into the fire of the two sections he had deployed on the north side of the re-entrant, overlooking the two huts so far detected. He accepted my offer to lead this activity and with my loyal signaller, Gunner 'Midge' Rogers and Corporal Bob Ziemski's section we proceeded further up the re-entrant. As we carefully climbed up along the re-entrant's rocky northern side it became steeper and we shortly came upon a third hut which was brilliantly sited under almost complete protection by a huge projecting rock slab and backed hard up against a 4-metre-high rock face. The hut was open-sided and from our right a clearly defined track crossed our front and entered the northern end of the structure. Moving carefully, we became aware of one and then a second trip-wired US .30 calibre Garand rifle, both of which were loaded and set to warn of any approach along this track from the north. This hut was clearly the 'command post' of the encampment.

Bob Ziemski and I were crouched about 2 metres from the north end of the open-sided hut and concealed by quite thick foliage. Through the downpour we could see three VC sitting and standing at benches arranged inside the structure. At the southern side of this hut was an exit path which turned sharp left before a 4-metre cliff face and, by means of two small wooden bridges, crossed the stream which, by now, was noisily in full spate due to the continual downpour. Paralleling the stream, the path continued down to the sign-posted entry gate. Taking great care to avoid the booby-trapped rifles, we positioned Bob Ziemski's M60 machine gun team and most of his section on higher ground to our right, so they could cover us from above by firing into the lower two huts.

While this was occurring, Dennis deployed his second and third sections under Dave Babbage and Corporal Bob Bunting, together with his platoon headquarters, to cover the encampment from above and to the north of it. Here they would wait for the attack to be initiated by Bob Ziemski's section, which Midge Rogers and I were accompanying. Bob and I addressed ourselves to dealing with the three occupants of the

7. OPERATION QUEANBEYAN – OCTOBER 1966

'command post' hut, which we agreed would be the best way to trigger the attack. The nearest occupant appeared to be the senior of the three and was seated with a US .30 calibre M1 carbine on the bench by his right hand. The next VC was towards the middle of the hut and standing while he carefully wiped a rag over a US M3A1 45 calibre 'grease gun' mounted with a long, 30-round magazine. The third man was at the far end of the hut working on some poster artwork, with his rifle to his right leaning against the hut exit. By silent hand signals Bob and I agreed that I would deal with the two closest men and he would handle the third.

Time was racing on, so we both stood upright and, in accordance with the current 'rules of engagement', I called three times for the VC to '*chieu hoi*' (surrender)! Such was my nervous tension that the first challenge came out as a girlish squeak. No matter – my sounds were enough to warn Dennis that the assault he was commanding was commencing! To their great credit the three VC we confronted reacted with boldness and defiance; it was only the element of surprise that gave Bob and me the crucial advantage that we needed. I dealt with the middle man first because he was holding a weapon. However, he still managed to fire two rounds, which went through the thatched roof and into the rock overhang above the hut. The closest VC reacted instantly but the need to reach for and aim his rifle proved fatal. His movement obscured Bob's view of the furthest man who fled out of the far end of the hut but, when he turned left to cross the first bridge, Bob and I fired at him simultaneously. In seeking his target, Bob had moved to my left side and I expected a shower of hot ejected cartridge cases from his M16 on my shoulder. Instead I felt a small object strike me as his weapon suffered a stoppage caused by a separated case, where the base of the fired cartridge case detaches and is ejected, leaving most of the case jammed in the weapon's breech and halting the weapon's functioning. Fortunately, either Bob's single shot or my burst killed the escaping man.

The M60 machine gun, manned by Private Robbie Arnold, and the small group above us brilliantly added their weight of fire to ours, particularly into the two lower huts containing we knew not what. One VC tried to exit to our lower left but was quickly dealt with by Midge, my signaller. After this we had no further targets as the occupants of the two lower huts decamped to the north and downhill in what must have been a practised drill. Unfortunately for them, they immediately entered Dennis's killing ground at short range. A sustained fusillade by the two M60s and rifles of his group quickly sealed their fate. In the shortest time, their quiet rain-soaked haven had become a charnel house. The engagement had unfolded exactly as Dennis had planned. Every member had played his part with the patient stealth, iron nerve and ruthless discipline and confidence needed for success in this kind of very close combat.

The nervous tension and silence that followed the deafening noise gave way to the need to report the contact to 5 RAR HQ. Dennis reported the initial details of the contact on his radio net to Paul Greenhalgh and, turning the volume up on my radio, Midge provided our battery commander, Major Neville Gair, with an update of our location and a brief report on the situation. Since we were unsure what lay above us, Dennis agreed that Bob Ziemski's section should neutralise the booby-trapped rifles protecting the track leading uphill from the encampment and secure the approach from that direction. He then reorganised his whole platoon on the high ground on the northern side of the encampment and completed his detailed radio report of the action. At 1630 hours, because of our distance from the rest of D Company, the difficult terrain and the short amount of remaining daylight, we were ordered to secure all enemy weapons, ammunition and documents and return to D Company. A full search of the installation and burial of enemy dead would be conducted the next day. During this pause I busied myself by plotting the route we would follow back to D Company.

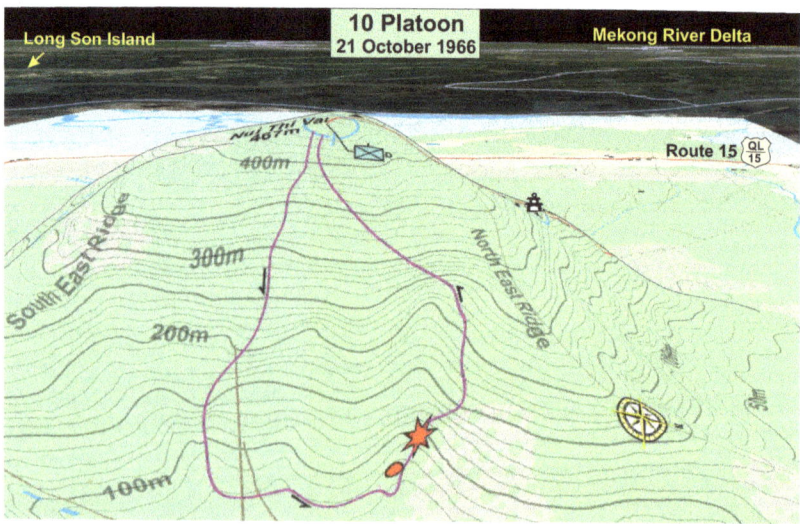

Map 13A: 10 Platoon attack: 21 October 1966.

Source: Designed by Ron Boxall and produced by Alan Mayne from circa 1966 US military maps provided by Bruce Davies.

In the interest of mobility in very difficult terrain we were patrolling without our full load-carrying equipment. We had to use toggle ropes to tie enemy weapons into small bundles to enable them to be carried with minimal hindrance. The light was already beginning to fade, as indeed was the sustained adrenaline rush and elation we had just experienced, as we clambered from escarpment to escarpment while trying to stick to the return route we had planned. Just after last light, and with waning confidence in our map reading, the welcome 'thumbs up' signal was passed back from our forward section and we passed into D Company's perimeter.

During that night the enemy encampment was engaged with artillery in case other VC elements tried to recover materiel from the site. The next day the whole of D Company returned to the encampment to search it thoroughly, bury the enemy dead and destroy the installation. My initial assessment of the difficulty of getting artillery fire into the encampment proved correct – overnight, rounds had fallen all around the narrow re-entrant, but none fell onto the installation itself. Ten enemy had died at our hands. We later heard that another had escaped but shortly afterwards surrendered at Duc Thanh, many kilometres away to the north-east.

Max Carroll

The single VC who escaped from this contact surrendered himself several days later to the ARVN at Duc Thanh and confirmed, under interrogation, that the group which 10 Platoon had attacked was part of the Chau Duc District Company. The subsequent D Company search of the area of the 10 Platoon attack discovered a quantity of clothing, a further cache of rice, packs of documents, medical supplies and several unserviceable weapons.

B Company's time in the ambush role had been as unproductive as that of D Company, so on 23 October 1966 they lifted their ambushes and, together with C Company, proceeded to allotted search areas on Nui Toc Tien. While moving, B Company sighted three VC at a considerable distance and engaged them with artillery fire with unknown results. The search of Nui Toc Tien over the next two days yielded little except for B Company's find of a platoon-sized camp, several weeks old, with some shallow graves close by.

While this Nui Toc Tien search was proceeding, D Company was continuing their similar task on the eastern slopes of Nui Thi Vai, again with little further result. At the same time, the north-west spur of Nui Thi Vai was being searched by A Company, the assault pioneers and our supporting sappers, with some useful finds being made. By 25 October 1966 we considered that the whole area of operations had been very thoroughly worked over and it was decided to terminate Operation Queanbeyan on the next day. The battalion had been continuously in the field for 21 hard days, spread over three consecutive operations. Our men, while still alert and effective, were tired.

It was expected that, at some time after our departure, the VC would move back to Nui Thi Vai, which had been an important base and sanctuary for them for a very long time. It was impossible to destroy the rocky structure of the mountain and its caves. However, we did what we could and made what was left of the caves, tunnels and the surrounding areas uninhabitable by seeding them with long-lasting tear gas crystals. We destroyed all surface installations with explosives.

A and D Companies linked up with BHQ at the pagoda during the afternoon of 25 October 1966 ready to fly out next morning. The helicopter lift of A Company and BHQ, less the Tactical Command Group, took place between 0645 and 0945 hours. The pagoda LZ was small and could only take one Iroquois at a time. B and C Companies swept south from their overnight harbours near Nui Toc Tien, to link up with armoured personnel carriers at an assembly area near Route 15, which had been secured by a 6 RAR platoon from the FSB. On their way to the assembly area, B Company apprehended a VC suspect, who had some explaining to do back at 1 ATF about why he had been where he was when captured. He was lucky he had not been shot. B and C Companies then moved back to Nui Dat between 1430 and 1530 hours, while the airlift of D Company and BHQ Tac (Tactical Headquarters) took place simultaneously. The FSB then moved back to Nui Dat between 1600 and 1700 hours.

What had we achieved? The operation was considered successful. We had discovered a large, occupied VC base area, with numerous above ground installations and caches, and an extensive multi-layered cave and tunnel system used for accommodation, storage of valuable documents, explosives, ammunition and equipment, as well as concealing many effective fire positions. All that we found had been destroyed or rendered untenable. We had also killed, wounded and dispersed VC elements occupying the hills, and found items of high intelligence value. We had hurt and disrupted the VC and it would take them much time and effort to recover, which gave us hard-earned satisfaction. We mourned our dead and felt for the seriously wounded who were evacuated to Australia. The other wounded recovered in-country and then rejoined us. We all appreciated that we were only halfway through our tour of duty and had another six months to go with many more operations to come, and it was a case of just getting on with the job. While there was little time for personal reflection, the essential post-operational analyses were carefully done, as after each operation, to evaluate our actions and procedures, always with the intent of improving our performance.

Editors' conclusion

It is appropriate to note that several gallantry awards were made for actions in the clearing of Nui Thi Vai and they appear among those listed in Appendix A. In those days, the British Honours and Awards system was used by Australia and it was normal for awards not cited as 'Immediate' to be promulgated several months after the event. When finally announced, they were received with much satisfaction and approval by the battalion. 5 RAR's determined incursions into the enemy's long-held sanctuary of Nui Thi Vai, soon after the Battle of Long Tan, served notice that the arrival of 1 ATF confronted him with a new opponent in Phuoc Tuy who was able to detect and contest his tenure of any piece of terrain. For the battalion, Operation Queanbeyan marked the point when it had found its measure as an Australian infantry battalion, liked what it found and moved forward with unalloyed confidence in its men and its methods.

8

A PLATOON COMMANDER'S WAR – PART 1

Roger Wainwright and Terry O'Hanlon

Editors' introduction

The saying that the Vietnam War was 'a platoon commander's war' derives, in part from the fact that our infantry platoon commanders were the peripheral nodes in a radio communication web which extended from the action happening at the point of battle, upwards and sideways, throughout a widespread network. Thus, command and support hierarchies were kept instantly informed of events and conditions faced by the soldiers entrusted with implementing their orders. In addition, the platoon commander's radio link and his professional knowledge, skills and cool-headed judgement enabled the risks of employing close artillery and air support to be accepted, as well as the rapid calling of life-saving aeromedical evacuation whenever his platoon suffered a casualty.

At the same time, platoon commanders were the infantry officers most personally enmeshed with their battalion's fighting soldiers – the diggers for whom they had the responsibilities of training, guiding and care. They were simultaneously boss, teacher and counsellor to their diggers. They were also their soldiers' champion, who maintained a close interest in their backgrounds, interests, talents and personalities. This relationship between the junior officer and his men was the lynchpin of success in Vietnam, as it has always been throughout Australia's lengthening military history. These things are evident throughout this book. Our Vietnam platoon commanders ranged in age from their early to mid-20s. Only in the warrior's field of life-and-death toil are such weighty expectations confidently heaped upon such young shoulders.

Roger Wainwright

As Field Marshal Viscount Slim of Yarralumla and Bishopston observed in the first paragraph of *Defeat into Victory*, his account of the Burma Campaign of World War II:

> the four best commands in the Service are a platoon, a battalion, a division and an army … A platoon, because it is your first command, because you are young, and because, if you are any good, you know the men in it better than their mothers do and love them as much.[1]

I had a military career spanning more than 35 years including service in four infantry battalions of the Royal Australian Regiment (RAR) and holding key roles in army training establishments and appointments in Defence operational and intelligence communities. The most satisfying and rewarding of these postings was the privilege of commanding a platoon of the Tiger Battalion on active service. Lamentably, the subsequent commands enjoyed by Viscount Slim passed me by!

I trust my recollections will give a reasonably clear description of the challenges facing the platoons of the 5th Battalion (5 RAR) in 1966. All 12 rifle platoons and the four platoons of Support Company had different experiences, but there was a common base for us all, including a depth of camaraderie that embodied strong support for each other. We were all required to work to the same standard operating procedures (SOP) of the battalion but there was still scope through our individual command and leadership traits to help each platoon to develop its own identity and character.

After graduating from the Royal Military College (RMC) Duntroon on 14 December 1965, I joined 5 RAR on 5 January 1966. I was allocated to command 8 Platoon, a position I proudly held for the next 17 months. Five infantry graduates of our RMC class had spent a two-week attachment with 5 RAR in August 1965 as part of our corps familiarisation training

---

1   Viscount Slim, *Defeat into Victory*, Cassell, London, 1956, p 3.

prior to graduation. The founding commanding officer (CO), Lieutenant Colonel Peter Oxley, gave us a warm welcome with a few appreciated fatherly pearls of wisdom and we were then placed under the guidance of the 'in place' platoon commanders. I recall that the battalion second in command (2IC), Major John Warr, was soon to assume command and the more junior company commanders were already calling him 'Sir'. At that stage in 1965 there was little talk that the battalion would soon have a pivotal role in the establishment of the 1st Australian Task Force (1 ATF) in Phuoc Tuy Province, Vietnam. John Warr assumed command of 5 RAR on promotion to lieutenant colonel on 1 September.

The very early days of 1966 were spent getting to know my platoon, receiving reinforcements, both regular and national service, supervising individual and section-level training, and assembling my platoon commander's notebook. This, after a time, seemed to be of limited value; although it was held to be a mandatory measure of a platoon commander's knowledge of his soldiers' qualifications, capabilities and personal details. We faced a very steep learning curve because we platoon commanders were recent graduates of RMC, the Officer Cadet School Portsea or the Officer Training Unit (OTU) Scheyville. Our OTU colleagues comprised five of the first class of national service officers to graduate from Scheyville. Two of them, John Deane-Butcher and Harry Neesham, joined C Company as my fellow platoon commanders.

The rumours of 5 RAR being sent to Vietnam were now rife but until we received formal notice, we were instructed to say in outside conversation '*If* we go to Vietnam', not '*when* we go to Vietnam'. During February and early March, all companies had rotated through the Jungle Training Centre at Canungra for some harsh but extremely valuable training. We also undertook mine warfare training at the School of Military Engineering at Casula. This involved daily forced marches in battle order from Holsworthy to Casula (7 km) to keep our fitness at a high level. By this time the platoons were generally settled and up to full strength, although I had two new section commanders join my platoon about this time to replace two who were just not up to the mark.

There is no doubt that junior non-commissioned officers (NCOs) are the backbone of a battalion, particularly in counter-insurgency operations. I was fortunate to have excellent stability with my section commanders, and we were together for almost our entire tour of duty in Vietnam. Whenever hard yards had to be covered, I had no hesitation in putting any of them forward as my point section. They were Corporals Russell Quinn of 4 Section, Leslie 'Doc' Urquhart of 5 Section and Holger 'Curly' Koblitz of 6 Section. Doc has since died but I am still in contact with Russ and Curly.

I had two platoon sergeants over this period: Keith 'Shorty' Mavin and, from September 1966, Ralph 'Rowdy' Hindmarsh. They were different personalities and both very good at their job. Shorty did not endear himself to some members of the platoon, but a platoon sergeant is not required to win in any popularity contest. Rowdy was a strong and supportive sergeant who went on to be a company sergeant major (CSM) on the battalion's second tour of Vietnam and later became a regimental sergeant major (RSM).

The battalion was formally warned for service in Vietnam on 9 March 1966. This was the official commencement of our involvement in Operation Hardihood, the deployment of 1 ATF to Vietnam and the establishment of the base at Nui Dat. Many people think that Operation Hardihood started on 24 May 1966 when the battalion deployed from Vung Tau into landing zone (LZ) Hudson to secure the area surrounding the nearby Nui Dat, but that was just the initial tactical phase. Hardihood was a sequential operation comprising the deployment of 1 ATF from Australia through to seizing and securing the site of the intended base at Nui Dat.

The very first entry in the 5 RAR Commander's Diary, the official record that all units are required to maintain after being warned for active service, states: '0900 hrs. CO (Lieutenant Colonel Warr) attended conference at 1TF. Unit warned for service in South Vietnam as part of 1ATF. Operation codenamed Hardihood'. Although our early training had been very busy it certainly picked up in intensity, with greater priority now being given to both our operational and administrative readiness.

On 11 March the battalion departed by air from the Holsworthy 'aero paddock' by Caribou aircraft for Exercises Ben Tiger and Iron Lady, to be held at Gospers Mountain in the Colo-Putty Field Training Area. These exercises provided the final opportunity for platoons to put the finishing touches on teamwork and tactics including an introduction to helicopter operations. The battalion returned to Gallipoli Barracks on 24 March and commenced pre-embarkation leave on 7 April.

The deployment to Vietnam began on 19 April with the departure of the advance party commanded by Major John Miller. Every platoon was represented on the advance party by either the platoon commander or the platoon sergeant so that they could feed off the experiences of their 1 RAR counterparts who were the third battalion of the US 173 Airborne Brigade at Bien Hoa. There were still formalities to complete at home and on 20 April a battalion ceremonial parade, including a traditional 'Beating the Retreat' ceremony, was held at Holsworthy and reviewed by the Minister for the Army, Malcolm Fraser. The following day the battalion marched through Sydney in a ticker tape farewell with the salute being taken by the Governor of NSW, Sir Roden Cutler VC, KCMG, CBE.

Lieutenant Colonel Warr and his party departed the Royal Australian Air Force (RAAF) Base Richmond by Qantas charter on 28 April. He was accompanied by elements of Battalion Headquarters (BHQ) and 36 members of 8 Platoon. We travelled via Townsville and Manila to Saigon. HMAS *Sydney* had departed on 22 April with 130 men of 5 RAR, comprising C Company less 8 Platoon, the Transport Platoon with their vehicles, and unit stores. HMAS *Sydney* anchored off Vung Tau on 4 May. The remaining subunits departed by air on alternate days from 30 April with the whole battalion being complete at Vung Tau on 13 May.

Our knowledge of the situation on arrival was tenuous and we had little awareness of the enemy's strength, locations or activities. The arrival of C Company became folklore as its officer commanding, Major Noel Granter, ordered all members to disembark from the landing craft at Vung Tau port with bayonets fixed, although the area was designated as secure. This event caused much merriment to the bystanders at the wharf, particularly the Americans, and became the subject of a cartoon in an Australian newspaper. Our company quartermaster sergeant, Staff Sergeant Bob Trenear, could not join the 'assault' as his bayonet was safely buried at the bottom of his kit bag.

Having travelled by air with my platoon and the CO's party to Saigon's Tan Son Nhut airport, John Warr took the opportunity to talk to me about the battalion's dearth of knowledge about our new situation. Before he went to visit the battalion's advance party, who were attached to 1 RAR at Bien Hoa, he reminded me that I was commanding the first platoon of the battalion to arrive in Vietnam and to ensure that, on arrival at Vung Tau, I took all security precautions including mounting clearing patrols at first and last light. Yes sir! My platoon flew to Vung Tau in a US Air Force C123 Provider and were then piled into a large US Army truck – a cattle truck. The route from Vung Tau airfield to our staging area at 'Back Beach' took us through sand dunes and scrub which to me seemed a likely place to be ambushed. Not being certain of the enemy situation, I ordered my machine gunners to load their weapons and mount positions on the corners of the truck.

As we moved into a clear area near the beach, I saw a makeshift camp comprising a large tent, some one-man shelters (hutchies) and some very basic facilities. I had my machine gunners unload and we were welcomed by a happy assistant adjutant, Lieutenant Ralph Thompson, who was clad only in shorts, boots and a hat and wearing a holstered pistol. He pointed us in the direction of some cold 'goffas' (canned soft drink) and showed us where we could pitch our hutchies. No clearing patrols were deployed although we did mount a sentry post. Over the next few days in the heat and humidity, with the sun beating down and reflecting off the white sand, 8 Platoon erected steel pickets and ridge wires for the following companies to erect their hutchies. On 1 May we also helped to develop four key sentry and observation posts that were being established on the outer perimeter of the Tigers' temporary home. It was a quick acclimatisation.

5 RAR Training Directive of 2 May 1966 aimed at finalising the training of the battalion in readiness for operations. Ralph Thompson had been given responsibility for coordinating this training with each company as they progressively arrived at Vung Tau. The program included helicopter operations, clearing operations, armoured personnel carrier training, small arms training including weapon live-firing out to sea, vehicle counter-ambush drills and house clearing. A communications exercise was also conducted for all officers which was aimed at overcoming the difficulties arising from differences between Australian and US radio voice procedures.

To relieve the intense activity and to reinforce bonding with our American allies, preparations were made in the form of an officers' formal dining-in night, with appropriate security. It was held at the Pacific Hotel, Vung Tau, on 20 May. Officers of the US Army's 68 Assault Helicopter Company, which was to support us during Operation Hardihood, were invited to attend. I had fallen foul of my company commander for some obscure reason so was appointed as duty officer and remained at Back Beach. It was an interesting sight to see my fellow officers return well lubricated from the dinner to the battalion's secure area. Several had a last swim in the balmy waters of the South China Sea, resplendent in their summer formal mess dress. It was the 'last supper' before insertion into operations.

5 RAR Operation Order Number 4 was issued on 22 May with the mission '5RAR is to destroy the enemy in the Tactical Area of Responsibility allotted as a preliminary to the establishment of 1ATF in the area'. Orders were passed down the command chain to platoon and section level and, while there was a nervous expectation in the air, there prevailed a quiet confidence that our training would hold us in good stead in the days to come. To give us a spiritual boost, a battalion church parade was held, the service being conducted by Father John Williams and Chaplain Ed Bennett.

My notes of the orders I gave to 8 Platoon for 24 May, the day the operation began, show reveille was at 0400 hours and, following breakfast and other final administrative preparations, we departed at 0610 hours for LZ Snakepit (Vung Tau airfield). Our company lift-off was scheduled for 0703 hours with an 0718 insertion into LZ Hudson which was secured by elements of the US 173 Airborne Brigade. The order of fly-in was: A Company, C Company with the CO and his tactical party, B Company and D Company. Seven hundred and seventy troops were airlifted using 30 UH-1D Iroquois helicopters, comprising four lifts of these aircraft with each chalk (passenger load) comprising either six or seven men. The men of both A Company and C Company carried a 5-kilogram 81-millimetre mortar bomb in addition to their normal combat load as the initial ammunition supply for the mortar platoon.

After the manoeuvre, with elements of the battalion deployed to LZ Hudson, the rifle companies commenced deployment into their designated areas of operations from 1200 hours. It was a day that I will always remember. At 1400 hours 8 Platoon had the first enemy contact of 5 RAR, when we were fired upon by one or two enemy who then fled. A short while later we again sighted two VC but, on both occasions despite having employed our well-rehearsed contact drills, we had no results.

The location of these two contacts was the small ground rise that became the home for 5 RAR's BHQ and those of subsequent battalions located on the northern side of the Nui Dat base during the next six years. C Company harboured a few hundred metres to the east of this location and commenced digging shell scrapes (shallow protective fighting pits for each soldier). Late that afternoon we heard small arms fire from about 500 metres away followed later by the sad news that Private Errol Noack of B Company's 5 Platoon had become the battalion's first casualty. This was sad news for several members of my platoon as they knew Errol well, having undergone recruit and early infantry training with him. Although he was a member of another company, such a loss hit hard particularly on our first day in operations. After two contacts and the loss of a mate the reality had well and truly sunk in that we were at war.

We stood-to (armed, fully equipped and alert) and sentries were posted for the night hoping that a night's rest would prepare us for the second day. This was not to be. The wet season was in full swing and we were drenched, with our shell scrapes becoming small swimming pools. At about 2150 hours we heard artillery rounds land close to our position, so close that shrapnel whipped through the trees above us. Regardless of discomfort, our water-filled shell scrapes were then a welcome refuge. It appeared that this fire came from US artillery, located near the province capital Ba Ria, as part of an H&I (harassing and interdiction) fire program about which we were not aware. At 2226 hours 5 RAR BHQ sent the following terse message to 173 Airborne Brigade: 'Please ensure no further unrequested H&I fire is put into my area without reference to this HQ. Fire received approximately 2150 was uncomfortable'. Our operations officer, Max Carroll, assured us later that the remonstration over the radio was far more explicit than that recorded in the battalion's operations log.

So ended our first day of operations. I recall thinking that we will need to get used to such activity and briefed my platoon accordingly the following morning – only '363 days and a wakey!' (363 days and one night's sleep to go before we can go home). I was a little more than 21 years and marginally older than the men of my platoon who were a mix of regular soldiers and national servicemen who were mostly from the first call-up. The only platoon members older than me were my three section commanders and my platoon sergeant.

When service in Vietnam was looming, I started to think about how I would perform as a young platoon commander with direct responsibility for training, commanding and leading my men and attending to their ongoing training and welfare. I still have some self-analysis notes that I wrote at the time and they address three fundamental questions. First, how would I react when giving orders to kill enemy soldiers?

Second, how would I react when members of my own platoon were killed or wounded in action? Third, how well would I react when we were in a particularly dire situation? There was to be only one way I would find the answers.

The construction of the base at Nui Dat while maintaining security was extremely difficult. Digging-in and coordinating defensive positions at section, platoon and company level was frustrating as it had to be combined with ongoing operations including some village cordon and search activities. In between the battalion's operations, all platoons undertook fighting and ambush patrols in our tactical area of responsibility (TAOR) as well as manning sentry positions on a 24-hour daily basis, along with the digging of bunkers with overhead protection and erecting defensive barbed wire obstacles. All these activities were conducted at the height of the wet season and there was no escape from the red mud churned up by vehicles and the digging-in process.

My platoon, where it was sited in C Company's area, occupied the most northern platoon position in the Task Force base. It felt like being the proverbial pimple on the pumpkin as the most likely enemy assaults were anticipated to come from the north. Our defences were boosted with the allocation of a .50 calibre heavy machine gun located in my platoon area, primarily to provide mutual support between us and B Company who were on our right flank. We constructed a fortified bunker for this gun. It became the major strong point for our position and continuously manned, 24 hours per day. It also housed the control mechanism for banks of M18A1 Claymore mines (aimed mines, each of which projected 700 steel balls in a 60° arc in front of the device at an initial velocity of 1,218 metres per second) which we laid in front of our perimeter.

The Nui Dat facilities for ablutions, messing (meals) and recreation were very basic until hard-standing (solid flooring) was provided as the tour progressed. Black-out conditions were in place but there was no electric lighting until much later. For months, the only light available was from flashlights, locally sourced candles or by wiring small fluorescent tubes to the part-expired batteries of our ANPRC 25 radio sets.

I will always admire the persistence of our soldiers and NCOs, who faced these circumstances with determination, humour and resilience. We were pioneers who, together with 6 RAR, established bases for follow-on battalions who would inherit a defendable base and facilities with reasonable amenities.

The pressure on platoons was great and after returning from Operation Sydney Two, the cordon and search of Duc My, and a quick shower my platoon was ordered out on a 48-hour patrol. On return to Nui Dat and before I went to BHQ for a debrief, I directed my platoon to rest, have a clean-up, write a letter home and, apart from the sentries on our .50 calibre machine gun, to generally unwind. On return from being debriefed I found about eight members of my platoon had been diverted to digging the large underground command post for Company HQ. I ordered them back to our platoon lines which led to a confrontation with our CSM, Warrant Officer Ross Wormald, about who was commanding 8 Platoon. I stood up for my men and won the point.

The second member of 5 RAR killed in action was Private John Sweetnam, a 19-year-old regular soldier of my 8 Platoon. Sadly, John died on 9 June when he moved while in an ambush position and was mistakenly shot by a member who had not long joined the platoon. He fired at unexpected movement within the ambush area. This incident also occurred during Operation Hardihood. It was the first occasion that a US Army helicopter had conducted a night *Dustoff* of an Australian soldier of 1 ATF. We used hexamine tablet (field cooking fuel) fires to illuminate the boundaries of a rice paddy field for an LZ with Corporal Russ Quinn guiding the helicopter in by torch and being fully illuminated by the landing-lights of the aircraft. A few hours later we received the news by radio that John had not survived. This incident hit the platoon hard as John was well respected, a fine soldier and a good mate of all in his section and 8 Platoon. I still have a copy of the letter I wrote to his mother at the time and tried to contact her when we returned home. The circuit road in C Company's area in Nui Dat base was named 'Sweetnam Crescent' in his memory and the name was retained by all following battalions that occupied the position.

Years later when I was an instructor at various army schools and had the benefit of hindsight, I concluded that the defences at Nui Dat were lacking, particularly in relation to those vital principles of defence – mutual support, depth, all-round defence and interlocking arcs of fire. This was exacerbated by the fact that 1 ATF had only two infantry battalions throughout 1966–67 instead of the three that were needed. Nor were the mobility and firepower of tanks available in the early and most vulnerable days of 1 ATF's seizure and occupation of its Nui Dat base.

8. A PLATOON COMMANDER'S WAR – PART 1

The early difficulties in protecting the Nui Dat base can be illustrated by the dearth of defensive capability during the Battle of Long Tan. On 17 and 18 August all 5 RAR rifle companies were deployed to the north or north-east of Nui Dat. The SITREP (situation report) for the period 1600–2000 hours on 18 August, at the time when the battle was at its most intense, lists the locations assigned to 5 RAR elements after most were quickly ordered back to Nui Dat. This was a very sparse, skeletal manning of those 1 ATF unit areas that had been denuded of men and weapons used to mount a reaction force to support 6 RAR's D Company at Long Tan. To make it worse, C Company was still deployed to the north at Binh Ba following the battalion's cordon and search of that village.

5 RAR's platoons were defending unfamiliar company positions. They were a thin red line with virtually nothing in reserve. No doubt this became an urgent consideration in 1 ATF eventually being bolstered by an additional infantry battalion and a squadron of tanks. These were considered necessary from the outset; but the third battalion was not added until December 1967 and the tank squadron did not arrive until early 1968. Questions remain in many minds about the likely outcome of the threat to 1 ATF in the early days if D Company of 6 RAR had not encountered the large enemy force at Long Tan on 18 August.

The constantly high tempo of our operations – patrolling, ambushing and building defences – during the early months led to the refinement of many of our procedures. We had also absorbed and proved many of the lessons learnt by 1 RAR, which had been a permanent part of the US 173 Airborne Brigade throughout 1965–66. These factors led to a major revision of our SOPs, which were reissued in early October 1966 prior to deployment on Operation Canberra.

It became common, particularly in very thick vegetation, for sections to use just one scout. This facilitated navigation by allowing closer communication between the leading section commander and his scout. It also became necessary when our sections were often reduced from 10 men to about seven or eight, and sometimes even fewer. Otherwise, there was no effective rifle group in each section. Eventually, I gave up employing a batman (orderly) as I felt he would be better used in one of the sections as a rifleman.

Harbour drills (moving into a stationary, defensive posture for an extended halt) at platoon level were automatic, ordered by hand signals alone and the layout quickly coordinated after all sections were in position. Similarly, drills for deploying a *reactive* quick ambush were refined so that the position could be rapidly and quietly occupied after a quick reconnaissance by myself. Conversely, a *deliberate* ambush was pre-planned and deployed in response to intelligence about known, anticipated or suspected enemy activity. Ambushing was a key tactic in maintaining the initiative in our TAOR. While deliberate ambushes were laid at selected locations based on intelligence and map reconnaissance, the final siting of any ambush was the prerogative of the ambush commander who assessed the site's features, likely enemy approaches and the ability to concentrate maximum fire into a selected killing ground.

A triangular ambush concept was developed which was not in accordance with current operational doctrine. A harbour is not an ambush nor is an ambush a harbour. This combination of a night-time ambush and a harbour was brought about by increasing fatigue caused both by constant daytime patrolling and diminishing platoon strengths. Platoons had to release men to attend courses, contribute to essential non-combat manpower needs, for rest and leave, illness or injury and numerous other reasons. In retrospect, we can only envy the rotational reinforcement concept that enables platoons deployed in present-day operations to be maintained at optimal strength during operations.

A strong relationship with my radio operator was paramount. A signaller with long whip-like aerials showing above him was a sure sign to the enemy that a 'boss' was nearby, so there prevailed a firm arrangement between us that he was far enough away so as not to attract unwanted attention, but near enough to provide me with quick access to the radio when needed. My first signaller was Private Ian Foran, a very capable first-intake national serviceman whom I had trained in Australia. Ian was a reluctant soldier who did not want to be in Vietnam but nevertheless did his duty. After a few months in Vietnam, Ian was poached by my company commander who had recognised his skills and made him his own signaller on the company command net. Rank hath its privileges! Private David Sharp then volunteered to become my signaller. He was another first-intake national serviceman who had been the forward scout for 4 Section. He learnt quickly and was an excellent signaller.

In training my NCOs, I placed a lot of emphasis on indirect fire support from artillery and mortars and made sure that their supporting fire was always available. I did this by showing them how artillery or mortar defensive fire tasks could be planned on the four key points of the compass at a safe distance from our location, so fire could be called for and adjusted at night without reference to maps, which needed the use of torchlight. It was a bit like an insurance policy – in place but, hopefully, not needed. By day, I would sometimes call for unplanned fire support during independent platoon TAOR patrols, when not in contact with the enemy. I knew it was a confidence booster to the platoon to know that this vital support was on hand if needed, and to see that all members of our leadership group were competent in its use.

After several months on operations, it was fair to say that we were at the top of our game. Confidence was high, our teamwork was excellent and we were winning in our contacts with the enemy.

And now to Operations Canberra, Robin and Queanbeyan. The background and effect of these operations have been covered in other chapters, so I will confine myself to some incidents involving my platoon. On the morning of 8 October, 8 Platoon was leading C Company up a steep ridgeline covered in very thick vegetation which afforded limited observation. The only option was to move carefully in single file. Doc Urquhart's 5 Section was leading, with his scout Terry 'Harry' Harris in front. In making his way through undergrowth, he badly cut his wrist, which later required stitches. I moved the other two sections forward with Curly Koblitz's 6 Section now in the lead, followed by me and Dave Sharp, then Russ Quinn's 4 Section with my platoon sergeant Rowdy Hindmarsh and Doc's section in the rear. At about 1030 hours we came across a recently used track and heard voices. I told C Company headquarters that I would investigate. Artillery fire was laid to the north and placed on call, ready to be fired at my request.

> **Private Daryl McCombe, forward scout, recalls this episode:**
>
> On 8 October our platoon was leading C Company in single file. 'Doc's' section was leading with 'Harry' Harris as the forward scout. Our section followed with Russ Quinn's section last with Bobby Box the scout. Word came back up the line that Harry had cut his hand badly and that our section was to move up front and take the lead. This placed Russ Quinn's section next after platoon headquarters and Doc's section, with the injured man, in the rear.
>
> I led the company down on to relatively level ground but still patrolling through thick jungle. I walked into a slightly cleared area and saw a freshly dug trench with some digging implements strewn about it. This was directly in front of me and about 10 metres away. I turned to signal to 'Curly' Koblitz but he was out of sight. I had developed a bad habit of getting too far out in front of the man behind me. I turned my back on the trench and took a couple of steps back from where I had paused when 'Curly' came in to view. I gave him the hand signal to indicate enemy up ahead and then went down on one knee facing the trench to wait for him to come up to me. Before he got to me a voice called out '*Uc Dai Loi*' [Vietnamese for Australian] and so they knew we were there. The voice came from my front but to my right at about the 2 o'clock direction. This was followed immediately by a couple of rifle shots. I believe it was the same person who yelled out, '*Uc Dai Loi*!' who fired the two shots.[1]

[1] Daryl McCombe, email correspondence with the author, 30 May 2017.

Several more shots were fired from another direction. I radioed this information back to my company commander, Major John Miller, who told me to clear the area. Curly's section was already positioned to provide fire support, so I moved forward and did a quick reconnaissance to the right flank which fell away steeply and was thickly covered by vegetation. The left was a better option, so I decided to take the other two sections with me on this flank and assault downhill through the position with Curly's section providing fire support. After we moved past the fire support section a booby trap exploded, which we later discovered was initiated by a tripwire.

We suffered seven casualties, two of which were serious. The immediate area was made secure and we started the difficult task of withdrawing the casualties about 300 metres back to C Company headquarters where there was a potential LZ. This took considerable time to clear of tall vegetation and was still a tight LZ, but large enough for a *Dustoff* helicopter to land. It was still relatively tight because of a large tree stump in the landing area. The evacuation involved two lifts by US Army Iroquois *Dustoff* helicopters and was not complete until after 1300 hours.

The two serious casualties were Private Bobby Box and Private David Riik, respectively the forward scout and a rifleman with Russ Quinn's section. Both were returned to Australia because of the seriousness of their wounds. Private Doug Bishop had also received leg wounds but returned to the platoon after 29 days convalescence at the US 36 Evacuation Hospital, Vung Tau. The policy was that any casualty requiring 30 days or more to recover would be returned to Australia. Doug was delighted to make it back to the platoon with a day to spare so he could participate in more adventures. Dave Sharp was not wounded but shrapnel did hit his radio which remained operable. I also received some minor shrapnel wounds to my left side which I didn't report until later, with John Miller insisting that I be evacuated to have the shrapnel plucked out. The main impact was worn by my ammunition pouch with shrapnel penetrating my M16 rifle's spare magazines.

Next day at about 1400 hours in the same area, 7 Platoon encountered more booby traps, suffering four casualties. It was clear that the area was laced with booby traps, many of which had been attached to vines and sited to create a channelling affect. The same LZ was used to evacuate these casualties.

During the next 24 hours C Company located some of the enemy's prepared but unoccupied positions within what appeared to be a large base camp area. It included training facilities, a hospital, ammunition, medical stores, a workplace for making booby traps, items of personal equipment, weapons registers, written reports of vehicle movement along Route 15 and an important map of foot track systems in the western part of Phuoc Tuy province.

On the early morning of 9 October with a few stitches inserted, I flew into an LZ being secured by B Company to await the arrival of C Company and rejoin my platoon. After a resupply of ammunition, explosives and rations, we continued the search of the western slopes of Nui Thi Vai, finding more enemy facilities, tunnels, ammunition and surgical equipment. The sappers (combat engineers) were kept very busy, destroying as many of these as they could and undertook the onerous task of delousing many of the booby traps and mines that were discovered. In addition to these enemy munitions, we also encountered very touchy unexploded US BLU3 cluster bomblets, many caught by their fins in the thick vegetation.

The Combat Engineer Teams of 1 Field Squadron that joined us were all extremely brave and skilful and a very welcome addition to any infantry company. We can only admire the skills and tenacity they showed in climbing into tunnels, searching for and delousing mines and booby traps, and using high explosives to destroy enemy facilities. They were a vital part of our operations and held in very high regard.

This pattern of searching continued into the next day but could not be completed as we had to move quickly to the north-western edge of Nui Thi Vai to LZ Michael for extraction by helicopter to Route 15 for the commencement of Operation Robin. We knew we were to return to Nui Thi Vai several days later, to continue with the clearing of enemy from it in another operation.

Details of Operation Robin to secure Route 15 for the arrival of 3 Brigade of 4 Infantry Division (US) have been recounted in Chapter 6. This operation passed relatively routinely for C Company except for the crash of a Sioux helicopter flying south along Route 15 as it approached C Company. We witnessed the helicopter's destruction as it bounced down the road before coming to stop about 30 metres from our perimeter.

Orders for Operation Queanbeyan, our return to Nui Thi Vai, were issued during Operation Robin and, to gain surprise, we departed from the roadside of Route 15 on foot at 0300 hours on 17 October. We harboured in the thick undergrowth to avoid detection prior to moving into our designated area of operations at first light. Essentially, this was the same area where we had suffered casualties and discovered numerous enemy facilities in the preceding week. Expectations were quite high that the battalion would be in for an interesting time.

It was hard going in the thick vegetation and steep rocky slopes and, in the afternoon, we heard continual gunfire and fire support from a US helicopter light fire team. We found out later this came from a major contact involving the Anti-Tank Platoon. The following morning, we reached the area where we'd had the enemy contact 10 days before and, after searching the area, we realised that we needed far more explosives to destroy the enemy facilities than we were carrying. Consequently, these were flown into us, along with two additional combat engineers.

The LZ to be used was the one that had been used to evacuate our earlier casualties. We were watching the approaching RAAF Iroquois when it appeared that the rear rotor clipped a tree during its descent. The helicopter then crashed nearby but just outside the area we had secured. It lost power, its nose collided with a tree and it slid down the tree crunching heavily onto the ground.

My platoon was closest to the crash, so I moved a section to the far side of the wreckage to provide additional security. Two members of 5 Section, Private Syd Shore and Private Bill Cavanagh, ran forward to assist. At this stage a small fire was burning inside the aircraft, on the right-hand side.

> **Syd Shore describes the incident:**
>
> Just as the helicopter was arriving, we had noticed another booby trap near the track we were on. I ran towards the helicopter just as it hit the ground after sliding down a tree. Some crew and passengers who were able were exiting the fuselage and I told them to move down the track but not to move off it. There was small fire which I would have been able to put out but couldn't work the fire extinguisher. Bill Cavanagh had now arrived. We noticed that one of the pilots could not get out as his right foot was pinned by the tree. Bill and I then worked together with a RAAF crewman, who was on the inside, to pull away the Perspex under the damaged nose of the chopper to free the trapped right foot of the unconscious co-pilot. We eventually got him free but by this time the chopper was well and truly alight. Thankfully everyone was clear from the site before its machine gun ammunition started to explode.[1]

[1] Syd Shore, email correspondence with the author, 16 August 2017.

The TNT on board burned fiercely and destroyed the helicopter. Syd and Bill were both recommended for awards and some months later we were advised that they were Mentioned in Dispatches for their prompt and courageous actions. If they had not intervened, as their citations state, the crash 'would most certainly have resulted in the incineration of the helpless second pilot in the ensuing fire in the nose section of the aircraft'.[2] Years later while researching this operation, I came across the official 'Recommendation for an Honour or Award' for Syd and Bill. Both Lieutenant Colonel Warr and Brigadier Jackson, the task force commander, had recommended them for the George Medal. The subsequent reduction in their awards occurred higher up the approval chain. The RAAF helicopter crewman involved in the incident was subsequently awarded the George Medal.

---

2   See 5th Battalion The Royal Australian Regiment Association website, *Citation accompanying the award of Mentioned in Dispatches to Pte. Shore*, www.5rar.asn.au/history/cite_shore.htm.

Maintaining alertness, efficiency and ongoing battle hardness was a challenge for all platoon and section commanders, particularly as our tour of duty progressed. My platoon was most proficient when it was in regular contact with the enemy or there was convincing intelligence to suggest that enemy were nearby. We went through some extended periods of little contact with the enemy. Slackness could creep in with inattention on sentry duty, laxity on patrol, weapon cleanliness dropping off and an element of boredom creeping in along with repetitive routines. All this was nipped in the bud by section and platoon commanders. Doug Bishop remembers, 'the mind-deadening tedium and discomfort of click-after-click [kilometre-after-kilometre] of patrolling the TAOR, and the ever-present tiredness'. On the positive side, it was strongly evident that we were gaining control of Phuoc Tuy Province and that the enemy was now very much on the back foot.

A small historical note associated with 5 RAR's Operation Queanbeyan is that it was possibly the last time that Australia's famous Second World War weapon, the Owen machine carbine (OMC), was used on active service by the rifle companies of an Australian infantry battalion. Many members had already transitioned to the US M16 5.56 mm rifle with very basic familiarisation lessons in the days prior to these operations. The OMC had little hitting power mainly due to old ammunition being fired from a weapon which used low velocity pistol ammunition.

The typical digger of the Tiger Battalion showed all the traits we have come to expect since the original Anzacs. He was brave, loyal and innovative. He could be outspoken and a straight shooter, but tolerant with a sense of humour. He was reliable on operations and always watched his mate's back. He would wind down and play hard whenever he could. He expected his leaders to face the same hardships as he did and respected them for doing so.

While I have focused on aspects encountered by the platoons of the rifle companies and Support Company, we were totally reliant on the timely support and commitment of the often-unheralded platoons of Administration Company. They provided the rations, both at Nui Dat and by putting together some nice surprises to send into the field via resupply helicopters. Our company cook, Sergeant 'Paddy' Cahill, and his small team were unstinting in providing the best culinary offerings they could, and he was famous for his bread rolls. Sergeant Mick Henrys and his armourers kept our weapons in a healthy state. The Medical Platoon gave us our devoted stretcher bearers who were infantrymen first but also had medical skills training. They were also morale-lifters as members of the Battalion Band. The Transport Platoon reliably maintained the battalion's fleet of vehicles under very difficult and rudimentary conditions. Successful operations would have been much more difficult to mount without the indefatigable support of the seldom-applauded men of Administration Company.

Terry O'Hanlon

In 1964 I was working for Australian Mercantile Land & Finance, a rural stock and station agency in the town of Charleville in south-western Queensland, when I was called up for two years of national service. I had no interest in joining the army. I thought it was a bloody nuisance, completely upsetting what I wanted to do with my life. Cattle and horse work, rodeo and camp-drafting, and life in the bush was where I was going. Work, parties and rugby league football were the go at Charleville in south-western Queensland and I was enjoying them all.

Upon being called up I was sent to 1 Recruit Training Battalion at Kapooka, near Wagga Wagga in south-central NSW. I arrived in the middle of winter still very unimpressed with the whole army thing. After a short time, national servicemen were asked if they wanted to apply for entry to an officer training course at the newly established OTU at Scheyville, just west of Sydney. I applied thinking that, as an officer, I would have at least some say in my destiny. This also gave me a goal, something to aim for and I really enjoyed what faced me in the next hectic, pressurised six months – the mates I made, the discipline, the personal standards demanded, the sense of challenge and achievement, the burgeoning self-confidence and the spirit of the first, ground-breaking class of OTU officer cadets – the whole tightly compressed challenge which was so different from the comfortable pace of my former life. On occasions I captained the OTU Rugby Team; I graduated third in my class and was awarded the Staff Prize for Tactics.

Five of our first OTU class were posted to 5 RAR which was a great honour, and I was one of them; posted to the first Australian Army unit chosen to take national servicemen into war operations. My fellow OTU graduates posted to 5 RAR were Melford Roe, Harry Neesham, John Deane-Butcher and Ted Pott. I had played rugby union at school and, interestingly, two fellows I played against and who became my friends when I played with them in a Combined Schools First Fifteen in 1962, were John Deane-Butcher and John Fraser. As mentioned, John Deane-Butcher and I became fellow platoon commanders in 5 RAR. John Fraser was a member of the second OTU class to graduate and he had nearly completed his two years of compulsory national service when he extended his service on learning that his battalion, 3 RAR, was to go to Vietnam. He died leading his platoon in the Long Hai Hills on 28 March 1968, when he stepped on an enemy mine.

On joining the battalion, I was assigned to 5 Platoon, B Company. This was a fortunate development for many reasons. Our CO, Lieutenant Colonel John Warr, was a man who cared deeply for his men and he had a band of very experienced company commanders and senior NCOs in his battalion. Most importantly for me, I had an outstanding platoon sergeant as my deputy, Sergeant Sam Hassall; and a great group of junior NCOs and soldiers. Sam's guidance and support were invaluable to a new and very raw second lieutenant given his first command in a battalion that had been warned for active service.

The officer commanding (OC) B Company, Major Bruce McQualter, was a very good leader in operations and was supported by his calm and thoughtful 2IC, Captain Bob O'Neill, who was a source of sage advice to us. Bruce and I didn't really hit it off, which was irrelevant as I respected his ability and authority. Bruce died of wounds late in the tour and Bob left B Company early in the tour, transferred to BHQ as the intelligence officer.

I was a volunteer for the battalion's advance party which preceded the main body into Vietnam. I volunteered because our adjutant, Captain Peter Isaacs, had awarded me 30 days as battalion duty officer and I wanted to escape the tedium of being virtually confined to barracks. Adjutants are the supervisors of the behavioural standards and social graces of junior officers; and Peter had taken a very dim view of my being late to our farewell, mixed (ladies attending), formal dining-in night. Volunteering was a clever move because it also gave me valuable experience of patrolling with 1 RAR who had preceded us to Vietnam and were part of the US Army's 173 Airborne Brigade, based in Bien Hoa Province.

The battalion was inserted, by air assault, into Phuoc Tuy Province and secured the area around the hill called Nui Dat, which was to become the 1 ATF base. Our war had begun with Operation Hardihood. Late on the first day B Company stopped for a water resupply from a stream. My 5 Platoon was in the lead on the eastern slope of a low rise just north of Nui Dat. Sam Hassall led our water party, which had just returned from a nearby stream in the fading light, when some shots rang out followed by a large volume of fire, both incoming and outgoing. One of our water party, Private Errol Noack, was hit in the first exchange of shots. Corporal George Gilbert was quick to realise that the incoming fire was from another company and was instrumental in stopping the firing from both sources. Errol, a national serviceman, was an exuberant soldier, keen and well-liked by his mates. I spoke with him before he was evacuated by *Dustoff* helicopter to a US Army hospital in Vung Tau, but he died on the way. Thus, as if underlining the perpetual controversy about sending conscripted men to war, the first national serviceman to be killed in action died on his first day in action.

The whole event had many parts. B Company was stationary. A Company was close by. One of the companies was not where it thought it was and there were VC between them. One of our machine gunners, Private Joe Devlin, who was positioned on our left, saw what he was sure were two VC moving from right to left across his front. He did not fire because he was unsure of where our water party was. I have always believed the VC were moving away from A Company after initiating the contact. The loss of Errol had a very profound effect on my men, but they soon rallied and pressed on with their tasks. The lessons from this incident resulted in the devising of procedures to be strictly followed when friendly elements were close to each other, or there was a danger of navigation errors in jungle which might lead to a clash between them.

For years, speculation endured about whether VC were involved at the scene or how difficulties of navigation in fading light and featureless, thickly wooded terrain might have combined to result in two companies being unaware of each other's proximity while on their first day in operations, and whether this might have triggered the incident. Such speculation conveniently ignores the overriding fact that war is a dangerous and unforgiving business in which innumerable factors are at play.

The men of 5 Platoon were smart, and it was my responsibility to keep them as fully informed as I could. I knew they would follow if I was straight with them. To us, our platoon was everything. Our first operation was difficult. We were inexperienced and had contacts with the enemy, including a platoon attack which is well described in Bob O'Neill's 1968 book *Vietnam Task*:

> Five Platoon was separated from the remainder of the company … They encountered a Viet Cong defensive position, which was occupied by five men. The platoon commander, Second Lieutenant O'Hanlon, ordered an attack which drove out the Viet Cong, who left a considerable trail of blood. On following this blood trail, voices were heard. One wounded Viet Cong attracted attention to himself and surrendered. Our chaps bandaged his wounded leg and splinted it in case it had been broken. He accepted a cigarette and a drink of water. Within twenty minutes of receiving his wound he was flying to the same hospital which we used at Vung Tau. Near the huts of the base Five Platoon discovered a cache containing 1,300 pounds [600 kg] of rice. Disposal of captured rice was always a problem when it is found in such large quantities as it was seldom possible to lift it out by helicopter or by road. Often the only expedient which could be used for denying the rice to the Viet Cong was to blow it up. Five Platoon were forced to do this because … no more helicopters were available.[3]

All operations were important, but Operation Hardihood was our baptism of fire and it fixed in our minds a clear idea of what the following 12 months were likely to encompass, very likely at an increasing tempo. Its experiences were invaluable; we really got to know and value each other and developed faith in our systems and our ability to adapt our techniques and procedures to meet any situation that arose. Our bonding began a journey that is yet to end.

In the first week we had lost one of our own men, killed four VC, captured one and destroyed a large quantity of enemy rations. After about two weeks of the battalion's clearing of Nui Dat and its surrounding areas, 5 Platoon was relieved to move into what was to become 1 ATF's base.

---

3   Robert J O'Neill, *Vietnam Task: The 5th Battalion, Royal Australian Regiment*, Cassell Australia, Melbourne, 1968, p 41.

Although it was far from secure at that time, at least the whole battalion was concentrated to commence construction of our part of the Task Force base.

In this chapter and Chapters 10 and 15, fellow junior officers have described the tests which confronted platoon commanders during the earlier part of 5 RAR's first tour of war service. Their narratives describe the heavy responsibilities which we shouldered as young men and the accompanying pressures of leadership while in continual danger, a situation which faced the army's infantry platoon commanders throughout the Vietnam War and other earlier wars. I have confined my narrative to the very earliest of our experiences to avoid the unneeded repetitiveness of a blow-by-blow description of many more incidents, the types of which are clearly described elsewhere.

In action, and sometimes while waiting for action, I believe all men experience some sort of fear. This is where training, mateship and a determination not to let down one's comrades or oneself all come into play and bestow an ability to suppress fear. With Australians, humour and a communal sense of bravado and aggressiveness spread confidence. It was noticeable how many more men attended church parades before each operation – for some, the doubters, the prudent precaution of an 'each-way' bet might have been at play or, more likely, comfort derived from another reassuring gathering of mates was the spur.

It was my honour to have served with such men who became, and remain, my brothers. I never considered myself as a national service officer, rather, I thought of myself as just another platoon commander. When, later in the tour, I seriously injured my knee and was returned to Australia, it was one of the worst times in my life – I'd had to leave my men.

Intermission: 'A Platoon Commander's War' continues in Chapter 10.

9

CONTACT WITH THE ENEMY – THROUGH SOLDIERS' EYES

Bob Kearney, Ted Harrison, Dan Riley
and John O'Callaghan

Introduction by Ron Boxall

The Nui Dinh hills and the adjacent Nui Thi Vai hills soon acquired the nickname of 'the Warburton mountains', then 'the Warbies', when spoken of by soldiers of 5 RAR (5th Battalion, the Royal Australian Regiment). A popular American song of the day told of the dangers of venturing into wild country, its first line being, 'They say don't go on Wolverton Mountain'. A soldier of D Company, Private Colin Illman, teased his mate Private Graham 'Nugget' Warburton with the amended line, 'They say don't go on *Warburton* Mountain'. The Australian diggers' liking for diminutives soon saw 'the Warbies' routinely applied to the looming hill complexes to the west of Nui Dat. This nickname quickly became widespread throughout the battalion and beyond. Its origins were later authenticated by D Company's commander Major Paul Greenhalgh and Second Lieutenant Dennis Rainer, the two soldiers' platoon commander. Alas, Graham Warburton was killed in action a few days before the battalion first set foot into 'the Warbies' to conduct Operation Canberra.

The Nui Thi Vai hills were the battleground for our three major operations in October 1966, and two of our junior non-commissioned officers (NCOs) and two privates have contributed vignettes of what it was like for them as individuals to engage in combat with the Viet Cong (VC) in our first six months in Vietnam. They are but four of the hundreds of

5 RAR's rank and file who thus shouldered the Australian infantryman's eternal burden of adding to the enviable reputation of the long line of those who had gone before them. Earlier generations had subscribed to that ancient military mantra, learned at Mother Army's knee:

> The role of the infantry is to seek out and close with the enemy, to kill or capture him, to seize and hold ground and to repel attack, by day or night, regardless of season, weather or terrain.[1]

It was now their turn.

Corporal Bob Kearney, section commander

Now, more than 50 years after returning from my tour of duty in South Vietnam with 5 RAR (1966–67), some of my memories of the war have been distorted or forgotten. The moments I would like to remember are now hazy and yet those I would like to forget are crystal clear. Among those I recall vividly are the tired young faces of the men I served alongside and the officers and senior NCOs who trained and led us into and out of situations on the dark foreboding range of steep hills later collectively referred to as the 'Warburton mountains'. On 24 May 1966 during the battalion's helicopter lift from Back Beach at Vung Tau to landing zone (LZ) Hudson, near the remains of a village named Ap An Phu in Phuoc Tuy Province, I saw the 'Warbies' for the first time and somehow knew the day would come when we would have to go there.

With increased enemy operations occurring in and around the villages along the road between Vung Tau, Bien Hoa, Long Binh and Saigon (Route 15), as well as charging a tax on all who dared use the road, a combined American and Australian operation was planned to make the road safe for the coming transportation of troops, materiel and equipment. In early October, our young national service platoon commander, Second Lieutenant John Deane-Butcher, informed us that on 6 October we were to climb up and clear the western edge of the range that dominated Route 15. As a corporal, I was only interested in what part our company (C Company) and platoon (9 Platoon) would play in this massive

---

1   Australian Military Board, *The division in battle*, nos 1–11, Pamphlet No 1: *Organisation and tactics,* Army Headquarters, Canberra, 1966, p 14.

9. CONTACT WITH THE ENEMY – THROUGH SOLDIERS' EYES

operation. Soon after our briefing I thought of the words to a song that had been sung or hummed in the lines after the completion of our first operation (Hardihood): 'They say don't go on Wolverton Mountain …'.

Knowing we now had to climb part of the steep black range of hills to the west of Nui Dat reminded me of an earlier operation during which we climbed a much smaller hill, Nui Nghe, and my section second in command (2IC) 'Titch' Tomas was fatally wounded. We had learned from Operation Hardihood – and all the operations since – to lighten our load so now, for the hard slog up and into the 'Warbies', the bins in the tents were full of discarded ration packaging and other items deemed too heavy for the work ahead.

My section was made up of young regular and national service soldiers, all of whom were good at their jobs. Each man was a character in his own right and, even now, I can see their faces as if it were only yesterday. Second Lieutenant John Deane-Butcher, our platoon commander, and Harry Neesham, the commander of 7 Platoon, and many of the NCOs and men they led, were 'nashos', whose lives had been put on hold or in some cases ended in Vietnam. Lieutenant Roger Wainwright, the only regular army platoon commander in the company, was their mentor and his leadership style and advice had a huge influence on both John and Harry. Whereas the platoon commanders were all about the same age, the standout among our officers was the company commander, Major John Miller. John, although older and far more experienced than his platoon commanders and anyone else in the company, was a calm, kind man who took every opportunity to improve the conditions of his men. John, our company sergeant major (CSM), senior NCOs and two of the corporals had previously served in Malaya and their knowledge and experience of living and patrolling in jungle was of great benefit to all.

Our intelligence officer, Captain (now Professor) Robert O'Neill, has covered the major contacts and incidents that occurred during Operation Canberra in his book *Vietnam Task*, written during the battalion's tour of duty. It was from *Vietnam Task* that I learned much about the detail of why each of our major operations was conducted and the parts the other platoons and companies played in them. Junior NCOs and soldiers have a very small circle of influence and if they, like me, concerned themselves only with what involved their section, platoon and company directly, they would have little understanding of the purposes of each operation. Notwithstanding the 'big picture' briefings before, during and after an operation, all these years later the incidents in which I had no direct involvement have been almost erased from my memory. It is only the events in which I was directly involved and the little things of which one takes mental snapshots that remain as clear in my mind today as they would be if they had happened last week.

During Operation Queanbeyan, one such mental snapshot I clearly recall is that of our CSM, Warrant Officer Ross Wormald, and myself standing together on 18 October as we watched a Royal Australian Air Force resupply helicopter steadily approach the LZ that had earlier been cut out of the jungle to evacuate the wounded men of 8 Platoon on 8 October during Operation Canberra. Of necessity, the LZ had been hastily cut and, in addition to being strewn with felled trees and foliage, still had, on the upper side, some tall trees which looked more like poles. The problem, as I recall it, was that the chopper carrying two combat engineers and loaded with their explosives had to approach the LZ from the lower end, meaning that all the pilots could see in front of them was the jungle-covered face of the mountain.

As the chopper hovered over the LZ, I asked the CSM and the others nearby 'do you reckon his blades are a bit too close to that large tree?' They all agreed and suddenly the chopper lifted and flew forward towards the face of the mountain, banking away to the right in what appeared to be an attempt to go around and come in again. Suddenly the helicopter appeared to lose power and, in what seemed like slow motion, it dropped into the trees where it immediately began tearing itself apart. The noise it made as it smashed through the heavy jungle sounded like that which I imagine would have been made by a wounded and dying dinosaur. The CSM yelled 'get back to your platoons!' Upon reaching my section area, I could see the flames and shortly thereafter, when I heard exploding ammunition, I imagined the crew and all aboard the chopper had been killed. Miraculously, as I learned later, none of the men were killed, however they were all badly injured and one of the pilots was trapped in the burning chopper. Had it not been for the courage and determination of the 9 Squadron crewman, Sergeant Gordon Buttriss, and Privates Bill Cavanagh and Syd Shore of 8 Platoon, the copilot would have undoubtedly suffered an excruciating death. For their actions during this perilous rescue, Sergeant Buttriss was later awarded the George Medal and both 8 Platoon diggers were Mentioned in Dispatches (MID).

Clearly, the next problem for Major Miller was the extraction of the injured men, so he quickly implemented a plan to get them out as soon as possible. It was not long before I saw above us an American army *Dustoff* chopper, marked on both doors with a red cross on a white background. The pilots who flew these specialist medical evacuation choppers and their crewmen were renowned for their skills and courage, and the crew of this chopper demonstrated the reasons behind their legendary status. As the chopper approached the LZ, the pilot was obviously not pleased by the tight, rough area he had to put his aircraft down onto, so he simply turned his chopper around and, guided by his crewman, slowly backed it safely onto a rocky outcrop not far from the original LZ. Once the patients were on board, the pilot lifted the chopper a few feet and flew off the mountainside towards the hospital at Vung Tau. That crew could not have known it, but that day they received a standing ovation from the diggers of C Company, 5 RAR.

The 'silence of soldiers'

Over the 50 years since we left Vietnam in 1967, I have been frequently asked 'what was it like in Vietnam?' For most of that half-century I lacked a suitable answer so would simply say something like 'not good' or 'sometimes boring, sometimes too exciting', or just change the subject. After seeing the film *Forrest Gump* starring Tom Hanks, I finally had the answer and now say as Forrest Gump did, 'well we walked a lot and it rained a lot'.

In October 1966, our battalion conducted four operations: Operations Crow's Nest, 1–3 October; Canberra, 6–10 October; Robin, 11–16 October; and Queanbeyan, 17–26 October. These were productive but costly and tiring operations, from which I, like all the blokes, retain numerous mental pictures of certain aspects; but others, like those of the diggers who, only 49 years before we left Vietnam in 1967, were fighting the Battle of Passchendaele, have faded over time. When asked by their children and grandchildren, 'What was it like in the war?', like all who have been to war since, they would find a way to change the subject. Recently when I was asked about the 'silence of soldiers' by some descendants of those heroes of the Great War and Second World War, I used the following analogy:

> Trying to explain what it is like to be in a war is akin to a blind person trying to explain to a sighted person what it is like to be blind. Your relatives were not being secretive; they simply find it is just too hard.

Some of my many mental snapshots of sights, smells and sounds in the 'Warbies' include:

- A well-established and highly organised enemy camp, trenches and huts covered by hand-sewn quilts of leaves.
- Russian and VC flags, stick grenades, ammunition and weapons.
- Milky (soapy) water in the streams.
- The dank wet smell of rotting vegetation and the continually moving shadows created by speckled sunlight through the ever-shifting dense leaf canopy.
- Massive bald, bullet and shell-scarred granite boulders that offered the enemy complete protection from the air.
- Ancient moss-covered rocks, lichen-covered trees and vines of all descriptions, large and small, that sometimes acted like a tripwire.
- A tree in an enemy camp that was lit up at night by iridescent fungi or insects.
- Fireflies, pigs, monkeys and unexploded butterfly bombs.
- Small sharp punji stakes embedded in both sides of a track leading up to a rock sangar (firing position) overlooking Nui Dat. An enemy machine gunner in the sangar would have forced all who were not immediately killed on the track to jump onto the punjis.
- The observers on the rock could have used binoculars to observe our every move as we built Nui Dat base from day one.
- Dried napalm residue on the rocks that reminded me of honeycomb.
- Huge rice caches and how we and our attached combat engineers destroyed them.
- The roar of close air support jet aircraft, the crack of artillery shells and mortar bombs impacting and, at night, the sound of wind through bamboo.
- The distant sound of a contact with the enemy in which we knew our mates could either be killed or wounded.
- The sweat-drenched, tired and haggard red faces of the great men in my section.

- The sounds and sight of the Bell Sioux helicopter as it crashed and bounced along Route 15, right in front of our company during Operation Robin.

These are some of the sights and sounds that I cannot forget from just one month during our tour of duty.

Lance Corporal Ted Harrison, section commander, 1 Platoon, A Company

My 10-man section was a good mix of regulars and national servicemen. As I remember, there was some disgruntlement at being conscripted, but over time and with training the discontent faded as we developed into a tightly knit platoon. My role, initially, was second in command of 1 Section, 1 Platoon, A Company, in control of the M60 machine gun team. We were very fortunate to be led by Lieutenant John Hartley, in my view a natural leader of men and a bloody good map-reader, which was very important in navigating heavily forested and jungle environments where accurate navigation was vital. Our section commander was Corporal Jim Mavromatis, and Douglas 'Douggy' Moles was our forward scout. Doug, a national serviceman from Tasmania, was a natural bush scout and we relied on his keen senses on many occasions.

The vital role of machine gunner was given to 'the big bloke', Private Bill Winkel, a regular soldier and a timber cutter from Queensland. Bill had a sardonic sense of humour and could always be relied on. Of course, all roles needed to be interchangeable due to attrition caused by illness and casualties and made worse by an occasional shortage of reinforcements. On one operation our section was down to four men. At this time Jim Mavromatis had been struck down with a serious and mysterious illness and returned to Australia, and I was acting section commander and machine gunner rolled into one. But like many of the understrength platoons, after a day's patrolling, sometimes including enemy contacts, our platoon was often tasked with setting up night ambushes on rice paddies and trails, when we were very fatigued. In my view, sleep deprivation was a major problem during operations and patrols.

Vietnam's wet season caused problems with feet and chafed skin, mould, rust and a level of weapon maintenance not experienced in training in Australia. The need to be able to move quickly at any time dictated that you kept your socks and boots on for the duration of the patrol or operation. Once, during the wet season, my feet were continually wet for several days and soon developed an intense itch. During a rest break, I removed my boots to examine my feet and discovered my toenails had loosened and turned dark yellow with the skin peeling away from my soles and heels. Modifications were necessary and many in the platoon did away with socks and underpants and drilled holes in the back of the heels of their boots to allow the water to drain. Back at Nui Dat, the downpours would fill our weapon pits and deep drains had to be dug around tents to prevent flooding. The roads and tracks through the battalion area turned to slush.

Vietnam's fauna is quite diverse, and we dealt regularly with spiders, scorpions, snakes and monkeys. On one occasion I was tasked with conducting a reconnaissance forward of our position, and Doug Moles accompanied me. We came across a clearing approximately 150 metres wide by 60 metres long, covered with waist-high grass. Normally we would skirt around the clearing but, being behind time, I decided to cover Doug while he crossed and cleared the far treeline. I saw his 'all clear' sign and commenced to cross when I noticed something moving parallel to me and parting the grass at speed. Then it turned and came straight at me, slamming into my leg and turning me around through 180 degrees. I looked back to what seemed to be a huge pig. I limped over to Doug and examined my leg to find no real damage. On returning we skirted the clearing in a very proper tactical fashion.

Cordon and search operations were opportunities to witness village life, and for a naive 19-year-old it was a real experience. We found the villagers to be unassuming and compliant. The CO developed a code of conduct for dealing with the locals and a cornerstone of that policy was to treat the villagers with respect and courtesy. I felt a deep compassion for the villagers, and especially the children caught up in the turmoil of war. We found the amount of cruelty the VC were capable of inflicting upon their own people to be incredible. Once, A Company was stationed in the village of Binh Ba to protect the village from VC incursions and, when possible, we would play soccer with the kids. We made friends with many of the children and adults and we would be invited into their homes for tea. I found their friendship warm and genuine.

In early October, the battalion was to mount Operation Canberra. John Hartley called together his O Group (Orders Group) and announced that the battalion was required to protect a lengthy stretch of Route 15. It was explained that an American army infantry brigade would travel in truck convoys from Vung Tau along Route 15 to Bien Hoa. Sections of the highway were still under threat and the VC were able to attack or mine many sections of the road. Prior to the convoy, we were ordered to clear a high hill complex called Nui Thi Vai, including a foothill called Nui Ong Trinh, as this was one of the areas thought to be a possible firing point for enemy mortars to attack Route 15. During this period, we were witness to an air strike on the western face of Nui Thi Vai. I was later to learn that B Company had spotted a large group of VC and an air strike had been called in to attack them. C Company also had clashes with the VC and took some casualties. We of A Company finally crossed the summit of Nui Thi Vai and then commenced the steep descent of its north-western face. We were then positioned strategically along Route 15 for the next few days as the American convoys proceeded north to Bien Hoa with few incidents.

On 16 October, A Company mounted armoured personnel carriers (APCs) and moved north-west along Route 15 to an area opposite the western face of Nui Thi Vai. We dismounted from the APCs and moved west, across and away from Route 15, into the treeline where we set up our company harbour. No cooking was allowed. A final O Group was conducted, and we were informed that we would be commencing Operation Queanbeyan in the early hours of next morning. We were informed that the aim of this operation was to kill or capture any VC remaining on Nui Thi Vai, destroy their bases and seize any documents, equipment or supplies they had left behind after the airstrikes of Operation Canberra.

By this stage of our tour, we were heading into the dry season and the nights were often rain-free. Many of us, when not on gun piquet, would simply lay down on a ground sheet with our backpack for a pillow, our weapon next to us and sleep. When on operations or patrols you never allowed your weapon to be further than arm's reach away. The only time you were separated from your 'best mate' was when you went on rest and recreation leave outside of Vietnam.

At 0300 hours, A Company broke harbour and we commenced the move east towards the western approaches of Nui Thi Vai. We were able to cross Route 15 and enter the treeline before first light. Just after dawn we harboured so that the company could bolt down a cold breakfast. We had climbed over the summit of Nui Thi Vai previously, so the thought of doing it again, humping a 30-kilogram load, caused me to shudder. 1 Platoon was given the task of leading the company with 1 Section in the lead. About mid-morning we were following a track when Doug, our forward scout, sighted a small concrete installation to the rear of what was first thought to be a disused garden. Our skipper, Lieutenant John Hartley, was called forward and he decided that 1 Section would cover both flanks while 2 Section would move forward and search the installation. After I had positioned the machine gun team, I turned to head back when almost immediately, there was a loud explosion. I felt a burning sensation down my left side as I was lifted off my feet and slammed into the ground. Lying on my side I began to pant like a dog, with a hole in my chest and with searing pain in my abdomen. The abdominal pain was so intense that all I could do was crawl into a foetal position to try to ease the pain. Big Bill Winkel and 'Nifty' Neville Thompson had also been wounded. Our attached combat engineers cleared a safe path to us and the battalion's medical officer, Captain Tony 'Doc' White arrived to ease the pain. Makeshift stretchers were made, and I was carried to a clearing, lifted into the bay of a *Dustoff* helicopter and flown to the American 36 Evacuation Hospital at Vung Tau. There I started to recover from a perforated oesophagus, multiple perforations of the left lung and multiple perforations of the small intestine. For me, the war against the VC was over. I returned to Australia in November 1966 but would have given my right arm to have seen it through and returned with the battalion in May 1967.

Dan Riley, machine gunner, Anti-Tank Platoon, Support Company

From 17 to 26 October 5 RAR was committed to Operation Queanbeyan. The CO had decided to move the battalion around the northern and western sides of Nui Thi Vai so that two companies could move up the western side. A third company could clear the ground immediately to the north of the hill and a fourth company could lie in ambush positions on the approach routes to the north of the hill, a little further out.

This company would hamper VC movement both towards and away from Nui Thi Vai by use of the track systems that had been shown on a captured enemy map. This task was assigned to D Company; B Company was to be its neighbour on the north, A Company was to search the central north section of the western slope, while Battalion Headquarters (BHQ), protected by the Assault Pioneer and Anti-Tank platoons, was to advance up the track to a pagoda and install itself in an area where good radio communications with the companies could be ensured. Our sister battalion, 6 RAR, assisted by providing its D Company to protect the gun position sited beside Route 15. We had no idea that the day would change us for the rest of our lives.

As the Anti-Tank Platoon moved up into position to begin the ascent, a message was passed that a booby trap had been tripped and the VC would know where we were or, at least, be aware of movement in the area. Our primary task was to move ahead of BHQ up a very steep and narrow track to a pagoda near the summit. The climb was exhausting, made worse by the heat and weight of the M60 machine gun, ammunition, equipment, rations and water. At one point when we paused for a breath, I took a salt tablet that stuck in my throat, but a quick drink cleared it and we continued to climb. It was obvious that all were feeling the physical stress. The probability that the VC were nearby heightened our alertness so there was no talking. Messages were passed by hand signals. The track was just wide enough for one man to walk along. Some boulders near the track were huge, well over 10 metres in length and several metres high. The vegetation was thick and provided shade from the hot sun and the rain, but it limited vision to a few metres. Our section finally reached the pagoda, checked for booby traps, cleared the immediate area and realised we were some distance from the top of Nui Thi Vai. However, the fellas were grateful to pause with the expectation that the worst was behind us. Then it all went sideways!

'Contact!' was shouted, and shots were fired at a VC soldier who disappeared behind one of the many rocks beside the track. Others were sighted higher up the slope. Messages followed in quick succession that BHQ, which was following us, had been ambushed, a captain was hit in the chest and the Anti-Tank Platoon was to move back down the track to clear out the VC. After a steep climb, the platoon was exhausted so the skipper, Second Lieutenant Mick Deak, ordered all backpacks to be dropped and the descent began with extreme vigilance. As we reached the ambush site, the realisation hit home that we had all walked through the enemy's location only minutes before!

The skipper ordered Corporal Norm Womal's section to move from the track across a steep gully to where the VC were located, while the other sections were to provide fire support. I was located near a large rock on the topside of the ambush site and positioned the M60 ready to fire. As I did this, a shot rang out and Norm fell! He had been shot through the throat but managed to give directions to the skipper. The skipper called several of us to him to see if there was any way to reach Norm. His extraction to a safe area presented problems for the platoon and the battalion. The VC knew where Norm lay and could fire at anyone moving to his assistance. Although the platoon could neutralise the VC with covering fire for a short time, it was doubtful we could keep the fire up long enough to extract Norm. Despite the skipper's orders to the contrary, our medic, Private Peter 'Doc' Fraser, crawled under enemy fire to Norm. He reached him and proceeded to dress his wound, placing his own body between Norm and the enemy in order to shield him from further fire. The enemy continued firing, missing Fraser by inches. In the meantime, a stretcher party moved forward under the control of our platoon sergeant, Ray 'Skinny' Calvert, while protected by covering fire from the remainder of the platoon.

During this time, I had managed to return to my position, and prepared to provide fire support. Peering out from the rock it was obvious I could not clearly distinguish where Norm, Doc Fraser and the stretcher party were located. The last thing needed was for me to blaze away at a target I could not see and hit mates with friendly fire. This frustration continued until I decided to move to where I could have a clearer shot. As I moved forward, the barrel lock of my M60 machine gun was caught and disengaged by the vines. The result was sheer desperation because the M60 was temporarily out of action, I was exposed and there was incoming fire while I scrambled for cover.

Skinny called for covering fire and the stretcher party managed to cross the killing ground in both directions without being hit, although the volume of enemy fire made movement extremely slow. Despite the odds, the extraction was successful, and the stretcher party struggled back to the cover of the rocks behind the remainder of the platoon.

Captain Tony White, the battalion's medical officer, moved forward to our position and was waiting to dress Norm's wound when the stretcher party met him. A few moments later our highly respected Pacific Islander mate died, and we had lost a very fine man and an outstanding section commander. The stretcher party clambered down the wet rocks to place Norm's body into a chopper.

The challenge was how to get a chopper into a very difficult area with limited places from which to extract Norm. Fortunately, efforts to extract the wounded captain from BHQ had earlier been successful and now the process was repeated. Despite the difficulties, the pilot managed to land the helicopter and collect Norm's body. Shrouded by a ground sheet, he was placed on the aircraft and flown out to Vung Tau. The impact of his death settled on those left behind on the hillside. The stretcher party laboured back over the rocks with tremendous weariness and dejection to rejoin the platoon.

After Norm had been extracted from where he was wounded, the skipper ordered the sections to move towards him and into a protected area. This was because helicopter gunships were to deliver suppressing rocket and gunfire onto the tunnel entrances where the VC were located. As I sat there with others, out of the line of fire, a crushing weight dropped onto my shoulders. We were not in the Land of Oz! These few hours had been lethal and there was no way to deflect the possibility that anyone in the platoon could have been killed. All the near misses, contacts or the loss of men in other parts of the battalion did not match the loss of our close mate.

The shock of these events was suppressed as the gunships blasted the tunnel system with rockets, followed by fire from their multi-barrelled machine guns, all within a stone's throw of our position. After the shooting had stopped and the dust settled, a section swept through the area and found that the VC were gone but had left booby traps. The thought that they could be waiting in deeper tunnels for nightfall to escape ensured that everyone's alertness remained on a razor edge.

Later that afternoon the Anti-Tank Platoon climbed back to the pagoda, checked for booby traps, picked up our packs and prepared to settle in for a disturbed night. One final task for the day was to escort, in the falling light, a section of combat engineers to the summit to record the location of the VC tunnel systems. It soon became impossible to see your hand in front of your face. When a soldier behind me slipped and became entangled in vines, I could hear him only a metre away. After a blunt exchange of suggestions on what to do, I tried to cut the vines with my machete and narrowly missed slashing him. Again, a message was hammered home to me; it was not about what you want to do: rather, it is about what has to be done to solve the problem. Finally, with greater care, the vines were severed, and we moved forward to the summit and said 'goodbye' to the engineers. The section then moved silently back to the pagoda, careful not to startle the sentries lying in wait for our return. The sentries were also on a knife edge and they all had fingers on triggers. Through experience, or just dumb luck, no one started shooting as we re-entered the platoon's position within the perimeter. Later that night as I lay next to the M60, I gave thanks for being alive.

In the following days, we learned a soldier of the Assault Pioneer Platoon had been killed and an officer wounded just 50 metres from our position. A few days later, D Company's 10 Platoon attacked 11 VC in a small, cleverly concealed installation and killed 10. Several weeks later many of us were to return as the newly formed Reconnaissance Platoon in another operation to check these same VC tunnel systems.

For their bravery and leadership in the operation, three members of the Anti-Tank Platoon were decorated. The Military Cross was awarded to Second Lieutenant Mick Deak, the Military Medal to Private Peter Fraser, and Corporal Norm Womal was posthumously MID. The national origins of these three soldiers were, respectively, German, Scottish and Pacific Islander.

John O'Callaghan, machine gunner, 5 Platoon

It was the beginning of Operation Holsworthy on 7 August 1966. Surrounding us was silence, except for the falling rain. It was hard to believe sometimes that there were many dozen riflemen, including myself, sliding through the jungle on the way to Binh Ba, a village we were to search the next day after surrounding it that night. This was a technique that 5 RAR helped to develop.

Since at this stage we were travelling in daylight, it was necessary to restrict any movement of villagers in the area, and various cover stories were used to accomplish this. If memory serves me, one was that our artillery would be firing into this area throughout the day and so it was declared a 'free fire zone' – that is, aside from ourselves, anyone out here would be assumed to be enemy. This had been widely notified to the surrounding population.

9. CONTACT WITH THE ENEMY – THROUGH SOLDIERS' EYES

We were proceeding through low scrub with a thin forest of young rubber trees extending away to our left and hard on our right was thick, high grass between overgrown banana trees whose fronds drooped to the ground like green tattered curtains. The rain was near-torrential. I was the machine gunner in our section and during training it was impressed on us that 'the M60 is the life or death of the section' – very true, and I never forgot it.

Something in that green mess drew my attention, the tip of a conical bamboo hat and maybe something black. It was not one of us – and therefore, probably, enemy! I gave the hand signal for 'enemy' and we hit the ground, but the rest of the platoon being in front and in the downpour, didn't realise what was happening behind them. Things were developing in seconds, if not microseconds, and I feared they were walking into an ambush. 'The gun is the life or death ...' – I dared not wait longer and fired several bursts, the silence was shattered and then – nothing.

Our platoon commander, Second Lieutenant Terry O'Hanlon, took a party forward to investigate the results of our firing and returned to tell me there were two villagers, a young boy, dead, and a woman dying. So much for the effectiveness of the 'free fire zone' notification. I collapsed and cried to rival the rain and told the skipper I would never be able to use the gun again. Softly but firmly and with compassion he assured me that when the time came, I would do my duty.

So, the war dragged on and in November we came to Operation Hayman, one which saw us in the good old American Hueys (Iroquois helicopters) doing an airborne assault on to Long Son Island, a VC haven, training and rest area. The island was not far off the coast and was surrounded by swamps and vast areas of thick mangroves – nature's little fortress.

During the operation, we of B Company wound our way up to the top of a high ridge overlooking a village and a wide waterway opening out to the South China Sea through the mangroves. Suddenly, from the right-hand side and in the distance, a squad of about 10 enemy dashed from the mangroves and headed for the other side slowed by the height of the tide.

Our 5 Platoon, being best positioned, was given the 'go' to engage them and the other two gunners and myself did so. I was very fortunate to have a large flat rock nearby, which was handy to use as a gun platform, so I made full use of it. Although at long range, we brought effective fire to bear. Some of the enemy squad made it to the other side, some did not.

I recalled what Lieutenant O'Hanlon had said. You were right Terry, thank you. Sometimes the 'fog of war' becomes very foggy indeed.

Conclusion by Robert O'Neill

These accounts of what it was like for individual Australian soldiers to face a well-armed, skilful enemy, on ground over which they had operated for several years, show how serious the battle for 'the Warbies' was. Our men, the privates, NCOs and officers of the battalion, met their challenges well. However, in November everyone had to keep in mind that there was still a further six months of our commitment to run. The war was becoming a strain on all of us, physically and mentally. But at the same time, we were gaining in knowledge and confidence, and we knew from our first six months' experience that we would make the grade as a battalion at war. But all members still had their own individual challenges to face, stimulated by the awareness that death could come rapidly with a single bullet, a mine blast or a shrapnel fragment.

10

A PLATOON COMMANDER'S WAR – PART 2

John Hartley and Harry Neesham

Editors' introduction

Two further narratives by platoon commanders continue after Chapter 9's interlude of recollections by a few of the diggers, who were typical of the hundreds who made up the men who served with the battalion's young officers.

John Hartley

I graduated from the Royal Military College (RMC) at Duntroon in December 1965. Australia's contribution to the war in Vietnam had increased significantly with the deployment of 1 RAR (1st Battalion, the Royal Australian Regiment) earlier that year. I think most of us hoped to see active service; I certainly did. At least half of the infantrymen in my class were off to the exotic Pacific Islands Regiment while the rest of us were rationed out to our nine infantry battalions.

Some weeks before graduation, I was summoned to see Captain Paul Greenhalgh, the adjutant. I think I enjoyed his confidence but, as the senior cadet of Sovereign's Company, most of our discussions had revolved around my company's and my own inability to satisfy his high expectations of us. I therefore approached his office with some trepidation. His first words were: 'What can I tell you that would make you happiest?' Without consideration, I immediately replied, 'You could tell me that I am going to Vietnam'. 'Congratulations', he said, 'you are posted to 5 RAR'. 5 RAR was to go to Vietnam in April to replace 1 RAR. Paul also told me that he, too, was posted to 5 RAR as a company commander.

I knew of no one who had been to Vietnam. We had, of course, studied the origins of conflict and our understanding of revolutionary warfare was, I think, quite comprehensive. Many of our instructors had served in the Malayan Emergency. We certainly understood the military/political nature of revolutionary warfare, the stages of a communist insurgency, Maoist doctrine and the concept of People's War. We had also studied the French experience in Indo-China. I received some prizes on graduation which included Bernard Fall's *Street Without Joy* and Jean Larteguy's *Yellow Fever*. So, I guess, at least psychologically, I was ready and most desirous of a posting to Vietnam.

In early January, after three weeks leave, I marched into 5 RAR. I was posted to A Company and, to my delight, appointed to command 1 Platoon. I went through the rare but memorable baptism of meeting my first platoon. My platoon sergeant, John Healy, was an experienced soldier who was the quintessential senior non-commissioned officer (NCO): demanding of standards, intolerant of any form of slackness, exemplary in his own personal performance, firm but extremely fair; he was also highly respected. To me he was a marvellous blend of coach, confidante and critic. I learnt from him every day. The company sergeant major (CSM), Warrant Officer Jock Stewart, was another old soldier and a rarity – he had seen service in the Australian Army Training Team Vietnam. Indeed, at that time he was the only man in the battalion who had seen service in Vietnam. I enjoyed his company immensely. He would regale us endlessly with stories of punji stakes (for more explanation about punji stakes, see Chapter 7). The CSM also talked about booby traps, mines and the cunning Viet Cong (VC) who appeared to have suborned most of the population. It was a land of snakes, aggressive ants, scorpions and bar girls who charged much, promised more but gave little. To me it all seemed remarkably exciting and extraordinarily exotic. And much of it was.

The soldiers were first rate. Three quarters of my platoon of about 35 were national servicemen – men of the first intake. They had been in the army for about nine months. All were about 21, they appeared to accept their lot as national servicemen, had shared recruit and early infantry training and, generally, were great friends. None were married; few had girlfriends.

They largely came from Victoria and Tasmania. I believe their age (about two to three years older than many of their Australian Regular Army colleagues who had to be 19 years old to be sent on operational service) was a telling factor; the difference made by this couple of years was quite remarkable. They were generally well educated; with most appearing to have completed Year 12. My three section commanders were an interesting mix. The oldest was 38 and the other two also had long service, much of it in a peacetime, garrison environment.

For the next four months training was intense. About half the time was spent at Holsworthy where we were based. Typically, we trained from six in the morning until six at night. Many evenings were taken up with administration: drafting wills, inoculations, receiving new dog tags (identity discs) and so on. Training involved much field-craft and shooting. Physical training was an everyday feature. We received lectures on the origin of the war, the history and customs of the people of Vietnam, the Geneva Convention and a lengthy session from a group of chaplains on character guidance. Soldiers were required to attend but not the officers. I thought this odd. I attended throughout not because I was particularly convinced of much of what I heard, but because I wanted to share my troops' experiences.

New weapons were introduced. The American M16 Armalite – lightweight, firing 5.56 mm ammunition and a vast improvement on the Second World War Owen gun, which I carried for the first few months in Vietnam. The M79 grenade launcher also made its appearance. We were intrigued by this weapon which looked a bit like a very large-bore shotgun and fired a 40 mm grenade to ranges up to 400 metres with little recoil. For those of us who had fired the much heavier Energa grenade from a projector fitted to the L1A1 self-loading rifle, the M79 was indeed a revelation. We were also introduced to the M18 Claymore anti-personnel mine and a new type of trip flare, the proper combination of which would prove highly lethal and effective when used in ambushes. The American VHF ANPRC 25 radio set made its appearance and replaced the cantankerous Korean War–era 9 and 9A sets which seemed forever to require tuning. We trained with M113 armoured personnel carriers (APCs), did much first aid work and, for a week, jogged to the School of Military Engineering and back where we were introduced to the vagaries of mines and booby traps. And all this time, I learnt more about my NCOs and soldiers.

We went to the Jungle Training Centre, which had a reputation for us to live up to. I had been there before as an RMC cadet and jungle-clad country held little in the way of surprises. But many soldiers had no experience of such tropical places and the sound and smell, the rain and heat, and the constant proximity to trees and scrub, frequently dense and almost impenetrable, needed to be mastered. Here we learned that the jungle was not a threat; it was at least neutral and, ideally, an ally.

Our last exercise at Canungra was held at Wiangaree State Forest in northern NSW. This was tropical rainforest at its best. We entered the long valley with dozens of ridge lines and smaller re-entrants running off them. Company headquarters and two of the platoons moved along the northern edge; my platoon was about 500 metres south and we moved along the southern side. For the next five days, I was seldom confident about where I was, and it was only when we finally emerged at the top of the valley to be met by our transport that I recognised my location.

Before going to Vietnam, we had a week's pre-embarkation leave. It was a time for some personal assessments. National service was a new reality and Australia had yet to suffer a national service battle casualty. Street marches were unknown. The Vietnam Moratorium protests had yet to emerge but the mother and girlfriend of one of my soldiers were part of the 'Save Our Sons' protest movement. I liked the soldier, but I thought he was being overly influenced by his mother and girlfriend. To keep an eye on him, I made him my batman; he was competent and cheerful from Tuesday to Friday. On Monday he appeared somewhat confused and concerned. I remember parading on the A Company parade ground on a Friday evening after a week's exercise, prior to going on weekend leave. I heard a shrill female voice shouting, 'Hey Batman, it's Robin here, I hope you poisoned the bastard!'. A day before we embarked, my batman declared himself a conscientious objector and was taken off the draft for Vietnam. We followed his court case with interest. He subsequently was declared not to be a conscientious objector, ordered to Vietnam but went AWOL (absent without leave), served a prison sentence and had not completed his national service until some 18 months after the soldiers in his intake had finished theirs.

It is difficult to describe our arrival in Vietnam. We flew via Manila on a Qantas charter flight. From the air, Saigon looked tropical and exotic. I noted, however, the numerous small waterholes which seemed to be

10. A PLATOON COMMANDER'S WAR – PART 2

everywhere. Subsequently, I recognised these were shell craters. We arrived at Tan Son Nhut airport, spent about two hours there and then flew by US Air Force transport aircraft to Vung Tau.

Vung Tau had been a seaside resort for wealthy French and Vietnamese families. Any sense of insecurity was more than compensated for by the sun, the beach and the very fine sand. We were introduced to the UH-1H, a larger version of the Iroquois helicopter than the UH-1B used by the Royal Australian Air Force (RAAF): the Huey, the mighty sky workhorse, and surely one of the icons of the Vietnam War. We did some short training operations. Platoons vied with each other to be the quickest at deplaning from helicopters. This resulted in our standing on the skids prior to landing and even jumping off before the helicopter had touched down. Battalion Headquarters (BHQ) soon put a stop to this unsafe practice.

Our time next to the South China Sea in Vung Tau was short. We rapidly acclimatised and gained some sense of the terrain – wading through delta mangroves in water up to the waist and clinging mud, open paddy fields with only low bunds for cover, bamboo scrub with thorns which gripped equipment and clothing, and flat, featureless scrub where navigation could only be conducted by 'dead reckoning'; sticking closely to a compass bearing and using cumbersome pace-counting to estimate distance travelled. With practice, experience and proficient map reading, the system proved surprisingly accurate. We also worked in sand dunes and quickly appreciated the importance of keeping our weapons clean.

There was little likelihood of contact with the VC in this area, but we saw signs of war all around us. Shortly, we were to be launched on a real operation. We worked with keen anticipation and listened with increasing focus to the lengthy artillery and air bombardment to our north in the general direction of our impending air assault. The night sky was lit with flashes, not dissimilar to a tropical storm, with a rumble of explosions which has long been the hallmark of armies on the eve of battle. Next morning, after repeatedly checking our webbing and weapons, we emplaned in about 40 helicopters and flew in tight formation to Landing Zone (LZ) Hudson, beside a rubber plantation which was secured by American soldiers of 173 Airborne Brigade. Although we had practised with helicopters, we had never experienced such a concentrated landing with so many at once. We moved off the helicopters, lay on the ground until they had flown off and then moved to our allotted position in the battalion assembly area near the edge of the LZ in anticipation of the remainder of the battalion arriving.

As I recall, 24 May 1966 was a stiflingly hot day. The wet season, with its monsoonal rain and soaring humidity, had started. We were constantly in a lather of sweat, and low scrub and tall grass added to our discomfort. My platoon led the move to the east along the small Song Cau River. The plan was for us to cross two re-entrants, move north along the second re-entrant and then lay a series of ambushes. The battalion's mission was to secure a small hill called Nui Dat and the surrounding countryside, ideally out to about 5 kilometres, to enable the establishment of the 1st Australian Task Force (1 ATF) base. I do not think anyone in my platoon knew this – it may have been kept from us because of operational security. We thought that Operation Hardihood was to be a five-day operation – it turned out to be nearly three times that long.

Some 20 minutes into the move, the forward scout of my forward section sighted and fired at an armed man. 'Contact front!' was shouted. I dashed forward while the forward section deployed with the machine gun group to the right and the rifle group to the left. It was as if we had done it a thousand times before: Canungra, Holsworthy, Wiangaree and Colo-Putty training areas all revisited. We were to have several more fleeting contacts with one or two armed men; I doubt that more than one or two of us caught a glimpse of any enemy, but they were there, and we saw enough evidence of their presence to be extremely alert.

We eventually reached the second re-entrant. 3 Platoon passed through us and headed north. The A Company platoon commanders gathered with our company commander to decide our next move. We were to do a series of ambushes. We were to return to the junction of the river and the re-entrant and to ambush the track we had made moving into the area. This was always a problem for us: wherever we moved, we left tracks.

Suddenly, some shots were fired. 3 Platoon was in contact. The volume of fire rapidly increased; heavy automatic fire started; bullets zipped through the trees overhead. We quickly dispersed. I ran back to my platoon. Without orders, or letting anyone know, I moved my platoon up to the firefight. We deployed into an extended formation, fixed bayonets and approached one flank of the firing. Some 10 metres from the flank, I heard Australian voices shouting to each other and I realised that the contact was between two groups of Australians. Just as I was to radio this information, the word came through the A Company radio net: 'Cease fire, cease fire, in contact with friendlies'. I backed off my platoon quietly and returned to our start point some 150 metres away.

Much controversy surrounded this incident which resulted in the death of Private Errol Noack, a South Australian and the first national serviceman to be killed in Vietnam. Some of us believe he was killed by friendly fire. The official version is that he was probably shot by a VC group which had interposed itself between A Company's 3 Platoon and B Company's 5 Platoon. The whole incident gave me much to think about. I believe that B Company, which was to come down the first re-entrant after my company had cleared the area, missed the first re-entrant and mistook the second re-entrant for the first. Certainly, navigation was difficult. What appeared on a map as a re-entrant very often was a very small depression. If you did not pace the distance accurately, then there was little confidence in knowing where you were with certainty.

I also thought seriously about my independent action. Had I been 30 seconds sooner, I should have opened fire from a few metres onto 5 Platoon with the likelihood that many casualties would have ensued. Clearly, I was too aggressive and was prone to act independently. I determined not to do this again. Decisive action was fine; but the consequences needed to be considered, and I thought how lucky I was to learn this lesson so early in the tour.

Operation Hardihood was a fascinating start to our Vietnam experience. The battalion quickly became frustrated. Small groups of VC were everywhere. We had numerous contacts with the enemy, but it was not until the third day that my platoon killed and recovered the first VC in the 1 ATF area of operations.

We'd had three contacts that morning; all were at long range. By now we were extremely alert and tense. We moved very quietly. Suddenly the forward section stopped. As always, when this happened I moved forward, trailed by my radio operator. The section commander and forward scout said they had heard voices to our front. We moved forward very cautiously to the edge of a small clearing. About 20 metres ahead, on the other side of the clearing, were four armed men in black, pyjama-type clothes. They were urgently packing and clearly about to move. I immediately opened fire and shouted to those around me to do the same. The VC disappeared, we quickly deployed into an extended line and swept the area. One body was recovered with a handful of ammunition, a Chinese grenade and some webbing.

We searched the body; he had an ID card. He was about 35 and clearly was a local VC. We buried him in situ. We were elated. 1 Platoon had done it. We were the envy of the battalion, or so we thought. I am now much older and have seen too much not to recognise that we were equally happy because we had survived. It is also a contemplative business to recognise that you have taken a life – an enemy, certainly, and someone who would have no compunction about killing us – but another human being, a friend or relative to someone, perhaps a father or husband.

We found a large rice cache (several tonnes I should think, bagged and stacked under a black tarpaulin); it was rice donated by the United States, as was identified by the branding on the bags. We were ordered to destroy it, and we simply split the bags and tipped their contents into a nearby river. It was hard work in the humid, overcast day. I fired my first artillery mission and called down mortar fire, both against fleeing groups of VCs who were some distance off.

Operation Hardihood was our baptism. There would be many similar operations – large, multi-unit sweeps, with a mix of supporting arms. But much of our time was spent on endless platoon-sized patrols, usually within 10 kilometres of the Task Force base. This was where platoon commanders learnt their trade – days on end of independent action, moving silently and alertly, constantly listening and watching, evaluating signs – all done patiently, but employing great speed and aggression when required.

There were several types of operation. The large-scale search and destroy operations I have partly described – in many ways, these were the most interesting. We invariably moved into new territory, usually in the areas where the VC was well established. Sometimes we even clashed with North Vietnamese Army Main Force or regular units. I recall very clearly our first contact with the latter. They were clearly several degrees better than the VC and prepared to stand and fight far more aggressively.

Another type of operation was the cordon and search. We would surround a village or hamlet, at night, isolating it before dawn, and searching it for arms, or caches of food or any signs of VC presence. These operations required great coordination, involvement of Vietnamese authorities,

10. A PLATOON COMMANDER'S WAR – PART 2

psychological operations (psyops) and civil affairs support. There is an apocryphal story of the psyops loud-speaker aircraft flying overhead and telling the people they are about to have their village searched. People were to report to the village square with their ID cards. They were to take food and water, as they may need to be there for some hours. The only problem was that the aircraft was a day early. I wonder how long the people might have waited patiently in the square.

An often-used tactic was ambushing, which could be employed as part of any of the operations. Ambushes could be quick, simply by moving off to the side of a track, or deliberate. The latter could involve extensive use of mines and flares, registration of artillery fire and even digging into defensive positions. As the year moved on, we found ourselves increasingly conducting ambushes. Some were overnight; others for several days. Soldiers would be sited in the ambush in groups of three with one fully alert the whole time. When we first went to Vietnam we tended to deploy in pairs, but as the year wore on and people became continually fatigued, we found that we needed to use groups of three to ensure that one person was fully alert the whole time, thus allowing the overall rest time for each soldier to be increased. Sometimes we would even relieve soldiers in an ambush site.

One of my platoon's notable incidents was at night, sitting on our packs while waiting to cross a wide paddy field. We were just inside the treeline which was parallel to a path. A group of about 20 VC, with weapons slung, making no attempt to be quiet or secure, walked past at about 4 metres distance. We could hardly believe what was happening. A wild firefight ensued. While we suffered no casualties, next morning while searching the area, we noted numerous blood trails. Major Max Carroll, our company commander, directed the company into several ambush positions, which resulted in some contacts and further VC casualties. On another occasion, the VC were obviously aware of our presence and initiated the contact by firing into the rear of the ambush position. We could clearly smell VC camps, particularly if they had been occupied for more than a couple of days. I dare say they could do the same with us. On the other hand, we were never ambushed. It was a golden rule never to move along tracks.

We flew initially with the US Army who impressed us as they were quite prepared to accept all manner of risks to evacuate casualties. They were also quite prepared to press home their fire support. Occasionally we had US Air Force strike aircraft in support and their forward air controllers in light aircraft were clearly very skilled. We also deployed on occasion, using their large twin-rotor Chinook helicopters. In hindsight, I suspect we equated their risk-taking and daring with professionalism. I am not nearly so sure that was always the case. I do not think they achieved quite the level of combined skill and professionalism that our Australian helicopter crews did in later years.

So, we quickly grew to admire and like our US Army helicopter people. On Operation Hardihood, for instance, it was not unusual in late afternoon to have a helicopter deliver our mail, another to bring us cold, chocolate-flavoured milk, another to deliver a hot box dinner and still another to take away the empty hot boxes. Of course, there were attendant security problems with all this air traffic. We wanted to find the VC and not frighten them off. When our own air force commenced helicopter operations we were disappointed. In our ignorance, we thought the RAAF pilots were extraordinarily cautious. They even wanted us to fly with closed doors. No self-respecting fighting soldier ever wants to fly in a helicopter with closed doors. On one occasion a door gunner carelessly discharged a belt of ammunition just as we were to be lifted from an LZ. Of course, we conveniently forgot the dozen or so similar incidents that we had had in our first three months. We never quite developed the same rapport with the RAAF as we did with the US Army aviation units, but later battalions certainly did. Our reluctance was something of a pity because I saw the RAAF in action some years later, during my second tour in Vietnam, and they were a very professional, fighting organisation. Indeed, after receiving a serious gunshot wound, I would not have survived if they had not successfully medically evacuated me.

I remember one incident which did not end happily, and which could have completely soured relations between our battalion and 9 Squadron RAAF. For nearly 40 days we had been in the field during the dry season, so we were not constantly wet. But we slept on the ground, never fully washed, ate hard rations the whole time, lost several kilograms in the process and had some casualties resulting from numerous contacts. We had been combing booby-trapped tunnels and it was all extraordinarily tiring and intense.

The operation finished on the top of Nui Thi Vai, a mountain 470 metres in height, with a pagoda on a ridgeline slightly below the summit. Most of the battalion were airlifted from the only available pad which could accommodate just one Iroquois at a time. The helicopters lined up, one behind the other, way off into the distance; each to land, load and depart in turn. This part of the operation required several hours. We were the last platoon to depart. Our job just before we were to be extracted was to protect a small combat engineer party which was to detonate some charges to release large amounts of CS (tear gas) powder in the caves near the top of the mountain. I had carefully rehearsed this with the engineer officer. I deployed my platoon to cover the area. The sapper would enter the cave, shout 'fire on' and come out through the entrance where I stood. We would then move smartly to an area some distance from the cave in case the CS powder spread out of the caves.

The engineer officer entered and a few minutes later I heard an explosion. My first thought was that he had prematurely set off the charge. I turned to move into the cave only to be overwhelmed by a cloud of CS powder. I could not breathe; my lungs were on fire. I fell to the ground and slowly the CS lifted. My radio operator was equally affected. My platoon sergeant, 'Shorty' Mavin, dragged us clear. The engineer officer and his offsider then appeared; they had become confused and exited safely by another tunnel. We then moved to the LZ and were extracted from the 470-metre high hill. The RAAF pilot complained of being gassed at an altitude of 500 metres! Instead of flying to Nui Dat, we flew to Vung Tau.

I asked why this was so and was told that the crew was going to afternoon tea and would return us to Nui Dat in 30 minutes. I protested with some passion. It was just as well I did because my six soldiers were furious. We duly flew on to Nui Dat in a very sombre mood. As we left the helicopter, I did not thank them or wave as I would usually do. Instead I walked away only to hear the noise of the rotor change dramatically. I looked back and saw a plume of purple smoke billowing from the helicopter. I knew who had discharged the smoke grenade as he exited the aircraft and grabbed the culprit. 'Why did you do that?' 'Because I had no bloody CS grenades left!' was the answer. It was something that all of us needed to forget. There is much more I could say about Vietnam. It was the high adventure of my youth. I am conscious of the aphorism that says we all refight the wars of our youth and that no two wars are ever the same.

A third of my platoon became casualties and about half did not finish their tour. Many suffered for years after with poor health and emotional discomfort. It was a long year. Of the first 100 days, we spent 92 on hard rations, we all lost considerable body weight and we were constantly wet. We had limited opportunity to develop an affinity with the local people and were intolerant of anybody else's war. I developed an enormous respect for the Vietnamese people, but it required another tour of duty in a different setting for it to happen.

I was very fortunate; I stayed on as a full-time soldier. The experience certainly coloured my attitudes to soldiering. Overwhelmingly, I was imbued with a sense of responsibility towards my soldiers; this required me to be fair and compassionate but also to demand high standards. I also respected the enemy. His was a very difficult life. For him there was no respite, no rest and recreation leave, no close air support or rapid evacuation of casualties to sophisticated medical facilities; he was a proficient, skilled, patient and committed foe.

It was a hard year. But I would not have missed it for anything. It was certainly the greatest privilege I have had – to command Australian infantrymen in war.

Harry Neesham

My journey to Vietnam began when prime minister Robert Menzies announced in November 1964 the introduction of national service for 20-year-old men, commencing on 1 July 1965. At the time, the announcement caused barely a ripple in my life. I was a Western Australian government auditor, had just completed the first year of my Diploma in Accountancy and had been voted the best first-year footballer in the Western Australian Football League (WAFL). It could not happen to me!

A letter from the Department of Labour and National Service in March 1965 advising of my call-up dramatically changed my circumstances. I was directed to present for a medical examination and then report to Irwin Barracks in Perth on 30 June for transfer to Puckapunyal in Victoria to commence my service. My first thoughts were not of my impending military training. This was a unique opportunity to further my football career in Victoria during my two years of army service. I contacted a few Victorian Football League clubs before signing a contract to play for the Geelong club.

Along with about 240 other Western Australians, I was transported by air and bus to Puckapunyal, arriving at 0700 hours on 1 July 1965. We were immediately introduced to army routine. Uniforms and weapons were issued, followed by inoculations and then a haircut, whether it was needed or not. While I had not experienced army cadet training at school, being the second eldest of 12 children, the concept of structure and discipline came naturally to me. I fell quite easily into army routine and enjoyed the following days that were filled with drill and sport. My first week in the army passed quickly.

At the end of the week, our platoon sergeant advised us that the army was seeking volunteers for officer training. He pointed out it would be a real challenge, but those chosen would be paid at corporal's rate during the officer training. Influenced both by the challenge and financial incentive, I applied, was subjected to a rigorous assessment process and accepted as one of the 97 national servicemen and eight army aviation cadets who comprised the first course at the newly raised Officer Training Unit (OTU) at Scheyville in NSW. The course began on 18 July 1965.

The army assembled its most experienced instructors, all with extensive active overseas service, to transform civilians into infantry platoon commanders in an intense 22 weeks of unrelenting activity. The training was both physically and mentally demanding and the attrition rate was high. I thrived on the physical challenges but found military history classes at the end of a 14-hour day very challenging. Few concessions were afforded to officer cadets; however, I was fortunate to be granted leave on three occasions to fly back to Perth on a Saturday morning to participate in the WAFL final series and helped to achieve a premiership for my club East Fremantle.

On 18 December 1965, 76 of the 107 officer cadets who began the course graduated as second lieutenants. I ranked sixth in graduation order and received the OTU Athletics Prize. Five members of this inaugural class, Melford Roe, Terry O'Hanlon, Ted Pott, John Deane-Butcher and myself were posted to 5 RAR. We became members of the first fully integrated unit of regular army and national service soldiers to undertake active service overseas and so became part of Australian military history.

I assumed my posting as the commander of 7 Platoon, C Company, in early January 1966 and immediately experienced a situation not covered in my training. Three members of my platoon were Western Australian national servicemen who had shared a hut with me at Puckapunyal before I was selected for officer training. One of these, Private John McShane, had worked with me in the Western Australia Department of Lands and we had spent the previous two years doing mid-week fitness training together. The potential for this familiarity to impact on discipline was real, but the situation was adroitly addressed by my deputy, Sergeant Ralph 'Rowdy' Hindmarsh. He called the men to attention, announced with a salute, 'The platoon is ready for inspection Sir!' By this simple action he firmly implanted in the minds of all platoon members the burden of authority which had been heaped upon me and signalled the need for them to respect it or, at least, to give me a fair go to show my wares.

Training at section, platoon and company level was intense and exhausting over the next three months. The men were subjected to regular rifle range practice, route marches and battle-runs to the School of Military Engineers to be trained in mine warfare. Pleasingly, all members of the platoon soon met the required battle-readiness fitness standard. Our training at the Jungle Training Centre at Canungra in south-east Queensland was challenging, as its tropical jungle conditions were like those we could expect in Vietnam. Competition between the 5 RAR rifle companies was fierce and a race over the notorious obstacle course was organised. I won the event for C Company and in the process set a course record which, I'm told, stood for quite a long time. At the completion of this closely assessed training, C Company was deemed to be fully prepared for overseas service.

I departed Australia by Qantas Boeing 707 from RAAF Base Richmond on 19 April 1966 as part of the 5 RAR advance party, which also included two other national service platoon commanders, John Deane-Butcher and Melford Roe. We arrived at the Bien Hoa US military base on 20 April and were attached to our 1 RAR counterparts. I joined Second Lieutenant John Dwyer on three 48-hour tactical area of responsibility patrols around the base area. The casual efficiency of his men in preparation for and execution of these patrols greatly impressed me. I wondered whether my platoon would develop this confidence and was subsequently delighted at the completion of our first combat experience, during Operation Hardihood, to see it on display so soon.

While most of the advance party returned by air to Vung Tau as their companies arrived in country, John Deane-Butcher and I were afforded additional time at Bien Hoa while our C Company mates travelled to Vietnam aboard HMAS *Sydney* and were the last 5 RAR troops to arrive. We were scheduled to fly on an American army UH-1D Iroquois helicopter to Vung Tau on 4 May. The helicopter was clearly overloaded at take-off and struggled to gain altitude. As we were approaching the Bear Cat US Army base, we lost power and altitude and the pilot made a forced landing, fortunately in a new base being constructed for a US Army infantry brigade. This event could well have prematurely ended our Vietnam tour. The pilot stated that two people would have to remain with the construction engineers until another chopper could pick them up. Being the most junior officers on board we were certain we would have to deplane. I can only assume our brass shoulder pips inferred a higher rank than second lieutenant because a US Army major and captain were directed to stay.

On rejoining my platoon, I was advised my platoon sergeant, Rowdy Hindmarsh, had contracted glandular fever just prior to the departure of HMAS *Sydney*. He had not made the trip and it was six weeks before I received a replacement platoon sergeant. As a result, I carried out the additional responsibilities of platoon sergeant during this period, with the help of my three section commanders. This added to the load on me and my men as we commenced operations.

Preparation for Operation Hardihood occurred from 5 May, with all troops warned about security and the need for vigilance. Amazingly, prior to the operation commencing, a photo of the 5 RAR camp on 'Back Beach' at Vung Tau, including the sentry post showing Corporal Leslie 'Doc' Urquhart of 8 Platoon, appeared in the Australian magazine *Pix*. Many diggers received copies from home requesting advice as to which was their tent.

During our time at Back Beach I was approached by an American who wore US Army greens but without insignia of any kind. He said he was part of a training team for Nungs, who were Chinese/Vietnamese operatives, but not of the South Vietnamese Army. He asked if I would like to see their training camp which was situated a few kilometres from Vung Tau. I sought and received permission to accompany him. The camp had two Nissen igloo huts that were chock-full of weapons from every part of the world and I suspected it might have been part of a CIA operation. The facility was impressive and as we were leaving he asked if there was any weapon I would particularly like to have. I indicated that the US .30 calibre M1 carbine had always impressed me. He laughed, saying he would bring a real weapon for me the next day. When he arrived next morning, he handed me a brand-new Armalite rifle and 5,000 rounds of ammunition for it. I thanked him and proceeded to advise my company commander. He said I should keep it and when we were established at Nui Dat the platoon could practice with it in anticipation of our Second World War–era Owen machine carbines possibly being replaced by similar weapons. The weapon was an early AR15 version of the lightweight US 5.56 mm M16 rifle, which was less unwieldy than our log 7.62 mm L1A1 rifle and could be fired as a fully automatic weapon. About 10 weeks later, during weapons test firing, I tried the weapon and allowed my sergeant and corporals to fire it. The weapon had good hitting power and was light and compact, but the gas cylinder caked with carbon and seized up due to excessive oil in the working parts of the weapon. I had my sergeant take it to the battalion's armourer and leave it with him. Sometime later we were issued with a newer, more effective version of this rifle which we soon learned not to over-lubricate.

The battalion commenced Operation Hardihood on the 24 May and C Company was airlifted to LZ Hudson. We were greeted by members of the US 173 Airborne Brigade who, despite their significant casualties in the weeks prior to our arrival, claimed there were no VC within miles. As we proceeded over the Song Cau River, we heard rifle fire from a contact involving B Company and proceeded cautiously into the rubber plantation surrounding Nui Dat. We travelled for about 2 kilometres as a company, with two platoons forward in a reverse-arrowhead formation, before harbouring and having an early meal.

My 7 Platoon was tasked that night with setting a half-platoon ambush on a track junction at the edge of the rubber plantation, about 1 kilometre from the rest of C Company. After a night lying in soaking rain, adjusting to the noises of the jungle, with no sleep and not seeing any VC, I sent out clearing patrols at first light and then set out to rejoin C Company after advising by radio that we were returning to their position. This was acknowledged by company headquarters, and 8 and 9 Platoons who then alerted their troops. We proceeded in staggered file towards our platoon position and what followed could have been disastrous. As we approached our position with 3 Section leading, we were fired on. We hit the ground with Corporal Ray Orchard yelling out 'contact front!' A couple of seconds later someone called out, 'It's Orch', and both groups called urgently for firing to stop. This incident highlighted a problem when a platoon was split for either patrolling or ambushing and the platoon radio was with the patrol or ambush group. As no provision had been made for a radio for the other element of my platoon, its members were unaware of our approach. In the early morning light our wet jungle green clothes appeared black. It being our second day on operations, it was only reasonable the uninformed sentry would expect the worst and open fire. The positive outcome from this experience was the immediate requirement for an extra radio to be provided in any situation where one element of a platoon was on patrol while the other element remained with the company main body.

My platoon suffered its first casualties on 17 June when Corporal Graham McCray and Private Uri Wolk were wounded by a booby trap. We were on the first day of a three-day patrol west of Nui Dat. Conditions were very hot, and we were travelling in tall, thick grass without shade. We were on a tight schedule to clear this area and didn't pause until 1330 hours. I tried to radio our location to Company HQ but was unable to make contact, so advised BHQ instead. We recommenced the patrol and discovered a VC camp comprising a series of weapon pits camouflaged with overhead protection from artillery fire. These showed no evidence of being recently used so we destroyed them and recorded the site as a future artillery fire task; then we commenced the 4-kilometre trek to our night harbour position. We were travelling in 150-centimetre-high kunai grass when the forward scout struck a tripwire, detonating a grenade.

This caused severe shrapnel wounds to Graham McCray's torso and Uri Wolk's legs. The platoon reacted in practised fashion, adopting an all-round defence stance. We were fortunate to have our stretcher bearer Private Ron Shoebridge with us and he immediately attended to the wounded. This incident occurred at 1430 hours and I tried to radio for a *Dustoff* helicopter, but the ANPRC 25 radio set, as we had experienced earlier on the patrol, was unreliable in thick country and contact could not be established with either C Company or BHQ. A rudimentary stretcher and a relay system were used to carry Graham while Uri walked assisted by Ron Shoebridge. We could only proceed at a rate that the forward scout determined was safe, and that the bearer party could manage.

It took three hours in stifling heat to reach the edge of LZ Hudson. We finally established radio communications at 1740 hours with BHQ and arranged a *Dustoff* chopper. When the chopper arrived at 1757 hours the pilot asked us to indicate our position with a coloured smoke grenade. We activated yellow smoke but again our radio failed and the pilot, unable to verify with us the colour used, requested we throw smoke again. This time we threw red smoke, the radio came good, we were able to confirm the smoke was ours and the chopper landed and took the wounded to the US Army 36 Evacuation Hospital in Vung Tau, a flight of 20 minutes.

Graham McCray's injuries were so severe he had to return to Australia. Uri Wolk rejoined the platoon after three weeks of recovering from his wounds.

After the *Dustoff*, we headed back into the jungle and harboured for the night, as we had insufficient daylight to rejoin the company position until next morning. I realised as we settled into night routine that my platoon had displayed, over the preceding five hours, a level of calmness and confidence that spoke well of their training and confidence in one another. We had experienced the shock of a booby trap exploding in our midst. The platoon had reacted well, going immediately into all-round defence. The men had then carried and assisted two injured mates and their weapons, ammunition and equipment for three hours in blistering heat through thick vegetation, with very little water, to place them on a *Dustoff* chopper. We were all aware Graham McCray's injuries were severe and hoped and prayed he would be OK. He had led 2 Section for our first month on operations as we continuously patrolled our designated search areas. He, like us, had grown used to living in wet clothes, spending hours staring into the black nothingness of the jungle while in ambush or on sentry picquet and dealing with mosquitoes, leeches and scorpions, but his short tour of duty was over.

We returned to base next morning where I was debriefed on the incident. I then received a briefing on my next patrol mission, was told to replenish rations and ammunition and ordered to move out after 8 and 9 Platoons returned from similar 48-hour patrols. We left base two days later, to return to the area where we had encountered the booby trap, with Private Don 'Tubby' Treloar stepping up from rifleman to machine gunner and Corporal Ted West becoming the commander of 2 Section. We were back to full fighting strength.

On 22 June we had covered over 8 kilometres within our designated search area before harbouring for an early evening meal at 1730 hours. This was to allow ample time for moving into an ambush position for the night. As we settled in, three VC moved across the front of 1 Section, about 200 metres away. Shots were exchanged before the VC escaped into the jungle. 1 Section moved out to sweep the area where the VC had been sighted but found no sign of casualties. A quantity of small arms ammunition was located during the sweep. Next morning, I was directed by company headquarters to provide an accurate grid reference for our contact to facilitate future artillery fire missions. This was done by taking compass bearings on two clearly identifiable geographic features. Where the reciprocal bearings from the two features intersected on the map would be an accurate indication of our location. (Oh, how we could have used a modern hand-held GPS!) The area we were in was covered in thick foliage, so I took my radio operator, Private Bill Parkes, and proceeded to a point 100 metres to the north of the platoon position where I was able to observe two peaks of the Nui Thi Via mountains. I stood on a rice paddy bund to take the compass bearings and, as I did, four shots rang out. I heard the first crack over my head as I dropped to the ground, rolled into a firing position and bumped into Bill Parkes who had the same immediate reaction to the shots. The shooter was in a creek bed and I believe this accounted for the shots going high. I learnt some lessons from this encounter, like the effectiveness of hours of training leading to an instant response to being shot at and, more importantly, the perils of standing in the open engrossed in a navigation problem with my platoon some distance away with the platoon's radio.

In early July the battalion commenced Operation Sydney to search the area around Nui Nghe, a prominent feature a few kilometres north-west of Nui Dat. C Company was tasked with searching the area north of this feature before sweeping over the hill to deal with any VC on the hill. During two days of patrolling in very thick jungle, many enemy camps and facilities were found and destroyed. The company was to move into position on the north-west slopes to advance on the hill summit, with 8 and 9 Platoons to lead, and my platoon to move behind them in reserve. We were returning at about 1700 hours from a patrol prior to moving my platoon into position when an artillery barrage was called onto the top of the hill from where shots were being fired at our spotter plane. Three rounds overshot the hill and one exploded in the tree canopy near 9 Platoon.

Lance Corporal Marinko 'Titch' Tomas received severe shrapnel wounds to his back from the tree burst. An urgent *Dustoff* was called and, as I had identified a suitable LZ about 150 metres from our position, I was directed to escort the stretcher party and secure the LZ with my 7 Platoon. As Titch was being placed on the chopper I patted his shoulder and told him he would be OK, but he died shortly after arriving at the hospital. He was the first Western Australian national serviceman killed in Vietnam. I knew him well, as we usually assisted Father John Williams, our battalion's chaplain, when he said mass prior to us going out on operations. Titch was a good bloke and his death deeply affected me. On my return to

Australia, I visited his family who had been targeted with hate mail. They were relieved I was with him when he was wounded, and the family and I have remained friends.

The battalion continued saturation patrolling of all areas adjacent to Nui Dat and conducted cordon and search operations on some villages throughout July. These resulted in regular contacts with the VC and finding and destroying their installations. As August approached, I considered how we had measured up to the challenges that had confronted us to date, and appreciated the human endeavour involved in carrying out infantry operations in jungle terrain with the physical and mental strain involved.

Soon after we first arrived at Nui Dat, stress and fatigue became our constant companions. C Company had lost men killed and wounded but, throughout these early months, I witnessed a subtle change in my men's demeanour. Every patrol deepened their solidarity. The skill of the forward scout or the alertness of the night picquet could mean the difference between life and death. My men uncomplainingly carried a 30-kilogram backpack plus a rifle, machine gun or radio set for kilometres in tropical heat, pressing quietly through thorny 'wait-a-while' vines and bamboo thickets with two-inch thorns, wading through streams, swamps and mud, all while staying alert and ready to react instantly; and then, at night, sat in inky blackness staring at nothingness during a tropical downpour while taking their turn at manning a machine gun. Such daily routines are but a few of the many parts of each man's slice of a shared burden. His mates know they can rely on him and he gains their total trust. Mutual trust and dependence increased as the process was repeated day after day; and the resulting deep bonds were evident in the cohesion, confidence and easy camaraderie that pervaded the whole platoon.

In early August prior to a cordon and search of Binh Ba, most of the battalion were in base. Various games were organised between the companies, tug-of-war and volleyball being the easiest to organise. However, on this occasion as a follow-up to an earlier contest in Australia, C Company participated in a game of Australian rules football. The venue was the red, laterite clay of the under-construction airstrip on the northern side of Nui Dat hill, later to be known as Luscombe Field. The goal posts were two stacked aviation gasoline drums with single drums for the behind posts. The game was played in jungle greens and boots, with C Company shirtless. The competition was played in earnest with many a bump and spill, but in the end C Company prevailed comfortably. While Roger

10. A PLATOON COMMANDER'S WAR – PART 2

Wainwright and I did well, the man of the match was C Company's centre half-back Private Syd Shore of 8 Platoon. This was possibly the first Aussie rules football game played in Vietnam and, sadly, not recorded in the official war history.

Binh Ba was the most significant village in our area of operations. On 7 August the battalion, reinforced by two companies from 6 RAR, commenced Operation Holsworthy to cordon and search the village. This was the most significant task undertaken by the battalion to date. Precise planning and efficient execution were essential to the success of this complex operation. After a long march to company assembly areas and a night insertion march through an old-growth rubber plantation, we waited in total darkness for the order to move into our respective blocking positions. There was no moon and inside the plantation was as black as pitch. To aid movement through the inky darkness we foraged in the leaf litter and found luminous lichen that we attached to each man's backpack. I moved forward to get the forward section to do this and while returning stepped into a depression and twisted my ankle. My concern was not for my ankle but for the noise I made when falling. As there was no reaction from the direction of the village, I quickly returned to my position.

The effectiveness of the tactical planning by the battalion and its precise implementation produced an outstanding result. Some VC village cadre and ARVN (Army of the Republic of Vietnam) draft dodgers were apprehended without casualties to the battalion, a most outstanding result for such a complex operation. However, a far greater victory was achieved by this operation. The local villagers were aware of our presence in Phuoc Tuy province but had no real understanding of us or our purpose. At various times individual villagers had been detained by platoon or company patrols as they tried to carry out their normal activities, which had in many instances been curtailed by our presence. The restriction on wood gathering and collection of fruit from gardens in some areas, along with the grazing of cattle, had all been a significant impost on the locals. We now had the village surrounded and the reaction we experienced as the people awoke was extraordinary. In our location an old woman came out of her house at daybreak to be confronted by four heavily armed Australians. She re-entered her house and reappeared 15 minutes later with a large kettle of lemongrass tea and proceeded to offer this to the men. I thought at the time, how would my or any Australian mother have reacted to this situation. Clearly, we had made a good impression to reinforce a reputation which had probably preceded us; and our presence was welcomed by many of the villagers.

Our indication that the battalion would have an ongoing association with the village was also appreciated. I was impressed when, after searching the village and during our distributing of rice and spare rations, the large number of villagers who lined up to receive food did so in a polite manner with genuine appreciation for our kindness. An action that positively impacted our goal of winning the hearts and minds of these people, and those of the locally deployed Vietnamese 1 Commando Company, who were under the control of Captain Ron Boxall and his small team, was a game of soccer. We were much bigger and stronger than our opponents but were instructed to ensure the match ended in a draw. A few heated moments occurred during the game as enthusiastic players from both sides clashed vigorously in attacking the ball; however, all parties were happy with the result and our standing in the village was enhanced.

After the village search was completed, Captain Tony White, the battalion medical officer, provided a clinic service to locals during his regular visits to our troops. I took the opportunity on one of these visits to have my ankle examined as it was quite sore. My leg was black from the knee down and swollen. A severely sprained ankle was diagnosed, and Tony indicated he would arrange for me to be restricted to light duties when we returned to base. True to his word, when I returned to Nui Dat base three weeks later, I was appointed commander of a 12-man squad to provide security for the headquarters, Australian Force Vietnam, in Saigon. On my return to Australia, I was found to have snapped my lateral ligament in this incident. While much of our issued equipment was substandard, the fact that I was able to continue with operational duties in the jungle and mountains for a further eight months confirms this was not the case with our excellent calf-length boots, known as boots GP (general purpose).

The VC mortaring of the Task Force base on 17 August resulted in the whole battalion, except for C Company, returning to base next morning. We were to provide support for Binh Ba village as promised. When the Battle of Long Tan commenced early that afternoon, we followed its progress on the radio network, seriously concerned for the men of D Company, 6 RAR, who, just 10 days before, had assisted us in the cordon and search of Binh Ba. We could hear the continuous roar of the artillery supporting D Company, 6 RAR, and then, at about 1600 hours, the APC troop supporting us was recalled to rejoin the relieving force. We were within artillery 105 mm gun range from Nui Dat and were directed to dig-in with overhead cover and expect an attack. We were on our own; however, I was proud of the quiet determination the men displayed as they set about preparing our defensive positions for an impending enemy attack. We spent a sleepless night on full alert, but no enemy came our way. I was pleased to greet the sun next day.

Following the Battle of Long Tan, all elements of the battalion were involved in intensive patrolling in the areas between Binh Ba and Nui Dat during the next four weeks to keep the VC off balance. As a result, we lived in filthy clothes for two weeks. This resulted in most of the men developing rashes and foot tinea due to the constant dampness. Our CO, John Warr, visited us regularly and introduced a rotation system for platoons to spend a day in Vung Tau swimming in the ocean. While the medical benefit may have been small, the impact on the men's morale was significant.

On 6 October, Operation Canberra was undertaken to commence securing Route 15 through Phuoc Tuy Province to allow newly arrived elements of the US 4 Infantry Division to move from their port of entry, Vung Tau, to their Bear Cat base in Bien Hoa Province to the north. To achieve this, we had to first clear the Nui Thi Vai hills which overlooked the road. My platoon led C Company from Route 15 for two days before 8 Platoon assumed the lead on the morning of 8 October. Just after 1030 hours, 8 Platoon was fired on and encountered booby traps. Eight men were wounded and because of the denseness of the jungle it took over two hours for us to hand-clear an LZ for the *Dustoff* chopper. Once the wounded were safely away, I was directed to clear an enemy installation 100 metres north of the LZ. This was a moment of truth. I was unsure of the extent of the installation to be cleared, the number of defenders, if any, and the layout of any fighting pits. It was my call, so I determined, after a brief reconnaissance, to have one section in a fire support position and to move through using one section up and the other behind in close support. 3 Section was to provide fire support and, as they moved into position, the section commander, Corporal Ray Orchard, screamed out, 'Stop' to Private Alex Bernotas, who was wriggling into place. Ray had seen the booby trap, but his warning was too late. Shrapnel struck Alex in the lower back and wounded another three men. I was standing next to Ray who was wounded with a piece of shrapnel the size of five cent coin embedded in his forehead. Ray was the first person in our company to spot a booby trap before it was detonated. A *Dustoff* helicopter was called and my wounded were taken to hospital. Alex Bernotas's wounds were so severe he was returned to Australia. After this incident we were withdrawn 500 metres while an airstrike and an artillery bombardment were brought to bear on the area in response to B Company contacting a large VC force on the Nui Thi Vai feature, further to our north.

Ray Orchard's bushcraft was exceptional. Later in our tour of duty, when we were moving through very dense jungle with 1 Section leading, because of the thickness of the foliage, I was forward with the lead section check-navigating for Corporal Alan McNulty. Suddenly, shots were fired directly behind by Ray Orchard who shouted, 'Contact left!'. The platoon went into a counter-ambush drill and Sergeant John Lee-Smith swept through the VC camp with 2 Section. The camp comprised about 50 weapon pits, a sandal factory and a kitchen with rice cooking. The VC had bolted into the thick scrub and we were unable to locate any sign of their having taken casualties. I quizzed Ray on how he had seen the VC sentry. He said, 'I just looked through the leaves.' Given that 10 people had stared into that area, it was his observation skills which certainly saved our lives. Ray Orchard was a special soldier who inspired men by his actions and leadership, he was a natural leader and he was Aboriginal. His section comprised a blend of older regular soldiers and young national servicemen; but Ray saw no difference between them. They were his boys and they respected his authority. His bushcraft was without peer in the company and some of us owed their lives to his skills. Respect and admiration for Ray extended throughout the whole battalion. I kept contact with Ray after we returned to Australia and saw both his anger when refused entry to a Queensland RSL (Returned and Services League) club and his joy at the 1987 national Welcome Home march. I was honoured to present his eulogy when he died in February 2013. Ray was an Australian soldier, which says it all. He was a man of courage, honesty and integrity and we loved and respected him as a brother.

Later that day we moved towards B Company's position to harbour for the night. We were located on the side of a very steep hill with only a small area of flat ground, which company headquarters occupied. It was impossible to set a perimeter due to the terrain, so the men were grouped in proximity to the gun positions to enable the night picquet to operate. I slept that night with my feet against a tree almost in the vertical position due to the steepness of the hill. Next day my platoon was leading the company as we moved back to the VC base complex where we had taken casualties. As we approached the installation, I observed a broken branch, a VC sign for a tripwire ahead. I called a halt just as my forward scout, Private Ken Warren, sent hand signals to indicate an obstacle and for me to come forward to see for myself. The tripwire was attached to a Chicom grenade and, as we looked for a place to get off the track, we realised both sides were heavily booby-trapped with vines attached to grenades. Our attached combat engineers were called forward. They disarmed a tripwire stretched across the track and we moved cautiously into the complex.

The enemy base contained a hospital, large quantities of drugs, 10 tonnes of rice and a booby trap workshop. With little time available we did our best to destroy the camp, but we were required to secure Route 15 the following day, so we left late in the afternoon for our new position along the road. It must have seemed strange to the incoming Americans to see us waving them on, in floppy bush hats and often shirtless. The American units moving along Route 15 wore flak jackets and steel helmets and the floors of their vehicles were sandbagged to protect against mines A major general stopped his jeep and expressed his thanks to me, saying how happy he was to be working with professionals. I looked at my men and realised that, while they did not match the fresh look of the new-to-country Americans, I'm sure there was something about their easy confidence and the way they carried themselves which attracted the compliment.

We did not completely leave the Nui Thi Vai hills to the VC, for we returned to the area after securing the road as part of the US Army Operation Robin. This new thrust into the same hills was called Operation Queanbeyan. It involved a lot of scrub-bashing as we searched further into the hills without any contact with the enemy, although other companies and BHQ had significant enemy contacts which are described in Chapters 7 and 15.

November 1966 saw the battalion just halfway into our 12-month tour of duty in Vietnam. There was much more to follow but such events extend beyond the period covered by this book. To round out my narrative as one of the first five national service officers to lead Australian soldiers in combat operations I shall close my tale with a brief description of my departure from 5 RAR and the men who remain my brothers to this day.

My tour of Vietnam ended on 12 April 1967 and the manner of its occurring deserves mention. At 1000 hours on that day, our CO, John Warr, flew from Nui Dat to the Horseshoe Hill feature in a Sioux helicopter and asked for me to join him. As kindly as it is possible, he told me my younger brother had been killed in a road accident and my parents had asked for my return to Australia. He said, 'Your tour here is completed, if you wish to go home I will make it happen.' He agreed that I should speak to my men as there was still one week of operations to go before our relief by 7 RAR. My men expressed sorrow at my losing a brother and told me to go.

I left the Horseshoe in the CO's Sioux at 1030 hours, returned to Nui Dat, changed into civilian clothes which had been 12 months in a tin trunk and was driven to the airstrip where I boarded an RAAF Caribou aircraft for Saigon. I was met at Tan Son Nhut airport by a consular official and handed a passport which included a signature copied from my pay book. I travelled by Air Vietnam to Singapore, boarded a BOAC (British Overseas Airways Corporation) aircraft and arrived in Perth at midnight. My total journey had taken 13 hours. To put this journey into perspective, John Warr, who at times had responsibility for almost 1,000 troops in combat, had taken the time to arrange my rapid return to Australia. He was compassionate and always showed empathy for his men. He was on outstanding CO and the results achieved by our battalion during its tour of duty attest to this.

Editors' conclusion

Chapters 8, 9, 10 and 15 provide comprehensive insights into the day-to-day experiences of 5 RAR's junior officers and their men in the operational environment which prevailed in the first six months of 1 ATF's deployment into Phuoc Tuy Province. Their narratives have been included in this book to convey an idea of the diverse hardships that confronted some of the nation's young men when they were among the first Australians to be committed into that challenging environment; and to show how they coped and settled into operations. For this reason, their stories have concentrated on the first six months of our battalion's first tour of duty in Vietnam. They are but a few of innumerable personal stories that can be drawn from within an infantry battalion at war.

11

ADVISERS? ACTIVITIES BEYOND THE BATTALION

Ron Boxall and Ron Bade

Introduction by Robert O'Neill

In taking part in the Vietnam War we were aware that once again Australia was providing a small contingent in a major conflict which our principal allies regarded as very important. We had played a similar role in the Second World War and the Korean War. We thought it very likely that Australia would be called upon to give similar service and support in future conflicts in this region, under US leadership. Therefore, we, as soldiers, wanted to test the effectiveness of our alliance partnership at the ground force level. We were keen to have direct personal experience of how it worked, and to draw our own conclusions for the future from a year of operating together.

Soon after 5th Battalion, the Royal Australian Regiment (5 RAR), had settled into its final perimeter within the newly established 1st Australian Task Force (1 ATF) base at Nui Dat, the battalion was required to provide personnel for tasks which were well beyond our normal range of responsibilities. One of our officers was detached to work with a CIA-sponsored activity and, later, another was detached to be an adviser to a South Vietnamese Army Regional Force company transferred from the Saigon area. The activities of both elements were confined to Phuoc Tuy Province, within 10 kilometres of 1 ATF's base at Nui Dat. Captains Boxall and Bade each describe their experiences and thoughts on these activities in this chapter.

Ron Boxall

In mid-to-late July 1966 I was going about my chores as second in command (2IC) of D Company, 5 RAR. Our company base within the 1 ATF perimeter at Nui Dat was on the upper eastern slopes of the Nui Dat hill feature. We were geographically separated from the rest of the battalion and in the enviable position of not being sited on the more vulnerable parts of the 1 ATF base perimeter. I suppose this was how I came to be selected as more readily available than others for a job detached from 1 ATF.

For a young temporary captain, the experiences I was about to have would prove intriguing, eye-opening and quite instructive. Despite any seemingly sour notes in the following paragraphs, I would not have missed the sojourn at any price. Its many lessons were pure gold.

My recall of dates throughout the period I describe is clouded because I didn't keep a diary, and second, the day-to-day activity of the group to which I was assigned wasn't required to be reported to Headquarters 1 ATF (HQ 1 ATF). From the start of my detachment from 5 RAR I maintained a radio on 1 ATF's command radio net, but I was never fed any information by it or required to furnish details of my day-to-day activities. On the few occasions when I offered information I thought was pertinent, my efforts drew what I took to be a mixture of confusion and indifference. So, I desisted, resolving to maintain radio communications to report only incidents of pressing operational importance and to ensure that I had a means of calling for artillery fire support. I seemed to be regarded as something of a wild card who was monitoring the 1 ATF command net to keep myself in the picture about what was going on around me. Thus, most details of my activities were not recorded either by myself or in the 1 ATF radio log. In retrospect I think that I was considered as working for an obscure foreign agency to whom my activities were of immediate importance and from which any relevant intelligence and other information would filter to 1 ATF through the US Phuoc Tuy provincial headquarters. Crazily, I had no means of communicating with my American civilian 'boss' in Ba Ria other than by visiting him; a one-way arrangement in that my visits were never reciprocated.

11. ADVISERS? ACTIVITIES BEYOND THE BATTALION

The events that followed gave me an insight into the pseudo-military shenanigans which some of our American allies seemed to hold in great store. I accept that there were probably some 'sneaky-Pete' triumphs they could claim, but my experiences of them left me with the conclusion that the results of such activities in Phuoc Tuy in the early days of 1 ATF's operations were quantifiable only in the negative. I have since concluded that, apart from insisting that a 1 ATF officer be assigned to a CIA intelligence operation in Phuoc Tuy, the commander of 1 ATF probably had no say in the presence or activities of a 'Combined Studies Group' (CSG) operation within his bailiwick; CSG being one of the flimsy *noms de guerre* used by the CIA during the Vietnam War. Additionally, it soon became clear to me that those directing the CSG were not happy with the arrangement which inserted an outsider into their cabal. Inevitably, I developed the view that its ongoing activities in the province had more to do with the preservation of US intelligence agency fiefdoms than being a seriously considered part of prosecuting the local shooting war. The concept of CSG efforts in Phuoc Tuy Province was arcane and its hard-to-glimpse rationale seemed little more than delusive chicanery – less macabre, but similar in mentality to the US military's lamentable predilection for inflating enemy body counts throughout the Vietnam War.

I left 5 RAR to report to HQ 1 ATF, awash with confidence that I would receive a detailed briefing and accompanying orders but was simply told that I was to replace another 1 ATF officer currently 'running' a Vietnamese 'outfit' presently located in the large village of Hoa Long, which was noted for the mixed loyalties of its inhabitants. It was the capital of Long Le district and located astride Route 2 between 1 ATF's base at Nui Dat and the provincial capital, Ba Ria. I was to contact this officer and he would brief me. I soon located him and his small team of three Australians, whom I will describe shortly.

Meeting him and seeing his 'headquarters', located in a disused schoolhouse roughly in the centre of Hoa Long, did little for my enthusiasm for what might lie ahead. The man I was to relieve was also a 1 ATF infantry captain who appeared slightly older than me. Surprisingly I did not know him, nor had I ever heard of him. He was a thin, sallow-complexioned man with a narrow, Hollywood-hero moustache. He sported a standard army bush hat which had been starched and carefully shaped into a version of a civilian pork-pie hat, which he wore perched squarely and set low on his brow. He had the appearance of a minor Damon Runyon character – rather like a fugitive from a race course betting ring. His general manner and lack of enthusiasm conveyed that he was not impressed with his current circumstances and was much looking forward to putting them behind him.

His 'briefing', though reasonably comprehensive, was unstructured and delivered mostly by responding to my queries or prompts by his team members. He thus conveyed that the non-ARVN (Army of the Republic of Vietnam) company-sized unit was recruited, equipped and paid by the CSG's chief agent in Phuoc Tuy Province who operated from Ba Ria. In effect they were civilians; a mixture of Nungs (Vietnamese Chinese) and Montagnards (aboriginal people from Vietnam's mountainous regions). Allegedly both groups had a deep-seated dislike of the Vietnamese. By joining this CSG program they were absolved from service in the ARVN and were paid more than their ARVN counterparts, but there was no rank structure as such. Their leaders at company, platoon and squad levels were described as having been elected by their peers and received a pay-loading for the honour. There were no apparent disciplinary arrangements or clear means of enforcing rules or orders other than the threat of dismissal. For the most part they were dressed in elaborately patterned camouflage uniforms and armed with a variety of weapons, many of which were of non-US origin. They sported berets with a badge depicting a rearing cobra and most wore M26 hand grenades on the chest straps of their equipment, while carrying about them a range of other military and civilian items which gave the appearance of an armed flock of itinerant hoarders. They were currently scattered in small groups among Hoa Long's many houses, supposedly as a deterrent to Viet Cong movement in and out of the very large village. There being no radio communications within the group, the only method of internal communication was by gatherings of platoon and squad 'leaders'. The senior member or 'company commander' was described as a mere figurehead who nodded wisely as instructions, all devised and coordinated by the 'advisers', were imparted.

The group went by two names. Depending on the speaker's preference, they were variously referred to as 1 Commando Company (1 Cdo Coy) or the Provincial Reconnaissance Unit. In other words, whichever took your fancy would do. In this narrative I will stick to 1 Cdo Coy which seemed to be the 1 ATF preference. At the completion of his 'briefing' my predecessor departed with a flippant farewell to me and his former team members, which we returned in kind. My new colleagues soon made it clear that they regarded his replacement as a relief in more than one sense of the word.

11. ADVISERS? ACTIVITIES BEYOND THE BATTALION

The small team of 'advisers' I was to head consisted of two Australian Army Training Team (AATTV) warrant officers (WO), Alan Seale and 'Squizzy' Taylor, and a Vietnamese linguist from HQ 1 ATF, Corporal 'Bondi' Bailey. Alan proved to be a crusty, no-nonsense Englishman with many years of service as an Australian infantryman. Squizzy was a steady ordnance WO having his first experience of more warrior-like duties. Both became great backstops for me and relieved many uncertainties with their wise counsel, versatility and remarkable adaptability. Bondi Bailey was another great operator; steady, reliable and a very accomplished interpreter.

The district chief, Dai Uy (Captain) Kim, had his district headquarters in Hoa Long but it proved hard to arrange a meeting with him until an incident occurred which caused our paths to cross, when he demonstrated that he was both perceptive and a man of action. He was very unhappy with the presence of 1 Cdo Coy in his district capital and had been so since they were first thrust into his domain. He claimed to have no say in their presence or their activities which were disruptive and resented by all villagers, irrespective of their political loyalties. By the time I met Kim this resentment had already become apparent to me through observing the clearly poor relations between the villagers and 1 Cdo Coy personnel. This seemed largely related to the pestering of village women, boozy behaviour and chicken rustling. I'm sure that the villagers' resentment included a strong element of fear of these interlopers.

A week or so after my arrival in Hoa Long a short succession of shots came from the village market place not far from our schoolhouse. Grabbing our weapons, we moved around the intervening houses to the market place where we found a relatively calm gathering of villagers milling around something which was holding their attention. Moving cautiously through the throng we met Kim and his adviser, a US Army captain. Both were armed with M16 rifles and before them lay the body of one of 1 Cdo Coy's members. Kim explained that the dead man had been drunk and threatening villagers with his weapons. He had been summoned to the scene and, after assessing the problem, applied his long-held policy of never arguing with a heavily armed drunk and promptly shot him. After we recovered the man's weapons and ammunition, Kim arranged the disposal of his body. The man's demise didn't seem to affect his comrades unduly; the villagers remained impassive. Clearly all had become inured to witnessing the swift justice which often went with the overt authoritarianism commonly practised at the lower levels of the South

Vietnamese government. When I reported the loss of this man to my CSG 'boss' it was dismissed with a verbal shrug and the conversation moved on to other matters.

This brings me to a description of how my interaction with the CSG in Phuoc Tuy Province played out. Immediately following the departure of my predecessor, I visited my 'boss' in his villa headquarters in Ba Ria. His name was Mathews and he claimed to be a former corporal in the US Marine Corps. He basically confirmed what my predecessor had told me. Throughout our conversation he was either unsure of the rationale behind the presence of 1 Cdo Coy in Phuoc Tuy or was being clumsily guarded about it. When I asked what type of operations they had been trained for, he became quite vague and spoke in circles about infiltration of Viet Cong village infrastructure and its subsequent elimination. Experience and events soon revealed that, apart from some basic weapons training, evidence of realistic training to those ends was not to be found. Apparently connected with his headquarters were three AATTV members, one captain and two WOs, who were unmistakeably reticent about conversing with me. It was never revealed to me exactly what they did, and I was left to speculate about their role. Their combined attitude and attire excited mild disdain. They were dressed in civilian clothes, with shirts tantalisingly unfastened at the top few buttons, and at hip level they wore low-slung leather holsters emblazoned with the bold letters 'US' and containing ubiquitous Colt .45 calibre automatic pistols. One of the WOs was overweight and looked particularly comical.

A short time afterwards I was advised that Mathews had been replaced so I went to Ba Ria to meet my new 'boss'. To the best of my memory his name was Buckley and he claimed to be a former US Army lieutenant colonel. He was a taciturn man who gave the impression that he had been sent in as a new broom to tidy up the local CSG operation. His first task for me was to fire a third of the 1 Cdo Coy's members and recover their weapons. On my return to Hoa Long our small team burned the midnight oil to devise a scheme for what might prove to be a very delicate administrative manoeuvre.

Our plan was simple and worked smoothly. We were to kick things off on the next pay day, beginning with an assembly parade in front of the school house which contained a few separate but interconnected rooms. The members were told that all weapons, ammunition and equipment were to be checked for serviceability or replacement on pay day. They were told to deposit their present weapons, ammunition and equipment in a large room at the end of the building via an external door and return to the 'pay parade' in front of the school house, and that payment would commence when this was completed. When all had complied, the large room was made secure and payment was commenced with individuals entering the pay room one at a time. The pay room was connected by doors to two other large rooms. After being paid, each of those who had been selected for retention were directed into one of the adjoining rooms and the 'discards' were directed to the other. Both groups were to remain in these rooms until pay was completed.

When all had been paid, the discards were released into the custody of Kim's ARVN soldiers who arranged their rapid removal from Hoa Long. The 'keepers' were then reissued with their weapons, ammunition and equipment, and organisational adjustments and reassignments to tasks were made. The operation was completed by returning most of the recovered weapons to CSG. Recovered ammunition and equipment items were retained as an immediate resupply pool. The reaction of the 'keepers' to dismissal of the 'discards' seemed to be one of general indifference – but, after all, they still had their jobs. I later heard that such rationalisations were an occasional feature of life in the employ of CSG in Phuoc Tuy Province. This must have been an ongoing depletion of the certitude and morale of 1 Cdo Coy's members, not to mention their loyalty.

After a few weeks at Hoa Long, 1 Cdo Coy was redeployed to the village of Binh Ba which was located on Route 2, some 7 kilometres north of the 1 ATF base at Nui Dat. No reason was given for the change of location, but their task remained to deter Viet Cong movement in and out of Binh Ba village, which was quite a different situation from Hoa Long. It was the location of a French-owned rubber plantation and processing factory. The operation's business name was Don Dien de Gallia. The village was adjacent to the factory and consisted of well-arranged, substantial dwellings for housing the factory employees and plantation workers. A fine Roman Catholic Church was a part of the village and it was served by a very canny, diminutive, French-educated priest called Pere Joseph. Slightly apart from the village and near the factory were a pair of large two-storeyed villas which housed two Frenchmen, the operation's manager, Jean-Jacques Pernes, and its engineer, Monsieur Moreau. A couple of hundred metres to the north of the village a large grass airfield extended 2,000 metres westwards from a satellite hamlet, Ap Ngai Giao, also located on Route 2. About a third of the way along its length, on its northern side, there was another villa which was unoccupied. Pernes and

Moreau both spoke Vietnamese and I communicated with them in that language through Bondi Bailey. A short time later, a French-born soldier from 5 RAR, Private Ron 'Frenchy' Delaurey-Simpson, joined our team to provide another avenue of communication.

It was clear that Pernes and Moreau did not want 1 Cdo Coy personnel living around the village houses as they had done in Hoa Long. Their reputation had probably preceded them. Instead, I had the use of the villa beside the airstrip and the 1 Cdo Coy 'troops' were deployed to its north in the adjacent rubber plantation. From there they went about various minor tasks associated with being a 'deterring presence'. Determining their tasks was complicated by the certainty that most of them couldn't be trusted out of sight; and it was not long before problems like those experienced at Hoa Long re-emerged. I had been told that the sudden redeployment from the Long Le district capital to this commercial operation's workers' village in Duc Thanh district was done at the request of the Phuoc Tuy province chief, Colonel Dat. In response to my queries, the upbeat yet slightly evasive way in which this information was confirmed by my usually taciturn CSG 'boss', Buckley, led me to suspect that there was more to the story. Subsequent events were to reinforce my suspicions.

One day a light aircraft landed on the village airstrip and taxied to the western end of Binh Ba, opposite 'my' villa. With some flying experience and a keen interest in light aircraft I recognised it as a Helio Courier, a relatively rare and highly capable American short take-off and landing aircraft. As I drove towards where the aircraft was parked I noted that it was unpainted and had no markings apart from a black serial number on the tail fin. As I got closer I saw that it had 'AIR AMERICA' in quite small letters on the side of the fuselage, just behind the wings. As I arrived near where it had parked, Pernes and Moreau also arrived in their small Citroen CV2. Two civilians wearing sidearms emerged from the aircraft and, after cursory nods to me, one of them engaged Pernes and Moreau in conversation in Vietnamese. Bondi Bailey wasn't with me and I could not follow what was said. After a short time, a tightly packed bundle, approximately 30x30x30 centimetres in size and neatly tied with some sort of binding wire or cord, was transferred from the aircraft to the Citroen. From about six or seven metres it looked to me like paper money. With nothing further said, and nods all round to me, the Frenchmen and the Americans departed in their respective machines. Assuming CSG would be aware of their Air America confreres' activities I thought no more about it until two days later when Pernes approached me. He asked whether I knew of any artillery tasks that might be fired during the next day or so to the north along Route 2 towards the Courtenay rubber plantation. I replied that I was not permitted give him any details of operational matters. He readily accepted my reply and I asked why he wanted to know such things. He replied, quite matter-of-factly, that he needed to go north along Route 2 to a rendezvous (with the Viet Cong) where he would 'pay the next of his company's "tax" instalments' which allowed its operations to continue unmolested. I knew it would be pointless to ask him to provide more details as it would be inviting him to possibly compromise himself and his workers. It was left for me to ponder why the CIA was delivering money to be paid to the Viet Cong via a French rubber plantation operation. I suspect the real answer would have been both mind-boggling in its complexity and deliciously absurd in its rationale.

At one point a jeep with three US Army communications specialists arrived unannounced to stay for a few days. They described themselves as a 'radio research team' whose equipment was used to obtain fixes on enemy radio locations. They were emphatic about removing their signals equipment, documentation and weapons from their vehicle and securely stowing them inside the villa but left numerous items in the unattended jeep. Some of these were promptly liberated by untraceable elements of 1 Cdo Coy. The new arrivals were particularly upset about the loss of some bourbon whisky, their other missing items being of comparatively small concern. Their marked attention to the security of their radio equipment seemed curious considering they were tasked to swan about the countryside in their lone-runner jeep, obviously prone to ambush and loss to the enemy of their sensitive equipment, not to mention their lives. Their parent organisation was obviously comprised of deep thinkers.

Around this time, I received a message from 1 ATF that Land Rover spare parts were in short supply. I was to return my Australian Army vehicle as soon as possible and should approach my CSG 'boss' about supplying me with another vehicle before I relinquished the Land Rover. I did so, and he gave me a completed US Army requisition form and told me to submit it to the US Army cannibalisation point at Cat Lo near Vung Tau where I was told to come back in a week's time and a jeep would be put together for me. When I returned, the non-commissioned officer (NCO) attending to me required a receipt for the 'bitzer' M38 A1 jeep. I was unsure of all the implications but, being an admirer of Major Stan Maizey's dubious but effective acquisition techniques, I supplied a signature; not my own, but a signature indeed. The NCO didn't care – he had a signature and was not interested in my *bona fides*. On the way back to Binh Ba I dropped off the Land Rover at 1 ATF, where I had its .30 calibre Browning machine gun and its mounting transferred to the jeep, before making my way back to Binh Ba.

Phase 1 of 5 RAR's Operation Holsworthy was a very successful cordon and search of Binh Ba on the night of 7/8 August 1966. Following the cordon and search, as I described earlier, 1 Cdo Coy was moved from Hoa Long to the area of the villa by the airfield at Binh Ba, while 5 RAR continued with Operation Holsworthy in and around Binh Ba. In his Commander's Diary for August, Brigadier Jackson 'propose[d] to maintain a [5 RAR] rifle company with sections of mortars and APCs [armoured personnel carriers] at Binh Ba until [he was] satisfied that the Province Chief can assure the security of the place'.

On 17 August the 1 ATF base at Nui Dat was mortared and Operation Holsworthy was terminated, with all elements of 5 RAR except C Company returning to Nui Dat. On the following day, 18 August, the Battle of Long Tan took place some 8 kilometres to our south-east. I and my small team listened intently to the 1 ATF command net throughout these events. Should the Viet Cong elements involved at Long Tan have moved in our direction, our survival plan was based on the reasonable belief that 1 Cdo Coy would decamp at the first hint of trouble. Fortunately, the enemy survivors of Long Tan retired in other directions and our self-extraction plan was shelved.

Over 50 years later I became aware of a 5 RAR operation order for Operation Woolloomooloo which is dated 17 August 1966, the day before the Battle of Long Tan. It was clearly prepared in haste as it was signed by Major Bert Cassidy and not 5 RAR's operations officer Major Max Carroll, who would have been flat out with other very pressing priorities as the first major Australian engagement of the war was unfolding. The purpose of Operation Woolloomooloo was to fulfil the Commander 1 ATF's diarised intention to maintain a rifle company with mortars and APCs (armoured personnel carriers) at Binh Ba on a rotation of seven to 10 days until the province chief could provide a suitable ARVN presence there. The operation order's mission paragraph reads, 'The 5RAR rifle company is to provide support to 1Cdo Coy at Binh Ba'. In its 'friendly forces' paragraphs it details 1 Cdo Coy's tasks at Binh Ba, none of which I had heard either formally or fully expressed 50 years earlier from any source. It also stated that '1 Cdo Coy operates through an Australian adviser and is under the tactical control of 5RAR'. These and many other revelations were contained in this operation order which I saw for the first time in late 2017 while checking facts for this narrative. With some bemusement and annoyance, I looked at its Distribution List and found that neither CSG, 1 Cdo Coy nor I appeared as recipients of any of its 70 copies.

5 RAR's operational files show that, following Operation Holsworthy, C Company remained in the vicinity. It was listed as the first of 5 RAR's rifle companies undertaking the rotation at Binh Ba from 23 August to 14 September, followed by A, B and D Companies until 4 October, when Operation Woolloomooloo concluded prior to the commencement of Operation Canberra in the Nui Thi Vai hills on 6 October. At no stage of my sojourn at Binh Ba was there any mention of an operation codenamed Woolloomooloo. It is interesting to note that it is not mentioned in the official history nor in Bob O'Neill's *Vietnam Task*. Understandably, the operation order was probably prepared in haste then de-prioritised and somewhat forgotten in the turbulence of Long Tan and its aftermath. It was to remain unmentioned by any recorder of 1 ATF's early history in Phuoc Tuy Province.

Shortly before Operation Woolloomooloo concluded, I was advised that 1 Cdo Coy was to be removed from Binh Ba and returned to CSG's fold for employment elsewhere. I was not given any reason for its withdrawal, but it was obvious to all that its effectiveness was non-existent, and its presence was disruptive. On the day before its withdrawal I was recalled to 5 RAR to be involved in Operation Canberra, commanding the defence component of a 103 Field Battery gun position beside Route 15 near Ap Ong Trinh Dp. My obvious means of movement was the jeep in my possession, so I drove it to Nui Dat, accepting that I might have to surrender it subsequently.

On my return to 5 RAR I made the mistake of driving through battalion headquarters on my way to D Company when I caught the eagle eye of Stan Maizey. Obeying his firm indication to pull up beside him I was confronted by his best quizzical and covetous scowl. 'Where did you get this?' was his opening gambit. I gave him the details. His response was, 'Well, I'll be having it!' I said, 'No sir!' He said, 'What? Come again!' I said, 'No sir – I scrounged it fair and square!' His frown softened, the corners of his mouth curved into a wisp of a smile and, with the merest hint of admiration, he conspiratorially asked, 'Can you get any more?' To his clear disappointment the gist of my reply was, 'Unlikely'. Next day he sent a message to D Company, 'In view of the scarcity of spare parts, and with the advent of Jack 1 [the jeep's new nickname], D Company is to return one of its two Land Rovers to the Battalion vehicle pool'. Stan was a hard man to beat – but he did like a trier. The jeep postscript is that I was never asked to surrender it and, when D Company left Nui Dat to occupy the Horseshoe hill feature 7 kilometres south-east of Nui Dat, it was bequeathed to the chaplains who usually had to cadge lifts to go about their ministrations.

Although the term was never used, I later presumed that 1 Cdo Coy may have been an experimental part of the so-called 'Phoenix Program' which was supposed to target and eliminate the Viet Cong infrastructure (VCI) at village level. In the American television series *The Vietnam War*, made in 2017, Tran Ngoc Chau, the South Vietnamese progenitor of the Phoenix (Phung Hoang) Program, spoke briefly. He disappointedly described it as 'his teenager who went astray and was lost to his foster parents' (the CIA?).

The Phoenix Program was rated poorly in the television series, with only a brief negative mention of it as an 'assassination and torture program'. Brigadier Chamberlain, the author of Appendix D, noted in January 2018:

> My experience of Phoenix when working in the Phuoc Tuy Provincial Intelligence Operations Centre in 1969, was that it was ineffectual due partly to distrust and little cooperation between the 'competing' agencies.

He also noted that, as late as June 1970, 1 ATF reports assessed that the Phoenix Program:

> achieved very few results … there had been a reduction in the VCI (Viet Cong Infrastructure) resulting from 1ATF ambushes, contacts, air strikes and Hoi Chan (defectors), but remarkably little that can be attributed to the Phung Hoang (Phoenix) Program … Most VCI eliminations are a direct result of 1ATF operations, identification of VCI personnel from captured documents, defectors and prisoner of war interrogations … Few of those eliminated have been important cadres at village level, most being low level supply organizers … The (Allied) intelligence community is fragmented and uncoordinated.

11. ADVISERS? ACTIVITIES BEYOND THE BATTALION

Towards the end of Chapter 5, Bob O'Neill gives an insight into the jealousies and rivalries at play among and between the intelligence and operations staff of US military headquarters at various levels. One can only imagine, with some incredulity, what the relationships between the military intelligence communities and the US 'spook' agencies must have been like – somewhere between feigned and non-existent? In their military doctrine the Americans subscribe to nine principles of war. One of them, unity of command, is described as having the purpose of 'ensuring unity of effort under one responsible commander for every objective'.

Why then did the commander of 1 ATF, who had the overall objective of defeating the Viet Cong in his assigned area of operations, need to endure quasi-military activities by non-military US agencies, together with the presence of loosely controlled ARVN elements within areas in which he was conducting operations without having at least temporary control over them? An ARVN artillery incident during Operation Robin, which is described by George Bindley towards the end of Chapter 12, illustrates both the perils and diseconomies of not addressing this need. Such issues raise obvious questions about why peripheral CIA intelligence activity with its associated quasi-military operations needed to be sequestered from the primary military effort, and why inability or failure to coordinate effectively all contributions to warfighting at the operational and tactical levels seemed to pervade the way in which the Vietnam War was conducted.

The resulting confusion was exacerbated by the cynical obfuscation that the Government of South Vietnam was in command of the war, supported by allies, principally the United States. No amount of window dressing could conceal that it was America's chosen war and that her military were directing its operations, albeit alongside an apparently separate battlefield involvement of the CIA.

Our American friends might say that poor ARVN reliability imposed an imperative need for strict adherence to other US principles of war, like security and surprise, which outweighed need for unity of command. Perhaps so, but the routine, continual sidelining of any fundamental principle is a form of fraudulent self-deception. It is often held that fraud is a virtue in war; but only when it is practised against the enemy and not allowed to become a delusory and energy-consuming internal malady.

While reflecting on the broader Vietnam War during the many months of this book's gestation, I came across a commentary in the *Time* magazine issue for 9 April 2018. It was written by Admiral James Stavritis, US Navy, a former supreme allied commander of NATO. He drew attention to a book, *Dereliction of Duty*, by Lieutenant General HR McMaster, US Army. Published in 1997, it was based on a very highly rated doctoral thesis which McMaster had prepared as a major and graduate student at the University of North Carolina. *Dereliction of Duty* became a bestseller and has been studied in many US military colleges and research institutes. In his comments, Admiral Stavritis opined that:

> *Dereliction of Duty* is in many ways a stinging indictment of the Washington culture of deceit, hidden agendas and backstabbing that helped pull the US into a quagmire in Vietnam. It tells the story of the malfeasance of the uniformed senior military in misleading the nation and the President about the true state of affairs as the war spiralled down to defeat.[1]

The propagation and scattering of 'private armies', inimically discrete intelligence operations and loosely controlled ARVN elements among overarching military operations without responsibility for overall command, control and coordination being vested in one military commander at each appropriate level was bound to become nugatory. There is much to question about why the CIA was not confined to clandestine activity elsewhere than on the battlefield, and denied any right to meddle thereon. Mine was only a brief exposure to one of the CIA's widespread, tacked-on warfighting schemes; one which seemed to lack definition, credible reputation or incisiveness. During a second tour of duty five years later, again with an RAR battalion, I perceived no changes to what by then had become a stalled formulaic prosecution of the broader war. Thus, the Vietnam War stands as a beacon of political and military failure to adapt and revise failing strategy.

Before concluding, I should not forebear from rating the peripheral and puny 1966 contributions to warfighting within Phuoc Tuy province by 1 Cdo Coy and its parent organisation. In the interests of brevity and clarity I borrow the incomparable pragmatism of the Australian digger to say, 'The whole idea was about as much use as tits on bacon – zero out of ten!'

---

1   James Stavridis, 'H.R. McMaster worked for me: His retirement from the military reveals a lot about President Trump', *Time*, 9 April 2018, available at: time.com/5212570/hr-mcmaster-trump/.

11. ADVISERS? ACTIVITIES BEYOND THE BATTALION

I was to be followed later at Binh Ba by a fellow 5 RAR officer, Captain Ron Bade, whose experiences are related in the following section of this chapter. His circumstances were different to mine and neither of us became aware of each other's time at Binh Ba until many months had passed. Nonetheless, both of us drew conclusions early in our separate experiences that there was a need for astute caution when working at the lower level of US – South Vietnamese relations in Phuoc Tuy Province.

Ron Bade

My one big regret about my time in Vietnam was that I did not keep a diary. For some reason I thought that keeping a diary with reference to operations would be a security risk. Now, as I sit and attempt to recall the events of more than 50 years ago, my one thought is, 'If only!' This means that some of my recollections about date/time details and names may not be precise; but I trust that I may be allowed some leeway. When I consider my time at Binh Ba as a temporary adviser to a Regional Force (RF) company, my only substantive date reference point is that I was there when I received news of my son's birth. He was born on 10 October 1966 and a day or so afterwards a Royal Australian Air Force Iroquois landed on the airfield beside the compound and our CO, John Warr, accompanied by Tony White, Peter Isaacs and Bob O'Neill, jumped out of the helicopter, shook my hand, congratulated me, gave me a copy of the telegram and promptly departed. It was a shame they couldn't have stayed that night as the birth of my son was celebrated with great gusto by the Vietnamese troops. Having a son as first-born is considered very auspicious in Vietnamese culture. The troops expended short air-bursts of small arms fire and coloured flares in lieu of fireworks. My concern that night was that the celebrations would have been a beacon for any enemy operating in the vicinity. Fortunately, nothing happened.

How and when did I get to Binh Ba? I have trawled through the battalion's operations logs as they appear on the Australian War Memorial website and I can find little that indicates dates or the events preceding my moving to Binh Ba. However, looking through the battalion's list of operations, the dates of Operation Darlinghurst or Operation Toledo are the most likely. I was operating the administration cell located forward with battalion HQ, which was harboured in the rubber plantation to the south of Binh Ba. As officer on watch in the APC-mounted command post during the night, my signaller received a call from Task Force HQ to 'Fetch Sunray' (John Warr). After speaking with Task Force HQ, John Warr told us of the impending arrival of an ARVN RF company at Binh Ba the following day. He also said that as advisers from the AATTV were not immediately available, the battalion was to provide a liaison officer (LO) for 48 hours. When I asked who was to be the LO, I was not surprised that it was to be me. At that stage I did not know that my 48 hours was to extend to more than two months!

The next day it struck me that there was a singular lack of communication between the various parties involved in the move of the RF company. What was the mission of the company? If I recall correctly, no formal operation order existed or, if it did, it had not percolated to my level. It seemed that, although Task Force HQ had requested 5 RAR to provide an LO, command of the RF company was to be exercised by the local district chief, Dai Uy (Captain) Nguyen Van Be, based at subsector HQ in Duc Thanh. Also in Duc Thanh was a US Army adviser, Major Bill Prescott, and his team which included US enlisted men and Australian WOs. However, Major Prescott was obviously confined to an advisory role. My team consisted of Warrant Officer 'Sooty' Smith from the Task Force Civil Affairs Unit, a 5 RAR signaller, Private Ron 'Frenchy' Delaurey-Simpson, my batman, a Land Rover with driver and an interpreter, Sergeant Mick Henry (not to be confused with the 5 RAR armourer Sergeant Mick Henrys). My role as an LO was somewhat unclear. Was I simply there for liaison or was I to assume an advisory role? Sooty Smith and I quickly determined that self-preservation dictated that we needed to act as advisers – welcome or not!

When the RF company arrived, I was surprised to see that the soldiers were a pretty rag-tag bunch and that many had arrived with accompanying wives and children. What on earth does one do with wives and children in a defence compound? The company commander, Second Lieutenant Truong, told me that the company had been based not far from Saigon and, being a RF company, it had not expected to be moved out of the district in which it had been raised. Consequently, many of the troops and their families were very upset at moving to Binh Ba. The extent of their upset became very evident during the next couple of days!

The site chosen for the RF company was the vacant villa on the north side of the Gallia plantation airfield on the northern edge of Binh Ba. The site comprised a two-storey masonry villa with a long single-storey building

11. ADVISERS? ACTIVITIES BEYOND THE BATTALION

behind. I decided that my team would occupy the villa and that the RF company could utilise the other building. This was reluctantly agreed to by Truong. The immediate task was to determine how the company would occupy the site. I discussed the defensive position with Truong and talked about all-round defence and mutual support. However, he was committed to the old, discredited French concept of a triangular redoubt. Despite my remonstrations about his decision, a triangle it was. I thought to myself 'Thank goodness I will only be here for 48 hours!' How wrong was I.

Next morning, I discovered that some of the troops had deserted during the night. I reported this to John Warr and said that the company commander had told me that it would be difficult to prevent further desertions as the troops were very unhappy about the move. Next day, a few more had deserted so John came to the villa in an APC and had me parade the company before him. He spoke through my interpreter telling the RF personnel that anyone else who deserted would be shot. As he spoke, Lieutenant Ross Guymer, in the cupola of his APC, traversed his .50 calibre machine gun back and forth across the assembled company. We had no further desertions!

Forty-eight hours had elapsed and there was no sign of advisers arriving to relieve my team. It was time to discuss roles and routines with Truong. The placement of the company in Binh Ba was obviously designed to deter Viet Cong activity in the village and to provide a measure of protection for the inhabitants. Our first task was to develop the defensive position. Digging weapon pits and a perimeter communication trench commenced, but progress was extremely slow. When we discussed the lack of progress with individuals, the response was always that they were very tired from their move. Of more concern for troops with families was the erection of some form of shelter for their families behind the weapon pits – a novel concept. When it came to daily routine in the position, Truong had little idea of morning or evening stand-to (changing between day and night routines) or the need for clearing patrols to clear the area outside the perimeter. He did agree that he would give this a try, but it was a dismal failure. The chatter from the compound during stand-to was non-stop and the clearing patrols would not venture further than keeping in sight of the compound.

If our activity extended beyond the compound there was obvious potential for conflict between the RF company and elements of 5 RAR operating at the same time in the Binh Ba area. Consequently, Task Force HQ gave the RF company a mini-TAOR (tactical area of responsibility) within the Task Force TAOR. This was a large part of the Gallia plantation area north of the airfield. Now, with a defined TAOR, it was my task to get the company out on operations. This turned out to be far more difficult than I expected.

One of the first operations was a cordon and search of a part of Binh Ba village. Truong and I agreed that we would leave our compound and be in place before daybreak. When the day came, the troops milled around the gate of the compound and it was obvious that they had no desire to move out of the compound in the dark. We eventually left the compound as dawn broke. Inevitably, the troops were seen moving into the cordon, so the operation was fruitless. However, Truong was quite excited that they had completed the operation and invited Sooty Smith and me to join his officers and NCOs for a belated breakfast in one of the village food stalls. I can still remember the portions of duck hacked with a cleaver and the splinters of bone therein.

Patrols of our mini-TAOR were pretty much as disappointing as the cordon and search. I had the feeling that the troops had no desire to be outside the compound and they invariably made lots of noise. One wonders if the noise was just ill-discipline or made in the hope that any enemy would hear them and avoid contact. My concern, when I was with them, was that their noise would attract enemy that they were not capable of engaging effectively.

Once I was told that the AATTV advisers would not be coming for some time, we decided to make the old villa as liveable as possible. Our first task was to clear the villa floors of an accumulated ten-centimetre layer of dead black beetles. Happily, we discovered that the toilet on the upper floor would flush by using a bucket of water. The original wooden 'thunder box' latrine that we had purloined from somewhere was no longer useable after troops and their families had 'kangarooed' on the seat with muddy feet! With US steel fence pickets that we obtained from Major Prescott's team, and the help of a welder from the Gallia plantation workshop, we fashioned a frame from which we could suspend a canvas shower bucket. The frame had a base made from pickets that allowed us to shower above

11. ADVISERS? ACTIVITIES BEYOND THE BATTALION

the mud. We slept on breath-inflated mattresses on the tiled floor. This was quite comfortable, but we did bounce around somewhat when there was a B-52 bombing raid anywhere nearby.

While we were settling in, the company continued to develop our compound. Beyond their original concertina wire obstacle, they built barbed wire fences and then proceeded to lay a minefield of M16 'jumping jack' anti-personnel mines. These were armed and connected to tripwires which would be the undoing of a couple of the troops a short time later. One afternoon I heard several shots from within the compound. They turned out not to be accidental discharges, as had occurred several times already, but were attempts to kill one of the dogs which had strayed in from the Gallia plantation. Two soldiers ran out the front gate of the compound and around the minefield perimeter fence to where an apparently dead dog was laying. As one of them picked up the dog it latched on to one of the men – it was only stunned by the bullet! To get away from the dog, the men ran headlong towards the compound – straight into the minefield! Some mines were triggered but, miraculously, both men escaped unhurt. As we watched from the upstairs balcony of the villa, we were dumbfounded.

We were visited quite often by the district chief, Dai Uy (Captain) Be, usually accompanied by some of Major Prescott's team from Duc Thanh. However, information on what was going on around the district was generally scarce. Sooty Smith and I made periodic visits to Messieurs Pernes and Moreau, the manager and engineer at the Gallia plantation, but, although these visits were always cordial, they were of little intelligence value. One got the impression that both men were intent on appearing 'neutral' to be able to carry on business at the plant. As far as information from the Task Force HQ or 5 RAR was concerned, I was kept informed of any plans that might impact my TAOR, but otherwise we were on our own and we felt a bit like the forgotten few. We also visited Father Joseph, the Catholic priest at Binh Ba. He was able to provide limited helpful information on what had been going on in the village, but he was always concerned that he would be branded an informer by local Viet Cong.

Working through an interpreter is always difficult so I knew that I was lucky to have Mick Henry with me. I knew I could guarantee he would tell me what he understood of Be's or Truong's statements, not what a local interpreter might be inclined to pass on – probably what they thought I wanted to hear. Unfortunately, one day Mick said something to Dai Uy

Be that Be felt was an insult, so he declined to communicate any further through Sergeant Henry. Fortunately, my French-speaking signaller, Ron Simpson, was able to communicate with both Be and Truong in French. This also forced me to resurrect my Year 12 schoolboy French when Be insisted in addressing me in French. Mick Henry, being of no further use, returned to Task Force HQ.

Administrative support from 5 RAR was quite minimal. I resorted to doing a run back to 5 RAR down Route 2 about once a week in my Land Rover, hoping to not run into an ambush. Doing this was a little scary but we were lucky and encountered no problems. We were able to collect clean clothes, pick up our mail and, with the help of the caterer, Warrant Officer Peter Roby, we were able to scrounge rations to keep us alive for another week. It is interesting to note that, during the year after 5 RAR returned home, the AATTV advisers at Binh Ba were ambushed doing the same run as I had done, and I understand that at least two were killed.

Another aspect of the RF company came to light one evening when I was moving around the weapon pits during stand-to. Several families stated that they were very hungry and that they had little or no food. This surprised me as I had seen sacks of rice arriving in the compound and I had seen troops supplementing the rice with fish and greens from the local market as well as plants foraged outside the compound. I raised the issue of hunger with Truong and he informed me that he received the salaries and rice ration for all members of the company and he then distributed both as he saw fit. It was obvious that if any member dissented they were punished with reduced salary or rice ration or both. I said that I felt that restricting rice ration was hardly fair, but my comments fell on deaf ears. Perhaps this was the only real sanction available to him to maintain discipline over his coterie of soldiers and their dependants, but one unlikely to reinforce either his popularity or his personal safety.

Later, I was invited to travel to Sector HQ at Ba Ria with Truong and some of his officers. We braved Route 2 once more with arms bristling out of several vehicles. The conference at Sector HQ gave me the impression that the US advisory staff there were not really interested in the RF and that little was expected of my RF company other than to be a presence at Binh Ba. Following the conference, Truong invited me to his home in Ba Ria for lunch. I hadn't expected that he would have had a house in Ba Ria – maybe the real reason to visit Sector HQ was to be able to see his wife and family! His home was a modest house, but it was nicely furnished and extremely well kept. Lunch was an extremely tasty Vietnamese banquet served by his domestic staff while his troops kept guard outside. On the run back to Binh Ba, I started to wonder about how much of the salary and sustenance moneys entrusted to him went to his troops.

It would be remiss of me to conclude this story without mentioning the disciplinary regime in the company. One day in a corner of the compound some troops built a strange structure. It was a collection of short steel pickets driven into the ground and then interlaced with barbed wire to form a box shape about 2 metres square and 30 centimetres high. This was the lockup for troops being punished. They were made to crawl into the structure and the entrance sealed. They could do no more than lie on the grass and were often left there overnight or for several days. Often, when they were released, they were subjected to a beating with a long cane wielded by a couple of burly troops. Those notables gave the impression of being Truong's bodyguard. This was not a form of justice found in the Australian Army!

In my opinion the establishment of the RF compound at Binh Ba did little to assist the effort to engage and destroy the Viet Cong. In many ways it was just a waste of valuable resources. I suspect that enemy activity in Binh Ba continued unhindered despite the arrival of the RF company. My tenure at Binh Ba ended when a team of AATTV advisers finally arrived unannounced with a truckload of home comforts and told us that we could return to 5 RAR. My 48 hours there had extended to over two months!

Many years later, in 2008, my wife and I toured Vietnam. We went to Vung Tau for two nights and engaged a local guide to take us to Nui Dat. Our female guide was quite knowledgeable but when we got to Binh Ba she was not familiar with the old village as it now nestles west of the new town. We eventually got a couple of local boys to guide us through the old village and through a cashew plantation to where our RF compound had been. It looked totally different. The villa had been demolished and the building materials used by the locals. The airstrip had gone and the whole area had been replanted with small rubber plants. A very bright blue shack had been erected on the base of the old villa by an old couple who were replanting the rubber. As we spoke with them, he took me around the base of the villa describing the columns of the porch and where the stairs to the upper floor had been. It was without doubt the site of my villa.

As we posed for a photo with the couple, he declared that he had been a Viet Cong supporter, and his wife then added, 'Me too'. We shook hands and agreed that we were enemies no more. When I asked what had happened to the minefield, one of the many onlookers who had gathered around us raced off and came back with an unbelievably rusty M16 mine. After suggesting he take it well away I asked how the minefield had been cleared. The wife straightaway grabbed a stick, got down on her knees and demonstrated how she and others had prodded for the mines and neutralised the firing mechanisms – a very dicey undertaking but, perhaps, a demonstration of the futility of laying mines! However, it was great to have gone back 40 years later and reminisced about a significant chapter in my army career.

Conclusion by Robert O'Neill

Although they produced little of measurable effect on warfighting efforts in Phuoc Tuy province, the sojourns of Captains Boxall and Bade early in 5 RAR's tour were useful in that they provided the battalion with a close insight into life at the village level as well as better awareness of the machinations of disparate military and civil authorities in and around 1 ATF's bailiwick. It was a complex war, particularly at the level of South Vietnamese – US relations. Australia was a clear step down from this top layer of interaction, so it was important for us to have the direct assessments that could be derived only from the personal experience of two young officers inserted into this structure – particularly as it was a structure that did not fit together anywhere near as smoothly as its makers had intended.

23. 5 RAR soldiers patrolling through the secondary growth of an unworked rubber plantation.
Source: Neil Ordner.

24. A platoon of C Company filling water bottles from a jungle stream while the surrounding area is secured by the rest of the company. Each platoon would take it in turns to resupply with water while protected by the others.

Source: Neil Ordner.

25. November 1966: Helicopter insertion into Long Son Island on Operation Hayman. A US Army UH Iroquois helicopter is carrying 5 RAR soldiers who are not strapped in, some sitting on the floor. This was to effect quick emplaning, maximum passenger loading, and quick exiting at destinations. The rearmost passenger (facing outwards) is one of the aircraft's two door gunners. The altitude of the aircraft indicates that these aircraft were transiting above the range of effective small arms ground fire.

Source: Neil Ordner.

26. Lance Corporal Gordon Meredith leading 9 Platoon in the shake-out after dismounting from Armoured Personnel Carriers into open terrain during the dry season. The battlefield was not all dark, dank and wet. The hills in the distance are the rocky, jungle-clad Nui Thi Vai and Nui Dinh complexes.

Source: Neil Ordner.

27. October 1966: Preparing for the evacuation by Sioux helicopter of Captain Brian Le Dan who was wounded during Operation Queanbeyan (see Chapter 7). The aircraft later returned to the same difficult landing site to recover the body of Corporal Norm Womal. The picture shows (left to right) the pilot Second Lieutenant Bob Askew, Captain Bob Supple and Captain Brian Le Dan holding a fresh wound dressing to his chest.

Source: Unknown.

28. November 1966: Captain Ron Boxall, in command of D Company during Operation Hayman.

Source: Ron Boxall.

29. Second Lieutenant Bob Askew and Captain Jim Campbell DFC. Two of 161 (Independent) Reconnaissance Flight's Sioux pilots who gave outstanding service to 5 RAR throughout 1966–67 (see Chapters 7 and 14).

Source: Bob Askew.

30. November 1966: D Company's artillery forward observer, Lieutenant Barry Campbell, and 10 Platoon's commander, Second Lieutenant Dennis Rainer MC, who had worked closely together during 10 Platoon's attack on 21 October (see Chapter 7).

Source: Ron Boxall.

31. Second Lieutenant Michael Deak MC at work.

Source: Darryl Henry.

32. This photograph of the Reconnaissance Platoon typifies the fighting soldiers of 5 RAR's first tour of Vietnam in 1966–67. The list of absentee names shows that platoons were usually deployed understrength. *Rearmost man*: Daniel 'Bluey' Riley; *Fourth Row*: Dave Western, Robert 'Bobby' Godfrey, John 'Macca' McLaren, Darryl 'Butch' Moroney; *Third Row*: Walter 'Jock' Brannan, Robert 'Dogs' Kearney, Robert 'Bob' Searl, Barney Gambold, David 'Maxy' Campbell, Glen 'Moose' Benham; *Second Row*: Ken 'Scaisey' Scaysbrook, John 'Scalesy' Scales, Wayne 'Pagey' Page, Denis 'Millsey' Mills, William 'Suave Harve' Harvey, Gary 'BG' Nottage; *Front Row*: John 'Blah' Williams, John 'Blue' Edwards, David 'Blue' Wollner, Mick 'Skip' Deak MC, Raymond 'Ferret' Ferrier, John 'Blue' Mulby, Robert 'Bobby' Egan (Brandt), Bruce 'Jacka' Aitken; *Absent*: John Lea-Smith, Bernie Smith, Peter 'Doc' Fraser MM, Ray 'Skinny' Calvert, Trevor 'Taffy' Cheeseman, Anthony 'Bluey' Twaits, William 'Billy' Evans.

Source: Mick Deak (Michael von Berg).

33. January 1967: The officers of 5 RAR at Nui Dat: *Rear*: 2Lt L O'Dea, 2Lt MJ Roe, Lt DJF Rowe, Capt. RB Milligan, Capt. WJ Molloy, Capt. JE Taske (on exchange with Capt. HAD White), Lt TJ Sheehan, Capt. RW Bade, Capt. RJ O'Neill, Lt GR Wainwright, 2Lt RR Gunning, 2Lt DG Lovell, 2Lt HT Neesham, 2Lt AE Pott; *Standing*: Capt. RT Shambrook, Lt J Carruthers, 2Lt MGJ Deak, Chap JF Williams, Mr J Bentley (Salvation Army), Capt. RW Supple, Lt GN Negus, 2Lt JD Mcaloney, Capt. KG Mallinson, Capt. RG Thompson, Capt. BG Le Dan, 2Lt DC Rainer, Capt. RE Boxall; *Seated*: Maj. PG Cole, Maj. JF Miller, Maj. OM Carroll, Maj. IRJ Hodgkinson, Lt Col. JA Warr, Capt. PJ Isaacs, Maj. MB Mcqualter, Maj. PN Greenhalgh, Maj. RD Hamlyn. *Absent*: Capt. HAD White, Lt JC Hartley, 2Lt JH Deane-Butcher, 2Lt RJ Davis.

Source: The 5 RAR Association website, www.5rar.asn.au.

34. November 1966: Dai Uy (Captain) Nguyen Van Be and Captain Ron Bade at Binh Ba. Private Ron 'Frenchy' Delaurey-Simpson is standing between the two bare-chested soldiers on the left (see Chapter 11).

Source: Ron Bade.

35. Late 1966: Second Lieutenant John Deane-Butcher on patrol with his platoon. They had just located an enemy cache of new shovels which they are retrieving. The men are carrying outdated 1937 pattern backpacks.

Source: Terry Tomassi.

36. October 1966: Battalion Headquarters on operations on Nui Thi Vai. Major Max Carroll is on the radio in the front trench (right) with the battalion's senior command post signaller, Corporal Dave Western, recording his conversation. Assisting in the rear trench are Captain Bob Supple (left) and a 1 ATF signaller.

Source: Bob O'Neill.

37. February 1967: Major Ivor 'Blue' Hodgkinson (5 RAR's second in command from December 1966), Captain Bob O'Neill (intelligence officer), Captain Peter Isaacs (adjutant) and Major Ron Hamlyn (officer commanding Administration Company) after a conference with the Commanding Officer, Lieutenant Colonel John Warr.

Source: Bob O'Neill.

38. 5 RAR's Operations Officer, Major Max Carroll, and the commander of 103 Field Battery, Major Neville Gair, at a time when that battery was allocated in direct support of the battalion.

Source: Bob O'Neill.

39. July 1966: Wet season conditions were experienced for several weeks during construction of 5 RAR's base at Nui Dat.

Source: Terry Tomassi.

40. Intelligence Officer Captain Bob O'Neill briefing soldiers in 5 RAR's open-air theatre, 'The Mayfair'.

Source: Terry Tomassi.

41. October 1966: Pilot Second Lieutenant Bill Davies, being stretchered to a waiting aeromedical evacuation helicopter for transportation to a US neurosurgical facility in Saigon after being shot down in his Sioux Helicopter, the wreckage of which is strewn along Route 15 (see Chapter 14).

Source: Terry Tomassi.

42. 'The Rat Pack', a group of 9 Platoon members: (left to right) Private John Reynolds, Private Neil Selleck, Private Bob Antonio, Private Roger Sinclair, Lance Corporal Gordon Meredith, Private Danny Cross and Lance Corporal Peter Blanch.

Source: Terry Tomassi.

43. Late 1966: Corporal Bob 'Dogs' Kearney, reflecting while on a break from patrolling in the jungle.

Source: Unknown.

44. December 1966: The Commanding Officer serving Christmas dinner to men of C Company. Lieutenant Colonel John Warr is discussing the menu (designed by Lance Corporal Brian Budden) with Lance Corporal Warren Burns. Sitting directly opposite is Private Danny Cross, and at bottom right is Private Barry Delsar. At left of Burns is Corporal Terry Tueno. On his left, with glasses, is Private John Buhagiar. Standing behind the Commanding Officer is Private Tom Brand. The men at the left foreground are Privates Roger Sinclair and John Fitzgerald.

Source: Australian War Memorial, COL/66/1023/VN.

12

FIRE SUPPORT: 103 FIELD BATTERY ROYAL AUSTRALIAN ARTILLERY IN ACTION

George Bindley, John Griggs, Peter Aspinall,
Doug Heazlewood and Brian Mortimer

Editors' introduction

This chapter is an integration of five contributions by members of the artillery battery which directly supported 5th Battalion, the Royal Australian Regiment (5 RAR), operations in October and November 1966, 103 Field Battery of 1 Field Regiment, Royal Australian Artillery (RAA). The Vietnam War relationship between an Australian infantry battalion and its directly supporting artillery (usually a battery in support of each battalion) was extremely important for both. For the infantry, the artillery was a powerful mobile defence against an attacking enemy and an aggressive multiplier of combat power. For the artillery, their security depended partially on protective infantry, both located with their gun positions and in maintaining control of the battlefield more widely. It was very important for both sides of this partnership that they had high confidence in each other. Lives hinged on how well this mutual dependence was accepted, valued and practised.

We, 5 RAR, had had four months of working with 103 Field Battery, and they had our fullest confidence. The battery was equipped with six Italian-designed OTO Melara L5 105 mm pack howitzers. These guns were compact and could be disassembled for transportation by Iroquois helicopter. They could be relied upon to deliver accurate fire over ranges up to 10,000 metres. They were capable of firing in the upper register (i.e. at barrel elevations of over 45 degrees), which made them particularly useful for giving support in hilly or mountainous country. They could be fired against enemy positions and his attacking or reconnoitring forces, by day or by night. One defect was that their sights could mist up in rainy weather. Another was their relative lightness of construction, which made the gun trails liable to fracture when rounds were fired at maximum charge of propellant.

Within each of our companies, 103 Battery embedded forward observer (FO) officers, each with a bombardier assistant (FO Ack), two artillery signallers and a batman – collectively known as an FO Party. The FO Parties became an integral part of each company headquarters and shared every danger and hardship, trod every weary kilometre and were, in the deepest sense, our brothers-in-arms. When the battalion was not deployed on operations they lived with our companies in the 1st Australian Task Force (1 ATF) base at Nui Dat, and not with their own battery – they were absolutely of our ilk.

The FO Parties, moving with each of our companies when we were out on operations, kept themselves fully in the picture with every aspect of our tactics and procedures, and learned about their many nuances – to the extent that they were able to instinctively anticipate our needs and be instantly ready to call for supporting fire from their battery's guns. The FOs also had access to more powerful firepower, delivered by US heavy artillery (155 mm and 8-inch guns), and even to naval gunfire from warships within range. Through coordination with US Air Force (USAF) airborne forward air controllers, the full orchestra of integrated close air support and artillery and mortar fire could play under their batons, should this level of firepower be needed. FOs were appropriately skilled and conveniently positioned – at the side of the infantry commanders in the forefront of battle.

Another integral element of our fire support was the battalion's own Mortar Platoon. The 81 mm mortars fired a less powerful round than the 105 mm guns, but they were man-portable and could be deployed in action close to the troops they were supporting. On these operations up in the hills, our Mortar Platoon rendered great service because of their high angle of fire. This meant they were not as limited as some artillery guns which required a flatter trajectory for their shells and could have their fire masked by some of the steep, high ridges that our infantry had to fight over. Mortars have been lobbing their bombs over crests into masked terrain for hundreds of years. Nonetheless, they could not match the destructive power of our 'nine-mile snipers'.

With that age-old, infantry-conferred and affectionate sobriquet, let us now look at the problems of fighting from the gunners' perspective. First is the view of a young lieutenant who was initially a gun position officer (GPO), in charge of the guns at the point of firing, and, later, an FO.

Overview: Lieutenant John Griggs

In subsequent paragraphs, my colleagues add touches to an artillery collage of which I apply the first layer. For our esteemed infantry brothers of 5 RAR, who so often sought our wares, we hope that our group effort will reveal much about the dark art of what is now rather ancient gunnery. Some facets may have had them wondering for more than 50 years!

To start the composition, I briefly look at activity in five different gun positions, including those we used in Operations Canberra, Robin and Queanbeyan (gun positions 3, 4 and 5), to show how we operated in each of them.

Gun position 1 – Duc Thanh

I remember this village as it was the most northerly area we occupied during my time as GPO. From Duc Thanh we could cover the northern, eastern and western approaches to Nui Dat, and give support to the individual company positions occupied during patrolling operations and village cordon and search operations through the northern half of Phuoc Tuy. From memory, Duc Thanh was occupied by people resettled from North Vietnam. It wasn't a busy time firing close support missions, but I spent a considerable time in the command post (CP), getting target records up to date. Thank heavens CP lighting, via small battery-powered fluoro tubes, had improved by the time we arrived, as all target records were written in HB pencil into target record books and much of that work was done at night. These included defensive fire tasks (nicknamed tin trunks) for the troops we were supporting, and counter-mortar target records. The call for the latter fire was 'Bombard' and employed six rounds per gun FFE (fire for effect) on each suspected enemy mortar position.

'Bombard' was used powerfully during the night before the Battle of Long Tan by the whole of 1 Field Regiment, when the 1 ATF base at Nui Dat was attacked by enemy mortar fire. Each application delivered 108 rounds of HE (high explosive) 105 mm artillery shells onto each suspect location.

During each night, harassing and interdiction (H&I) missions were fired, generally being one or two guns firing one or two rounds at predetermined times on tracks or targets selected by the intelligence staff. Viet Cong (VC) prisoners stated during interrogation that they feared our unpredictable H&I fire. This was welcome feedback because the tasks were very tiring and disruptive at night for gun detachments (crews) which generally were under-manned by tired and weary gunners.

Gun position 2 – Nui Dat Base

After deployments to remote gun positions, reoccupying the 1 ATF base gun position was a time-consuming procedure. Here the battery was occupying and defending an unprotected and open approach to the Task Force headquarters (HQ) across a vast paddy field. When deployed to a gun position elsewhere, we needed to leave behind a sizeable rear detachment, thus reducing the numbers serving the guns on operations. We also did three other things: (1) set up dummy (make-believe) guns to give the impression that our base position was occupied; (2) maintained a standing patrol forward of our sector of the base's defensive wire obstacles; (3) readied the gun position for the returning guns. There were also a myriad of other tasks including preparing ammunition, unloading stores and personal gear and being ready to respond to calls for fire at all times.

Gun position 3 – Ap Ong Trinh Dc

From memory, we occupied this position during the afternoon after a road trip from Nui Dat. As I recall, the regiment's 2IC (second in command) selected the area after an air reconnaissance. Imagine my reaction later, when I found he had allocated an area for six gun platforms and a CP which was under water. From the air the water was hidden by long grass. I never forgot that episode and later as an instructor in gunnery and a battery commander I drove the lesson home to others: reconnaissance for gun positions MUST always be conducted on foot. We were quite busy in this position, but it was not suitable for a long stay and the commanding officer (CO), Lieutenant Colonel Richmond 'Dick' Cubis, had us move further along Route 15 a couple of days later.

Actually, on the day we moved, Cubis flew in around 1000 and chipped me for not having shaved. I told him how I had been busy and was yet to arrive at the shaving point in my morning routine. (The CO wasn't noted for his sense of humour.) My mornings were hectic from stand-to (the time each day, before first light, when all personnel come to an armed and fully alert status) until around 1000. My duties in changing from night to day routine included checking gun parallelism (a detailed procedure involving a theodolite to ensure that guns were aligned exactly parallel to each other), changing CP staff, giving briefings, maintaining gun records and so on. So, around 1000 was my 'birdie-bath' time, when a section commander stood in for me in the CP.

Gun position 4 – Ap Ong Trinh Dp

We moved 2 kilometres south-east into an area where we stayed for some time, in company with some larger 155 mm guns from Battery A, 2/35 US Artillery Battalion. Their H&I tasks at night were purgatory for us, as we felt the full force of the blast across our gun position when they fired. The shock wave and noise would wake the dead.

While 5 RAR was busy up in the hills, we were worried somewhat by crests (simply put, where targets might not be able to be engaged because there was a hill or ridgeline in the way). However, our howitzers were able to fire at high angle (like a mortar) so, generally, we were able to answer any call for fire. The steep hilly ground did affect the fall of shot, but that's what FOs were trained to handle.

Being alongside Route 15, we inevitably attracted local vendors selling food and drinks. We also set up showers through which our soldiers were rotated, much to the delight of locals passing by in crowded buses, which slowed down to allow passengers a good look. Incoming US troops were trucked past in convoys every day for hours at a time during daylight, but it was at night when things got a bit tricky.

For whatever reason, some South Vietnamese gunners in the village of Phu My took a dislike to the area surrounding us and the area in which 5 RAR was operating. They sent more than a few rounds our way, apparently once too often. On one occasion Lieutenant Colonel Cubis ordered my guns to load and lay on the village. Receiving this fire mission from my CO made the hairs on the back of my neck stand. I knew the location was designated as a 'no fire zone', occupied by friendly troops and civilians. I contacted our battery captain, George Bindley, and our battery commander, Major Neville Gair, for clarification. We had our signallers try to contact the US Army advisers in the Phu My area by radio to no avail. I had two signallers carefully record all fire orders and conversations, for evidence purposes, as there would have been quite an inquiry had we fired.

We did not fire, and the circumstances in which a potential catastrophe was averted are explained later in this chapter by George Bindley. A lot can go wrong in war when coordination and liaison are not up to required standards; and a hasty, unhelpful interference in operational events by a senior commander rears its head.

The return to Nui Dat after Operation Queanbeyan saw my time as GPO of 103 Field Battery come to an end. I handed over to Lieutenant Mike Langley and joined C Company, 5 RAR, (under Major John Miller) as their FO, replacing Lieutenant Kerry Mellor.

Gun position 5 – Lang Phuoc Hoa

This was my first operation as an FO. My assistant was Bombardier Dave Rose who later worked for me as a warrant officer at the School of Artillery and rose to the rank of major. Dave and I learnt a very salutary lesson while searching the village on the edge of the Rung Sat (Special Zone) before we assaulted the island of Long Son. There were calls for illumination rounds to be fired in order to light up an area offshore. Major Miller and I were standing next to an armoured personnel carrier (APC) observing over the water, which was being lit up, when we heard a strange buzzing noise. It got louder and suddenly there was a great CLANG on the APC. The noise was made by the steel inserts or sleeves which were carried in the illumination shells, to assist in ejecting the flares and parachute without damaging them. The inserts simply fell to the ground while the empty carrier shell continued in its trajectory. The firing tables would tell where the empty carriers would fall, but there was no mention of the sleeves. The lesson we learnt was 'do not have illumination rounds burst overhead'.

On that gun position the guns used a very effective deception plan to convince the enemy that 5 RAR was going to assault north into the hills rather than south onto the island. Just before H hour (the time at which an operation commences) the guns, which had been pointing north and firing H&I in that direction during the night, suddenly turned around to face the island just as the first wave of the air-mounted assault was landing.

Life as a gun section commander: Lieutenant Doug Heazlewood

I joined 103 Field Battery after a period as assistant adjutant for the first two months of 1 Field Regiment's tour of duty in Vietnam, a role for which I felt untrained and comparatively lacking in motivation. But as a section commander in 103 Battery, I felt like Brer Rabbit safe in the briar patch – happy and comfortable in the only role for which I had in any way been fully trained.

On reflection, I may have had more reason to be daunted. 103 Battery was a team in every sense of the word, being possessed of a very dedicated group of competent and professional officers and a leavening of some of the finest non-commissioned officers (NCOs) I would ever know. Many already had a grounding in active service and went on to achieve distinguished careers. The complement of gunners included many we considered to be the pick of the regular soldiers of the regiment and about 30 or more men of the first intakes of conscripted national servicemen. Their readiness training in Australia had made them into the best-performing team that I encountered, before or since. By the time I joined them, I could not discern any differences between regular and national service soldiers – I always had to ask whether a soldier was the one or the other. One of the 'nashos', Bombardier Graeme Sutherland, had already developed the competence and confidence to serve as a gun detachment commander during the most challenging task of our entire tour, the Battle of Long Tan.

Although I was their officer, and they ultimately would have to do what I said, I needed to be accepted into *their* team before my opinion was thought to matter. A vivid memory is that my first ever deployment with an artillery battery, operational or otherwise, was motoring up the 'black' route to Binh Ba as the battery leader!

I was also very pleased to learn that we were to become the direct support (DS) battery for 5 RAR, where I knew some of the officers. My belief then, borne out by the experience, was that they were a formidable team and we would have to perform very well to match them. I was greatly heartened, when it came time for us to 'rotate' from being their DS battery back to the general support role, that 5 RAR had made the very generous gesture of requesting that we be allowed to remain their DS battery until the end of their tour. I shared the pride, felt by everyone on the gun line, in the knowledge that we had earned their trust and gratitude.

With the help of our HQ battery comrades, we had played a leading role in fire support for the Battle of Long Tan, all on the gun line gaining some salutary lessons to be applied later in our tour. 5 RAR's first major excursion into the long-term task of clearing and establishing control over Phuoc Tuy Province came about in October. It was the series of operations described in this book that forced us to extend our capacity to overcome the unique problems of effective fire support for infantry offensive operations in very difficult terrain and at the further reaches of our allotted area of operations.

From the perspective of the gun line, the special problems brought about by the nature of these operations that we needed to meet and overcome included:

Optical sights

Constant, unpredictable instances of gunsights 'fogging up' had to be managed. Being called for a fire mission, only to find your sight suddenly fogged up, thus rendering the gun useless until it cleared, was not to be countenanced. This problem was accentuated during prolonged operations far away from the replacement or repair readily available at Nui Dat. Sergeant Reg Matheson's remedy was the preventive measure of making sure that his sight, when not on the gun, was in his bed, whether he was there or not.

Unstable gun platforms

This was especially a problem in the gun position first occupied for Operation Canberra, where the ground was so wet that we had to enlist the aid of APCs to get some guns into position. Once settled, they became very difficult to traverse through the large switches in bearing we needed to accommodate, with the trails burying and needing to be dug out. (The trails are the rearmost parts of the gun by which it is towed and, when in action, they 'anchor' the gun to the ground and prevent it being driven backwards when fired.) Foresight, anticipation and cooperation between gun detachments were the key elements in dealing with this problem.

Gun aiming points

The restricted size of a gun position's defensive perimeter would make it difficult to deploy gun aiming posts far enough from the gun to maintain accurate laying of the gun onto the target. We were often reduced to using paralleloscopes as the primary method of laying the guns on target, and this brought other difficulties. Innovative ways of illuminating the gunsights had to be found to accommodate the amount of night firing that was called for, and large traverses of the gun would bring the 'scope' to the 'wrong' side of the gun – very slick drills for changing and recording aiming points at night had to be perfected. The gun moving about on a soggy 'platform' added to this difficulty.

Fatigue

Gun position defensive perimeters were not fully occupied in daytime and this required the gun crews to man double sentry shifts during the day. Work required to establish and develop the gun position, the strenuous nature of engaging planned and opportunity targets and the requirement to engage in very active H&I programs during the night combined to restrict us to about four hours sleep per day for the duration of these operations.

Other hazards

In the first gun position occupied to support Operation Canberra, we were the unhappy recipients of two incoming rounds, travelling straight towards us at high velocity, and landing as close as 200 metres outside our perimeter. This happened at regular intervals for a few days. We were slightly, but not entirely, relieved to eventually learn that they were 'friendly' – coming in error from two Army of the Republic of Vietnam (ARVN) 105 mm guns located in their military compound at the village of Phu My, a few kilometres north on Route 15. They were a powerful nuisance and communication difficulties led to a predicament which could have had calamitous results, but for the calmness of John Griggs and the initiative of George Bindley. They recount their respective dilemmas, and the actions they took, elsewhere in this chapter.

These were not the only hazards encountered in providing safe and effective fire support to 5 RAR. The possibilities for error are ever-present in the application of artillery fire anywhere. They assumed an extra dimension in the very intimate support we were usually required to provide to our infantry comrades. Knowing the accurate location of the target, as well as those of the observer and the guns, was affected by the uncertain quality of the maps. Also, we had no way of knowing whether the meteorological information we were given to allow for wind, humidity and temperature was accurate. The steep slopes encountered in the Nui Thi Vai hills, exacerbated by the variety and height of the timber covering, added to the challenges of the laws of physics. It seemed that any error arising from factors beyond our control (as opposed to 'mistakes') was magnified and had the propensity to detract from the mutual trust and confidence we strove to achieve with our infantry comrades. Inevitably, there were instances of people being wounded, killed and frightened by our fire. In my memory, on no occasion during our whole tour was anyone injured by a round from our guns through a mistake in calculating firing data or in applying sight settings to the guns. The causes of such casualties were inherent hazards of the dangerous game of war; a fact that in no way diminished the devastated feelings of all involved. 103 Battery was able to maintain a good record. This was not only due to the depth of knowledge and training of all ranks, but also the dedication that I witnessed, time and again. These traits were manifested by a determination not to risk applying expedient solutions to difficult issues. The problems were there to be solved and we worked through them by applying ourselves to solutions based on application and adaption of the long-established orthodox practice which had been developed into our doctrine over generations.

Sustaining the effort

I lived on the gun position for 10 months of my tour. The unique fact of gun position life was that you were 'in action' for every hour and day of the tour. If Long Tan had taught us anything, it was that our state of readiness needed to be just as high at all times in the Nui Dat base as it was when deployed elsewhere. While the psychological pressure of being a gunner on the gun line was not the same level of that of a rifleman on patrol, it was constant – without relief. The only true rest for gun line soldiers was to get away from the gun position altogether – opportunities were rare. We lived cheek-by-jowl, night and day, and natural tensions could and did arise. That these were never allowed to impinge on required group performance is great tribute to the 'level-headedness' of all the NCOs and soldiers in the battery. I came to know and respect their profound talent to defuse occasions of raised tension. I well remember, on our penultimate day, when a 'stand-down' of four hours was declared so that we could relax as a total group. Within a few minutes of the call to take posts again, a three-battery 'fire mission regiment' was called and we were able to be first to report 'ready' one more time. They were truly a great team, and I will remember them always.

Reflections by our medical assistant: Lance Corporal Brian 'Doc' Mortimer

As the 103 Battery medic, one of my monthly duties was to participate in the medical civil aid program, or MEDCAP. A helicopter flew us to a village for a working session of around four hours, after which the helicopter would return us to base. For these village calls, I would take my basic medical pannier with me, enabling me to conduct an army-type sick parade for the villagers.

I would see around 30 people, treating basic health problems such as cuts, sore throats and minor local infections. Children would sometimes feign a sore throat so they could get lozenges. Those I determined needed to be reviewed by a medical officer would be seen later by the regimental medical officer (RMO), Captain John Taske, or his replacement, Captain Ted Heffernan.

On one of these MEDCAP visits, an old Vietnamese gentleman had a cyst the size of a tennis ball on his chest excised by the RMO, Captain Ted ('When-in-doubt, Cut-it-out') Heffernan without any local anaesthetic. Sutures were not available, so the village tailor provided cotton to close the wound. On subsequent visits, I found the patient to have healed very well. On another visit, some of us had the pleasure of being guests at a Vietnamese wedding. The wedding feast included plenty of meat, but as it was probably dog, routinely consumed in villages throughout Vietnam, I stuck with the rice and 'risky' salad.

I recall our battery being deployed in support of 5 RAR in October 1966. We were located on Route 15, the main road to Saigon. It was a busy road and the guns were only metres from the traffic. Many buses would travel past, loaded with people, some strapped to the roof, along with produce and luggage. The traffic was nonstop until last light when a curfew came into effect. At stand-to one morning, I remember seeing in the half-light a lone figure on a bicycle. He was a local food vendor and his basket was loaded with the omnipresent, locally produced and ever-popular fresh bread rolls. We affectionately called them 'heppo [hepatitis] rolls'. I can't recall how we paid for them as we never took money with us on operations.

I had been with the battery for nearly 12 months before I observed the guns firing on charge one (the lowest propellant charge) with the barrels almost vertical as the guns engaged a relatively nearby target which was masked by terrain. In this case the muzzle velocity of the round was so low I could see the blurred shape of the projectile leaving the gun.

Finally, a gruesome sight I will never forget was when we came upon makeshift shallow graves of about six VC soldiers. Due to the heat and build-up of decomposition gases, two of the corpses were observed sitting up in their graves.

Operation Canberra, 6–10 October 1966: Captain Peter Aspinall

When 103 Field Battery was allotted in direct support of 5 RAR, my FO Party and I were attached to B Company. We arrived in the B Company tent lines at Nui Dat on Sunday 28 August 1966, immediately following the completion of Operation Smithfield, the battlefield clearance operation after the Battle of Long Tan. I had been involved in both actions as the FO for A Company, 6 RAR.

On arrival in B Company lines, I met the officer commanding (OC), Major Bruce McQualter, with whom I was to form a close working relationship. This was key to ensuring the most effective use of close artillery support on operations. Initially, while in the Nui Dat lines, I shared a tent with his 2IC, Captain Bob O'Neill. During the company patrols that followed,

12. FIRE SUPPORT

I came to know the OC's patterns of thought, including what Bruce might want of close fire support by both artillery and strike aircraft. By the time of Operation Canberra, the understanding between us was instinctive.

In Operation Canberra, B Company was tasked to clear the western side of the Nui Thi Vai hill. A major feature of this hill was a steep spur line, or ridge, running from west to east up to the crest of the hill to a height of 467 metres. This spur was very steep in places, at times with a gradient of 1 in 2 or 1 in 3, and it was thickly covered by trees, vines and bushes. C Company was similarly tasked to clear an area further east of us.

On 6 October, B Company was transported by APCs along Route 15 to a point north of the village of Ap Ong Trinh Dp where we dismounted to commence our advance north to the western side of Nui Thi Vai. Initial progress was slow as we were moving through very marshy ground, at times wading in waist-deep water. My artillery task in this early phase was limited to map-registering potential defensive fire targets along our planned track and to our east, the anticipated direction from which we might be contacted by the enemy.

By mid to late morning on 8 October, C Company to our east had advanced to the southern slopes of Nui Thi Vai and contacted the enemy, resulting in a number of casualties requiring evacuation. This action heightened the expectation of Major McQualter that B Company was likely to make contact as we moved around the south-western spur of Nui Thi Vai and approached the main west-to-east spur line from the south.

Not only did this spur rise steeply from west to east, it had steep slopes either side of the ridgeline. This posed a major difficulty in planning defensive fire targets, as the minor variations in the trajectory of each round fired, inherent in all artillery fire, could result in rounds impacting below the crest, or carrying over the spur's crest, well into the next gully or re-entrant. This problem was exacerbated by our west–east spur lying almost at right angles to the bearing from the gun position. A graphic demonstration of this situation occurred during a later operation when the FO attached to another company endeavoured to engage a target on a similarly placed spur line. When he ordered 'fire for effect', some rounds cleared the top of the spur line, only to fall into another company's area.

By mid-afternoon B Company was climbing the southern slope of the spur with the intention of crossing to the northern side. Major McQualter halted the company and called me forward and told me that the leading platoon had detected a group of VC estimated to be around 30 strong. He was sending reconnaissance groups to confirm the location and strength of the VC and, as it appeared that they might be preparing to depart, he was also anxious to deploy the company as quickly as possible to attack and prevent them escaping.

He gave orders to his platoons for a company attack and, although I was extremely concerned about the likely fall of shot for the reasons outlined, I rapidly created a comprehensive fire plan and sent it to the gun position. As the platoons deployed, the company headquarters moved to a more advantageous location. However, in doing so we found ourselves among booby trap tripwires that the VC had set. It was remarkable that none were tripped. When Bruce was comfortable with his company's dispositions, he radioed his CO, Lt Col John Warr, that he was about to commence the attack. But the CO ordered him to hold his position. After a delay the CO called off the attack. While I was located close to Bruce, I could not hear the CO's instructions; but the look of disbelief on Bruce's face was clear.

Though nothing was said, based on our close relationship, I was certain he was on the verge of ordering his platoons to attack anyway; and then advising the CO that it was too late to comply with his order to desist. McQualter's discipline prevailed and he ordered his platoons to withdraw. For a considerable time, his demeanour betrayed his frustration and disappointment, which he later conveyed to me after the company had harboured for the night.

The company headquarters had difficulty extricating itself from among the tripwires; however, it did so without incident. Once clear of the immediate vicinity of the enemy the area was comprehensively engaged with mortar and artillery fire, then with USAF airstrikes as described in Chapters 7 and 14. After these engagements, it was too late in the day for any follow-up action by B Company. The next day it was confirmed that any VC who might have survived the bombardment had left the area. Much damage had been done and important information, equipment and other materiel was recovered, along with evidence of significant enemy casualties.

5 RAR's task of securing a part of Route 15 by clearing the Nui Thi Vai hill feature had been successful. However, it was not the success that might have been achieved had Bruce McQualter bowed to what I think was his first instinct, to disobey his CO. On the other hand, very recent intelligence from credible sources had been hand delivered to CO 5 RAR,

by the Task Force HQ's intelligence officer. It revealed that the enemy strength was probably more than the 30 that B Company estimated to have been present. If this information was correct, the task was too big for a company attack in terrain where it would be extremely difficult for 5 RAR's other companies to move rapidly to B Company's assistance if it was needed.

Operation Hayman: Captain George Bindley

While Operation Hayman took place shortly after 5 RAR's operations in the Nui Thi Vai hills, the following narrative is included as a sequel to illustrate the tensions that can develop between commanders who are each intent on doing their job, often under considerable pressure and amid a host of complexities. These tensions, sometimes exacerbated by personality conflicts extending over a series of incidents, can result in a senior officer being relieved of his command in battle – as was the outcome here.

Operation Hayman started on 8 November with 5 RAR flying in to Long Son Island from a landing zone close to Lang Phuoc Hoa village on the mainland. Crucially for some, this was the first time 1 ATF Tactical HQ deployed away from Nui Dat. I was battery captain, 103 Field Battery RAA. We were located on the mainland, close to Lang Phuoc Hoa, in direct support of 5 RAR. Two days later I flew to the island to join 5 RAR's HQ and take over as acting battery commander.

I arrived at 5 RAR's HQ, located adjacent to the Task Force HQ, where I joined the CO, Lieutenant Colonel John Warr, and Major Stan Maizey, his operations officer. C Company, 6 RAR, commanded by Major Brian McFarlane, was deployed to provide local defence for the Task Force HQ complex. The Task Force HQ's Defence and Employment (D&E) Platoon was also placed under McFarlane's command. 1 Field Regiment's Tactical HQ, under Lieutenant Colonel Cubis, was also making its first operational deployment, and was located with the Task Force HQ group.

During the night 10/11 November, the D&E Platoon sergeant reported that there was a largish number of enemy to his front moving towards his position. Brian McFarlane decided to use guns rather than mortars to engage them. His FO, Captain Tony Wales of 161 Field Battery RNZA (Royal New Zealand Artillery), opened fire adjustment a safe distance away on a point previously recorded by US Army medium artillery that afternoon. I switched my set onto the battery radio net to monitor progress with the fire mission. With overhead fire, artillery rounds at the end of their trajectory are moving away from the force they are supporting. By contrast, if a target is between our own troops and the guns, as it was in this case, the noise of rounds heading straight for you can be unnerving. The sky was overcast with a low cloud base amplifying the roar of rounds approaching the target. An idea of the experience is provided by Brian McFarlane in his book *We Band of Brothers – A True Australian Adventure Story*:

> The Sergeant gave me a clear indication of how much to drop the fire towards him and we did it, and again, and again. He told me that the fire was approaching the area where the enemy troops were and we agreed on a small drop in range and to 'Fire for Effect' … by this time all those in the various headquarters and in my company were wishing they had dug deeper trenches as the noise of the rounds exploding on the rocky ground was horrendous and some shrapnel and bits of rock were whistling through the air but not too desperately for those of us who were used to such things.[1]

Soon after the fire mission started, I received a call from 1 Field Regiment's Tactical HQ duty officer. He said the CO was unhappy with how the mission was being controlled. I explained that it was normal observed fire, and control was the FO's responsibility. And, although the sound of incoming shells might be a bit uncomfortable, that too was normal. The mission continued with, of course, **drop** corrections for range, which took the point of impact further away from the HQ complex.

Then, shortly afterwards Lieutenant Colonel Cubis called me by field telephone: 'What net are you on?' 'Battery sir.' 'You bloody idiot, MET – Mike Echo Tango!' 'Oh, you mean met [meteorological data]. We are not using any. None is available.' 'Apply a drop correction of 200 metres [to the range between guns and target] and tell the FO I want to see him in the morning.' Still fuming, he hung up. I did not relay this message to Tony Wales. He had enough on his plate. I passed the 'meteorology' correction to the GPO, Lieutenant Mike Langley, and ordered clinometer laying to improve accuracy.

---

1   Brian McFarlane, *We Band of Brothers – A True Australian Adventure Story*, Brian W. McFarlane, Sydney, 2000, pp 309–10.

12. FIRE SUPPORT

Because the OT line (from the location of the observer, Tony Wales, calling for the fire to the target) was east to west and the guns were firing from the north, the 'met' correction effectively reduced the guns' range by 200 metres but had little effect on the real culprit which was the bearing the guns were laid on. The fire was still coming almost directly towards the headquarters agglomeration, and each OT drop correction made by Tony swung the line of fire east and closer to those headquarters. When satisfied with his fire adjustments, Tony Wales then ordered, 'fire for effect' and *nothing happened*! Then, on the battery radio net, the GPO reported, 'End of mission'. Tony had not ordered it, and I certainly didn't. I asked the GPO who had terminated the fire mission. He said that it was ordered by Colonel Cubis on the regimental radio net.

I told Colonel Warr, who was furious. Stan Maizey offered the battalion mortars, but Brian McFarlane declined, preferring the more accurate guns with such a close target. Being a mere bearer of bad news did not stop me getting a good ribbing from John Warr and Stan Maizey. Again, from his book, Brian McFarlane takes up the story from his end:

> As soon as Tony Wales gave the order, 'Fire for Effect' on the artillery regimental net, another call was broadcast:
>
> 'This is 95 Alpha [Cubis]. STOP.' The guns did not fire.
>
> Tony replied, 'My Foxhound Sunray [My infantry commander, Major McFarlane] wants to know why.'
>
> 'Because <u>my</u> Sunray says so.' replied Cubis's **operator**.[2]

Brian McFarlane's question had been ignored. He wondered how the CO of the regiment located at Task Force HQ could veto an order for fire from a forward company commander in contact with the enemy and, when asked to explain, refused to do so. The D&E Platoon reported there was still enemy movement between where the last shell had fallen and themselves. McFarlane called Brigadier Jackson, whose HQ he was defending, and explained what was happening. He was told he would get his fire. His book records:

> Again, Captain Wales ordered 'Fire.'
>
> Again, 95 Alpha ordered 'STOP.'

---

2   McFarlane, *We Band of Brothers*, pp 309–310. Emphasis added.

Again, McFarlane called the Brigadier and received the same assurance.

Again, Captain Wales ordered 'Fire.'

Nothing was heard from 95Alpha; and **the guns fired**.[3]

The reality of who was running the battle had apparently eluded Lieutenant Colonel Cubis. His intervention clearly implied a lack of confidence in the professional competence of his officers and an unwillingness to state it. He had a reputation for intervening in matters simply because he could. Others felt that, because he had been acknowledged for a good effort commanding the artillery support for the Battle of Long Tan, he believed that his pronouncements on artillery matters were incontestable, irrespective of their context, timing or effect – perhaps a sad case of incipient egomania. Whatever the cause, his actions were both faulty and dangerous.

Next morning Brigadier Jackson asked Brian McFarlane to come and see him. The brigadier apologised for what had happened and said that Cubis had been relieved of his command and when asked by Brigadier Jackson why he had intervened, he argued that, in his professional opinion, the fire was unsafe. The brigadier was not persuaded. This was not the first time that Brigadier Jackson had intervened to stop Cubis from doing something strange.

Earlier, during Operation Canberra, Cubis visited the gun position and found its siting unsuitable. He ordered a move to a better site. However, he neglected to inform or liaise with the battery commander located with HQ 5 RAR so that the move could be coordinated with the battalion's operational needs. This naturally upset the CO of 5 RAR. At the time the battalion was in sporadic contact with the enemy in the hills, and the move left them without their dedicated fire support for the significant amount of time needed to relocate the guns. Leaving aside technical reasons for relocating the guns to a better site, Cubis's arbitrary and precipitate order caused immediate concern and anger, and ongoing doubts in the minds of 5 RAR. When questioned about his intervention without consulting 5 RAR, Cubis insisted the movement/deployment of the guns was his prerogative. He would not retreat from this belief and the disputation inevitably involved Brigadier Jackson.

---

3   Ibid. Emphasis added.

12. FIRE SUPPORT

A short time later, during Operation Robin, there had been an incident that could have been catastrophic. The ARVN had two M2A2 105 mm howitzers in their compound at Phu My. During the night they were firing H&I into the Nui Thi Via hills to their south-east, uncomfortably close to 5 RAR. Despite attempts to stop it, the fire continued. Cubis decided the solution was for 103 Battery to fire a few warning rounds at the Vietnamese gunners in their compound.

I was called to the battery CP and briefed by the GPO, Lieutenant John Griggs. The guns were laid on the target ready to fire, but the Phu My area had been declared a 'no fire zone'. The implications were very serious. A series of questions sprang to mind in rapid succession: What if we received counter-battery fire in return? What if we, the ARVN or local civilians took casualties? Would we be headline news? How could we explain to an investigation that, despite being given an order we knew to be a serious violation of rules by which we were bound, we had fired on friendly troops and civilians? How could I stop it happening?

It came to me that I had seen a similar situation before. The film *Paths of Glory* (1957), Stanley Kubrick's antiwar epic, has a scene where an angry general gives an order to an artillery battery commander to fire on his own trenches. The battery commander refuses to fire unless given a written order. The general, fearing the consequences of his action and being unable to deny responsibility, backs down. This was worth a try. I spoke to the 1 Field Regiment duty officer at Nui Dat and said that I would not fire unless I received a written order. As it was the middle of the night and I was in an unsecured, remote area, my request was clearly impossible to satisfy. The alarm was raised. Brigadier Jackson was called, stepped in and stopped the rot. Thank heavens.

Now, in Operation Hayman on Long Son Island and with such recollections in mind, I called Artillery Tactical HQ next morning to ask when Cubis wanted to see Tony Wales. I was told that he had returned to the mainland and was not available. Stan Maizey then handed me a message addressed to all 1 ATF units written in longhand and signed by Major Dick Hannigan, the task force operations officer. It concluded, 'Major McDermott, 2IC of 1st Field Regiment, has assumed administrative command of the Regiment.'

It was Remembrance Day, 11 November 1966. I will never forget it!

13

THE MEDICAL PROBLEMS OF OPERATIONS IN THE HILLS

Tony White and Ian McDougall

Introduction by Ron Boxall

The aesthete Morihei Ueshiba, a veteran of the Russo–Japanese war of 1904–05 and who later became famous as an enlightened martial artist, once said, 'Loyalty and devotion lead to bravery. Bravery leads to the spirit of self-sacrifice. The spirit of self-sacrifice creates trust in the power of brotherly love'.[1] No more needs to be said to introduce a chapter which showcases men who were routinely called upon to put the welfare of mates before all else – the reader will find threads of Morihei's sentiments as a recurring theme among the following paragraphs, and in other parts of this book.

Tony White

By October 1966 – after five months in Vietnam – the battalion's physical and mental health was at its peak. The soldiers were now well acclimatised. The wet season, with its endless mud, mould and misery, was over. The incidence of fever and skin disease and the rates of non-casualty hospital admissions had fallen. Hygiene practices, including malaria prophylaxis,

---

[1] Morihei Ueshiba, *Meditation and the martial arts*, Shambhala Publications, Colorado, US, 2005, p 67.

were accepted and practised. Conditions back in the battalion lines at Nui Dat were more comfortable with amenities such as company canteens, the outdoor cinema and the Task Force concert area (the 'Dust Bowl') providing welcome distractions from relentless duty. The troops were getting used to the rhythm of one or two weeks out on operations followed by a week or two of physically demanding base development tasks and defensive patrolling. During their 12-month tour of duty, they were able to look forward to a two-day break of rest and convalescence on the beach at Vung Tau as well as one spell of five days rest and recreation elsewhere in Asia.

Medical cover for the battalion was provided by the Medical Platoon. This comprised the regimental medical officer (RMO), two staff sergeants (Mick Seats (medical) and Ayb Brown (hygiene inspector)), five corporal medical assistants (trained to basic nursing level) and the stretcher bearer/bandsmen. The RMO, staff sergeants and one corporal constituted the regimental aid post (the medical centre) at Battalion Headquarters (BHQ) when in the base area. The other corporals were distributed one for each of the four rifle companies, taking care of day-to-day medical problems. By this stage of the year, medical personnel at every level were becoming more confident in handling both casualties and sickness. Pharmaceutical resupply when out on operations was working well, ably handled by Mick Seats who remained in the regimental aid post at our Nui Dat base. Above all – for both the troops and their medical attendants – was the peace of mind from having a superb and timely helicopter aeromedical evacuation *Dustoff* system. This could enable casualties to be in hospital care within an hour of an incident, service far superior to what was available for the general population in Australia at the time.

By any measure, I was grossly under-prepared for the role of RMO of an infantry battalion on active service. At the age of 25, I had only just completed my intern year, where my surgical experience had been limited to suturing drunks in the Emergency Department and to serving as a very junior assistant in surgical operations at Sydney Hospital. I had no first aid training. A teaching hospital is no place to learn the bread-and-butter medicine that constitutes the bulk of an RMO's work; such experience is gained over a couple of years in a general practice setting. My knowledge of tropical medicine was a textbook on the subject plus a hazy recollection of one term's lectures during the medical course at Sydney University. My posting to the battalion was as a rushed, last-minute replacement, two months before our deployment to Vietnam. This meant that I was plucked out of the six-week Indoctrination Course at the School of Army Health at Week 2. The course was designed to ease the transition of young civilian doctors into the army system. Here one was taught not only aspects of military medicine, kit, uniforms and the rank structure, but also basic tactics, living in the bush, handling of weapons and so on. Missing out on this part of my education was a major handicap. I had been in my school Sea Cadets in Kenya and a pilot officer in the Cambridge University Air Squadron, but there were huge gaps in my knowledge of the military culture at the time I joined the battalion. For example, I was unsure whether it was I who was to salute the regimental sergeant major or the other way around. Fortunately, I was generously supported by my fellow officers throughout.

The life of a battalion RMO on active service is one of unremitting humdrum toil punctuated by episodes of intense, sometimes extremely stressful, activity. But I was never idle. When in the Nui Dat base area between battalion operations, the day began with a sick parade which could last all morning. The most common disorder seen was skin disease, particularly fungal and bacterial infections. This was not surprising considering the relentless heat and humidity, friction from clothing and webbing equipment, and minor cuts and scratches. The troops often went days without an opportunity for showering and a change of clothes. Other common conditions included respiratory infections, orthopaedic problems (knees, backs, ankles), sexually transmitted diseases and fevers. Malaria was held in check by rigorous application of preventive measures.

My other routine duties in the base area included inspections of the battalion area with the hygiene staff sergeant. Attention to proper standards of food-handling, garbage disposal, latrines and so on may sound unglamorous but, if neglected, has often resulted in outbreaks of disease which can impact more on manpower than battle casualties. Other duties included reporting on the health situation in the battalion and among the civilians attending village clinics. There were debriefing and training sessions with medical assistants and stretcher bearers, discussions with the commanding officer and company commanders and – transport permitting – trips to the hospitals in Vung Tau to visit battalion members and liaise with the doctors. As RMO, I understood the importance of getting out of the regimental aid post as much as possible and taking every opportunity to visit companies to discuss medical problems, debrief after incidents and get to know – and be known by – the soldiers. A large commitment of time and effort was the Medical Civic Action Program in which I ran clinics for civilians in neighbouring villages.

This relatively routine schedule back in the base area could be shattered on occasion, calling for an adrenaline-filled sprint. One such instance was early one morning when two grenades were accidentally discarded into a pit in which a fire was burning. There was an impressively loud explosion but fortunately the injuries to bystanders were slight. At the other extreme was a horrific accidental shooting. I was engaged in paperwork at the regimental aid post one afternoon when I was summoned by an out-of-breath runner. I ran flat out up to a tent in B Company lines to find a soldier with a massive gaping wound in his chest. He was beyond help. Close by on the floor lay his mate, pounding the ground with his fist and howling with grief. They had been handling a non-issue shotgun when it discharged, with a disastrous consequence. The two were close friends and the dead soldier had been the other's best man at his wedding before they embarked for Vietnam. On return to Australia the dead man was to have married his mate's sister-in-law. There was a sequel to compound this tragic event. Three months later, the survivor of the shooting was himself to lose his life when the patrol of armoured personnel carriers in which he was travelling ran into a minefield. Six other soldiers were also killed and 27 wounded. Two of these – the company commander and platoon commander – were to die of their wounds over the following week. It was an utterly harrowing scene, with the casualties spread over an area the size of a tennis court. Assisted by the one surviving medic – himself wounded – I found myself almost overwhelmed by the needs of the casualties and their sheer number. Of course, the knowledge that we were walking and working in a minefield made for an hour of terror pending the arrival of *Dustoff* casualty evacuation helicopters and sappers to clear the remaining mines. This catastrophe – the biggest minefield incident in Australia's involvement in the Vietnam war – was certainly the worst incident of my army service. I found all encounters with casualties extremely distressing. A summons to 'fetch Starlight' (the radio call sign of the RMO and medics) would fill me with dread. There was no knowing what lay in wait except the certainty that it would be awful.

13. THE MEDICAL PROBLEMS OF OPERATIONS IN THE HILLS

In any discussion of the Medical Platoon, the Battalion Band merits special mention. Numbering 25 and under the command of bandmaster Warrant Officer Bob Taylor, they were a disparate group. Eight had served an apprenticeship at the army School of Music; others had musical experience at school, church or in community bands. Their instruments were cornets, horns, trombone, euphonium, tuba, saxophone and percussion. When not out on operations the band was in constant demand, playing at ceremonial parades, church services, memorials, hospitals and, on visits to villages, as part of the civic action program.

As well as their infantry and musical duties, bandsmen also had basic first aid training to provide care for casualties when out on operations. Allocated one per platoon (30 men), they were officially known as stretcher bearers, a hangover from the 19th century when the retrieval of casualties from the battlefield was becoming formalised. At that time any non-combatant, including bandsmen, would be mustered to the task of clearing the dead and wounded from the battlefield.

The practice was taken up by the fledgling Australian Commonwealth Military Force and a General Order in 1902 ordained that 'all bandsmen, in addition to their duties as such, should be trained as stretcher bearers and should be allocated to companies in time of war'.

In past wars – and even to some extent within the battalion in the early days – there was an initial widespread belief that bandsmen/stretcher bearers were shirkers, not real soldiers. The fact that they were musicians may have further contributed to this attitude. Such disdain was soon banished once their dedication and courage became common knowledge. They were fully armed to protect themselves and the casualties in their care. During our year of service in Vietnam, two of the battalion's stretcher bearers received bravery awards, one was killed and four were wounded. In the trying conditions of the October 1966 operations in the hills they again acquitted themselves with honour.

The skills of the medical assistants and stretcher bearers were soon to be put to work. It was on Day 3 of Operation Canberra that two platoons were hit in separate booby trap incidents, wounding eleven soldiers, three of them seriously. First aid was administered and helicopter evacuation effected after a minimal landing zone had been cleared. One disappointing defect in the medical system was that first responders did not receive any follow-up on the casualties they had cared for until the RMO, in the days or weeks ahead, was able to find an opportunity to visit the hospitals to which they had been evacuated.

The five-day road-holding task (Operation Robin) that immediately followed Operation Canberra was an opportunity to carry out Medical Civic Action Program clinics (MEDCAPs) at villages on Route 15 along which the battalion was strung. MEDCAPs were staged during operations whenever time and the tactical situation permitted. The team consisted of the RMO, a Royal Australian Army Medical Corps (RAAMC) non-commissioned officer, one or two stretcher bearers and an Army of the Republic of Vietnam interpreter. Clinics were conducted in any suitable building or under a marquee. In wartime Vietnam, the civilian population had very limited access to medical care. Road travel to clinics and hospitals was perilous. The last time the inhabitants of Long Cat village had seen a doctor was three years previously, when an American army unit had passed through. Consequently, MEDCAPs were invariably extremely popular with villagers. Sometimes as many as 75 patients would be seen in three hours.

If the situation was suitable the bandmaster assembled the stretcher bearer/bandsmen and arranged for their instruments to be brought out by truck from Nui Dat. A brass band concert – a rare experience for the locals – ensued, greatly lightening the atmosphere.

The MEDCAPs had immense public relations value and were recognised as a useful contribution to counter-insurgency. For the battalion medics, they provided welcome contact with Vietnamese civilians and an understanding of their health problems. However, their medical utility was extremely limited. The main problems were the language barrier – even with interpreters – and the lack of privacy to permit an effective physical examination. These factors, as well as a total absence of laboratory help, rendered accurate diagnosis almost impossible. When a confident diagnosis could be made, the range of medications available for their treatment was limited. Above all was the huge burden of chronic disease – malaria, tuberculosis and hookworm – prevalent in the population. These diseases require long-term treatment under close supervision; a flying visit by a well-intentioned team was utterly ineffective and could only engender false hope.

13. THE MEDICAL PROBLEMS OF OPERATIONS IN THE HILLS

Even though the MEDCAPs could be tiring, I always found them interesting and the civilian contact a lively counterpoint to military life. Sometimes this could be a challenge. The priest at Long Cat village kindly invited me to lunch. The main dish was smashed duck in a bowl of blood with spicules of bone for consistency. Not wishing to offend, I managed to get through it with the aid of rice whisky which was somewhat redolent of aviation gasoline.

One afternoon I was standing at the roadside at the C Company position, having done a 'house call' and awaiting a ride with the Sioux reconnaissance helicopter to take me back to BHQ. The chopper sped towards us, flying just a metre above the road surface, when it suddenly hit the ground, cartwheeling down the bitumen, pieces of the aircraft flying off, until the shattered wreck came to rest metres from where we were standing. The pilot, Second Lieutenant Bill Davies, had a head injury and was unconscious. We stunned onlookers had no idea as to what had caused the crash, although the possibility of sniper fire was raised. His passenger was Staff Sergeant 'Sailor' Mealing, a Korean War veteran and colourful battalion identity. He had several fractures and his evacuation to hospital in Vung Tau was expedited. Because of Davies' head injury, I decided to call for a second *Dustoff* helicopter and escorted him to a hospital with neurosurgical facilities in Saigon. Both casualties survived and were evacuated to Australia in the weeks ahead. Bill Davies relates the story of his crash and his evacuation and recovery in Chapter 14.

Leaving the roadside for the second excursion into the hills (Operation Queanbeyan) meant a return to the toughest terrain most of us had ever encountered. The going was steep with an average gradient of 1 in 3, on a track slippery from the tail end of the wet season. The troops were carrying kit, ammunition and rations totalling some 30 kilograms. The hillside was littered with giant granite boulders, some as big as shipping containers, riven by clefts and caves, and overlain with tall trees and dense undergrowth, perfect for snipers. This setting and our awareness of the presence of the enemy and booby traps along the track raised the level of tension considerably.

On the morning of the first day of Operation Queanbeyan (17 October), four soldiers of A Company were wounded by one such booby trap. That same afternoon the Reconnaissance Group, 100 metres or so uphill from where BHQ had paused, had come under fire and its leader, Captain Brian Le Dan, was reported as wounded. I took off up the track to join him. He was a lucky man: the bullet had struck his Owen gun and he received only a flesh wound on the chest wall from fragments. Bleeding was readily controlled with a shell dressing. We settled down in the shelter of a large rock until he felt confident enough to walk back down the track with me to where it was possible for him to be extracted in a remarkable piece of helicopter piloting (Chapter 14) and conveyed to hospital. Shortly afterwards, Corporal Norm Womal was shot leading his section to clear the area. He lay in a very exposed position. In the time-honoured tradition, stretcher bearer Private Peter Fraser – against orders – crawled forward under fire, dressed the wound, shielded Womal from enemy fire and assisted a carrying party to bring him to me further down the slope. Womal had a bullet entry wound above the collarbone and it was obvious that he was bleeding freely from a major vessel within the chest. There was no way to stop the bleeding. The small amount of albumin that I was carrying and administered intravenously could not keep pace with his blood loss and he died within 20 minutes. (Details of this engagement are described in Chapter 7.)

The next two days were taken up with assaults on caves along the track. These actions were costly, with the death of Private Gordon D'Antoine on 18 October and the serious wounding of two soldiers by a booby trap grenade the following day (Chapter 7). One of the wounded was Private Trevor Lynch. Non-medical people often think that medics are quite unfeeling and able to go about their duties focusing only on the technical task that lies before them. Corporal Ian McDougall RAAMC was attached to the Pioneer Platoon that afternoon and had to deal with the two casualties. Ian was the only national service corporal in the Medical Platoon. His account gives some insight into the toll that casualty management can impose on those charged with tending to those in their care.

Ian McDougall

Trevor Lynch and another soldier had been detailed to make the actual assault with the backpack flame-throwers. We did not see their initial approach, but suddenly there was the almighty crack of a mine detonation, followed by loud screaming. With clearance from the section commander I was with, I made my way back to the track and down then out to where the wounded lay.

To say I was scared stiff would be a gross understatement. The two men lay immediately in front of the caves which had numerous entrances with little cover. I recall feeling very lonely and totally exposed.

I turned my attention to Trevor, who was screaming in a demented fashion and writhing on the ground. He had sustained multiple wounds; in fact, his was the most mutilated human body I had ever seen and ever want to. I had great difficulty deciding where to start as he had dozens of bleeding wounds, some of them very serious, broken limbs and many facial injuries. The front of his body was a mass of puncture wounds. I remember, as I started applying wound dressings, that I had to tie Trevor's hands together to stop him dislodging dressings and doing himself more damage. I recall that I was crying at one point due to the frustration I felt in trying stop blood loss from so many wounds at once. I doubt if Trevor was aware at that time of anything, and his wild screaming continued unabated, but I do recall that Captain Tony White, the 5 RAR RMO, joined me at some stage. I have tried hard since to forget that incident, and have obviously partially succeeded, as I do not recall how or when my patient was evacuated, or what happened to the other soldier or even if I had treated him.

Tony White

Trevor Lynch survived but was totally and permanently incapacitated, losing both eyes and being confined to a wheelchair until his early death at the age of 51. Ian McDougall, despite being plagued by post-traumatic stress disorder, went on to have a successful career in the Australian Federal Police. No medic can erase the memory of the maimed soldiers for whom he did his best and that memory is rendered more painful by the flood of emotions that accompanies it.

The Nui Thi Vai hills operations were an intense, physically and mentally demanding 20 days of almost continuous and varied activity. Aside from the steady stream of medical problems – bronchitis, twisted knees, sprained ankles, crotch rot and so on – there were the fearful and intensely stressful battle casualties with which to contend. I am proud of all in the Medical Platoon who acquitted themselves so well in such trying circumstances.

Editors' conclusion

At war, all infantrymen are continuously mindful of the inescapable likelihood of casualties. How well they function effectively for extended periods depends on an individual's confidence in himself, his training, the systems within which he operates and others who support him. Much of this confidence emanates from a sense of being part of the hierarchical entity which includes his platoon, his company and his battalion. This cossets him in a brotherhood of identity, acceptance, obligation, shared danger, mutual dependence and pride. Deep interpersonal bonds which become unshakeable lifelong friendships are inevitable. To Australians the phenomenon is just 'mateship' – long held to be among the foremost of our distinctive national traits.

Much is written of such things; often without good, firsthand examples of the many factors which are at play in moulding the resilience of those whose duty is to seek out and destroy an enemy. The words of Tony White and Ian McDougall give a hint of the many facets of an infantry battalion at war which are sparsely aired in most postwar accounts. Notably, they vividly impart the morale effects of having members of our battalion's dedicated medical team, including our RMO, deployed at the forefront of danger.

The impact of rapid aeromedical evacuation of casualties to sophisticated surgical facilities during the Vietnam War has deservedly been hailed for its effects on survivability and morale. But the comfort of having, right at hand, known mates who were trained to be casualty first responders was a pearl beyond price.

Our medical team, in providing that response on the battlefield, first had to reach the soldiers who had been wounded, lying immobile on the ground, often still under direct enemy observation. As they moved forward to help those in need, they had to make hard choices on whom to treat first. They had to shed normal concerns for their own safety and frequently accept a very high degree of personal risk over short periods. We never saw any of our Medical Platoon members hesitate as they entered a danger zone. Such areas were particularly threatening when they included hidden mines and booby traps, activated by barely visible tripwires, concealed pressure switches or remote-control wires laid underground and reaching back to a control point where the firer could lie, hidden from view and in relative safety. They entered and moved about areas where mines or booby traps had been encountered, or where the enemy was in close proximity, to treat first those wounded whom they judged to be in greatest need.

A second difficult scenario that our medics had to face was the constant pressure to give effective assistance to the people in the villages through which we had to operate, and with whom we wanted to develop good relations. The locals trusted us, and that made our awareness of the limited nature of the medical assistance that we could provide particularly worrisome. This awareness arose first and foremost in the minds of our medical team, who could see the consequences of being able to provide only very limited assistance more clearly than any of us.

Many share the view that our medical team's devotion to our casualties, with the special risks that such devotion entailed, was worthy of very high recognition. Similarly, their vital role in helping us gain the trust and confidence of local villagers merited special mention. Our confidence in their bravery, knowledge and compassion made a huge difference to our battalion's effectiveness in counter-insurgency operations.

14

THE CHALLENGES OF AIR SUPPORT

Jim Campbell, Bob Supple, Bob Askew,
Robert O'Neill and Bill Davies

Editors' introduction

Air support played an important part in most operations that 5th Battalion, the Royal Australian Regiment (5 RAR), undertook during the Vietnam War. Helicopters were ideally suited to the type of warfare and difficult terrain of Vietnam and they provided a level of air mobility, close fire support, air resupply, air reconnaissance and casualty evacuation that had not been seen in earlier conflicts. Army pilots, who were allocated in direct support of infantry battalions during operations from the beginning of 1 ATF's (1st Australian Task Force) deployment into Phuoc Tuy Province, provide this chapter's narratives. They show the robust mutual regard which rapidly developed and long endured between them and those they supported.

Jim Campbell

No aircraft other than the helicopter could have provided ground forces with the various types of intimate air support which were essential to the nature of operations undertaken in Vietnam. The Bell UH-1 models, officially named 'Iroquois' but commonly referred to as the 'Huey', were particularly important. Troop and cargo-carrying versions, with two M60 machine guns operated by side-door gunners, were known as 'slicks'. Heavily armed ground support versions with rapid-fire, multi-barrelled machine guns and high explosive (HE) rockets, were known as 'gunships'. In operations, slicks inserted and extracted small patrols or entire infantry units like 5 RAR, using clear areas called landing zones (LZ). They then kept them resupplied. The casualty evacuation version of the Huey was code-named *Dustoff*. Larger helicopters such as the Boeing CH-47 Chinook were able to lift artillery units into and out of remote jungle and hilltop fire base locations in support of the battalion.

Slicks could provide close fire support from their side-mounted M60 machine guns. This could prove vital in infantry insertions into, and extractions from, unsecured LZs. In jungle or high rugged areas like the mountainous areas of Phuoc Tuy Province, suitable LZs were few and far between. Any suspected of being under Viet Cong surveillance could either be secured by ground forces or be 'prepared' by artillery or gunships immediately before the landing of troop-carrying slicks.

In its *Dustoff* role, the Iroquois could extract wounded soldiers from even the most inaccessible LZs. In thick primary jungle, casualties could be extracted by lowering, by winch cable, a vertical stretcher called a 'jungle penetrator'. With the casualty secured he could then be winched, upright, out of the jungle into the *Dustoff* helicopter. Casualties could be transported, in less than 30 minutes, to either the Australian Army's 1 Field Hospital or the US Army's 36 Evacuation Hospital at Vung Tau; or, if necessary, to specialist US medical facilities in Saigon within an hour. *Dustoff* support added greatly to the confidence and morale of our soldiers during operations.

Iroquois from both American and Australian units supported 1 ATF. 9 Squadron Royal Australian Air Force (RAAF) provided the Australian Iroquois and their aircraft used the radio call sign *Albatross*. US Army Aviation units provided the US Iroquois gunships and usually used lurid and macho call signs. Later in the war RAAF gunships became available and used the call sign *Bushranger*. So successful was the Iroquois in the Vietnam War that it endures as an iconic symbol for veterans of the air-mobile operations in which it was so extensively used.

In addition to the Iroquois, the battalion was supported by the smaller three-seat Bell Sioux 47G 3B1 helicopters. Australian Army pilots of 161 (Independent) Reconnaissance Flight (161 (Indep) Recce Flight) flew this type, forever associated with the Korean War. They used the radio call sign *Possum* and their primary roles were to provide air reconnaissance, forward air control of close air support and artillery fire and casualty evacuation using two exterior mounted stretchers. The latter capability was very important in cases where the combination of a tight extraction LZ and limited time precluded the use of the larger Iroquois *Dustoff*.

The battalion could task air-delivered fire; this was called close air support. The US Air Force provided close air support with its fixed-wing propeller-driven aircraft or jet fighter ground attack aircraft. The US Army's ground attack helicopters could also be used. The aircraft could deliver a range of ordnance including HE bombs, cluster bombs and napalm to surface targets. The US Army's gunships had very high rates of fire from both machine guns and automatic 40 mm grenade launchers, as well as volley-fired rockets. Close air support was invaluable against hardened installations and enemy targets outside the range of artillery. Also available for tasking was the destructive power of US Air Force B-52 strategic bombers and the high potency fire from the many rapid-fire, multi-barrelled machine guns mounted on converted C-47 transport aircraft (the Second World War military version of the venerable 1930s civilian DC3). These were then redesignated AC-47; the added 'A' to indicate their attack role. The radio call sign used by these aircraft was *Spooky*. Their popular nickname was 'Puff the Magic Dragon' because the 'red rain' of their voluminous tracer fire, particularly at night, suggested a fire-breathing, flying beast.

5 RAR made greater use of the different types of air support available to it during the period of Operations Canberra, Robin and Queanbeyan than at any other time during the battalion's tour of duty in Vietnam. These operations commenced with the battalion making its initial movement into the Nui Thi Vai and the Nui Toc Tien Hills areas on foot. Insertion by foot rather than helicopter was necessary to conceal the deployment of 5 RAR rifle companies from the Viet Cong. After the Viet Cong became aware of the presence of the battalion in the area, close air support was called in by the battalion as described in Chapters 6 and 14.

The Sioux from 161 (Indep) Recce Flight provided continuous daily air support for the battalion during these operations. The helicopter section of the flight had been operating with 6 RAR on the eastern and north-eastern side of the Nui Dinh hills in September 1966 so the pilots were reasonably familiar with the area. Each day a pilot was assigned to 5 RAR for the whole day to fly whatever tasks the battalion required. The pilot would be briefed the evening before, by the previous day's pilot, on the location of Battalion Headquarters (BHQ) and the fire support base (FSB) and where they could land. The new pilot would also be advised of all current company locations and any other relevant information for the following day.

Bob Supple

Prior to their experiences in Vietnam, all army pilots had worked or served with infantry battalions on exercises in Australia. Captain Jim Campbell DFC, who commanded the 161 (Indep) Recce Flight's helicopters, had been posted to 1 RAR for three years in Australia and Malaysia before becoming a pilot. Jim Campbell was awarded the Distinguished Flying Cross due largely to his actions during 5 RAR Operation Renmark when, on 21 February 1967, he flew Captain Tony White, the 5 RAR medical officer, into a minefield to assist our wounded personnel. Jim landed time after time in the minefield until all the wounded were evacuated to where the larger *Dustoff* aircraft could safely collect them. This was necessary because the stronger rotor downwash of the larger aircraft was likely to activate the sensitive anti-personnel mines.

161 (Indep) Recce Flight had operated out of Vung Tau until the end of February 1967. Then after their workshops and aircraft parking areas in the 1 ATF base were completed, they relocated alongside 5 RAR at Nui Dat. Sioux helicopters did not spend the night in the field with battalions during operations because the helicopters did not have any protection from enemy mortar attack or other action. Also, because they were difficult to conceal, their presence could give away the location of the unit they were supporting to the enemy.

Operation Canberra from 6 to 10 October 1966 involved 5 RAR's preliminary clearance of the Nui Thi Vai hills prior to Operation Robin where the battalion was tasked to secure a section of Route 15 directly overlooked by the Nui Thi Vai hills. Operation Robin was mounted to ensure the safe passage by road of 3 Brigade of the US 4 Infantry Division from Vung Tau to Bien Hoa. Sioux helicopters completed discreet aerial reconnaissance of the Nui Thi Vai area for Operation Canberra by 5 October 1966. On the following day the rifle companies and BHQ of 5 RAR commenced an approach on foot through the jungle towards the

14. THE CHALLENGES OF AIR SUPPORT

foothills of Nui Thi Vai. Late in the morning of 8 October, C Company suffered casualties from booby traps. The casualties were evacuated by a *Dustoff* Iroquois from an LZ hand-cut into the jungle by their mates.

In the early afternoon, B Company sighted a group of about 30 Viet Cong and a fire plan employing mortars, artillery and air support was prepared. B and C Companies were pulled back a safe distance from the Viet Cong location and artillery and mortar fire was directed onto the Viet Cong position. Then Iroquois gunships were called in and fired rockets and machine guns directly onto the Viet Cong position.

Following the gunship attack an airstrike was used to destroy any Viet Cong still occupying hardened bunkers. This airstrike was coordinated by BHQ and commenced with the arrival overhead of the US forward air controller in a light aircraft. I briefed the US forward air controller, nicknamed *Birddog*, on the target details and the locations of all friendly forces. When the F-100 Super Sabre ground attack aircraft arrived and started circling overhead, the forward air controller identified both enemy and friendly locations to the ground attack aircraft by means of coloured smoke grenades, which they used to help him identify their locations in the jungle. This involved somewhat lengthy radio communications between the rifle companies, BHQ and *Birddog*, followed by further radio communications between *Birddog* and the strike aircraft.

The air strike entailed an attack by two waves of F-100 jet aircraft using 500-pound bombs, napalm and cluster bomb units (CBUs). CBUs were large containers which exploded above the ground, scattering many smaller bomblets through the surrounding jungle to detonate on impact. Once the intricacies of identifying the enemy and friendly locations to the F-100s were successfully completed, the attack began. The airstrike produced thunderous engine roars, deafening explosions and clouds of dust and smoke, concluding not long before daylight ended; with a ground force follow-up then impossible before the following morning. During the afternoon of the airstrike, 1,000 rounds of mortar ammunition had been flown in by Iroquois to the mortar base plate position close to BHQ and, that night, the two Mortar Platoon sections (four 81 mm mortars) fired 960 rounds as a follow-up to the air strike. The ground follow-up of the air strike which took place next morning is described in Chapter 6.

On the afternoon of 10 October, Iroquois airlifted the battalion to positions along Route 15 to commence Operation Robin which was conducted from 11 to 16 October. It involved searching for mines and booby traps and intensive patrolling along Route 15 and its conduct is described in Chapter 6. A near-tragic event during this operation was the crash of the Sioux helicopter then supporting the battalion. The pilot, Second Lieutenant Bill Davies, was flying at low level beside Route 15 when his main rotor blades appeared to strike a power pole; his aircraft crashed and was destroyed. Bill relates this incident and its aftermath later in this chapter.

The US 4 Infantry Division convoy with its own armoured vehicle and helicopter gunship support completed its passage along Route 15 by 16 October. Australian Iroquois and Sioux helicopters had once again provided command and control, reconnaissance, resupply and casualty evacuation missions for 5 RAR throughout Operation Robin. The battalion immediately readied itself for Operation Queanbeyan – the much-anticipated return to the Nui Thi Vai hills. This commenced on 17 October 1966 and was designed to destroy any Viet Cong remaining in or returning to their sanctuary. Intelligence reports had indicated that the Viet Cong were still active on Nui Thi Vai and the battalion knew that there were more installations to be dealt with.

After the deception measures described in Chapter 7, the rifle companies of the battalion moved on foot into their assigned areas around Nui Thi Vai and BHQ commenced its move to occupy the area surrounding a pagoda near the top of Nui Thi Vai. On that same afternoon BHQ with its protection elements, the Anti-Tank Platoon and the Assault Pioneer Platoon, came into heavy contact with the Viet Cong while ascending a spur of Nui Thi Vai. The contact lasted for several hours and helicopter gunships were called on to play an important role in assisting the heavily engaged Anti-Tank Platoon.

During this engagement, Second Lieutenant Bob Askew piloted a Sioux helicopter to evacuate casualties on two separate occasions, each under very difficult circumstances. Bob had to land his small helicopter on a rocky projection on the side of the steep hillside slope, in a position where the surrounding trees allowed little scope for any error in judgement. The Sioux was also at a very real risk of being shot down by enemy ground fire during its approach and departure. Despite these risks, Bob completed

14. THE CHALLENGES OF AIR SUPPORT

both casevac (casualty evacuation) missions. This feat of exceptional flying is covered both in Chapter 7 and in the following paragraphs, which include Bob's own description of his difficulties.

Robert O'Neill

On the first day of the operation, in the very difficult terrain of the Nui Thi Vai hills, Captain Brian Le Dan and Corporal Norm Womal were wounded, with Norm dying of his wounds before he could be evacuated to hospital. Trees and bushes were cleared around a fairly flat rock ledge to form an LZ barely large enough for a Sioux helicopter to complete the extraction of the casualties. Second Lieutenant Bob Askew performed this very difficult flying feat twice. He first picked up the wounded Brian Le Dan and flew him to where a larger *Dustoff* Iroquois could land. He returned later that day to retrieve Norm Womal's body. Bob's amazing skills and committed flying achieved these casevacs on this day. The challenges he faced are described below by Bob and Jim Campbell who both operated in and out of this rudimentary LZ.

As soon as Brian Le Dan was wounded, *Possum 5* (Bob's call sign) was alerted. He had been repositioned from Nui Dat to an FSB alongside Route 15 where he waited until the area was made sufficiently secure for him to attempt to find an LZ. When the only available option was improved and secured, he was called forward. Captain Bob Supple, 5 RAR's assistant operations officer, guided *Possum 5* onto the tiny LZ, while crouching low to avoid decapitation by its whirling rotor blades.

Bob Askew

I recall being on standby at an FSB beside Route 15 when the request came through for the first casevac. After the second one I returned to the FSB on standby for the rest of the day. With both missions the difficulties of the LZ were only part of the deal; the possibility of being exposed to Viet Cong fire by having to make my lengthy approach over steeply sloping ground, all of which could not be secured by the troops below, was the biggest concern for me. As I approached, the sounds of the fighting were plainly audible. Even while wearing a flying helmet and despite the chopper's noise, the distinctive 'whap' sound of a close one lent clarity to the term 'aimed ground fire'. Hearing gunfire close at hand was considered normal; being under fire wasn't – not by me! At the end of the day, sitting quietly somewhere and thinking over what I had learned, it was satisfying to know that when I was hard pushed, I was up to the job – something most of us have wondered about.

On landing to collect the first casualty I exited 'the plastic helicopter' (as it was sometimes affectionately described) for a couple of reasons. One, to check the main rotor blades as I had cut my way through some small vegetation on the approach. Two, I was sure my green pants might have turned brown during the approach. They hadn't, but I did have an urgent call in the other department. I can remember thinking at the time, while standing urinating against the rock, under the now green-tipped rotor blades, a thousand feet up on the edge of a mountain, with a rather large and noisy firefight happening close by, that this was rather a different setting for having a pee! The third and most compelling reason for stepping out of 'the office' was that I felt somewhat exposed waiting in a prominent plexiglass bubble when a nice secure rock face was close at hand.

After lifting out Brian Le Dan I delivered him to the *Dustoff* helicopter which was waiting in a clear area beside Route 15. As there was no direct security there, the pilot had chosen the largest cleared area he could find with the nearest treeline about 300 metres away. I landed in front of him, not beside him, in case his side-door gunners needed to defend our exposed situation. I also asked if he would delay his departure until I had shut down and inspected my aircraft for damage. I didn't want to be left stranded on the ground with an unserviceable aircraft. To my surprise no damage was readily visible. After a second approach and departure to pick up Norm Womal's body, I returned to my standby location where our engineers thoroughly inspected the chopper and found no damage apart from about 120 centimetres of green foliage stains along the outer leading edges of both blades. I was amazed, and thankful, that the pilot had acquired no additional apertures.

Fifty years later I'm pleased to repeat my congratulations to the 5 RAR men who were involved that day. The organisation and execution needed in preparing the LZ, the coordination required to get the right people into the right place at the right time, while fighting was ongoing, was superb; as was Bob Supple's tricky and dangerous task of guiding me in. Their efforts made the very difficult landing and departure of my aircraft achievable and contributed greatly to the success of my tasks.

14. THE CHALLENGES OF AIR SUPPORT

Bob Supple

The Anti-Tank Platoon remained pinned down under the weight of Viet Cong fire coming from caves and rocks further up the slope of Nui Thi Vai. The Viet Cong were too close for mortar or artillery fire to be used and supporting machine gun fire from a distant rifle company had proved ineffective and dangerous in trying to dislodge the enemy from their positions. Our commanding officer (CO) then decided to employ two US Army Iroquois gunships who were in support of the battalion to help clear the enemy from their rocky positions.

Once all elements had marked their position with coloured smoke, the gunships commenced their attack. The direct rocket and machine gun fire of the gunships was able to penetrate the caves and rock positions from which the Viet Cong were firing their weapons, and this finally caused them to withdraw. BHQ was then able to resume its move up the Nui Thi Vai slopes to reach its objective near a hilltop pagoda. The full story of the Anti-Tank Platoon's engagement is described in Chapter 7.

Air support in the form of airborne command and control facilities, reconnaissance, resupply and casualty evacuation missions continued to be flown for the battalion throughout Operation Queanbeyan. LZs in the Nui Thi Vai area were mainly too small and hazardous for Iroquois, but they could fly water, rations and ammunition for the rifle companies to a larger LZ at battalion HQ or to the artillery FSB beside Route 15, for on-ferrying to the rifle companies by Sioux.

Jim Campbell

When I was about to take off in my Sioux from the BHQ pad at the pagoda with a load of supplies for one of the companies, the warrant officer directing my take-off gave the thumbs down signal and pointed to the side of the helicopter opposite the pilot's seat. When I got out of the aircraft to investigate, I found the exhaust pipe had cracked and broken off at the supercharger and hot exhaust discharge was going straight onto the oil lines of the Sioux. An engine failure could have occurred if I had continued with the flight, so I aborted the take-off. A mechanic was immediately flown in from Vung Tau, a replacement part was fitted, and I was back flying within an hour.

During the clearance and search of caves encountered on the Nui Thi Vai slopes, I flew into the same difficult landing spot Bob Askew had twice used to evacuate casualties on 17 October. Bob had briefed me on the landing site, saying:

> It requires a curved approach and you are committed to a landing. The rock surface is very uneven, and the rotor blades just miss the tree branches. To take off, you need to hover backwards about 30 metres and then rotate through 180 degrees and follow the same curved path out of the LZ.

I had to use this landing site over several days, to deliver bags of tear gas crystals to be used by the battalion to make the caves on Nui Thi Vai hills uninhabitable. I had already felt the effect of a slight leakage from the bags in flight on a previous day. On what I think was the last day of this mission, I made an approach to a pad near the top of the mountains on the north-west side. During the approach, I heard a dull bang and noticed a cloud of dust come out of the entrance to a cave not far from the LZ. The cloud came across the chopper as I came to a hover and my eyes became very irritated and breathing became difficult. I abandoned the approach and with laboured breathing and blurred vision, swaying through the sky for some time until the company on the ground advised that everything was back under control at the landing area. When my senses started to return to normal, I was able to return and land to complete the mission.

Ron Boxall

On 10 October 1966 Second Lieutenant Bill Davies was flying a Sioux helicopter in support of 5 RAR. He was involved in a serious crash which destroyed the helicopter and he and his passenger were injured, Bill very seriously. Since that time the incident has been the subject of speculation, with two conflicting versions of the cause. Was it 'pilot error', as some eyewitnesses inexpertly claimed, or was he shot down? After 50 years of frustration, Bill now has an opportunity to bring idle conjecture to a close. In doing so, he provides another insight into the mettle of our *Possum* brothers.

14. THE CHALLENGES OF AIR SUPPORT

Bill Davies

My first association with 5 RAR was in October 1965 during a training exercise in the Colo-Putty Training Area north-west of Sydney. The exercise in early 1966 was one of the battalion's final tests before it embarked for Vietnam in April. This was my very first job as an operational army pilot after receiving my 'wings'. In May 1966 I was posted to Vietnam as a replacement for Captain Bev Smith who, while flying a Sioux in Bien Hoa Province, had been shot in the left hand. The left hand normally operates the controls for climbing or descending and for varying engine power to suit either manoeuvre. Without the use of his left hand he made a remarkably skilful landing without further damage to the aircraft or its occupants. I visited him in the Military Hospital at Yeronga in Brisbane before I embarked for Vietnam where I found him negotiating with doctors to have his shattered left hand formed into a 'grip', so he could operate the twist-grip throttle on the collective lever of a Sioux. Subsequently, he rejoined the ranks of the army's operational helicopter pilots.

On arrival in Phuoc Tuy Province I soon encountered the familiar faces of my 5 RAR acquaintances, remembered from when I had flown in support of their exercise earlier that year. I immediately felt at home. Soon I was in the thick of incessant demands for support by the humble Sioux, officially designated a light observation helicopter. While that was the primary role of the aircraft, the versatility and reliability which made it a legend in the Korean War was reinforced by the many diverse tasks we were called upon to perform. On one occasion I was tasked with the evacuation of a Vietnamese woman from the Binh Ba rubber plantation. She had been haemorrhaging for some days after childbirth. Captain Tony White, the regimental medical officer of 5 RAR, decided that she should be evacuated to the Vietnamese hospital in Ba Ria. We secured her in the external litter on my side of the aircraft where I could keep an eye on her as we flew to Ba Ria, the province capital. I fitted her with headphones with voice connection to the flight deck. This would slightly muffle the engine noise. In the passenger seat I carried an interpreter, so the patient could be kept informed to reduce her anxiety as much as possible. A bonus was that the interpreter would help to balance the helicopter laterally. I don't recall this precaution being covered on our unit's standard operating procedures (SOPs). I delivered her to Ba Ria airstrip where a Vietnamese ambulance was to meet us. None arrived and alternative transport had to be arranged hastily. I never heard whether the woman or her child survived.

Another evacuation, carried out about 10 kilometres north-east of Nui Dat, involved the recovery of an injured 5 RAR soldier. I made an initial attempt to fit the helicopter into a very tight landing site, but the rotor blade tips began striking tree leaves and twigs and there was no way I could safely persist with the approach. I radioed to 5 RAR personnel on the ground about cutting down a large, centrally placed tree. Its removal would give me a better chance of landing. I stayed nearby while this was undertaken but ran low on fuel before it could be accomplished. When I returned after refuelling the tree had been felled with a waist-high stump remaining. The approach was still a Rubik's Cube juggling job to get the Sioux onto the ground. With the casualty on one of the outside litters, the helicopter's reaction to the extra weight made the trees on our exit path look impossibly tall and their proximity masked any possibility of using any headwind for additional lift; all of which heightened my attention to the task. We scraped out of that one and it has been the stuff of nightmares since. The CO of 5 RAR, Lieutenant Colonel John Warr, was kind enough to commend my efforts by radio to my boss, Major Laurie Doyle, whom I omitted to tell about the hairiness of the extraction in case it was considered in breach of SOPs. However, when there was an urgent request to free heavily laden infantry from having to carrying a casualty and his equipment, a balanced, on-the-spot decision by the tasked pilot was clearly required. There was also the need to show the infantry, who constantly bore the brunt, that we were always there for them and that we were prepared to take any calculated risk to support them.

On 10 October I was flying in support of 5 RAR's part in Operation Robin. I was tasked to carry captured enemy materiel and the company quartermaster sergeant of B Company, Staff Sergeant 'Sailor' Mealing, to a designated site beside Route 15. I remember flying very low along the road but nothing more of what followed. When I awoke in a US military hospital I was being visited by my unit commander, Laurie Doyle, and my section commander, Jim Campbell. They commiserated with me and asked me a few questions which I tried to answer, unaware that the conversation was part of an investigation being conducted into the crash.

Although I had no idea what had happened to place me in hospital, I wasn't particularly curious. There was a war on and I knew I'd find out soon enough. As far as I was concerned, I would be back piloting choppers in a few days – a week at the most! I felt quite guilty about not being back at 161 (Indep) Recce Flight pulling my weight in flying duties with my fellow pilots. My optimism and guilt both proved to be wide of the mark. The bones of my face and around my eyes had been broken in many places. Significant nerve damage caused sensory and muscle anomalies and I suffered severe double vision, among other problems. I vaguely understood that all this might mean the end of my flying career, only a couple of days after my 21st birthday.

As I lay in bed my tongue felt a strand of 'spaghetti' in my mouth between my upper gums and my top lip. I tentatively began pulling at this strand with my fingers but, fortunately, an alert nurse intervened and snipped it off close to the gums. Apparently, it was medical grade 'Silastic' used to fill the sinus cavities to keep the cheekbones in place after they had been repositioned. The Red Cross handed out care packages to us patients and I can remember a toothbrush and some toothpaste that remained unused for some time. More so, I remember the efforts that the American Red Cross made to get telegrams to and from my family in Australia. This was especially gratifying for a foreign patient like me in an American hospital in Saigon. The resulting two-way communication was ultra-sweet. Eventually, as the fog cleared, I amended my news to family members from, 'I'll be flying again next week' to 'I'll be coming home for Christmas, just so you won't miss me'. Invaluable reassurance – for correspondents at both ends!

I found out from one of my fellow pilots who managed to visit me in the Saigon hospital that the wreckage of my helicopter was 'wrapped around a steel telegraph pole'. I felt terrible at this news. No pilot wants to think that they have collided with an obstacle or flown into the ground. I told my friend that I understood that all the roadside poles in the crash area were on the western side of Route 15 and, if there had been one or two on the eastern side of the roadway, maybe I had collided with one of them; but I could not imagine colliding with one on the western side. When he confirmed that the pole concerned was on the western side it gave me some small satisfaction, because I was sure that, while I had undoubtedly struck one of them, it was unlikely that the crash was due to 'pilot error'. Nonetheless, I experienced an intense feeling of shame and failure with no way of explaining what else might have contributed to the crash.

Left wondering, and in an information vacuum, I was moved to another US military medical facility at Saigon's Tan Son Nhut airport where patients were tended on camp stretchers while awaiting evacuation from Vietnam. In a journey of many legs, I was flown by RAAF C130 Hercules to an overnight stay in Butterworth in Malaysia, thence to Christmas Island and through the RAAF bases in Western Australia, South Australia and Richmond near Sydney. From RAAF Richmond I was transported to the army hospital at Ingleburn. Subsequently I was flown from RAAF Richmond to RAAF Amberly and transported to 1 Military Hospital at Yeronga in Brisbane. I promised myself I would do whatever it took to fly again. This was the beginning of 15 months of anguish and frustration, but I did fly again as an operational pilot. In fact, I flew once again in support of 5 RAR in 1968 as the battalion exercised in preparation for its second tour of duty in Vietnam.

During that exercise, on Holsworthy firing ranges, I was marshalled into an LZ by a 5 RAR soldier who obviously knew what he was doing. After shutting down the Sioux, I chatted to the soldier giving him some well-deserved feedback. At one point he said, 'Yes, I was on the battalion's first tour of Vietnam – I saw a chopper go in [crash].' 'Whereabouts?' I asked, thinking mine might have been the incident he was recalling. 'On Highway 15', he said, confirming that he was speaking of my crash. 'Do you know what happened to the pilot?' I asked. 'Oh, he's a vegetable, I think', he replied. It was a pleasure to introduce myself as a non-vegetative survivor.

Years later, in Perth, I met two former 5 RAR soldiers who also had witnessed to my crash. I was eager to hear anything from eyewitnesses and, although they were cautious with their opinions, they were pretty sure that, for whatever reasons, I had just flown into the steel pylon. I suggested that I knew well the siting of the poles in relation to the road and was careful to keep clear of them. I also told them that when Major Doyle and a fellow Sioux pilot, Second Lieutenant Bob Askew, inspected the wreckage they found Perspex shards with bullet holes in them on the approach to the impact site. Bob Askew had told me this, after I had returned to flying, pointing out that there was also a projectile hole which was in the remains of the rear part of the helicopter's cockpit bubble which would have been right behind where I was sitting.

Further, in January 1967, I received a letter from the commander of 1 ATF, Brigadier David Jackson, telling me the cause of my crash was my having been fired upon. He hoped I wouldn't be too inconvenienced by my injuries and that my Christmas had not been spoiled. While I was very pleased to receive such a letter from our task force commander confirming that I had been brought down by ground fire, my principal concern remained the severe double vision which persisted. Was I ever going to get back to aircrew medical standard?

My hunger to learn all I could about the crash led me to trawl later through the evidence of the Army Court of Enquiry which began three days after the crash. I was relieved to read in its report that my lingering fears about 'pilot error' were unnecessary. The enquiry found, *inter alia,* that:

- Small arms automatic fire was heard just prior to the impact and in the direction from which the aircraft was approaching. This was reported by three individuals from C Company, 5 RAR, who were deployed along the road adjacent to the crash site.
- One of my facial injuries was caused by a high-velocity fragment, identity unknown. The attending surgeon from the US 3rd Field Hospital, Saigon, had recorded that my facial injuries appeared to have been caused by a high-velocity fragment which entered on the lower left side of my head and exited on the upper right. The impact would have tended to throw my body to the right and the resulting shock wave would have rendered me unconscious.
- Damage to the Perspex bubble showed possible bullet holes.

Speculation about the cause of my crash has persisted for more than 50 years despite the evidence taken by a Court of Enquiry and its findings. I was glad to learn that my passenger, Staff Sergeant 'Sailor' Mealing, made a full recovery from his injuries and went on to serve another tour of duty in Vietnam. I will always be indebted to those members of 5 RAR who swiftly came to our aid; particularly their medical officer, Captain Tony White, who made an on-the-spot decision that I should be flown directly to a US neurosurgical facility, bypassing the usual casualty evacuation chain. His fortuitous presence nearby and his quick decision probably saved my life.

Editors' conclusion

Air support played a vital and dynamic part in what 5 RAR achieved during Operations Canberra, Robin and Queanbeyan. The difficulties imposed by the steep jungle terrain of the Nui Thi Vai hills and the constant threat of Viet Cong ground fire were severe tests of the professional skills and courage of the pilots. On completion of operations in the Nui Thi Vai hills our CO, John Warr, conducted a debriefing during which he commended 161 (Indep) Recce Flight on the magnificent job their pilots had done flying in support of the battalion throughout these operations. The closeness of their support in the most trying of conditions demonstrated that, being army pilots, they enjoyed a natural affinity for, and a detailed understanding of, an infantry battalion's needs in operations. Their narratives clearly show a magnificent level of devotion to comrades who were locked in ground operations. Understandably, this was an outlook that was inherently more difficult for their RAAF counterparts to acquire. Much more could and should have been done, at all levels in both army and air force hierarchies, to narrow the 'cultural divide' which fuelled the initial and lingering poor understanding of each other's operational imperatives (described in other chapters).

15

THE DEVELOPMENT OF THE RECONNAISSANCE PLATOON

Michael Deak (Michael von Berg)

Editors' introduction

In Chapter 5 it was noted that the conversion of the Anti-Tank Platoon to the Reconnaissance Platoon was a way of finding more useful employment for the platoon in the absence of a role for its anti-armour capabilities (the enemy having no armoured elements in Phuoc Tuy Province). The Australian Army had reorganised in 1965 to structure units for their roles in the Vietnam War and reformed its infantry battalions along the lines of those it had deployed during the Malayan Emergency and the Indonesian Confrontation of Malaysia. However, an Anti-Tank Platoon was added, probably because of the availability of large anti-armour weapons as hand-me-down items from the previous Pentropic organisation. This encompassed large, infantry-based, so-called 'Battle Groups' which could be brigaded to form a 'Task Force'. For obscure reasons, this was modelled on a US Army five-sided Pentomic organisational structure for Cold War scenarios. By 1964 the Australian Army had deemed its Pentropic battle groups to be unsuited to operations in South-East Asia; and, with the advent of Australia's new commitment to Vietnam, the concept was promptly abandoned. But, in brigading combat and combat support elements, the designation 'Task Force' was retained in preference to 'Brigade Group' which had previously been used for many years.

Thus, the Anti-Tank Platoon was armed with large US M40 106 mm recoilless rifles (RCL) which were vehicle-mounted or could be fired on the ground, but only from a solid footing. Their use in a perimeter defence role at the Nui Dat base or at fire support bases, employing canister (grapeshot) ammunition, seems never to have been considered. They were not readily man-portable and their unwieldy weight of 210 kilograms and length of 3.4 metres rendered these RCL of no use against enemy bunkers in close jungle or cave systems in the mountains. A lightweight substitute for such purposes, the US M72 66 mm LAW (light anti-armour weapon), a telescoping rocket launcher of 2.5 kilograms and 0.63/0.88 metres long when folded/extended, were later carried in each rifle section. Consequently, the M40 RCLs remained in storage at Nui Dat, with two being deployed as decorative 'sentries' in front of the Battalion Headquarters (BHQ) facilities, and their crews and their cut-down transport vehicles put to other uses.

Michael Deak

My conversation with Lieutenant Colonel Warr took place a few days after Second Lieutenant Dennis Rainer, a handful of soldiers and I arrived back after marching as a part of the Australian contingent through Saigon on Vietnam's National Day, 1966. We'd gone because after Operation Queanbeyan our commanding officer (CO) thought we deserved a break in Saigon. The march through Saigon, though, was anything but peaceful with the Viet Cong dropping mortar bombs on the forward elements of the marchers. While a little disconcerting, we completed the march without any further disruptions. On returning to Nui Dat I was summoned to see our CO. I was worried that he may have heard of some of the escapades that Dennis and I had got up to in Saigon after the parade and that mortar attack, when some soothing and relaxing elixir was in order. When I reached BHQ and saw the CO, our intelligence officer Captain Bob O'Neill, our operations officer Major Max Carroll and others, my mind went into overdrive and I thought, 'This might not be good'. It wasn't the first time I had fronted the CO for some social infraction or other misdemeanour. When it was explained to me that the battalion was keen to establish its own Reconnaissance Platoon and that I had been selected to form and command this new entity, a wave of relief swept over me.

15. THE DEVELOPMENT OF THE RECONNAISSANCE PLATOON

A detailed briefing followed, in the style of a fireside chat about the new platoon's role, the selection and training of its personnel, its operational support requirements and administrative and logistics issues. I was given instructions to plan and conduct a selection process and training program to be held over a two-week period in the Vung Tau sand hills and the surrounding area. It was envisaged that the Anti-Tank Platoon, which had fought so valiantly up in the Nui Thi Vai hills, would take on the role of the battalion's Reconnaissance Platoon. This would avoid disruption to any of the rifle companies. Because the enemy did not have tanks in our area of operations, the CO decided the employment of the Anti-Tank Platoon should be changed to something more needed. The originator of the idea, I discovered later, was Major Stan Maizey, our battalion's second in command (2IC). 'Stan the Man', as he was affectionately called, was a keen punter like me, and on more than one occasion we tried our luck on a race at Rosehill or a game of seven-card stud.

I don't know what the battalion would have done without Stan the Man's industrious, far-reaching and occasionally questionable procurement methods in those early days of inadequate equipment and supplies. Supply in those first three months in Vietnam was a nightmare, and there were those who referred to 5 RAR as the 'Hydraulic Battalion – will lift anything'. Maizey, although a senior major, was very much our own 'Sergeant Bilko', who believed very little was unprocurable. He was an amazing man who served us extremely well before his talents were identified and he was poached by the Task Force HQ.

After the briefing I went back to the tent I shared with my platoon sergeant, Ray 'Skinny' Calvert. Despite details of the proposal being restricted to a 'need-to-know' basis, I told him much of what was said in the briefing. The CO still had to gain the support and approval of the task force commander, but I knew I could rely on Skinny and wanted his views and recommendations about which of the men in the current Anti-Tank Platoon might be suitable, and his thoughts on how we might carry out our new role. Skinny was an excellent senior non-commissioned officer (NCO), but, unfortunately, he developed a major medical condition which resulted in his return to Australia shortly after the completion of the platoon's training course for its new role. I was sorry to lose him at that stage because I liked and trusted him. I had also served with him before I was commissioned. Clearly, he was disappointed at having to return to Australia but his well-being and ultimately that of the platoon came first. I was pleased I was able to get his thoughts about the proposed changes as his input and suggestions proved invaluable.

To enable me to look at a suitable structure for our new Reconnaissance Platoon it was arranged that I should spend some time with our 3 Squadron, Special Air Service (SAS). Thankfully I knew many of the NCO patrol commanders but was still a little apprehensive about meeting them on their turf. I assumed there might be some suspicion or resentment of a young, recently graduated platoon commander having the temerity to consider conducting small-manned reconnaissance patrols using conventionally trained diggers from an infantry battalion. How wrong I was! Major John Murphy, the officer commanding 3 SAS Squadron, and his officers and some of his hardened and experienced NCO patrol commanders could not have been more relaxed and helpful in supporting what we were trying to achieve. I think they were relieved that, with the advent of reconnaissance platoons which were organic to infantry battalions, they would be able to concentrate more on the stealthy, long-range patrols deep into enemy sanctuaries, which was their primary role in Vietnam. Unlike them, we would operate much closer to our own forces (within 10,000 metres) and never out of artillery range. After these discussions I was heartened by John Murphy and his team's encouragement and knew that with the right training and equipment, we could fulfil the role that our battalion had in mind. These discussions also enabled me to decide on our patrol composition, command structure, weapons, communications systems and the numbers of NCOs and soldiers required in the platoon.

I was very happy with the advice that I had been given and the support 3 SAS Squadron was going to provide in conducting the personnel selection course and training. I felt that although we would operate in a different way to the SAS patrols, we needed their advice and support before we embarked on selection and training. In a two-week training period it could not be an SAS selection course, which would have entailed far too much for us to absorb. We needed a course suited to our competence levels and our small talent pool, half of whom would be national servicemen with barely 18 months of service under their belts. This is not meant to be derogatory in any way because our 'nashos' throughout the battalion were outstanding; but there is a thing called training overload which can do more harm than good, and all we needed were the basic reconnaissance patrol skills and specialist SAS contact drills which were not practised in the battalion. Thankfully, our SAS advisers agreed with my rationale. My proposed platoon structure and outline operating procedures were then discussed with our CO and his HQ team, and they agreed with my suggestions. I was then left to my own devices to

15. THE DEVELOPMENT OF THE RECONNAISSANCE PLATOON

prepare the training syllabus, selection process, equipment and weapons lists, communications arrangements and the platoon's modus operandi. For a recently graduated officer this task was daunting, but having the trust of the CO, the operations officer and the intelligence officer gave me tremendous confidence, a clear sense of purpose and a determination not to let the battalion down. To establish and operate a platoon in a totally new and demanding role in war is difficult, but we were helped by having the advantage of selecting NCOs and soldiers from within the battalion, who were battle-hardened and experienced through six months of patrolling, ambushing, cordon and searches of villages and contact with the enemy. Some had lost mates so there really wasn't much for me to do in scene-setting or preparing them for what they could expect. They had all been living with these realities since the battalion was inserted into Phuoc Tuy. With this experience behind them, I knew there was not much the men needed in the way of telling them what to expect. This meant the SAS instructors and I could concentrate on specialist reconnaissance tactics and techniques and on operating in small self-sufficient groups capable of gaining information and, importantly, staying alive to bring it back.

Because it was only a matter of weeks since one of my section commanders, Norm Womal, had been killed during a contact in the Nui Thi Vai hills, I was still feeling his loss and made a commitment I would do everything possible to ensure that all members of the Reconnaissance Platoon came home. Notwithstanding my determination, I knew that, even with the best intentions, there was only so much I could do and I resolved to select the best available men for the role. I was seeking men who could be moulded into a tight, efficient, fighting platoon; who shared the values of caring, supporting, helping and respecting one another; but who also had the determination and ruthlessness needed to close with and kill the enemy. This embodied the ethos that we would never leave anyone, wounded or dead, behind. Although many who had applied to join the platoon were former rugby and beer-drinking friends of my soldiering days before being commissioned, there is a big difference between protecting a mate's back in a rugby ruck and protecting a mate in a firefight. A friend protects his mate's back in a rugby ruck; a brother protects his mate's back in a firefight. There is a big difference between friendship and brotherhood, which is not understood by many except those who have served in war and have experienced the death or wounding of men to whom they have grown so close. I was determined to instil strong notions of leadership throughout the platoon and a sense of 'brotherhood'. We would not only be protecting each other's backs, but looking after each other mentally and spiritually as well. If a brother was feeling down, we could all pitch in to make a difference. This was generally done through some wicked prank or black humour which created lighter moments to help lift the spirits of any individual who was feeling below par. This approach was applied in abundance and I still laugh when recalling some of the antics.

Captain Peter Isaacs, the adjutant, promulgated a message throughout the battalion seeking volunteers for the new platoon while I canvassed the soldiers of the Anti-Tank Platoon and was delighted that many chose to try for selection. After interviewing volunteers, 40 soldiers and NCOs were named to attend the selection course. When told the course was to be conducted at Back Beach near Vung Tau, many thought that the course was going to be a beach holiday with barbecues, and would be a bit of a junket. How wrong were they!

I was absolutely delighted with the NCOs who had volunteered because I had served with many of them as a soldier, played rugby with them and engaged in the frivolities and mischief that young soldiers get up to. I considered them to be my mates. Of course, this can work for you or against you and, during the selection process, I marked my NCO mates very hard, for they would determine the success or otherwise of the platoon. Corporal Bernard 'Bernie' Smith was a very experienced NCO who had previously served in Malaya and possessed solid leadership skills. Corporal Bob 'Dogs' Kearney, the youngest section commander in the battalion at 20 years of age, had been in my section in 1 RAR. Corporal John 'Blue' Mulby was an outstanding soldier, hard as nails, with an infectious black sense of humour. Lance Corporal William, or Bill, 'Suave Harve' Harvey was another great soldier, who could make masterful sidesteps on both the rugby field and the dance floor. Platoon Sergeant John Lea-Smith, who was relatively new to the battalion, very quickly became my trusted 2IC, confidante and friend and, like Blue Mulby, also possessed a warped sense of humour. All the men who applied were characters, and all good blokes. Many I knew well, so it was a challenge to ensure I assessed everyone fairly based on the standards that the SAS instructors and I wanted them to achieve. I professed an attitude of transparency and inclusiveness, which embraces all fairly and equally, and has no hidden agenda. Not being honest with soldiers is the quickest way to lose their respect and so I led with an approach of 'what you see is what you get', not asking anyone to do anything I was not prepared to do myself. During the selection course I occasionally thought this was not such a good policy.

15. THE DEVELOPMENT OF THE RECONNAISSANCE PLATOON

We had men from every part of the battalion and many did not know one another. A good way to get to know each other quickly is over a beer or something stronger; and that we did whenever we had no night training. Bonding and camaraderie was established within a short period of time and, in part, this was the making of the new platoon. To make sure the bonding sessions did not get out of hand, I would wake the whole team every morning at about 0500 hours and run through the beaches and sand hills of Vung Tau until all dropped – myself included. After a night of 'bonding', this was almost torture. It took me back to my early days of rugby and water polo where I had coaches who instilled in me an almost masochistic bent to drive my body until I was able to push through pain barriers and actually enjoy it. There wasn't a lot of joy in this exercise but we pushed on and the men did extremely well, helped by the fact that all were already extremely fit through time already spent 'in country', where there were very few fat infantrymen. Our normal regimen was light rations, long periods on operations in sauna-like conditions, patrolling while heavily laden, going over and under natural obstacles, all with adrenaline pumping while being hyper-alert. These ensured an inability to accumulate fat or lose physical fitness. There were a few early drop-outs and they were sent back to where they came from in the battalion. As the numbers declined and the remaining individuals got to know each other better, I could see and feel the pride, confidence and cohesive spirit this group of individuals was developing. Over the period of the course this grew stronger and stronger so that, towards the end, they were champing at the bit to get out on operations in their new role.

My hardest task was to select the final members of the platoon, which I did in consultation with the SAS instructors. Those who were not selected were counselled about why they were not successful. In all cases the unsuccessful were good soldiers but not selected because of some characteristic which made them unsuitable for working as a member of a small reconnaissance patrol. All of these men did an amazing job and went back to their platoons and companies as better soldiers; which was of benefit both to them and the battalion. Not being suited for the reconnaissance role in no way diminished them as soldiers and valued members of the battalion. Importantly, getting a pat on the back for having a crack at something different was some compensation for not being selected.

We needed to adopt many specialist skills of the SAS and some of their standard operating procedures. Achieving this in a two-week course was very demanding, but by adapting we adopted! Many of these changes centred on navigation, night movement, communications, observation and deduction skills, breaking-contact drills, medical support, demolitions, calling in supporting fire, bushcraft and survival. Only so much could be achieved in two weeks and, although the SAS instructors were very generous in sharing their knowledge and experience, there was a lot to learn and, in retrospect, our real learning was gained 'on the job', in operations. This on-the-job training aspect became a very important part of our post-operations debrief procedure, where lessons learned or mistakes made were shared, as a reinforcing part of our learning process.

The structure of the Reconnaissance Platoon was three five-man patrols, each commanded by a corporal and one six-man HQ patrol, commanded by me as platoon commander. The equipment carried by each patrol was a PRC-25 VHF radio and an M60 7.62 mm machine gun. Each soldier carried a personal weapon of choice, either a 5.56 mm M16 or 7.62 mm self-loading rifle. Each patrol also carried an M79 40 mm grenade launcher, M26 hand grenades, smoke grenades, ammunition, a medical kit and food, water, maps and compass. The patrol would consist of a forward scout (a duty shared by rotation), the corporal patrol commander, a radio operator, a machine gunner and a 'tail-end-charlie', who was also the patrol medic. My HQ patrol would consist of a forward scout, myself, two radio operators, my platoon sergeant and the tail-end-charlie who was also the platoon medic. The two radios of my HQ patrol were to provide control of the three five-man patrols and a separate radio to link with BHQ and to call for artillery or close air support. Because my HQ patrol had the additional weight of an extra radio and batteries, a machine gun was not carried, but we had everything else when it came to small arms, grenade launchers and ammunition. This platoon structure required a full complement of 26 individuals to be available for putting all patrols into the field at once. To allow for absences due to illness or leave, a total of 28 personnel were selected for the newly established platoon.

My reasoning for the patrols to be armed with the heavy M60 general purpose machine gun, at a small cost to mobility in fluid situations, was both tactical and psychological. When a small reconnaissance patrol contacted the enemy, the M60's ability to put down fire at a cyclic rate of 550 rounds per minute would keep the enemy occupied and their heads down, while the patrol extricated itself and rapidly departed the scene to

15. THE DEVELOPMENT OF THE RECONNAISSANCE PLATOON

report on the enemy's presence. Encountering machine gun fire could cause the enemy to think that the small five-man information-gathering patrol was actually a much larger unit, such as a platoon or company, which always employed M60s. This rationale proved to be sound, for it certainly worked for us.

Although we now had the Reconnaissance Platoon, we did not have all the equipment necessary to fulfil our new role. I had learned a lot from our battalion 2IC Stan the Man, so what we didn't have we begged, borrowed, traded or found unattended until our requirements had been met. On our first operations we had to learn on the job, until we became comfortable with the standards achieved. Becoming familiar with the new platoon structure and the unusual benefit of having internal radio communications as well as direct contact with BHQ and fire support agencies for when we encountered serious trouble were significant changes for us. Of course, there was some concern about the risk of losing a patrol or even the entire platoon due to enemy action. It was not an unrealistic possibility and we needed to gain our 'reconnaissance legs' slowly, building up a record of competence and success.

The patrols would all be mobile, moving together on the one axis with HQ patrol in the centre, the best position for radio signals reception, with a patrol to the left, two to the right; or one on a piece of ground not necessarily on axis but of tactical importance. The key requirement was radio contact at all times, and although long periods of radio silence were encouraged, it was necessary that all were always on radio alert so that messages could be acknowledged by simply pressing the transmit switch using a simple, intermittent, on-off code without speaking; and the radio carrier wave could be silently detected by all radios operating on the frequency being used. If a patrol was in trouble, they could let it be known quickly so that assistance could be provided.

As we developed both skills and confidence, we were deployed further afield. Our tactics were determined by enemy activity, the terrain and the task in hand. After being silently inserted into the area of interest, slow movement of 400 to 1,000 metres maximum per day was involved. Where smaller enemy numbers were suspected or assumed, the platoon would be split into its small patrols to operate independently. If we were operating well away from the battalion and the likelihood of encountering a large enemy force was high, we would operate as a full platoon, concealing indications that the enemy would associate with this size of group. Once we had perfected our methods, we were fully utilised by the battalion in a multitude of tasks which changed through necessity or innovation.

There was always the risk of death or wounding by booby traps or mines and, like the rest of the battalion, we did not wear or carry any personal protective equipment such as body armour or helmets. In our case, even if it had been available, it is questionable whether, loaded down by protective equipment, we could have operated effectively in a jungle environment. The heat, humidity, monsoonal rains and densely vegetated terrain would have made it almost impossible to move freely and quietly, or quickly when the need arose. We wore mostly US-style combat clothing (because it had more pockets and was more durable), bush hats and our personal webbing and backpacks which were made up of a mixture of Australian, UK, US and ARVN (Army of the Republic of Vietnam) gear. We went without underwear and socks. Being constantly wet through from sweat and rain, the less clothing worn the quicker a man would dry out. This also proved a good way of reducing our proneness to the ever-present skin problems of ringworm and tinea. We had a job to do and we needed to feel comfortable and able to move freely for long periods of time through different types of thick foliage and dense jungle, while remaining alert and effective. I remember one incident where a senior officer who had recently joined the battalion disapproved of the camouflage paint we had applied in irregular patterns to our weapons. I told him that on patrol the weapons' plastic furniture and metal surfaces, when covered with our sweat or rain, glistened and could reflect light to indicate our presence to the enemy – at which he laughed. I respectfully told him I would not be removing our camouflage paint from our weapons and if he had a problem with that he should take it up with the CO. I never heard more from him and we kept our camouflage paint. With our individual outfits and machine gun ammunition belts across each man's chest we looked not dissimilar to Pancho Villa's bandits.

Weapon cleanliness was not a problem because all took great pride in their weapons. Like every platoon in the battalion we test fired all weapons before operations to ensure they were in good working condition. Everyone in the Reconnaissance Platoon was permitted to carry as much ammunition as he wanted and all were well loaded-up in case we deliberately engaged an enemy force, as happened when we ambushed them.

15. THE DEVELOPMENT OF THE RECONNAISSANCE PLATOON

Adequate water supply was always at the top of our minds. Without it, soldiers soon become less effective and at risk of becoming heat casualties, jeopardising both their security and the mission. Personally, I carried seven water bottles and most others did the same. Some dumped certain large cans of food, especially the despised US ham and lima beans, to make room for a water bladder inside their pack. It is possible to operate in hot tropical environments without surplus food but not without adequate water. One of the major benefits of having the Reconnaissance Platoon was that it enabled the battalion to deploy us to the high ground of the Nui Dinh hills, west of Nui Dat, and the steep Long Hai range to the south-east where we were the first Australians to patrol there. We could scale these features quicker than a company, and it enabled the CO to fully utilise his rifle companies on other major operational tasks. Because many of our platoon tasks were on high ground in the dry season, the only water resupply we could expect was by helicopter at a tactically suitable time. Hence the need to carry as much as we could in case opportunities for resupply proved scarce.

Usually, the platoon managed to get on to high ground without being detected by the enemy or the local civilians, and water rationing needed to be strictly applied. In the dry season, if we were operating a platoon-sized fighting patrol to seek deliberate contact with the enemy, we would move parallel to creek lines (but not in them because the enemy were usually then located close to water). Here we had fewer problems in keeping up with our water requirements. But at night, if not ambushing, we would head back up to the high ground to harbour securely.

Our combat rations consisted of a mixture of dehydrated and canned US or Australian rations. Many carried an onion or fresh chillies to spice up a good curry mixed with rice. However we could only make curry in a relatively safe area because of its strong cooking smells.

It is amazing how little food is needed to survive but, without tea or coffee, hunger pangs are accentuated. A good brew is a great morale booster and nerve calmer. The platoon was normally inserted into search areas by helicopter, armoured personnel carriers (APCs) or on foot. If on foot, insertion would normally be from a secure area like a fire support base in first or last light, into a jungle area that was well covered from view. If deploying by helicopter, either Royal Australian Air Force or US Army Aviation units were used. As a deception measure, several dummy runs were done in and out of areas so that the enemy had great difficulty in knowing exactly where the helicopters had landed and whether any troops had alighted. Extractions were mostly done in a similar manner, after we had been able to secure an area for the helicopters to touch down.

Insertion by APCs, although noisy, was used as a tactic to confuse the enemy. The platoon would be inside the APCs and out of sight, with some other troops or some of our own who were not being deployed carried openly on top of the vehicles to give the impression that it was just a routine APC patrol with some infantry protection. At a predetermined alighting spot in a well concealed area, while the APCs were still moving, keeping their engine revolutions high, the loading ramps would slowly be lowered while still moving; the patrol would quickly alight without any changes to the sounds and movements of the APCs. This was a very successful insertion tactic from fire support bases, where the enemy thought these were the regular APC-mounted clearing patrols providing security to the fire support base. Because they saw soldiers on top of the carriers going out and going back, they were unaware we had dismounted while on the move.

While patrolling, no one spoke aloud and hand signals were used for communicating. When in close proximity to another man, whispers were used. This was the standard form of communications for all Australian platoons on operations and was very effective, both for security and in keeping everyone informed at all times. Breakfast was light, mostly a brew with a biscuit, lunch was eaten cold with water, and a late afternoon meal was a good, morale-boosting cook up. Although cooking created smells, it didn't matter much because we always moved away to another area just on last light.

Whether we were operating as a platoon or as small patrols, in any contact with the enemy we could call for artillery to drop initial rounds onto ground near the enemy's position from where the fire could be adjusted onto the enemy or his likely withdrawal routes. This could be executed in about five minutes because wherever we were, there was always an artillery battery allotted in direct support (DS) which meant that its fire was guaranteed to the battalion. Working in isolation, with perhaps a backup force being some two to three hours away, the possibility of encountering a larger, well-equipped enemy force was a reality. If such a situation occurred, having artillery support immediately available, and able to be quickly adjusted to suit the circumstances, was a tactical advantage and huge morale booster.

15. THE DEVELOPMENT OF THE RECONNAISSANCE PLATOON

Both Australian and New Zealand artillery batteries were marvellous in these DS roles. Also readily available were the heavier guns of our US allies, whose 155 mm, 175 mm and 8 inch batteries could be called on through the battalion's DS battery commander. He was always located with BHQ and, when we requested them, these fire support assets came on line quickly.

Naval gunfire was used in one incident to silence an enemy mortar which was creating havoc in a major enemy attack on the defended ARVN village of Lo Gom, located east of the Long Hai hills near the larger coastal village of Lang Phuoc Hai. The Reconnaissance Platoon, in an ambush position some 5,000 metres away, had identified the mortar position and engaged it with Australian and US artillery without success. 1 ATF HQ, through C Company's artillery forward observer, offered US naval gunfire support from a vessel cruising on station in the South China Sea. Although we were about 5 kilometres from the target, the naval 5 inch shells sounded like freight trains passing our ambush position. The enemy mortar was silenced very effectively.

Like the rifle companies we also had access to gunships, airstrikes, flare ships, 'Puff the Magic Dragon' (Dakota C47 cargo aircraft using the call sign *Spooky* and armed with several multi-barrelled machine guns with very high cyclic rates of fire), and *Dustoff* helicopters. I cannot speak highly enough of our operations team at BHQ and the rifle company commanders for the incredible support they provided us when in trouble. Their unfailing support gave us the confidence and encouragement to be more enterprising and daring, knowing when the 'proverbial' hit the fan, the battalion would look after us.

We soon noticed that many of us had started to develop a sixth sense. There was often a feeling of something being not quite right where the hair, for whatever reason, stood up at the back of the neck and, in many cases, these feelings proved to be correct. In situations of danger, isolation and highly elevated alertness with constant adrenaline rushes, survival instincts seemed to kick in, like some form of human radar, to warn of danger or hint that something wasn't quite right.

Another skill we developed was tracking. The entire platoon acquired this ability; some were better than others. Signs which others might not notice were quickly picked up and told a story – how many people had passed, how long ago, enemy or villager, what size loads were they carrying, running or walking, travelling in which direction? These were all very important bits of information passed back for analysis. Dogs are great for detection and tracking, but they can't make assumptions or draw conclusions!

Although we were getting very good at our game and were used extensively by the battalion, having only a day or two in base every month, we had to recognise any signs of burnout. When we were in base we would play hard. What was wonderful when coming back into base was to be met by the CO and the Salvation Army's John Bentley, with a kind word from the CO and a hot cup of tea from John the 'Salvo'; although most of the blokes were looking forward to something a bit cooler. The CO knew all my NCOs and soldiers by name and nickname and greeted them in that way, which for us was quite special. They thought the world of 'Wingy' as the diggers affectionately called the CO, knowing how much he cared and what he stood for.

Our other tasks included assisting in the training of the ARVN Regional Force NCOs with Captain George Mansford at Binh Ba, leading the 5 RAR rifle companies into cordon positions on village cordon and search operations, surveillance cover for the rifle companies during minefield construction, riding on the splash boards of APCs while clearing roads, reinforcing D Company on the Horseshoe feature, and frequent patrolling and ambushing tasks throughout a large patch of jungle known as The Long Green. The lighter moments of the platoon and how this group of different personalities, backgrounds and experience became such a close-knit family are worthy of mention. When in base, where alcohol was permitted, we all defused, using the time-honoured Australian cure-all of a relaxing drink with close mates. After a quick shower and getting rid of a month's dirt I would go up to be debriefed by Captain Bob O'Neill, our intelligence officer, or sometimes the CO or operations officer. I would usually go to the diggers' boozer where my blokes had already started with a beer or two and have a very informal chat with them about the operation. What did we do well and not so well, and what we could do better in the future? Sometimes the best ideas and innovations come from an unlikely quarter and my diggers and NCOs were not backward in coming forward with a couple of beers under their belt. The ideas and suggestions were not all good but they were being heard; and that was vitally important to them. Once the boozer had closed we moved to my tent and the conversations would continue until the early hours of the

15. THE DEVELOPMENT OF THE RECONNAISSANCE PLATOON

morning. No matter how loosened the tongues became there was never a harsh word or disagreement and, 50 years later, those who have not passed away keep in touch.

The day following an operation or task was always spent getting ready for the next time we were to leave the base. In preparation, before attending the battalion Orders Group to receive my orders, I would warn out the platoon to attend a later briefing and platoon Orders Group at the back of my tent where I would use a terrain mud map to assist me in giving orders. I wanted every member of the platoon to know as much as I did by providing a good overview of the enemy situation, the terrain and area where we were going to be operating. I did this by giving them a description of our mission, how I saw it developing and where we fitted into the battalion's overall scheme before assigning tasks to my patrol commanders. At the end of my briefing and orders, the patrol commanders went away with their patrols to conduct their own Orders Group, giving the detailed instructions on how each man in their patrol was to participate in the platoon's part in the operation. I did it this way to personally pass on as much information as I could to every soldier, and to encourage interaction and input from them. Our lives depended on each other and I wanted them to understand this reality and for each of them to foster it. I would say to the platoon that if anyone was hit we would aim to get him out and on his way to hospital in Vung Tau within 30 minutes. Whatever we were doing, our primary objective would instantly become getting our man out, the operation or patrol objectives becoming secondary. Many of my ex-soldiers at reunions have told me that this policy really resonated with them because they knew they would never be abandoned. The positive effect this had on platoon morale cannot be overstated.

To gain information we would spend time in Vietnamese villages mixing with the villagers, particularly with the children. For these tasks I had the services of an interpreter who did a terrific job for us in engaging with the locals. This was as much a hearts and minds exercise as an information-seeking operation, and although we never really knew who was friend or foe, I felt it best in these circumstances to look for the good, not the bad, and respect the villagers' customs, culture and hospitality. At times, the latter was unbelievable. A poor village chief's family offering you a Vietnamese delicacy of roasted pigs ears with '*nuoc mam*', a very pungent fermented fish sauce laced with sliced bullet chillies. With a swig or two of rice whisky this was not hard to accept, but when the chief was getting into his '*mot, hai, ba, yo*' mood (one, two, three, down!), it was time to bid farewell. After all, we were on duty and I needed to debrief our interpreter and others in the platoon about what they had observed or heard. These things would not have been possible without the platoon being friendly and respectful of women and children. The lives of kids in the midst of a dirty war about which they understood little would have been made a lot worse if we, the foreign '*Uc Dai Loi* round-eyes' (Australian Caucasians), treated them badly. The Reconnaissance Platoon had a lot to do with locals and always treated them with compassion and respect.

The antics and sense of the ridiculous of everyone in the platoon were an immensely important relief valve. Some might say this bordered on being immature and irresponsible, and today I might agree, but at the time these lighter moments are what kept us sane. We worked hard and just loved each other's company and all that it provided during a dangerous period in our lives. By the end of our tour we all had that blank 'thousand-yard stare' and, although we had become very good at what we were doing, we were mentally exhausted. The intensity, anxiety, mental concentration and enemy contacts were telling; and the relief when we all boarded HMAS *Sydney* for our trip home was not only felt, it could be seen.

It's very difficult to touch on everything that the platoon went through from start to finish. The unique and gifted people with whom I served and who contributed enormously to our success made the platoon and its experiences very special to me. I was honoured to select, establish and lead a specialised infantry reconnaissance platoon and was humbled to have the privilege of leading an outstanding group of individuals who became brothers for life. In Vietnam they were ordinary young men doing extraordinary things. More than that cannot be asked.

Today, when I am asked to speak or give a presentation to a battalion's reconnaissance platoon or to the Advanced Reconnaissance Course at the Infantry Centre, I look with great pride at the young men who have decided to take on this role knowing we, of the first infantry battalion reconnaissance platoon, spawned a legacy which is being kept alive and built upon by the magnificent young soldiers who are serving today.

Editors' conclusion

The availability of the Anti-Tank Platoon's members as a basis for manning, equipping and training a desirable alternative capability was fortuitous. In the early days of 1 ATF in Phuoc Tuy Province, 3 SAS Squadron members were heavily committed to building up their knowledge of a new operational environment and honing their highly specialised tactics and techniques to suit any unfamiliar conditions which confronted them. Quite properly, they were not employed on reconnaissance tasks that were within the infantry battalions' capabilities. For a battalion CO to detach a platoon from a rifle company to undertake specific missions meant reducing the capability and flexibility of that company, which restricted its employability. In 5 RAR, having available an organic component which was selectively manned, equipped and trained for intelligence missions meant that the CO could separately task it for reconnaissance, surveillance, selective ambushing or civic action tasks without cannibalising one of his four manoeuvre companies. This was a great advantage. It made a huge difference to the amount of accurate short-term intelligence information available to the battalion, for which our intelligence officer was extremely grateful.

The Reconnaissance Platoon was a very successful development but, surprisingly, it was not followed up by the battalions which came after 5 RAR in Vietnam. Some retained the designated Anti-Tank Platoon and employed it as an extra rifle platoon, as 5 RAR had done initially. In others it was replaced by a Tracker Platoon which employed war dogs to detect enemy presence and to follow up their withdrawing elements. Perhaps the reconnaissance platoon idea required a particular combination of perceptive, adaptable people who could work well together, from CO to riflemen, in order for it to become feasible.

16

JOHN WARR AS COMMANDING OFFICER: HIS APPROACH TO THE WAR

Max Carroll, Peter Isaacs,
Michael Deak (Michael von Berg) and Mark Warr

Editors' introduction

In any infantry battalion the key person is the commanding officer (CO). His position is very challenging to hold, demanding knowledge, operational skill, judgement and humanity in directing the efforts of several hundred men in a complex and dangerous environment. COs vary in their effectiveness and how they are regarded by the men under their command. In 5th Battalion, the Royal Australian Regiment (5 RAR), the overwhelming consensus, both while we were on operations in Vietnam and over the several decades since then, was that we were very lucky to have had John Warr to lead us. In this chapter, three of the officers who related most closely with him on operations, and one member of his family, present their views from different perspectives to make clear the reasons for his high place in our esteem and affection. His personality and his leadership are discussed by those who knew him best as our commander in war.

Max Carroll

I was still at the Staff College, Queenscliff, when my posting to 5 RAR as a company commander was promulgated in late 1965. I was very satisfied. I had been requesting a return to regimental duties as I had not served in a regular battalion since late 1959. I had done my time as a Citizens Military Forces adjutant, an instructor at an Army Headquarters School and a Grade 3 staff appointment before Staff College. It was common knowledge that 5 RAR was the logical replacement for 1 RAR in Vietnam, so I also had active service to look forward to. Many of my infantry student colleagues, who were destined for a variety of Grade 2 staff appointments on various headquarters, were rather envious.

On one of my visits to Canberra, where my family had remained while I was at Queenscliff, I paid my respects to the Directorate of Infantry at Army Headquarters. I had the dual intent of not only saying 'thank you very much', but also of finding out all I could about my new CO, Lieutenant Colonel John Warr, who was a complete stranger to me. I learnt as much as the guarded staff officers were prepared to tell me, but it was enough to establish that he had a good reputation, otherwise he would not be commanding an Australian Regular Army battalion. He was an Royal Military College graduate of 1947, had served in Japan in the British Commonwealth Occupation Force and then in Korea with 3 RAR, where he had been badly wounded. He had also done an exchange appointment with the Canadian Army. I was looking forward to meeting him.

It was Wednesday morning, 5 January 1966, when I reported for duty with 5 RAR at the old Holsworthy Barracks. It was like coming home. I had last been there in 1957 with 3 RAR before going to Malaya. The immaculately turned out regimental policeman who gave me directions at the front gate was a clear indication of the high standard of this battalion, and this in turn meant a good CO. I was duly ushered in to meet John Warr and he came around from behind his desk to greet me. I knew that he was appraising me, as I was him, but his keen eyes, ready grin and firm handshake made for a relaxed first meeting. I instinctively liked this bloke and knew I would enjoy working with him. In easy chairs over a cup of coffee he briefed me on all aspects of the battalion. We discussed current strength, reinforcements due, the likelihood of going to Vietnam, and the heavy training ahead. Then he got around to telling me what I would be doing. I was to be officer commanding (OC) Support

Company. He must have noticed my disappointment, as I badly wanted a rifle company. He went on to say that, in addition to Support Company, I would be battalion operations officer and battle second in command (2IC). This was a system that 1 RAR had necessarily adopted from being part of 173 Airborne Brigade. As we would be replacing 1 RAR, we would also be following the same system. He added that the job would be demanding and meant writing all the battalion operation orders, for which staff training was essential. When we were deployed, I would be running the battalion command post and the operational radio command net. He concluded by saying that as only himself, Stan Maizey – the 2IC – and I were Staff College graduates, perhaps I now understood why I had arrived straight from Staff College. This latter remark was delivered with his disarming grin! And I had been checking him out before joining. It was obvious to me then that he had been in close liaison with the Director of Infantry and subsequently I had won the lottery! And so began a very close, professional relationship, as well as a lifelong friendship.

John Warr was a commander with high standards, which is as it should be. He knew what he wanted, clearly expressed this in his orders and expected his subordinates to ensure these standards were met. Training for war is always at a hard, ruthless tempo, particularly so when it is known that in several months' time shooting to kill will be the norm. The time from when we were officially warned in late January 1966 for deployment to Vietnam, until when our advance party left on 20 April 1966, was short and so could not be wasted. Between late January and early February we had several hundred reinforcements march in who had never worked together at their final platoon or company levels, let alone as a battalion. Several new officers marched into the battalion, including myself, who had to get a grip rapidly on things. This was the time to get things right because errors here could be corrected without loss of life. We succeeded because John Warr was everywhere: observing, talking and listening to all ranks, and quietly and shrewdly assessing their strengths and weaknesses. He was a good manager who got the best out of people. He rode with a loose rein, but God help anyone, who, after a fair warning, didn't measure up. They left! This particularly applied to officers, warrant officers and senior non-commissioned officers (NCOs), as his soldiers' lives depended on these people. He also continued this policy in Vietnam and we were a tightly welded unit, efficient, confident and proud when we departed from Australia; and our CO was held in high esteem by all ranks.

Vietnam put all the training to the test; we hit the ground running and never looked back. There were difficult, often tense periods, particularly during prolonged operations, when strain and weariness were constant companions; it was then that the CO's calm leadership prevailed. He led by example and I, as his senior operations officer who worked closely with him in the planning and execution of our war, often saw his coolness under stress. I admired him greatly and learned a lot from him. He had an easy, laid-back style with not only me but other officers on the headquarters who worked closely with him, such as Stan Maizey, the 2IC, Peter Isaacs, the adjutant/assistant operations officer, and Bob O'Neill, the intelligence officer. He would often pose questions which invited discussion, during which he would pick our brains. Obviously, he was testing a plan he had in his head for weaknesses when exposed to other viewpoints, and he always listened carefully to what was said. After he had formulated his plan for an operation he would then pass it to me to work out the fine detail, coordination and writing of the draft operation order. This I then cleared with him before the final production of the order, which he then issued at his Orders Group. I liked working for him.

I only disagreed with one of John Warr's operational decisions, and that was during Operation Canberra, referred to in Chapter 6 and by Peter Isaacs in this chapter. I felt then and still do, that he should have allowed Bruce McQualter's B Company attack to proceed. 'The Role Of An Infantry Battalion', published in *The Division in Battle Pamphlet No 1* is unequivocal, and reads:

> To seek out and close with the enemy, to kill or capture him, to seize and hold ground and to repel attack, by day or night, regardless of season, weather or terrain.[1]

B Company had successfully found the enemy, were undetected and were ready to go in. Bruce was bitterly disappointed at being pulled back. We shared his disappointment, particularly as he had the key element of surprise in his favour. I knew him well, having served together twice before. He was a competent leader, with a superb company which he had trained well. If he said he could successfully attack, I believed him. However, the CO's decision was final, so we obeyed and got on with the war, without recriminations.

---

1   Australian Military Board, *The division in battle*, nos 1–11, Pamphlet No 1: *Organisation and tactics,* Army Headquarters, Canberra, 1966, p 14.

16. JOHN WARR AS COMMANDING OFFICER

John Warr's relations with the task force commander, Brigadier David Jackson, were good and easy, as the task force commander allowed both of his battalion commanders a fair bit of latitude. David Jackson was well experienced in Vietnam, having commanded the Australian Army Training Team Vietnam, then the Australian Army Force Vietnam, before assuming command of 1st Australian Task Force (1 ATF). He ran a good Task Force, although he was severely restricted in terms of what could be done by only two battalions. His successor, Brigadier Stuart Graham, inherited the same problems. He too was easy to work with; our relations with the Task Force headquarters staff also improved when our 2IC, Stan Maizey, moved there to become the task force operations officer.

I feel I must offer some words of support for Stuart Graham, who has been maligned by a host of armchair warriors with perfect hindsight, for his decision to build the barrier minefield from Dat Do to the sea. In the planning stage, he sought the opinions of both John Warr and Colin Townsend, his two battalion COs, plus Brian Florence, the OC of 1 Field Squadron, Royal Australian Engineers. All were against it, pointing out the time-honoured principle that an obstacle must be covered by observation and fire. However, the Vietnamese province chief guaranteed to provide this cover. Graham next put his proposal to higher headquarters, both Australian and US, and NO ONE OBJECTED! His hope was that the obstacle would free his limited infantry resources for use elsewhere. In the event, the Vietnamese failed to fulfil their commitment, which was a bitter lesson learnt! The Army of the Republic of Vietnam (ARVN) let him down! Again, I am not aware of any resultant ill feelings between Graham and his subordinate unit commanders. We, including John Warr, accepted his decision and got on with the job.

A few closing words on John Warr. He was a gentleman in his dealings with others, and was a gentle man by nature, although there was a strong band of steel beneath the quiet, smiling exterior. It was indeed remarkable that a man who did not drink alcohol, smoke, swear or lose his temper should be held in such high regard and esteem by the rather wild, hardened and at times 'hairy-heeled' bunch of officers, warrant officers, NCOs and men who were 5 RAR. We all respected his professional competence, but we also knew that he cared deeply for his battalion, and this was reflected in our sincere feelings for him. We all agreed that we were indeed lucky to have him as CO.

Peter Isaacs

I joined the Australian Army from the UK in January 1963 and was posted to 1 RAR at Holsworthy, NSW. At the time, John Warr was OC B Company. As I was a platoon commander in E Company, I didn't really get to know him at all, although I do remember him arranging for a Sydney stockbroker to come and address the officers one evening in our mess at Gallipoli Barracks. It was at a time when the darling of the Sydney Stock Exchange was the Kalgoorlie-based mining company Poseidon, and everyone with a few bob to invest was hoping to make a fortune in Australia's burgeoning mining industry. I think it did, however, indicate John's interest in business, an interest that he was to develop after he retired from the army.

It wasn't really until 1964 that I got to know him. He had been appointed the senior administration and logistics staff officer on 1 RAR Battalion Headquarters (BHQ, which was multi-functionally organised and staffed to operate as a Battle Group HQ within the Pentropic divisional structure) where I had become a junior operations staff officer. In late 1964, orders were received to reform 1 RAR into a smaller 750-man infantry battalion suitable for operations in South-East Asia, and create 5 RAR from the 'leftovers', it was largely John's responsibility to bring this upheaval about. As was his nature, he set about it with his customary enthusiasm and eye for detail but was probably as disappointed as I was when informed that neither of us would remain with 1 RAR during its forthcoming deployment to South Vietnam, scheduled to occur in April 1965.

I'm sure that John was doubly disappointed to learn that he was not to become 5 RAR's first CO; that honour going to Peter Oxley who was then the military attaché in Saigon and not due to join the battalion until May 1965. 1 RAR and 5 RAR separated at the beginning of 1965 and John assumed 'administrative command' of 5 RAR when the battalion was formally established on 1 March. This arrangement continued after 1 RAR's departure for South Vietnam in April and until Peter Oxley joined and assumed command in May.

Recognition of John's hard work and unstinting efforts came with the announcement that he was to be promoted to command of the battalion in September. Although it was assumed that 5 RAR would relieve 1 RAR in South Vietnam in April 1966, this was not confirmed until January.

John prepared the battalion for war with a combination of realism for the complexity of the task at hand, toughness when necessary and an understanding of the strengths and weaknesses of his officers, warrant officers and senior NCOs. Of the 16 officers who had formed the battalion in March 1965, only nine of the originals remained when the full complement of 37 embarked with the battalion for South Vietnam in April a year later. This enormous throughput of officers and a seriously understrength cadre of experienced warrant officers and senior NCOs occurred at a time when the battalion was being brought up to strength with the first drafts of partly trained national servicemen. By the time the battalion embarked for Vietnam, these comprised approximately 50 per cent of the unit's strength. It was a severe handicap that John overcame through persistence with the various tiers of higher headquarters. He was able to obtain for the battalion the personnel and the equipment needed from what turned out to be a chronically under-resourced ordnance system. The reality was that in 1965–66, the Australian Army was ill-prepared for the task of mobilising the forces that politicians were committing to a war in South-East Asia.

As adjutant and assistant operations officer, it was my privilege to serve John closely and to develop a friendship that continued until he died in 1999. I don't ever recall seeing John lose his temper, nor do I recall him raising his voice. He had an easygoing style and, unlike some COs I have known, was always approachable. He encouraged discussion, the exchange of views and ideas. We who served him did so to the best of our abilities because we all recognised his decent human nature, understood what he wanted to achieve and were determined to achieve it with him.

I have heard it said by a former senior NCO that he considered 5 RAR to have been outstanding because John Warr commanded the battalion and his officers led from the front. He cited the unusually high number of fatal officer casualties as evidence for this. His view of our officer casualties, although quite widely held, does not reflect the reality of the actual circumstances. The best infantry officers lead from the front when circumstances demand, but the five who were killed were all victims of mines which are indiscriminate. Nevertheless, they were certainly among the best officers we had.

In Chapter 6 there is an account of a near collision on 8 October 1966 between B Company and some 30 members of the Viet Cong (VC) 274 Regiment. In deciding not to allow B Company to attack what was probably the headquarters of this VC Regiment, but rather to call in massive artillery and offensive air support, I believe John was following the advice he had been given by Major General Tom Daly on the eve of our departure for South Vietnam.

Had we attacked and killed or captured 274 Regiment, it would have been an outstanding tactical victory, but would it have had a major impact on the war? Of course not, but we would certainly have taken casualties, possibly in significant numbers if, as 11th-hour intelligence had revealed, B Company had encountered a much stronger force than was revealed by their initial contact. Men are alive today and their descendants too because of John Warr's decision on that day. It was not a war of Australia's national survival, nor of great strategic importance. At the time, I thought John's decision was wrong, but with the benefit of hindsight, I cannot now criticise him for that decision.

Like any man, John favoured some people more than others and, in my opinion, he was at times hard on some of his officers who were the least deserving of criticism. Nevertheless, he dealt decisively with those officers, warrant officers and senior NCOs who, prior to embarkation and in the early months of our deployment, failed to meet the high standards he set. Within BHQ John had several gifted individuals, namely his successive seconds in command Stan Maizey and Ivor 'Blue' Hodgkinson, operations officer and OC Support Company Max Carroll and, from August 1966, intelligence officer Bob O'Neill. Stan and Blue ran the administration of the battalion with energy and flair, and relieved John of what was a major headache prior to and during the first six months of our deployment. Max was a master of staff duties and wrote the complex plans to implement John's operational concepts. He drove the operations and provided the 'aggression'. Bob was the analyst and thinker, and was highly influential on John's decisions as to the concept of operations. This was significant because until the arrival of Brigadier Stuart Graham as 1 ATF Commander in January 1967, Brigadier David Jackson had permitted both battalion commanders considerable freedom of action in deciding on their operational priorities. From the army's experiences in the Malayan Emergency, John had developed a good understanding of the concept of counter-revolutionary warfare. He did not believe that pursuing VC Main Force units all over the province was either feasible at the time, or likely to produce the necessary results in terms of bringing security to the population and separating them from the VC.

16. JOHN WARR AS COMMANDING OFFICER

5 RAR developed the concept and procedures for cordon and search operations and conducted several highly effective examples. They were not dramatic, headline-grabbing events. Barbed wire enclosures containing fearful and uncooperative villagers morphed into white cloth tape enclosures in which villagers awaiting questioning were fed and entertained with music played by the Battalion Band! It was not because John necessarily believed that Vietnamese civilians should be treated gently; after all, many, if not most, were VC sympathisers and some were active supporters. It was mainly because better results were obtained by treating them with kindness, and many embedded VC cadre members were thus successfully rooted out of the communities which they had hitherto controlled.

Towards the end of our tour, we began the construction of what became the infamous 'fence'; the 11-kilometre, mined wire barrier between the Horseshoe feature and the coast. John had misgivings about the concept and raised them with Brigadier Graham, but I don't recall his expressing them within the battalion. We got on with it and built the fence with the assistance of our supporting Engineer Field Squadron who had the unenviable task of laying more than 30,000 mines. Brigadier Graham's plans were fully supported by his operations and intelligence staff and approved by the Commanding General of II Field Force Vietnam (IIFFV) to whom he reported. So far as I am aware, no objection was raised by Commander, Australian Force Vietnam, in Saigon. If the Vietnamese military authorities had fulfilled their obligations, the VC might have been prevented from lifting so many mines and using them against our successors. Graham didn't have the benefit of hindsight that his many critics have enjoyed.

During the year, we took 26 fatal casualties, some the results of our own errors, and a further 79 were wounded in action. Our grief was expressed through battalion parades at which our padres gave thanks for the lives of the fallen and their service to Australia. If John was affected by the casualties, he didn't show it. Perhaps he drew strength from his Christian Science faith.

It was a privilege to have served John for almost two years in both peace and war. I learned much from his example and from those individuals I mentioned earlier. Battalions reflect their commander's style and hence

John Warr led a battalion that was second to none. The late Ron Hamlyn, who commanded both Administration Company and B Company after Bruce McQualter was killed, summed it up when he said:

> Every night for the next few years I used to thank the Lord for giving 5 RAR John Arnold Warr as commanding officer; the most compassionate and caring man I ever met.

Michael Deak (Michael von Berg)

Lieutenant Colonel John Warr and I go back to the days of 1 RAR (1962–64) before I was commissioned. On more than one occasion I was a source of some concern in the battalion for the occasional social indiscretion and being somewhat high spirited. When I was selected for the Officer Cadet School, Portsea, it surprised John Warr and many others, but none more so when I graduated in December 1965 and was posted to 5 RAR in January 1966 where John Warr was now the CO. Although now commissioned, my past exploits could have very easily curtailed my new career before it had time to start. The CO, with one phone call or stroke of the pen, could have banished me from the battalion to some lesser role, as the battalion was going to war, but he didn't and that's where our journey really began. He must have seen something in me despite my past misdemeanours. A CO with less patience and understanding may not have been as accommodating.

Once deployed in Vietnam, I took my responsibilities as a platoon commander in A Company very seriously, particularly on operations and in looking after my men, who were a great bunch. But there was friction between the OC A Company and myself, mostly on tactical and operational issues that I will not go into. Suffice it to say that my time in the company was limited after the OC A Company reported me for gambling with the troops. This resulted in my fronting the task force commander. The CO could have once again dispensed with my services but instead transferred me to Support Company and the Anti-Tank Platoon under the watchful eye, guidance and inspirational leadership of Major Max Carroll, for whom I had enormous respect. Respect is paramount in the relationship between any company commander and his platoon commanders. Where there is no respect there is no trust, and happily these two very important characteristics in Max were there in abundance, which assisted me enormously in my new role.

16. JOHN WARR AS COMMANDING OFFICER

When the CO tasked me to establish the battalion's Reconnaissance Platoon, I was delighted and honoured to be given the opportunity and determined to do whatever was possible to not let him or the battalion down. My fellow officers and the battalion deserved nothing less. In many ways that task, its responsibilities and the wonderful men I had the honour to lead have made me what I am today.

The CO was respected and admired by the soldiers in the battalion, who referred to him affectionately as 'Wingy', because as a platoon commander in Korea a mine incident had left him with a right arm unable to be fully extended. Given the penchant for Australian soldiers to give everyone and everything a nickname, Wingy was born. The soldiers not only respected and admired Wingy, they were very fond of him because they knew he cared and no matter where he came across the soldiers, he would always have that wry smile to put diggers at ease. More importantly, he would engage with them meaningfully in asking about their families and about themselves. He always placed a gentle hand on the shoulder when thanking someone for a job well done.

What I really respected about John Warr as a battle commander and as a leader was that the BHQ group was always in the field with us, doing the hard yards, the same as everyone else in the battalion. They shared with us liana and thorny 'wait-a-while' vines that were very difficult to get through, bamboo thickets and impregnable jungle that were just as much a hindrance and as annoying to the CO as they were to us in the rifle companies. As the battle commander, if one of the companies said it was facing rough going, the CO didn't have to be convinced, sitting back in a static command post or floating about in a Sioux helicopter. He led from the front and when we were wet, tired, exhausted and miserable there was a good chance the CO shared our discomforts.

In the Reconnaissance Platoon debriefs that I underwent with the CO and Bob O'Neill, at times I was disappointed that our patrols had not revealed anything of major importance. They both advised me that negative information is often positive information, and Bob O'Neill would put it into an intelligence-gathering context. All information, positive or negative, was appreciated and the CO would take this all on board and then question me about my men, their health and disposition. This would be followed by a beer in the mess where the CO, as a teetotaller, would have a can of Coke before I went down to have a drink with my blokes in the diggers' boozer. I have had many commanders who claimed they cared for their soldiers. With John Warr there was no doubt or ambiguity; I knew he really did care. A huge difference!

This feeling of someone really caring is particularly relevant when you are out on patrol somewhere and all hell breaks loose. Knowing that all available support is there for you to use when needed gives you great confidence as a young platoon commander in fighting the fight and extracting your blokes from a tough situation if warranted. After a very difficult contact where 'Bluey' Twaits was badly wounded, resulting in the loss of his leg below the knee, the very next day John Warr arranged for me to fly over to see Blue in 36 Evacuation Hospital, because John knew we were all very concerned about him.

It's very difficult to describe the fondness and enormous respect I have for John Warr still to this day. Although he saved my arse on more than one occasion, I think the basis for my feelings is much more than that. It's both spiritual and humanistic, where John epitomised everything that is so special and unique about old Christian values. Forgiveness, empathy, compassion and a brotherly love that was evident in so many ways. This brotherly love was felt throughout the battalion, whenever we lost good officers and men. I know John Warr felt it deeply, but through his strong personal beliefs, strength of character and quiet leadership, he kept us together to continue in our respective roles. He certainly had a major effect on me, and some of his principles and ethics have remained with me to this present day. Don't always look for the bad, look for the good; don't close your mind off because it's not your idea; if you believe in something, pursue it strongly; be approachable and honest with your subordinates; and, most importantly, be fair in your judgements. It was a great honour and a lot of fun, mostly at my expense, in serving a very special CO, mentor and leader.

Mark Warr

My father, the man the battalion got to know in Vietnam and after, I believe was very much the same man within his family. His motives and thoughts were always first for those around him, be it battalion or family, and was constantly considering how he could help improve things for them. In the last 10 years I have become more interested in the Vietnam War, and the more I read and learn about it, the more impressed I am by

16. JOHN WARR AS COMMANDING OFFICER

how and what 5 RAR achieved while there. When I see photographs of John in Vietnam, he seems particularly content, and while there was much sadness and devastation experienced, John was given pretty much free rein on how best to do the job. Every decision was motivated to help not only his men, but also the Vietnamese people. Some publications I have read mention the differences of view that John had about Brigadier Stuart Graham's decision, when Graham had decided to lay land mines. John's primary concerns would have been not only for his men and the Australian battalions that would come after, but also for the local Vietnamese people, who he felt would be adversely affected by this development.

John never liked how some in the media, particularly in America, would gauge military success by the highly inflated enemy body counts. He didn't see this fraudulent approach as helpful to winning the war in Vietnam. While he could be confrontational if necessary, his decisions were intended primarily to win the Vietnamese people over and to protect his men.

I think his refined cordon and search operations exemplify his thinking on how to conduct this kind of war. Under the circumstances, he saw it as the safest way of sifting the VC out of the villages, and protecting the men of 5 RAR, while bringing the villagers onside. When I see film footage and hear about the battalion's band playing in the villages during these operations, I think, yep, that's John. He's doing whatever he can to make the situation more tolerable for the Vietnamese, but I've sometimes wondered what the villagers thought of the music.

Another incident that showed his need to protect his men was covered in Bob O'Neill's book *Vietnam Task*.[2] B Company had about 30 VC covered, in the Nui Thi Vai hills, and were in a perfect position to attack them. Bruce McQualter was waiting on the order from John to go ahead when John was given intelligence at that very moment that a large unit of VC could be in the vicinity. It was fresh intelligence and his mind would move quickly in situations like this. I understand that it only took a few moments for him to consider the implications and decide that the task was likely to be too big for the isolated B Company alone. He would never put his soldiers' lives unnecessarily at risk.

---

2   Robert J O'Neill, *Vietnam Task: The 5th Battalion, Royal Australian Regiment*, Cassell Australia, Melbourne, 1968.

Another incident that I learnt about was related in the battalion's medical officer Tony White's book *Starlight*.³ C Company were performing a cordon and search in An Nhut village when a mine was set off, killing three and wounding five more. John was bending over Major Don Bourne, talking to him and giving him words of comfort. Tony knew that Don had already died but didn't have the heart to tell John. It was apparently quite a few moments until he realised Don was dead. In the words of Tony, 'the look of pain and dismay that came over his face at that moment was, for me, one of the most poignant moments of the war'.⁴

How John felt doesn't surprise me. The achievements of 5 RAR during this tour I think are very much still a great unsung story. The operations of the Australian Army, and its tactics and strategies, had to change to meet a new kind of warfare. But on top of that, 5 RAR were the first in Vietnam to be manned by a high proportion of conscripted national servicemen. The controversy over using these men in this war was very divisive in Australia and there were also problems caused, for example, by the Seamen's Union when they refused to load ships with supplies necessary for the war front. 1 ATF eventually needed to beg, borrow and occasionally 'liberate' from the Americans some of the equipment they needed. When 5 RAR arrived at Vung Tau in 1966, it was estimated that about 70 per cent of the population of Phuoc Tuy Province in South Vietnam was effectively under some form of VC control. By the time they left, one year later, that level of control had been reduced to about 15 per cent. John always supported the doctrine that it is difficult to win a counter-insurgency war without winning the hearts and minds of the people. The battalion began that process very effectively in the relatively short time they were in Vietnam.

John was an extremely empathetic person who would never back down from a challenge but would take it on enthusiastically. He would revel in the situation, and he gave any chance he could to the people in his battalion to do the same. He would work with them and create clear goals that met the challenges of the battalion as a whole. It was all the things that I learned to believe a good leader should do. But knowing John as my father, I do not find this surprising.

---

3   Tony White, *Starlight: An Australian Army Doctor in Vietnam*, CopyRight Publishing, Brisbane, 2011.
4   White, *Starlight*, p 144.

16. JOHN WARR AS COMMANDING OFFICER

In my opinion, I can't imagine a better person to lead 5 RAR through so many challenges, from before the time they left Sydney until their return, having achieved so much. I vividly remember attending Government House in Sydney when John was presented with the insignia of the Distinguished Service Order. From the moment John received that award I can remember him telling anybody who asked about it that it recognised the achievements and work done by the whole battalion. Whenever I was with him, and the same question was asked, he would give the same or similar answer for the next 30 years. He never stopped praising the efforts of the whole battalion and making light of what he had done.

Bruce Ruxton was the president of the Victorian Returned and Services League (RSL) for many years after the war. He was John's brother-in-law and my maternal uncle. I noticed over the years that Vietnam veterans were negative towards the RSL and complained that it had done little for them on their return. I used to think that it must be something to do with the branch to which they belonged. In Bruce's later years he was living in Noosa, and I visited him. I remember telling him that I found the Vietnam War extremely interesting and asked if he knew anybody I could visit, to tell me more about events there. He looked at me sheepishly and appeared somewhat embarrassed. Anybody who knows Bruce, or knows of him, is aware that it takes plenty to move him. Looking quite moved, he answered, 'I don't know much about that period at all, Mark'. I think he realised the lack of recognition he and the RSL had given Vietnam veterans, and it had become a cause for deep regret to him.

I was fortunate enough to travel to Vietnam several years ago, and even more fortunate to have been taken around the old base of Nui Dat, and to have visited the original site of the Battle of Long Tan and the port of Vung Tau, by Graham 'Breaker' Cusack. Graham was a second lieutenant with 6 RAR and had been that battalion's command post duty officer on the afternoon of the Battle of Long Tan. He was the first to hear 'contact' by D Company and listened in to the constant radio communications with them during the battle. When he took me and my partner Sue to Long Tan, he could still remember word for word the radio conversations he had had that day. It was 2011, almost 45 years later, but he described it like it was yesterday. I am very grateful to Graham for the experiences of that day, but even more grateful to have been given the father I had in John Warr, and to have learnt so much about the extraordinary 5th Battalion of the Royal Australian Regiment that he commanded in 1966–67.

17

CONCLUSION: THE DEVELOPMENT OF A 5 RAR APPROACH

Robert O'Neill

By November 1966, 5th Battalion, the Royal Australian Regiment (5 RAR), had developed its own approach to the conflict and the battalion's role in it. We could see that the Viet Cong, while powerful, did not yet fully control the civil population of South Vietnam: it was for the people's support that the war was being waged by both sides. Despite the importance of the psychological battle for hearts and minds, military operations were still critical. The Viet Minh had achieved success against the French by meeting them in major engagements such as the battles in the highlands of 1951–53, and at Dien Bien Phu in the north in 1953–54. While the North Vietnamese and Viet Cong did not have forces powerful enough to defeat the Americans in the Tet Offensive in 1968, they soon realised that the American position depended on the willingness of the American people to keep their forces engaged and well supplied with men and materiel. Eventually this realisation became the key to the North Vietnamese successful strategy of protracting the war until well into the 1970s, by which time they had well and truly undermined American public willingness to continue the conflict.

While we, and particularly our commanding officer John Warr, were aware of the sensitivity of Australian public and political opinion to casualties, our soldiers continued to operate with high morale and plenty of spirit, despite the significant risks of losses that they faced. There was no way of wholly avoiding these risks. However, the dangers could be managed by being on the alert ourselves and clearly able to win engagements with the Viet Cong, despite our relatively small forces. Had the Viet Cong come to believe that we were averse to fighting, or unable to fight well, they would have constantly harassed us. Our main objective in tactical engagements was to avoid having the battalion, or even a company, cut to ribbons. Offensive action, such as our operations in the Nui Thi Vai hills, had an important role to play. But we had to keep casualties within strict limits to remain effective over the long haul in this kind of war.

To this end, the battalion was helped greatly by the quality and training levels of our soldiers. It was gratifying to see how quickly and effectively our national servicemen had made the transition from their civilian occupations to become effective infantrymen over a period of less than a year. In February 1966, while watching some of our men shoot on a field firing range near our barracks at Holsworthy in western Sydney, I remarked to our company sergeant major, John Bates, on the skill of their shooting. He replied, 'Just wait until they are on the two-way range. In Vietnam, the target fires back at you!' It was a salutary thought and I never forgot it. Hence, I was profoundly relieved at seeing how quickly and effectively our soldiers swung into action from the outset in May 1966 when the Viet Cong first opened fire on them. Men who a year previously had been automechanics, hairdressers, clerks and shop assistants had become very proficient infantry soldiers. They showed that they could hold their own with confidence, and they achieved a high rate of success against experienced guerrillas, fighting on their own soil and not willing to give way.

During 1966–67 we worked and fought hard, hoping that our actions would contribute in the long term to a successful outcome to the war. For those who followed us, that prospect changed after the Tet Offensive of 1968. Thereafter, public confidence in eventual victory progressively declined, as it became apparent that the Americans, and hence the South Vietnamese, were not going to prevail. The Royal Australian Regiment battalions who followed us ruminated little on such matters. In the immutable tradition of their forebears they applied their Regiment's motto, 'duty first', in fine spirit until the day in 1972 when the last RAR company was withdrawn. However, this is not a book about our postwar experience and concerns. Suffice to say that after our return to Australia, the problem of readjustment in a world which did not value our efforts and sacrifices in Vietnam was formidable for all of us. However, it has had the long-term effect of promoting unity and comradeship among former 5 RAR members.

17. CONCLUSION

There was no feeling within 5 RAR in 1966–67 that we were going to have an easy year. We were aware of the Viet Cong and North Vietnamese superiority in numbers, and their long, successful record in warfare since 1946. They had a capacity to do us real harm in ambushes and raids, and by continually laying mines and setting booby traps in areas through which we had to move. They also fought well in defence of their own forward positions and base camps. They had their own political system which was partially in effect in much of Phuoc Tuy at the time of our arrival. They had access to local people who could provide reinforcements, food, money and intelligence when called upon to do so. They knew our movements because their supporters saw us coming to and going from Nui Dat and other places that we held, especially when we used helicopters or surface vehicles.

The one form of movement that our enemies could not always detect was when we went on foot, especially during hours of darkness. So we became accustomed to peering into the darkness, operating off tracks and footpaths, or through jungle and rubber plantations, moving our feet slowly and carefully, preventing metal items of equipment from clanging, and speaking to each other in whispers or by hand signal when there was some light. Our soldiers had to get used to operating without much sleep at night, and to the tensions which built up naturally as we strove to be stealthy. We never could be entirely sure that there was not an armed enemy crouching in the darkness behind the base of a tree or behind a rock, lining us up in his weapon sights or preparing to detonate a mine or bomb. The Viet Cong soon learned that we could be equally or more adept at their tactics. Our companies set ambushes and sent out clearing patrols around their positions at every morning and evening stand-to. Moving silently at night became a very familiar experience to most 5 RAR soldiers.

Other challenges our men had to contend with were fatigue, the weather and shortages in some important items of weaponry and equipment. When we were out on operations, a normal carrying load was around 30 kilograms. This included a lightweight, foldable shelter, water, food for up to five days, a weapon, claymore mines for ambushing, grenades and, heaviest of all, ammunition both for one's own weapon and for the heavy consumers such as our general purpose machine guns. Often there were additional heavy items to be portered such as bombs for our mortars. Patrols and platoons had to carry radios (for tactical communications, not entertainment) and their heavy batteries to be shared around whatever group needed them. The prevailing heat and humidity caused copious sweating, and the pressure of pack straps gave us sore shoulders as a constant accompaniment to patrolling.

Our infantrymen had to be young and fit to cope with these pressures, and they stood the test well. Commanders had to take all these factors into account and seek to mitigate them by practical measures such as establishing a pack-dump where soldiers' heaviest loads could be kept secure while their owners moved to get to grips with the enemy. For our first few months in Phuoc Tuy we had to contend with the wet season, when on most afternoons, and frequently at night, we were subjected to heavy rain. Had the weather been cold, the rain would have been a health hazard, but in the warmth of the tropics it was more of an inconvenience than a danger. The climate did, however, lead to the added problem of skin complaints of various kinds, creating a major challenge for Tony White and his medical team in keeping us all fit for operations.

While learning to live with these various problems and pressures, we felt a special confidence in the leadership of John Warr. I shall not repeat what has been conveyed in Chapter 16, but simply observe that, having studied battalion commanders of the wars of the 20th century, he is in the upper bracket. By the time that he had appointed me to work with him directly as intelligence officer, I knew that he was thinking hard about how to use our capacities most effectively throughout the following nine months. In November 1966, when the pressure of operating in the hills had eased, John gave me the task of making a detailed analysis of the results of all our operations in Vietnam to that date. He particularly wanted a balance of results – of gains versus costs. The gains were to be measured in terms of our effectiveness in weakening the Viet Cong, while the costs were to be assessed in terms of our own casualties and time taken to achieve results.

My analysis first focused on eight conventional operations, in which we were opposing Viet Cong main force and provincial mobile units. We had suffered six killed and 31 wounded, while the Viet Cong had lost 33 killed, an unknown number of wounded and two captured. The analysis then moved to our five cordon and search operations, in which we had suffered one killed in action and none wounded, while the Viet Cong had lost 16 killed, 47 captured and 112 suspects apprehended. Clearly, the cordon and search method was the more effective way of operating. This conclusion was reinforced when the amount of time that had been spent on operations was taken into account. We could spend days patrolling in the jungle with only occasional contact with the enemy, whereas in a well-planned and prepared

17. CONCLUSION

cordon and search operation, the numbers of Viet Cong apprehended per day of operational time were several times greater. And, more importantly, the weakening of Viet Cong political authority in the villages that we searched and then developed friendly contact with was far greater than would have been achieved by battles deep in the jungle between opposing forces.

After discussion with Max Carroll, Peter Isaacs and myself, John put his thoughts onto paper, and proceeded to develop them for publication in the *Australian Army Journal* when we returned to Australia. It appeared in No. 222 of the *Journal*, published in November 1967, under the title 'Cordon and Search Operations in Phuoc Tuy Province'. It is included in this volume as Appendix C. The article was essentially an argument for greater use of these operations, based on a careful appraisal of all the various types of operations that we had undertaken. John stressed the point that the essential nature of the war was the competition to win the lasting support of the Vietnamese civilian population. Therefore, it was of paramount importance to help the local people and not to add to their burdens by destroying what little they had by way of houses and means of food production. John much preferred to offer help with activities such as the building of dispensaries and school rooms, and to provide support for visits to the villages by our medical specialists. Our regimental medical officer, Tony White, had a very full agenda in looking after the health of some 800 young Australians and then trying to give medical assistance to the local population, many of whom had rarely seen a doctor in their lifetimes.

John's article received a wide circulation, not only though the Australian Army, but also through other armies who exchanged their journals with us, especially the Americans, the British, the Canadians, the Irish and the New Zealanders. As well as identifying 5 RAR with a preferred modus operandi, he raised our army's reputation for taking a thoughtful, committed approach to a difficult set of military problems. It was very fitting that his contribution to the improvement of methods of counter-insurgency was recognised by his receipt of the Distinguished Service Order. His citation referred particularly to his development of the cordon and search method:

> The techniques for these later operations were developed so successfully by Lieutenant Colonel Warr that they have been accepted as standard procedures in the First Australian Task Force.[1]

---

1 See 5th Battalion The Royal Australian Regiment Association website, *Citation accompanying the award of the Distinguished Service Order to Lt-Col. Warr*, www.5rar.asn.au/history/cite_warr.htm.

In a field where it is hard to be original, he fostered a fresh approach which was both more effective as a means of limiting the influence of the Viet Cong and more economical in terms of the casualties suffered by our own soldiers. It also demonstrated to villagers that Australians were firm, fair and determined in rooting out our enemy, and careful of the local people's welfare and property in doing so.

When I became intelligence officer John also appointed me to be the battalion's civil affairs officer. The two jobs went well together because I could often gather some useful intelligence while visiting a village for civil affairs purposes, and I could give better advice on the civil affairs program based on what I had learned through intelligence gathering and analysis. The first stage in establishing a civil affairs program was to gain the trust and cooperation of the villagers. This took time, but John gave it high priority. Individual platoons, especially the Anti-Tank Platoon under Mick Deak (von Berg), were stationed in villages for several days at a time. There were some villages where the Viet Cong influence was high, and others where government policies had not helped them as much as they might have. But there were yet others where the people were keen to make friendly contact with us, and accept assistance, offering information on local Viet Cong activities in return. Mick's platoon combined the essential skills required for counter-insurgency because they had much more to offer than simply intruding on the villagers and applying restrictions to their way of life.

In conducting cordon and search operations, the local police sometimes caused problems for us. We were dependent on them doing their job of identifying known Viet Cong supporters fairly and accurately, and we had to face the possibilities that justice could be dispensed on an arbitrary basis, or sometimes abused to settle old scores. We tried to limit these problems by following up with visits to those who had been arrested, to see how they were being treated and what was happening to them in terms of legal process. The fact that local officials knew that we would take an interest in whatever action followed our apprehension of a Viet Cong suspect made a difference to the way they were treated, but it was far from perfect in ensuring that justice was meted out evenly to everyone.

The Viet Cong, for their part, had to accept that in late 1966 they lost substantial control over western Phuoc Tuy, thereby enabling South Vietnamese and allied forces to pass freely between Vung Tau, Ba Ria and the base complexes around Bien Hoa. The Viet Cong could still take

17. CONCLUSION

offensive action by raiding villages and South Vietnamese military posts along Route 15, but they could not stay in the area for any lengthy period. Government and allied forces, especially the 1st Australian Task Force (1 ATF), were now able to respond quickly and powerfully. The Viet Cong therefore had to turn their attention elsewhere in the province to be able to strike effectively, and at a reasonable cost in terms of their own lives and resources.

From late 1966, the Viet Cong focused on strengthening their presence in the eastern part of Phuoc Tuy, and this resulted in an increasing number of Australian operations there, especially in the Long Hai Hills in the south-eastern corner. The Viet Cong had positions of real strength in this part of the province, and they remained able tacticians. We suffered nine deaths in a 19-day period in February and early March 1967, chiefly due to mines and booby traps. By the time we had completed our operational tour in Vietnam on 26 April, the Viet Cong had lost military control in central and western Phuoc Tuy, but they had retained and probably increased control in the east. Our replacement battalion, 7 RAR, and its successors still had formidable challenges ahead of them, both in Phuoc Tuy and beyond, as the Americans drew more on our resources to resist a growing North Vietnamese and Viet Cong military presence in the crucially important area east of Bien Hoa and Saigon.

The Viet Cong retained and reconstructed their political network in the central part of Phuoc Tuy. It may not have been as strong as it had been before we began our cordon and search operations, but nonetheless it remained a formidable asset to them. In February and March 1968, when the Tet Offensive burst into the media headlines around the world, it became obvious that the Viet Cong and North Vietnamese had retained a substantial degree of control in South Vietnam, and it would take a major and prolonged effort to break that grip. Public opinion in the United States and other allied countries turned against making this kind of commitment, and so the war ground on for seven more years before ending in defeat for the United States and its allies.

One of the key challenges of the war was the development of smooth and effective inter-allied relations. For us in Phuoc Tuy, that meant essentially our cooperation with the Americans and the South Vietnamese Army. Although other nations were taking part in the conflict, we had little to do with the South Koreans, Filipinos and Thais. We also worked closely with the New Zealand gunners, but we never felt that they were foreigners.

The Americans were our closest partners from the day of our arrival. As Max Carroll and Peter Isaacs have related, they accepted us as valued allies and immediately invited some of our key people to directly observe their operations. They helped us to settle in and gave us a quick feel for what it was like to work in the Vietnamese environment. They supported us closely with helicopters and ground attack aircraft when we needed them. They based heavy artillery elements right alongside us at Nui Dat. They were particularly good to work with because they respected our national sovereignty. Occasionally, when supporting their operations, we were placed under their command, but they did not give us unusually dangerous or difficult missions. Nor did they relegate us to a safe corner because they did not think we could handle the more challenging assignments. It was a good working relationship, based on close cooperation and mutual respect formed in the two World Wars and the Korean War.

During our first few months in Vietnam, and before our supply system was functioning properly, the Americans were very helpful in meeting some of our needs. Soon various members of our battalion, from the second in command downwards, knew where the main American stores in our vicinity were located, and they bargained and traded for badly needed items ranging from tents and furniture to heavy machine guns. Another area in which the Americans were willing to be particularly helpful was that of intelligence cooperation. Given their excellent signals interception capability, we always felt confident that if the Viet Cong or North Vietnamese were planning a major operation against us, such as their attack at Long Tan, we would receive warning from the Americans. However, the major American headquarters, such as that of II Field Force Vietnam (II FFV) near Bien Hoa, were vast and the routine passage of intelligence down to our level could be slow. Fortunately, American common sense enabled less formal ways of communicating to develop, enabling me to have some very fruitful visits to II FFV for direct personal briefing on the latest intelligence available. As Max Carroll has said, generally we found the Americans to be good working partners and they had our respect. We did not always agree with their methods. There was a need, we felt, for a little more understanding of the fragility of Vietnamese rural communities. But our allies were learning as they went along, as we also had to do in different fields.

Our contact with the armed forces of South Vietnam was not as close as it was with the Americans. The principal South Vietnamese forces in Phuoc Tuy were the Regional Force and Popular Force companies. They were scattered widely but thinly across the province. They varied considerably in effectiveness. They sometimes had to fend off strong Viet Cong attacks on their remote compounds, and the outcomes of such clashes showed that some of the South Vietnamese were brave and would fight hard. But sometimes we also saw that such performance by the South Vietnamese could not be relied on, and we suspected that there was sometimes outright collusion between the two opposing sides. This possibility gave us a security problem in that we had to judge very carefully how far we disclosed our own intentions to South Vietnamese military personnel, and how fully we shared our intelligence information with them. Similarly, we had to be careful about how much credence we gave their reports on their own and Viet Cong activities, especially in the northern and eastern parts of Phuoc Tuy.

This is not to say that we did not receive any worthwhile help from the South Vietnamese military or their local civilian administration. Our working relations with them, which began in the area around Binh Ba and Duc My, developed considerably in following months while we were securing the area around Route 15. Nonetheless, the South Vietnamese military effectiveness in Phuoc Tuy was on the low side, and for most of the operations described in this book, we did not factor the Army of the Republic of Vietnam into our planning as a major asset.

Just as the South Vietnamese had problems in maintaining morale and commitment among their soldiers, so also did the Viet Cong and North Vietnamese. The South Vietnamese Chieu Hoi (or returnee) program encouraged some of their enemies to come forward and surrender in return for cash, resettlement opportunities and, hopefully, ending up on the winning side in the war. This program caused the Viet Cong leaders real problems. As they admitted themselves, in the period from January to October 1966 they lost 66 cadre personnel and soldiers to the Chieu Hoi program in Phuoc Tuy. The actual number of returnees was probably greater. However, this program was badly resourced and often given low priority by the South Vietnamese authorities.

Another scheme developed by the South Vietnamese Government was the Revolutionary Development Cadre Program. These cadres were trained groups of young men who were sent out to help individual villages with development and local defence projects. We called them the 'Rev Devvers' and often they appeared to us as the gilded youth of Saigon, sent out on relatively safe assignments to the countryside for periods of a few weeks at a time. Some of them appeared on their own smart motorcycles, with guitars slung across their shoulders. During 1966 they were not so noticeable, although we did work with them occasionally. On one fence-building project, when the Rev Devvers were not making rapid progress, we were able to have a platoon of Viet Cong returnees sent in to help. The comparison between the effectiveness of the two groups was not a bad indicator of the final result of the war!

During the period focused on in this book, September–November 1966, we were too busy up in the hills and along Route 15 to have had much contact with these activities of the South Vietnamese. We needed, however, to keep them in mind because they did show that the Saigon government recognised the political nature of the war. But for us on Nui Thi Vai and the Nui Dinh hills, the war still posed strong military demands because that was the way in which the Viet Cong had come to control western Phuoc Tuy. We had to clear the enemy off the dominating high ground or they could frustrate everything we attempted.

Once the high ground had been taken and the Viet Cong driven away, we had some resources free with which to establish a friendly and helpful presence in and around the villages. It was a good opportunity to enjoy some more relaxed operations in which we were not carrying 30-kilogram loads several hundred feet up steep slopes, while under fire from enemy in well-chosen positions. Our platoons sometimes deployed alongside several of the larger villages. Their inhabitants were friendly and seemed good-humoured towards us, and our soldiers reciprocated. We set about getting to know those in the leading positions in the villages, explaining what we were trying to do, asking how we could help them and gaining useful information in return.

We could not take for granted that the Viet Cong would stay away from the high ground. Reconnaissance and fighting patrols remained necessary, but they were lighter operations than the ones we had mounted to gain control of the heights. The continuing process of maintaining surveillance over the dominant ground was greatly helped by 3 SAS Squadron's regular patrol operations in the province's hill complexes.

We also had to think about the low ground between the hills and the Rung Sat, the extensive area of mangroves to the west and south-west of Phuoc Tuy, which the Viet Cong used to conceal their supply routes along which equipment, weapons, ammunition and other useful items were brought into the area east of Bien Hoa and south of War Zone D. In November 1966, we followed Operation Queanbeyan with two further operations in this area: Operation Yass, which was a cordon and search of the village of Phuoc Hoa; and Operation Hayman to clear the Viet Cong off Long Son Island. This sweep concluded a very intense period of 37 days of operations which changed the way in which Phuoc Tuy was shared between the Government of South Vietnam and the Viet Cong. Route 15 was now open as a secure road for reinforcements and supplies to use from Vung Tau to the crucial Saigon–Bien Hoa area. The important villages of western Phuoc Tuy were now able to receive medical and dental assistance, more schoolrooms and other community facilities, and to know thereby that their welfare was one of our major concerns.

This was a major transformation. The effectiveness of our drive against the Viet Cong was recognised by the awards of several decorations to 5 RAR members. These are listed in Appendix A. All of us had learned a lot about the complexities of counter-insurgency warfare. Given the changes that have taken place in warfare and conflict during the following 50 years, the year that we spent in Phuoc Tuy in 1966–67 gave us all a very relevant education, and a set of practical insights which still enlighten the Australian Army's operational methods.

Readers may decide whether and to what extent the lessons that we learned in Phuoc Tuy are relevant to the present and future problems of national and international security. Perhaps most will agree that Australia needs to take preparation for international military commitments much more seriously in times of peace than we have done in the past. In the cases of the two World Wars it took the best part of two years to raise, train and equip our forces for service abroad. We sent them off in less time than that, but they had to learn on the battlefield. Similarly, in the Korean War we were not able to field a second battalion of troops until mid-1952, two years after the war had begun, despite having a large number of veterans of the Second World War on which to draw. To raise a force of two battalions for service in Vietnam, Australia had to introduce a very controversial national service scheme in 1965. It was not until late 1967 that a third battalion could be provided to make up a full, brigade-sized force. And regarding essential equipment, as Stan Maizey has stated in

Chapter 3, the two battalions sent to Vietnam in 1966 went without some of their key items, and we had to beg or borrow what we needed from our allies in the field.

Numbers of troops available were not the only manpower problem confronting 1 ATF. To fight wars successfully, much depends on the quality of tactical leadership available on the battlefield. Company commanders and platoon commanders do not grow on trees. The latter take about a year to train properly, and company commanders take much longer. Shortage of trained company commanders is probably the key bottleneck in mobilising our army for operations. Similarly, non-commissioned officers take a year to train at the junior levels, and several years at the most senior. Given the normal size of Australia's army in time of peace, these are powerful limitations on our ability to raise and deploy other than token forces for service with allies. One can imagine the reaction of a long-term major ally, upon whose power our national security was predicated, being told by a present or future Australian prime minister, 'Sorry, one battalion is all we can field initially; 12 months later we can make it two battalions and after another year we can add a third'. This was the prevailing scenario when an expanded Australian Army involvement in Vietnam was implemented in 1965. Starting in 1945, 20 years of governmental lip service to military defence was its progenitor.

This history of the operations of a single Australian battalion in the Vietnam War offers food for further thought on how we might fight another war, either abroad or in Australia, and how we ought to approach this possibility in terms of anticipation, preparation, training, operational methods and equipment. This book also stands as a memorial to the service of several hundred young Australians, volunteers and national servicemen, who, in 5 RAR, showed the bravery and commitment to have done as well as they did in Vietnam. They established a strong mateship in battle which has endured over the past 54 years. We are not about to forget those who paid with their lives, or endured severe incapacity, as a result of their service in Vietnam! Nor shall we forget the love and support of our wives, families, fiancées and other close friends during our year in Vietnam. It was a very big team effort!

APPENDIX A. 5TH BATTALION DECORATIONS AND AWARDS: VIETNAM 1966–67

Distinguished Service Order

Lieutenant Colonel **John Arnold Warr**

Military Cross

Second Lieutenant **Michael Joseph Gunther Deak** (Michael von Berg)
Second Lieutenant **John Douglas McAloney**
Second Lieutenant **Dennis Claude Rainer**

Military Medal

Private **Colin John Cogswell**
Private **Peter Fraser**

British Empire Medal

Sergeant **Robert George Armitage**

Commendation for Distinguished Service

Sergeant **Robert George Armitage** (gazetted in Vietnam End of War List 3 June 1998)

Mentioned in Dispatches

Major **Owen Maxwell Carroll**
Major **Paul Netherton Greenhalgh**
Major **Ivor Ronald John Hodgkinson** MBE
Major **Stanley John Maizey**
Major **Malcolm Bruce McQualter***
Captain **Peter James Isaacs**
Captain **Harold Anthony Duckett White**
Captain **Robert John O'Neill**
Lieutenant **John Curtis Hartley** (two awards)
Lieutenant **John Carruthers***
Second Lieutenant **Dennis Claude Rainer**
Warrant Officer Class 2 **Brian Malcolm Hughson**
Sergeant **Robert George Armitage**
Corporal **Norman James Womal***
Private **William Roy Cavanagh**
Private **Sydney Lawrence Shore**
Private **Arthur Douglas Hillier**
Private **Lawrence Victor Lewis**

* posthumously

Citations accompanying these awards can be found on the 5 RAR Association website: www.5rar.asn.au/history/awards.htm.

APPENDIX B. AUTHORS' BIOGRAPHICAL NOTES

213017 Second Lieutenant Robert William Askew, aged 26, of Guildford, New South Wales. Australian Regular Army – helicopter pilot of 161 (Independent) Reconnaissance Flight; he was awarded a Queen's Commendation for Brave Conduct. He enlisted as a soldier in 1959 and was commissioned after qualifying as an army pilot. Post-Vietnam his military flying appointments included an exchange posting with the British Army in Malaysia. After resigning as a captain in 1970 his civilian aviation career included flying helicopters, small and large VIP jets and airliners throughout Australia, Papua New Guinea (PNG), South-East Asia and the Middle East. As a senior aircraft captain, his passengers included the Prince and Princess of Wales and Middle Eastern royalty, presidents, prime ministers and other potentates; and he was seconded from Air Niugini to the PNG Prime Minister's Department for four years of world-wide assignments.

54154 Captain Peter Clive Aspinall, aged 24, of Sydney, New South Wales. Australian Regular Army – 103 Field Battery forward observer with A and B Companies. An Officer Cadet School, Portsea, graduate (June 1961) with a 29-year career in unit, training and staff postings. Leaving the army in Sydney 1988, he gained a postgraduate qualification in strategic marketing leading to a position in the International Marketing Institute of Australia. He returned to the financial services sector prior to retiring to the Blue Mountains in 2000. In 2003 he relocated to his home town of Albany in Western Australia where he has served as president of the Albany Aero Club, the Albany Returned and Services League (RSL) sub-branch and chair of the Albany Centenary of ANZAC Alliance. Currently president of RSL Western Australia, he was appointed a Member of the Order of Australia in 2018.

17089 Captain Ronald William Bade, aged 24, of Brisbane, Queensland. Australian Regular Army – second in command of A Company and, subsequently, acting as officer commanding Administration Company, 5 RAR (5th Battalion, the Royal Australian Regiment). Graduating from the Royal Military College, Duntroon, in 1963, his career spanned 28 years, retiring as a colonel. He graduated into the Royal Australian Electrical and Mechanical Engineers (RAEME) and, in 1966, he was seconded to infantry and posted to 5 RAR. Post-Vietnam he returned to RAEME. He is a graduate of the British Royal Military College of Science and the Australian Joint Services Staff College. He held senior appointments in the army's Logistic Command, including commanding officer of 4 Base Workshop Battalion, and in the Maintenance Engineering Agency. Post-army he joined Kodak as logistics manager in Melbourne, Singapore and Hong Kong until retiring in 2004.

235167 Captain George Bindley, aged 29, of Sydney, New South Wales. Australian Regular Army – battery captain of 103 Field Battery. A 1959 Royal Military College, Duntroon, graduate, his early postings included two years with the British 26 and 45 Field Regiments in Malaya and a tour of duty in Vietnam. Returning to Australia in 1967, on promotion to major, he was appointed Artillery Instructor, Senior Instructor of Military Arts Wing and Coordinator of Training at the Officer Cadet School. On resigning from the regular army in 1970, he transferred to the Citizen Military Force and joined a prominent stockbroking firm in Melbourne as a private client adviser. In 1977 he became a director of the Capel Court Corporation and, in 1984, managing director of ANZCAP Management. Since 1990 he has been principal and director of his family business.

14967 Captain Ronald Edward Boxall, aged 25, of Toowoomba, Queensland. Australian Regular Army – second in command of D Company, 5 RAR. An Officer Cadet School graduate (December 1959), leading to a 31-year army career. His early appointments were mostly in infantry battalions and army schools. He completed a second tour of Vietnam in 1971 as a rifle company commander with 4 RAR/NZ (ANZAC) and was awarded the South Vietnamese Cross of Gallantry. A graduate of Australian and Canadian defence staff colleges, his mid-career postings included concepts and doctrine development staff appointments. Following these he became chief instructor of the Infantry Centre and then chief instructor of the army's Command and Staff College. In 1983, on promotion to colonel, he was appointed the first director of military education and training at the Australian Defence Force Academy after which he was promoted to brigadier and appointed commander of 4 Military District. Then followed his only appointment in Army Office, Canberra, as deputy chief of operations until he left the army in 1990. Post-army, he was a businessman and held several tyre industry company directorships and chairmanships until retirement in 2006.

61597 Lieutenant Barry John Campbell, aged 30, of St Helens, Tasmania. Joined the Australian Regular Army on completing national service in 1955. He served in the Malayan Emergency 1957–59 and was commissioned in 1964. He was awarded the Royal Humane Society's Stanhope Gold Medal in 1965 for saving a life. He deployed to Vietnam in 1966 with 1 Field Regiment as survey officer and then as forward observer attached to D Company, 5 RAR. He completed a second tour in Vietnam as battery captain and, subsequently, battery commander of 106 Battery in 1970–71, for which he was Mentioned in Dispatches (MID). Post-Vietnam, he served in various appointments including on the Australian Army Staff, London. He graduated from the Army Staff College in 1973. In 1981, as a lieutenant colonel, he left the army and worked for Hawker de Havilland (Australia) until retiring in 1992.

18548 Captain James Douglas Campbell, aged 28, of Gympie, Queensland. Australian Regular Army – helicopter pilot of 161 Independent Reconnaissance Flight. Trained as a motor mechanic at the Army Apprentice School in 1954–56, he served with 1 RAR during the Malayan Emergency in 1959. Selected for flying training in 1961, he graduated first in his course at Royal Australian Air Force (RAAF) Point Cook and completed training as a helicopter pilot at RAAF Amberley in June 1962, when he was commissioned and posted to 16 Army Light Aircraft Squadron. Later that year he flew for the UN in Irian Jaya. He qualified as an Iroquois instructor in the United States and returned to be a helicopter instructor with 16 Army Light Aircraft Squadron in 1964. In 1966–67 he was the rotary wing section commander in 161 Independent Reconnaissance Flight, part of 1 ATF (1st Australian Task Force). For his performance during numerous hazardous missions he was awarded the first Distinguished Flying Cross of the Vietnam War. Postwar he had a wide range of flying and non-flying appointments and graduated from the Australian Staff College in 1975. Leaving the army in 1980, he was involved in setting up and operating three permanent helicopter rescue services on the Sunshine Coast, the Gold Coast and at Bundaberg. The recipient of many awards for community service, in retirement he has continued his involvement in a wide range of activities and still competes in outrigger paddling titles at both state and national levels.

52680 Major Owen Maxwell Carroll, aged 35, of Perth, Western Australia. Australian Regular Army – 5 RAR's operations officer (while also commanding Support Company) and, later, commanded A Company. A 1953 graduate of the Officer Cadet School, Portsea, he previously had served as a rifle platoon and tracker team commander in 3 RAR during the Malayan Emergency and was MID. He graduated from the Army Staff College in 1965 and was immediately posted to 5 RAR. Post-Vietnam, he served on loan to the Malaysian Army, and as an instructor at the Officer Cadet School, Portsea, and the Royal Military College, Duntroon. He held multiple staff appointments including on the Australian Army Staff in London. Retired as a colonel after 31 years service. Post-army pursuits included rural interests, executive assistant to the Australian Federal Police Commissioner and on the staff of the Australian War Memorial.

215835 Captain Ernest Chamberlain, aged 25, of Sydney, New South Wales. A Vietnamese linguist, Australian Regular Army. A 1965 graduate of the Officer Cadet School, Portsea, in 1969–70 he was an intelligence officer in Ba Ria and Nui Dat, at the Australian Embassy, and as a staff officer/aide on an Army of the Republic of Vietnam Headquarters. He was later the Vietnam desk officer in the Australian Joint Intelligence Organisation, revisiting Vietnam in 1974. In his 36-year military career, he was the Army's Director of Military Intelligence and Director of Studies at its Staff College. He also served in Singapore and the UK, as Defence Attaché in Cambodia (awarded the Conspicuous Service Cross) and as Head of Australian Defence Staff in Jakarta as a brigadier. Retired, he worked in East Timor for several years, including as strategic policy adviser to the Timor-Leste Defence Minister. He has written seven published books on Timor and five on the Vietnam War.

19991 Second Lieutenant William Davies, aged 20, of Brisbane, Queensland. Australian Regular Army – helicopter pilot, 161 Independent Reconnaissance Flight. Straight from high school, he was commissioned after completing flying training as an officer cadet. He was evacuated from Vietnam to Australia after being shot down and, after a long rehabilitation, he returned to flying duties as an army pilot. He then served as an army recruiting officer in Perth, Western Australia, for 16 months before resigning his short service commission and travelling extensively throughout the world. On return to Australia he completed six years of full-time study in psychology and was appointed to the foundation staff of the Vietnam Veterans Counselling Service in Perth. After several years of counselling, recurring ill health and infirmity due to his injuries led to his retiring and settling in Perth.

216701 Second Lieutenant Michael Gunther Deak, aged 23, of Adelaide, South Australia. He enlisted as a soldier in 1962 and, in December 1965, graduated from the Officer Cadet School, Portsea, and was posted to A Company, 5 RAR. He later transferred to the Anti-Tank Platoon and was awarded the Military Cross for his actions as its platoon commander. He was later tasked to establish the battalion's Reconnaissance Platoon in Vietnam. Postwar, he served in the Special Air Service Regiment, 2 Commando Regiment, various staff appointments and again in 5 RAR as adjutant. In 1973 he resigned his commission, took up his rightful name and title as Michael Baron von Berg. On his return after 12 years overseas, he was appointed group marketing director of the Hardy Wine Company. In 1991 he established his own consultancy, operating globally for some 20 years until his retirement. He was awarded the Order of Australia Medal for services to rugby in 2015.

235277 Lieutenant John Henry Griggs, aged 23, of Sydney, New South Wales. Graduated from the Royal Military College, Duntroon, in 1964 – gun position officer of 103 Field Battery until attached to C Company, 5 RAR, as forward observer in October 1966. He completed the gunnery staff course at Larkhill in the UK in 1968–69, then was posted as an instructor in gunnery at the School of Artillery, and, later, as a battery commander. He served in Headquarters, PNG Defence Force, graduated from the Australian Staff College in 1975 and then was a senior instructor (trials and development) before promotion to lieutenant colonel in 1979. His last appointment was in operational doctrine development. He left the army in 1982 to become a hotelier for 30 years, before retiring.

215812 Lance Corporal Edmund William Dennis Harrison, aged 19, of Lewisham, New South Wales. Australian Regular Army – posted to 5 RAR on its formation in early 1965. Second in command of 1 Section, 1 Platoon of A Company until seriously wounded on 17 October 1966 and evacuated to Australia. He served for another 13 years in various postings until 1979, then formed a career in middle management within the printing industry before retiring in 2000 due to ill health caused by his war service. He is the long-serving webmaster of the 5 RAR Association's multi-award-winning website and a Life Member of the Association.

17105 Lieutenant John Curtis Hartley, aged 22, of Woombye, Queensland. A 1965 graduate of the Royal Military College, Duntroon, he was commander of 1 Platoon, A Company throughout 5 RAR's first tour in Vietnam. During this tour, he was twice MID and twice wounded. In 1970, he returned to Vietnam as an adviser with the Australian Army Training Team Vietnam when he received the Vietnamese Cross of Gallantry and two US awards for valour. Seriously wounded, he was evacuated to Australia where he recovered and served in the army for nearly 40 years, achieving the rank of major general. He was appointed an Officer of the Order of Australia in 1992 for his service. His senior appointments included head of the army's Training Command, Director of the Defence Intelligence Organisation, Deputy Chief of the Army and Land Commander Australia. Post-army he has been head of the Royal United Services Institute, national president of the National Rifle Association, chairman of the Battle Honours Committee and is presently CEO and director of the not-for-profit research institute, Future Directions International.

335162 Lieutenant Douglas James Heazlewood, aged 22, of Warrnambool, Victoria. Australian Regular Army – section commander and, later, gun position officer of 103 Field Battery, he graduated from the Royal Military College, Duntroon, in 1965. Post-Vietnam, he underwent advanced training in the UK and held various unit and instructional appointments. After commanding a field battery, he attended long-term training at the UK Royal Military College of Science and completed an exchange appointment in the UK Ministry of Defence. There followed materiel acquisition, intelligence and Australian Army Staff Washington appointments and a period on the Joint Plans staff at Defence Headquarters. Leaving the army in 1987, as a lieutenant colonel, he was marketing manager of the Small Arms Factory in Lithgow, becoming general manager until 1993 when he returned to Warrnambool and retired in 2011 as finance manager of a human services agency.

47056 Lieutenant David Murray Horner, aged 23, of Adelaide, South Australia. Australian Regular Army – a platoon commander in 3 RAR in Vietnam in 1971. A graduate of the Royal Military College, Duntroon (1969) and of the Australian Army Staff College, he had regimental and staff postings before transferring to the Army Reserve and becoming an academic. Later, as a colonel in the Army Reserve, he was the first head of the army's Land Warfare Studies Centre. He was professor of Australian defence history at The Australian National University for 15 years and is now an emeritus professor at that university. The author or editor of 35 books on Australian military history, defence and intelligence, he is also the Official Historian of Australian, Humanitarian and Post-Cold War Operations. He was appointed a Member of the Order of Australia in 2009 for services to higher education in Australian military history and heritage as a researcher, author and academic.

311478 Captain Peter Isaacs, aged 25, of the Isle of Wight, UK. Ex-British Army and Australian Regular Army – adjutant and assistant operations officer 5 RAR, then an instructor at the Officer Training Unit Scheyville, before returning to the UK in 1968. In 1975 he was a company commander, then second in command of a Baluch infantry battalion during the Dhofar war in Oman. Wounded by a mine in 1976, losing a leg and an eye. Awarded a Sultanate of Oman Commendation for Brave Conduct. From 1986 he was director of several international security companies followed by management of UN mine clearance operations in Angola, Bosnia-Herzegovina and Tajikistan and border management and counter-narcotics programs in Central Asia including Northern Afghanistan. Latterly, director of a British company providing armed guards at US military bases and embassies in Afghanistan and in the Middle East. Retired in 2016, he lives in the United Kingdom.

43268 Corporal Robert Stanley Kearney, aged 20, of Adelaide, South Australia. Australian Regular Army – section commander in 9 Platoon 5 RAR. He joined the army at the age of 17 in 1963. He served a second tour in Vietnam in 1971 when he was a platoon sergeant throughout 3 RAR's second tour. Following retirement as a warrant officer in 1983, he gained a commission in the Army Reserve and was employed by South Australia Correctional Services and, later, the South Australia Country Fire Service. Since retirement in 2014, he volunteers with the Virtual War Memorial Australia (vwma.org.au). He is the author of three books about the First World War, and co-author of two about Vietnam. He received an Order of Australia Medal in 2001 for services to military history preservation, and to the community. In 2019, the History Council of South Australia named him the South Australian Historian of the Year for his ongoing work.

4717396 Corporal Ian Alexander McDougall, aged 20, of Basket Range, South Australia. A national serviceman of the first intake in 1965, he served as a medic with artillery and then with all companies of 5 RAR, being the first national service medic to serve with an Australian infantry battalion in operations. He joined the Australian Federal Police in South Australia and served also in the Northern Territory and New South Wales; at times in charge of various substations and squads before returning to South Australia in 1987 as a detective sergeant. After 31 years, he retired as detective station sergeant in charge of the General Crime Branch (Commonwealth Investigations Branch) in Adelaide. He completed numerous periods of higher duties as inspector or superintendent and received Commendations from three different Commissioners.

235023 Major Stanley John Maizey, aged 36, of Sydney, New South Wales. Australian Regular Army – second in command of 5 RAR. A 1951 graduate of the Royal Military College, Duntroon, he attended the Army's Staff College in 1963. Being a Staff College graduate, he was transferred from 5 RAR to 1 ATF headquarters in December 1966 to be the operations officer. As a junior officer he served in Japan and Korea with 1 RAR and 2 RAR, in Malaya with 2 RAR and in training and staff assignments in Australia. He was later chief instructor of the Officer Training Unit. On promotion to colonel he was commanding officer of 2 Recruit Training Battalion, head of Operations Branch in Headquarters Training Command, and commander of a District Support Group. He retired in 1979. Post-army, in Sydney, he was manager of Randwick Racecourse and then the Royal Motor Yacht Squadron. Later, in Kempsey, he was manager of the childhood cancer charity, the Challenge Foundation. He died in 2018.

15878 Corporal Brian Edward Mortimer, aged 23, of Blacktown, New South Wales. Australian Regular Army – medical assistant of 103 Field Battery. Post-Vietnam, his army career extended to 38 years, retiring as a major. His career highlights included medical sergeant of 1 RAR in Malaysia and Singapore, an instructor at the Australian Army School of Health, an attachment to the British Army School of Health at Aldershot in the UK, and regimental sergeant major of 9 Field Ambulance in Townsville and 1 Military Hospital in Brisbane. Commissioned in 1985, he was adjutant of 10 Field Hospital in Hobart, administration officer of the Army Malaria Research Unit and of 1 Military Hospital. In a headquarters staff appointment, he coordinated army support for Northern Territory Aboriginal communities. He retired in 1999.

5713701 Second Lieutenant Henry Thomas Neesham, aged 21, of Palmyra, Western Australia. A national serviceman, he commanded 7 Platoon, C Company, for all but a few weeks of 5 RAR's first tour of Vietnam. A member of the first class (1965) to graduate from the Officer Training Unit, Scheyville. Post-Vietnam, he rejoined the Western Australia public service in late 1967. In a 43-year career, his prominent positions included 23 years as CEO of the Western Australia Workers' Compensation and Rehabilitation Commission, including three years as chairman of the Australian Heads of Workers' Compensation Authorities. In 2001 he attended the Cole Royal Commission into the Building and Construction Industry as an expert witness. A founding director, in 2000, of the Clontarf Foundation, which fosters the education, self-esteem and life skills of indigenous boys, he remains a member of the board.

2781397 Private John Patrick O'Callaghan, aged 21, of Leichhardt, New South Wales. A national serviceman of the first intake in 1965 – machine gunner of 5 Platoon, B Company, and later a member of the Regimental Police Section in Battalion Headquarters. After completing his national service obligation, he returned to Sydney and worked as a waterboard maintenance crew member and a vehicle serviceman, truck driver, transport manager and plant operator in the earth-moving and horticulture industries until his retirement.

1731021 Second Lieutenant Terrence Harold O'Hanlon, aged 21, of Boonah, Queensland. National serviceman – commander of 5 Platoon, B Company. A member of the first class to graduate from the Officer Training Unit, Scheyville. Returning injured from Vietnam, he completed his service obligation as a member of the staff of the Officer Training Unit. On leaving the army, he returned to his family's property at Boonah where he ran cattle and bred horses. He has a lifetime commitment to breeding working horses and has judged at many Royal Shows. He has been a director and president of the Australian Quarter Horse Association and a director of the National Cutting Horse Association. He has owned and partnered in cattle stations in the Northern Territory and hotels and motels in central Queensland. In retirement he still breeds horses.

335113 Captain Robert John O'Neill, aged 29, of Melbourne, Victoria. Australian Regular Army 1955–68, graduate of the Royal Military College, Duntroon, in 1958, Bachelor of Engineering, University of Melbourne, 1960, Master of Arts and Doctor of Philosophy, Oxford University, 1965. Second in command of B Company, 5 RAR, January–

August 1966, battalion intelligence officer, August 1966 – May 1967. Transferred to the academic staff at the Royal Military College, Duntroon, in 1968; Head of the Strategic and Defence Studies Centre, The Australian National University, 1971–82. Official Historian of Australia's Role in the Korean War 1970–82, director of the International Institute for Strategic Studies, London, 1982–87, Chichele Professor of the History of War and Fellow of All Souls College, Oxford, 1987–2001. Chairman of the Council of the International Institute for Strategic Studies, 1996–2001. Trustee of the Imperial War Museum, London, 1990–2001, Chairman of Trustees, 1998–2001. Member Commonwealth War Graves Commission, 1991–2001. Honorary colonel, the 5th Battalion, the Royal Green Jackets, 1993–99. Honorary Doctor of Letters, The Australian National University, 2001. Chairman of the council, Australian Strategic Policy Institute, 2000–05. Chairman of the board, Menzies Centre for Australian Studies, London, 1990–95. Author of *The German Army and the Nazi Party 1933–39,* 1966, *Vietnam Task, the Fifth Battalion, The Royal Australian Regiment,* written during operations in Vietnam 1966–67 and published in 1968, *General Giap – Politician and Strategist,* 1969. *Australia in the Korean War 1950–1953,* 2 vols, 1981 and 1985. Honorary Fellow, Australian Institute for International Affairs, 2008. Jubilee Fellow, Academy of the Social Sciences in Australia, 2018. He was MID in 1967 and appointed an Officer of the Order of Australia in 1988.

2412265 Private Daniel Eric Riley, aged 19, of Granville, New South Wales. Australian Regular Army 1965–68 – served in the Anti-Tank Platoon and subsequently the Reconnaissance Platoon. Upon return to Australia he trained as a paratrooper and became a corporal in 5 RAR. Post-service, he completed teacher training with postings to rural and regional New South Wales before completing a doctoral program in the United States. Throughout his tertiary qualifications, experience and publications, he maintained links with both Australian and New Zealand defence forces as part of his tertiary responsibilities. His study of professional learning included visits to the US Army and Canadian defence staff colleges, post-2001. In addition to tertiary appointments, his career included service as an educational consultant with school systems in New South Wales and Western Australia's Kimberley region. He retired in 2010.

214040 Captain Robert William Supple, aged 24, of Cowra, New South Wales. Australian Regular Army – second in command of A Company, 5 RAR, and assistant operations officer on Battalion Headquarters during some major operations. An Officer Cadet School Graduate (December 1962), he served as the platoon commander of the Royal Australian Regiment's Airborne Platoon before joining 5 RAR in 1965. Upon leaving the battalion in 1967, he served as the adjutant/training officer of the Citizen Military Force's 1 Commando Company in Sydney and was later an instructor in Tactics Wing of the Officer Training Unit, at Scheyville in New South Wales, involved in training national service officer cadets for service in Vietnam. In 1971 he resigned from the army to commence a career in business.

47046 Lieutenant George Roger Wainwright, aged 21, of Adelaide, South Australia. Australian Regular Army – he commanded 8 Platoon, C Company, for the duration of 5 RAR's tour of Vietnam in 1966–67 and was wounded in action. His 1965 graduation from the Royal Military College, Duntroon, was followed by a 35-year military career, retiring as a colonel. He served in four RAR battalions and several army schools. He is a graduate of the Australian Army Staff College and the US Armed Forces Staff College. His later career involved senior postings in training environments, including Director of Military Art at the Royal Military College, Duntroon; and in strategic operational and intelligence appointments. Post-army, he was contracted to conduct several Australian Defence Force personnel projects. He has been president of the 5 RAR Association since 2005 and is an inaugural director of the RAR Corporation.

Lieutenant Colonel John Arnold Warr, aged 41, of Mosman, New South Wales. Australian Regular Army – commanding officer of 5 RAR (see Chapter 16). A 1947 graduate of the Royal Military College, Duntroon, he served as a junior officer with the British Commonwealth Occupation Forces in Japan post–Second World War and was seriously wounded during the Korean War, while serving with 3 RAR. As a major he served with the Canadian Army as an exchange officer in 1960–62. In 1967 he was awarded the Distinguished Service Order for his command of 5 RAR in 1966–67. He resigned from the Army in 1972 as a colonel. There followed a period as Assistant Registrar of the University of New South Wales, during which time he appeared before the Senate Standing Committee on Foreign Affairs and Defence, assisting with its examination of the Australian Army's future roles. He later spent many years as a businessman in the swimming pool industry. He instigated the 5th Battalion, the Royal Australian Regiment Association, in 1967 and served as its president until his death in May 1999.

J. Mark Warr of Sydney, New South Wales, son of Lieutenant Colonel John Warr. In his early 20s, Mark was assistant export manager for a timber milling company and a meat processing company in NSW. In his late 20s, he developed a business publications business that imported and published specialised publications for Australian and New Zealand companies. Mark sold this business in the late 1980s, married and had two children. During this time, he bought, with his father, a retail swimming pool business comprised of two shops and three service vans on Sydney's North Shore. This grew to three stores and 17 service vans and was servicing and maintaining 80 per cent of the major commercial swimming pools in Sydney's CBD. With 28 staff, a program to restructure the company was undertaken, which successfully franchised 13 service vans, before being sold to Poolwerx in 2006. Since then, Mark has undertaken new business ventures.

216799 Captain Harold Anthony Duckett White, aged 26, of Sydney, New South Wales. Australian Regular Army (five-year short service commission) – 5 RAR's regimental medical officer. A graduate of Cambridge and Sydney universities. He served, post-Vietnam, as regimental medical officer of 1 Recruit Training Battalion at Kapooka in New South Wales and with the British Military Hospital in Singapore. Back in civilian life, he qualified as a dermatologist, and was in private practice and a visiting medical officer at Royal Prince Alfred Hospital, Sydney, as well as a senior lecturer at the University of Sydney. As a colonel in the Army Reserve in Army Office, Canberra, he served as a consultant dermatologist. He was appointed a Member of the Order of Australia for remote area dermatology and medical education in Australia and the Pacific Islands. He retired in 2010. He published a book on his experiences in Vietnam in 2011: *Starlight: An Australian army doctor in Vietnam*.

APPENDIX C. CORDON AND SEARCH OPERATIONS

John Warr

This article was originally published in the *Australian Army Journal* No. 222, in November 1967. Note that all images and maps included in this reproduction are modern reconstructions.

Introduction

The war in South Vietnam is being fought with the aim of controlling the people, as the side which controls the people must eventually control the government and the country.

As a basis for achieving this aim, the communists, wherever possible, have established their own administration at village and hamlet level. This is achieved by creating in each village a cadre, usually composed of dedicated communists, whose tasks are to discredit the government, indoctrinate the villagers with communist propaganda and build an organization to support the Viet Cong forces in the field. The methods used by the cadres to obtain the co-operation and support of the villagers are, brutal but effective. The headmen, schoolteachers, policemen and local administrators are either eliminated or their families killed or tortured it they fail to co-operate. The cadre is also used to recruit young men and women into the Viet Cong forces and to provide labour when required.

The French Army in Indo-China found it almost impossible to operate in such an environment where they were like goldfish in a bowl with the Viet Minh almost invariably being aware of their intentions and all movement being reported. Ho Chi Minh considered that the establishment of the cadres was of prime importance as they would allow his guerrilla forces to operate like fish in a sea of peasants. It is suggested that if the village cadres were eliminated and the people secured against Viet Cong influence, the major advantages enjoyed by the Viet Cong would disappear. Unable to use the villages as operational bases the Viet Cong forces would be isolated from the people and their military effectiveness reduced as their ability to obtain food, tax and intelligence decreased. The Viet Cong would not be able to visit their homes and families and their morale would be reduced accordingly. In addition, the villagers would not be subjected to communist propaganda.

If the Viet Cong lost their ability to use the villages for their own purposes, they would be compelled to operate from bases in the mountains, swamps or thick jungle and, while they remained in such bases, would be unable to achieve their aim and would therefore be ineffective except as a threat. To become effective, the Viet Cong would have to leave their bases and seek battle with the government forces. Such battles would, as a result, almost certainly be in areas where the great fire power of the Allied forces could be employed most effectively. If the Viet Cong chose to remain in their bases they could, be harassed by air and artillery which, as has already been illustrated in South Vietnam, will reduce their morale and Increase the number of *Hoi Chanh* (Viet Cong who surrender).

With the elimination of the Viet Cong cadres, government armed forces and police (but not Allied troops) must be employed to secure the villagers against Viet Cong activities and the movement of the people and distribution of food must be controlled. Then the government will be positioned to re-establish local administration, including medical services, education and transport; civil aid can also be commenced.

The re-establishment of government control should also convince the villagers that the Viet Cong lacks the ability to secure, administer and assist the people. Once the villagers have been convinced this will be passed onto the Viet Cong through their families in the villages and the number of *Hoi Chanh* will further increase.

In addition, with the added security gained by the elimination of Viet Cong support in the villages, increased intelligence gained from the *Hoi Chanh* and the villagers, more effective operations can be mounted against the Viet Cong bases. Such operations should not be mounted until the Viet Cong cadres are destroyed and the people secured.

During its service in Vietnam in 1966–67, 5 RAR cordoned and searched villages on nine occasions in order to remove Viet Cong cadres. From these operations, 5 RAR devised sympathetic methods and techniques for controlling civilians. This article will describe cordon and search operations in three villages, each of which produced different problems in its planning and execution. The operations were:

- Operation SYDNEY TWO – The cordon and search of Duc My village on 20 July 1966
- Operation HOLSWORTHY – The cordon and search of Binh Ba village on 9 August 1966
- Operation YASS – The cordon and search of Phuoc Hoa village on 7 November 1966

Map 1 [located in Acknowledgements section] illustrates the location of these villages in Phuoc Tuy Province.

Cordon and search of Duc My Village

The Village of Duc My is one of the Binh Ba estate villages situated on Route 2 about 3 miles north of the First Australian Task Force base of Nui Dat. These villages are

- Duc Trung – population approximately 700,
- Binh Ba – population approximately 1,800, and
- Duc My – population approximately 500.

Duc My is separated from Binh Ba to the north by 500 yards of clean rubber plantation. Before the operation it was known that 97 Viet Cong had relatives or friends in these Binh Ba villages and, of these, 26 visited Duc My occasionally. The attitude of the local population was pro-Viet Cong due to the absence of government control for several years.

Operation SYDNEY ONE, which required 5 RAR to clear the area to the west of Duc My, commenced on 4 July and continued until 14 July. For this operation, a base (code-named *Tennis*) was established about a mile south of the southern part of Duc My village. *Tennis* was occupied by battalion headquarters, one rifle company, the assault pioneer platoon, anti-tank platoon, the mortar platoon, less one section, 105 Field Battery and one troop of 1 Armoured Personnel Carrier Squadron. As a preliminary to the cordon and search of Duc My village, the establishment of the base at *Tennis* had the following advantages:

- It allowed 13 days (later increased to 16 days) for the Viet Cong and villagers in Duc My to become accustomed to the presence of the battalion so close to the village and lulled them into a false sense of security.
- It permitted easy air and ground reconnaissance of the village and approach routes without unduly arousing Viet Cong suspicions.
- It allowed the battalion to concentrate at *Tennis* immediately before commencement of the operation without affecting the operation's security.

Duc My consisted of about 80 houses, widely scattered on the west side of Route 2. The villagers were mainly Montagnards and the majority were employed as rubber tappers on the Binh Ba estate. Banana plantations and mixed gardens located in and around the village made movement difficult at night. The perimeter of the village was poorly defined except on the north side where a broad track ran along the edge of the rubber plantation. Air reconnaissance indicated some bunkers in the village.

Forces Available. The following forces were available for the operation: 5 RAR about 550 strong; the remainder were required to defend the battalion base area, or were in hospital, on leave, or attending language courses.

Under 5 RAR command were one troop of 1 Armoured Personnel Carrier Squadron with one of its mortar sections and elements of 3 Field Engineer troop. 105 Field Battery was allocated 'In Direct Support' and allocated 'In Support' were D Company of 6 RAR; two Sioux aircraft; four RAAF Iroquois; six Vietnamese policemen and some Vietnamese interpreters.

Considerations. Duc My village was scattered over an area of 600 metres from east to west and 1,200 metres from north to south. It was considered that each rifle company in the cordon could cover approximately 450 metres, with two platoons forward in the cordon, each with all three sections forward, and men positioned in pairs at 22 metre intervals. A platoon would be held in depth some 75 to 100 metres in rear of the forward two platoons of each company. Thus, if all four rifle companies were used, the complete village could not be cordoned. It was therefore decided to place the cordon as indicated in Map A.1. This plan had the disadvantage of excluding from the cordon a small number of scattered houses to the east and south but would permit most of the cordon to be along easily located tracks and tree lines.

The use of all rifle companies in the cordon required that:

- 105 Field Battery (Major P. Tedder) be returned to Nui Dat base area as troops would not be available to protect the gun area at *Tennis*.
- One of the rifle companies be relieved by armoured personnel carriers or other troops after the cordon had been closed to allow the rifle company to search the village and apprehend suspects.
- One of the rifle companies be held as battalion reserve while the cordon was moving into position. A Company (Major AP Cassidy), mounted on armoured personnel carriers was nominated for this task.

The next problem was to determine the time that the cordon would be in position. It was decided that the final movement of the companies into their cordon positions should be carried out immediately after first light. This would permit the movement to be carried out with the greatest possible speed and reduce the danger of companies clashing with each other as they closed the cordon. If the cordon companies commenced moving into their positions at 0545 hours, the time of first light, it was estimated that the cordon would be completed by 0615 hours. A move at first light into the final positions permitted the use of armoured personnel carriers, armed helicopters, Sioux helicopter and a Cessna light aircraft fitted with loud-speakers to advise the villagers to remain calm and stay in their houses etc. However, the operation taught that a cordon must be in position before first light for at that time the normal life in the villages commences with people moving out to begin tapping rubber trees, moving goods to market and cattle to adjacent areas.

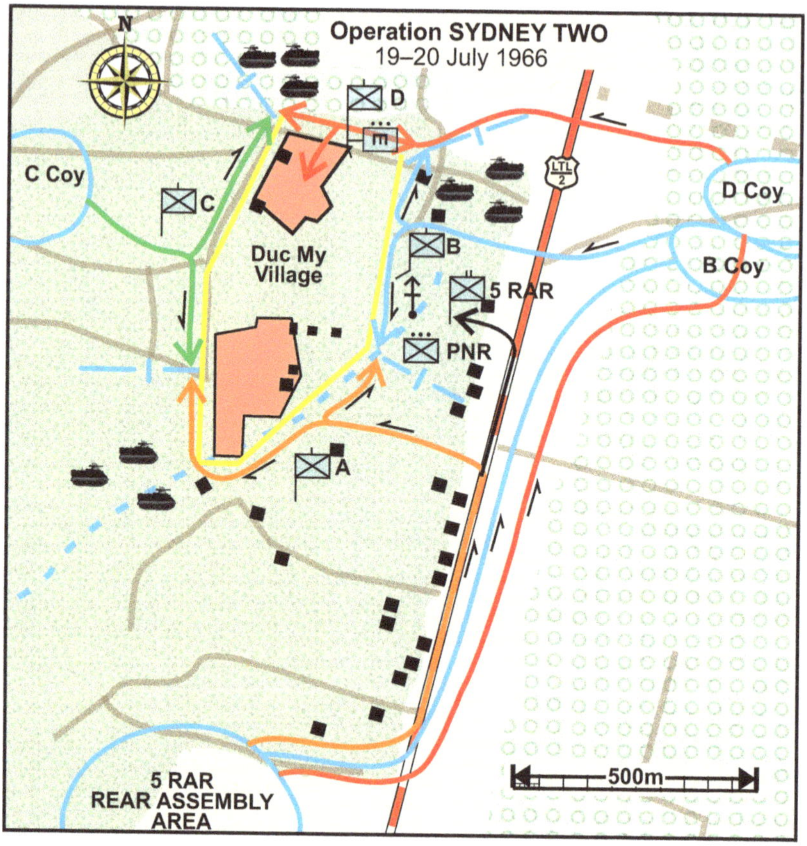

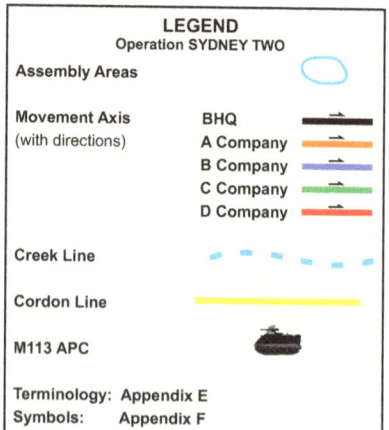

Map A.1: Operation Sydney Two: 19–20 July 1966.

Source: Designed by Ron Boxall and produced by Alan Mayne from circa 1966 US military maps provided by Bruce Davies.

APPENDIX C

The next consideration was the choice of approach routes to the village. As the cordon was to be completed just after first light it was necessary for most of the movement to be at night. While this produced problems, it also increased the likelihood of achieving surprise for, at that time, the Viet Cong accepted that Allied troops did not move at night.

The main problems posed by the move were seen to be:

- The need for reconnaissance to confirm routes into assembly areas and into the final cordon positions. In some areas the eastern and southern cordons would pass between houses.
- Control at night when hand signals could not be used. This problem was partly overcome by using a toggle rope tied to equipment on the back of each soldier for the soldier following behind to hold. Radio was used to control and confirm the movement of companies. All radio users spoke in whispers and the use of radio was kept to a minimum.
- Control and deployment of the battalion if a major contact occurred while the companies were moving into position (when it would not be in the best posture to meet such a threat). The CO's party (CO, BC, IO, batmen and operators) moved immediately behind the leading company. In addition, A company, mounted on armoured personnel carriers, was made the battalion reserve and in an emergency could have moved in the vehicles at night along Route 2 to support B Company. (Major B. McQualter) and D Company (Major P. Greenhalgh).
- Security. If the Viet Cong learnt of the intention to cordon and search the village, they would not only have left it, but might also have laid booby traps and ambushes on the probable approach routes.

The initial plan was to move all the companies, except the one which was to cordon the north side, into position via a re-entrant running into the village from the south-west as this route would have assisted in navigation and provided covered approach. The final company was to move by armoured personnel carrier along Route 2 and close the cordon on the north side at the last minute.

On the night 14–15 July, reconnaissance parties of company seconds-in-command (Captains Bade, Milligan and Boxall) under command of Captain O'Neill and including company guides and representatives from the armoured personnel carrier troop checked the proposed routes to assembly areas and cordon positions. As a result, the proposed route along the re-entrant was found to be unsuitable for the movement of large numbers of troops at night due to thick undergrowth and fallen dead timber which would have made silent movement Impossible.

Plan. From the reconnaissance it was decided to move C Company (Major N. Granter) into its cordon position from the west. B and D Companies and the CO's party would from the east and A Company with battalion headquarters (under Major M. Carroll), with the mortars and the anti-tank platoon on armoured personnel carriers would move from the south at the last possible moment. A Company would also be battalion reserve unit the cordon was closed, when the armoured personnel carrier troop and anti-tank platoon would take over this role. Once A Company was in position, the armoured personnel carrier troop would relieve D Company of cordoning the north side of the village.

Two sections of mortars were to move in mortar armoured personnel carriers to an area between the village and Route 2 while the Assault Pioneer Platoon was to provide protection for Battalion Headquarters and construct enclosures for suspects and villagers awaiting interrogation.

On 15 July the operation was deferred when B and C Companies retuned to the 1 ATF base to participate in 6 RAR's Operation BRISBANE. On the night of the 16–17 a further reconnaissance was carried out to confirm the proposed new routes. On the 19th B and C Companies rejoined 5 RAR at *Tennis* and the Battalion moved that afternoon to cordon Duc My next morning.

Security. The following precautions were taken to ensure that the intention to cordon the village was not disclosed to the Viet Cong:

- No movement of ground forces north of *Tennis* towards the village was permitted except for the reconnaissance parties of 14–15 and 16–17 July.
- 105 Field Battery was returned to Nui Dat from *Tennis* during the afternoon of 19 July inside armoured personnel carriers. While the battalion base was located at *Tennis* there had been frequent but irregular movement of personnel carriers to and from the base. The movement of 19 July should not therefore have caused undue concern to any Viet Cong who observed it as the guns were concealed within the armoured personnel carriers. Tyres from the Italian-made pack howitzers were placed onto the larger field guns used by 105 Field Battery on this operation to permit the guns to be carried inside

the APCs. It should be noted that the introduction of the twin .30 calibre machine-gun turret has restricted the interior space of the APC and, as a result, it cannot transport the 105-mm field gun as an internal load.
- Air reconnaissance by all company and platoon commanders was permitted over the village up to 16 July. There was a risk that this would alert the Viet Cong despite each flight being allowed to pass over the village only once and then to fly westwards to the area where the battalion operated until 14 July. The deferment of the operation for three days assisted in reducing any suspicion aroused by the air reconnaissance.
- The Vietnamese police and interpreters who were to assist with the search of the village joined the battalion at *Tennis* during the afternoon of 19 July and were not briefed about their tasks until that time.
- A rear battalion assembly area was selected about 800 metres south of the cordon area. This allowed the battalion less C Company to move from *Tennis* late in the afternoon of 19 July and arrive in the rear battalion assembly area just at last light when the possibility of contact with woodcutters and other civilians in the area would be reduced. From the battalion assembly area, it was comparatively easy for B and D Companies to move after last light to their forward assembly areas as the going was through a clean rubber plantation. The rear battalion assembly area was considered sufficiently far from Duc My to allow the armoured personnel carrier troop to move into it just before last light, at low speed without being heard. Next morning, however, when the armoured personnel carriers started up at first light, the noise of their motors would be heard by the CO's party 1,400 metres to the north-east. However, at that time, speed was more important than quietness. The direction of movement of the vehicles could not be determined from their sound. C Company was allocated a forward assembly area about 800 metres to the west of the village. The company could occupy the area by last light on 19 July and the area and the routes into it were such that detection was most unlikely.

Execution. To assist the movement by night, all back-packs were moved in armoured personnel carriers, daylight rehearsals were held at *Tennis* and companies used toggle ropes to assist soldiers in following the man ahead.

Everything went according to plan until about 0100 hours on 20 July when the leading soldier of D Company, Private F. Clark, fell 50 feet down a disused well. Fortunately, he was rescued unhurt within about 15 minutes. At 0545 hours B Company commenced to move into its cordon position. Soon afterwards, 4 Platoon (Second Lieutenant J. Carruthers) met six Viet Cong moving towards them. One Viet Cong was killed, four were wounded (of whom three were captured) and one was captured unhurt; 4 Platoon was unscathed. The captured and wounded Viet Cong were handed over to the reserve platoon and B Company closed its portion of the cordon on time.

A Company in armoured personnel carriers moved at full speed along Route 2 but experienced some difficulty in crossing the re-entrant to the south-west of the village and one of the armoured personnel carriers became bogged. Some troops then dismounted and ran into position.

The mortars and battalion headquarters (less the CO's party who were with D Company) arrived on time.

The Battalion Second-in-Command (Major S. Maizey) flew overhead at 0615 hours in a Sioux helicopter with two armed Iroquois helicopters and the Cessna loud-speaker aircraft.

Minor resistance was encountered in the village. At 0630 hours C Company, on the west side of the cordon, killed one Viet Cong trying to move through the cordon. At 0730 hours another Viet Cong who tried to break the cordon in C Company area was wounded and later he was flushed from a nearby bunker. About 1130 hours an armed Viet Cong, who had been hiding in thick undergrowth in the village, suddenly stood up and ran. He was killed by a soldier in the A Company cordon with one round.

These contacts emphasized the need for good fire discipline, the ability to recognize our own soldiers quickly, and observation of the following rules of engagement which were issued before the operation:

- Fire only
    a. When fired at.
    b. When a suspect is about to commit a hostile act.
    c. If a suspect attempted to run through the cordon and fails to halt after being challenged.

APPENDIX C

- Don't fire into the cordoned area unless the fire is controlled, and the target can be clearly seen.
- If fired on from a house:
  a. Take cover.
  b. Call an interpreter forward.
  c. Have the interpreter advise the occupants by means of a loud hailer to surrender.
  d. If this fails, call in the village chief and have him speak to the householder.
  e. If the occupants still refuse to surrender, burn the house (this is the only circumstance under which houses will be burnt).
- If in doubt, don't shoot.

D Company, with engineers, seven interpreters, six policemen, the Battalion's medical officer, the bandmaster, the stretcher-bearer sergeant and a medical team from 1 ATF commenced to clear the village about 0630 hours. By this time the cordon was in place and the loud-speaker aircraft had advised the villagers that they were surrounded and to remain in their houses and obey directions. The village was divided into platoon areas tor the search. Half section groups cleared each house in turn, evacuating the males and directing sick villagers to company headquarters for medical treatment. The clearance of the village was completed about 1400 hours.

The Assault Pioneer Platoon constructed three separate barbed wire enclosures at Battalion Headquarters. Two of the enclosures were provided with screened toilet facilities and the third had a screened interrogation area. The Battalion's Regimental Police and Intelligence Section guarded the cages. All males of Viet Cong military age (12 to 45 years) were evacuated by the clearing company to the north end of the village where the anti-tank platoon and a section of armoured personnel carriers evacuated them to the enclosures.

The Intelligence Officer (Captain D. Willcox), assisted by Vietnamese interpreters, interrogated the men, and suspects were evacuated to the 1st Australian Task Force base by armoured personnel carriers for further interrogation.

The battalion withdrew from the village area late in the afternoon and four ambushes were laid around the village that night, but no further contacts occurred.

Lessons. As this was the first cordon of a village undertaken by troops of the 1st Australian Task Force in South Vietnam, a great number of lessons were learnt:

- The success of such an operation depends on meticulous preparation at all levels, sound security and good reconnaissance. As a guide, it is considered that seven clear days are required to plan, prepare and execute a cordon and search of a village.
- The cordon must be in position before first light as this is the time that the Viet Cong leave the villages and rubber tappers commence work. All later cordons undertaken by 5 RAR were in position at least one hour before first light; all were successful, and no enemy contacts were made while the cordon was moving into position. The time for the completion of the cordon must also be varied. In December 1966 it was learnt that the Viet Cong at Quang Giao, east of Binh Gia, were leaving their village each morning an hour before first light as they believed the battalion cordons were always completed at that time.
- A more efficient interrogation system was required. In all later cordons Vietnamese interrogation teams were provided and had marked success in locating Viet Cong cadre and sympathizers in the villages.
- Medical, dental and civil aid teams must be available to give assistance to the villagers once the initial search bas been completed. Arrangements were improved with each cordon and the final organization is described below.
- Food, water, shelter and latrines must be provided for villagers awaiting interrogation.
- Barbed wire should not be used for compounds as this creates the wrong atmosphere.
- In later cordons, white tape was used, sentries were kept as inconspicuous as possible and, to assist in creating a friendly atmosphere, the Battalion Band played popular Vietnamese and other music.
- Twelve Vietnamese police for each rifle company used to clear the village are required and should be used to give orders to the villagers and to move them about. The use of Vietnamese police provides evidence to the villagers that their government is actively engaged in clearing the Viet Cong from their village.

APPENDIX C

Organization for Interrogation, Distribution of Civil Aid etc.
The diagram below illustrates the layout used by 5 RAR in the final cordons in 1967. The whole layout could be established by a platoon in about an hour, by which time the first suspects would be arriving from their houses. The main features to be accommodated were:

- The battalion command post should be established a little distance from the interrogation area.
- Where sick people and children are encountered and cannot be moved from their houses, battalion headquarters should arrange medical treatment and interrogation in the houses. Civil aid personnel should also visit such houses and assist if possible.
- Children should accompany their mothers to the interrogation area.
- Villagers must be allowed time to have breakfast before moving to the interrogation area.
- When all the people are in the holding area and before interrogation begins, have a Vietnamese senior official explain to the people why they are being interrogated and the procedure to be followed. The use of *Hoi Chanh* to move among the villagers and talk to them has also assisted.

Results. The cordon and search of the village of Duc My resulted in the elimination of the Viet Cong cadre from the village, paved the way for the restoration of Government control and permitted the commencement of follow-up civil aid to the village.

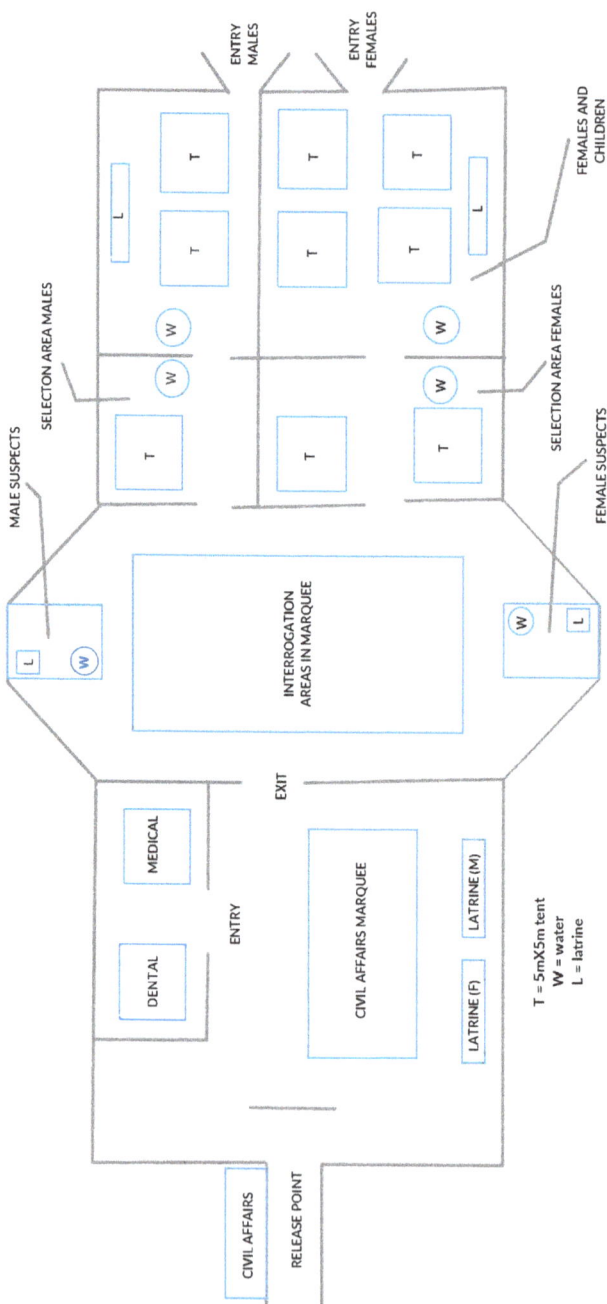

Figure A.1: 5 RAR Interrogation Compound.

Source: Redrawn from the original and produced by Ron Boxall.

APPENDIX C

Cordon and search of Binh Ba Village

The Government's influence in Binh Ba had been eroded gradually since 1961 and its forces were compelled to leave the village in 1964. From then on, the village had been controlled by the Viet Cong. It was estimated that perhaps 20 per cent of the population (particularly the younger men) were actively supporting or were sympathetic towards the hard-core Viet Cong cadre within the village.

It was accepted that most of the village would have collaborated with the Viet Cong and that many had become members of the civil or political organizations or of the military elements. As a matter of personal survival, the villagers would have had little choice but to pay their taxes and provide food and labour. In 1965 one of the village leaders who refused to co-operate with the Viet Cong was taken from his bed late one night and killed on the village soccer field. Several others who had resisted conscription disappeared without trace. It was considered that the political allegiance of most villagers probably was more related to military strength than to ideology.

The enemy force in the area was believed to consist of:

- **Main Force.** 5 Division comprising 274 and 275 Regiments. It was considered unlikely that Main Force units would be uncounted initially in strength in or near Binh Ba during the cordon and search phase of the operation. Small reconnaissance elements might be encountered at any time. It was possible that during the pacification stage, the Main Force units (in conjunction with the Provincial, District and Guerrilla Forces) could quickly launch a major attack unless a sizeable force actively patrolled the area surrounding Binh Ba.

- **Provincial Force.** It was believed that the Viet Cong Provincial Headquarters was based in an area a few miles south-east of Binh Ba. The Provincial Mobile Battalion (D445) was considered unlikely to be encountered in strength in or near Binh Ba in the cordon and search phase of the operation. It was believed possible that small reconnaissance elements could be encountered at any time. The 50th Platoon was known to consist of three squads each of eight to 10 men and to be in the area and directly subordinate to the Viet Cong Provincial Headquarters. The platoon was armed with Soviet 7.62-mm M1944 rifles, US .30 calibre carbines, possibly three Thompson Sub-machine-guns and M26 grenades. The area of responsibility of the platoon was the forest area on each side of the Inter-Provincial Route 2 near Binh Ba and was about 6 square kilometres in extent.

- **District Forces.** It was considered unlikely that the Duc Thanh District (C20) Company would be encountered in strength; however, if the cordon force achieved surprise, it could encounter elements of the Binh Ba Village Guerrilla Platoon within the village. This platoon consisted of three squads each of twelve men and was armed with 10 Soviet 7.62-mm M1944 rifles, eight US .30 M1 carbines, two German rifles (possibly Mauser 7.92 mm) and four M26 grenades. The task of the platoon was to exercise military control over Binh Ba village.

The intelligence available was far more detailed than that provided in July for the cordon of Duc My village. The additional information was obtained from Viet Cong prisoners and documents taken at Duc My and other Viet Cong captured during Operation Sydney, together with information from other sources.

Apart from the cultivation of minor fruit and vegetable crops, the major source of income for the Binh Ba villagers was the Gallia Rubber Plantation which surrounds the village. The plantation was under French ownership and management. To keep the plantation operating the French owner had agreed to pay tax to the Viet Cong.

The clearance of the Viet Cong cadres from Binh Ba and Duc Trung and the subsequent pacification of the villages were aimed at:

- Permitting the Province Chief to re-establish government control in the village and, as a result, depriving the Viet Cong of tax, food and intelligence. The Viet Cong in the village had been taxing the villagers one day's pay and two litres of rice per month.
- Opening the road from Binh Ba to the Catholic (and therefore anti-communist) village of Binh Gia to the north-east to permit the people of Binh Gia to have access to the Ba Ria market. Binh Gia had a population of some 6,000 and the Viet Cong had not permitted them to use Route 2.
- Allowing a large quantity of rubber stored in the processing plant at Duc Trung to be moved to Saigon via Ba Ria.

Late in July '66, 5 RAR was ordered to carry out a simultaneous cordon and search of the adjacent villages of Binh Ba and Duc Trung, to make a second search of the village of Duc My and later to open and secure the road from Binh Ba to 1 Australian Task Force base. There was also a requirement to secure the village area to allow a Vietnamese commando company to be established on the village outskirts. This was to be Operation HOLSWORTHY.

Forces Available. The following forces were allotted to assist 5 RAR in the cordon and search: 2 Armoured Personnel Carrier Squadron, less one troop; 105 Field Battery; 161 Battery, Royal New Zealand Artillery; A Battery 2/35 Artillery (USA) equipped with 155-mm self-propelled guns; one troop from 1 Field Engineer Squadron; C and D Companies of 6 RAR; one section of 1 Transport Platoon; one Sioux helicopter of 161 (Independent) Recce Flight; one Iroquois helicopter of 9 Squadron RAAF; a Light Fire Team (two USA armed Iroquois helicopters); a Cessna aircraft equipped with loud-speaker; a Psychological Warfare detachment; a Forward Air Controller Detachment; interpreters from 1 Australian Task Force Linguist Section; six Vietnamese policemen; and an additional Medical Officer (for civil aid assistance). In addition, elements of 3 Special Air Services Squadron were to operate well to the north-west and north-east of the villages to give early warning of large-scale Viet Cong movements.

Considerations. Duc Trung village was about 800 by 850 metres and surrounded by a high wire fence with a deep ditch outside the fence. Its total length of 1,300 metres could be cordoned in the clean rubber plantation by two rifle companies. Binh Ba was approximately 600 metres by 300 metres with well-defined sides. This would require a company on each of the larger sides and approximately two platoons on each of the shorter sides to complete the cordon. It was therefore decided to cordon each village as follows:

- Duc Trung: D Company 5 RAR (Major P. Greenhalgh) and D Company 6 RAR. (Captain I. McLean-Williams)
- Binh Ba: A Company (Major Maizey) less one platoon to cordon the west side. B Company (Major B. McQualter) to cordon the east side. (After first light two sections of 1 Armoured Personnel Carrier Squadron were to relieve B Company of the cordon task and allow the company to search the village.) C Company 5 RAR (Major J. Miller) to cordon the north side of the village. C Company 6 RAR (Major B. McFarlane) to cordon the south side of the village.

The rubber plantation was worked daily and therefore the cordon force could approach only to the edge of the plantation by daylight. Thus, the final approach had to be under cover of darkness. An approach from the east would have required the force to move through thick country outside the plantation. This was often frequented by woodcutters and to conceal the 900-man force would have been difficult. An approach from the south was not possible due to the location of Duc My village. Consequently, an approach from the west appeared to be the best and offered the following advantages:

a. A covered approach to the south-west corner of the plantation through an area regularly patrolled by our forces and in which no civilians were allowed.

b. The edge of the rubber plantation and the air strip could be used to assist night navigation, particularly since the air strip led directly to both villages.

The western approach was therefore selected for the cordon force, less B Company, which was to cordon the east side of Binh Ba village. B Company was given the eastern approach to reduce the number of companies on the western route, to give flank protection to the main force, to cut off any Viet Cong who may have received warning of the approach of the cordon and fled to the east and to enable the cordon to be placed around Binh Ba as quickly as possible early on 9 August.

It was considered that one rifle company on the east route could move into position undetected and, if it was seen by Viet Cong trail watchers, its size would not indicate its cordon task.

Plan. The outline plan is illustrated on Map A.2.

APPENDIX C

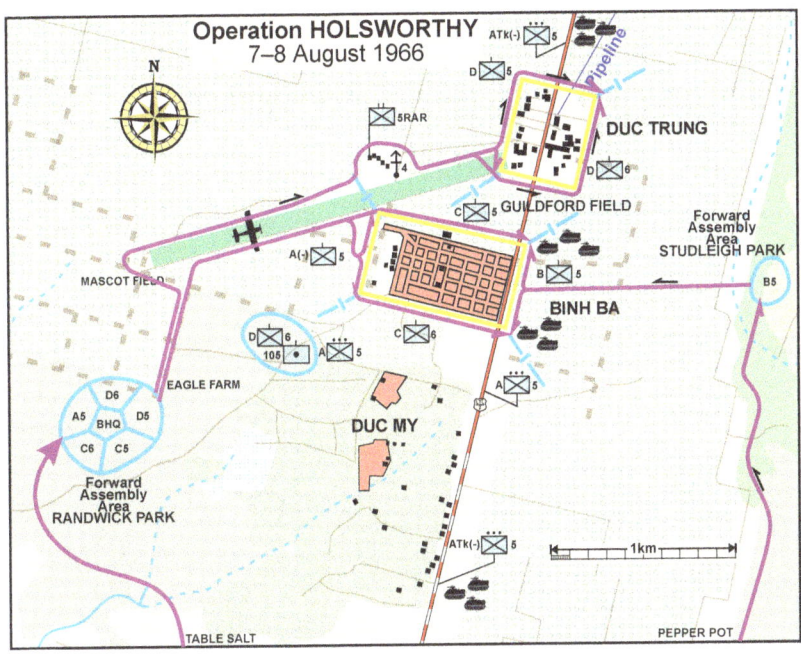

Map A.2: Operation Holsworthy: 7–8 August 1966.

Source: Designed by Ron Boxall and produced by Alan Mayne from circa 1966 US military maps provided by Bruce Davies.

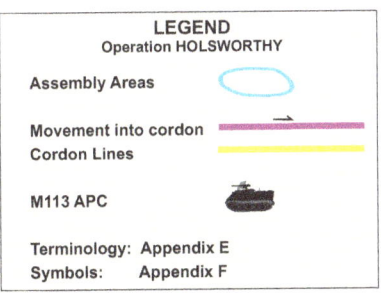

The cordon was to be in place by 0530 hours which was one hour before first light. In addition to the cordons by the six rifle companies, ambushes were sited on the likely exits towards Duc My village and north of Duc Trung to stop any Viet Cong who tried to escape. These ambushes were to be in position before the cordon was closed and would be able to give protection and early warning to the cordon companies of the presence of any Viet Cong forces. Four ambushes each equipped with radios were to be established by the A Company platoon not included in the cordon and by the Anti-Tank Platoon.

379

The village of Duc Trung was to be searched by the platoon of A Company after it lifted its ambushes near Duc My on the morning of 9 August. This platoon was to be assisted by engineers of 1 Field Engineer Squadron during the ambushes and search of the village.

It was estimated that the search of the village of Duc Trung would be completed by midday, as both the area and the population were small. The greater part of Duc Trung was covered by the rubber processing plants. As soon as the search of Duc Trung was completed, and all males of Viet Cong military age had been evacuated, D Company 5 RAR was to move to Duc My village and search it while D Company 6 RAR moved to an area south-west of Binh Ba village to secure a gun area for use by 105 Field Battery and A Battery of the 2/35 Artillery (US). Armoured personnel carriers were to block off possible escape routes from Duc My while D Company 5 RAR searched the village.

The Assault Pioneer Platoon was to provide protection for Battalion Headquarters during the approach march and in cordon, and was then to construct, enclosures in the Battalion Headquarters area and secure suspects until they were evacuated by road transport to Ba Ria for interrogation. The vehicles were to be escorted by armoured personnel carriers. All males of ages between 12 and 45 years were to be taken for interrogation. In all later cordons, women 15 to 35 years were also screened, and some female Viet Cong cadre members were apprehended. On this occasion it was considered undesirable to take both the women and the men from the village as it may not have been possible to return them to their homes for a day or two in which case their young children would have been neglected.

A light aircraft equipped with loudspeakers was to be over the villages at 0615 hours using prepared tapes to inform the villagers that they were surrounded, that a house curfew had been imposed and that they were to obey directions. Leaflets were also prepared by the 1 Australian Task Force to be distributed during the search of the village and the ensuing civic action.

The mortar platoon, less one section, was to come forward in mortar armoured personnel carriers at first light on 9 August. Armoured personnel carriers were also to take over the cordon from B Company, block Route 2 north of Duc Trung and provide a reserve from shortly after first light on 9 August. The Battalion Headquarters Group under Major M. Carroll, together with the CO's party, moved in rear of D Company 6 RAR.

Execution. On 5 August, C Company established a base some 1,000 metres due south of the south-west corner of the airfield and on the night 5–6 August reconnaissance parties from all companies except B Company operated from the base to check routes and timings. During this reconnaissance it was discovered that the proposed battalion assembly area for the evening prior to the cordon would be unsatisfactory and it was therefore decided to move the cordon force into the rubber plantation just at last light.

C Company and the reconnaissance groups returned to 5 RAR on 6 August and orders were issued the following morning. On the 8th at 0800 hours, the Adjutant, Captain P. Isaacs, who had the task of laying out the battalion assembly area together with company guides, departed from Nui Dat and the remainder of the battalion group departed at 0930 hours. The battalion group, less B Company, were in the selected area by 1700 hours and just at last light moved into the rubber plantation. The companies were then laid out ready to move later that night.

Toggle ropes were to be used to assist movement in the dark by troops tying the toggle rope of the soldier ahead of them to a piece of their equipment which they placed on the ground while resting. The leading company (D Company 5 RAR) was scheduled to depart from the assembly area at 2300 hours. Troops were alerted in time and minor movement, including closing-up, occurred in preparation to move off, with the result that, in some instances, equipment attached to toggle ropes of the man ahead suddenly took off between the rubber trees in the dark, much to the consternation of the owners. In this way the Forward Air Controller lost his radio and one officer lost a bag containing maps and papers. (These were recovered in the assembly area next day.) As a result, the move commenced 15 minutes later than planned but, because of the bright moonlight, the easy going through the plantation along the side of the airstrip and the time reserve which had been allowed, all companies and ambush parties arrived in their allotted areas on time. No contact was made with any Viet Cong forces. At 0615 hours the voice aircraft arrived over Binh Ba and 45 minutes later the armoured personnel carriers relieved B Company of its cordon task. At 0730 hours the search of Binh Ba and Duc Trung began. By the end of that day the searches of the villages of Duc Trung and Duc My were completed and the search of Binh Ba and evacuation of males was completed by midday on 10 August.

Pacification. The pacification programme which followed over a period of months was just as important and significant as the operation on 9 August. Unlike the operation at Duc My village in July, the battalion did not leave the area immediately after the search of the villages but remained until 16 August patrolling and Searching the plantation area and approaches. On 11 August the road to Ba Ria was opened for the first time in more than three months and picqueted to prevent interference from the Viet Cong. The opening of the road had a remarkable effect on the morale of the people. In the first two days, 1,500 people travelling on Lambretta taxis, ox carts, bicycles, tractors and army transport moved south to Ba Ria.

During the period 9 August to 16 August, effective contact was made with the villagers in the following ways:

- Companies organized football matches with the villagers, particularly with the Children.
- Medical and dental teams from 1 ATF gave regular treatment. The French doctor from the head office of the plantation recommended regular weekly visits by aircraft to the plantation.
- Civil affairs section of 1 ATF distributed food and clothing.
- 5 RAR's Roman Catholic padre (Chaplain John Williams) conducted services with the village priest in the village church and some soldiers attended services with the villagers on a voluntary basis.
- Above all, the soldiers were courteous to the villagers, respectful to the women and elderly folk and did their best to treat the Vietnamese as equals.

1 Australian Task Force arranged for a newly raised Vietnamese Commando Company (with Captain R. Boxall of 5 RAR as adviser) to be moved to Binh Ba to give security to the village after the withdrawal of our forces. To support this Vietnamese company, C Company and later other companies from the Battalion, together with a section of mortars, remained at Binh Ba for the next two months.

Lessons. The lessons learnt during the cordon of Duc My were applied, but other lessons emerged:

- Ample time must be allowed in a night move to ensure that all soldiers are awake and have checked their equipment before moving.
- The need for Australian interpreters was vital.

- All tinned food issued to villagers must first be opened to prevent it being stored and later given to the Viet Cong. It is better to deliver gifts of food to each house to ensure an equal distribution or give the food to the village chief (if reliable) or the village priest to distribute.
- Never throw food or gifts to crowds of children or adults. The resultant scramble or fight among themselves for the items on the ground destroys their self respect.
- Do not give food to children as their parents generally disagree with such action. It destroys parental discipline and makes beggars of the children.

Results. A total of 168 males of military age were apprehended and interrogated and of these, 17 Viet Cong were captured, and 77 suspects detained. Thus, without a shot being fired, the Binh Ba village guerrilla platoon and the Viet Cong cadre in the village was eliminated. There is little doubt that to have killed or captured these Viet Cong in ambushes and search and destroy operations would have required several months of constant patrolling and would probably have resulted in casualties to us. The cadre members employed in the villages could not have been captured by any other means.

The psychological effect on the villagers of the operation was tremendous for they saw the Viet Cong taken from the village, the re-establishment of government control and a return to a more normal life.

The road from Binh Ba to Ba Ria has not been closed since the operation and the Viet Cong have not attempted to interfere with its traffic.

Reports late in 1966 indicated that some Viet Cong had infiltrated back into the village so, early in January 1967, 5 RAR again cordoned and searched Binh Ba village during Operation CALOUNDRA and 9 Viet Cong were apprehended.

Cordon and search of Phuoc Hoa Village

The area of flat ground to the west and south-west of Phuoc Tuy was of considerable importance to the Viet Cong. This region linked the sea transport routes of the Rung Sat, a marshy low-lying area to the west, with a system of foot and cart tracks which ran through to the Hat Dich area, the main Viet Cong base in the northwest of Phuoc Tuy, and to other bases further north.

Viet Cong activity was concentrated in the area between the villages of Phu My, Phuoc Hoa and Long Huong and Long Son Island. The island was situated near the junction of several sea routes leading into landing points and was ideally situated for use as a refuge and a rest centre. The main routes for water-borne traffic were the rivers which fanned out on the northern side of Long Son Island. The most direct route for the Viet Cong into Phuoc Tuy Province was through the fishing village of Phuoc Hoa. This village was also the one best served by land and sea routes and simple harbour facilities. It was therefore the scene of the most significant Viet Cong activity which passed through into western Phuoc Tuy Province.

The western strip of the Province was also of interest to the Viet Cong because of Route 15, the main road between the major port of Vung Tau, the provincial capital, Ba Ria, and Saigon. The Viet Cong had made attacks in the area to dominate their supply routes by crushing villagers who resisted them and by exploiting people who were sympathetic.

Along Route 15 were located a few military posts garrisoned by the Army of the Republic of Vietnam (ARVN). These were largely ineffective because, at that time, the troops did not patrol sufficiently or ambush at night. In addition, the Viet Cong intelligence net invariably obtained details of any activities initiated from these posts. The Viet Cong, however, had a regular patrol system which covered the whole area at night, usually with platoon strength patrols although company-sized patrols had been reported.

The Viet Cong also used the area for gaining intelligence concerning Allied movements by observing road movement along Route 15, air movements to and from Vung Tau airfield and shipping arriving at Vung Tau or moving along the river to Saigon.

There was much civilian activity in the area; woodcutters moved far inland with ox carts and fishermen covered the waterways. Theoretically, night movement was forbidden but this was rarely policed along Route 15 and never policed on the water. Many fishermen worked at night and it was impossible to tell a Viet Cong sampan from an innocent one. Because of the impracticalities of enforcing the night curfew, the area was not a free-fire zone and fire could not be opened unless direct physical contact occurred with the Viet Cong. This situation was of tremendous assistance to the Viet Cong.

APPENDIX C

In September 1966 Brigadier O. D. Jackson, the Commander, 1 Australian Task Force, indicated that 5 RAR would be required to clear Long Son Island, later in the year. In October 5 RAR conducted Operations CANBERRA, ROBIN and QUEANBEYAN in the area along Route 15 and in the Nui Thi Vai hills nearby; and, as a result, came to know the whole area quite well. During Operation ROBIN, A Company (Major P. Cole) established a company base 800 metres east of Phuoc Hoa village and a study was made of the village layout in case it might be required later. Documents captured during Operation QUEANBEYAN, together with information from other sources, confirmed that Phuoc Hoa village, despite having an ARVN Popular Force Company located in it, was the centre of Viet Cong activity in the area. 1 Australian Task Force therefore directed that 5 RAR would cordon and search Phuoc Hoa village (Operation YASS) immediately before it carried out the operation to clear Long Son Island (Operation HAYMAN). Some troops could then be located in Phuoc Hoa village to block any movement of Viet Cong from Long Son Island to the village during Operation HAYMAN.

The main Viet Cong unit known to be in the area was the C20 guerrilla company which had three platoons, each of three squads with a total strength of 110 men. They were armed with 1 medium machine-gun, 4 light machine-guns, 19 sub-machine-guns, 2 revolvers and the remainder of the company carried US .30 calibre carbines or AK44 long rifles. The members of the company were drawn from Long Son Island, Phuoc Hoa and Long Huong villages. The morale of the company was fair.

It was considered probable that some water transportation (sampan) members would be at Phuoc Hoa overnight. It was also feasible that a medium sized Viet Cong force could be staging through the area at the time of the operation. It was thought that once the operation commenced the C20 company might harass the Battalion by sniping and setting booby traps. Other Viet Cong in Phuoc Hoa would probably try to flee by sampan into the mangroves or by the track to the north-east.

Phuoc Hoa had a population of about 700 adults who were engaged mainly in woodcutting or fishing. Many sampans used the small boat harbour and several families lived on these sampans permanently. The village area was well defined with Route 15 on the north-east side, and a high embankment and ditch on the other sides; in addition, mangroves bordered the village on the south-west side.

Forces Available. Additional forces were allotted to assist 5 RAR in the operation. These comprised: 1 Armoured Personnel Carrier Squadron, less a troop; 103 Field Battery, one platoon of A Battery 2/35 Artillery Battalion (USA); one troop of 1 Field Engineer Squadron (30 all ranks); C Company 6 RAR; elements of 3 Special Air Service Squadron; 30 Vietnamese policemen; six interpreters; one light fire team (two armed Iroquois helicopters); one Sioux helicopter of 161 (Independent) Reconnaissance Flight; and one Cessna aircraft equipped with loud speaker.

Considerations. The sides of the village were between 550 and 650 metres long. One company would therefore be allocated to cordon each side, and C Company 6 RAR (Major B. McFarlane) would secure the gun area. A detailed ground reconnaissance of the village immediately prior to the operation was not possible, but it was believed that booby traps and mines were probably laid along the ditch on the outskirts of the village. It was therefore decided that the cordon companies on the north-west side (B Company, Major B. McQualter) and south-east side (D Company, Captain R. Boxall) would not approach closer to the ditches than 20 metres.

The village was beyond the range of field artillery at the 1 ATF base and so the supporting artillery had to be moved to a suitable location nearby. This would make it impossible to hide the fact that an operation was to be undertaken in the general area. It was therefore decided to move the force via Route 15 in armoured personnel carriers and trucks. If the cordon was to be in position about an hour before first light, the force would have to be moved to an area east of Route 15 where it could be concealed by day and able to establish the cordon by night. A, B and D Companies and the Battalion Headquarters group would therefore dismount from vehicles in the general area of Phuoc Hoa village and move on foot to harbour areas about 1,000 metres east of Route 15.

C Company (Major J. Miller) was to cordon the south-west side of the village adjacent to the mangroves. Air reconnaissance indicated that even at low tide it would be impossible to move this company in the dark through the mangroves quickly enough to ensure that the cordon was closed before any Viet Cong in the village had an opportunity to escape by sampan into the mangroves.

It was therefore decided to use the armoured personnel carriers to move C Company through the village from Route 15 to the boat harbour area at maximum speed when the other sides of the cordon were in position and to establish the cordon along the top of the embankment while simultaneously securing the boat harbour area to prevent sampans escaping.

It was also considered that two assault boats would be required in the Rach Tre river channel to the west of the village to ensure that there was no movement from the village in sampans. 3 Special Air Services Squadron was given the task of providing the assault craft, crews and radios for this task. Consideration was given to moving the boats into position along the Rach Tre channel to the west of the village, but this was ruled out due to difficulty of navigation at night in the mangrove waterways and the possible loss of surprise. C Company with the assault boats was to harbour some 1500 metres north of Phuoc Hoa and off Route 15 where there was reasonable cover. The outline plan for the movement of the cordon force and detailed cordon positions are shown in Map A.3.

Security and Deception. 103 Field Battery and the platoon of A Battery 2/35 Artillery were required to support both Operation YASS and Operation HAYMAN, including the air assault onto Long Son Island, at first light the day after Operation YASS. It was therefore desirable that the selected gun area meet the requirements of both operations. The general area was flat and muddy and there were only a few likely sites. The gun area selected by 1 Australian Task Force was on the west side of Route 15 about 500 metres south of Phuoc Hoa. As the gun area was to be occupied on November 6, the day preceding the cordon, a cover plan was necessary to convince the Viet Cong that the activity in the area was not related to Phuoc Hoa village or Long Son Island. The proximity of the gun area to the village should have convinced most Viet Cong that the guns were not intended to support activities in the immediate vicinity of the village.

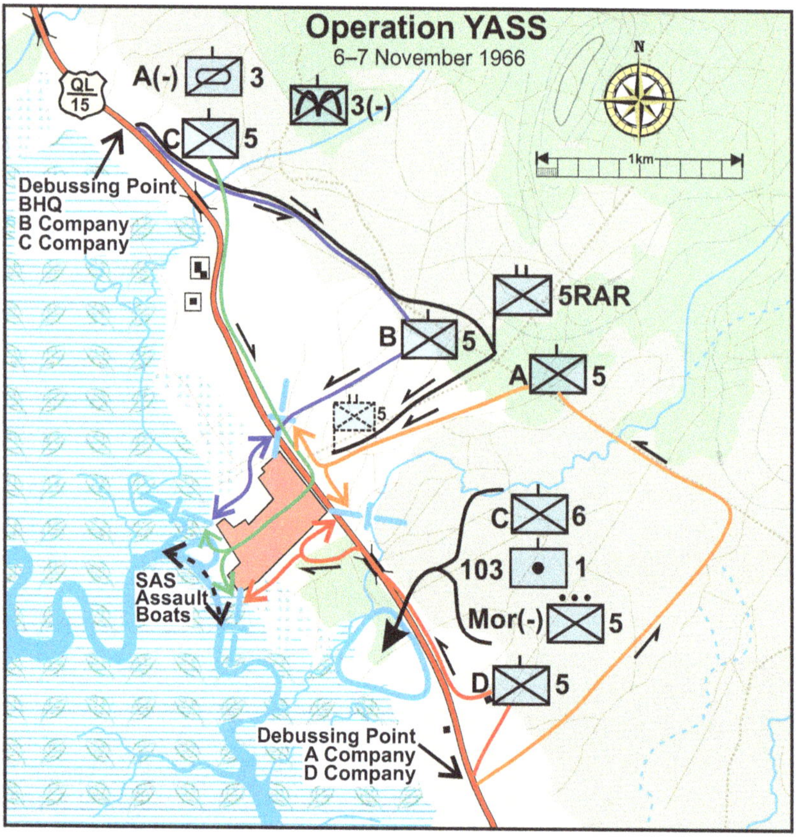

Map A.3: Operation Yass: 6–7 November 1966.

Source: Designed by Ron Boxall and produced by Alan Mayne from circa 1966 US military maps provided by Bruce Davies.

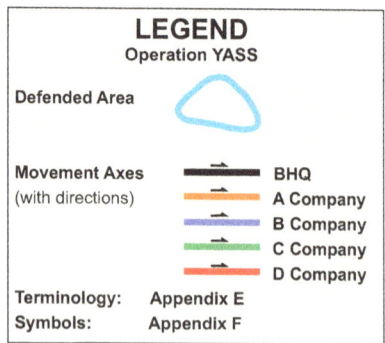

APPENDIX C

A cover plan was issued by 1 Australian Task Force one week before the operation and the actual details of both Operation YASS and Operation HAYMAN were restricted so that in the Battalion only four officers (Commanding Officer, Second-in-Command, Operations Officer and Intelligence Officer) were informed. The cover plan gave the exact details of Operation YASS as they were to occur, including times, dates and method of movement up to the stage where the troops debussed on Route 15 and moved east. Here the cover plan varied from the true plan and indicated that the battalion would continue to move east to the Nui Dinh hills to carry out a clearing operation. The cover plan was given a wide distribution.

In addition, two 'teams' (Second Lieutenants J. McAloney and J. Carruthers, and WO2 B. M. Hughson and Sergeant T. Witheridge) were provided with money and sent on two occasions to Vung Tau to spend the evenings in the bars talking about the 'forthcoming' operation in the Nui Dinh hills.

The four members knew only the details of the cover plan and no members other than the four officers mentioned above knew of the tasks of the teams in Vung Tau. During their 'tour of duty' in Vung Tau, the NCO team had their conversation recorded on tape by a Vietnamese barman in one establishment, were questioned at length about the operation by Vietnamese girls in another bar and on another occasion were followed from a bar for some distance by a Vietnamese civilian. The four concerned all agreed that it was the most enjoyable task ever given to them.

An ARVN Popular Force company located In Phuoc Hoa village raised the problems of either moving the company or risking a clash with it while the cordon was being placed in position.

As C Company was required to move through the middle of the village to establish the south-west side of the cordon, contact with the Popular Force company was inevitable and it was necessary therefore to move the company without arousing the suspicions of the villagers. The Province Chief, who was the only Vietnamese to know of the operation, agreed to direct the Popular Force Company to move to an adjacent ARVN post on 6 November for training purposes and to remain there for the night. Apparently, it was not uncommon to move these companies to other ARVN posts for training.

It was essential that the two assault boats to be used by the Special Air Services soldiers should be hidden from view and so the boats were moved inside 2 ½ ton vehicles with their cargo canopies closed.

On 6 November, the initial movement was carried out according to the cover plan and the troops left the vehicles near Phuoc Hoa and moved about 1,000 metres east as shown in Map A.3.

An hour after this eastward movement commenced, 103 Field Battery fired artillery missions to the east on the Nui Dinh Hills where the falling rounds were clearly visible for many miles and a Sioux helicopter made flights over the same area to convince any Viet Cong observers that the battalion was moving towards and intended to operate in the Hills.

The Vietnamese policemen and interpreters allocated to assist in the clearance of the village were not informed of their tasks by the Province Headquarters until early on the morning of 7 November.

Execution. On 6 November (the day preceding the cordon) everything went according to plan until 1530 hours when B Company, while moving into its harbour area, met 35 civilians from Phuoc Hoa. B Company sent the villagers back to their village and continued moving east, harbouring a little further east than had been planned.

When C Company, in armoured personnel carriers, passed the entrance to Phuoc Hoa village they noticed a large moveable barbed wire barricade with M26 grenades hung on it at the village entrance. It seemed possible that the barricade might be placed across the entrance each night and as this would have delayed movement of the APCs by the minute or two needed to enable Viet Cong in the village to escape into the mangroves, the company commander Major Miller, returned to the village later that afternoon on the pretext of arranging for a medical team to visit the village next morning. During his visit, Major Miller leant that the barricade was not placed across the entrance each night.

By 0400 hours next morning, all companies of the cordon except C Company were in position. The curfew along Route 15 was supposed to be enforced until 0530 hours daily, but at 0430 hours the civilian traffic began to move. A little later A Company observed movement in the village. So, at 0500 hours, 30 minutes earlier than planned, C Company was ordered to move. The APCs carrying C Company and escorting the two trucks carrying the assault boats came down Route 15 at maximum speed, with headlights on, and turned in straight through the middle of the village. Within minutes the SAS assault boats had been launched into the boat harbour and the cordon completed. 103 Field Battery fired illumination rounds over the western end of the village and APCs with spotlights on each turret lit up the boat harbour and mangroves so that any movement by Viet Cong would have been easily detected. Some APCs were then moved back to Route 15, where all traffic had been stopped, and their headlights and spotlights were used to light up the ditches on the north-west and south-east sides of the village.

The voice aircraft; which was not due to fly until first light (0630 hours), did not arrive at all, because of mechanical failure. Interpreters, with loud hailers and mounted on armoured personnel carriers, were then used to advise the villagers of the procedures to be followed.

At 0800 the first of the villagers departed by truck and APCs for interrogation in Ba Ria and by midday the last of the 700 villagers to be screened (men 12 to 45 years and women 15 to 35 years) had departed. Fifteen members of the Popular Force company who had remained in the village were also apprehended.

Results. 16 Viet Cong were captured in the cordon, again without loss to the battalion. One of the captured Viet Cong was a cadre leader who had been sought for many months by the Vietnamese Government authorities. These results would indicate that the cover plan and deception activities were successful.

The Battalion Reconnaissance Platoon (Second Lieutenant M. Deak), formerly the Anti-Tank Platoon which had been retrained for a reconnaissance role remained in Phuoc Hoa village until 12 November to prevent Viet Cong using the village as an escape route from Long Son Island. In this period a sound, friendly relationship was established with the villagers by the Platoon's members. Medical aid for the villagers was also provided.

Conclusions

In the seven-month period, July 1966 to February 1967, 5 RAR carried out nine village cordon and search operations. These resulted in 14 Viet Cong killed, 5 wounded, 224 prisoners and detainees for the loss of 4 men killed and 5 wounded. Except for one, all casualties suffered by the Battalion were caused by one booby trap.

When 1 Australian Task Force commenced operations in Phuoc Tuy in May 1966, the Viet Cong controlled the entire province except for the capital Ba Ria, which was expected to fall to the Viet Cong at any time. 1 ATF operations in 1966–67 resulted in a majority of people in the province being brought under effective government control.

The speed with which the Viet Cong cadres can be eliminated by cordon and searches must be adjusted to the capacity of the government forces to secure the villages against the return of the enemy. Once village security is established certain restrictions is necessary. A detailed census of all people in each village is required. Daily road-checks are essential to ensure that the Viet Cong are unable to move as civilians on the roads and use public transport. Food control needs to be established so that all rice is collected, accounted for and secured centrally in each village, and issued weekly to villagers in accordance with the number of people in each family. Daily checks are required by the police in the village to ensure that villagers take with them only enough cooked rice (which cannot be stored) for their midday meal. In this way the villagers will be protected against Viet Cong demands for food. Where farmers live outside a village and cannot be protected, a resettlement programme needs to be initiated before cordon operations are undertaken. A poor resettlement program can quickly nullify all other efforts.

Cordon and search operations and follow-up pacification programmes are the only effective means of re-establishing effective village control and such operations are an essential preliminary to the defeat of the Viet Cong main force.

APPENDIX D. THE ENEMY: UNCONTESTED TENANCY PRIOR TO THE ARRIVAL OF 1 ATF

Ernest Chamberlain

The Saigon government's Phuoc Tuy Province was about 55 kilometres from east to west and about 35 kilometres from north to south (an area of some 1,958 square kilometres – 2.86 per cent of the size of Tasmania). The province capital, Phuoc Le/Ba Ria Town, was about 110 kilometres by road south-east of Saigon via Route 15 (nowadays Route 51). In mid-1966, the official population of the province was about 105,000, including Ba Ria Town's population of about 10,000. Vung Tau (Cap St Jacques), 22 kilometres south-west of Ba Ria Town, had a further population of 42,000. Phuoc Tuy comprised six districts (early 1966 populations shown in brackets): Long Le (31,800), Long Dien (24,500), Dat Do (24,700), Duc Thanh (12,650) and Xuyen Moc (6,260). There were 29 villages and 129 hamlets in the province.

As the deep-draft river port at Saigon – the only one in the III Corps Tactical Zone – had a limited capacity, Route 15 was an important strategic route linking Saigon and Bien Hoa with the limited berthing facilities at Vung Tau port. The Route had been completed in 1896 during the French colonial period.[1]

---

1 A second, different 'Route 15' in southern North Vietnam was a major infiltration route from Vinh to the Mu Gia Pass (the principal entry point to the Ho Chi Minh Trail through Laos). During the war, US and South Vietnamese forces also conducted operations along Route 15 in the Kampong Cham area of Cambodia.

An early 1966 US Military Assistance Command, Vietnam (MACV), technical survey described Route 15 as: 'an all-weather highway with an intermediate bituminous surface … with well-compacted macadam in good condition. … and limited off-road dispersal possibilities'.[2] The road surface was from 4.2 to 4.9 metres wide. With 11 significant bridges[3] on Route 15 within Phuoc Tuy Province, and many minor bridges and culverts, the route was highly vulnerable to interdiction by anti-government forces. Heavy rains during the wet season (May to October) could flood sections of the roadway and also restrict daytime vehicle passage. The route was overlooked by ranges of wooded and jungle-covered hills covering an area of about 80 square kilometres comprising, from the north-west to the south-east: the Nui Thi Vai – 467 metres high; the Nui Toc Tien – 221 metres high (2 kilometres east of Route 15); the Nui Ong Trinh – 504 metres high; and, reaching to the north-western outskirts of Ba Ria Town, the Nui Dinh – 491 metres high (whose summit is about 4 kilometres to the north of Route 15). Many caves and larger caverns were scattered throughout these granite hills – with crevasses and rock falls of larger boulders covered with vines and tree roots. These natural features and tunnels had been used by resistance elements over many decades. Several small isolated Buddhist temples and shrines were scattered throughout the hills.

To the west of Route 15 lay the Rung Sac/Sat ('Salty Jungle'), an area of about 1,250 square kilometres of tidal swamp, mangroves and nipa palm bordering Can Gio District of Gia Dinh/Bien Hoa Province. The Rung Sat encompassed villages within Can Gio and Quan Xuyen Districts, and the large island of Long Son[4] within Phuoc Tuy Province. The Long Tau River and the Soai Rap River ran through the Rung Sat and connected Vung Tau and South China Sea with Saigon.

---

2   USMACV/JGS Combined Intelligence Center Vietnam (CICV), 'Area Analysis Study 66-36 – National Route 15', 1 March 1966.
3   The Song (River) Dinh flows through Ba Ria Town and is bridged within the town at coordinates YS 375610.
4   Long Son Island (population 5,300) was dominated by Nui Nua Hill – 183 metres. 1 ATF conducted its 'first combat assault' and a 'search and destroy' operation (Operation Hayman) into Long Son Island, adjacent to the Rung Sat, in the period 8–12 November 1966; 1 ATF, 'OPORD 1/14/66', 4 November 1966, Australian War Memorial (AWM), AWM95 1/4/16.

APPENDIX D

The first Indo-China War

On 9 February 1946, the French forces reoccupied Ba Ria Province[5] – with columns advancing along Route 15 through Long Thanh and also through Xuan Loc, down Route 2 to seize Ba Ria Town. En route, the French briefly engaged a Viet Minh 'Republican Guard' force on Route 15 at Phuoc Hoa. Government machinery was re-established in the province under Bui The Kham as the province chief and Lieutenant Colonel Pougin de la Maissoneuve as the sector commander.[6] A small Viet Minh guerrilla unit – the Quang Trung force – was formed at Long Phuoc village in 1946, and by the end of that year had reportedly grown to 25 'secret self-defence guerrilla units'[7] covering 40 villages across the province. Rubber plantation workers in the Route 2 area provided recruits, and further units were raised: the 16 Detachment, the 307 Regiment (established in May 1948) and the 397 Regiment (December 1949, combining the 307 and 309 Regiments). During this period, the Viet Minh were mostly active in the central and eastern areas of Ba Ria Province – principally in the Dat Do area, and from their Minh Dam Secret Zone bases in the Long Hai hills. However, the 700-strong Viet Minh 300 Battalion operated against Route 15 – principally interdicting the route in the Phu My area on the Ba Ria Province/Bien Hoa border and to the north. In September 1947, the route was cut by the Viet Minh for almost five years. Road traffic from Saigon to Vung Tau was forced to travel eastward along Route 1 to Xuan Loc Town, and then south down Route 2 to Ba Ria and on to Vung Tau – a total distance of 155 kilometres, or to Long Hai on the shore of the South China Sea.

---

5   In October 1956, the Saigon Government of President Ngo Dinh Diem retitled their Ba Ria Province as Phuoc Tuy Province, which included the adjacent Can Gio District and Vung Tau. However, the communist side preferred the earlier title of Ba Ria Province. While the province capital was officially titled Phuoc Le (until 1982), it was commonly referred to as 'Ba Ria Town' by both sides.
6   Trần Văn Khánh (et al.) and the Executive Committee of the Bà Rịa-Vũng Tàu Party, *Lịch sử Đảng bộ tỉnh Bà Rịa-Vũng Tàu 1930–1975* [*The history of the Party in Bà Rịa-Vũng Tàu Province 1930–1975*], Vol I, 1930–1954, Nhà Xuất bản Chính trị Quốc gia [National Political Publishing House], Hà Nội, 2000 (hereafter 'the Ba Ria History'), and Le Thanh Tuong, *Monographie de la province de Baria Sud Vietnam*, Saigon, 1950.
7   EP Chamberlain, *The Viet Cong D445 Battalion: Their story*, E Chamberlain, Point Lonsdale, 2016, p 12, fn 39.

According to the Viet Cong (VC) Long Dat History: 'At the beginning of 1951, all the Viet Minh elements were forced to move into the Minh Dam base area.'[8] However, on 15 March 1953, the Main Force Battalion 300 and the Long Dat local unit attacked Route 23 – and captured a French officer (Fardel, the commander of Dat Do). In late February 1953, French forces retook Phu My village, re-established a subsector there, and cleared Route 15. They then moved east of Ba Ria Town and cleared Route 23 to Dat Do. The Chau Duc History records that:

> In the first months of 1953, 96% of populated area [104 villages] was temporarily seized by the enemy, and our guerrillas were under great pressure. Co Trach village [i.e. the centre of Chau Duc District] was one of the only villages held by the Party.[9]

However, in early May 1953, a French officer, Captain Joseph Suacot (called '*la Panthère noire*' by the Viet Minh[10]), led elements of the 64 Vietnamese Infantry Battalion on a sortie into the Hat Dich.[11] The force was ambushed by the Viet Minh's 3 Company/300 Battalion – and Captain Suacot was killed. Six months later, on 5 November 1953, 3 and 4 Companies of 300 Battalion attacked a French convoy 2 kilometres from Binh Ba Subsector and killed Lieutenant Colonel de la Maissoneuve, the sector commander, a captain, a number of officers, and 60 soldiers of the local '65ᵗʰ BVN Battalion [sic]'[12] (BVN: *Bataillon Vietnamien*).

---

8   Phan Ngọc Danh and Trần Quang Toại, *Lịch Sử Đấu Tranh Cách Mạng Của Huyện Long Đất* [*The history of the revolutionary struggle in Long Dat district*], Nhà Xuất Bản Đồng Nai [The Dong Nai Publishing House], Đồng Nai, 1986, hereafter 'the Long Dat History', p 70.
9   Le Minh Duc and Ho Song Quynh (eds), *The history of the armed forces of Chau Duc District (1945–2014)*, The Truth – National Political Publishing House, Hanoi, 2014, hereafter 'the Chau Duc History 2014', p 81.
10   Nguyễn Công Danh and Lê Minh Nghĩa (et al.), *Lịch sử Đấu Tranh Cách Mạng Của Đảng Bộ Và Nhân Dân Huyện Châu Đức (1930–2000)* [*The history of the revolutionary struggle of the Party Chapter and the people of Châu Đức District (1930–2000)*], Nhà Xuất Bản Chính Trị Quốc Gia, [National Political Publishing House], Hà Nội, 2004, hereafter 'the Chau Duc History 2004', p 84.
11   The small village of Hat Dich was located in the vicinity of YS 3477, about 11 kilometres west of the Duc Thanh District Sub-Sector. The Hat Dich area was defined in a US 9 Infantry Division report as an area of 190 square kilometres, bounded by coordinates YS 2693, YS 4093, YS 4078 and YS 2478, containing the jungle area south of the Binh Son Rubber Plantation and east of Route 15 to Route 2, with the Thi Vai Mountains on the south. G. McGarrigle, '9th Div Operations', Vietnam Center and Archive Texas Tech (VCAT), Item No. 1071514010, Chapter 9, p 3 (Map).
12   Hồ Sĩ Thành, *Đặc Khu Rừng Sác* [*The Rung Sac Special Zone*], Nhà Xuất Bản Trẻ [Youth Publishing House], Ho Chi Minh City, 2003, p 10.

The river route between Vung Tau and Saigon – via the Saigon, Long Tau and Soai Rap rivers – was only occasionally interrupted. On 26 May 1951, the Viet Minh's 300 Battalion sank the 8,000-ton French vessel *Saint Loubenbier* on the Long Tau River using limpet mines – this was the largest French vessel sunk during that conflict.

On 21 July 1952, a Viet Minh commando and security element, disguised as auxiliary troops, attacked the *Le Centre de Repos* officer recreation centre in Vung Tau. Twenty French were killed and 23 wounded – including women and children.

Post-Geneva

Under the Geneva Accords of 20 July 1954, large numbers of Viet Minh were 'regrouped'[13] from the South to North Vietnam. Over a 300-day period, about 90,000 Viet Minh reportedly regrouped, in phases, to North Vietnam from six assembly areas, including the Ham Tan-Xuyen Moc area (10,700). Many ex-Viet Minh, including men born in Phuoc Tuy, later infiltrated back into the South beginning in the early 1960s. In 1955, large numbers of Vietnamese Catholics moved from the North and were settled in the South. The government of Ngo Dinh Diem settled many of these refugees in Phuoc Tuy – principally in the villages of Binh Gia, Binh Ba and Phuoc Tinh, but also in villages along Route 15 including Phu My, Ong Trinh South, Phuoc Hoa, Lang Cat and Long Huong. The Saigon government established posts along Route 15 manned by the Civil Guard/Civil Defence Force (*Bao An* – later the Regional Forces) and the paramilitary Self-Defence Corps (*Dan Ve* – later the Popular Forces), but bandits from the Rung Sat continued to harass travellers and commercial traffic on Route 15. As noted, night movement was not possible along the route.

The Ba Ria History relates:

> In 1956, after many armed clashes with the Saigon government's armed forces, the Binh Xuyen[14] [a paramilitary gangster group in Saigon driven out by president Diem] were defeated, fled, and

---

13 Chamberlain, *The Viet Cong D445 Battalion*, p 9 and fn 24.
14 The Binh Xuyen were formed in the early 1920s as a loose coalition of gangs and contract labourers. From 1945, Binh Xuyen forces fought against the Viet Minh and from 1949, having been allowed to monopolize gambling in Saigon-Cholon and the trucking industry, became a self-funded element of the Vietnamese National Army. In 1955, the Binh Xuyen were almost wiped out by the National Army in the Rung Sat region. In 1956, a number of Binh Xuyen fighters joined the then nascent communist forces in Ba Ria Province.

lodged their troops scattered throughout the Rung Sac (Long Thanh), the Nui Thi Vai Mountains, and the Giong Chau Pha jungle ... At the beginning of 1957, the Eastern Region Inter-Provincial Committee deployed the unit led by Nguyen Quoc Thanh from the Rung Sac (Long Thanh) to the Giong jungle (Hat Dich) to build a base ... in the Bung Lung (Hat Dich) area.[15]

At the beginning of 1958, the Military Committee of the communists' Eastern Region appointed Le Minh Thinh to take a section and a radio to Ba Ria and organise an armed force. After more than '20 days of cutting through the jungle and crossing hills, the group of Eastern Region military cadre safely reached central Phuoc Tuy'.[16] In June 1958, a provincial 40-strong VC C-40 Company was established with a base in the Bung Lung (Hat Dich) area in the west of the province.[17]

North Vietnam's Politburo Resolution No. 15 of January 1959 stated: 'The Way for the Vietnamese Revolution in the South' directed a 'violent revolution in the South'.[18] On 12 March 1960, as part of the broader Dong Khoi ('Simultaneous Uprising') movement, the Ba Ria Province Committee's C-40 Company attacked Binh Ba village on Route 2. This attack reportedly 'began the armed uprising movement across the whole Province'.[19] In April 1960, a second VC company, C-45 Company, was raised and operated to the west of Route 2 as a mobile unit to defend the Hat Dich base and to harass both Route 2 and Route 15. These elements operated under the communists' Chau Thanh District (retitled Chau Duc District in 1965).[20] With declining security, in 1960 the Saigon government established a Route 15 Security Task Force to protect commerce on the route and provide safety for Saigon elites travelling to their villas in Vung Tau and Long Hai. Nguyen Van Buu, a Vung Tau businessman, reportedly funded 300 quasi-official paramilitary soldiers to ensure his seafood shipments reached Saigon on Route 15.[21] In Phuoc Tuy, a 50-man Political Action Unit – the forerunner to the 1 Commando

---

15   The Ba Ria History, p 13.
16   Chamberlain, *The Viet Cong D445 Battalion*, p 11.
17   While C-40 was established in August 1958, to maintain secrecy it was only officially announced in February 1960. Later, C-40 became C-440 and subsequently joined with C-445 to form D445 Provincial Battalion in early 1965.
18   Lien-Hang T. Nguyen, *Hanoi's war: An international history of the war for peace in Vietnam*, University of North Carolina Press, Chapel Hill, 2012, pp 39–43. See also Tai Sung An, 'Hanoi's 15th Plenum Resolution – 1959', VCAT, Item No. 23130010009.
19   Chamberlain, *The Viet Cong D445 Battalion*, p 12.
20   VC Chau Duc District was formed from Chau Thanh and Duc Thanh Districts on 24 May 1965.
21   S. Methven, *Laughter in the shadows: A CIA memoir*, Naval Institute Press, 2014, pp 105–106.

Company/Province Reconnaissance Unit – operated in concert with these 'shrimp soldiers'.[22] However, commercial enterprises in Vung Tau utilising Route 15 to Saigon continued to pay the VC for safe passage. While strategically important for the movement of cargo to Saigon, also any 'closure to Saigonese holiday-makers due to enemy action tended to lower morale in the capital and serve as an indicator of Viet Cong encroachment'.[23]

According to the communist Tan Thanh District history, at this time 'the revolutionary movement along Route 15 was weak', and the senior communist cadre Tran Ngoc Buu was dispatched to the area to conduct 'armed propaganda' and develop an 'infrastructure' network.[24] Soon after, in July 1960 at Ben Tau near Hat Dich village, C-45 Company attacked and destroyed a 55-strong Civil Guard (i.e. Regional Force) force from the Phu My Special Sector, seizing 50 weapons including three machine guns. Hat Dich village became the first 'liberated village' in the province. The Chau Duc History relates that in December 1962:

> the C-45 Provincial Unit combined with village guerrillas to attack and destroy the Binh Ba post, seized a large number of weapons, ammunition and food, and captured three Western commercial managers … [who] were taken to the base for education and urged to pay taxes to the Front for their exploitation of the rubber.[25]

In 1962, the population of the province, excluding Vung Tau, was reportedly about 117,000. The Route 15 area was only lightly populated, with the villages and hamlets astride the route dependent on rice cultivation, fishing in the Rung Sat, salt processing, charcoal production and wood gathering in the foothills. The villagers along Route 15 were forbidden by the government to move more than 1,000 metres from the road. From Ba Ria Town north-west to the Bien Hoa Province border – a distance of 28 kilometres – the settlements were: Long Huong village, Phu/Chu Hai hamlet, Kim Hai hamlet, Long Cat hamlet, Phuoc Hoa village, Ong Trinh hamlets (north and south) and Phu My village

---

22   Methven, *Laughter in the shadows*, p 106.
23   Ian McNeill, *To Long Tan: The Australian Army and the Vietnam War 1950–1966*, Allen & Unwin, St Leonards, 1993, p 11.
24   Unknown authors, *Lịch sử Đấu Tranh Cách Mạng Của Nhân Dân Huyện Tân Thành* [*The history of the people's revolutionary struggle in Tan Thanh District*], Vung Tau, 2014.
25   The Chau Duc History 2014, p 112.

(2 kilometres from the border with Long Thanh District of Bien Hoa Province). The total population along Route 15 within Phuoc Tuy was about 18,000 – 15 per cent of the province's population.

In 1962, the VC's C-40 and C-45 Companies were reportedly combined as the C-445 Provincial Company (D445 Battalion's predecessor), and, with the C-20 Chau Thanh District Company, continued to operate principally in the more populated central and eastern regions of the province in the Binh Ba, Long Phuoc, Dat Do and Long Hai areas. In early 1962, the Saigon government established the headquarters of the Phuoc Bien Special Zone in a camp beside Route 15, 2 kilometres north of Phu My village, to control security across Bien Hoa, Long Khanh and Phuoc Tuy provinces. To improve security on Route 15, artillery detachments of 105 mm howitzers were based at Phu My, Ong Trinh and Ba Ria; and six of the province's 23 strategic hamlets[26] were developed along Route 15 (at My Xuan, Hoi Bai, Kim Hai, Chu Hai, Phuoc Hoa and Phu My). Subsequently, from October 1962, strategic hamlets were also developed at Ong Trinh, Phuoc Loc and Lang Cat, and the strategic hamlet at Phuoc Hoa was further strengthened and incorporated the villagers of Hoi Bai.

The VC also developed fortified 'combat villages' with complex tunnel systems – the largest at Long Tan and Long Phuoc. On 5 March 1963, Army of the Republic of Vietnam (ARVN) and Regional Force (RF) forces – with supporting M113 armoured personnel carriers (APCs) and 105 mm artillery – attacked the fortified VC village of Long Phuoc. Exploiting the extensive system of tunnels, the VC forces (the C-45 Provincial Company and the C-20 District Company) reportedly held out for 44 days before withdrawing.

In November 1963, president Ngo Dinh Diem was overthrown in a military coup and a period of significant instability began with rapidly changing governments. The strategic hamlet program faltered, and the VC made significant gains in the countryside.[27] In February 1964, a high-

---

26 In 1962, the focus of the strategic hamlet program was on the six provinces around Saigon (including Phuoc Tuy) and Kontum Province. Initially, 11,316 strategic hamlets were planned country-wide. In Phuoc Tuy, as at 31 July 1963, reportedly 135 of the province's planned 162 strategic hamlets had been completed – covering 121,000 (87 per cent of the province's population), and 171 hamlet militiamen had been trained: see US Operations Mission (USOM), 'Notes on Strategic Hamlets', 15 August 1963, VCAT, Item No. 239070130036.

27 On 23 February 1964, the program was 'revitalized' as the 'New Life Hamlets' ('Ap Doi Moi') program – and in 1965 retitled 'Secure Hamlets' ('Ap Tan Sinh' – i.e. still 'New Life Hamlets', but in Sino-Vietnamese).

level CIA report for the US Administration noted that 'a recent report from COMUSMACV [the commanding general of MACV] estimates that in 23 of the Republic of Vietnam's 43 provinces, the Viet Cong dominate more that 50 percent of the area'. The same report states that 'the Viet Cong exercise 80% control in Phuoc Tuy. It thus appears that Phuoc Tuy should be considered as a possible addition to the list of [13] critical provinces'.[28]

Security responsibility for Phuoc Tuy fell to the ARVN III Corps Zone's 33 Tactical Zone – with its major force as the 5 ARVN Infantry Division, under Colonel (later president) Nguyen Van Thieu, headquartered in Bien Hoa. In the period 1963–66, the VC Ba Ria Province Committee group (up to 60 strong) and its special action element was centred in their Bung Lung base in a treed valley between the Nui Ong Trinh and the Nui Dinh, in the far south of the Hat Dich zone. Also at this time, to escape security forces, communist youth activists from Saigon – the Thanh Doan Saigon-Gia Dinh – established operating bases in the Nui Thi Vai and Nui Dinh hills.

The 'Sea Trail' from the north and the Battle of Binh Gia

The communist headquarters south of the Central Highlands – the Central Office for South Vietnam (COSVN)[29] – began preparations in 1962 to receive arms and ammunition by sea from the North at two principal locations – Loc An/Ho Tram on the Phuoc Tuy coast north of Phuoc Hai village, and at Ben Tre (Kien Hoa Province) in the northern Mekong Delta. From Ben Tre, the off-loaded materiel – principally arms and ammunition – was moved north to Can Gio (in the Rung Sat), then via the Thi Vai River to Route 15, where porters of the Group 445B unit moved the loads across Route 15 (principally near Phu My) and up into the Hat Dich base area, and northward into the major VC base area of

---

28 Central Intelligence Agency (CIA), 'Memorandum/Weekly Report OCI No.1061/64: The Situation in South Vietnam', 28 February 1964, VCAT, Item No. 0410102003.
29 COSVN: directed from Hanoi and located in the Cambodia/South Vietnam border area northwest of Saigon, COSVN was the communist political and military headquarters responsible for South Vietnam south of the Central and Southern Highlands – an area termed 'Nam Bo' (equating to the French colonial 'Cochin China' region). The COSVN area covered 32 of the South's 44 provinces and nominally 69 per cent of its population.

War Zone D.³⁰ Landings were also made near Phuoc Hoa farther south on Route 15, and materiel was portered northward on the track between the Nui Toc Tien and the Nui Dinh into the Hat Dich base. The activities of Group 445B reportedly developed the Hac Dich base area, including Base Area 303, as a 'Thanh Địa' ('Citadel') of COSVN's Eastern Nam Bo Region.³¹ On 3 October 1963, the first shipment of 20 tonnes was landed on the coast at Loc An north of Phuoc Hai from a 40-tonne vessel – including 1,500 rifles, 24 machine guns and two 75 mm recoilless rifles (RCLs). By November 1963, the 'Sea Trail' to Loc An and Ben Tre regularly moved large tonnages, supplying the VC multi-regimental force with weapons for the Battle of Binh Gia (18 kilometres north of Ba Ria Town) in December 1964 and January 1965 – including AK-47s, B-40s and ammunition. The VC force at the Battle of Binh Gia, under a 'Campaign Headquarters', comprised the 271 and the 272 Main Force Regiments and the local C-445 and C-440 Companies. The communist victory at Binh Gia was a significant defeat for the Saigon government. Three ARVN ranger battalions (30, 33 and 38) suffered heavy casualties, and the 428-strong 4 Marine Battalion suffered 112 killed and 71 wounded. Three US advisers were captured: a captain, a sergeant and a private first class.

Route 15 insecure – and 'accommodation'

On 24 November 1964, an element of the 274 VC Regiment ambushed a four-vehicle ARVN convoy on Route 15 near Phuoc Hoa village – 15 ARVN/RF were killed (including a major) and 10 were wounded. A US Army sergeant was also killed. Four vehicles were destroyed – including two armoured vehicles – and three .30 calibre machine guns, one 60 mm mortar, 27 individual weapons and two radios were seized by the VC force. The MACV account summarised: 'VC activity along the heavily-travelled Route 15 is sporadic; the area of the ambush is, however,

---

30   Located about 40 kilometres north-west of Saigon, War Zone D was the VC designation for a major base area encompassing roughly 2,000 square kilometres that in 1965–66 was a haven for the 271, 272 and 273 Regiments – and, occasionally, the 274 Regiment. In the last days of June 1965, the US 173 Airborne Brigade – including 1 RAR – conducted a major search and destroy operation into the western area of War Zone D.
31   Chamberlain, *The Viet Cong D445 Battalion*, p 31, fn 108, for a detailed explanation of Group 445B and its activities.

prone to such incidents'.³² On 17 December 1964, the 272 VC Regiment reportedly destroyed six ARVN armoured vehicles on the route – but this may have been the foregoing ambush of 24 November 1964.

During 1964, the senior Chau Thanh District communist cadre reportedly negotiated an 'accommodation/local détente' with the ARVN officer based at Phuoc Hoa responsible for the security of Route 15, Major Nguyen Van Phuoc, who provided 50 M26 grenades and 2,000 rounds of ammunition to Vo Van Lot (the commander of VC Intelligence Unit 316). According to the Dat Do History:

> Thanks to our winning over of Major Phuoc,³³ we were able to render ineffective a whole Ranger Group (nine companies – more than 800 men), completely control Route 15, and safely move hundreds of tons of weapons from the Rung Sac across the Route to the Hat Dich.³⁴

Such 'accommodation' arrangements – sometimes euphemistically referred to as 'mutual self-limitations' between isolated Territorial Forces along Route 15 and the VC were not uncommon.³⁵

---

32 US MACV, 'Military Report, 21–28 November 1964', 30 November 1964, VCAT, Item No. F015800030978.
33 The suborning of Major Phuoc is also related in Trần Văn Khánh (et al.) and the Executive Committee of the Bà Rịa-Vũng Tàu Party, *Lịch sử Đảng bộ tỉnh Bà Rịa–Vũng Tàu 1930–1975* [*The history of the Party in Baria–Vung Tau Province 1930–1975*], Nhà Xuất bản Chính trị Quốc gia [National Political Publishing House], Hà Nội, 2000, hereafter 'the Province Party History'. The Long Dat History refers to Major Phuoc's activities as lasting until January 1965, and also notes that Phuoc had formerly been a Binh Xuyen commander. Formed in the 1920s, the Binh Xuyen was a militarised group of heavily armed criminal gangs. The Binh Xuyen were almost wiped out by the Saigon government in 1955, but their forces were later used against the Vietnamese communists.
34 The Dat Do History relates: 'Our military proselytising cadre assigned a cadre to his [Major Phuoc's] unit to explain the Revolution's policies to Phuoc and his soldiers, and sent two Province reconnaissance cadre to be introduced to Phuoc – and proposed that Phuoc take them into the Phuoc Bien Commando Base [i.e. the Ranger base at Phu My airfield] to assess the situation.' (Trần Quang Toại and Đặng Tấn Hương (eds), *Lịch Sử Đấu Tranh Và Xây Dựng Của Đảng Bộ, Quân Và Dân Huyện Đất Đỏ (1930–2005)* [*The history of the struggle and development of the Party Committee, the forces and the people of Dat Do District (1930–2005)*], Nhà Xuất Bản Tổng Hợp Đồng Nai [Dong Nai Collective Publishing House], Biên Hòa, 2006, hereafter 'the Dat Do History'.)
35 The Territorial Forces (RF and PF) elements totalled about 4,000 men: all were understrength, some PF platoons had only 18–20 men, some RF Companies had only 30–80 men. The personal weapons of the RF and PF soldiers were the Second World War–vintage M1 and M2 carbines and the heavier Garand rifle. These Territorial Force troops were not capable of engaging VC Main Force regiments armed with AK-47 and SKS automatic rifles, RPD light machine guns and B-40 rocket-propelled grenades. Main Force VC elements were equipped with AK-47s from very early January 1965.

The 10 ARVN Division was formed in May 1965 and, headquartered in Xuan Loc, had responsibility for the 33 Tactical Zone. Its 52 Regiment often deployed into Phuoc Tuy Province. On 1 January 1967, the division was retitled the 18 ARVN Division. On 10 July 1965, 1st Battalion of the 274 VC Regiment[36] ambushed a 14-vehicle convoy – including two armoured vehicles – on Route 15 in the Phu My area. Some of the captured weapons were reportedly passed to local VC forces.

In July 1965, the US Provincial Representative reported that:

> The security situation in the districts of Duc Thanh and Xuyen Moc continues to remain critical as only the district towns [capitals] are under GVN control. All roads leading into the district capital of Duc Thanh and Xuyen Moc are cut and under VC control … The cutting of Hwy #15 has caused an economic pinch on incoming supplies and out-going marketings of fish. Much of the economy of this Province is based upon the fishing industry, and the cutting of Hwy #15 has stopped the flow of this commodity to the Saigon markets.[37]

---

36 Based on the 800 Dong Nai Battalion, and with infiltrated cadre from the 308 NVA Division, the 274 Regiment was founded in War Zone D north-east of Saigon in January 1964. The Dong Nai River flows south from the Central Highlands, through Bien Hoa, and joins the Saigon River 29 kilometres north-east of Ho Chi Minh City. In October 1964, the 274 Regiment assisted with the movement of arms and materiel landed on the coast north of Phuoc Hai for the Binh Gia Campaign. The regiment's principal battlefield was in southern Long Khanh Province – ambushing Route 20, attacking the railway line and strategic hamlets – including at Vo Su and Gia Ray. On 24 November 1964, its 800 Battalion attacked an ARVN convoy on Route 15 near Phu My, inflicting heavy casualties. In 1965–66, the regiment developed base areas in the Hat Dich and in the east of Route 2 in northern Phuoc Tuy Province. On the founding of the 5 VC Division in September 1965, the 274 and the 275 Regiments were subordinated to that formation. In October 1965, the 274's strength was 1,977. The 274 Regiment also ambushed ARVN troops on Route 15 on 1 August and 10 August 1966. Based on captured documents, in June 1966, the strengths of the Regiment's battalions were: 800 Battalion (formerly D1 unit) – 411; 265 Battalion (D2) – 401; 308 Battalion (D3) – 316. The Regimental Headquarters and its support companies (C16 to C23 inclusive) and the convalescent unit numbered about a further 660 personnel, for a total regimental strength of about 1,790. Seasonally, effective combat strength was seriously depleted by malaria (e.g. in August 1968, of 141 hospitalised 274 Regiment troops, 113 patients had malaria, 14 were for 'other causes', and four were wounded in action (WIA)).
37 USOM, 'Reports of USOM Provincial Representatives for the Month Ending 31 July 1965', 31 July 1965, VCAT, Item No. 6-20-19B7-116-UA17-95_001492. Also available at: spartanhistory.kora.matrix.msu.edu/files/6/32/6-20-19B7-116-UA17-95_001492.pdf. The next report for August 1965 noted the 'spurt of inflation caused by the closing of Route 15 to Saigon'.

APPENDIX D

At the end of August 1965, MACV assessed that 62.6 per cent of Phuoc Tuy's population were within 'dark blue' areas – that is, under government control – but 12.5 per cent were in 'red' areas under VC control.[38]

In early September 1965, COSVN formed the 5 VC Infantry Division under its Military Region 1 to command the 274 and the 275 Main Force Regiments – the 275 Regiment had originally been raised in the Mekong Delta. The division's base was in the May Tao Mountains with its initial area of operations in Long Khanh, Binh Tuy and Phuoc Tuy Provinces. The D445 Provincial Mobile Battalion was officially formed on 19 September 1965 – and only rarely operated in the Nui Dinh and Nui Thi Vai hills, and is not known to have harassed Route 15.[39]

In mid-October 1965, VC Military Region 1 (later Military Region 7 from late 1967) issued an 'Intelligence Order' directing province military intelligence staffs to provide information on the movement and deployment of enemy troops. Ba Ria was specifically cited: 'Observe the enemy movements on Route 15, especially on the route from Cap [i.e. Vung Tau] to Ba Ria and Phu My.'[40] In Bien Hoa Province, the Intelligence Order directed the observation of 'III Corps and the American and Australian troops [i.e. 1 RAR Battalion Group]'. Observation posts – 'Special Detachment – Route 15' – were established on the Nui Thi Vai and Nui Dinh features, manned by local VC elements, who reported to intelligence cadre equipped with high-frequency (HF) radios (US AN/GRC-9 or Chinese Communist 102E, 71B, transceivers). The US military signals intelligence (SIGINT) organisation in South Vietnam intercepted VC HF Morse communications and determined VC locations with direction-finding equipment.[41]

---

38   US MACV, 'US MACV Monthly Report of Rural Reconstruction Progress: 25 July – 25 August 1965', 11 September 1965, VCAT, Item No. F01570001007.
39   The battalion was actually formed earlier, on 23 February 1965, as the 'Ba Ria Province Concentrated Unit' with Bui Quang Chanh (aka Sau Chanh) 'as the "Battalion Commander". For a detailed history of D445, see Chamberlain, *The Viet Cong D445 Battalion*.
40   The Intelligence Order by the G2 staff of Military Region 1 was captured by the US 25 Infantry Division on 18 May 1966, and the English translation can be found: 'Captured Documents (CDEC): Intelligence Order Stating That C2 Personnel Must Know the Enemies Tactical Position', VCAT, Item No. F034600110656, p 2.
41   For example, the headquarters of the 5 VC Division – nicknamed 'Fred' – was 'fixed' 25 times in the two months to 17 February 1966 in north-eastern Phuoc Tuy, south-eastern Long Khanh and in Binh Tuy Province.

The Rangers' victory on Route 15 at Kim Hai

On 11 November 1965, 3rd Battalion of the 275 VC Regiment attempted to ambush an ARVN convoy on Route 15 (the 52 Ranger Battalion and RF elements) at Kim Hai hamlet, Phuoc Hoa village (about 10 kilometres north-west of Ba Ria Town). However, forewarned, the ARVN force drove off the 275 Regiment elements and inflicted heavy casualties on the VC force.[42] However, the account in the 5 VC Division History relates a VC victory:

> From the beginning of November, Comrade Nguyen Thoi Bung [the 275th Regiment's commander – who later commanded the Regiment at the Battle of Long Tan in August 1966], together with Battalion Commander Hai Phung, engaged directly in the preparations for the battle on Route 15.[43] On 4 November, the 3rd Battalion deployed from its base at Song Ray to Long Thanh for the engagement. After three days of difficult and tiring movement, and avoiding discovery by enemy commandos and outposts, on 7 November the 3rd Battalion reached its fighting positions at the base of the Nui Thi Vai Mountain [sic]. The fighting strength of the battalion at this time was still low[44] – a company only had 40 weapons. The 1st Company (of the 1st Battalion) with a strength of only 45 was attached to the 3rd Battalion as a reinforcement. As a consequence, the problem required that the ambush had to be truly secret and a surprise if the intention to completely destroy two enemy companies and their vehicles was to be

---

42 The Ranger Force – the 3 and 4 Companies under the battalion executive officer – and the RF force were returning along Route 15 from an ambushing operation when they were warned by Phuoc Tuy Sector Headquarters and halted 2 kilometres short of the 275 Regiment ambush site. Air support from F-100 jet aircraft struck the VC positions. The Rangers reportedly recovered the first B-40 captured in South Vietnam.

43 This was the only significant engagement west of Route 2 involving the 275 VC Regiment during the period 1966 to early 1970. The ambush is mentioned briefly in 1 ATF's 'INTSUM No 1/66: Vung Tau', 21 May 1966 (AWM95 1/4/1) (as is the later 11–12 April 1966 battle against US forces during Operation Abilene at Tam Bo north of Nui Dat involving elements of the 274 VC Regiment, in a subsequent Intelligence Review: '1 ATF Intelligence Review No. 2', 29 October 1966, AWM95 1/4/14). See also 1 ATF, 'Troops Information Sheet No. 31, 13–19 February 1967', AWM95 1/4/30. The Kim Hai/Phuoc Hoa ambush is related in the Australian Army's official history, but the location is incorrectly cited as occurring at 'Binh Gia', and the outcome is incorrectly described as a win for the VC: 'The Viet Cong demonstrated their capacity to mount regimental-sized ambushes on 11 November 1965, when 275 Regiment ambushed and virtually destroyed the elite ARVN 52 Ranger Battalion near Binh Gia' (McNeill, *To Long Tan*, p 222).

44 However, captured 274 Regiment documents detail the strengths of the regiment's battalions in October 1965 as: 1st Battalion – 404; 2nd Battalion – 684; and 3rd Battalion – 486. The regiment's strength was 1,977.

achieved ... After a day of fierce fighting, the 3rd Battalion and the 1st Company of the 5th [i.e. 275th] Regiment had killed a large number of the enemy, inflicting heavy casualties on the 52nd Ranger Battalion and a Phuoc Tuy Sector provincial company, destroyed two helicopters, 16 mechanised vehicles, a jeep, captured six enemy and seized 12 weapons and two radios. We lost 16 comrades and a further 32 were wounded.[45]

According to a contemporary VC pamphlet titled *Victories in November 1965*, two Ranger companies were wiped out and 16 vehicles destroyed on 11 November 1965. However, as related in the 275 Regiment History,[46] a 'Traitor S' had defected and revealed the 275's ambush plans to the Ba Ria sector headquarters. Thus warned, the 52 Ranger Battalion force, the 701 RF Company, and the 31 RF Mechanised Platoon attacked and drove the compromised VC ambush force back into the hills. For defeating the 3rd Battalion/275 Regiment and 1 Company of its 1st Battalion at Kim Hai, the Vietnamese forces were awarded a US Presidential Citation on 18 November 1966.[47] A mid-November Saigon press report cited 'VC Piles Up Phuoc Le Ambush Toll for Burial: 150 Bodies Spotted in Village',[48] and a Joint US Public Affairs Office Report of 30 November 1965 noted '300' VC were killed in the action at Kim Hai.[49]

Soon after that engagement, US aircraft increased Operation Ranch Hand chemical defoliation missions in Phuoc Tuy Province[50] – spraying 60,000 litres in the period 18 December 1965 to 30 January 1966. This included missions to reduce roadside cover along Route 15 and the banks of the principal waterways in the Rung Sat.[51] In mid-December 1965,

---

45 Hồ Sơn Đài (ed.), *Lịch sử Sư đoàn Bộ binh 5 (1965–2005)* [*The history of the 5th Infantry Division (1965–2005)*], Nhà Xuất Bản Quân Đội Nhân Dân [The People's Army Publishing House], Hà Nội, 2005, hereafter 'the 5 VC Division History', pp 59–60.
46 Ho Son Dai – Senior Colonel (ed.), *The history of the 5th Infantry Regiment (1965–2015)*, The People's Army Publishing House, Hanoi, 2015.
47 Lyndon B. Johnson, 'Presidential Unit Citation Awarded to the 52d Ranger Battalion, Army of the Republic of Vietnam, and Attached Units', 18 November 1966.
48 *The Sunday Post*, Saigon, 14 November 1965.
49 JUSPAO Field Representative, 'Reports of USOM Provincial Representatives for Month Ending 30 November 1965', VCAT, Item No. 23970103001, p 30.
50 The inaugural Ranch Hand operations in South Vietnam were flown along Route 15 by US Air Force C-123 aircraft in the period 10–16 January 1962 at 150 feet and covering a 500-foot swathe – but avoiding crops.
51 After Operation Vaucluse, on 21 September 1966 1 ATF requested approval from Province Chief Lieutenant Colonel Le Duc Dat for defoliation in the Nui Dinh Hill mass because 'the foliage in this area provides concealment for VC movement and base areas'.

Chau Duc District ordered a five-day campaign on Route 15 of 'striking strategic hamlets, laying mines, digging holes on the road, and setting up mounds in the form of crocodiles' teeth'.[52]

1966: Route 15 queried in Washington – D445 into action – Vung Tau shelled

In US Senate Appropriation Hearings in late January 1966, the US Secretary of Defense, Robert McNamara, was queried on the 'status of Route 15'. He responded: 'It is, I believe, closed at the present time, and if it isn't actually closed today it is closed off and on.' Senator Mansfield asked: 'Closed to the Americans?' Secretary McNamara responded: 'Well, it is not closed to a military convoy. We can fight our way through and over any road in the country, as a matter of fact. But it is closed to unarmed and unescorted traffic.'[53]

At the end of January 1966, the 2 Brigade/1 US Infantry Division conducted Operation Mallet – ambitiously described as 'a search and destroy operation to open Route 15'.[54] However, Phase 2 of the operation was conducted in the Binh Son area of Long Thanh District and did not extend into Phuoc Tuy Province.

On the other, eastern, side of the province, near the Minh Dam/Long Hai hills at Da Giang on Route 44 (Upper), the D445 Local Force Battalion ambushed a large group of ARVN trainees from the Long Hai non-commissioned officer (NCO) school on 8 January 1966. A MACV report noted 31 ARVN soldiers killed and 30 wounded – and three US advisers killed.[55] On Route 15, in January 1966, D445 Battalion reportedly ambushed and destroyed six trucks of the 'South Korean forces'.[56]

---

52   Captured document: 'Chau Duc District Directive', December 1965, USMACV/JGS Combined Document Exploitation Centre (CDEC), Saigon, Item No. 10-2287-66.
53   US Armed Services Committee, 'Appropriations, 89th Congress, S2792', 2 February 1966, VCAT, Item No. 2184815002, p 143.
54   A.G. Traas, *Engineers at war*, US Government Printing Office, Washington, 2010.
55   US MACV Military History Branch, 'Chronology of Significant Events during 1966', 27 April 1967, VCAT Item No. 13370149004.
56   Chamberlain, *The Viet Cong D445 Battalion*, p 56 and fn 197. That mention of South Korean troops may be a reference to the major RVNAF Operation Dan Tam 36 (late February – early March 1966) that extended into the Minh Dam Mountains. A Republic of Korea engineer company participated in that operation, part of the Republic of Korea's 'Dove Force' based at Bien Hoa from late February 1965.

On 12 March 1966, a force comprising VC sappers (240C Company) and an artillery element from 5 VC Division moved from the Minh Dam base and attacked and shelled the Vung Tau airfield and the Chi Linh Rural Development Cadre Training Centre in Vung Tau. According to a rallier from the 240C Sapper Company, the unit incorporated a platoon from D445 Battalion and had undergone training directed by Sau Chanh, the commander of D445 Battalion, prior to the attack on Vung Tau. According to the 5 VC Division History:

> In only 45 minutes of combat, 138 rounds of 82mm mortar and 75mm RCL were fired – together with 70 other rounds, and 25 B40s. The artillery and sappers of the 4th Regiment [274 Regiment] killed and wounded a large number of the enemy – including a senior officer [of major to full colonel rank], and destroyed nine enemy aircraft.[57]

The biography of Tong Viet Duong – the commander of the '70-strong sapper company', claimed 'almost 300 Americans were killed at the airfield while watching an outdoor movie – including a colonel'[58] and 37 aircraft (C130, AD6, T28 and L19s) were destroyed. The Royal Australian Air Force Caribou Flight at Vung Tau reported a shelling by 60 mortars on that date – four bombs impacted near the flight's hangar, and two DHC-4 Caribou were damaged.

About 17 per cent living under VC Control in Phuoc Tuy

According to a US military report in March 1966, of Phuoc Tuy and Vung Tau's population of 138,000 (Phuoc Tuy, 100,000; Vung Tau, 38,000), 87,000 lived in government-controlled areas, 22,000 in areas 'undergoing pacification', 12,000 in areas considered 'relatively free of VC', and 17,000 'living in VC-controlled areas'.[59] A curfew was in effect between 10 pm and 4 am – but was 'not rigidly enforced' and the 'VC infrastructure was established down to village and hamlet level'.[60] 'Approximately 32% of the population is Pro-GVN, 12% Pro-VC, and

---

57 The 5 VC Division History, p 74.
58 Xuan Bao, *The story of a war hero: Tong Viet Duong*, Dong Nai On-Line, 6 September 2012.
59 US 1st Infantry Division, 'Combat Operations After Action Report – Operation Abilene, April 1966', Defense Technical Information Centre (DTIC), AD387599.
60 Ibid.

56% are neutral'.[61] The VC had 'a high degree of control over the rural population and had little difficulty moving throughout the Province'.[62] The CIA assessed the VC 'militia and political cadre' in the province's 35 villages numbered '2.956'.[63]

In the period 30 March – 15 April 1966, the US 1 Infantry Division (with 173 Airborne Brigade that included the Australian 1 RAR Battalion Group) conducted Operation Abilene in Phuoc Tuy and Long Khanh Provinces. Operation Abilene had the aim of 'destroying the 94th [i.e. the 274] VC Regiment, the 5th [i.e. the 275] VC Regiment, and the May Tao Secret Zone'.[64] Support bases were established in the Courtenay Plantation area near the Long Khanh/Phuoc Tuy border from 29 March and subsequently farther south at the Binh Ba airstrip. In a 'southern' phase of Operation Abilene, on 4 April 1966, two US battalions conducted a search and destroy operation north and north-east of the VC-controlled village of Long Tan while an ARVN force searched the village – and then moved the villagers to Dat Do, Long Dien and Hoa Long.

VC victory at Tam Bo

1 RAR returned to Bien Hoa from Operation Abilene's Binh Ba logistic base area on 8–9 April 1966 by road and air to prepare for Operation Denver in the Song Be area of Phuoc Long Province.[65] On 11 April, Charlie Company/2nd Battalion of 16 Regiment of the US 1 Infantry Division engaged a VC force that included '800 Battalion' (i.e. 1/274 VC Regiment) in north-eastern Phuoc Tuy – about 5 kilometres south of the Long Khanh/Phuoc Tuy border and about 8 kilometres east of

---

61   Ibid.
62   Ibid. The US MACV 'Monthly Report of Revolutionary Development Progress: Population and Area Control' for May 1966 (dated 15 June 1966, VCAT, Item No. F01500010098), later showed Phuoc Tuy as 65 per cent 'controlled', with 24 per cent 'undergoing clearance' and 11.5 per cent 'under VC control'. At the end of June 1966, according to MACV, 70 hamlets in the province were classified as 'secured', six 'undergoing securing' and 35 'undergoing clearing'. Of the province's population, 65,900 were deemed 'secure' – that is, 64.3 per cent. US MACV, 'MACV Monthly Report of Revolutionary Development Progress: 1–30 June 1966', 15 July 1966, VCAT, Item No. F015700010112.
63   However, these figures were not considered 'completely accurate' due to 'input limitations'. CIA, Director of Current Intelligence Memorandum, 'Viet Cong Strength by Village', 12 May 1966, VCAT, Item No. F02920030138.
64   1 RAR, 'OPORD 7/66, Bien Hoa', 24 March 1966, AWM95 7/1/69.
65   US 1st Infantry Division, 'Combat Operations After Action Report – Operation Abilene, April 1966', DTIC, AD387599. On 8 April 1966, D445 Battalion's 4 Company mortared the US 1 Division support base at Binh Ba airstrip.

Route 2. Initially unsupported by other US companies, the 134-strong Charlie Company suffered 48 killed in action (KIA) and 58 wounded in action (WIA). Reportedly, the bodies of 41 VC were found on the battlefield, and 100–150 VC were assessed by MACV as having been killed or wounded in the engagement. That engagement on 11 April 1966 is known as the Battle of Cam My in US records and as the Battle of Tam Bo in Vietnamese communist accounts.[66]

Increased interdiction on Route 15 and in the Rung Sat

In late April 1966, the VC Chau Duc District directed their guerrilla elements on Route 15 in Chu Hai, Phuoc Hoa and Phu My villages to develop 'American Killing Belts' along Route 15. On 19 May 1966, the Ba Ria Province Unit assigned demolition tasks on Route 15 and on Route 2 to the Chau Duc District Unit – to counter US operations. West of Route 15, by early 1966, COSVN had established the Rung Sat Special Zone (Group 10/T.10) – with a reported strength of 600, to support the movement of materiel from Ben Het in the upper Mekong Delta and to interdict shipping transiting the Rung Sat. On 26 August 1966, Group 10 sappers attacked a US vessel, the *Baton Rouge Victory* (8,500 tons), on the Long Tau River with two limpet mines. Seven American civilian sailors were killed, and the vessel's captain was forced to run the ship aground.[67]

Clearing Long Phuoc and Long Tan – mid-1966

In the period 17–21 May, in the first phase of Operation Hardihood, the US 173 Airborne Brigade (without 1 RAR) and 3/43 Battalion of the ARVN 10 Division cleared the tunnels and bunkers of the VC's fortified

---

66 The battle took place at YS 5408620 – about 4 kilometres east of the site of the late September 1971 'Battle of Nui Le', when 4 RAR/NZ engaged elements of the 33 NVA Regiment. Detailed VC accounts are available in the captured notebook of the second in command of the 274 Regiment, Nguyễn Nam Hưng: see VCAT, Item No. F03460056029 (CDEC Log 11-1253-66 – with the Vietnamese text in CDEC Log 11-1259-66). The Battle of Tâm Bố is also recounted in Hưng's 2006 memoir: Nguyễn Nam Hưng – Major General, *Một Đời Chinh Chiến* [*A life at war*], Nhà Xuất bản Chính trị Quốc gia, Hà Nội, 2006.
67 Group 10 – later the 10 Sapper Regiment – reportedly lost 631 personnel killed during the war (319 Northerners and 312 Southerners).

Long Phuoc village. Elements of D445 and the Chau Duc District's 21 Company (C-21) resisted strongly, and the 173's 1/503 Battalion lost 19 killed and 90 wounded in the battle.[68] Half of Long Phuoc's 3,000 villagers were moved to Hoa Long, and others to Dat Do and to Long Dien.

The 1st Australian Task Force arrives

The 1st Australian Task Force Headquarters (HQ 1 ATF) was formally activated in Vung Tau on 20 May 1966. As agreed in the 17 March 1966 Military Working Arrangement with MACV, its directive included 'to conduct operations related to the security of Highway 15, as required'.[69] On 12 May 1966, Lieutenant General JO Seaman, commander II Field Force Vietnam (II FFV), issued his Campaign Directive for the 1966 wet season that included a task for 1 ATF: 'to clear and secure route QL15 from Vung Tau to Ba Ria [sic] and LTL2 [i.e. Route 2] within sector in coordination with appropriate ARVN commanders'.[70] On 19 May 1966, the Australian Chief of the General Staff expanded on 1 ATF's role, stating:

> The military reason for the deployment of the Australian Task Force in Phuoc Tuy Province under national command was to improve the military situation so that Route 15 from Vung Tau to Bien Hoa can be used for major military movements. This is required to allow the development of the port of Vung Tau in order to relieve the congestion of military shipping in the Saigon area.[71]

---

68 According to accounts of the fighting by the Ba Ria Province Headquarters dated 3 June 1966: 'In the period 17–25 May 1966 D445 Battalion – in coordination with Chau Duc District troops and the Long Phuoc guerrillas, killed 556 Americans and 45 wounded.' VC losses were reportedly 10 killed and 25 wounded. Captured Documents CDEC Log 09-1885-66, 29 August 1966, VCAT, Item No. F034600822587.
69 Mc Neill, *To Long Tan*, pp 238–240.
70 McNeill, *To Long Tan*, p 240 and endnote 36, p 534.
71 McNeill, *To Long Tan*, p 238.

APPENDIX D

Vietnamese Government security forces in Phuoc Tuy in mid-1966

In June 1966, government troops in Phuoc Tuy and Vung Tau comprised 3rd Battalion of the 43 Regiment/10 ARVN Infantry Division, the 52 Ranger Battalion, 16 RF companies, 22 Popular Force (PF) platoons, and the 1 Commando Company (later the Provincial Reconnaissance Unit – PRU). The ARVN National Training Centre was located at Van Kiep on Ba Ria's eastern edge, and an ARVN NCO Training Centre operated near Long Hai village.

Along Route 15, the 701 RF Company was at Phu My, and the 673 RF Company was distributed between Ong Trinh North and Ong Trinh South. PF platoons had been established at Phuoc Hoa and Long Huong villages.[72] The RF and PF were under the command of the province chief/military sector commander, Lieutenant Colonel Le Duc Dat,[73] and those along Route 15 were under the control of Long Le district subsector at Hoa Long, commanded by Lieutenant Tran Tan Phat.[74] The 40-strong MACV Team 89 advisory team – headed by a lieutenant colonel – included Captain Mike Wells (AATTV) from early June 1966 as the operations and training adviser at sector headquarters in Ba Ria. Team 89 advisers also served in the subsectors at Long Le (Hoa Long), Long Dien and Dat Do; and 20 Team 78 personnel were assigned to the National Training Centre at Van Kiep and the NCO Training School at Long Hai. The 3rd Battalion of the ARVN 43 Regiment was located on Route 2 on Ba Ria's northern outskirts.

At the end of June 1966, according to MACV, 70 hamlets in the province were classified as 'secured', six 'undergoing securing' and 35 were 'undergoing clearing'. Of the province's population, 65,900 (i.e. 64.3 per cent) were deemed 'secure'; 3,800 of the population

---

72   By early October 1966, prior to 5 RAR's Operation Canberra/Robin, RF deployments on Route 15 were 578 RF Company at YS 285630 (Phuoc Hoa village); 609 RF Company at YS 264673 (Ap Ong Trinh); and 701 RF Company at YS 252745 (Phu My village). An ARVN unit occupied the Phu My post, 2 kilometres north of the village.
73   Lieutenant Colonel Le Duc Dat (born 1928) was the province chief from early 1964 until September 1967, when he was replaced by Lieutenant Colonel Nguyen Ba Truoc. Subsequently, in April 1972, during the communist Nguyen Hue Offensive, Colonel Le Duc Dat was killed at Tan Canh in the Central Highlands when commanding the 22 ARVN Infantry Division. Posthumously, he was appointed brigadier.
74   Phat was replaced in the second half of 1966 by Captain Vo Sanh Kim.

(i.e. 3.7 per cent) were reportedly under VC control.⁷⁵ This was a significant improvement over the MACV assessments for previous months. At the end of March 1966, VC control of the population had been reported as 17.1 per cent, at the end of April 15.6 per cent, and at the end of May 11.5 per cent. The resettlement of the villagers from Long Tan and Long Phuoc – and the location of 1 ATF adjacent to Hoa Long – significantly reduced the extent of the population under VC control.

The VC in Phuoc Tuy in mid-1966⁷⁶

Subordinate to the VC's Military Region 1, the Ba Ria Province⁷⁷ Unit had approximately 16 subordinate elements and entities. The principal elements of the Province Unit's headquarters were a 'Staff' (73 members),⁷⁸ 'Political' personnel (27) and military staff (46). The Province Unit's operative elements were D445 Battalion (about 380 strong), a Ba Ria Town Special Action Unit (C610/982 – 34 members), the Long Dat District Unit (159), the Chau Duc District Unit (about 110), the Xuyen Moc District Unit (29), a small province reconnaissance unit, a rear services element, a medical element (46), a prisoner of war camp (14) and a military training school (18). Additionally, the Ba Ria Province Unit commanded, through its three district units, several village guerrilla units and militia elements (including at Phu My, Phuoc Hoa and Phu Hai

---

75   US MACV, 'MACV Monthly Report of Revolutionary Development Progress: 1–30 June 1966', 15 July 1966, VCAT, Item No. F015700010112. The report noted that the areas on the map depiction were 'not precise' and were only a 'rough approximation'.
76   The figures provided here have been compiled from captured documents in Chamberlain, *The Viet Cong D445 Battalion*, Annex J, p 1, fnn 1–6.
77   In the following years, several reorganisations occurred that modified the geographic extent of 'Ba Ria'. In late 1966, the Viet Cong Military Region 1 (T1 – Eastern Nam Bo) was re-organised to comprise three provinces: Tay Ninh, Thu Dau Mot and Ba Bien. Ba Bien Province then comprised the former Ba Ria Province together with three districts of Bien Hoa Province (Long Thanh, Trang Bom and Binh Son) and districts of Long Khanh Province (including Dinh Quan).
78   'Staff' included the Finance and Economy Section that managed the budget – including tax collection. For example, in Chau Duc District, 10 per cent of farm produce was to be collected as tax in 1970. The Viet Cong also levied 'industrial taxes' on shops, vehicles, brick kilns, timber, sand, alcohol, etc.

on Route 15), and the VC Infrastructure[79] (VCI – including the Party and front entities). The VC province headquarters had encrypted HF Morse communications with Military Region 1 (later Military Region 7), and with its principal subordinate military units and districts. However, a primary means of contact within the province was by courier ('commo-liaison') and employing a postal system utilising 'cover designators' and 'Letter Box Numbers'.[80] Also subordinate to VC Military Region 1, the 274 and 275 VC Main Force Regiments of 5 VC Division were the VC Main Force elements that operated within the province.

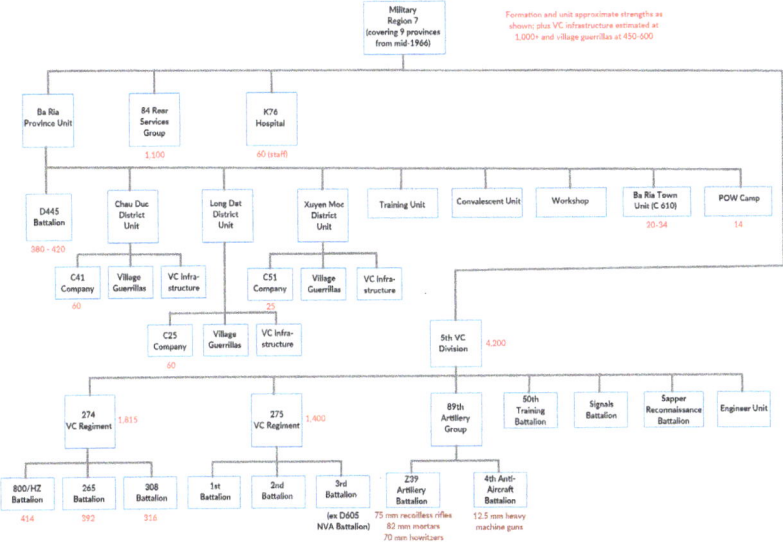

Figure A.2: VC organisation in Phuoc Tuy Province in mid-1966.
Source: Drawn and produced by Ron Boxall from details provided by Ernest Chamberlain.

---

79 The primary agency that directed communist efforts in the South was the People's Revolutionary Party – the southern arm of the Vietnam Workers' Party (VWP). The VWP managed the war in the southern half of South Vietnam through its Central Office for South Vietnam (COSVN), reinstituted in January 1961 to replace the Xu Uy Nam Bo (Nam Bo Regional Committee). Party structures controlled all geographic entities, military units and front organisations. In the South, the 'umbrella' front organisation was the National Liberation Front of South Vietnam, formed in December 1960. Subsequently, a Provisional Revolutionary Government (PRG) was formed on 8 June 1969.
80 Chamberlain, *The Viet Cong D445 Battalion*, fn 200.

A 1 ATF view of the enemy

Reviewing VC activity in Phuoc Tuy in May 1966, Brigadier David Jackson declared that the province 'was not a backwater'.[81] 1 ATF's first intelligence summary (INTSUM),[82] supporting Operation Hardihood in central Phuoc Tuy, did not report any VC elements in the Route 15 area – but noted that the route 'was subject to VC interdiction'. Enemy forces listed as operating in the province comprised the 2,000-strong 274 VC Main Force Regiment (also known as the Dong Nai Regiment, 4 Regiment, 94 Regiment, Group 94, Q764 and Q4) and the 275 VC Main Force Regiment (1,800 troops – also known as the 5 Regiment, Group 45, Group 54, Q765 and Q5) – both formations of the 5 VC Division – and the D445 Local Force Battalion (550 troops). Several VC local companies were also listed in the INTSUM: C-20, C-300, C-70 and C-610 (the Baria Special Action Unit – located on the southern slopes of the Nui Dinh); and 'an estimated 400 local guerrillas, lightly armed were operating throughout the Province in 5 to 15-man groups'.[83] That INTSUM briefly referenced the 275 Regiment's failed ambush on Route 15 on 11 November 1965 against the 52 ARVN Ranger Battalion.

Having deployed to its Nui Dat base, the initial operations of the 4,500-strong Task Force[84] focused on securing its immediate Tactical Area of Responsibility, including 'reclearing' the villages of Long Phuoc and Long Tan. In June, a brief 1 ATF terrain survey of 'Zone Cherry' (Route 15) noted reliable indications of observation posts on the

---

81 Taped interview, Dr Bruce Horsfield, 20 August 1990, Burradoo NSW, AWM: AWM 3849628, Tape 1. During US operations in Phuoc Tuy Province in the period April to mid-September 1966, US forces reportedly lost 87 personnel KIA and 408 WIA – in Operations Abilene, Hardihood, Hollandia and Toledo. MACCORDS (MACV Civil Operations and Rural Development) Team 89 – based in Van Kiep, lost three KIA in a D445 ambush on 6 January 1966.
82 1 ATF, 'INTSUM No 1/66', 21 May 1966, AWM95 1/4/1.
83 In mid-July 1966, the CIA reported confirmed communist strength in the South as: Viet Cong Main Force combat strength at 59,035 (83 battalions) with 17,553 support personnel; North Vietnamese combat troops as 34,910 (55 battalions); and 103,600 'paramilitary combat personnel' (with a further 40,000 armed political cadre). A further 23 combat battalions were unconfirmed (six VC, 17 NVA). More than one-half of the 138 confirmed combat battalions were organised into 29 regiments (13 VC, 16 NVA), with most of the regiments controlled by five divisional headquarters. The confirmed infiltration rate from the North for June 1966 was 10,460 troops (both Northerners and Southerner 'regroupees'). CIA, 'The Status of North Vietnamese Infiltration into South Vietnam', 24 February 1967, VCAT, Item No. F029200040263.
84 At the end of June 1966, Australian forces in Vietnam totalled 4,487 with 2,830 personnel at Nui Dat and 1,011 with 1st Australian Logistic Support Group (1 ALSG) at Vung Tau. US military personnel in the Republic of Vietnam numbered 278,810. Others were: 'New Zealand – 150; Philippines – 57; Republic of China – 20; and Thailand – 19'. The 12-strong Spanish military medical team arrived in September 1966.

eastern heights of the Nui Ong Cau (part of the Nui Dinh complex and overlooking Route 2), and that VC mortars had been fired on 10 June 1966 from the eastern slopes of the Nui Dinh hills (from YS 361671 and YS 372670).[85]

A VC view of 1 ATF

The 2004 Chau Duc History described the introduction of Australian troops into the province as follows:

> The Australians – who were very experienced mercenaries having fought a counter-guerrilla war in Malaya, were given the task by their American masters to conduct pacification 'trials' in Ba Ria, in order to create a key defensive barrier for them for Saigon and to directly protect the military port of Vung Tau. The Australian military were very expert in ambush tactics, small-scale raids, moving in scattered half-section and section groups, and striking deep into our bases. They quickly adapted to the climate and the tropical jungle. They also bore hardship – and would conceal themselves in the marshy swamps for hours – and would put up with the heavy wind and rain throughout the night in order to ambush us. They could cross streams and swamps – and even traverse jungles of new bamboo that was thick with thorns in order to secretly approach their objective. Most dangerous of all was their ambush tactic in which they 'assimilated' into the terrain – and this cost us many killed and other losses. Cay Cay and Bau Lung were routinely under fire – and the hills and jungles, the villages and hamlets, and the base areas were torn apart and crushed.[86]

In September 1966, a rallier from the 274 Regiment's 1st Battalion related to his MACV debriefers that:

> The VC were very cautious in confrontations with the Australians ... The Australians had considerable combat experience from the Korean War ... In addition, the Australians were strongly supported by artillery and air force firepower – therefore the VC dared not cause the engagement to last long.[87]

---

85   'Area Analysis of Zone Cherry, Appendix 2 to Annex A (Intelligence) to Op Plan 1-66', June 1966, AWM95 1/4/3.
86   The Chau Duc History 2004, pp 148–149.
87   Le Van Sang (rallied at Binh Gia, 28 September 1966), 274 VC Regiment, US MACV/JGS Combined Military Interrogation Centre (CMIC) Interrogation Report 1325.

A high-level defector, North Vietnam Army (NVA) Lieutenant Colonel Le Xuan Chuyen (chief of staff/chief of operations of the 5 VC Division),[88] had a similar view:

> The Australian forces have much experience in conducting operations, bivouacking troops and attacking, but because they are too tall and big, it is difficult for them to keep from being seen and thus being shot at and wounded. The US forces have strong firepower, but because they are big and tall, they are easy to see. Their operation regulations are followed almost as if they were fixed and their attack capability lacks activeness and speed.[89]

VC observers in the hills

NVA Lieutenant Colonel Le Xuan Chuyen disclosed in his mid-1966 debrief that there 'was an observation post equipped with a 15-watt radio on the Thi Vai Mountain to conduct air observation and observe RVNAF [Republic of Vietnam Air Force] activities along Route 15'.[90]

In July 1966, 1 ATF's 547 Signals Detachment, a SIGINT element, intercepted VC Morse communications – including the HF transmissions of the VC observation groups overlooking Route 15 and including one post that was nicknamed 'Dodo'.[91] At the end of July, the commanding general of MACV (COMUSMACV) General WC Westmoreland had personally urged that the VC observation and reporting posts monitoring the vulnerable Route 15 be eliminated ASAP – a 'Priority One Alfa task'.[92] On deployment to Vietnam, 547 Signals Detachment had no integral

---

88   Le Xuan Chuyen had defected on 2 August 1966, and was debriefed extensively.
89   US MACV/JGS CMIC, 'Interrogation of Le Xuan Chuyen, Saigon', 7 August 1966, VCAT, Item No. 4080124002, p 11.
90   Ibid, p 6, para 46.
91   Dodo's SIGINT 'station identifier' was RAD1963 and its 'notation' was VNGB (Vietnamese Guerrilla Morse) M7178. Another station, called 'Leech' (RAD255A, VNGB M7191) and probably associated with Dodo, also operated in the Thi Vai area. These stations were usually 'secure' in caves – with observers of Route 15 providing information to them by courier.
92   'ATF [was] ordered by General Westmoreland to capture VC radio station in our area (substation on Priority One Alfa).' Captain TJ Richards (OC 547 Signal Detachment), signal to DMI-A(Mi8) (Directorate of Military Intelligence-Army (Military Intelligence 8)), 2 August 1966, DMI-A, Army Headquarters. The Australian official history cites a later date for General Westmoreland's interest: 'In late [sic] July, 547 Signal Troop [sic] began picking up powerful Viet Cong radio transmissions from the Nui Dinh hills … General Westmoreland … seemed to attach particular importance to it. In October, he [General Westmoreland], sent word personally to the task force to "take it out"' (McNeill, *To Long Tan*, p 395).

APPENDIX D

radio direction-finding (DF) capability, either land-based or airborne, to determine the location of NVA/VC radio stations. Initially, 'fixes' on the location of Dodo were acquired by EC-47 aircraft of the US Air Force's 6994 Security Squadron.

From mid-July, patrols from 1 ATF's 3 SAS (Special Air Service) Squadron were tasked to eliminate Dodo – that is, tasked against the 'special target (a communications station)', the 'OPs and comms station', or the 'special target area' on Nui Ong Trinh Mountain (YS 680688) closely overlooking Route 15, and in the Nui Dinh hills (YS 3365). 'Fred' – a US vernacular term for an unidentified enemy radio transmitter – was also used in SAS reporting as a nickname for Dodo.[93]

On the return of SAS Patrol No 22 on 23 July, the 1 ATF commander and the operations officer spoke with the patrol commander (Sergeant E Tonna) on the deployment of further patrols to the 'special target area'. On 27 July, SAS Patrol No 31 led by Sergeant AG Urquhart killed five VC, including two VC women, in the Nui Dinh hills (at YS 351668). Captured documents indicated that the two women were couriers and food suppliers for the VC's Dodo observation posts and its radio team.[94]

However, Dodo was not silenced. The US airborne direction-finding (ARDF) 'fixes' were often unreliable – at times out by several kilometres: 'ARDF has been found wanting so far as its accuracy is concerned'.[95] In late July 1966, in order to more accurately locate Dodo, two AN/PRD-1 ground-based DF sets of equipment were allocated on loan to 547 Signal Detachment by the US 17 Radio Research Group at Long Binh, specifically to 'fix' Dodo, which would then be attacked and eliminated by 1 ATF SAS patrols. The PRD-1s were initially sited on Nui Dat hill within the 1 ATF base and at the ARVN National Training Centre at Van Kiep on the eastern outskirts of Ba Ria Town – and the fixes acquired were more accurate than the locations reported by the US ARDF.

Dodo was eventually eliminated on 24 October 1966, when a female VC radio operator (To Thi Nâu – also known as Ba Hoang, alias Minh Hoang – Military Proselytising Section, Hoa Long village) was captured

---

93 3rd SAS Squadron, 'Commanders Diary – Narrative', July 1966, AWM95 7/12/2. Also discussed in Chamberlain, *The Viet Cong D445 Battalion*, Annex E, p E-14.
94 D Horner, *Phantoms of the jungle: A history of the Special Air Service*, Allen & Unwin, 1989, p 190.
95 Captain TJ Richards, transcript of an audio tape to DMI (Mi8), 13 September 1966, DMI-A, Army Headquarters, received October 1966.

by B Company, 6 RAR, on Nui Dinh Mountain (at YS 332657) together with a US Type RT-77 AN/GRC-9 radio.[96] In early August, SAS patrols were also conducted on the eastern-facing slopes of the Nui Dinh and in the Chau Pha Stream area – including a squadron-level raid on 10–11 August.

Securing Route 15

The limited capacity of port facilities to receive the incoming build-up of US forces into southern South Vietnam was of serious concern to MACV. While the Saigon Port could accommodate the unloading of materiel, a large number of US vehicles and personnel were planned to be landed at Vung Tau and moved via Route 15 to US military complexes at Bear Cat, Long Binh and Bien Hoa. The principal formations planned to arrive were the 196 Light Infantry Brigade (mid-August), the 4 Infantry Division (expected 2–16 September – its 2 Brigade had already arrived), the 11 Armored Cavalry Regiment (scheduled to disembark at Vung Tau beginning on 7 September),[97] the 199 Light Infantry Brigade (expected late November), and the 9 Infantry Division (expected late November).[98] As noted, General Westmoreland understandably took a close personal interest in the security of Route 15.

On 9 July 1966, the VC's Chau Duc District issued a directive for increased offensive activity to commemorate 20 July – the anniversary of the 1954 Geneva Accords. Village VC committees were ordered to organise 'special units to attack RVNAF on Route 15, sabotage roads and bridges, and build obstacles to block road traffic'.[99] A 'High Point' was scheduled for 23 July 1966. On 3 August, the military intelligence staff

---

96   1 ATF, 'Intelligence Review, Nui Dat', 29 October 1966, AWM95 1/4/14. Ms Nau was subsequently interrogated at 1 ATF – and was the object of the infamous 'water torture' incident – see McNeill, *To Long Tan*, pp 395–98; Ian McNeill and Ashley Ekins, *On the Offensive: The Australian Army in the Vietnam War, January 1967–June 1968*, Allen & Unwin, Crows Nest, 2003 (including endnotes); and AWM file AWM98, R670/1/7.

97   With Route 15's security not guaranteed, the 11 Armored Cavalry Regiment personnel were flown from Vung Tau to Long Binh in US Air Force C-130 aircraft. The Regiment's advance party and equipment landed at Saigon on 18 August. The remaining eight vessels disembarked equipment at Saigon between 16 September and 9 October (499 wheeled vehicles, 483 combat full-tracked vehicles and 22 helicopters).

98   II FFV, 'Operation Report for Quarterly Period ending 31 October 1966, Saigon', 15 November 1966.

99   Nam Tien, 'Directive No. 73CV', 9 July 1966, MACV/JGS CDEC, VCAT, Item No. F0346/0003-0443-000.

of Chau Duc District sent a directive to VC village committees at Phu My, Phuoc Hoa and Chu Hai requiring them to collect intelligence on 'Route 15, the local terrain, and enemy elements'. These reports were to be submitted by 30 August 1966 in order to develop plans to 'to disrupt enemy lines-of-communications – Route 15'. The directive included examples of information required and a format.

In mid-July 1966, a report from HQ II FFV had indicated that elements of the 274 VC Regiment had occupied areas of the Nui Toc Tien and Nui Dinh hills, and threatened movement on Route 15.[100] On 16 July, 1 ATF launched Operation Brisbane – 6 RAR with an APC squadron and artillery support – into the area.[101] However, no enemy were found, and on 18 July, B/6 RAR conducted an uneventful three-hour APC-borne 'Road Runner' operation along the length of Route 15 from Ba Ria to Phu My. This was the first of 1 ATF's Road Runner operations, aimed at securing the main and secondary roads in the province – with the Route 15 area designated 'Road Runner West'.[102]

Heightened concerns – 274 VC Main Force Regiment

The captured diary of Nguyen Nam Hung – the second in command/chief of staff of the 274 VC Regiment (whose diary was captured by 5 RAR on 21 October 1966 in the Nui Thi Vai hills), indicated that in June and July 1966, elements of the Regiment were engaged in observing Route 15 in preparation for attacks in the Phu My area and interdicting the route.[103] As a light infantry formation, elements of the regiment could move swiftly from their base areas east of Route 2 and in the Hat Dich to

---

100 II FFV, 'HQ 1ATF Log Sheet 476', 15 July 1966, AWM95 1/4/4.
101 At 2020 hours on 15 July, a VC battalion was reported at YS 2963. The order for Operation Brisbane (16–18 July 1966) noted: 'recent intelligence reports indicate that the VC will attempt to ambush a convoy on Route QL 15 between mid-July and 30 July 1966', FRAG O 1-3-66, 18 July 1966. The mission was to 'search and destroy the enemy in GR 3164 … with a suspected enemy battalion located at YS 313649'. The 1 ATF Commander's Diary reported that the operation did 'not find trace of any large VC force … a very useful ground mobility exercise … and introduced SAS patrols secretly into the hills'. The official history noted: 'Airstrikes in the area prior to the operation may have forced the enemy away.' McNeill, *To Long Tan*, p 446.
102 Road Runner operations were formally initiated under 1 ATF, 'Op Plan 2/66', 24 July 1966, AWM95 1/4/5.
103 Chamberlain, *The Viet Cong D445 Battalion*, Annex N, p N-4, fn 14. See also, 1 ATF, 'Troops Information Sheet No. 31', 13–19 February 1967, AWM95 1/4/30.

the Route 15 area with little chance of detection. On 1 August 1966, the 274 VC Regiment attacked the base of the 2nd Battalion/48 Regiment at Phu My and ambushed an ARVN convoy nearby on Route 15 just north of Phu My.[104] ARVN casualties were 32 KIA (23 in the base, and nine in the convoy), 14 WIA and five missing in action (MIA); with 21 individual weapons and two crew-served weapons lost to the VC.

Soon after, on 10 August, the 274 Regiment's 265 (i.e. 2) Battalion attacked an ARVN 48 Regiment convoy of 15 trucks on Route 15 about 14 kilometres south of the border with Bien Hoa Province (YS 270660); and on 11 August an estimated VC battalion attacked the ARVN compound at Phu My on Route 15 (YS 237766). The ARVN sector headquarters in Ba Ria reported 18 VC killed and three ARVN killed and five wounded.[105] From mid-August 1966, the 274 Regiment observed Route 1 in Long Khanh Province, planning attacks on the strategic hamlets of Hung Nghia and Hung Loc, before conducting rice-portering operations in late August.

Clearing the way

Route 15 through Phuoc Tuy Province from Ba Ria to the developing US Bear Cat base in Bien Hoa Province (YT 155015 – about 30 kilometres north of the Phuoc Tuy/Bien Hoa border) had been classified as 'red' – meaning 'route is VC-controlled and a major military operation or engineer effort is required to clear it'. To secure the road deployment of 3 Brigade/4 US Infantry Division from Vung Tau along Route 15 to its Bear Cat base, II FFV mounted a corps-level operation, Operation Robin,

---

104 The ARVN convoy was ambushed on Route 15 at YS 236784. The ARVN 2/48 Battalion base was located at YS 238773 beside Route 15 – beside the Second World War airstrip about 2 kilometres north of Phu My village. The ARVN base was shelled by 57 mm RCLs, and the ARVN reaction force was reportedly ambushed by a VC battalion. Lost weapons included a .30 MG, a 60 mm mortar and 21 small arms; 10 trucks were damaged. See 1 ATF, 'INTSUM No. 62', 2 August 1966, AWM95 1/4/6, Part 2. The 5 VC Division History relates: 'In August, the 4th [i.e. 274th] Regiment organised an ambush of mechanised vehicles on Route 51 [i.e. previously Route 15], destroying seven military vehicles, 50 enemy, shooting down an aircraft and seizing two weapons.' Liberation Radio reported that on 1 August, 'the Liberation Armed Forces attacked an enemy military convoy on Highway 15 (Bien Hoa – Ba Ria). Two companies of the puppet Regiment 48 of Division 10 were put out of action after 10 minutes of fighting.' – 'One Puppet Company wiped out east of Saigon', *Vietnam Courier*, Hanoi, 8 November 1966.
105 1 ATF, 'Log Sheet 666', 10 August 1966, AWM95 1/4/6, Part 1: 'a battalion of 48 Regt ambushed on road near Phu My – 4 ARVN KIA, 6 WIA, 38 VC (BC) – claimed.'

APPENDIX D

beginning on 3 October 1966.[106] Route security for the three-hour move of the 3 Brigade to Bear Cat was provided by 1 ATF within Phuoc Tuy and by the US 173 Airborne Brigade in Bien Hoa Province.[107] Subsequent Route 15 security operations directed by Headquarters II FFV were titled Operation Duck and Operation Canary.

These operations were acknowledged in General Westmoreland's 1968 'Report on the War in Vietnam':

> After a brief training period, the task force came under the operational control of the U.S. II Field Force and moved to Phuoc Tuy Province with the mission of supporting pacification operations along Highway 15 and in the eastern portion of the critical Rung Sat Special Zone.[108]

Today Route 51 – previously Route 15 – is a four-lane highway, built up along its length from Ba Ria to Phu My.[109] With a population of over 23,000, Phu My is a large industrial town and the district capital of Tan Thanh District. Industries in Phu My include a steel mill, chemical plants and electricity generation – reportedly providing 35–40 per cent of Vietnam's total electricity requirements. Phu My also includes the major Thi Vai-Cai Mep deep-water container port that is also visited regularly by international tourist liners. An international airport is being constructed north of Phu My in the Long Thanh area. There are smaller ports along Route 51, including on the Dinh River at Ba Ria Town. Particularly on weekends, traffic on Route 51 from Ho Chi Minh City/Bien Hoa is extremely heavy with domestic tourists travelling to Vung Tau and Long Hai. Popular tourist attractions in Phuoc Tuy Province include the former 'resistance bases', and temples and shrines in the Nui Thi Vai and Nui Dinh hills.

---

106 The equipment and cargo of the 3 Brigade arrived by ship at Saigon, with personnel moving in 50-vehicle truck convoys from Vung Tau along Route 15 to Bear Cat – a three-hour journey.
107 An 11 Armored Cavalry Regiment report related that: 'On 4 October, the 2nd Squadron conducted a route reconnaissance of Route 15 from Bien Hoa to Baria … During the period 10-17 October, the 1st Squadron was under the operational control of the 173d Airborne Brigade participated in Operation Robin.' 11th Armored Cavalry Regiment, 'Operational report lessons learned', 31 October 1966, DTIC, AD386101.
108 General WC Westmoreland, 'Report on the War in Vietnam (as of 30 June 1968)', Section II, VCAT, Item No. 168300010017. p 222.
109 Until recently, most road travel from Saigon/Ho Chi Minh City to Vung Tau was via Bien Hoa and then via Route 51. However, since February 2015 the shortest and fastest route is the tolled Ho Chi Minh City – Long Thanh Expressway, which joins Route 51 at Long Thanh.

For decades, the insecurity of South Vietnam's major highways had been a major impediment, frustration and embarrassment to governments in Saigon – suggestive of a failing state. In September 1966, following the arrival in country of further significant allied military formations, the securing of the strategic Route 15 to Vung Tau – to at least 'amber' status – was in prospect. The newly arrived 1 ATF was to play a key role in that operation.

APPENDIX E. GLOSSARY OF MILITARY TERMS

ANPRC radio	American Pack Radio Communications radio
Aslt Pnr Platoon	Assault Pioneer Platoon
ATk Platoon	Anti-Tank Platoon
battle order	A soldier's full range of personal fighting equipment
breaking harbour	Moving out of a temporarily secured area
cannabilisation point	A US Army salvage unit's location
casevac	Casualty evacuation
contact	A skirmish, joining with the enemy in battle.
delousing	Rendering safe a mine or booby trap
Dustoff	A casualty evacuation, the code word for casevac helicopters
enfilade fire	Gunfire directed from the side across a front
fire for effect (FFE)	Artillery fire applied after initial fire has been satisfactorily adjusted
fire support base	A secured location in which supporting artillery is temporarily based
gun line	An assemblage of artillery within a base
harassing and interdiction (H&I)	A type of artillery fire designed to aggravate more than destroy
hutchie	A soldier's individual shelter from weather
in country	In Vietnam
insertion	Delivery of troops into an area by foot, vehicle or aircraft

interdict	To impede or intercept
KIA	Killed in action
Mentioned in Dispatches (MID)	An award for commendable service
MIA	Missing in action
movement axis	The centre line of movement of a body of troops, some of whom might be deployed some distace from the axis
moving by fire and movement	A tactical drill in which designated troops maintain covering fire, while others move forward to take up firing while the first group then moves forward to repeat the process
on net	Mutual understanding
Orders Group	A formal gathering at which orders are imparted by commanders
Pentomic	US Army scheme of organisation for Cold War nuclear scenarios
Pentropic	Australian Army short-lived scheme of organisation for tropical warfare scenarios
pogo	A non-combatant soldier
punji stakes	Sharp metal or wooden stakes used by the Viet Cong in mantraps
re-entrant	A gully between ridgelines
rock sangar	A protective embrasure constructed with rocks
search and clear axis	See: movement axis
SLR	Self-loading rifle
sortie	A single aircraft mission
strafing	Fire applied against ground targets by aircraft using cannon or machine guns
tropical studded	Fitted with brass studs for improved grip in wet tropical terrain (Second World War Australian Army boots)
warn out	Give prior notice to
WIA	Wounded in action

APPENDIX F.
MAP SYMBOLS

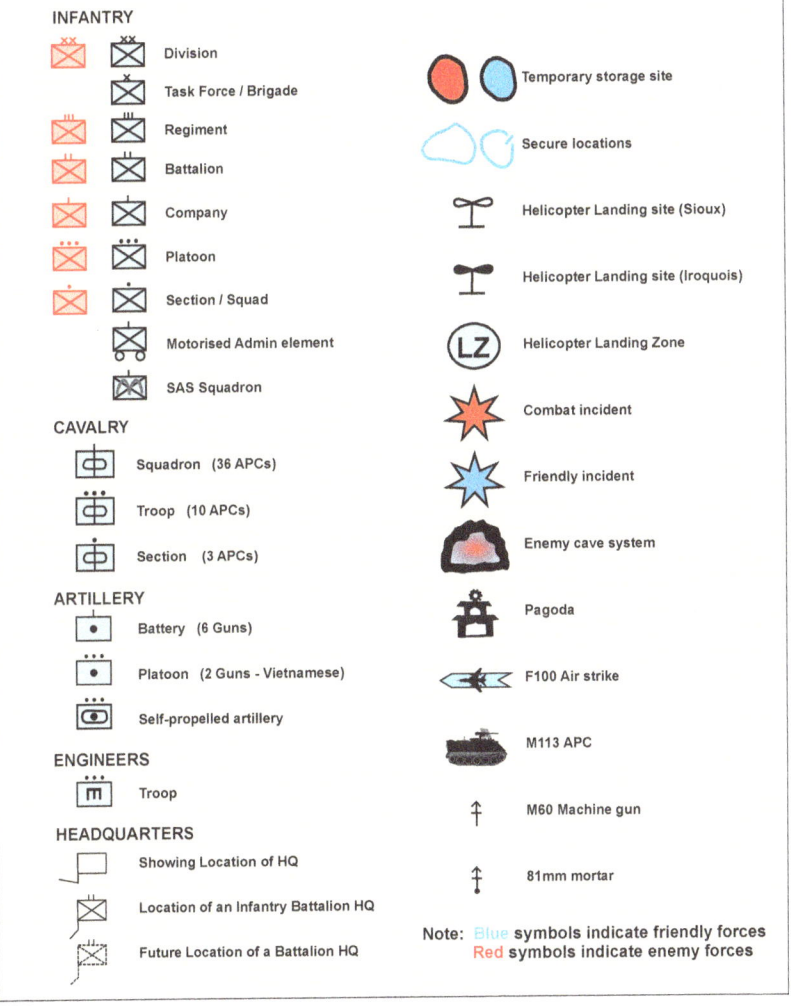

Source: Designed by Ron Boxall and produced by Alan Mayne.

APPENDIX G.
BIBLIOGRAPHY

The Vietnam War as a Whole

Hastings, Max, *Vietnam: An Epic Tragedy, 1945–1975*, William Collins, London, 2018

Australia's Part in the War

Edwards, Peter, *Australia and the Vietnam War*, NewSouth Publishing, Sydney, 2014

Ham, Paul, *Vietnam: the Australian War*, Harper Collins, Australia, 2007

Horner, David, *Strategic Command: General Sir John Wilton and Australia's Asian Wars*, Oxford University Press, South Melbourne, 2005

Odgers, George, *Mission Vietnam: Royal Australian Air Force Operations 1964–1972*, Australian Government Publishing Service, Canberra, 1974

The First Australian Task Force in Vietnam

Chamberlain, Ernest, *The Viet Cong: D445 Battalion*, Ernest Chamberlain, Point Lonsdale, 2016

Davies, Bruce with McKay, Gary, *Vietnam: The Complete Story of the Australian War*, Allen & Unwin, Crows Nest, 2012

Fairhead, Fred, *A Duty Done: A Summary of Operations by The Royal Australian Regiment in the Vietnam War 1965–1972*, The Royal Australian Regiment Association SA Inc., Linden Park, 2014

Gower, Steve, *Rounds Complete: An Artillery Forward Observer in Vietnam,* Big Sky Publishing Pty Ltd, Newport, 2017

McNeill, Ian, *To Long Tan: The Australian Army and the Vietnam War 1950–1966,* Allen & Unwin in association with the Australian War Memorial, St Leonards, 1993

McNeill, Ian and Ekins, Ashley, *On the Offensive: The Australian Army in the Vietnam War, January 1967–June 1968*, Allen & Unwin, Crows Nest, 2003

O'Neill, Robert J., *Vietnam Task: The 5th Battalion, Royal Australian Regiment*, Cassell Australia, Melbourne, 1968

Richardson, Thomas, *Destroy and Build: Pacification in Phuoc Tuy, 1966-72*, Cambridge University Press, Cambridge, 2017, doi.org/10.1017/9781316995648

White, Tony, *Starlight: An Australian Army Doctor in Vietnam,* CopyRight Publishing, Brisbane, 2011

Articles

O'Neill, Robert, 'Three Villages of Phuoc Tuy', *Quadrant,* January–February 1967

O'Neill, Robert, 'Australian Military Problems in Vietnam', *Australian Outlook,* April 1969

Warr, John A., 'Cordon and Search Operations in Phuoc Tuy Province', *Australian Army Journal* No. 222, November 1967

INDEX

Note: Page numbers in **bold** refer to images.

A Company, 5 RAR
   'Alvenia', 125
   Binh Ba, 182, 227
   casualties, 125, 184, 279
   Deak, 328
   discovery of *Birddog*, 63
   Duc My, 70
   1 Platoon, 181–4, 192–202
   Operation Canberra, 95, 100, 105
   Operation Hardihood, 157, 171
   Operation Holsworthy, 377–9
   Operation Queanbeyan, 124–5, 131, 133–4, 137, 140, 148, 185
   Operation Robin, 105–6, **116**
   Operation Sydney Two, 365, 367, 370
   Operation Yass, 386, 390
   3 Platoon, 196–7
AAFV *see* Australian Army Force Vietnam
AATTV *see* Australian Army Training Team Vietnam
AC-47 aircraft, 287
Administration Company, 5 RAR, 50, 168–9, 328
Agent Orange, 19
air support, 285–300
airborne direction-finding 'fixes', 419
airstrikes, 89, 105–6, 183, 214, 266, 289, 313
Aitken, Bruce 'Jacka' (Private), **245**

Albatross call sign, 286
American Red Cross, 297
An Nhut, 332
ANPRC 25 radio sets, 159, 193, 207
Anti-Tank Platoon
   becomes Reconnaissance Platoon, 85–6, 301–17
   Deak, 328, 340
   FSB Tennis, 66
   Operation Canberra, 95
   Operation Holsworthy, 378
   Operation Queanbeyan, 124–5, 127, 132, 134, 136–7, 139–40, 185, 187, 290, 293
   Operation Robin, 166
   Operation Sydney, 70, 73
   weapons, 47
Antonio, Bob (Private), **251**
Ap An Phu, 176
Ap Ngai Giao, 223
Ap Ong Trinh Dc, 256–7
Ap Ong Trinh Dp, 94–5, 107, 227, 257–8, 265
Armitage, Bob (Sergeant), **116**
Army Court of Enquiry, 299
Army of the Republic of Vietnam (ARVN)
   Binh Ba, 226
   casualties, 402, 407–8, 422
   CIA and, 230
   Commando Company, 382
   defeat at Binh Gia, 402

disliked by Montagnards and Nungs, 220
draft dodgers, 211
Duc Thanh outpost, 75
18 Division, 404
failure to defend Graham's minefield, 323
52 Ranger Battalion, 406–7, 413, 416
52 Regiment, 404
5 Infantry Division, 401
5 RAR advisors, 74
43 Regiment, 413
48 Regiment, 422
4 Marine Battalion, 402
'friendly fire', 261
headquarters Ba Ria, 76
Kim (Captain), 223
Lo Gom, 313
National Training Centre, 413, 419
NCO Training School, 413
1 Commando Company, 212, 220–8, 230, 398–9, 413
Operation Queanbeyan, 144
Operation Robin, 229, 271
Popular Force companies, 343, 385, 389, 391, 397, 413
Provincial Reconnaissance Unit, 413
Regional Force companies, 231–7, 314, 343, 397, 400, 407, 413
relations with 5 RAR, 343
Route 15, 94
search operations, 77
2nd Battalion, 422
701 RF Company, 407
10 Division, 404, 413
3rd Battalion, 413
31 RF Mechanised Platoon, 407
3/43 Battalion, 411
III Corps, 401, 405
Viet Cong and, 17, 32, 147
Arnold, Robbie (Private), 145

ARVN *see* Army of the Republic of Vietnam
Askew, Bob (Second Lieutenant), **242**, **244**
on Davies' helicopter crash, 298
161 (Independent) Reconnaissance Flight, 5, 133, **244**
Operation Queanbeyan, 290–2, 294
service history, 349
Aspinall, Peter (Captain), 264–7, 349
assassination, 228
Assault Pioneer Platoons
casualties, 188
FSB Tennis, 66
McDougall, 280
Operation Holsworthy, 380
Operation Queanbeyan, **121**, 124, 128, 132, 134, 137–40, 185, 188
Operation Sydney Two, 368, 371
Australian Army Force Vietnam (AAFV), 25, 34, 323, 327
Australian Army Journal, 5, 72, 339
Australian Army Training Team Vietnam (AATTV)
advisors, 232, 236–7
assumes Bade's role, 74
CSG, 222
earlier Vietnam experience, 17, 21, 23
Jackson, 25, 323
reputation, 56
Seale and Taylor, 221
Stewart, 192
Wells, 413
Australian Commonwealth Military Force, 277
Australian Force Vietnam, Saigon headquarters, 212
Australian Logistic Support Group, 21, 37
Australian rules football game, 210–11

INDEX

B Company, 5 RAR
  air support for, 289
  Binh Ba, 227
  'Blanche', 125
  casualties, 170–1
  Duc My, 70
  5 Platoon, 98–9, 158, 170–2,
    188–90, 197
  4 Platoon, 370
  Hamlyn, 328
  landing zone secured, 165
  national servicemen, 1
  Nui Dat, 159
  Operation Canberra, 95, 98–101,
    104–5, 183, 265, 267, 289,
    322, 325–6, 331
  Operation Hardihood, 157, 171
  Operation Holsworthy, 73,
    377–8, 380–1
  Operation Queanbeyan, 124–5,
    134, 138, 140–1, 147–8, 185
  Operation Robin, 105–7
  Operation Sydney Two, 366–70
  Operation Yass, 386, 390
  reconnaissance patrols, 73
  support from 103 Field Battery,
    264
B Company (US), 57
B-52 bombers, 235, 287
Ba Hang, 419
Ba Ria
  ARVN Headquarters, 422
  Ba Ria Province Unit, 414
  'Combined Studies Group', 220,
    222
  doctor, 140
  location, 393
  population, 393
  Province Committee, 401
  provincial capital, 13, 17, 158
  proximity to Nui Dat, 38
  Route 2, 76
  Route 15, 53, 93–4, 399, 405
  Sector HQ, 236

Viet Cong, 400
Viet Cong supporters, 40
Viet Minh activity, 395
Babbage, Dave (Corporal), 143–4
'Back Beach', 156, 176, 205, 306
Bade, Ron (Captain), **246–7**
  advisor to Regional Force, ARVN,
    74, 231–8
  Binh Ba, 231–7
  Operation Sydney Two, 367
  service history, 350
  2IC A Company, 8
Bailey, 'Bondi' (Corporal), 221, 224
Balmoral Fire Support Base, 2
Bang Lung, 398
Base Area 303, 402
Bates, John (Sergeant Major), 336
Baton Rouge Victory, 411
Battalion Band, 169, 277, 327, 372
Battalion Band (US), 49
Battalion Command Group, 58
Battalion Headquarters, **248**
  airstrike organised, 289
  arrival in Vietnam, 155
  FSB Tennis, 66
  'Heidi', 125
  immersed in operations, 329
  message to 173 Airborne Brigade,
    158
  Nui Dat, 157
  Operation Canberra, 95, 97, 106
  Operation Holsworthy, 73, 380
  Operation Queanbeyan, 124–5,
    127–8, 130, 132–4, 137, 148,
    185, 293
  Operation Yass, 386
  Reconnaissance Party, 127–8, 132
  regimental aid post, 274
  staff officers, 55, 57, 78, 91
  Tac, 148
  visit from Smith, 59
Bau Lung, 417
Be, Nguyen Van (Captain), 74, 77,
  232, 235–6, 247

433

Bear Cat, 83–4, 93–4, 205, 213, 420, 422–3
Ben Het, 411
Ben Tau, 399
Ben Tiger Exercise, 154
Ben Tre, 401
Benham, Glen 'Moose' (Private), **245**
Bennett, Ed (Chaplain), 157
Bentley, John, **246**, 314
Bernotas, Alex (Private), 213–14
Bien Hoa
   airbase, 7, 25, 57, 63, 93
   1 RAR, 21, 26–8, 31, 48
   173 Airborne Brigade (US), 155
   Operation Canberra, 176
   Province, 94
   rejected as 1 RAR base, 36–7
   Route 15, 394
   II Field Force Vietnam (US), 342
   II Vietnamese Corps, 36, 55
   US position, 83–4, 420, 422
   Viet Cong, 341, 400
Bindley, George (Captain), 5, 258, 262, 267–71, 350
Binh Ba
   A Company, 5 RAR, 182
   ARVN, 232
   C Company support for, 212
   cordon and search operations, 75, 210–12, 226
   CSG, 223
   Duc My estate village, 363
   Guerrilla Platoon, 376
   intensive patrolling, 213
   mine clearance, 238
   1 Commando Company, ARVN, 223, 226
   Operation Holsworthy, 73–4, 188, 375–83
   plan to attack, 72
   public interest in battle, 2
   reconnaissance patrols, 76
   Regional Force base, 232–3
   2008, 237–8
   Viet Cong, 363, 375, 400
   Viet Minh, 397
   working with ARVN, 343
Binh Gia, 75, 77, 372, 376, 397, 402
Binh Son, 408
Binh Tuy, 36, 405
Binh Xuyen, 397
Birddog, 63, 101, 289
Birtles, Robert (Private), **111**
Bishop, Doug (Private), 165, 168
Blamey, Sir Thomas (General), 22, 34, 43
Blanch, Peter (Lance Corporal), **251**
'Bombard', 255–6
bombardier assistants, 254
Borneo, 10
Bourne, Don (Major), 332
Box, Bob (Private), **118**, 164–5
Boxall, Ron (Brigadier), **246**
   CIA operation, 74, 218–28, 230
   co-editor, 4
   D Company, 5 RAR, **243**
   Maizey and, 227–8
   Operation Canberra, 95
   Operation Hayman, **243**
   Operation Holsworthy, 382
   Operation Sydney Two, 367
   Operation Yass, 386
   2IC D Company, 218
   service history, 350
   soccer game, 212
   work with Provincial Reconnaissance Unit, 74
Brand, Tom (Private), **251**
Brannan, Walter 'Jock' (Private), **245**
Brinnon, Charles (Lieutenant), 19, **116**
British Commonwealth Occupation Force, Japan, 25
Brogan, Mervyn (Major General), 33
Brooke, Alan (Field Marshal) (British Army), 25
Brown, Ayb (Staff Sergeant), 274
Browning machine guns, 65, 226
Bryan, David 'Stretch' (Lance Corporal), **111**

INDEX

Buckley (CIA), 222, 224
Budden, Brian (Lance Corporal), **251**
Buhagiar, John (Private), **251**
Bui The Kham, 395
Bung Lung, 401
Bunting, Bob (Corporal), 144–5
Burge, Brian (Corporal), 137
Burns, Warren (Lance Corporal), **251**
Bushranger call sign, 286
Buttriss, Gordon (Sergeant), 136, 178

C Company, 5 RAR, **240**
   Binh Ba, 76, 161, 227
   casualties, 106, 137, 164–5, 177, 207–8, 213
   'Christine', 125
   commanders, 153
   departure for Vietnam, 48
   Duc My, 70, 72
   8 Platoon, 98, **111**, **116**, **118**, 135–6, 152–3, 155–7, 163, 178, 206, 211, 213
   under Neesham, 203–16
   9 Platoon, 176, 206, **241**, **251**
   Nui Dat, 157–9
   Operation Canberra, 95, 98, 100–1, 104, **115**, 176, 183, 265, 289
   Operation Hardihood, 157
   Operation Holsworthy, 73, 211, 377, 381–2
   Operation Queanbeyan, 124–5, 134–5, 138, 140–1, 148, 166
   Operation Robin, 106, 166
   Operation Sydney Two, 366, 368–70
   Operation Yass, 386–7, 389–90
   7 Platoon, 66, 68, 165, 177
C-47 transport aircraft, 287
Cahill, 'Paddy' (Sergeant), 168
call signs, 286–7, 291, 313
Calvert, Ray 'Skinny' (Sergeant), 129–30, 186, **245**, 303
Cam My, 411

Campbell, Barry (Lieutenant), 141–7, **244**, 351
Campbell, David 'Maxy' (Private), **245**
Campbell, Jim (Captain), 5, **244**, 285–8, 293–4, 296, 351
Can Gio District, 394, 401
Canungra Jungle Training Centre, 11, 46, 153, 194, 196, 204
Caribou aircraft, 409
Carroll, Max (Colonel), **246**, **248–9**
   BHQ staff officer, 55
   Deak and, 302, 328
   Long Tan, 226
   Malayan Emergency, 87
   officer commanding Support Company, 55
   Operation Canberra, 101
   Operation Hardihood, 58, 61, 199
   Operation Holsworthy, 74, 380
   Operation Queanbeyan, 123–7, 132–41, 147–9
   Operation Robin, 104
   Operation Sydney, 69
   operations officer, 4, 8, 53, 65–6, 79, 158, 321
   relations with US forces, 342
   service history, 320, 352
   Support Company, 320–1, 326
   Vietnamese casualties, 59
   Warr and, 66, 320–3, 339
Carruthers, J (Lieutenant), **246**, 370, 389
Cassidy, AP 'Bert' (Major), 59, 85, 226, 365
casualties 5 RAR, 106, 125, 164, 188, 213, 215, 327, 332, 338, 341
   AATTV advisors, 236
   Bernotas, 213–14
   Bishop, 165
   Bourne, 332
   Box, 165
   D'Antoine, 137, 280

435

Davies, 107, **250**, 296–9
Deane-Butcher, 170
Goodman, 138
Harrison, 184
helicopter crash, 178–9, 279
Le Dan, 128, 132–3, 279–80, 291–2
Lynch, 138, 280–1
McAloney, 137
McCray, 207–8
McQualter, 170, 328
Mealing, 107, 299
Noack, 158, 171, 197
Orchard, 213
Riik, 165
Sweetnam, 160
Thompson, 184
Tomas, 177, 209–10
Twaits, 330
Warburton, 175
Winkel, 184
Wolk, 207
Womal, 129–30, 132, 186–7, 280, 291–2, 305
Cat Lo, 225
Catholic clergy, 18
Catholic villages, 75, 107, 397
Cavanagh, Bill (Private), **116**, 136, 167, 178
Cavanagh, Kevin (Private), **112**
Cay Cay, 417
Central Office for South Vietnam, 401–2, 405, 411
Centre de Repos, Le, 397
Centurion tanks, 64
Cessna light aircraft, 365, 370, 377
CGS Exercise, 36
Chamberlain, Ernest (Brigadier), 17, 81–2, 228, 352
Charlie Company, 2nd Battalion (US), 410
Chau Duc, 398, 408, 411–12, 414, 420–1
Chau Duc History, 396, 399, 417
Chau Pha, 420

Chau Thanh, 398, 400, 403
Chau Tran Ngoc, 228
Cheeseman, Trevor 'Taffy' (Corporal), **245**
Chi Linh Rural Development Cadre Training Centre, 409
Chief of the General Staff (CGS), 21–3, 33, 36, 39, **116–17**, 412
Chiefs of Staff Committee, 27–8, 33, 42–3
Chieu Hoi program, 343
Chu Hai, 400, 411, 421
CIA, 74, 217, 219–30, 401
Civil Guard, 397, 399–400
Clarke, Fred (Private), 70, 370
Claymore mines, 49, 159, 193, 337
cluster bombs, 100, 102, 165, 287, 289
Co Trach, 396
Coad (Lieutenant Colonel), 57
Cogswell, Colin (Private), 98–100
Cole, Peter (Major), 131, **246**, 385
Colo-Putty training area, 154, 196, 295
COMAFV *see* Commander, Australia Force Vietnam
Combat Engineer Teams, 166
'Combined Studies Group' (CSG), 219–20, 222–7 *see also* CIA
Commander, Australia Force Vietnam (COMAFV), 36, 39–41, 43, 51, 53
C123 Provider transport aircraft, 48
conscientious objectors, 194
conscription, 1, 12–13, 171, 181, 259, 332
Coral Fire Support Base, 2
cordon and search operations
    Binh Ba, 74–5, 210–12, 226, 234
    contact with villagers, 182
    Duc My, 69–70, 363–74
    5 RAR, 72, 327, 331, 338–9, 361–92
    Nui Dat, 210

INDEX

Phuoc Hoa, 53, 345
results, 392
'Country Fair' operations, 77
Courtenay Hill, 42, 410
Criss, Dick (Private), **116**
Cross, Danny (Private), **251**
CSG *see* 'Combined Studies Group'
Cubis, Richmond 'Dick' (Lieutenant Colonel), 257–8, 267–71
Cusack, Graham 'Breaker' (Second Lieutenant), 333
Cutler, Sir Roden, 100, 155

D Company, 5 RAR
   Binh Ba, 227
   Boxall, Ron (Brigadier), 218
   casualties, 106, 175
   'Doda', 125
   Duc My, 70, 72
   11 Platoon, 95
   Operation Canberra, 95
   Operation Hardihood, 157
   Operation Holsworthy, 377, 379, 381
   Operation Queanbeyan, 124–5, 134, 141–2, 146–8, 185, 188
   Operation Robin, 106
   Operation Sydney Two, 364, 366–71
   Operation Toledo, **116**
   Operation Yass, 386
   support from Reconnaissance Platoon, 314
   10 Platoon, 141–2, 147, 188, **244**
   Warburton, Graham (Private), 77
D Company, 6 RAR
   attacked, 82
   Battle of Long Tan, 14, 52, 76, 135
   Long Tan, 161
   Operation Queanbeyan, 124, 185
   reconnaissance patrols, 73
   Route 15, 94
Da Giang, 408

Dalat, 52
Daly, Tom (Major General), 27, 39, 101, **116–17**, 326
D'Antoine, Gordon (Private), 136–7, 280
Dat (Colonel), 224
Dat Do, 323, 393, 395–6, 400, 403, 410, 412–13
Davies, Bill (Second Lieutenant), **250**
   helicopter crash, 107, **250**, 279, 290, 294, 296–9
   161 (Independent) Reconnaissance Flight, 5
   Vietnam service, 295–6, 352–3
Davis, RJ (Second Lieutenant), **246**
DC3 aircraft, 287
de la Maissoneuve, Pougin (Lieutenant Colonel), 395–6
De Puy, William (Brigadier General), 29–30
Deak, Michael 'Skip' (Second Lieutenant) (later von Berg), **244–6**
   A Company, 5 RAR, 328
   Anti-Tank Platoon, 328, 340
   Carroll and, 328
   Military Cross, 188
   O'Neill and, 329
   Operation Queanbeyan, 127–32, 185
   Reconnaissance Platoon, 85, 301–17, 329, 391
   Royal Australian Regiment Association, 8
   service history, 353
   Support Company, 328
   Warr and, 328–30
Deane-Butcher, John (Second Lieutenant), **246–7**
   national serviceman, 204
   OTU graduate, 153, 169, 203
   platoon commander, 177
   rugby union, 170
   'Warburton mountains', 176

Defeat into Victory (Slim), 152
Defence and Employment (D&E) Platoon, 267, 269
Defence Committee, 24–5, 29, 34
Delaurey-Simpson, Ron 'Frenchy' (Private), 224, 232, 247
Delsar, Barry (Private), **251**
Dereliction of Duty (McMaster), 230
Derringer, 101
Devlin, Joe (Private), 100, 171
diary of Nguyen Nam Hung, 90
Dien Bien Phu, 9, 335
Dinh River, 423
direct support, 312–13, 364
Directorate of Infantry, 320
Division in Battle Pamphlet No 1, The (Australian Military Board), 322
Doda, 125
'Dodo', 418–19
Dohle, Cliff (Flight Lieutenant), 135
'Domino Theory', 10
Don Dien de Gallia, 223
Dong Khoi movement, 398
Doyle, Laurie (Major), 296, 298
Drennan, Bill 'Sharpe' (Corporal), 128–9
drills, 162
Duc My, 69–71, 73, 160, 343, 363–74, 376, 378–9, 381–2
Duc Thanh, 74–7, 84, 147, 224, 232, 255, 376, 393, 404
Duc Trung, 73, 363, 376–81
Dunstan, Sir Donald (Lieutenant General), 39, 41
Dustoff evacuations, 46, 59, 98, 107, 133, 136, 160, 164, 171, 179, 184, 207–9, 213–14, 274, 276, 279, 286–9, 291–2, 296, 313
Dwyer, John (Second Lieutenant), 204
Eastern Command, 27
Eastern Region Inter-Provincial Committee, 398
Edwards, John 'Blue' (Private), **245**
Egan (Brandt), Robert 'Bobby' (Private), **245**

8 RAR, 33–4
11 Armored Cavalry Regiment (US), 420
Engineer Field Squadron, 327
equipment, 47–8, 51, 64–5
Exercise Sky High, 40

F-100 Super Sabre aircraft, 289
Fall, Bernard, 192
Fardel (French commander), 396
Ferrier, Raymond 'Ferret' (Private), **245**
field telephones, 50
Fifth Battalion, the Royal Australian Regiment, *see* 5 RAR
Filipino forces, 341
1st Australian Logistic Support Group, 47, 51, 102, 104
1st Australian Task Force *see* 1 ATF
1st Brigade, 46
First Battle of Britain, The (Fredette), 90
Fitzgerald, John (Private), **251**
5 RAR *see also* member Companies
  arrival in Vietnam, 48, 154–6, 194–5, 204
  Battalion Advance Party, 55
  Battalion Headquarters, 55
  casualties, 276–7, 280–1
  under 173 Airborne Brigade (US), 58
  raised for Vietnam service, 9, 29, 33, 154, 321, 324
  relations with South Vietnamese forces, 343–4
  relations with US forces, 342
  second Vietnam tour, 298
  structure, 3
  supported by 103 Field Battery, 253–71
  tactics, 335–46
  training for Vietnam deployment, 11, 46–8, 153–4, 194, 196, 202–4, 336
  weapons, 253

INDEX

5 RAR Association, 8
503 Airborne Infantry Regiment (US), 56–9
fixed-wing propeller-driven aircraft, 287
Florence, Brian (Major), 323
FO Parties, 254
Foale, Les (Warrant Officer), 132
F100 Super Sabre fighter-bombers, 101–2
food aid for villagers, **119–20**
food distribution rules, 383
foot problems, 181–2, 213
Foran, Ian (Private), **111**, 162
Forbes, Jim, 27
Forward Air Controller Detachment, 377, 381
forward observer officers, 254, 257, 264–5, 267
4 Infantry Division (US), 166, 213, 290, 420
4 RAR, 29, 33
France
    defeat in Indo-China, 9, 335, 395–7
    occupation of Ba Ria, 395
Fraser, John (Second Lieutenant), 170
Fraser, Malcolm, 35, 42, 155
Fraser, Peter 'Doc' (Private), 130, 132, 186, 188, **245**, 280
'Fred', 419
Fredette, Raymond, 90–1
Fridolf, Merv (Sergeant), 56
'friendly fire', 261
FSB Tennis *see* Tennis

Gair, Neville (Major), 95, 146, **249**, 258
Gallia rubber plantation, 232, 234–5, 376, 378
Gambold, Barney (Private), **245**
Geneva Accords, 397, 420
George Medals, 136, 167, 178
German Army and the Nazi Party, The (O'Neill, R), 90

Gia Dinh, 394
Giap, Vo Nguyen (General), 6
Gilbert, George (Corporal), 171
Godfrey, Robert 'Bobby' (Sergeant), **245**
Goodman, David (Private), 138
Gospers Mountain training area, 11, 46, 154
Gower, Steve (Major General), 8
Graham, Stuart (Brigadier), 323, 326–7, 331
Granter, Noel (Major), 155, 368
Greenhalgh, Paul (Major), **111**, **116**, **246**
    Commander D Company, 76, 141, 175
    Hartley and, 191–2
    Operation Holsworthy, 377
    Operation Queanbeyan, 146
    Operation Sydney Two, 367
Greville, Philip (Brigadier), 39
'grey funnel line', 19
Griggs, John (Lieutenant), 255–9, 262, 271, 353
'grunts', 104
gun aiming points, 261
gun platforms, 260–1
gun positions, 255–9
Gunning, RR (Second Lieutenant), **246**
gunships, 286–7, 289–90, 313
Guymer, Ross (Lieutenant), 233

H hour, 259
Hai Phung commander, 406
Hall, Jim (Corporal), 99
Ham Tan, 397
Hamlyn, RD (Major), **246**, **249**, 328
Hannigan, Richard (Major), **116**, 271
harassing and interdiction missions, 256–7, 259, 261, 271
Harris, Terry 'Harry' (Private), 163–4
Harrison, Ted (Lance Corporal)
    A Company, 181–4, 353–4

439

Operation Canberra, 183–4
wounded, 184
Hartley, John (Lieutenant), **246**
A Company, 5 RAR, 192–202
Operation Canberra, 181, 183–4
service history, 191–2, 353
Harvey, William 'Suave Harve' (Corporal), **245**, 306
Hasluck, Paul, 33
Hassall, Sam (Sergeant), 170–1
Hassett, Frank (Major General), 26–7
Hat Dich, 16, 383, 396, 398–9, 401–3, 421
Hay, Bob (Brigadier), 35, 41
HE 70 mm Mighty Mouse rockets, 101–2
Healy, John (Sergeant), 192
Heazlewood, Doug, 259–63, 354
Heffernan, Ted (Captain), 263
Helio Courier, 224
Henry, Mick (Sergeant), 232, 235–6
Henrys, Mick (Sergeant), 47, 168
Heroic 445 Battalion: Its History and Tradition, The, 17
Hicks, Sir Edwin, 24, 30–1, 33–4
Hill Jan, 102, **118**
Hill Julie, 102, **118**, 125
Hillier, Doug (Private), 98–9
Hindmarsh, Ralph 'Rowdy' (Sergeant), **116**, 154, 163, 204–5
HMAS *Jeparit*, 51
HMAS *Sydney*, 19, 48, 155, 204, 316
Ho Chi Minh, 6, 361
Ho Chi Minh City, 423
Ho Chi Minh Trail, 14, 16
Ho Tram, 401
Hoa Long, 219–24, 226, 410, 412–13, 419
Hodgkinson, Ivor 'Blue' (Major), **246**, **249**, 326
Hoi Bai, 400
Hoi Chanh (defectors), 228, 362, 373
Holsworthy, 9, 46, 153–5, 193, 196, 298, 320, 324, 336

Holt, Harold, 35
Hopper, Colin (Sapper), 136
Horner, David (Colonel), 354–5
Horseshoe Hill, 42, 215–16, 228, 314, 327
'Huey' helicopters, 19, 189, 195, 285–6
Hughson, Bruce 'Hughie' (Warrant Officer), 128, 132, 389
Hulme, Alan, 30, 33
Hung Loc, 422
Hung Nghia, 422
Hunter, Alan, **116**

Illman, Colin (Private), 175
Indo-China War (first), 395–7
Indonesian confrontation with Malaysia, 10, 23, 301
inter-allied relations, 341
interpreters, 73, 232–3, 295, 315–16, 364, 369, 371, 382, 386, 390–1
ARVN, 278
Bailey, 221
Henry, 235
1 Australian Task Force Linguist Section, 377
interrogation, 373–4
Iron Lady Exercise, 154
Irwin Barracks, 202
Isaacs, Peter (Captain), **246**, **249**
adjutant, 8, 56–7, 78, 87, 306, 322, 325
appreciation of 5 RAR, 80
Bade and, 231
BHQ staff officer, 55
O'Hanlon and, 170
Operation Canberra, 98–101
Operation Holsworthy, 73, 381
service history, 324, 355
Warr and, 324–8, 339
work with US forces, 56, 59

Jackson, David (Brigadier), **113**, **117**
AAFV, 323

AATTV, 323
Commander AAFV, 25
Commander AATTV, 25
Commander 1 ATF, 38, 61
Cubis and, 269–71
on Davies' helicopter crash, 298
leadership style, 88–9
Lockhart on, 40
McFarlane and, 269–70
medal recommendation for Privates, 167
Operation Holsworthy, 226
Operation Queanbeyan, 89
Operation Yass, 385
permission to return to Nui Thi Vai, 109, 123
on Phuoc Tuy, 416
relations with US command, 34
selection of Nui Dat, 38, 41
Warr and, 61, 109, 323, 326
Westmorland and, 27, 31, 84
Wilton and, 27–8, 31, 34–5, 37, 40
jet fighters, 287
Johnston, Lyndon, 29–30
Joint Chiefs of Staff, 25
Joseph (Pere), 223, 235
J2 division, MACV, 91
J3 (Operations) division, MACV, 91

Kapooka, 169
Kearney, Bob 'Dogs' (Corporal), 176–8, **245**, **251**, 306, 355
Kellor, Kerry (Lieutenant), 258
Kim Dai Uy (Captain), 221, 223
Kim Hai, 399–400, 406–7
Koblitz, Holger 'Curly' (Corporal), 154, 163–4
Korean War
  Australian experience, 417
  Australian and US cooperation, 342
  Bell Sioux helicopters, 286–7, 295
  5 RAR, 217
  Hassett, 26
  manpower, 345
  Mealing, 279
  radio sets, 193
  Warr, 88, 320
  Wilton, 22–3, 26
Kubrick, Stanley, 271
Ky, Nguyen Cao (Air Marshal), 33, **121**

Landing Zone Hudson, 57–8, 157, 176, 195–6, 206–7
Landing Zone Michael, 105, 166
Landing Zone Snakepit, 157
Lang Cat, 397, 400
Lang Phuoc Hoa, 258–9, 267, 313
Langley, Mike (Lieutenant), 258, 268
Larteguy, Jean, 192
Le Dan, Brian (Captain), **117**, **242**, **246**
  helicopter operations, 56
  Operation Queanbeyan, 127–8
  signals officer, 57, 78
  wounded, 127–8, 132–3, **242**, 279–80, 291–2
Le Duan, 6
Le Duc Dat (Lieutenant Colonel), 413
Le Duc Tho, 6
Le Minh Thinh, 398
Le Xuan Chuyen (Lieutenant Colonel), 418
Leaman, John (Sergeant), 57
Lea-Smith, John (Sergeant), 214, **245**, 306
Leslie, Gary (Corporal), 143
Lestrange, Robin (Private), **116**
Light Fire Team, 377
Lo Gom, 313
Loc An, 401–2
Lockhart, Greg, 40, 42
Long Binh, 83–4, 93, 176, 420
Long Cat, 107, 278–9, 399
Long, Charles, (Major General), 33
Long Dat, 40, 396, 414
Long Dien, 393, 410, 413

Long Green, The, 314
Long Hai, 77, 400, 413
Long Hai hills, 16, 40–1, 61, 170, 313, 341, 395, 408
Long Huong, 383, 385, 397, 399, 413
Long Khanh, 400, 405, 410, 422
Long Le district, 219, 224, 393, 413
Long, Phil (Private), **116**
Long Phuoc, 59, 64, 395, 400, 411–12, 414, 416
Long Son Island
    clearance, 53, 258, 385
    location, 394
    map, 146
    Operation Hayman, 189, **240**, 267, 271, 345, 385, 387
    Viet Cong escaping from, 391
    Viet Cong haven, 189, 384
Long Tan
    clearing, 411–12
    D Company, 6 RAR, 14, 52, 76, 212, 333
    Nguyen Thoi Bung, 406
    Operation Abilene, 410
    Operation Smithfield, 264
    public interest in battle, 2
    reclearing, 416
    role of artillery, 259–60
    significance of Nui Dat location, 41, 161
    6 RAR, 16
    survivors, 226
    tunnels, 400
    village levelled, 59
    villagers resettled, 414
Long Tau River, 394, 397, 411
Long Thanh, 395, 398, 400, 406, 408
Lovell, DG (Second Lieutenant), **246**
Luscombe Field, 210
Lynch, Trevor (Private), 138, 280–1

M16 rifles, 48, 99, **118**, 137, 145, 165, 168, 193, 206, 221, 308
M2A2 105 mm howitzers, 271

M18 Claymore mines, 159, 193
M26 grenades, 99, 220, 308, 375–6, 390, 403
M40 recoilless rifles, 302
M60 machine guns, 48–9, 51, 64
M72 light anti-armour weapon, 302
M79 grenades, 137, 193, 308
Mackay, Ken (Major General), **112**, **117**
    Commander, Australia Force Vietnam, 35, 40, 51
    Director of Military Operations and Plans, 24, 35
    Nui Dat, 40–1
    Phuoc Tuy, 30, 36
    service history, 24–5
    visits to Vietnam, 25, 29, 32, 51
    Westmorland and, 32
    Wilton and, 25–6
Madden, Ernie (Sergeant), 88
Maizey, Stan (Major), **118**
    artillery support, 267
    Bindley and, 269
    Boxall and, 227–8
    Cubis and, 271
    Deak and, 303
    Operation Holsworthy, 377
    Operation Sydney Two, 370
    Reconnaissance Platoon, 303, 309
    service history, 45, 356
    2IC 5 RAR, 46, 53–4, 56, 65, 321–2, 326
Malaya, 10, 12, 22, 29, 107, 177, 306, 417
Malayan Emergency, 10, 22, 87, 192, 301, 326
Mallinson, KG (Captain), **246**
Mansford, George (Captain), 314
Mason, Bruce (Private), **116**
Matheson, Reg (Sergeant), 260
Mathews (CIA), 222
Mavin, Keith 'Shorty' (Sergeant), 154, 201
Mavromatis, Jim (Corporal), 181
May Tao Mountains, 76, 405, 410

INDEX

May Tao Secret Zone, 16
'Mayfair, The', 52, **250**
McAloney, John (Second Lieutenant), **121**, 134, 136–8, **246**, 389
McCombe, Daryl (Private), **116**, 164
McCray, Graham (Corporal), 207–8
McDermott, Arthur (Major), 271
McDougall, Ian (Corporal), **114**, 138, 280–2, 356
McFarlane, Brian (Major), 267, 269–70, 377, 386
McGregor, Don (Warrant Officer Class 2), **111**
McLaren, John 'Macca' (Private), **245**
McLean, Allan (Corporal), 128–9, 131
McMaster, HR (Lieutenant General), 230
McNamara, Robert, 30, 408
McNeill, Ian, 41
McNeill, Robert, 2, 58
McNulty, Alan (Corporal), 214
McQualter, Bruce (Major), **246**
    B Company, 331, 367, 377, 386
    Operation Canberra, 100, 264–6, 322
    Operation Holsworthy, 377
    wounded, 170, 328
McShane, John (Private), 203–4
Mealing, 'Sailor' (Staff Sergeant), 107, 279, 296, 299
MEDCAP, 263, 276, 278–9
Medical Civic Action Program, 263, 276, 278
Medical Platoon, 168–9, 274–83, 382
Mekong Delta, 31–2, 53
Mentioned in Dispatches, 132, 136, 167, 178, 188, 348
Menzies, Robert, 25–6, 202
Meredith, Gordon (Lance Corporal), **241**, **251**
Middleton, Peter (Flight Lieutenant), 136
Military Crosses, 85, **121**, 188, 347

Military Medals, 99–100, 132, 188, 347
Military Region 1, 405, 414–15
Military Region 7, 405, 415
Military Working Arrangement, 25, 42, 412
Miller, John (Major), **246**
    advance party, 155
    C Company, 5 RAR, 164–5, 177, 179, 258, 377, 386, 390
    Operation Canberra, 98
Milligan, RB (Captain), **246**, 367
Mills, Denis 'Millsey' (Private), **245**
Minh Dam, 16, 395–6, 408–9
Minh Hoand, 419
Mission Vietnam, Royal Australian Air Force Operations 1964–1972 (Odgers), 135
Moles, Douglas 'Douggy' (Private), 181–2
Molloy, WJ (Captain), **246**
Monash, Sir John (General), 34
monsoons, 50, 63, 83, 143, 181–2, 196, 310
Montagnards, 69, 74, 220
moratoriums, 12
Moreau (Monsieur), 223–4
Moroney, Darryl 'Butch' (Private), **245**
Morse code, 140, 405, 415, 418
Mortar Platoon, 95, 254–5, 289
Mortimer, Brian 'Doc' (Lance Corporal), 263–4, 356
Mulby, John 'Blue' (Sergeant), **245**, 306
Murphy, John (Major), 304
My Xuan, 400

Nam Bo Region, 402
napalm, 102, 180, 289
National Liberation Front *see* Viet Cong
national servicemen
    B Company, 5 RAR, 1
    Deane-Butcher, 177, 204

5 RAR, 11, 332
  Foran, 162
  Holsworthy training, 46
  Moles, 181
  Neesham, 177, 202–3
  Noack, 59, 61, 158, 171
  officer training, 203
  O'Hanlon, 169
  1 Platoon, 192–3
  Roe, 204
  Sharp, 162
  Tomas, 209
NATO, 230
naval gunfire, 313
Neesham, Harry (Second Lieutenant), **246**
  C Company, 5 RAR, 153, 203–16
  national service, 202
  Operation Canberra, 213
  Operation Hardihood, 204–7
  Operation Holsworthy, 211
  Operation Queanbeyan, 215
  Operation Sydney, 209
  OTU graduate, 169, 203
  service history, 357
  7 Platoon, 177, 203–16
  Warr and, 215–16
Negus, GN (Lieutenant), **246**
New Zealand forces, 33, 267, 313, 341, 377
Ngai Giao, 77
Ngo Din Diem, 397, 400
Nguyen Nam Hung (Colonel), 90, 140, 421
Nguyen Quoc Thanh, 398
Nguyen Thoi Bung, 406
Nguyen Van Buu, 398
Nguyen Van Phuoc (Major), 403
Nguyen Van Thieu, 401
night operations, 78–9
9 Infantry Division (US), 420
9 RAR, 43
9 Squadron RAAF, 21, 286

Noack, Errol (Private), 59, 61, 158, 171, 197
non-commissioned officers (NCOs), 153–4, 346
North Vietnamese Army, 198, 418
Nottage, Gary 'BG' (Private), **245**
Nui Dat
  Battalion Headquarters, 157
  chosen for Australian base, 21, 38–43
  construction of base, 39, 159, 173
  cordon and search operations, 210
  defences, 14, 160–1
  'Dust Bowl', 274
  gun position 2, 256
  inhabitants removed, 58
  Luscombe Field, 210
  'Mayfair, The', 52
  mortared by Viet Cong, 196, 256
  Operation Hardihood, 19, 49, 58, 60–3, 65, 82, 170–2
  Task Force holdings, 102
  Viet Cong presence, 16
Nui Dinh hills
  capture of radio operator, 420
  D445 Provincial Mobile Battalion, 405
  5 RAR stationed, 13
  mortar attacks, 417
  103 Field Battery, Royal Australian Artillery, 390
  Operation Queanbeyan, 89
  Operation Vaucluse, 77
  Reconnaissance Platoon, 311
  'resistance bases', 423
  Route 15, 94, 394
  6 RAR, 84
  274 Regiment, 421
  Viet Cong, 401–2
  'Warburton mountains', 175
  White, Tony, 7
Nui May Tao, 16
Nui Nghe, 63, 65–6, 68, 77, 177, 209
Nui Ong Cau, 417
Nui Ong Trinh, 94–5, 183, 394, 401, 419

Nui Thi Vai, **121**
  D445 Provincial Mobile Battalion, 405
  equipment flown to, 52
  Landing Zone Michael, 105
  Operation Canberra, 98, 183, 213, 289
  Operation Hardihood, 200
  Operation Queanbeyan, 85, 89–90, 123–49, 184–8, 290, 293–4
  Operation Robin, 106, 109
  'resistance bases', 423
  Route 15, 94, 394
  Viet Cong, 401
  Viet Cong route through, 53
  'Warburton mountains', 175
Nui Toc Tien, 94, 141, 147–8, 394, 402, 421
Nungs, 74, 205, 220

O'Callaghan, John (Private), 188–90, 357
O'Dea, L (Second Lieutenant), **246**
Odgers, George, 135
Officer Cadet School Portsea, 153
Officer Training Unit, Scheyville, 46, 153, 169, 203
O'Hanlon, Terry (Second Lieutenant)
  B Company, 5 RAR, 170
  5 Platoon, 170
  injury, 173
  1 RAR, 170
  Operation Hardihood, 171–2
  Operation Holsworthy, 189–90
  OTU graduate, 203
  service history, 169, 357
1 ALSG *see* 1st Australian Logistic Support Group
1 Armoured Personnel Carrier Squadron, 364, 377, 386
1 ATF
  C Company location, 107
  CIA activities, 219–30

Civil Affairs Unit, 232, 382
Dental Unit, 107
547 Signals Detachment, 418–19
Headquarters, 45, 53, 84, 89, 232, 234–6, 256, 267, 412
leaflets, 380
Linguistic Section, 377
manpower, 345–6
mortared by Viet Cong, 196, 256
Nui Dat base, 21, 38–43, 48–9, 68, 81–2, 154, 196, 217–18
103 Field Battery, 254
Operation Hayman, 389
Operation Yass, 389
operational control, 35
Phuoc Tuy Province, 24, 42
role of 5 RAR, 153, 412, 417
roles, 36–7
Tactical Area of Responsibility, 77
two battalions, 84, 88
2/35 Artillery Regiment, 94
1 Commando Company, ARVN, 212, 220–8, 230, 398–9
1 Field Engineer Squadron, 377, 386
1 Field Hospital, 286
1 Field Regiment, 95, 98, 271
  Tactical HQ, 267–8, 271
1 Field Squadron, 166
1 Infantry Division (US), 410
1 RAR
  AATTV, 17
  arrive in Vietnam, 23
  Battalion Group, 405
  Bien Hoa, 21, 26
  deployment, 24–8, 33–4
  deployment with US forces, 56
  173 Airborne Brigade (US), 16, 55, 161, 321, 410
  Operation Denver, 410
  Operation Silver City, 42
  replaced by 5 RAR, 46–8
1 Transport Platoon, 377
101 Field Battery, Royal Australian Artillery, 5

103 Field Battery, Royal Australian Artillery, 5, 94, 227, 253–71, 386–7, 390–1
105 Field Battery, Royal Australian Artillery, 66, 363–5, 368–9, 377, 380
161 Field Battery, RNZA, 267, 377
161 (Independent) Reconnaissance Flight, 133, **244**, 286–8, 296, 299–300, 377, 386
173 Airborne Brigade (US)
　assessment of Viet Cong, 16
　Bien Hoa, 31, 55, 170
　5 RAR, 56–9, 61, 63, 82, 158
　Landing Zone Hudson, 157, 195, 206
　1 RAR, 25, 27, 55, 57, 155, 161
　Operation Abilene, 410
　Operation Hardihood, 49, 411–12
　Operation Hollandia, 61
　Operation Robin, 94
　Route 15, 423
　War Zone D, 42
196 Light Infantry Brigade (US), 420
199 Light Infantry Brigade (US), 420
O'Neill, Robert (Captain), **246, 249–50**
　Bade and, 231
　civil affairs officer, 340
　Deak and, 302, 314, 329
　intelligence officer, 78, 84–91, 105, 177, 322, 326, 340
　Operation Queanbeyan, 291
　Operation Sydney Two, 367
　service and academic history, 357–8
　2IC B Company, 5 RAR, 1, 12–13, 84, 170, 264
　Warr and, 338–9
Ong Trinh, 397, 399–400, 413
Operation Abilene, 410
Operation Brisbane, 368, 421
Operation Caloundra, 383

Operation Canary, 423
Operation Canberra, **118**
　A Company, 5 RAR, 95, 100, 105
　air support, 287–8
　airstrikes, 183
　B Company, 5 RAR, 95, 98–105, 183, 265, 267, 289, 322, 325–6, 331
　Battalion Headquarters, 106
　C Company, 5 RAR, 95, 98–101, 104, **115**, 161, 176, 183, 265, 289
　casualties, 277–8
　dates, 179
　8 Platoon, 178
　5 RAR, 385
　follow up actions, 123, 134
　gun positions, 255, 260–1
　Harrison, 183–4
　Hartley, 181
　map, 96, 103
　Neesham, 213
　Nui Thi Vai hills, 109, 227
　103 Field Battery, 264–7
　Route 15, 94
　Vietnam Task (O'Neill, R), 177
　'Warburton mountains', 175
Operation Crow's Nest, 77, 94, 179
Operation Darlinghurst, 76–7, 231
Operation Denver, 410–11
Operation Duck, 423
Operation Enoggera, 64–5
Operation Hardihood
　A Company, 5 RAR, 157, 171, 196–7
　B Company, 5 RAR, 157, 171, 197
　C Company, 5 RAR, 157
　D Company, 5 RAR, 157
　duration, 196
　intelligence summary, 416
　multi-unit sweep, 198
　Neesham, 204–7
　Nui Dat, 19, 58, 60–3, 65, 82, 154

Nui Thi Vai, 200
O'Hanlon, 171–2
173 Airborne Brigade (US), 49, 411–12
68 Assault Helicopter Company, 156
Sweetnam, 160
Operation Hayman, 189, **240**, **243**, 267–71, 345, 385, 387, 389
Operation Hobart, 72
Operation Hollandia, 61
Operation Holsworthy, 73–5, 188–9, 211, 226–7, 363, 375–83
Operation Mallet, 408
Operation Queanbeyan, **122**, **242**
   A Company, 5 RAR, 124–5, 131, 133–4, 137, 140, 148, 185
   air support, 287, 290
   Anti-Tank Platoon, 124–5, 127, 132, 134, 136–7, 139–40, 185, 187, 290–1, 293
   ARVN, 144
   Askew, 290–2, 294
   Assault Pioneer Platoons, **121**, 124, 128, 132, 134, 137–40, 185, 188
   B Company, 5 RAR, 124–5, 134, 138, 140–1, 147–8, 185
   Battalion Headquarters, 124–5, 127–8, 130, 132–4, 137, 148, 185, 293
   C Company, 5 RAR, 124–5, 134–5, 138, 140–1, 148, 166
   Carroll, 123–7, 132–41, 147–9
   D Company, 5 RAR, 124–5, 134, 141–2, 146–8, 185, 188
   D Company, 6 RAR, 124, 185
   dates, 179
   Deak, 127–32, 185
   5 RAR, 385
   Greenhalgh, 146
   Jackson, 89
   Le Dan, 127–8
   Medical Platoon, 279

Neesham, 215
Nui Dinh hills, 89
Nui Thi Vai, 52, 85, 89–90, 109, 123–49, 184–8, 290, 293–4
Owen machine carbine, 168
Route 15, 125
Wainwright, 135–6
Wormald, 178
Operation Ranch Hand, 407
Operation Renmark, 288
Operation Robin
   A Company, 5 RAR, 105–6, **116**, 385
   air support, 287–8, 296
   Anti-Tank Platoon, 166
   ARVN, 229, 271
   B Company, 5 RAR, 105–7
   C Company, 5 RAR, 106, 166
   Carroll, 104
   D Company, 5 RAR, 106
   dates, 179
   5 RAR, 385
   helicopter crash, 181
   map, 108
   MEDCAP, 278
   'no fire zone', 78
   Nui Thi Vai, 106, 109
   1 ATF, 423
   Route 15, 94, 166, 215, 290
   II Field Force Vietnam, 422–3
   White, 107
Operation Silver City, 42
Operation Smithfield, 264
Operation Sydney, 65–7, 69, 72, 209, 363
Operation Sydney Two, 69, 71–2, 160, 363–74, –374
Operation Toledo, 76–7, **116**, 231
Operation Vaucluse, 77, 94
Operation Woolloomooloo, 226–7
Operation Yass, 345, 363, 383–91
operational capability, 53
Operations Order Number 4, 157
optical sights, 260

Orchard, Ray (Corporal), 206, 213–14
Orders Group, 109, 183, 315, 322
OTO Melara L5 105 mm pack howitzers, 253–4
Owen machine gun, **118**, 133, 168, 193, 206, 280
Oxley, Peter (Lieutenant Colonel), 153, 324

Pacific Islands Regiment, 191
Page, Wayne 'Pagey' (Private), **245**
'Palace Guard', 95
Paltridge, Shane, 28, 30
Panthère noire, la, 396
Parker, Ken, 90
Parkes, Bill (Private), 209
Paths of Glory [film], 271
Pernes, Jean-Jacques, 223–4
Phan Rang, 32
'Phoenix Program', 228
Phu Hai, 414
Phu My
    ARVN, 261, 271, 413
    B Company, 5 RAR, 124
    Ba Ria Province Unit, 414
    D Company, 5 RAR, 124
    'no fire zone', 257–8
    Operation Robin, 106
    population, 423
    Post-Geneva, 397
    Route 15, 93–4, 395, 400, 421–2
    Special Sector, 399
    taken by French forces, 396
    Viet Cong, 384
    Viet Cong attack, 422
Phu/Chu Hai, 399
Phung Hoang, 228
Phuoc Bien Special Zone, 400
Phuoc Hai, 401
Phuoc Hoa
    ARVN, 413–14
    cordon and search operations, 53, 383–91
    1962, 399–400
    Post-Geneva, 397
    Route 15, 402
    Viet Cong, 411, 421
Phuoc Loc, 400
Phuoc Tinh, 397
Phuoc Tuy Province
    ARVN, 401, 404
    defoliation, 407
    economy, 13
    government control, 405, 413
    location, 393
    main Australian base, 21
    map, xxiii
    map Viet Cong locations, 15
    Operation Albinene, 410
    population, 393, 413
    Provincial Intelligence Operations Centre, 228
    selection as field of operation, 5
    Viet Cong, 1, 31, 81–3, 332, 340–1, 344, 401, 405, 409–10, 414–15
    Viet Minh, 397
Piper, Alex (Major), 89, 100
Pix magazine, 205
platoon commanders, 151–2, 173
Plimsoll, Sir James, 24
'pogos', 104
police relations, 340, 372
Politburo (North Vietnam), 398
Political Action Unit, 398
Possum call sign, 287, 294
Possum 5 call sign, 291
post-traumatic stress disorder, 19, 281
Pott, Ted (Second Lieutenant), 169, 203, **246**
Prescott, Bill (Major), 75–7, 232, 234–5
Presidential Citation, 407
Provincial Intelligence Operations Centre, 228
Provincial Reconnaissance Unit, 74, 220

Psychological Warfare detachment, 377
Public Affairs Office (US), 407
public opinion
  after the war, 336
  American, 335, 341
    opposing conscription, 12, 332
    opposing the war, 1–2, 6, 12
    supporting the war, 12
Puckapunyal, 202–3
'Puff the Magic Dragon', 287, 313
punishment cages, 237
punji stakes, 143, 180, 192

QM Platoon, 49
Quan Xuyen, 394
Quang Giao, 372
Quang Trung force, 395
Quinn, Russell (Corporal), **118**, 154, 160, 163–5
RAAF
  army relations with, 200–1
  base Richmond, 48
  Bell Sioux helicopters, 180, 215–16, 279, 286, 288, 290, 295–6, 298, 377
  Caribou Flight, 409
  C130 transport aircraft, 51
  helicopter crash, 166–7, 178, 180, 279, 290, 294, 296–9
  Iroquois helicopters, 21, 28–9, 34–5, 52–3, **122**, 134–5, 166–7, 195, 285–8, 290, 364, 377
  9 Squadron, 135, 286, 377
Rach Tre river channel, 387
radios, 50
Rainer, Dennis (Second Lieutenant), 141, 143–6, 175, **244**, **246**, 302
'Rat Pack, The', **251**
rations, 46, 51–2, 64, 168, 200–1, 311–12
Reconnaissance Platoon, 85, 188, **245**, 279, 301–17, 329, 391

Red Cross, 59
Republic of Vietnam Air Force, 418, 420
'resistance bases', 423
Returned and Services League (RSL), 214, 333
Revolutionary Development Cadre Program, 344
Reynolds, John (Private), **251**
Riik, David (Private), **111**, **118**, 165
Riley, Daniel 'Bluey' (Private), 184–8, **245**, 358
'Road Runner' operations, 77, 421
Roby, Peter (Warrant Officer), 236
Roe, Melford (Second Lieutenant), 169, 203–4, **246**
Rogers, 'Midge' (Gunner), 144–6
Rose, Dave (Bombadier), 258
Route 1, 395
Route 2
  Ap Ngai Giao, 223
  Binh Ba, 223
  defence of, 412
  Dong Khoi attack, 398
  Duc My, 70, 363
  French forces, 395
  Long Le district, 219
  map, 68
  opened to civilian traffic, 74–5
  Viet Cong, 421
Route 15
  ambushes of ARVN convoy, 402–3, 406, 416
  ambushes of South Korean forces, 408
  'American Killing Belts', 411
  Ap Ong Trinh Dp, 227
  ARVN, 413
  ARVN posts, 384
  Ba Ria, 405, 411
  closure, 408
  defence of, 93–5, 412, 420–3
  defoliation, 407
  gun positions, 257

location, 94
Operation Canberra, 176, 183, 213, 215, 266
Operation Mallet, 408
Operation Queanbeyan, 89–90, 125, 166
Operation Robin, 109, 166, 290
Phuoc Hoa, 53
population, 400
Route 51, 423
Saigon to Vung Tau, 13
secured, 345
Security Task Force, 398
surface, 13, 394
traffic, 264
US presence, 83–4
Viet Cong, 107, 341, 399, 402–4, 416
villages, 399
White, Tony, 7
Route 23, 396, 410
Route 44, 77, 408
Route 51, 423
Rowe, DJF (Lieutenant), **246**
Royal Australian Air Force *see* RAAF
Royal Australian Army Medical Corps, 278–9
Royal Australian Artillery, 253–71
Royal Australian Engineers, 39
Royal Australian Regiment Association, 8
Royal Military College (RMC), 22, 24, 152, 153, 191, 194
Rung Sac, 397–8, 403
Rung Sat, 258, 345, 383, 394, 398–9, 401, 407, 411, 423
Ruxton, Bruce, 333

Salvation Army, **246**, 314
SAS, 23, 34, 304, 308, 317, 344, 377, 387, 390–1, 419–20
'Save our Sons', 12, 194
Scales, John 'Scalsey' (Sergeant), **245**
Scaysbrook, Ken 'Scaisey' (Lance Corporal), **245**

Scherger, Sir Frederick (Air Chief Marshal), 27, 29, 33–5
School of Army Health, 275
School of Military Engineering, 48, 204
School of Music, 277
Schubert, Dennis (Sapper), 136
'Scrounging Platoon', 50, 65
'sea channel', 14, 16
Seale, Alan (Warrant Officer), 221
Seaman, JO (Lieutenant General), 412
Seamen's Union, 332
Searl, Robert 'Bob' (Corporal), **245**
Seats, Mick (Staff Sergeant), 274
2nd Battalion, 503 Airborne Infantry Regiment (US), 55
Self-Defence Corps, 397
Selleck, Neil (Private), **251**
Senate Appropriation Hearings (US), 408
7 RAR, 29, 33, 65, 341
17 Radio Research Group (US), 419
Shambrook, RT (Captain), **246**
Sharp, David (Private), 162–3, 165
Sheehan, TJ (Lieutenant), **246**
Shoebridge, Ron (Lance Corporal), **111**, 207
Shore, Syd (Private), 136, 167, 178, 211
Sinclair, Roger (Private), **251**
6 RAR
  A Company, 94, 264
  air support for, 287
  B Company, 420
  C Company, 377, 386
  D Company, 377, 380
  history, 58
  Long Tan, 52
  Nui Dinh hills, 84
  Operation Brisbane, 368, 421
  Operation Enoggera, 64–5
  Operation Hobart, 72
  Operation Holsworthy, 73, 211
  Operation Vaucluse, 77, 94

INDEX

Phuoc Tuy, 63
reconnaissance, 76
selection for Vietnam, 29, 33
Vung Tau, 61
16 Regiment (US), 410
68 Assault Helicopter Company (US), 19, 49, 56
64 Vietnamese Infantry Battalion, 396
6994 Security Squadron (US), 419
skin complaints, 53, 181–2, 273, 275, 310, 338
'slicks', 286
Slim, Sir William, Viscount (Field Marshal), 152
Smith, Bernie (Sergeant), **245**, 306
Smith, Bev (Captain), 295
Smith, Paul (Brigadier General), 59, 61
Smith, 'Sooty' (Warrant Officer), 232, 234–5
Soai Rap River, 394, 397
soccer game, 212
Song Be, 410
Song Cau River, 196, 206
Song Ray, 406
South Korean forces, 341, 408
South Vietnamese Army, 217
South Vietnamese government, 229
South-East Asia Treaty Organization, 22
Sovereign's Company, 191
Special Air Service *see* SAS
Spooky call sign, 287, 313
'Sports Cars', 47, 50
Staff College, 321
'Starlight', 276
Starlight: An Australian Army Doctor in Vietnam (White), 7, 332
Stavritis, James (Admiral), 230
Stewart, Jock (Warrant Officer), 192
Street Without Joy (Fall), 192
stretcher bearers, 129–30, 132, 169, 207, 274–5, 277–8, 280, 371

Stretton, Alan (Lieutenant Colonel), 35, 38
Stringer, Max (Private), **111**
Suacot, Joseph (Captain) (France), 396
Suckling, Alan (Private), **116**, **118**
Supple, Bob (Captain), **242**, **246**, **248**
  on air support activities, 288–91
  guiding *Dustoff* helicopter, 133, 291
  service history, 359
  2IC Support Company, 98
Support Company, 106, 128, 134, 184–8, 328
Sutherland, Graeme (Bombadier), 259
Sweetnam, John (Private), 160

Tactical Area of Responsibility (TAOR), 77, 159, 162–3, 168, 234–5, 416
Tactical Command Group, 148
Tam Bo, 410–11
Tan Thanh, 399, 423
TAOR *see* Tactical Area of Responsibility
Task Force Civil Affairs Unit, 232
Task Force Dental Unit, 107
Task Force HQ, 232, 234–6, 267, 269, 303
Taske, JE (Captain), **246**, 263
Taylor, Bob (Warrant Officer), 277
Taylor, 'Squizzy' (Warrant Officer), 221
Tedder, P (Major), 365
Tennis (FSB), 66, 70, 95, 98, 363–5, 368–9
Tet Offensive, 335–6, 341
Thai forces, 341
Thanh Dia, 402
Thanh Doan Saigon-Gia Dinh, 401
Thi Vai Mounain, 418
Thi Vai River, 401

451

Thi Vai-Cai Mep, 423
3rd Field Hospital (US), 299
33 Tactical Zone, 404
36 Evacuation Hospital (US), 165, 184, 207, 286, 330
Thompson, Neville 'Nifty' (Corporal), 184
Thompson, RG (Captain), **246**
Thompson, Ralph (Lieutenant), 56, 156
3 Brigade, 4 Infantry Division (US), 94, 422–3
3 RAR, 23, 29, 33, 107
3 Squadron, SAS, 304, 317, 344, 377, 387, 390–1, 419
III Corps Tactical Zone, 27, 36, 393
Throckmorton, John (Lieutenant General), 29
Tiger Battalion, 152, 156, 168
Time magazine, 230
To Long Tan: The Australian Army and the Vietnam War 1950–1966 (O'Neill, I), 58, 106
To Thi Nau, 419
Tomas, Marinko 'Titch' (Lance Corporal), 68, 177, 209–10
Tong Viet Duong, 409
Tonna, E (Sergeant), 419
torture, 228
Townsend, Colin (Lieutenant Colonel), 323
Tran Ngoc Buu, 399
Tran Tan Phat (Lieutenant), 413
Transport Platoon, 155, 169
Treloar, Don 'Tubby' (Private), 208
Truong (Second Lieutenant), 232–7
Tueno, Terry (Corporal), **251**
tunnels, 64, 105, 131, 137–8, 187, 200, 400, 411
Twaits, Anthony 'Bluey' (Private), **245**, 330
2 Armoured Personnel Carrier Squadron, 377
2 Brigade (US), 420
2 Camp Hospital, Ingleburn, 48
2 RAR, 33
2/35 Artillery Regiment (US), 94–5, 257, 377, 380, 386–7
II Corps Tactical Zone, 27, 36
II Field Force Vietnam (US), 35, 84–5, 327, 342, 412, 421–3
II Vietnamese Corps, 36

Ueshiba, Morihei, 273
Urquhart, AG (Sergeant), 419
Urquhart, Leslie 'Doc' (Corporal), 154, 163–4, 205
US forces
 B Company, 57
 Battalion Band, 49
 casualties, 58, 402, 408–11
 Charlie Company, 2nd Battalion, 410
 11 Armoured Cavalry Regiment, 420
 503 Airborne Infantry Regiment, 56–9
 4 Infantry Division, 166, 213, 290, 420
 Iroquois helicopters, 19, 101, 135–6, 164, 189, 204, **240**, 285–8, 293
 killed in action, 58
 9 Infantry Division, 420
 1 Infantry Division, 408, 410
 173 Airborne Brigade, 16, 25, 27, 31, 55–9, 61, 63, 82, 155, 157–8, 161, 170, 195, 206
 196 Light Infantry Brigade, 420
 199 Light Infantry Brigade, 420
 Operation Abilene, 410
 Operation Hardihood, 49, 411–12
 Operation Hollandia, 61
 Operation Robin, 94
 Pentomic structure, 301
 Public Affairs Office, 407
 Route 15, 423

INDEX

2nd Battalion, 503 Airborne Infantry Regiment, 55
17 Radio Research Group, 419
SIGINT, 405
16 Regiment, 410
68 Assault Helicopter Company, 19, 49, 56
6994 Security Squadron, 419
3rd Field Hospital, 299
36 Evacuation Hospital, 165, 184, 207, 286, 330
3 Brigade, 4 Infantry Division, 94, 422–3
2 Brigade, 1 Infantry Division, 408
2/35 Artillery Regiment, 94–5, 257, 377, 380, 386–7
II Field Force Vietnam, 35, 84–5, 327, 342, 412, 421–3
    US Air Force, 254, 266, 287
    War Zone D, 42
    working with, 342
    wounded in action, 58
US MACV *see* US Military Assistance Command, Vietnam
US Military Assistance Command, Vietnam (US MACV), 25, 29, 90–1, 394, 401–2, 405, 408, 411–14, 418, 420

Van Kiep, 413, 419
Vien, Cao Van (General), 35
Viet Cong
    assessment of Australians, 417–18
    Ba Ria Province Committee, 401
    Ba Ria Province Unit, 414
    Baria Special Action Unit, 416
    base areas near Saigon, 13
    bases in Phuoc Tuy, 16
    Bien Hoa, 341
    C-20 Company, 385, 400, 416
    C-40 Company, 398, 400
    C-45 Company, 399–400
    C-70 Company, 416
    C-300 Company, 416
    C-440 Company, 402
    C-445 Company, 402
    C-610 Company, 416
    casualties, 57, 72, 77, 82–3, 138, 145, 147, 172, 188–9, 197–8, 338, 370, 392, 407, 411, 419, 422
    Chau Duc District Company, 147
    conscripts, 13
    control of Phuoc Tuy, 13
    defectors, 228, 362, 373
    defences, 16
    D445 Local Force Battalion, 408–9, 412, 416
    D445 Provincial Mobile Battalion, 16–17, 59, 82–3, 405
    District Forces, 376
    Dong Nai Regiment, 416
    800 Battalion, 410
    equipment, 14, 16–17
    female, 380, 419–20
    Fifth Infantry Division, 14, 16
    5th Battalion, 407
    1st Battalion, 406
    5 Infantry Division, 405–6, 409, 415–16, 418
    5 Regiment, 416
    4 Regiment, 416
    Group 45, 416
    Group 54, 416
    Group 94, 416
    Group 445B unit, 401
    Guerrilla Platoon, 376
    Hoi Chanh, 362
    Infrastructure, 415
    local support, 17–18, 40–1, 69, 81, 84, 86, 327, 332, 361–2, 392
    Long Dat History, 396
    'Loyal Forces', 59
    Main Force, 14, 16, 38, 63, 76–7, 82, 84, 89, 198, 375, 396, 405, 415–16

Military Region 1, 405
Military Region 7, 405
94 Regiment, 416
Phuoc Tuy, 81–3, 341, 344
prevalence, 401
prisoners, 59, 72, 77, 148, 172, 228, 256, 383, 391–2
Provincial Force, 375–6
Q4, 416
Q5, 416
Q764, 416
Q765, 416
reconnaissance patrols, 82
relations with ARVN, 17
Route 15, 399
7th Military Region, 42
Tet Offensive, 6
3rd Battalion, 406–7
threats to Binh Ba, 76
threats to Nui Dat, 76
21 Company, 412
240C Company, 409
275 Regiment, 16, 65, 82–3, 375, 405–7, 410, 415–16
274 Regiment, 49, 63, 65, 77, 82–3, 89, 100, 140, 326, 375, 402, 404–5, 409–10, 415, 417, 421–2
Victories in November 1965, 407
Vietnam's National Day, 302
weapons, 375, 385, 402
Viet Minh, 9, 81, 335, 361, 395–7
Vietnam Task: The 5th Battalion, Royal Australian Regiment (O'Neill, R), 2, 58, 66, 172, 177, 227, 331
Vietnam veterans, 333
Vietnam War background, 9–10, 335, 361, 393, 395–412
Vietnam War, The [TV series], 228
Vietnamese Joint Chiefs of Staff, 35
Vietnamese, learning, 18
Vietnam's National Day, 302
Vo Van Lot, 403
Vung Tau

airfield shelled, 409
Australian Logistic Support Group, 37
Centre de Repos, Le, 397
considered for 1 ATF base, 38–9, 41
initial camp, 19, 25, 48–52, 55
Landing Zone Snakepit, 157
logistical support area, 13
No 9 Squadron RAAF, 21
Pacific Hotel, 49, 156
population, 399
proximity to Nui dat, 38
36 Evacuation Hospital (US), 165, 184, 207, 286
US Supply Depot, 50
Viet Cong, 409–10

Wainwright, Roger (Colonel), **116**, **246**
5 RAR Association, 8
C Company, 5 RAR, 153–69, 177
8 Platoon, 152–4
football game, 210–11
Operation Queanbeyan, 135–6
service history, 152, 359
Warr and, 155
wounded, 165
Wales, Tony (Captain), 267–9, 271
War Zone D, 42, 55, 345, 402
Warburton, Graham 'Nugget' (Private), 77, 175
'Warburton mountains', 175–7, 180, 190
Warner, Denis, 12
Warr, John (Lieutenant Colonel), **113**, **116**, **246**, **251**
appoints O'Neill intelligence officer, 84
arranges ocean swimming days, 213
arrival in Vietnam, 155
artillery support, 267

INDEX

Australian Army Journal article, 339, 361
Bade and, 231, 233
Bindley and, 269
Carroll and, 66, 320–3, 326, 339
Commanding Officer, 5 RAR, 5–7, 153, 319–33, 339–40
commends 161 (Indep) Reece Flight, 298–9
cordon and search operations, 69, 72, 361–92
Daly and, 101
Davies and, 296
Deak and, 302, 328–30
Distinguished Service Order, 333, 339
5 RAR, 80
historical perspective on conflict, 12, 88
Hodgkinson and, 326
Holsworthy, 46
Isaacs and, 324–8, 339
Jackson and, 109, 323
McQualter and, 266
medal recommendation for Privates, 167
Neesham and, 215–16
O'Hanlon on, 170
O'Neill and, 88, 338–9
Operation Canberra, 95, 100–1
Reconnaissance Platoon, 85
service history, 320, 324, 359–60
son Mark on, 330–3
'Sunray', 232
2IC 5 RAR, 153
Vietnamese casualties, 59
Wainwright and, 155
'Wingy', 314, 329
Warr, Mark, 330–3, 360
Warren, Ken (Private), 215
We Band of Brothers – A True Australian Adventure Story (McFarlane), 268
weapons, 47–8, 50–1, 53, 64–5, 193, 205–6

Welcome Home march, 214
Wells, Mike (Captain), 413
West, Ted (Corporal), 208
Western, Dave (Corporal), **245**, **248**
Westmorland, William (General), 25–7, 31–3, 35–6, 42, 83–4, **112**, 418, 420, 423
Whillas, Bob (Corporal), **111**
White, HAD (Captain), **246**
White, Tony (Captain), **114**, 332
  Bade and, 231
  Operation Renmark, 288
  Operation Robin, 107
  regimental medical officer, 7, 87, 273–82, 338–9
  service history, 360
  treated Davies, 299
  treating Le Dan, 128, 133
  treating villagers, 107, **122**, 212, 276, 278–9, 295
  treating wounded, 184, 273–81
Wiangaree State Forest, 194, 196
Willcox, Don (Captain), 13, 84, 89, 371
Williams, John 'Blah' (Private), **245**
Williams, John (Chaplain), **111**, 157, 209, **246**, 382
Wilton, Sir John (General)
  Chairman of the Chiefs of Staff Committee, 43
  changes to army structures, 23
  chief of the general staff, 21–3
  expanding the Vietnam force, 28–31
  military service, 22–3
  selection of Nui Dat, 38–42
  selection of Phuc Tuy as field of operation, 5, 21, 23–43
  'Sir Jovial', 23
  'Smiling Jack', 23
  two-battalion task force, 21, 30, 33–4, 36
Winkel, Bill (Private), 181, 184
Witheridge, T (Sergeant), 389

455

Wolk, Uri (Private), 207–8
Wollner, David 'Blue' (Private), 245
Womal, Norman (Corporal)
   section leader, 128
   wounded, 129–30, 132, 186–8, 280, 291–2, 305
Wormald, Ross (Warrant Officer), 160, 178

Xuan Loc, 395, 404
Xuyen Moc, 393, 397, 404, 414

Yellow Fever (Larteguy), 192

Ziemski, Bob (Corporal), 144, 146
Zone 33, 401
Zone Cherry, 416

www.ingramcontent.com/pod-product-compliance
Lightning Source LLC
Chambersburg PA
CBHW041732300426
44116CB00019B/2958